CORE TAX ANNUALS
Corporation Tax 2006/07

CW01572390

CORE TAX ANNUALS
Corporation Tax 2008/09

Juliana Watterston MSc FCA CTA (Fellow)

Series General Editor: Mark McLaughlin CTA (Fellow) ATT TEP

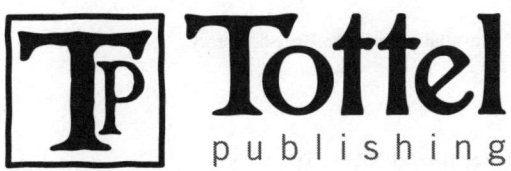

Tottel Publishing Ltd, Maxwelton House, 41–43 Boltro Road, Haywards Heath, West Sussex, RH16 1BJ

© Tottel Publishing Ltd 2008

Cover illustration © Marcus Duck 2008

Marcus Duck is a Brighton-based graphic designer and photographer. Contact:marcus@marcusduckdesign.com

A CIP Catalogue record for this book is available from the British Library.

ISBN: 978 1 84766 119 7

Typeset by Kerrypress Ltd, Luton, Beds

Printed in the UK by CPI William Clowes Beccles NR34 7TL

Preface

Introduction

This book aims to provide an up-to-date guide to the principles and practice of UK corporation tax for tax practitioners, company directors and all business persons. It is one of Tottel Publishing's six Core Tax Annuals.

A cost to business

Corporation tax is a cost to business. Responsible directors will monitor this cost and minimise the risks associated with poor compliance. Corporation tax is very much a boardroom topic, and one on which directors should ensure they are adequately informed to enable them to provide shareholder value. The commentary is supported by over 100 worked examples and is cross-referenced to case law, statute law and HMRC practice. The law is stated as at 1 August 2008. Tax planning and cost cutting ideas are detailed alphabetically in Chapter 22. The retail price indices used in capital gains calculations are given in appendix 1. Reference copies of forms CT600 are included in appendix 2.

Corporation tax reliefs

The UK has shifted from an industrial to a knowledge-based economy. Increasing importance is given to the economy's effect upon the environment. The capital allowance system that gives relief for the cost of fixed assets against profits is gradually being withdrawn and being replaced with allowances that concentrate on fostering knowledge, preserving the quality of the environment and the rejuvenation of neglected areas. The withdrawal of the traditional plant and machinery and industrial buildings allowances and the introduction of the annual investment allowance are covered in Chapter 6, together with the new energy savings reliefs, business renovation allowance and the flat conversion allowance. Of key importance are the reliefs available for new research and development. Enhanced relief is covered in Chapter 8 and tax credits in Chapter 9. Reliefs for the remediation of contaminated land are also to be found in Chapter 8. As a mature economy, the UK requires investment in new businesses and decaying infrastructure. The special reliefs for the corporate venturing scheme and the community investment scheme are addressed in Chapter 12. The company's own property and infrastructure investment may bring its activities within the ambit of the Construction Industry Scheme. These rules are discussed in Chapter 21.

Preface

Going international

International trading is often the norm. The main rate of corporation tax was reduced to 28% in order to retain the UK's international competitiveness. The substantial shareholdings exemption is an attractive relief for overseas investors. The changes to the controlled foreign companies rules are covered in Chapter 13. When considering intra-group and more especially international intra-group trading a company must not neglect its transfer pricing issues. Chapter 14 discusses transfer pricing.

Staying close to home

The vast majority of UK companies are shareholder owned and managed. Chapter 4 deals with the specialised matters affecting a close company. Of interest to busy proprietors are the self-assessment rules, the new penalty provisions, the new HMRC powers, the accounting and taxation issues and any *Companies Act 2006* changes that may have a bearing on corporation tax. These topics are referred toin Chapters 1, 2, 3 and 17. Important also are the computational rules and the loss reliefs available to single companies and groups, which are to be found in chapters 5, 7, 9 and 10 respectively. The corporate finance and investment rules will also be of interest and are covered in chapters 11 and 12.

Firm foundations

The company's fundamental structure must not be forgotten because it has a direct impact on the company's wealth generating powers. The initial formation is discussed in Chapter 1 and reorganisations and demergers are discussed in chapters 15 and 16. Chapter 19 deals with liquidations and the eventual winding up of the company, whilst chapters 18 and 20 deal with the anti-avoidance pitfalls and capital gains tax issues.

And finally

Needless to say, it has not been possible to cover all areas, and readers will need to turn to additional texts for in-depth coverage of certain areas such as leasing and specialised businesses. Nevertheless, I hope that you find that this book is useful to you!

Once again many thanks to the Tottel Publishing staff especially Sarah Blair and Heather Saward for their assistance in producing this book.

Juliana Watterston
watterston@mac.com
August 2008

Contents

Preface   *v*

Table of Statutes   *xiii*

Table of Statutory Instruments and Codes of Guidance   *xxix*

Table of European Legislation   *xxxviii*

Table of Cases   *xxxix*

List of Abbreviations   *xlvii*

Chapter 1: Introduction to corporation tax   **1**
    Formation of a UK company   1
    Companies Act 2006   2
    The basis of corporation tax   2
    Liability to corporation tax   3
    Company accounts and director duties   4
    Taxation and accounts   7

Chapter 2: Self-assessment   **11**
    Introduction   11
    Contacting HMRC   12
    Company records   13
    Company tax return   15
    Filing date   18
    Online filing   19
    Payment   20
    Failure to deliver a return by the filing date   21
    Enquiry   22
    Completion of enquiry   28
    Appeals procedures   31
    Determinations and discovery assessments   34
    Fraud   36
    Penalties for errors   37
    Destruction of documents   46
    Reasonable excuse   47
    Right of appeal   47
    Offence   47

Chapter 3: Rates and payment of corporation tax   **49**
    Rates of corporation tax   49
    Payment dates   52
    Interest   54

Contents

Repayments	55
Quarterly instalments	57
Group payment arrangements	59
Quarterly accounting	59

Chapter 4: Close companies and connected issues **62**
Introduction	62
Close companies	62
Close investment holding companies	74
Associated companies	77
Statutory exceptions	77

Chapter 5: Income **83**
Receipt of income and being within the charge to corporation tax	83
Sources of income	83
Trading income	84
Case law	85
Self-assessment of trading income	87
Capital v revenue	88
Schedule D Case I computational provisions	91
Expenditure charged against profits in the accounts but not allowable as a deduction for tax purposes	91
Allowable and disallowable deductions	97
Appropriations of profit	116
Employee incentives	117
Pension contributions	122
Capital allowances computation	125
Valuation of stock and work in progress	126
Schedule A income	130
Bodies granted exemption from corporation tax on trading income	132
Mutual companies	134
Members' sports clubs	135
Community amateur sports clubs (CASCs)	135
Corporation tax self-assessment	136

Chapter 6: Tangible fixed assets **138**
Accountancy treatment	138
Taxation treatment	138
Qualifying expenditure	141
Plant and machinery	144
Rates of allowances	154
First year allowance	156
Expenditure on which an FYA may not be claimed	161
Computation of capital allowances	161
Writing down allowance from 1 April 2008	163
Special rate expenditure and the special rate pool	166

The annual investment allowance 'AIA'   168
AIA claims   169
Interaction with capital allowances   172
Industrial buildings allowances   180
Business premises renovation allowances   197
Flat conversion allowances   204

Chapter 7: Intangible assets   **210**
Scope pre and post 1 April 2002   210
Meaning of an intangible asset   212
Corporation tax treatment   214
Prescribed debit and credit adjustments   216
Sale of an intangible asset   220
Groups   223
International aspects   227

Chapter 8: Research and development   **229**
Introduction   229
Capital expenditure   229
Revenue expenditure   233
Definition of an SME   237
Basis of Definition of an SME   238
Small or medium-sized company   239
Large company   241
Specialist HMRC units for R&D tax credit claims   244
Relief for expenditure on remediation of contaminated land   246

Chapter 9: Single company trading losses   **254**
Schedule D Case I trading losses   254
Carry forward of trading loss against future trading profits   254
Corporation tax computation   257
Relief for a trading loss against total profits of the preceding
      accounting periods when a company ceases to trade   267
Loss relief restriction   269
Self-assessment   271
HMRC amendments to tax returns and claims and elections   272
Repayments   273
Unrelieved loss   276
Clawback of first-year tax credit   279

Chapter 10: Groups   **283**
Business structure   283
Accounting and taxation requirements   284
Reliefs available to groups   284
Group relief   285
Availability of group relief   290

Contents

Chapter 11: Corporate finance   **303**
Company finance 303
Loan relationship 304
Money debt 304
Corporation tax treatment 308
Trading loan relationships 309
Unallowable purpose 310
Non-trading loan relationships 313
Relief for non-trading deficits 314
Trading and non-trading loan relationships 321
Connected persons 323
Consequences of connection 325
Groups and consortia 329
Loan relationships, derivatives and foreign exchange gains
   and losses (FOREX) 330
Company tax return 335

Chapter 12: Investment business   **336**
Introduction 336
Corporation tax computation 336
Management expenses 337
Investment in property 344
Schedule A income 344
Schedule A losses 350
Investment in other limited companies 350
Investment in company or government loan stock 361
Community investment tax relief 361

Chapter 13: Overseas matters   **368**
Introduction 368
Company residence 368
UK resident company with overseas income 369
Non-UK resident company carrying on a trade in the UK 369
Non-resident company becoming liable to UK corporation tax 371
Non-UK resident company not carrying on a trade in the
   UK but with other UK income 372
UK company becoming non-UK resident 372
Dual resident company 374
Overseas dividends 375
Controlled foreign companies 383

Chapter 14: Transfer pricing   **394**
Introduction 394
The UK transfer pricing rules 394
Small and medium-sized enterprises 397
Self-assessment 404

Chapter 15: Reconstructions and amalgamations   **412**
    Buying and selling a company   412
    Company reconstructions and amalgamations   414
    Capital gains tax   414
    Trading losses   422
    Later events   426
    Practical effects of section 343 relief   426

Chapter 16: Distributions   **431**
    Introduction   431
    Meaning   431
    Payments classed as a distribution   431
    Non-qualifying distribution   434
    Small company dividend payments   434
    Surplus ACT   436
    Exemptions from the distribution rules   437
    Demergers   437
    Purchase of own shares   442
    Distributions in a winding up by ESC C16   445

Chapter 17: Accounting and taxation   **450**
    Generally accepted accounting standards   450
    Accounting policies   450
    UK GAAP   451
    International GAAP   453
    Interaction of accounting and taxation principles   455
    FRSSE   455
    Accounting for tax   464

Chapter 18: Avoidance   **473**
    Introduction   473
    UK anti-avoidance legislation   475
    Existing corporation tax avoidance legislation   475
    Disclosure of tax avoidance schemes   477
    Notification   478
    Disclosable arrangements   478
    Corporation tax self-assessment   482
    International tax avoidance   482
    Capital losses   483
    Husband and wife companies   488
    Disclosure of tax avoidance schemes   489

Chapter 19: Liquidations   **492**
    Insolvency   492
    Administration proceedings   493
    Liquidation proceedings   495

Contents

Chapter 20: Capital gains   **499**
  Introduction   499
  Basic capital gains computation   500
  Relieving provisions   503
  Intra-group asset transfer   506
  Anti-avoidance   511
  Losses attributable to depreciatory transactions   515

Chapter 21: The construction industry scheme   **518**
  Introduction   518
  Construction contract   518
  Deductions on account of tax from contract payments to
    sub-contractors   521
  Registration   525
  Company change of control   526
  Cancellation of registration for gross payment   526
  Gross payment tests   531
  Application of sums deducted from contract payments   534

Chapter 22: The year end   **536**
  Corporation tax computation   536
  Planning   538

Appendix 1: Retail price index   **546**

Appendix 2: Company tax return forms   **548**
  Company Tax Return form CT600 (2008) Version 2   549
  Company – Short Tax Return form CT600 (Short) (2008)
    Version 2   557
  Company Tax Return form – Supplementary Pages –
    Loans to participators by close companies CT600A (2006)
    Version 2   561
  Company Tax Return form – Supplementary Pages –
    Controlled foreign companies CT600B (2006) Version 2   565
  Company Tax Return form – Supplementary Pages –
    Group and consortium CT600C (2006) Version 2   568
  Company Tax Return form – Supplementary Pages –
    Charities and CASCs CT600E (2006) Version 2   572
  Company Tax Return form – Supplementary Pages –
    Corporate Venturing Scheme CT600G (2006) Version 2   576
  Company Tax Return form – Supplementary pages –
    Cross-border royalties CT600H (2006) Version 2   580
  Company Tax Return form – Supplementary pages –
    Disclosure of tax avoidance schemes CT600J (2006)
    Version 2   583

Index   *585*

Table of Statutes

[All references are to paragraph number]

Capital Allowances Act 2001 ...... 9.40
  Pt 2–4 .... 6.6
  Pt 4A 6.6
  Pt 5–10 .... 6.6
  s 1 .... 5.35, 6.4
   3(1) 6.4
   4(5) 6.5
   5(1) 6.5
   5(4) 6.5
   6(1) 6.46
    (b) 6.4
   11(1) 6.7
   11(4) 6.7, 6.46
   11(4)(b) 6.40
   11(5) 6.46
   12 .... 6.19
   13 .... 6.19
   15 .... 6.7, 6.16
   18 .... 12.8
   21(1) 6.9
   21(3) 6.9
   23(2) 6.9
   25 .... 6.12
   26 .... 6.12
   28 .... 6.17
    (1) 6.16
    (2) 6.16
    (2B)(a) 6.16
   29 .... 6.14
   31ZA 6.16
   33A(1), (2), (4), (5) 6.17
   33B(1)–(5) 6.17
   34A 6.50, 6.57
   35 .... 6.16, 12.16
   38A(3) 6.46, 6.47
   38B 6.47
   45D 6.27
   45E 6.28
   45G 6.29
   45H 6.25
   45J 6.25

Capital Allowances Act 2001 – *contd*
  s 48(2)(b) 6.23
   49(2) 6.23
   49(4) 6.23
   51A(1) 6.48
    (5) 6.46
    (6) 6.46, 6.51
    (7) 6.46
   51C(3), (5) 6.49
   51D(3) 6.50
   51E(1), (3) 6.50
   51F(1) 6.50
   51L(2) 6.52
   52 .... 6.31
   52A 6.53
   55 .... 6.34
   56 .... 6.38
    (10), (11) 6.35
   56A 6.36
   58(1) 6.33
    (4A) 6.33, 6.53
    (5) 6.33
   61(1) 6.34
   64 .... 6.34
   65 .... 19.7
   67 .... 6.39
   67(1)(a) 6.40
   68 .... 6.39
   70 .... 6.59
   70G 6.57
   70H 6.57
    (1A), (1B) 6.57
   70I 6.58
   70J(3) 6.60
    (4) 6.60
    (6) 6.60
   70K 6.59
   70N 6.59
   70O 6.59
   70P 6.59
   70R 6.62

Capital Allowances Act 2001 – *contd*

s 70U............................... 6.63
70YE............................. 6.59
70YD............................. 6.52
71........................ 5.20, 6.15
72, 73............................ 5.20
74................................. 6.32
81................................. 6.47
83(b)............................. 6.36
86........................ 6.32, 6.36
91................................. 6.37
93................................. 6.37
96................................. 6.37
98................................. 6.37
101................................ 6.32
104B.............................. 6.41
104C.............................. 6.41
104D.............................. 6.45
104E.............................. 6.42
105................................ 6.56
173(1)(a)........................ 6.88
177................................ 6.30
176................................ 6.30
180A.............................. 6.26
186................................ 6.83
198................................ 15.2
205................................ 6.54
208................................ 6.34
210................................ 6.54
217........................ 6.31, 6.54
230................................ 6.31
236................................ 6.54
253................................ 12.8
260(1)–(3)....................... 9.21
266................................ 15.2
269................................ 6.31
271................................ 6.65
272................................ 6.71
272(1)–(3)....................... 6.71
273................................ 6.71
274................................ 6.70
274(1)............................ 6.66
275................................ 6.71
276(3)..................... 6.66, 6.51
277(1)............................ 6.71
279(1)............................ 6.72
285................................ 6.58
286................................ 6.65
292................................ 6.71
294................................ 6.71

Capital Allowances Act 2001 – *contd*

s 295.............................. 6.71
296................................ 6.71
297................................ 6.71
309................................ 6.78
310................................ 6.74
311................................ 6.82
313A.............................. 6.77
319(5)............................ 6.82
323................................ 6.82
343ZA............................ 6.77
352................................ 5.21
354................................ 19.7
356................................ 6.71
360A.............................. 6.86
360B(3).......................... 6.88
    (4))......................... 6.88
360C.............................. 6.89
360D.............................. 6.91
    (2)........................... 6.91
360E.............................. 6.93
360F....................... 6.86, 6.93
360G.............................. 6.94
360H.............................. 6.94
360I............................... 6.95
360J............................... 6.95
360L.............................. 6.95
360M............................. 6.96
360N.............................. 6.96
360Q.............................. 6.96
360P.............................. 6.97
360R.............................. 6.98
360S.............................. 6.99
360T.............................. 6.100
360U.............................. 6.100
360V.............................. 6.100
360X.............................. 6.100
360Z–360Z1................... 6.86
360Z3............................ 6.101
393A.............................. 6.102
393B.............................. 6.104
393C.................. 6.105, 6.106
393D.............................. 6.106
393E.............................. 6.107
393F.............................. 6.102
393I............................... 6.108
393J............................... 6.109
393N.............................. 6.110
393Q.............................. 6.111
393R.............................. 6.108

Capital Allowances Act 2001 – *contd*
s 393S............................ 6.111
437................................ 8.2
438................................ 8.6
438(2)............................ 8.6
438(4)............................ 8.6
439(1)............................ 8.2
439(5)............................ 8.4
441(3)............................ 8.7
442................................ 8.7
445................................ 8.9
448................................ 8.9
449................................ 8.9
450................................ 8.7
531................................ 6.92
559................................ 15.25
567............................ 6.5, 6.77
569............................ 6.5, 15.2
569(1)............................ 22.5
574(2)............................ 6.50
575............................ 6.34, 6.43

Companies Acts 1.10, 2.1, 16.30
Companies Act 1985 ... 2.12, 3.8, 5.53,
10.4, 13.31, 15.6,
16.19, 17.1, 17.2,
17.4, 17.8, 17.11
s 17................................ 16.32
153(3)(a)....................... 15.4
221................................ 2.3
226........................... 1.7, 10.2
226B............................. 1.10
227............................... 10.2
227B............................. 1.10
247(3)........................... 6.22
249(3)........................... 6.22
258............................... 6.23
(2)(c)...................... 6.23
259............................... 6.23
259(1)........................... 10.2
262............................... 10.2
263............................... 20.27
277............................... 4.18
382B............................. 5.16
425.................... 5.20, 15.8, 15.6
426–427A..................... 15.6
652............................... 16.26
652A.......... 16.27, 16.32, 19.14
654.................... 16.29, 16.31
741(1), (2)..................... 5.16

Companies Act 1985 – *contd*
Sch 4................................ 6.1
para 36A 1.8
Companies Act 2006 ..... 2.4, 6.1, 11.1,
16.9, 22.6
Pt 23................................ 16.1
s 19................................ 16.9
19CA............................ 5.16
30–36........................... 16.9
45A.............................. 9.31
45H.............................. 9.31
155............................... 1.4
170............................... 1.14
170(4)........................... 1.14
171............................... 1.14
172............................... 1.14
(1).......................... 1.14
173–181........................ 1.14
226(2)–(6)...................... 1.9
236............................... 9.31
237............................... 1.9
250............................... 5.16
251.................... 2.45, 5.16
270............................... 1.4
271............................... 1.4
356............................... 5.16
382, 383........................ 6.22
386............................ 1.9, 2.3
387............................... 2.3
393(1)........................... 1.9
394............................... 1.9
395........................ 1.9, 1.10
395............................... 1.10
396...................... 5.39, 7.6
(1).......................... 1.10
397............................... 1.10
414............................... 5.16
436(2)........................... 8.30
465, 466........................ 6.22
498............................... 1.9
652............................... 16.28
652A............................. 16.28
681(2)(a)....................... 15.4
709............................... 16.32
830............................... 20.27
895–898........................ 15.6
899............................... 15.6
900–941........................ 15.6
1000........... 16.28, 16.29, 16.32
1001............................. 16.26

Companies Act 2006 – *contd*
s 1003. 16.27, 16.28, 16.29, 16.32, 19.14
1012.................... 16.29, 16.30
1161............................. 6.23
1162.............. 2.53, 6.23, 6.49
Enterprise Act 2002 .... 19.4
Finance Act 1945 .... 6.2
Finance Act 1988
s 66................................ 13.2
73(2)............................. 5.20
130.............................. 13.12
(2)(a).......................... 18.5
Finance Act 1989
s 43(1)............................ 5.15
44................................ 12.4
102..................... 10.17, 10.18
Finance Act 1993
s 92.............................. 17.10
92A-92D..................... 17.10
Finance Act 1996
s 80–105.......................... 11.2
80(2)........................... 11.10
81(1).............. 11.3, 11.5, 11.8
81(2)............................ 11.4
81(3)............................ 11.5
82.............................. 11.11
82(7)........................... 11.11
83(2)........................... 11.17
83(2)(a).............. 11.17, 11.19
83(2)(c). 3.19, 9.28, 11.17, 11.18
83(3A) 11.17, 11.19, 11.20, 11.21
83(6)................... 11.17, 22.5
83(7)........................... 22.5
84(3)................. 11.11, 11.23
84(4)................. 11.22, 11.23
84A............................ 11.36
84A(1)......................... 14.20
84A(3)(b)...................... 14.20
85.............................. 11.9
85A............................. 11.9
85A(1)......................... 11.11
85B................. 11.33, 17.19
86.............................. 11.9
87................. 11.29, 11.35
87(1)........................... 11.25
87(2)........................... 11.28
87(2A)......................... 11.29
87(2B)......................... 11.29
87(2C)......................... 11.29

Finance Act 1996 – *contd*
s 87(3).......... 11.25, 11.26, 11.27
87(5)................. 11.25, 11.27
87A(1), (2).................... 11.27
88.............................. 11.29
88(5)........................... 11.29
91A............................ 11.7
91B............................ 11.7
100............................. 11.6
100(7).......................... 11.6
103(1).......................... 11.28
103(2).......................... 11.10
Sch 8–15...................... 11.2
Sch 8
para 1 .... 11.18
3 .... 11.17, 11.19
4(3) 11.21
Sch 9
para 1 .... 11.6
2 .... 11.30
5 .... 11.33
5A 11.35
5A(5) 11.35
6 .... 11.34
6(3A) 11.34
6(4) 11.34
6A 11.34
6B(1)–(7) 11.34
11 .... 11.34
13 .... 11.15
13(1) 11.14
13(2) 11.12
13(3) 11.12, 11.13
13(5) 11.13
14 .... 11.24, 17.14
17, 18 .... 11.31
Finance Act 1998
s 32.............................. 16.11
36.............................. 3.21
42..................... 1.12, 17.19
42(1)................. 1.14, 5.3
42(2)................. 1.12, 17.2
83ZA(4), (5).................. 9.43
Sch 18
para 2 .... 2.1
3 .... 2.36, 2.51
3(1) 2.1
3(3) 2.1
4 .... 2.1
5(1) 2.4

Finance Act 1998 – *contd*
Sch 18 – *contd*
para 7 .... 2.1
8 .... 3.7
9 .... 3.16
11 .... 2.1
14 .... 2.9, 2.14
15 .... 2.9, 9.23
16 .... 2.9
17 .... 2.12
18 .... 2.12
19 .... 2.12
20 .... 2.12, 2.24, 4.18
21(3) 2.3
21(5) 2.3
21(6) 2.3
22(2) 2.3
(3) 2.3
23(1) 2.3
23(3) 2.3
24 .... 2.13, 2.51
24(1) 2.16
25 .... 2.14, 9.5
26 .... 2.16
27 .... 2.20
29 .... 2.17
30, 31 .... 2.22
31A–31D 2.27
32 .... 2.23
33 .... 2.27
34 .... 2.23, 2.27
34(2)(a) 9.26
35 .... 2.22
36 .... 2.13, 2.26, 2.32
37 .... 2.32
39 .... 2.32
40 .... 2.32
41 .... 9.26
41(1) 2.14
42 .... 2.32
43 .... 9.5, 2.32
44 .... 2.26, 2.32
45 .... 2.32
46 .... 2.26, 2.32
(2) 2.32
48 .... 2.28
52(2), (5) 8.50
53 .... 2.32
54 .... 9.27
54–59 .... 9.22

Finance Act 1998 – *contd*
Sch 18 – *contd*
para 61 .... 9.26
62(1) 9.26
62(3) 9.26
64 .... 9.26
65(1), (2) 9.26
74 .... 11.17, 22.5
76 .... 9.26
77 .... 10.16
82 .... 6.4, 22.5
83L 8.50
Finance Act 1999
s 54 .... 12.18
85 .... 14.29, 14.30
Sch 6 .... 12.18
Finance Act 2000
Sch 15 .... 12.31
para 5–8 .... 12.33
18 .... 12.36
26 .... 12.35
36 .... 12.35
42 .... 12.33, 12.36
47 .... 12.40
(7) 12.40
67–71 .... 12.42
89 .... 12.38
Sch 20 .... 8.1, 8.10, 8.32, 9.35
para 1 .... 8.20
2 .... 8.18
3 .... 8.13
4 .... 8.12
5 .... 8.12, 8.13
7 .... 8.14
8A-8E 8.16
9–12 .... 8.17
13, 14 .... 8.21
17 .... 8.21
18A 8.30
22 .... 8.21
Sch 27
para 4 .... 10.6
Finance Act 2001
s 70 .... 8.33
85 .... 10.20
Sch 22 .... 8.33, 9.35, 9.36
para 1 .... 8.34
2 .... 8.35
3 .... 8.36
4 .... 8.37

Finance Act 2001 – *contd*
Sch 22 – *contd*
para 5 .... 8.38
6 .... 8.39
7 .... 8.40
8 .... 8.41
9 .... 8.42
10 .... 8.43
11 .... 8.44
12 .... 8.45
16 .... 8.48
17 .... 8.46
15 .... 8.47
18 .... 8.47
19 .... 8.49
29 .... 8.33
31 .... 8.34
(1) 8.36
(4) 8.42
Sch 23 .... 8.33
Finance Act 2002 .... 11.2
s 64 ...... 17.1, 17.13, 17.17, 17.20,
17.23, 17.26
79 .... 11.36
83 .... 11.36
96 .... 10.20
103(5) 1.12, 5.3
Sch 5 .... 9.35
Sch 12 .... 8.1, 8.10, 8.32
para 1 .... 8.21
3 .... 8.21
4 .... 8.13
(4) 8.12
5 .... 8.21
6 .... 8.21
9 .... 8.21
9(3) 8.12
10 .... 8.21
17(d) 8.16
Sch 13 .. 8.1, 8.21, 8.31, 8.32, 9.35
para 18A 8.31
Sch 16
para 2 .... 12.45
4 .... 12.47
7 .... 12.47
9 .... 12.47, 12.48
10 .... 12.49
11 .... 12.50
12–14 .... 12.51
16 .... 12.45

Finance Act 2002 – *contd*
Sch 16 – *contd*
para 18 .... 12.45
20 .... 12.46
21–23, 24 .... 12.52
24 .... 12.47
25 .... 12.47
27–29 .... 12.53
30, 31 .... 12.54
32 .... 12.55
35 .... 12.56
40–42 .... 12.57
Sch 18
para 1 .... 5.55
2(1) 5.55
3 .... 5.55
4–8 .... 5.56
16(b) 5.56
Sch 22 .... 5.41, 17.1, 17.20
para 6 .... 17.20
8, 9 .... 17.20
Sch 23 .... 11.36
Sch 26 .... 11.36
para 16 .... 11.36
27 .... 14.22
Sch 27 .... 11.36
Sch 28 .... 11.36
Sch 29
para 1 .... 7.10
paras 2–5 .... 7.6
6 .... 7.10
7(1) 7.10
8(3) 7.11
9 .... 7.15
10 .... 7.12
11 .... 7.12
12 .... 7.16
13 .... 7.17
15 .... 7.17, 7.18
16, 17 .... 7.17
22 .... 7.18
26 .... 7.18, 7.20
28 .... 7.18
29 .... 7.19
35 .... 7.13
39–41 .... 7.21
43 .... 7.21
50 .... 7.23
56 .... 7.24
57 .... 7.24

Finance Act 2002 – *contd*
Sch 29 – *contd*
para 58 .... 7.25
　　71 .... 7.25
　　72–77 .... 7.7
　　73A 17.17
　　75(2) 7.7
　　76 .... 7.8
　　82 .... 7.9
　　83 .... 6.15, 7.8
　　84–86 .... 7.26
　　84 .... 7.26, 15.11
　　87(2) 7.26
　　88 .... 7.26, 15.11, 18.5
　　92 .... 7.27
　　92(4C) 7.27
　　94 .... 7.11
　　96, 97 .... 7.28
　　99 .... 7.28
　　101 .... 7.29
　　102 .... 7.30
　　104 .... 7.31
　　108 .... 7.19, 7.32
　　116 .... 7.33
　　116A-116H 17.17
　　117 .... 7.2
　　118(1), (2) 7.3
　　118(3) 7.2
　　121 .... 7.4
　　137(1)(a) 7.3
Finance Act 2003 .... 5.28, 5.29
s 148............................. 13.6
　148(1), (2)...................... 13.7
　148(4), (5)...................... 13.8
　150............................. 13.10
　151............................. 13.11
Sch 6............................. 6.90
Sch 23............................ 5.26
para 1 .... 5.30
　　8 .... 5.26, 5.27
　　15 .... 5.27
　　16 .... 5.26, 5.27
　　21(3) 5.28
　　23 .... 5.26
Sch 24............................ 5.30
Finance Act 2004 .... 11.2, 11.28
s 50, 51........................... 17.1
　53............................... 17.17
　55.............................. 2.2, 5.1
　57............................... 21.1

Finance Act 2004 – *contd*
s 57(1), (2)....................... 21.2
　58–77........................... 21.1
　58........................ 21.1, 21.3
　59........................ 21.1, 21.5
　　(1)(b)–(l)).................... 21.8
　60........................ 21.1, 21.7
　61, 62.................... 21.1, 21.8
　63–77........................... 21.1
　64(5)........................... 21.12
　74(2), (3)....................... 21.4
　196............................. 5.32
　　(2)(b)........................ 5.31
　197............................. 5.32
　199............................. 5.40
　306............................. 18.6
　　(1)(a), (b)................... 18.9
　307............................. 18.6
　308–313.................... 18.6, 18.7
　314–319........................ 18.6
Sch 11............................ 21.1
Sch 12............................ 21.1
Finance Act 2005
s 24.............................. 13.31
　81.............................. 17.1
Sch 10
para 4 .... 11.7
　　9 .... 11.7
Sch 15........................... 17.18
Finance Act (No 2) 2005 .... 11.2
s 12.............................. 5.30
　40.............................. 11.36
Sch 2............................. 5.30
Sch 7............................. 18.16
Finance Act 2006 .. 2.7, 5.28, 11.2, 11.4
s 26(1), (2)....................... 3.1
　28.............................. 8.5
　29.............................. 8.29
　56.............................. 5.41
　57.............................. 5.49
　69.............................. 18.19
　70(12).......................... 18.20
　76.............................. 18.6
　77.............................. 7.8
　81.............................. 6.56
　93.............................. 5.26, 22.5
　93(2)........................... 5.28
　100(7).......................... 2.11
Sch 1
para 1 .... 10.8, 10.9

Finance Act 2006 – *contd*
Sch 1 – *contd*
  para 4(1), (2) 10.10
     6(4) 10.10
     7 .... 10.11
  Sch 2 .... 8.5
  Sch 3 .... 8.29
  Sch 6 .... 18.6
  para 6 .... 11.11
     10(2) 11.4
     10(6) 11.4
     16 .... 11.32
  Sch 8 .... 6.56, 6.49
  Sch 9
  para 12 .... 11.35
  Sch 10
  para 6, 7 .... 6.64
  Sch 15
  para 10 .... 5.41
     12 .... 5.41
Finance Act 2007 .... 4.18
  s 2 .... 3.1
   17 .... 12.22
   33 .... 5.30
   34 .... 13.27
   35 .... 6.4, 2.32
   36 .... 6.81, 22.6
   37 .... 6.49
   47 .... 13.29
   50 .... 8.18
   81 .... 2.31
   82, 83 .... 2.35
   94 .... 2.11
   95(3), (4) 2.15
   96 .... 2.32
     (3), (4) 2.15
   97 .... 2.36
   108 .... 4.5
   419 .... 2.34
  Sch 5 .... 18.16
  Sch 6 .... 6.64, 18.16
  Sch 13
  para 2 .... 11.37
     3 .... 11.38
     5 .... 11.39
     4 .... 11.39
     6 .... 11.39
     7 .... 11.40
     8 .... 11.41
     10 .... 11.42

Finance Act 2007 – *contd*
Sch 13 – *contd*
  para 9 .... 11.42
    11(5) 11.42
    12 .... 11.43
  Sch 15 .... 13.29
  para 22A 12.32
  Sch 16 .... 12.32, 12.35
  para 5 .... 13.46
    7 .... 13.41
    8 .... 13.36
  Sch 24 .... 2.36
  para 1, 1A 2.36
    2 .... 2.37
    3 .... 2.37
    5 .... 2.38
    5(4) 2.38
    6 .... 2.39
    7(1), (2), (4), (5) 2.40
    8 .... 2.41
    9 .... 2.42
    11 .... 2.42
    12 .... 2.42
    13(1)–(4) 2.43
    14 .... 2.44
    15, 16 .... 2.44
    17 .... 2.44
    18 .... 2.36
    19 .... 2.45
     (3) 2.45
    21 .... 2.45
  Sch 26
  para 1 .... 4.5
Finance Act 2008 .... 6.2
  s 6 .... 3.1
   .... 3.2
   22 .... 8.30
   29 .... 8.22
   30 .... 8.31
   37 .... 5.43
   59 .... 13.3
   64(2) 13.34
    (3) 13.35
    (4) 13.37
    (5) 13.38
   72 .... 6.14
   73 .... 6.3
   74 .... 5.35, 6.3
   79 .... 6.3
   .... 6.3, 6.35

Finance Act 2008 – *contd*
s 81(3)............................ 6.36
83................................ 6.3, 6.37
84................................ 6.65
85...................... 6.3, 6.75, 22.6
87................................ 6.77
89................................ 6.77
114(3), (6)........................ 2.48
119(4)(b)......................... 2.9
(6)............................. 2.23
124.............................. 2.31

para 1 .... 8.20, 8.21
Sch 9
para 1 .... 8.30
2 .... 8.31
Sch 15............................ 5.43
para 5(2), (3) 5.43
6(2) 5.43
7–10 .... 5.43
11(2), (3) 9.35
Sch 20
para 1 .... 6.61
8 .... 6.57
Sch 24
para 5 .... 6.33, 6.53
para 6 .... 6.54
23(3) 6.46
Sch 25
para 1(4) 9.32
2(1), (2) 9.33
3 .... 9.31
11(2), (3) 9.35
12(2), (3) 9.36
13(2) 9.37
15(2), (3) 9.38
17 .... 9.34
(6) 9.39
(1)–(5) 9.39
19 .... 9.30
23 .... 9.39
24 .... 9.40
25 .... 9.40
(10) 9.40
26 .... 9.41
27 .... 9.42
28 .... 9.42, 9.43
29 .... 9.43
Sch 26............................ 6.41
para 2 .... 6.41, 6.45

Finance Act 2008 – *contd*
Sch 26 – *contd*
para 15 .... 6.43
16 .... 6.44
17 .... 6.44
Sch 27
para 5 .... 6.83
31 .... 6.85
Sch 36
paras 1–5 .... 2.47
8 .... 2.47
(1) 2.56
10 .... 2.49
15 .... 2.50
16 .... 2.50
17 .... 2.50
18 .... 2.51
19 .... 2.53
20 .... 2.51
21 .... 2.53
23 .... 2.51
24 .... 2.51
25 .... 2.51
29 .... 2.29
30 .... 2.52
31 .... 2.52
32 .... 2.53
35 .... 2.52, 2.53
35(3) 2.52
36 .... 2.54
39 .... 2.55
40 .... 2.55
42, 43 .... 2.56
44, 45 .... 2.57
47, 50, 51 .... 2.58
53–54 .... 2.59
62 .... 2.52
Sch 37
para 8(3) 2.3
9 .... 2.3
Sch 39
para 37–42 .... 2.32
48 .... 12.53
Sch 40............................ 2.36
Sch 41............................ 2.36
**Financial Services and Markets
Act 2000** 11.1
**Income and Corporation Taxes
Act 1988**
Pt XVII, Chs 1-VI.............. 18.4

Income and Corporation Taxes Act
1988 – *contd*

s 6(1)	1.5
6(4)(a)	1.6
9(1)	1.6
9(3)	1.6
11	13.5
11(1)	9.6
11(2A)	1.5
11AA	13.9
(2)–(4)	13.9
12	1.6, 2.4
12(3)	19.7
12(3)(da)	19.6
12(4)	12.5
12(7)	19.11
12(7A), (7B)	5.41
12(7ZA)	19.6
13	3.5
13(1)	13.9
(b)	4.23
13(2)	3.5
13(3)	3.5, 3.9
13(4)	4.27, 4.30, 19.16
(4A)–(4C)	4.29
13A(1)–(3)	4.24
13A(2)	19.16
13A(2)(b)(ii)	4.26
13A(4)	19.16
15(1)	12.15
18(1)(ii)	5.4
24	12.25
31ZA	12.22
31ZA(5)	12.22
31ZB	12.22
31ZC	12.22
34	5.20, 12.17
35	5.20
55	6.7
70(1)	1.13
(2)	12.17
74	11.11, 12.4
74(1)	5.13, 5.20
74(1)(a)	5.20
74(1)(d)	5.20
74(1)(da)	6.17
74(1)(j)	5.20
74(1)(m)	5.20
74(2)	5.20
75	5.26, 11.19, 12.23

Income and Corporation Taxes Act
1988 – *contd*

s 75(1)	12.4, 12.12
75(2)	12.4
75(3)	9.21, 12.8, 12.12
75(4)(a)	12.4
75(6)	12.4
75(7)	12.4
75(9)	9.38, 12.12
75A	12.4
75B	12.4
76	5.26
79	5.20
79A	5.20
79B	5.20
83(1)	5.4
83A	5.52
84A(3ZA)	5.26
85A(3)	5.26
86	5.20
87	12.17
88D	5.20
90	5.20
91A, 91B	5.12
93	5.20
94	15.24
95	11.7
98	5.20, 12.22
100	17.24
100(1)(c)	22.5
100(1C)	19.7
105	19.7
105(1)	5.40
114	10.1
130	12.3, 12.25
131, 132	13.12
139, 140A	7.26
208	1.6, 12.7
209	13.33, 16.28
209(1)	16.2, 19.12, 19.16
209(2)(a)	16.1, 16.4
209(2)(b)	16.5, 16.19
209(2)(c)	16.8
209(2)(d)	11.6
209(2)(da)	14.27
209(2)(e)	11.6
209(4)	5.49, 16.4, 16.5, 19.12
209(5), (6)	16.4, 16.5, 19.12
210	16.6
210(1)	16.6

Income and Corporation Taxes Act 1988 – *contd*

s 211............................ 16.6
213.... 16.12, 16.13, 16.14, 16.16
213(3)(a), (b)................. 16.14
213(4), (5).................... 16.17
213(6)(a)...................... 16.14
213(6)(b)...................... 16.15
213(8)(a)-(e)................. 16.15
213(10), (11)................. 16.17
213(12)....................... 16.15
    (a).................... 16.15
214............................. 16.16
214(1A), (1B)................ 16.18
215.............. 16.18, 18.5, 18.12
216............................. 16.18
219............ 16.12, 16.19, 16.20
219(1)(a)...................... 16.20
220(1)......................... 16.21
220(5), (6)................... 16.21
221(1), (2)................... 16.22
221(4), (5)................... 16.22
222(4)......................... 16.22
222(7)......................... 16.22
223(1)......................... 16.22
225.............. 16.23, 18.5, 18.12
226............................. 16.23
227(8)......................... 16.24
229(1)......................... 16.19
234(5).......................... 16.8
254(8).......................... 16.7
271(3)............................ 1.4
337.............. 13.9, 13.12, 15.15
337(1)......................... 15.25
338............................. 11.19
338A............................ 9.15
338A(2)......................... 9.8
339............................. 5.49
339(7AA)....................... 5.40
342(2)(a)...................... 19.11
342(3A)........................ 19.11
342(6)......................... 19.11
342A............................ 19.6
343.. 6.23, 6.64, 6.84, 9.5, 13.34,
          15.2, 15.11, 15.4,
          15.12, 15.15, 15.17,
          15.20, 15.23, 15.24,
          15.25, 19.12, 21.6
343(1)......................... 15.19
343(1)(a)...................... 15.13

Income and Corporation Taxes Act 1988 – *contd*

s 343(1)(b)..................... 15.14
343(2)......... 13.15, 15.15, 15.25
343(3)........................... 9.5
343(4)................. 15.15, 15.24
343(7)......................... 15.23
343(8)................. 15.14, 15.19
343(9)......................... 15.24
344............................. 15.17
344(2)................. 15.17, 19.11
344(2)(a), (b)................. 15.17
344(3)(a)...................... 15.16
344(3)(b)...................... 15.17
344(5)(a), (b)................. 15.24
344(6)......................... 15.24
344(7)......................... 15.24
344(11)........................ 15.24
344(12)........................ 15.24
349(1B)......................... 5.50
349(2)......................... 14.28
392A................. 8.46, 12.23
    (1)................ 9.36, 11.18
    (2)................. 8.46, 9.36
392B(1)......................... 9.37
393..................... 9.20, 22.5
393(1)..... 8.46, 9.2, 9.3, 9.4, 9.7,
          9.10, 9.12, 9.13,
          9.14, 9.15, 9.21,
          9.35, 10.7, 11.19,
          15.24
393(7)........................... 9.1
393(8)........................... 9.9
393(9)........................... 9.8
393(10).......................... 9.6
393A....... 3.19, 9.14, 9.21, 9.28,
         11.19, 12.12, 22.6
393A(1)..... 9.2, 9.13, 9.16, 9.22,
         9.24, 11.18
393A(1)(a)........ 8.46, 9.15, 9.35
393A(1)(b) 6.64, 8.21, 8.46, 9.12,
         9.15, 9.35
393A(2A)........................ 9.16
393A(2B)........................ 9.16
393A(3)......................... 9.20
393A(8).......................... 9.8
393A(9)(a)....................... 9.1
393A(9)(c)....................... 9.6
393B(3)......................... 9.35
395............................. 9.35

**Income and Corporation Taxes Act
1988** – *contd*

s 397............................ 9.2, 10.7
400... 9.21, 9.35, 9.36, 9.37, 9.38
401.. 5.20, 8.20, 8.21, 8.21, 12.22
401(1AB)....................... 11.22
402....... 9.21, 10.7, 10.17, 12.12
402(2)............................ 10.8
402(2A), (2B)................. 10.9
402(6).......................... 10.15
403.............. 7.13, 10.7, 11.17
403(1)..... 8.46, 9.35, 9.36, 9.38,
12.12
403A.................. 10.9, 10.13
403C............................ 10.14
403F............................ 10.10
403G............................ 10.10
403ZA.......................... 10.7
403ZB.......................... 10.7
403ZD.......................... 10.7
403ZE.......................... 10.7
404............................. 13.15
410.................. 10.12, 19.6
410(1)(b)(ii)........... 19.6, 19.12
413(3)........................... 10.5
413(5)........................... 10.5
413(7)........................... 10.6
414(1)..................... 4.3, 4.5
415(5)............................ 4.6
  (6)............................ 4.7
416............................... 16.5
416(1)....................... 4.4, 6.64
416(2).................... 4.25, 11.26
416(3).................... 4.9, 11.26
416(4).......................... 11.26
416(5)........... 4.4, 4.28, 11.26
416(6)....... 4.4, 4.28, 4.29, 4.31,
11.26
417............................... 7.28
417(1)........................... 4.10
417(3)........................... 4.12
417(3)(a)......................... 4.29
417(3)(b)......................... 4.31
417(4)........................... 4.12
417(5).......................... 4.8
417(7)........................... 4.11
418.................... 16.7, 19.12
418(2)........................... 4.13
418(3)........................... 4.13
418(4)........................... 4.13

**Income and Corporation Taxes Act
1988** – *contd*

s 419.. 2.20, 4.10, 4.15, 4.16, 4.17,
4.18, 4.19, 4.21,
4.22, 22.5
419(1)...... 4.16, 4.17, 4.21, 4.22
419(2)(a), (b).................. 4.17
419(4).................... 4.15, 4.18
419(5).................... 4.16, 4.21
419(6).......................... 4.22
419(7).......................... 4.10
420(1), (2)..................... 4.17
421.............................. 4.20
422.............................. 4.22
444............................. 18.12
488............................. 9.32
489............................. 9.32
503............................. 5.45
505...................... 5.40, 9.32
505(1)(e)....................... 5.40
505(1)C(ii).................... 5.40
508............................. 9.32
519(2)........................... 1.4
573............................ 12.25
573(2).......................... 22.5
576............................ 12.25
  (4)........................... 12.25
577................. 5.14, 5.20, 12.4
577(5).......................... 5.14
577(9).......................... 5.20
577(10)......................... 5.14
577A............................ 12.4
577A(1)......................... 5.20
577A(1)(a), (b)................. 5.20
577A(2)......................... 5.20
578A............................ 5.20
579............................. 5.20
580............................. 5.20
589A............................ 5.20
589B............................ 5.20
617(3)–(5)...................... 5.20
707...................... 18.5, 18.12
731–738....................... 11.37
747...................... 7.33, 13.30
747(1).......................... 13.28
747(6).......................... 13.34
747A........................... 13.31
748............................. 13.36
748(4), (5).................... 13.31
749.................... 13.30, 13.33

Income and Corporation Taxes Act 1988 – *contd*

s 749A	13.30
749B	13.33
751A	13.46
752	13.33
755D	13.35
765	13.12, 18.4
766	13.12, 18.4
767	18.4
767A–769	18.4
768	9.5, 9.17, 15.12
768(4)	9.19
768A	9.17, 15.12
768B	12.13
768B(3)	12.13
768C	15.12
768D	12.23
769	2.54, 9.18, 12.13
770A–774	18.4
770A	14.1, 14.29
774	12.14
785B	6.61
785E	6.61
788(3)	13.9
790	13.16, 13.17
793	13.16
793A	13.16
795A	13.18
799(5)–(7)	13.19
801A	13.17, 13.20
803A	13.19
804ZA–804ZC	13.30
806	13.21
806B	13.20, 13.23
806D	13.20, 13.21
806E	13.21
806F	13.21
806H	13.26
815C	18.15
815ZA	12.3
826	3.17, 8.50
826(2)	3.17
826(4)	4.15
826(7A)	3.17, 9.28
826(7BB)	3.17
826(7C)	3.17, 9.28
832	1.4, 7.29, 15.16
832(1)	1.4, 5.1, 6.46, 8.10
834(3)	4.18

Income and Corporation Taxes Act 1988 – *contd*

s 834(4)	2.5
837A	8.3
838	10.5
839	6.31, 6.34, 6.43, 8.42, 9.18, 15.2
839(5), (6)	4.25
839(8)	4.26
840	11.27, 12.36, 14.4, 19.6
Sch 4AA	
para 7	5.26
Sch 16	3.23, 14.28
para 2	3.22
Sch 18	
para 1A	10.10
5	10.12
20	14.23
Sch 18A	10.9
para 11	10.11
15	10.11
Sch 20	5.51
Sch 24	
para 1–5	13.34
8–10	13.34
12	13.34
Sch 25	
para 1–4A	13.37
4A–4D	13.37
5	13.38
6	13.38, 13.39
7	13.45
8–12A	13.38
13–15	13.39
16–19	13.38
Sch 26	
para 1	13.43
(5)	13.43
4	13.44
Sch 28AA	14.1, 14.27, 14.29
para 1	14.3, 14.20
1A	14.3
1B	14.3
2	14.6
3	14.6
4(7)	14.4
5	14.6
5A	14.11, 14.14
5B	14.7
5C(1)	14.7

Income and Corporation Taxes Act 1988 – *contd*

Sch 28AA – *contd*

para 6 .... 14.15, 14.20
6D 14.21
7 .... 14.15
7A 14.16
8 . 14.16, 14.19, 14.20, 14.22
9 .... 14.16
12 .... 14.17
13 .... 14.18

Sch A.... 1.6, 5.2, 5.20, 5.22, 5.24,
5.26, 5.41, 5.43,
9.7, 9.11, 10.7,
10.11, 11.18, 11.19,
11.20, 12.2, 12.12,
12.14, 12.16, 12.17,
12.22, 15.15, 17.19,
22.3

Sch C
case I 5.20
case II 5.20

Sch D................. 1.6, 5.26, 15.15
case I 5.2, 5.4, 5.9, 5.12, 5.20,
5.24, 5.25, 5.26,
5.32, 5.45, 5.54,
7.10, 8.13, 8.21,
9.1, 9.7, 9.15, 9.20,
9.28, 10.7, 11.2,
11.11, 11.17, 11.19,
11.36, 12.4, 12.7,
12.12, 12.14, 12.17,
12.18, 12.22, 13.4,
17.20, 22.2, 22.3
case II . 5.4, 5.9, 8.13, 10.7, 11.19
case III . 5.2, 5.24, 5.45, 9.7, 9.11,
9.15, 10.7, 11.2,
11.16, 11.17, 11.19,
11.20 11.21, 11.36,
12.2, 12.12, 22.3
case V 5.2, 9.20, 10.7, 11.17,
11.20, 11.21, 13.19,
13.20, 13.24, 13.44,
17.19, 22.3
case VI 5.2, 5.24, 7.13, 12.4,
18.4, 22.3

Income Tax Act 1945 .... 6.2

Income Tax Act 2007

s 914 .... 2.23

Income Tax (Earnings and Pensions) Act 2003 ..... 5.15, 5.16, 5.20, 16.1

s 18 .... 4.18
67 .... 5.16
68 .... 4.17
175 .... 2.20
225 .... 5.20
431 .... 5.28
476 .... 5.27, 5.28
488 .... 5.27
530 .... 5.27, 5.28
531 .... 5.28
Sch 2 .... 5.27

Income Tax (Trading and Other Income) Act 2005

s 81 .... 5.20
384 .... 16.1
619–648 .... 15.4
758 .... 3.23
761, 762 .... 3.23
Sch 1
para 72 .... 5.20
para 77 .... 5.20

Industrial Development Act 1982

s 7, 8 .... 5.20

Inheritance Tax Act 1984

s 12 .... 5.30
94 .... 16.4

Insolvency Act 1986 .... 5.20
s 73 .... 19.1, 19.8
110 .... 15.6, 15.11

Limited Liability Partnerships Act 2000 .... 10.1

Pensions Act 1995

s 75 .... 5.31

Plant Varieties Act 1997

s 7 .... 7.6

Police and Criminal Evidence Act 1984

s 114 .... 2.35

Proceeds of Crime Act 2002 .... 18.2

Rent Act 1977 .... 6.92

Taxation of Chargeable Gains Act 1992

s 1 .... 20.1
1(7) 20.34
2A 18.19
8 .... 1.6, 9.21

Taxation of Chargeable Gains Act 1992 – *contd*

s 8(2)............................ 18.19
8(3)......................... 2.5, 12.5
10................................ 13.5
16A............................ 18.19
21............................. 20.24
24............................. 19.16
29–34......................... 20.24
29(2)......................... 20.25
(3)......................... 20.25
30..................... 20.29, 20.31
(1)........................... 20.26
(2)................... 20.26, 20.31
31..................... 20.27, 20.28
31(3)......................... 20.28
31(6)–(9)..................... 20.27
31(10)........................ 20.28
31A........................... 20.28
(9)........................... 20.28
32............................. 20.27
(2)........................... 20.29
(3)........................... 20.29
(5)........................... 20.29
33(2)......................... 20.31
A........................... 20.25
34A........................... 20.30
38..................... 5.45, 20.2
39............................. 8.49
44............................. 20.9
53(1)(b).................. 5.45, 20.4
53(2A).................. 5.45, 20.4
54..................... 5.45, 20.4
58(1)......................... 20.26
62(4)......................... 20.26
100(1)......................... 12.7
106........................... 18.16
117........................... 11.5
122..................... 15.7, 16.16
127...... 12.30, 15.7, 15.8, 16.16, 20.30
128............... 15.7, 15.8, 16.16
129–131......... 15.7, 15.8, 16.16
135.............. 12.30, 15.8, 20.16
(3)......................... 20.30
136..................... 15.1116.16
137........................... 15.9
138..................... 15.9, 18.12
138(1)......................... 18.5
139...... 15.11, 18.5, 18.12, 18.22

Taxation of Chargeable Gains Act 1992 – *contd*

s 140........................... 18.22
140A................. 15.11, 18.22
140B................. 18.5, 18.12
140D................. 18.5, 18.12
140E........................... 18.22
152..... 18.22, 20.6, 20.21, 20.22
152(5)......................... 20.7
153..................... 18.22, 20.8
155........................... 20.6
156........................... 20.6
(4)......................... 20.10
157........................... 20.13
161(3)......................... 20.18
165........................... 7.27
170................. 18.20, 20.15
170(11)......................... 19.12
171... 12.26, 12.28, 12.30, 13.15, 15.11, 19.12, 20.16
171(1) 20.26, 20.27, 20.29, 20.31
171A................. 20.17, 22.5
175........................... 20.21
175(2)......................... 13.15
176–181....................... 20.24
176..................... 10.15, 20.32
(1)......................... 20.32
177..................... 20.32, 20.33
178.... 20.26, 20.27, 20.30, 20.31
(7)......................... 20.30
179.... 10.1, 15.11, 20.22, 20.26, 20.27, 20.30, 20.31
179(2)......................... 15.11
179(3)......................... 20.22
(9)......................... 20.30
179(10)......................... 15.11
179A........................... 20.22
179B........................... 20.22
184(3), (4).................. 18.19
184A.......... 18.16, 18.19, 18.20
184B................. 18.16, 18.21
184C........................... 18.20
184D........................... 18.20
184E........................... 18.22
184F................. 18.19, 18.22
184G.......... 18.16, 18.23, 18.25
184H.......... 18.16, 18.24, 18.25
185.......... 13.13, 13.14, 18.22
187........................... 13.14
192............ 12.27, 16.12, 16.16

**Taxation of Chargeable Gains Act
1992** – *contd*
s 251(3)............................ 5.20
Sch 5AA......................... 15.11
para 2–5 .... 15.8
Sch 7
para 20 .... 12.30
Sch 7A................. 18.19, 18.20
para 2(8) 20.34
Sch 7AA................ 18.19, 20.34
Sch 7AC......................... 12.27
para 2 .... 12.27
3 .... 19.16
7 .... 12.27
10 .... 12.27, 12.30
11–15 .... 12.27
16 .... 12.27
18 .... 12.28
19 .... 12.29
20 .... 12.30
26 .... 12.27
Taxes Management Act 1970
s 9(A)............................ 2.16
9A....................... 2.17, 2.20
19A............................. 2.20
19A(2)......................... 2.20
20............................. 2.20
(3)........................... 2.20

Taxes Management Act 1970 – *contd*
s 59D............................. 3.8
(1)........................... 3.7
(2)......................... 10.18
59DA(4), (5).................. 9.27
70A............................ 2.11
87............................. 14.28
87A............................ 3.14
87A(1).......................... 4.15
87A(4A)........................ 3.19
90(2)........................... 2.11
98............................. 2.36
98(1), (2), (3).................. 2.2
100............................. 2.17
100(1)......................... 14.23
100C........................... 2.17
103A........................... 2.12
108(3)................... 2.1, 19.15
109............................. 4.15
109(3A).......................... 4.15
Sch 1A....... 4.19, 9.23, 9.24, 9.25
para 3(a) 9.25
5 .... 9.25
**Town and Country Planning
Acts** 12.20
**Tribunals, Courts and
Enforcement Act 2007** 2.31

Table of Statutory Instruments and Codes of Guidance

[All references are to paragraph number]

Business Premises Renovation
Allowances Regulations 2007,
SI 2007/945 .... 6.87
Capital Allowances
(Energy-Saving Plant and
Machinery) (Amendment)
Order 2007, SI 2007/2165 ..... 6.25
Capital Allowances
(Environmentally Beneficial
Plant And Machinery)
Order 2003, SI 2003/2076 ..... 6.25
Capital Allowances
(Environmentally Beneficial
Plant And Machinery)
(Amendment) Order 2006,
SI 2006/2235 .... 6.25
Capital Allowances (Leases of
Background Plant or
Machinery for a Building)
Order 2007, SI 2007/303 .... 6.62
Community Investment Tax Relief
(Accreditation of Community
Development Finance
Institutions) (Amendment)
Regulations 2008,
SI 2008/383 .... 12.47
Community Investment Tax Relief
(Accreditation of Community
Development Finance
Institutions) Regulations 2003,
2003/96 .... 12.47
Companies (Tables A-F)
Regulations 1985, SI 1985/805
reg 82 .... 5.16
Table A 16.9
arts 102, 103 .... 4.18, 16.9
Companies Act 1985 (Accounts
of Small and Medium-Sized
Enterprises and Audit
Exemption) (Amendment)
Regulations 2004, SI 2004/16 . 6.22

Companies Act 1985
(International Accounting
Standards and Other
Accounting Amendments)
Regulations 2004,
SI 2004/2947 .... 1.7

Controlled Foreign Companies
(Excluded Countries)
Regulations 1998,
SI 1998/3081
Pt II 13.41
reg 4 .... 13.41
reg 5 .... 13.39, 13.41

Corporation Tax (Finance Leasing
of Intangible Assets)
Regulations 2002,
SI 2002/1967 .... 7.31

Corporation Tax (Implementation
of the Mergers Directive)
Regulations 2007,
SI 2007/3186 .... 15.26

Corporation Tax (Instalment
Payments) Regulations 1998,
SI 1998/3175 .... 3.10
reg 6 .... 10.18, 10.19
reg 7 .... 3.20
reg 8 .... 3.20
reg 9 .... 10.18
reg 9(5C) 10.18
reg 9(5D) 10.18
reg 9(5E) 10.18
reg 10, 11 .... 10.19

Corporation Tax (Instalment
Payments) (Amendment)
Regulations 1999,
SI 1999/1929
reg 3 .... 10.18

Corporation Tax (Notice of
Coming Within Charge –
Information)
Regulations 2004,
SI 2004/250 .... 2.2

Corporation Tax (Simplified
Arrangements for Group
Relief) Regulations 1999,
SI 1999/2975 .... 10.16

Corporation Tax (Treatment of
Unrelieved Surplus Advance
Corporation Tax)
Regulations 1999,
SI 1999/358 .... 16.11

Double Taxation Relief
(Surrender of Relievable Tax
Within a Group)
Regulations 2001,
SI 2001/1163 .... 13.25
reg 9 .... 13.25

Education (Student Loans)
(Repayment)
Regulations 2000, SI 2000/944
reg 39(1), (3) 21.12

Energy-Saving Items (Corporation
Tax) Regulations 2008,
SI 2008/1520 .... 12.21

European Communities
(Definition of Treaties)
(Cooperation Agreement
between the European
Community and its Member
States and the Swiss
Confederation to Combat
Fraud) Order 2006,
SI 2006/307 .... 18.15

European Public Limited-Liability
Company Regulations 2004,
SI 2326/2004 .... 1.1

Finance Act 2006, Section 28
(Appointed Day)
Regulations 2008,
SI 2008/1878 .... 8.18

Finance Act 2007, Section 17(2)
(Corporation Tax deduction for
Expenditure on Energy-Saving
Items) (Appointed Day)
Order 2008, SI 2008/1520 .... 12.21

Finance Act 2008, Section 2
(Appointed Day) Order 2008,
SI 2008/1933 .... 8.20, 8.21

Finance Act 2008, Section 27
(Appointed Day) Order 2008,
SI 2008/1830 .... 8.13

Finance Act 2008, Section 28
(Appointed Day) Order 2008,
SI 2008/1929 .... 8.30

Finance Act 2008, Section 29
(Appointed Day) Order 2008,
SI 2008/1928 .... 8.22

Finance Act 2008, Section 30
(Appointed Day) Order 2008,
SI 2008/1925 .... 8.31

Financial Reporting Standards ... 1.10
FRS 1 Cash flow statements ... 17.5
FRS 2 Accounting for
subsidiary undertakings ... 10.1,
17.5
FRS 3 Reporting financial
performance 17.5, 17.20,
17.28
FRS 4 Capital instruments 11.9,
17.5
FRS 5 Reporting the Substance
of Transactions 1.10, 1.13,
17.5, 17.18
note G 17.18
FRS 6 Acquisitions and
mergers 17.5
FRS 7 Fair values in
acquisition accounting 7.15,
17.5
FRS 8 Related party
disclosures 17.5
FRS 9 Associates and joint
ventures 17.5
FRS 10 Goodwill and
intangible assets 7.6, 17.5,
17.17
FRS 11 Impairment of fixed
assets and goodwill 17.5
FRS 12 Provisions, contingent
liabilities and contingent
assets ... 5.16, 5.20, 17.5, 17.15
para 14 .... 17.16
para 19 .... 17.16
para 23 .... 17.16

Financial Reporting Standards – *contd*
FRS 12 Provisions, contingent
   liabilities and contingent assets –
   contd
   para 73 .... 17.16
FRS 13 Derivatives and other
   financial instruments:
   disclosures 7.7, 17.5
FRS 14 Earnings per share 17.5
FRS 15 Tangible fixed assets ... 6.1,
                 17.5, 17.13, 17.14
   para 97 .... 17.13
FRS 16 Current tax 17.5, 17.28,
                        17.29
FRS 17 Retirement benefits ... 17.5,
                        17.21
FRS 18 Accounting Policies ... 1.10,
              1.13, 17.5, 17.12
   para 26 .... 17.12
FRS 19 Deferred tax ... 17.5, 17.30,
            17.31, 17.32, 17.33,
            17.34, 17.35, 17.36,
                      17.38
   para 23 .... 17.37
   para 47 .... 17.36
   para 52 .... 17.36
FRS 20 Share-based payment . 5.26,
                      17.5
FRS 21 Events after the
   balance sheet date .. 5.16, 5.20,
               17.5, 17.11
FRS 22 Earnings per share 17.5
FRS 23 The effects of changes
   in foreign exchange rates . 17.5,
                   17.10
FRS 24 Financial reporting in
   hyperinflationary
   economies 17.5
FRS 25 Financial instruments:
   disclosure and
   presentation 11.9, 17.5
FRS 26 Financial instruments:
   measurement 11.9, 11.28,
            11.33, 11.36, 17.5,
                    17.9
FRS 27 Life assurance 17.5
FRS 28 Corresponding
   amounts 17.5

Financial Reporting Standards – *contd*
FRS 29 Financial instruments:
   disclosures 17.5
Financial reporting standard for
   smaller entities FRSSE (2002,
   2005) .. 1.10, 1.12, 6.1, 11.9, 11.11,
             11.28, 17.1, 17.5,
                    17.8
General Insurance Reserves (Tax)
   (Amendment)
   Regulations 2005,
   SI 2005/3289 .... 17.16
HMRC
A Modern System for
   Corporation Tax Payment.
   A Guide to Quarterly
   Instalment Payments
   (CTSA/BK3) 3.13
Application for a Group
   Payment Arrangement –
   Notes for Guidance 3.21
Business Income Manual
   BIM 31019 .... 1.12
   BIM 31032 .... 1.13
   BIM 31040 .... 1.13
   BIM 31047 .... 1.13
   BIM 31055 .... 1.13
   BIM 31060 .... 17.13
   BIM 31070 .... 17.13
   BIM 35000 .... 5.10
   BIM 35510 .... 5.20
   BIM 35595 .... 5.20
   BIM 37840 .... 5.20
   BIM 38220 .... 5.20
   BIM 38230 .... 5.20
   BIM 40070 .... 5.7
   BIM 42060 .... 5.20
   BIM 42070 .... 5.20
   BIM 42140 .... 5.20, 12.6
   BIM 42510 .... 5.20
   BIM 42515 .... 5.20
   BIM 42531 .... 5.20
   BIM 42540 .... 5.20
   BIM 42551 .... 5.20
   BIM 42555 .... 5.20
   BIM 42560 .... 5.20
   BIM 42565 .... 5.20
   BIM 42601 .... 5.20
   BIM 42605 .... 5.20

HMRC – *contd*
  Business Income Manual – *contd*
    BIM 42701 .... 5.20
    BIM 42710 .... 5.20
    BIM 42720 .... 5.20
    BIM 42730 .... 5.20
    BIM 42740 .... 5.20
    BIM 42750 .... 5.20
    BIM 42950+ 5.20
    BIM 43100+ 5.20
    BIM 43101 .... 5.20
    BIM 43105 .... 5.20
    BIM 43115 .... 5.20
    BIM 43160 .... 5.20
    BIM 43250 .... 5.20
    BIM 43251 .... 5.20
    BIM 43255 .... 5.20
    BIM 43260 .... 5.20
    BIM 43265 .... 5.20
    BIM 44000+ 5.20
    BIM 44155 .... 5.30
    BIM 44270 .... 5.20
    BIM 44290 .... 5.26
    BIM 44295 .... 5.26
    BIM 44350 .... 5.20
    BIM 44450 .... 5.26
    BIM 44501+ 5.30
    BIM 44550 .... 5.30
    BIM 45032 .... 5.20
    BIM 45070 .... 5.20
    BIM 45071 .... 5.20
    BIM 45072 .... 5.20
    BIM 45080 .... 5.20
    BIM 45101 .... 5.20
    BIM 45301 .... 5.20
    BIM 45305 .... 5.20
    BIM 45351 .... 5.20
    BIM 45355 .... 5.20
    BIM 45360 .... 5.20
    BIM 45365 .... 5.20
    BIM 45451 .... 5.20
    BIM 45455 .... 5.20
    BIM 45501 .... 5.20
    BIM 45505 .... 5.20
    BIM 45510 .... 5.20
    BIM 45515 .... 5.20
    BIM 45520 .... 5.20
    BIM 45525 .... 5.20
    BIM 45530 .... 5.20
    BIM 45755 .... 5.20

HMRC – *contd*
  Business Income Manual – *contd*
    BIM 45850+ 5.20
    BIM 45901 .... 5.20
    BIM 45905 .... 5.20
    BIM 46015 .... 5.31
    BIM 46210 .... 5.20
    BIM 46251 .... 5.20
    BIM 46255 .... 5.20
    BIM 46260 .... 5.20
    BIM 46265 .... 5.20
    BIM 46351 .... 5.20
    BIM 46405 .... 5.20
    BIM 46410 .... 5.20
    BIM 46415 .... 5.20
    BIM 46420 .... 5.20
    BIM 46450 .... 5.20
    BIM 46452 .... 5.20
    BIM 46460 .... 5.20
    BIM 46510+ 5.20
    BIM 46515 .... 17.15
    BIM 46535 .... 17.15
    BIM 46545 .... 17.15
    BIM 46801+ 5.20
    BIM 46900 .... 5.20
    BIM 46904 .... 5.20
    BIM 47001 .... 5.20
    BIM 47080 .... 5.20
    BIM 47115 .... 5.20
    BIM 47120 .... 5.20
    BIM 47200+ 5.20
    BIM 47301+ 5.20
    BIM 47400+ 5.20
    BIM 47600+ 5.20
    BIM 47610 .... 5.20
    BIM 47205 .... 5.20
    BIM 47210 .... 5.20
    BIM 47215 .... 5.20
    BIM 47705 .... 5.20
    BIM 47710 .... 5.20
    BIM 47715 .... 5.20
    BIM 47715–47720 .... 5.20
    BIM 47717 .... 5.20
    BIM 47720 .... 5.20
    BIM 51400 .... 5.20
    BIM 51420 .... 5.20
    BIM 51425 .... 5.20
    BIM 51430 .... 5.20
    BIM 57600–57620 .... 5.20

HMRC – *contd*

Capital Allowances Manual

CA 11140	6.4
CA 11520	6.92
CA 11800	6.5
CA 20070	6.8
CA 21010	6.11
CA 21100	6.10
CA 21120	6.10
CA 21130	6.10
CA 21140	6.11
CA 21190	6.12
CA 21880	6.11
CA 22070	6.11
CA 22080	6.11
CA 23115	6.29
CA 23135	6.25
CA 23110	6.23
CA 23170	6.22
CA 23350	6.40
CA 26150	6.30
CA 31050	6.65
CA 31110	6.65
CA 31400	6.71
CA 31410	6.71
CA 32210	6.67
CA 32224	6.52
CA 32800	6.79
CA 37600	6.73, 6.82
CA 60400	8.5
CA 60750	8.9

Capital Gains Tax Manual

CG 33920A	16.16
CG 52720/1	16.16

Code of Practice COP 9
suspected fraud (2005) 2.33

Code of Practice 10
information and advice .. 11.15

Code of Practice COP 14
corporation tax self
assessment enquiries 2.16,
2.24, 2.25

Company Taxation Manual

CTM 01405	2.6
CTM 03750	4.28, 4.31
CTM 03770	4.31
CTM 03810	4.32
CTM 04150	9.5
CTM 04200	9.10

HMRC – *contd*

Company Taxation Manual – *contd*

CTM 04510	9.14
CTM 04540	9.12
CTM 04550	9.13
CTM 04250	9.9
CTM 06020	15.17
CTM 06030	15.18
CTM 06060	15.19, 15.22
CTM 08040	12.3
CTM 08050	12.3
CTM 08260	12.8
CTM 08320	12.9
CTM 08420	12.8
CTM 20095	4.18, 16.9
CTM 36220	19.14
CTM 60780	19.16
CTM 61515	4.16
CTM 61520	4.16
CTM 61525	4.16
CTM 61535	4.17
CTM 61540	4.17, 4.21
CTM 61550	4.18
CTM 61605	4.18
CTM 61670	4.21
CTM 61680	4.21
CTM 90625	9.23
CTM 90650	9.26
CTM 90665	9.26
CTM 92110	9.27
CTM 92440	10.17
CTM 92740	10.18

Corporate Finance Manual

CFM 5151	11.28
CFM 5203a	11.11
CFM 5210	11.23
CFM 5230	11.24
CFM 5230a	11.24
CFM 5230b	11.24
CFM 5421c	11.29
CFM 6214	11.12
CFM 6215a	11.13
CFM 6216a	11.15
CFM 6224	11.14
CFM 6228	11.15
CFM 16025	11.28
CFM 16025a	11.29

HMRC – *contd*
Corporate Intangibles Research
and Development Manual
CIRD 10145 .... 7.4
CIRD 60130 .... 8.34
CIRD 60135 .... 8.36
CIRD 81200 .... 8.10
CIRD 81300 .... 8.11
CIRD 81900 – R&D tax
relief: conditions to be
satisfied: DTI guidelines
(2004) – text 8.11
CIRD 84100 .... 8.16
CIRD 84200 .... 8.17
CIRD 92850 – flowchart 8.10
Disclosure of Tax Avoidance
Schemes, June 2006 .... 18.7
Double Taxation Relief Manual
DT 2150 *et seq* 13.15
Employment Income Manual
EIM 42290 .... 5.16
EIM 42300 .... 5.16
Enquiry Manual
EM 8205 .... 2.18
EM 8207 .... 2.18
EM 8210 .... 2.18
EM 8211 .... 2.19
EM 8215 .... 2.27
EM 8565 .... 4.18
Extra Statutory Concessions
ESC 16 .... 16.26, 16.28, 19.14
ESC C9 .... 4.31, 4.32
Guidance: *The Corporate*
Venturing Scheme:
www.hmrc.gov.uk/guidance/t2s43
Insolvency Manual
INS 1203 .... 19.4
INS 1520 .... 19.10
International Manual
INTM 120070 .... 13.2
INTM 164130 .... 13.18
INTM 432112 .... 14.11
INTM 432114 .... 14.11
INTM 542010 .... 14.28
INTM 574000 .... 14.30
INTM 4340200 .... 14.36
Investigations Handbook 5525 ......
14.24
IR 160 .... 2.16, 2.24, 14.24

HMRC – *contd*
IR Statements of Practice
SP 13/80 .... 16.14, 16.15
SP 5/94 .... 4.31
SP 4/07 .... 14.30
Property Income Manual
PIM 2205 .... 12.20
PIM 4300 .... 12.22
Tax Bulletin
Issue 10 .... 12.22
Issue 37 October 1998 ...... 14.24
Issue 38 December 1998 ... 14.24
Issue 58 April 2002 .... 17.2
Income and Corporation Tax
(Electronic Communications)
Regulations 2003,
SI 2003/282 .... 2.10
Income Tax (Construction
Industry Scheme)
(Amendment No. 2)
Regulations 2008,
SI 2008/1282 .... 21.28
Income Tax (Construction
Industry Scheme)
Regulations 2005,
SI 2005/2045
reg 5 .... 21.5
reg 7 .... 21.10, 21.12
reg.8 .... 21.12
reg 9–11, 13–17 .... 21.10
reg 18, 19 .... 21.8
reg 20 .... 21.2
reg 22 .... 21.5
reg 25 .... 21.13
reg 46–49 .... 21.11
Income Tax (Pay As You Earn)
Regulations 2003,
SI 2003/2682
reg 68 .... 21.12
International Accounting
Standards 1.9, 1.10, 11.9, 17.1,
17.4
IAS 1 Presentation of financial
statements 17.6, 17.19
IAS 2 Inventories . 5.38, 17.6, 17.24
IAS 7 Cash flow statements 17.6

International Accounting Standards – *contd*

IAS 8 Accounting policies, changes in accounting estimates and errors 17.6, 17.20

IAS 10 Events after the balance sheet date 17.5, 17.6, 17.11

IAS 11 Construction contracts 17.6, 17.24

IAS 12 Income taxes ... 17.6, 17.29, 17.38, 17.39

IAS 14 Segment reporting 17.6

IAS 16 Property, plant and equipment 6.1, 17.6, 17.13

IAS 17 Leases 17.6, 17.22

IAS 18 Revenue ... 5.42, 17.6, 17.18

IAS 19 Employee benefits 17.6, 17.21

IAS 20 Accounting for government grants and disclosure of government assistance 17.6, 17.25

IAS 21 The effects of changes in foreign exchange rates . 17.5, 17.6, 17.10

IAS 23 Borrowing costs 17.6, 17.14

IAS 24 Related party disclosure 17.6

IAS 26 Accounting and reporting by retirement benefit plans 17.6

IAS 27 Consolidated and separate financial statements 17.6

IAS 28 Investments in associates 17.6

IAS 29 Financial reporting in hyperinflationary economies 17.5, 17.6

IAS 31 Interests in joint ventures 17.6

IAS 32 Financial instruments: presentation 11.9, 17.5, 17.6

IAS 33 Earnings per share 17.5, 17.6

IAS 34 Interim financial reporting 17.6

International Accounting Standards – *contd*

IAS 36 Impairment of assets ... 17.6

IAS 37 Provisions, contingent liabilities and contingent assets 17.6, 17.15

IAS 38 Intangible assets .. 8.3, 8.11, 17.6, 17.17

IAS 39 Financial instruments: recognition and measurement 11.9, 11.28, 11.33, 11.36, 17.5, 17.6, 17.9

IAS 40 Investment property 6.1, 17.6, 17.23

IAS 41 Agriculture 17.6

International Financial Reporting Standards 1.9, 1.10

IFRS 1 First-time adoption of international financial reporting standards 17.6, 17.17, 17.26

IFRS 2 Share-based payments . 17.5, 17.6

IFRS 3 Business combinations . 17.6

IFRS 4 Insurance contracts 17.6

IFRS 5 Non-current assets held for sale and discontinued operations 17.6

IFRS 6 Exploration for and evaluation of mineral assets 17.6

IFRS 7 Financial instruments disclosures 17.5, 17.6

IFRS 8 Operating Segments 17.6

Large And Medium-Sized Companies And Groups (Accounts And Reports) Regulations 2008, SI 2008/410 .... 5.39, 6.1, 7.6, 12.8

Loan Relationships and Derivative Contracts (Disregard and Bringing into Account of Profits and Losses) (Amendment No. 2) Regulations 2007, SI 2007/3431 .... 11.36

Loan Relationships and Derivative
Contracts (Disregard and
Bringing into Account of
Profits and Losses)
Regulations 2004,
SI 2004/3256
reg 3 .... 14.20

Loan Relationships and Derivative
Contracts (Disregard and
Bringing into Account of
Profits and Losses)
(Amendment) Regulations,
SI 2005/2012 .... 11.36

Loan Relationships and Derivative
Contracts (Disregard and
Bringing into Account of
Profits and Losses)
Regulations 2006, SI 2006/843
reg 5 .... 14.19

Loan Relationships and Derivative
Contracts (Disregard and
Bringing into Account of
Profits and Losses)
(Amendment)
Regulations 2006, SI 2006/936
reg 5 .... 14.19

Pensions (Northern Ireland)
Order 1995, SI1995/3213
art 75 .... 5.40

Police and Criminal Evidence
Act 1984 (Application to
Revenue and Customs)
Order 2007, SI 2007/3175 ..... 2.35

Small Companies and Groups
(Accounts and Directors'
Report) Regulations 2008,
SI 2008/409 .... 5.39, 6.1, 12.8

**Statements of Standard
Accounting Practice** 1.10
SSAP 4 Accounting for
government grants . 17.5, 17.25
SSAP 5 Accounting for value
added tax 17.5
SSAP 9 Stocks and long-term
contracts 5.37, 5.40, 5.41,
17.5, 17.15, 17.24
para 22 .... 17.24
App 1 paras 19, 20 .... 17.24

**Statements of Standard Accounting
Practice** – *contd*
SSAP 13 Accounting for
research and development . 8.3,
8.11, 17.5, 17.17
SSAP 17 Accounting for post
balance sheet events 1.13,
17.5, 17.11
SSAP 19 Accounting for
investment properties 6.1,
17.5, 17.23
SSAP 20 Foreign currency
translation 14.20, 17.5
SSAP 21 Accounting for lease
and hire purchase
contracts 17.5, 17.15, 17.22
SSAP 24 Accounting for
pension costs 17.5, 17.15,
17.21
SSAP 25 Segmental reporting .. 17.5

Statutory Maternity Pay
(Compensation of Employers)
Amendment Regulations 1994,
SI 1994/592
reg 4–6 .... 21.11

Statutory Paternity Pay and
Statutory Adoption Pay
(Administration)
Regulations 2002,
SI 2002/2820
reg 3, 5 .... 21.11

Tax Avoidance Schemes
(Prescribed Descriptions of
Arrangements)
Regulations 2006,
SI 2006/1543 .... 18.6, 18.9

Tax Avoidance Schemes
(Prescribed Descriptions of
Arrangements)
Regulations 2004,
SI 2004/1863 .... 18.6

Tax Avoidance Schemes
(Information)
Regulations 2004,
SI 2004/1864 .... 18.6
para 5 .... 18.12

Tax Avoidance Schemes
(Promoters, Prescribed
Circumstances and
Information) (Amendment)
Regulations 2004,
SI 2004/2613 .... 18.6
Tax Avoidance Schemes
(Information) (Amendment)
Regulations 2005,
SI 2005/1869 .... 18.6
Tax Avoidance Schemes
(Information) (Amendment)
Regulations 2006,
SI 2006/1544 .... 18.6
Tax Avoidance Schemes
(Promoters and Prescribed
Circumstances)
Regulations 2004,
SI 2004/1865 .... 18.6
Tax Information Exchange
Agreement (Taxes on Income)
(Jersey) Order 2005,
SI 2005/1261 .... 18.15
Tax Information Exchange
Agreement (Taxes on Income)
(Guernsey) Order 2005,
SI 2005/1262 .... 18.15
Tax Information Exchange
Agreement (Taxes on Income)
(Isle of Man) Order 2005,
SI 2005/1263 .... 18.15
Tax Information Exchange
Agreement (Taxes on Income)
(Virgin Islands) Order 2005,
SI 2005/1457 .... 18.15

Tax Information Exchange
Agreement (Taxes on Income)
(Aruba) Order 2005,
SI 2005/1458 .... 18.15
Tax Information Exchange
Agreement (Taxes on Income)
(Montserrat) Order 2005,
SI 2005/1459 .... 18.15
Tax Information Exchange
Agreement (Taxes on Income)
(Netherlands Antilles)
Order 2005, SI 2005/1460 .... 18.15
Taxes (Interest Rate)
Regulations 1989,
SI 1989/1297
reg 3ZA 3.18
reg 3ZB 3.18
Taxes (Interest Rate) (Amendment
No 2) Regulations 1998,
SI 1998/3176
reg 6 .... 3.18
UITF Abstracts 17.1, 17.4, 17.8
UITF Abstract 40 .. 5.40, 5.41, 5.42,
17.18
UK GAAP 1.8, 1.10, 1.12, 1.13, 5.3,
5.16, 5.20, 5.23,
5.25, 5.37, 5.41,
6.1, 7.6, 8.3, 8.11,
8.16, 8.17, 10.1,
11.9, 11.24, 17.1,
17.2, 17.4, 17.8,
17.10, 17.16, 17.17,
17.26

Table of European Legislation

[All references are to paragraph number]

Commission Recommendation 2003/361/EC concerning the definition of
    micro, small and medium-sized enterprises OJ (2003) L124/36 . 8.18, 14.7, 14.8
Directive 90/434EEC 15.26
Directive 2005/19/EC 15.26
EC Press Release of 10.11.2005 – MEMO/05/414 Code of Conduct on
    transfer pricing documentation in the EU – Frequently Asked Questions .. 14.25
EC Press Release of 10.11.2005 – IP/05/1403 Company taxation: Commission
    adopts Code of Conduct concerning transfer pricing 14.25
Regulation (EC) 1606/2002 of the European Parliament and of the Council of
    19 July 2002 on the application of international accounting standards 17.1
Regulation (EC) 1893/2006 .... 6.50
EC Treaty (Treaty of Rome)
    Art 43 .... 10.9, 13.28
    Art 48 .... 10.9, 13.28
    Art 49 .... 8.27
OECD Model Tax Convention 14.6
    Art 7(2) 13.8
    Art 9 .... 14.1, 14.5
OECD Transfer Pricing Guidelines
    Ch V 14.25

Table of Cases

Allen v Farquharson Bros & Co (1932) 17 TC 59, KBD 5.20

Allum v Marsh (Inspector of Taxes) SpC 446 [2005] STC (SCD) 191, Sp
  Comm 16.20

Anglo-Persian Oil Co Ltd v Dale (Inspector of Taxes) (1931) 16 TC 253,
  [1932] 1 KB 124, [1931] All ER Rep 725, CA 5.20

Atherton (Inspector of Taxes) v British Insulated & Helsby Cables Ltd
  (1925) 10 TC 155, [1926] AC 205, [1925] All ER Rep 623, HL 5.10, 5.20,
                                                                                            5.39

Ayerst v C & K (Construction) Ltd (1975) 50 TC 651, [1975] STC 345,
  [1976] AC 167, [1975] 2 All ER 537, HL 19.12

Baldwins Industrial Services plc v Barr Ltd [2003] BLR 176 .... 6.31

Balloon Promotions Ltd v HMRC [2006] SpC 524 .... 7.6

Bamford v ATA Advertising (1972) 48 TC 359, [1972] 1 WLR 1261,
  [1972] 3 All ER 535 .... 5.20

Bank Line Ltd v CIR (1974) 49 TC 307, [1974] STC 342; sub nom Bank
  Line Ltd v Lord Advocate [1974] TR 115, Ct of Sess 9.9

Beauchamp v F W Woolworth (1989) 61 TC 542, [1989] STC 510,
  [1989] 3 WLR 1 .... 5.10

Ben-Odeco Ltd v Powlson (1978) 52 TC 459, [1978] STC 460,
  [1978] 1 WLR 1093, [1978] 2 All ER 1111 .... 6.8

Benson v Yard Arm Club Ltd (1979) 53 TC 67, [1979] 1 WLR 347,
  [1979] 2 All ER 336 .... 6.10, 6.18

Bentleys, Stokes and Lowless v Beeson (1952) 33 TC 491, [1952] WN
  280, [1952] 2 All ER 82 .... 5.14

Bestway (Holdings) Ltd v Luff (Inspector of Taxes) (1998) 70 TC 512,
  [1998] STC 357, [1998] BTC 69, ChD 6.69

Bolam v Regent Oil Co Ltd (1956) 37 TC 56, [1956] TR 403, 35 ATC
  499 .... 5.20

Bolands Ltd v Davis (1925) I ITC 91, (1925) 4 ATC 532 .... 9.3

Bourne v Norwich Crematorium Ltd (1967) 44 TC 164, [1967] 1 WLR
  691, [1967] 2 All ER 576 .... 6.68

Brennan (Inspector of Taxes) v Denby Investment Co Ltd (2001) 73 TC
  455, [2001] STC 536, CA (NI) 4.16

Bristow v Dickson (William) & Co Ltd (1946) 27 TC 157, [1946] KB 321,
  [1946] 1 All ER 448 .... 5.20

Briton Ferry Steel Co Ltd v Barry (1939) 23 TC 414, [1940] 1 KB 463,
  [1939] 4 All ER 541 .... 15.21

Brown v Burnley Football & Athletic Co Ltd (1980) 53 TC 357,
  [1980] STC 424, [1980] 3 All ER 244 .... 5.10, 5.20

Buckingham v Securitas Properties Ltd (1979) 53 TC 292, [1980] STC
  166, [1980] 1 WLR 380 .... 6.68

CIR v Alexander von Glehn & Co Ltd (1920) 12 TC 232, [1920] 2 KB
  553, 123 LT 338, KBD 5.20

Table of Cases

CIR v Lambhill Ironworks Ltd (1950) 31 TC 393, [1950] TR 145, 1950
SLT 251 .... 6.71
CIR v Scottish & Newcastle Breweries Ltd (1982) 55 TC 252, [1982] STC
296, [1982] 1 WLR 322, [1982] 2 All ER 230 .... 6.10, 6.11, 6.18
CIR v Williams' Executor (1944) 26 TC 23 .... 5.20
CIR v Willoughby (1997) 70 TC 57, [1997] STC 995, [1997] 1 WLR
1071, HL 18.2
Cadbury Schweppes plc v Inland Revenue Commissioners (Case-196/04)
[2007] Ch 30, [2006] 3 WLR 890 .... 13.28
Cape Brandy Syndicate v CIR (1921) 12 TC 358, [1921] 2 KB 403, CA 5.6
Capital and National Trust Ltd v Golder (1949) 31 TC 265,
[1949] 2 All ER 956, [1949] TR 359, CA 12.8
Carr (Inspector of Taxes) v Sayer & Sayer (1992) 65 TC 15, [1992] STC
396, [1992] STI 458, ChD 6.68
Celtic Football and Athletic Club Ltd v Customs & Excise Commrs
[1983] STC 470, Ct of Sess 5.14
Centaur Clothes Group Ltd v Walker (2000) 72 TC 379, [2000] STC 324,
[2000] 1 WLR 799, [2000] 2 All ER 589, HL 5.1
Coates v Arndale Properties Ltd (1984) 59 TC 516, [1984] STC 637,
[1984] 1 WLR 1328, [1985] 1 All ER 15). 20.19
Cole Bros v Phillips [1982] STC 307, [1982] 1 WLR 1450,
[1982] 2 All ER 247, 55 TC 188 .... 6.11, 6.18
Coltness Iron Co v Black [1881] 6 AC 315, 1 TC 287, HL 6.2
Cooke v Beach Station Caravans Ltd (1974) 49 TC 514, [1974] STC 402,
[1974] 1 WLR 1398, [1974] 3 All ER 159 .... 6.18
Copeman (Inspector of Taxes) v William Flood & Sons Ltd (1940) 24 TC
53, [1941] KB 202, KBD 5.15
Copol Clothing Ltd v Hindmarsh (1983) 57 TC 575, [1984] STC 33,
[1984] 1 WLR 411 .... 6.70
Craven v White (1988) 62 TC 1, [1988] STC 476, [198] 1 AC 398, HL 18.2
Crusabridge Investments Ltd v Casings International Ltd (1979) 54 TC
246, ChD 6.70
Curtis v Oldfield (J & G) Ltd (1925) 9 TC 319, (1925) 94 LJKB 655, 133
LT 229 .... 5.20
Darngavil Coal Co Ltd v Francis (Surveyor of Taxes) (1913) 7 TC 1, 1913
SC 602, Ct of Sess (1 Div) 5.20
DCC Holdings (UK) Ltd v Revenue and Customs Comrs [2007] STC
(SCD) 592, [2007] STI 1649, SpC 611 .... 11.37
Dispit Ltd v Revenue and Customs Comrs [2007] STC (SCD) 194, [2007]
STI 349, SpC 579 .... 5.12
Dixon v Fitch's Garages Ltd (1975) 50 TC 509, [1975] STC 480,
[1976] 1 WLR 215, [1975] 3 All ER 455 .... 6.18
Duke of Westminster v CIR (1935) 19 TC 490, [1936] All ER 1,
[1935] All ER Rep 259, HL 18.2
Duomatic Ltd, Re [1969] 2 Ch 365, [1969] 2 WLR 114, [1969] 1 All ER
161 .... 5.16
E Bott Ltd v Price (Inspector of Taxes) (1986) 59 TC 437, [1987] STC
100, ChD 5.30
ECC Quarries Ltd v Watkis (1975) 51 TC 153, [1975] STC 578,
[1975] 3 All ER 843 .... 5.20

Earlspring Properties Ltd v Guest (Inspector of Taxes) (1995) 67 TC 259,
  [1995] STC 479, [1995] STI 433, CA 5.20
Ellerker (Inspector of Taxes) v Union Cold Storage Co Ltd; Thomas
  Borthwick & Sons Ltd v Compton (Inspector of Taxes) (1938) 22 TC
  195, [1939] 1 All ER 23, KBD 6.67
Ensign Tankers (Leasing) Ltd v Stokes (Inspector of Taxes) (1992) 64 TC
  617, [1992] STC 226, [1992] 1 AC 655, HL 18.2
Executive Network (Consultants) Ltd v O'Connor [1996] STC (SCD) 29,
  Sp Comm 5.20
Falmer Jeans Ltd v Rodin (Inspector of Taxes) (1990) 63 TC 55,
  [1990] STC 270 .... 15.21
Farmer (Inspector of Taxes) v Bankers Trust International Ltd
  (1990) 64 TC 1, [1990] STC 564, ChD 10.16
Felix Hadley & Co v Hadley (1897) 77 LT 131 .... 5.16
Ferribly Construction (UK) Ltd v Revenue & Customs Commissioners
  (2007) SpC 635 .... 2.16
Fleming v Associated Newspapers Ltd (1972) 48 TC 382, [1973] AC 628,
  [1972] 2 All ER 574 .... 5.14
Furniss (Inspector of Taxes) v Dawson (1984) 55 TC 324, [1984] STC
  153, [1984] 1 AC 474, HL 18.2
Garforth v Tankard Carpets Ltd (1980) 53 TC 342, [1980] STC 251,
  (1980) TR 29 .... 5.20
Gascoignes Group Ltd v Inspector of Taxes [2004] EWHC 640 (Ch),
  [2004] STC 844, 76 TC 623, ChD 4.31
Gaspet Ltd v Ellis (1987) 60 TC 91, [1987] STC 362, [1987] 1 WLR 769 .... 8.4
George Wimpey International Ltd v Rolfe (Inspector of Taxes)
  (1989) 62 TC 597, [1989] STC 609, ChD 13.15
Girobank plc v Clarke (1997) 70 TC 387, [1998] STC 182, [1998] 1 WLR
  942, [1998] 4 All ER 312 .... 6.68
Golder v Great Boulder Proprietary Gold Mines Ltd; IRC v Same
  (1952) 33 TC 75, [1952] 1 All ER 360, 31 ATC 61 .... 5.20
Gordon & Blair Ltd v CIR (1962) 40 TC 358, 1962 SC 267, 41 ATC 111 .... 9.3
Grant (Andrew) Services Ltd v Watton (Inspector of Taxes) (1999) 71 TC
  333, [1999] STC 330, [1999] BTC 85, ChD 4.16, 4.17
Gray (Inspector of Taxes) v Penrhyn (Lord) (1937) 21 TC 252,
  [1937] 3 All ER 468, KBD 5.20
Grays (Inspector of Taxes) v Seymours Garden Centre (Horticulture)
  (1995) 67 TC 401, [1995] STC 706, [1995] EGCS 99, CA 6.18
Green (Inspector of Taxes) v Gliksten (J) & Son Ltd (1929) 14 TC 364,
  [1929] AC 381, [1929] All ER Rep 383, HL 5.20
Gresham Life Assurance Society v Styles (1890) 2 TC 633, (1890) 3 TC
  185, [1892] AC 309 .... 5.20
Greycon Ltd v Klaentschi (Inspector of Taxes) [2003] STC (SCD) 370, Sp
  Comm 5.20
HMRC v Salaried Persons Postal Loans Ltd [2006] EWHC 763 (Ch),
  [2006] STC 1315, ChD 4.30
Hampton v Fortes Autogrill Ltd (1979) 53 TC 691, [1980] STC 80, (1979)
  TR 691 .... 6.18
Harding v Revenue and Customs Comrs [2008] EWHC 99 (Ch),
  [2008] STC 1965, [2008] BTC 109 .... 11.5

Table of Cases

Harrods (Buenos Aires) Ltd v Taylor-Gooby (1964) 41 TC 450, 108 SJ
117, [1964] TR 9, CA 5.20
Heather v P-E Consulting Group Ltd (1972) 48 TC 293, [1973] Ch 189,
[1973] 1 All ER 8 .... 5.10, 5.30
Hinton v Madden & Ireland Ltd (1959) 38 TC 391, [1959] 1 WLR 875,
[1959] 3 ALL ER 356 .... 6.10, 6.18
Hoechst AG Case C-410/98 .... 18.27
Hong Kong Commissioner of Inland Revenue v Cosmotron
Manufacturing Co (1997) 70 TC 292, [1997] STC 1134, [1997] 1 WLR
1288 .... 5.20
Hughes de Lasteyrie du Saillant v Minisère de l'économie, des Finances et
de l'Industrie Case C-902/02 .... 13.12
Hyett v Lennard (1940) 23 TC 346, [1940] 2 KB 180, [1940] 3 All ER
133 .... 5.20
J Lyons and Co Ltd v Attorney-General [1944] Ch 281, [1944] 1 All ER
477, 113 LJ Ch 196, ChD 6.10, 6.18
Jade Palace Ltd v Revenue and Customs Comrs [2006] STC (SCD) 419,
[2006] STI 1623, SpC 540 .... 2.27
Jarrold v John Good & Sons Ltd (1962) 40 TC 681, [1963] 1 WLR 214,
[1963] 1 All ER 141 .... 6.10, 6.18
Jeffs v Ringtons Ltd (1985) 58 TC 680, [1985] STC 809, [1986] 1 WLR
266, [1986] 1 All ER 144 .... 5.30
JG Ingram & Sons Ltd v Callaghan (1968) 45 TC 151, [1969] 1 WLR 456,
[1969] 1 All ER 433 .... 9.3
Jones v Garnett (Inspector of Taxes) [2005] EWHC 849 (Ch), [2005] STC
1667, [2005] All ER (D) 396 (Apr), ChD 18.26
Jowett (Inspector of Taxes) v O'Neill and Brennan Construction Ltd
[1998] STC 482, 70 TC 566, [1998] BTC 133, ChD 4.30, 12.10
Kawthar Consulting Ltd v HMRC. See Netlogic Consulting Ltd v HMRC;
Kawthar Consulting Ltd v HMRC
Kealy v O'Mara (Limerick) Ltd [1942] 21 TC 265; [1942] IR 616 .... 5.20
Keir & Cawder Ltd v CIR (1958) 38 TC 23 .... 5.20
Kilmarnock Equitable Co-Operative Society Ltd v CIR (1966) 42 TC 675,
[1966] TR 185, 1966 SLT 224 .... 6.69
LG Berry Investments Ltd v Attwooll (1964) 41 TC 547, [1964] 1 WLR
693, [1964] 2 All ER 126 .... 5.15, 12.4
Laboratoire Fournier SA v Direction des Verifications Nationales et
Internationales Case C-39/04, [2006] STC 538, [2005] ECR I-2057,
ECJ 8.27
Law Shipping Co Ltd v CIR (1923) 12 TC 621, 1924 SC 74, Ct of Sess (1
Div) 5.10
Laycock v Freeman Hardy and Willis Ltd (1938) 22 TC 288, [1939] 2 KB
1, [1938] 4 All ER 609 .... 15.21
Leach v Pogson (1962) 40 TC 585, [1962] TR 28, 41 ATC 298 .... 5.6
Leeds Permanent Building Society v Proctor (1982) 56 TC 293,
[1982] STC 821, [1982] 3 All ER 925 .... 6.10, 6.18
Leeming v Jones 1930 [1930] AC 415, 15 TC 333, HL 6.2

Lloyds UDT Finance Ltd v Chartered Finance Trust Holdings plc and
  Others (Britax International GmBH and Another, Pt 20 Defendants)
  [2002] EWCA Civ 806, (2002) 74 TC 662, [2002] STC 956 .... 5.20
MacDonald (Inspector of Taxes) v Dextra Acessories Ltd [2005] UKHL
  47, [2005] STC 1111, [2005] All ER (D) 85 (Jul), HL, ... 5.30
McKnight (Inspector of Taxes) v Sheppard (1999) 71 TC 410, [1999] STC
  669, [1999] 1 WLR 1133, [1999] 3 All ER 491 .... 5.13, 5.20
Malayam Plantations Ltd v Clark (Inspector of Taxes) (1935) 19 TC 314,
  KBD 15.19
Mallandain Investments Ltd v Shadbolt (Inspector of Taxes) (1940) 23 TC
  367, KBD 5.20
Mann Crossman & Paulin Ltd v Compton (1947) 28 TC 410,
  [1947] 1 All ER 742 .... 5.20
Marks & Spencer v David Halsey C-446/03, [2006] STC 237,
  [2006] Ch 184, [2006] All ER (EC) 255, ECJ 10.9, 10.10
Marshall Hus & Partners Ltd v Bolton (1980) 55 TC 539, [1981] STC 18,
  [1980] TR 371, DC 2.6, 9.12
Marson v Morton (1986) 59 TC 59, [1986] STC 463, [1986] 1 WLR
  1343 .... 5.6
Martin v Lowry (Inspector of Taxes) (1926) 11 TC 297, [1927] AC 312, 43
  TLR 116, HL 5.6
Mawsley Machinery Ltd v Robinson [1998] STC (SCD) 236, Sp Comm 5.30
Mesco Properties Ltd, Re (1979) 54 TC 238, [1979] STC 788,
  [1980] 1 WLR 96, [1980] 1 All ER 117 .... 19.15
Milnes v J Beam Group Ltd (1975) 50 TC 675, [1975] STC 487, [1975]
  TR 127, ChD 5.20
Moore (A & G) & Co v Hare (Surveyor of Taxes) (19141) 6 TC 572, 1915
  SC 91, Ct of Sess (1 Div) 5.20
Morgan v Tate & Lyle Ltd (1954) 35 TC 367, [1954] AC 21,
  [1954] 2 All ER 413 .... 5.20
Morley v Lawford & Co (1928) 14 TC 229, 140 LT 125 .... 5.20
Munby v Furlong (1977) 50 TC 491, [1976] 1 WLR 410, [1976] 1 All ER
  753 .... 6.18
National Provident Institution v Brown (Surveyor of Taxes) (1921) 8 TC
  57, [1921] AC 222, 125 LT 417, HL 5.1
Netlogic Consulting Ltd v HMRC; Kawthar Consulting Ltd v HMRC SpC
  477, [2005] STC (SCD) 524, [2005] SWTI 1237, Sp Comm 5.14, 9.3
New Zealand Commr of Inland Revenue v Challenge Corpn Ltd
  [1986] STC 548, [1987] 1 AC 155, [1987] 2 WLR 24, PC 18.2
Nuclear Electric plc v Bradley (Inspector of Taxes) (1996) 68 TC 670,
  [1996] STC 405, [1996] 1 WLR 529, CA 9.9, 11.10
Odeon Association Theatres Ltd v Jones (1971) 48 TC 257,
  [1973] Ch 288, [1971] 1 WLR 442, [1972] 1 All ER 681 .... 5.10
O'Grady (Inspector of Taxes) v Bullcroft Main Collieries Ltd
  (1932) 17 TC 93, KBD 5.10
O'Keefe (Inspector of Taxes) v Southport Printers Ltd (1984) 58 TC 88,
  [1984] STC 443, (1984) 81 LS Gaz 1685 .... 5.20
Owen v Southern Railway of Peru Ltd (1956) 36 TC 602, [1957] AC 334,
  [1956] 2 All ER 728 .... 5.20
Pickford v Quirke (Inspector of Taxes) (1927) 13 TC 251, KBD 5.6

Pyrah v Annis & Co Ltd (1956) 37 TC 163, [1957] 1 WLR 190,
[1957] 1 All ER 196 .... 5.20
RTZ Oil & Gas Ltd v Ellis (Inspector of Taxes) (1987) 61 TC 132,
[1987] STC 512, [1987] 1 WLR 1442 .... 5.20
R v CIR ex parte Newfields Developments Ltd [2001] UKHL 27, (2001)
73 TC 532, [2001] STC 901, [2001] 1 WLR 1111, HL 4.10, 4.31
Ransom v Higgs (1974) 50 TC 1, [1974] STC 539, [1974] 1 WLR 1594,
[1974] 3 All ER 949 .... 5.20
Redkite Ltd v Inspector of Taxes [1996] STC (SCD) 501, Sp Comm 5.20
Revenue and Customs Comrs v Bank of Ireland Britain Holdings Ltd
[2008] EWCA Civ 58, [2008] STC 398, [2008] BTC 126 .... 11.37
Revenue and Customs Comrs v Household Estate Agents Ltd
[2007] EWHC 1684 (Ch), [2008] STC 2045 .... 2.32
Revenue and Customs Comrs v Maco Door & Window Hardware
(UK) Ltd [2006] EWHC 1832 (Ch) 6.70
Robert Addie & Sons, CE 1875, 1 TC1,12 SLR 274 .... 6.2
Robinson v Scott Bader & Co Ltd (1981) 54 TC 757, [1981] STC 436,
[1981] 1 WLR 1135, [1981] 2 All ER 1116 .... 5.20
Rolfe (Inspector of Taxes) v Wimpey Waste Management Ltd
(1989) 62 TC 399, [1989] STC 454, CA 5.10
Rolls Royce Motors Ltd v Bamford (Inspector of Taxes) (1976) 51 TC
319, [1976] STC 152, ChD 15.21
Rose & Co (Wallpapers & Paints) Ltd v Campbell (1967) 44 TC 500,
[1968] 1 WLR 346, [1968] 1 All ER 405 .... 6.18
Rowntree and Co Ltd v Curtis [1925] 1 KB 328, [1924] 8 TC 678 .... 5.39
Rutledge v CIR (1929) 14 TC 490, 1929 SC 379, Ct of Sess (1 Div) 5.6
Rutter v Charles Sharpe & Co Ltd (1979) 53 TC 163, [1979] STC 711,
[1979] 1 WLR 1429 .... 5.30
Samuel Jones & Co (Devondale) Ltd v CIR (1951) 32 TC 513, [1951] TR
411, 1952 SC 94 .... 5.10
Schofield v R & H Hall Ltd (1974) 49 TC 538, [1975] STC 353, CA (NI) 6.18
St John's School (Mountford and Knibbs) v Ward (1974) 49 TC 524,
[1975] STC 7, [1974] TR 273, CA 6.18
Sharkey v Wernher (1955) 36 TC 275, [1956] AC 58, [1955] 3 All ER
493 .... 5.43, 17.24
Shepherd (Inspector of Taxes) v Law Land plc (1990) 63 TC 692,
[1990] STC 795, ChD 10.12
Small (Inspector of Taxes) v Mars UK Ltd [2007] UKHL 15
[2007] 1 WLR 1448, [2007] 2 All ER 440, [2007} All ER (D) 459
(Mar) 5.21
Smith v Revenue and Customs Commissioners SpC 680 .... 2.20
Snell v HMRC Commissioners SpC 532, [2006] STC (SCD) 296, Sp
Comm 15.9
Southern v Borax Consolidated (1940) 23 TC 598, [1941] 1 KB 111,
[1940] 4 All ER 412 .... 5.20
Southwell (Surveyor of Taxes) v Savill Bros (1901) 4 TC 430, [1901]
2 KB 349, 70 LJKB 815, KBD 5.20
Stott and Ingham v Trehearne (Inspector of Taxes) (1924) 9 TC 69, KBD 5.20
Sun Life Assurance Society v Davidson 37 TC 330, [1958] AC 184,
[1957] 3 WLR 362, HL 12.8

Symons (Inspector of Taxes) v Weeks (as personal representatives of
  Lord Llewelyn Davies) (1982) 56 TC 630, [1983] STC 195, DC 1.13
Tanfield Ltd v Carr (Inspector of Taxes) [1999] STC (SCD) 213, Sp
  Comm 5.20
Tapemaze Ltd v Melluish (HM Inspector of Taxes) (2000) 73 TC 167,
  [2000] STC 189, ChD 1.12
Threlfall v Jones (HM Inspector of Taxes); Gallagher v Jones (HM
  Inspector of Taxes) (1993) 66 TC 77, [1993] STC 537,
  [1993] Ch 107, CA 1.12
Transco plc v Dyall [2002] STC (SCD) 199 .... 5.20
Tucker v Granada Motorway Services Ltd (1979) 53 TC 92,
  [1979] 1 WLR 683, [1979] 2 All ER 801 .... 5.10
Vibroplant Ltd v Holland (1981) 54 TC 658, [1982] 1 All ER 792, [1981]
  TR 485, CA 6.69
Vodafone Cellular v Shaw (Inspector of Taxes) (1997) 69 TC 376,
  [1997] STC 734, [1997] BTC 247, CA 5.20
WT Ramsay Ltd v CIR (1981) TC 101, [1981] STC 174, [1982] AC
  300, HL 18.2
Wadsworth Morton Ltd v Jenkinson (1966) 43 TC 479, [1967] 1 WLR 79,
  [1966] 3 All ER 702 .... 15.19
Walker v Cater Securities Ltd (1974) 49 TC 625, [1974] STC 390,
  [1974] 1 WLR 1363, [1974] 3 All ER 63 .... 5.20
West v Phillips (Inspector of Taxes) (1958) 38 TC 203, [1958] TR 267, 37
  ATC 270, ChD 5.6
Weston v Garnett (Inspector of Taxes) [2005] EWCA Civ 742, [2005] STC
  1134, [2005] SWTI 1098, CA 11.5
William Grant & Sons Distillers Ltd v CIR [2004] STC (SCD) 253, Sp
  Comm 5.21
Wisdom v Chamberlain (1968) 45 TC 92, [1969] 1 WLR 275,
  [1969] 1 All ER 332 .... 5.6
Wimpy International Ltd v Warland (Inspector of Taxes) (1988) 61 TC 51,
  [1989] STC 273, CA 6.11, 6.18
Wood v Holden (Inspector of Taxes) [2006] EWCA Civ 26, [2006] STC
  443, [2006] 2 BCLC 210, [2006] All ER (D) 190 (Jan), CA 13.2
Wood Preservation Ltd v Prior (1969) 45 TC 112, [1969] 1 All ER 364, 57
  LJQB 7, 36 WR 281, CA 15.18
Yarmouth v France (1887) 19 QBD 647, 57 LJQB 7, 36 WR 281, CA 6.10, 6.18

List of Abbreviations

ACT	advance corporation tax
ADP	acceptable dividend policy
AIM	alternative investment market
APA	advance pricing agreement
APR	agricultural property relief
ARC	Accounting Regulatory Committee
ASB	Accounting Standards Board
BA	balancing allowance
BMT	bereaved minor trust
BPR	business property relief
CA	Companies Act
CAA 2001	Capital Allowances Act 2001
CFC	controlled foreign company
CIHC	close investment holding company
CTF	child trust fund
CTO	Capital Taxes Office
CTT	capital transfer tax
EEA	European Economic Area
EIS	enterprise investment scheme
ESC	Extra-statutory Concession
EUFT	eligible unrelieved foreign tax
FA	Finance Act
FRS	Financial Reporting Standard
FRSEE	Financial Report Standard for Smaller Entities
FYA	first year allowance
GWR	gift with reservation
HMRC	HM Revenue and Customs
IA	initial allowance
IA 1986	Insolvency Act 1986
IAS	International Accounting Standards
IASB	International Accounting Standards Board
IBA	industrial building allowance
ICTA 1988	Income and Corporation Act 1988
IFRS	International Financial Reporting Standards
IHT	inheritance tax
IHTA 1984	Inheritance Tax Act 1984
IHTM	Inheritance Tax Manual
ITEPA 2003	Income Tax (Earnings and Pensions) Act 2003
ITTOIA 2005	Income Tax (Trading and Other Income) Act 2005

LLP	limited liability partnership
OECD	Organisation for European Cooperation and Development
PCTCT	profits chargeable to corporation tax
PET	potentially exempt transfer
POA	pre-owned asset
R & D	research and development
SDLT	stamp duty land tax
SE	small enterprise
SI	Statutory Instrument
SME	small and medium-sized enterprise
SSAP	Statement of Standard Accounting Practice
SSCBA 1992	Social Security Contributions and Benefits Act 1992
TAAR	target anti-avoidance rule
TCGA 1992	Taxation of Chargeable Gains Act 1992
TMA 1970	Taxes Management Act 1970
TSI	transitional serial interests
UITF	Urgent Issue Task Force
UK GAAP	UK Generally Accepted Accounting Principles
UTR	Unique Taxpayer Reference
VCT	venture capital trust
VOA	Valuation Office Agency
WDA	writing down allowance
WDV	written down value

Chapter 1

Introduction to corporation tax

FORMATION OF A UK COMPANY

1.1   Corporation tax is charged on the profits of UK resident companies (*ICTA 1988, s 6(1)*); the vast majority of which are formed in the UK.

A UK company is formed by providing Companies House with details of its Memorandum and Articles of Association, directors, company secretary and members and registered office. The registrar of companies checks the documents and if approved retains them for public inspection. The new company may be a private company that is limited by shares, or by guarantee or it may be unlimited. Alternatively the company may be a public company limited that is also limited by shares. If limited by shares the members will subscribe to the company's share capital, which in turn forms their initial investment in the company. The liability of each member is restricted to the amount of his or her investment. A public company can offer its shares to the public, whereas a private company cannot. If a company is to be limited by guarantee the members make no contribution upon formation or during the company's lifetime, but agree instead to contribute an amount to the company's assets upon winding-up. Members of a private unlimited company have unlimited liability and the company need not necessarily have a share capital. A company limited by shares is by far the most common structure, and is the arrangement on which the commentary in this book is based. From 8 October 2004, it has been possible to establish a European company or Societas Europaea 'SE' in Great Britain (England, Scotland and Wales) (SI 2326/2004) and an SE is treated much like a PLC.

The company has a separate legal personality to its members. A company is required to maintain statutory books to record its constitution and structure and books of account to record its transactions. Documents notifying changes in structure must be filed at Companies House. Statutory accounts must be prepared annually and filed at Companies House. A company is also required to file an annual return with the Registrar of Companies every year.

COMPANIES ACT 2006

1.2   The *Companies Act 2006* received Royal Assent on 8 November 2006. Under the new Act public companies have more regulation whilst deregulation is the order of the day for private companies. This may encourage more companies to remain or convert to being private; which may bring even more UK companies within the close company status (see Chapter 4).

Certain *Companies Act 2006* provisions have already been introduced and all parts of the Act will come into force by 1 October 2009. With effect from 1 October 2008, the format of the Memorandum of Association will change. It will contain less information than it does currently with further information being supplied to the Registrar in the form of a series of statements made in the application for registration or in the articles. Also, with effect from 1 October 2008, a company must have at least one director who is a natural person (*CA 2006, s 155*). With effect from 6 April 2008 a private company is no longer required to appoint a company secretary, but may appoint a company secretary if they so wish (*CA 2006, s 270*). The requirement is maintained for public companies (*CA 2006, s 271*). See www.companieshouse.gov.uk for subsequent changes.

THE BASIS OF CORPORATION TAX

1.3   The UK operates a free enterprise economy and any person or persons can subscribe to a company. The shareholder reward for his, her or their investment in the company is a distribution of profits, commonly known as a dividend.

The profits of a company are brought to charge to tax under the corporation tax regime. Corporation tax is directly levied on the profits of companies and is payable by the company. Profits are the company's income less expenses, together with its chargeable gains. A dividend payment is not an expense of the company; it is a distribution payment. There is no relief for corporation tax. Instead, each qualifying distribution to a shareholder who is an individual carries a tax credit of 1/9 of the distribution; which effectively satisfies the liability of a basic rate taxpayer, but not a higher rate taxpayer. Company shareholders are not chargeable to corporation tax on distributions from other UK companies.

Corporation tax rates have varied over the years but generally speaking current UK corporation tax rates are at their lowest. See Chapter 3. The main rate of corporation tax is set to decrease even further, whilst the small company rate is set to increase. The tax base is also subject to characteristic annual *Finance Act* changes to target avoidance or to provide incentives.

LIABILITY TO CORPORATION TAX

Definition of a company

1.4   A company is not the only 'person' that is liable to corporation tax. This is because a company is defined as 'any body corporate or unincorporated association' (*ICTA 1988, s 832(1)*). Therefore members' clubs, societies and trade and voluntary associations will find themselves within the ambit of corporation tax (see **5.45–5.56**). The *s 832* definition of a company excludes a partnership, a local authority or a local authority association. Therefore partnerships, trustees, local authorities and local authority associations are not chargeable to corporation tax. Please see *Income Tax 2008/09* from Tottel for partnerships and *Trusts and Estates 2007/08* from Tottel for trustees. Local authorities and local authority associations are exempt from corporation tax, income tax and capital gains tax (*ICTA 1988, s 519(2)* and *TCGA 1992, s 271(3)*).

The extent of the corporation tax charge

1.5   It is immaterial where and how a UK company earns its profits because all UK resident companies are liable to corporation tax on their profits wherever they arise and whether or not they are received or transmitted to the UK (*ICTA 1988, s 6(1)*).

The UK (United Kingdom) for these purposes includes Great Britain and Northern Ireland but not the Irish Republic, the Isle of Man or the Channel Islands.

A company is UK resident if it is incorporated in the UK, i.e. registered at Companies House. If it is not incorporated in the UK but is managed and controlled from the UK it will most likely be resident in the UK for corporation tax purposes. These concepts are discussed in Chapter 13.

If a non-UK resident company carries on a trade in the UK through a permanent establishment, it will be liable to corporation tax on the profits directly attributable to the permanent establishment. A permanent establishment could amount to an overseas company's UK branch, UK office or UK agency. Such profits may emanate directly or indirectly from the permanent establishment and will include income from trades, property, intangibles and gains (*ICTA 1988, s 11(2A)*).

Taxation of company profits

1.6   *Section 6(4)(a)* of the *Taxes Act 1988* brings a company's profits into charge to corporation tax by stating that the profits that are chargeable to corporation tax consist of income and chargeable gains. Dividends and distributions received from UK resident companies are excluded (*ICTA 1988, s 208*). The profits for each accounting period are then chargeable to corporation tax at the appropriate rate (*ICTA 1988, s 12*). Corporation tax rates are fixed for financial years. The financial year (for corporation tax) commences on 1 April in one year and ends on 31 March in the next year and is known as the calendar year on which it commences e.g. the financial year 2008 commences on 1 April 2008 and ends on 31 March 2009.

In principle, company income and gains are calculated using income tax and capital gains tax principles (*ICTA 1988, s 9(1)* and *TCGA 1992, s 8*). The rules of Schedule A and the cases of Schedule D apply to corporation tax unless modified elsewhere in the legislation (*ICTA 1988, s 9(3)*).

COMPANY ACCOUNTS AND DIRECTOR DUTIES

Duty to prepare accounts

1.7   The company's financial results are presented in a company's accounts. Preparation of accounts is a duty of the directors. With effect from 6 April 2008 the *Companies Act 2006, s 394* (previously *Companies Act 1985, s 226* as amended by *SI 2004/2947*), states that the directors of every company shall prepare accounts for the company for each of its financial years. The accounts may be prepared either under the 'Companies Act individual accounts' accounting framework or under the 'IAS individual accounts' framework (*CA 2006, s 395*)(previously *CA 2005, s 226 (2)–(6)*).

Directors of a company must not approve accounts unless they are satisfied that those accounts give a true and fair view of the assets, liabilities, financial position and profit or loss of a company (*CA 2006, s 393(1)*). The *Companies Act 2006, s 386* states that every company shall keep adequate accounting records for the company for each of its financial years. Under Companies Act 2006 with effect from 6 April 2008, the auditor will also report on whether the company has maintained 'adequate records' (*CA 2006, s 498*). Prior to this the auditor had to report on whether proper accounting records were kept (*CA 2005, s 237*).

Companies Act accounts

1.8   *Companies Act* individual accounts comprise a balance sheet as at the last day of the financial year, and a profit and loss account for each financial year, which are known as individual accounts (*CA 2006, s 396 (1)*). The balance sheet must give a true and fair view of the state of the company's affairs as at the end of the financial year, and the profit and loss must give a true and fair view of the profit or loss of the company for the financial year. The individual accounts may be prepared in accordance either with Companies Act or IAS frameworks (*CA 2006, s 395*).

IAS individual accounts are accounts that comply with international accounting standards. If IAS are used the notes to the accounts must state that the accounts have been prepared in accordance with international standards (*CA 2006, s 397*) (*previously CA 1985, s 226B*)

Group accounts may be prepared on a similar basis, either *Companies Act* group accounts or 'IAS group accounts', which are in accordance with international accounting standards. Listed companies, as required by European law, must use IAS when preparing their consolidated accounts. If IAS group accounts are prepared, the directors must state in the notes to those accounts that they have been prepared in accordance with international accounting standards (*CA 2006, s 406*) (*previously CA 1985, s 227B*).

Accounting standards

1.9   The Accounting Standards Board (ASB), an independent body, sets the accounting standards that apply to all UK and Republic of Ireland entities that have not chosen to use International Financial Reporting Standards (IFRS). The Board has adopted a strategy of convergence with international standards.

The International Accounting Standards Board (IASB) sets the accounting standards to be used, with effect from 1 January 2005, by all listed groups. The standards are referred to as International Accounting Standards (IAS) or International Financial Reporting Standards (IFRS). UK companies may not use a standard as written by the IASB unless it has been adopted by the European Union. The European Commission set up the Accounting Regulatory Committee (ARC), which is chaired by the Commission and composed of representatives from member states. The ARC provides an opinion on Commission proposals of whether or not to endorse an international accounting standard (see **17.5–17.6**).

UK GAAP

1.10   The vast majority of UK companies apply UK GAAP. Over the past few years there have been many changes to UK GAAP. This is largely due to the ASB's focus to bring the UK's accounting standards in line with the international standards.

UK GAAP includes accounting standards, Urgent Issues Task Force (UITF) abstracts, the Companies Act and Stock Exchange requirements and other accepted industry practices. Until 1970 the *Companies Act* was the only regulatory force that governed the preparation of companies' financial statements. Since then accounting standards have developed commencing with statements of standard accounting practice (SSAPs), Financial Reporting Standards (FRSs) and latterly International Accounting Standards and International Financial Reporting Standards. The purpose of the accounting standards is to give an authority as to how a certain type of transaction should be recorded in the accounts to reflect a 'true and fair view'.

Smaller companies may adopt the Financial Reporting Standard for Smaller Entities (FRSSE), which is within UK GAAP. The FRSSE may be applied to small companies and groups as defined in the *Companies Act* (see **6.20** and **6.21**). Large or medium-sized groups cannot use the FRSSE. The FRSSE exempts the small company from complying with other accounting standards and UITF abstracts unless the company is preparing consolidated accounts. FRSSE embodies FRS 5 *Reporting the Substance of Transactions* and FRS 18 *Accounting Policies* (see **17.18**) principles amongst others. An International Accounting Standard for smaller entities has been proposed. The IASB issued Exposure Draft (ED) of the IFRS for SMEs on 15 February 2007, which is currently under review.

Companies Act directors' duties

1.11 Companies Act 2006 sets out seven statutory duties of directors (*CA 2006, ss 170–181*). These provisions, in the main, came into force on 1 October 2007 and are mainly legislating for principles already decided in existing case law. Companies Act 1985 imposed a statutory duty on directors to act in the interests of the company's employees and the interests of its members (*CA 1985, s 309(1)*). Companies Act 2006 provisions are more prescriptive and include:

- a duty to act within powers,

- a duty to promote the success of the company,

- a duty to exercise independent judgment,

- a duty to exercise reasonable care, skill and diligence,

- a duty to avoid conflicts of interest,

- a duty not to accept benefits from third parties, and

- a duty to declare interest in proposed transaction or arrangement.

(*CA 2006, ss 171–177*)

Time will tell how these new provisions will affect companies. The effect of the new provisions on the directors' responsibilities to corporation tax matters must also be considered. A requirement to promote the success of the company replaces the requirement to act in the interests of the employees' members (*CA 2006, s 172 (1)*). Previous legislation may not always have been clear but a more detailed format may again bring about the need to turn to the courts for guidance. Pre-existing case law on any issue still stands (*CA 2006, s 170 (4)*).

In promoting the success of the company it is stated that the director should consider:

- the likely consequences of any decision in the long term,

- the interests of the company's employees,

- the need to foster the company's business relationships with suppliers, customers and others,

- the impact of the company's operations on the community and the environment,

- the desirability of the company maintaining a reputation for high standards of business conduct, and

- the need to act fairly as between members of the company

(*CA 2006, s 172(1)*)

Directors are required to act responsibly in relation to all company dealings; this will include corporation tax compliance and corporation tax planning. In fulfilling their duties it is hoped that directors will not become too involved in the minutiae of making and recording decisions. Overall it is hoped that directors will be able to follow the spirit of the law by ensuring the 'long-term best interests of the company'. Therefore, it seems that strategic decisions, based on and around a business culture with clear policies supported by robust budgeting and forecasting may be more appropriate.

TAXATION AND ACCOUNTS

Legislation

1.12 A company may have many sources of income but the vast majority of UK companies carry on a trade of some sort. Over the years, the courts have applied GAAP as the rationale for determining the profits of a trade for taxation purposes. Accounts are treated as prepared according to GAAP for tax purposes even if they have not been so prepared: see *Threlfall v Jones (HM Inspector of Taxes); Gallagher v Jones (HM Inspector of Taxes)* (1993) 66 TC 77, [1993]

STC 537, [1994] 2 WLR 160, [1994] Ch 107 and *Tapemaze Ltd v Melluish* (*HM Inspector of Taxes*) (2000) 73 TC 167, [2000] STC 189. HMRC acknowledge that profits computed in accordance with UK generally accepted accounting practice, subject to adjustments, form the starting point for the computation of taxable profits (HMRC Business Income Manual BIM 31019). The accounts could be prepared under international GAAP but the occurrence is not as common as UK GAAP. Also, small companies are within the realms of UK GAAP if they choose to adopt the FRSSE.

The accounting basis was first embodied into statute by the *Finance Act 1998, s 42(1)* that introduced the principle that the profits of a trade must be prepared on an accounting basis that gives a true and fair view, subject to any adjustment required or authorised by law in computing profits for those purposes. *Finance Act 2002, s 103(5)* amended the *s 42* requirement so that now the profits of a trade must be computed in accordance with GAAP. The inference is of course that by using GAAP the accounts will continue to show a true and fair view. UK GAAP or international GAAP may be used and the legal override for accounting adjustments remains. .

HMRC practice

1.13 HMRC discuss FRS 18 *Accounting Policies* in HMRC Business Income Manual BIM 31032.

FRS 18 sets the framework for GAAP; IAS 8 being the international equivalent. The standard provides definitions of accounting policies, estimation techniques and measurement bases. Accounting policies are the manner in which certain types of transaction should be presented. Estimation techniques are the methods used to arrive at an estimated monetary amount. Measurement bases are the monetary attributes that are reflected in the accounts.

For example, if a company changed its method of stock valuation from average cost to FIFO, this would be a change of accounting policy. If, on the other hand, the company changed its method of ascertaining the cost of stock from a percentage of selling price to actual invoiced cost, this would only be a change in estimation techniques.

FRS 18, para 14 states that 'an entity should adopt accounting policies that enable its financial statements to give a true and fair view. Those accounting policies should be consistent with the requirements of accounting standards, Urgent Issues Task Force (UITF) Abstracts and companies legislation'.

The standard also states that a business must select those policies that 'are judged by the entity to be most appropriate to its particular circumstances for the purpose of giving a true and fair view'. What is 'appropriate' is left to each business to determine and is not defined in the standard. Instead the standard provides guidance on how the appropriateness of the accounting policies is to be judged. There are four objectives:

- relevance,
- reliability,
- comparability, and
- understandability (FRS 18, para 30).

Balancing the four objectives and the cost/benefit balance of providing the information constrains the four objectives. There are two bases of accounting in the preparation of financial statements and these are going concern and accruals. A going concern basis is always used unless the entity concerned has ceased trading or is to be liquidated. The accruals concept determines that transactions should be reflected in the accounts in the period they are incurred as opposed to the period in which they are received or paid. However, a deferral of costs under FRS 18 is not permitted unless the corresponding debit on the balance sheet meets the definition criteria of an asset under FRS 5 *Reporting the Substance of Transactions* (FRS 18, para 27).

HMRC particularly note that FRS 18 states that that prudence requires accounting policies to take account of uncertainty about the existence of assets, liabilities, gains, losses and changes to shareholders' funds or the amount at which they should be measured. FRS 18 also states that there is no need to exercise prudence where there is no uncertainty, nor should prudence be used as a reason to create, for example, hidden reserves or excessive provisions, deliberately understating assets or gains, or deliberately overstating liabilities or losses. To do that would mean that the financial statements are not neutral and therefore not reliable.

In Business Income Manual, BIM 31040, HMRC acknowledge the importance of SSAP 17 *Accounting for post balance sheet events*, by referring to comments in *Symons v Weeks (as personal representative of Lord Llewelyn-Davies)* (1982) 56 TC 630, [1983] STC 195. In this case it was commented that 'where facts are available they are preferable to speculative estimates'. For tax purposes it is not acceptable to ignore facts if by so doing an unreal loss is provided for. SSAP 17 has now been replaced by FRS 21 Events after the Balance Sheet Date (see **17.11**).

Although HMRC recognises that accounts are to be drawn up in accordance with GAAP, it seems uneasy with the notion of materiality, presumably because *ICTA 1988, s 70(1)* states that tax is to be charged on the full amount of any profits or gains.

Materiality is closely related to the relevance objective. Accounting practice considers that an item would be material to the financial statements if its mis-statement or omission might reasonably be expected to influence the economic decisions of the users of the statements. As such it acknowledges materiality as an accountancy concept and not as a taxation concept (HMRC Business Income Manual BIM 31047). Materiality is a judgment to be made in the light of the circumstances and the event. They suggest that the factual accuracy of any item in the accounts is not for the company, nor its accountants, nor indeed HMRC, but for the Commissioners to decide. Appeals before the Commissioners are discussed in Chapter 2 (see **2.23–2.27**).

The objective of FRS 5 *Reporting the substance of transactions* is to ensure that the substance of any transaction is reported in the financial statements. The commercial effect of all transactions is therefore recorded in the financial statements. The standard predisposes that economic substance takes precedence over legal form. HMRC consider that by and large FRS 5 is a sound basis for the preparation of accounts for taxation purposes (HMRC Business Income Manual BIM 31055).

1.14   The basic premise is that the accounting profits form the taxable profits, unless overridden by taxation law (*FA 1998, s 42(1)*). It is the overriding taxation law that we seek to examine in the following chapters. A further discussion of accounting and taxation is given in Chapter 17 together with a list of the UK and International Reporting Standards. Application of the accounting standards in relation to directors' remuneration and the valuation of work in progress is discussed in **5.16** and **5.37–5.42**.

Chapter 2

Self-assessment

INTRODUCTION

2.1   Companies report their liability to corporation tax to HMRC through the self-assessment procedures. Any notices served on the company should be served on the 'proper officer' that is the company secretary or the person acting as the company secretary (*TMA 1970, s 108(3)*). In cases of liquidation, the liquidator is responsible or any other person with implied or apparent authority. The treasurer or person acting as treasurer is responsible in the case of unincorporated associations. A company tax return includes a declaration by the person making the return that to the best of his knowledge and belief the return is correct and complete (*FA 1998, Sch 18, para 3(3)*).

Companies are also required to deliver a copy of their statutory accounts to HMRC (*FA 1998, Sch 18, para 11*). The company must also calculate its own 'self-assessment' (*FA 1998, Sch 18, para 7*). Companies will prepare a corporation tax computation to calculate the corporation tax due and submit this together with the corporation tax return including the supplementary pages and the statutory accounts to HMRC. A return is strictly not 'delivered' to HMRC unless it is accompanied by 'all the information, accounts, statements and reports' (*FA 1998, Sch 18, para 4*). The CT600 asks the company to confirm that the accounts and computations are included. HMRC reject returns where delivery is incomplete.

A complete company tax return should include:

- a completed form CT600;

- any appropriate supplementary pages;

- a set of accounts, appropriate to the type of company (if registered at Companies House the statutory accounts required under the *Companies Acts*); and

- a tax computation showing how the figures on the CT600 have been derived from the accounts (detailed trading and profit and loss accounts are usually included).

2.2 *Self-assessment*

If a company or a company's agent sends a CT600 without supporting accounts and tax computations, HMRC will return the CT600 to the company or the agent because it does not meet the legal return requirement (Working Together, Issue 18, November 2004).

HMRC may by notice require a company to deliver a corporation tax return to the issuing officer, together with any information and reports relevant to the tax liability (*FA 1998, Sch 18, para 3(1)*). If a company is chargeable to corporation tax for an accounting period, it is required to give notice to HMRC within 12 months of the end of the accounting period concerned that it is so liable. If the company fails to do so it will incur a penalty.(*FA 1998, Sch 18, para 2*).

The accuracy of the preparation of the corporation tax return and the completion of the Company Tax return is a prime management responsibility. Company Tax Return CT600 (2008) Version 2 and CT600 (Short) Version 2 are reproduced by kind permission of HMRC as Appendices. An outline corporation tax computation is included in **22.3**.

CONTACTING HMRC

2.2   A company or an organisation must inform HMRC within three months in writing when it comes within the charge to corporation tax (*FA 2004, s 55*). The information required is as follows:

- the company's name and registered number;
- the address of the company's registered office;
- the address of the company's principal place of business;
- the nature of the business being carried on by the company;
- the date to which the company intends to prepare accounts;
- the full name and home address of each of the directors of the company;
- if the company has taken over any business, including any trade, profession or vocation formerly carried out by another;
- the name and address of that former business;
- the name and address of the person from whom that business was acquired;
- the name and registered office of the parent company (if any); and
- the date that the company is required to register for PAYE.

(*Corporation Tax (Notice of Coming within Charge–Information) Regulations 2004, SI 2004/2502.*)

In practice, Companies House will inform HMRC of the formation of a new company and as a result HMRC will contact the company requesting information shown on form CT41G, which requests identical information as shown above. However, if HMRC does not contact the company for this information it is still the company's responsibility to supply the information and CT41G may be completed and submitted independently. For tax periods commencing prior to 1 April 2008, the original self-assessment penalty régime remains in force. The penalty for non-compliance is £300. There is also a £60 daily penalty (*TMA 1970, s 98(1)*). A false return can incur a penalty of £3,000 (*TMA 1970, s 98(2)*). Penalties cannot be imposed after the failure is rectified (*TMA 1970, s 98(3)*). For details of the penalty provisions applying for accounting periods commencing on or after 1 April 2008, see **2.36.**

If a company fails to inform HMRC, HMRC will assume that the first accounting period runs for 12 months from the date of incorporation.

HMRC will maintain the company's details on their database. HMRC use the database to issue returns and other communications to corporate taxpayers and it is important to keep HMRC informed of any changes in the company's accounting period or address.

COMPANY RECORDS

2.3   A company has a requirement to keep and preserve records together with supporting documents to enable it to deliver a complete and correct corporation tax return for each relevant accounting period.

If a company complies with *Companies Act 2006, ss 386 and 387 (formerly CA 1985, s 221)* it will maintain sufficient records to prepare its statutory accounts. Good accounting records should in most cases form good records for corporation tax purposes. Under self-assessment a company is specifically required to keep records of:

'(a) all receipts and expenses in the course of a company's activities and the matters in respect of which they arise and

(b) in the case of a trade involving dealing in goods, all sales and purchases made in the course of the trade.'

(*FA 1998, Sch 18, para 21(5)*)

The type of records retained will vary with the industry, but it is important to bear in mind that information must be available on how a matter arises. Current legislation and HMRC often look behind a transaction and it can be important to demonstrate how a business decision or transaction was actioned at the time.

2.3   Self-assessment

When self-assessment was first introduced, HMRC commented that if a company satisfied *CA 2006, ss 386* and *387* (formerly *CA 1985, s 221*) it will have satisfied the requirements to keep and preserve records for corporation tax self-assessment (*Revenue Tax Bulletin 37*, October 1998, p 587). Although that was some time ago, the article is still current.

In recent years, examinations of supporting vouchers by professionals acting for the company may have reduced due to the relaxation in the criteria for a statutory audit and also where the statutory audit concentrates on a risk-based approach. The onus for maintaining the supporting vouchers rests with the company and the supporting documents required are identified as 'accounts, books, deeds, contracts, vouchers and receipts' (*FA 1998, Sch 18, para 21(6)*)HMRC will accept alternative forms of records such as optical imaging systems. This is admissible evidence in Commissioner hearings (*FA 1998, Sch 18, para 22(2)*). As part of new HMRC powers (see **2.46** et seq.), *FA 2008, Sch 37, para 9* states that the records may be kept in any form and by any means subject to any exceptions made by HMRC in writing. Companies are not required to keep records relating to distributions and tax credits and details of gross and net interest payments (*FA 1998, Sch 18, para 22(3)*.The records must be kept for six years from the end of the relevant accounting period (*FA 1998, Sch 18, para 21(3)*).. With effect from 1 April 2009, as part of the new powers, HMRC may reduce this period below the six-year time limit (*FA 2008, Sch 37, para 8 (3)*). Records should be kept longer:

- if a return is under enquiry more than six years after the end of the accounting period;

- if the company makes its return late; or

- the records relate to a continuing transaction that may affect current years.

The maximum penalty for failing to preserve records has been £3,000 (*FA 1998, Sch 18, para 23(1)*), but this may be overridden by the new penalty regime effective for tax periods commencing on or after 1 April 2008 that are due to be filed on or after 1 April 2009, see **2.36.** There is no penalty for failing to keep or preserve records, which might have been needed, only for the purposes of claims, elections or notices not included in the return (*FA 1998, Sch 18, para 23(3)*).

Additional documentary evidence may be required to support arm's-length dealings under transfer pricing legislation. The records required to enable a company to deliver a correct and complete return in this instance go beyond the Companies Act requirements. This is discussed in **14.23** and **14.25.**

COMPANY TAX RETURN

Corporation tax accounting periods

2.4   Under the Companies Act 2006, directors of UK companies are required to prepare and file statutory accounts for every 12-month accounting period. Usually, from three to seven weeks after the end of the accounting period from information held in its database, HMRC will send the company a 'Form CT603 Notice to deliver its company tax return by the due date'. The notice will specify a 12-month period for which HMRC consider that a return is due (*FA 1998, Sch 18, para 5(1)*). In general, the corporation tax accounting period follows the statutory accounting period but for corporation tax purposes there are specific points at which an accounting period will begin or end.

A corporation tax accounting period first begins when a company comes within the scope of corporation tax by acquiring a source of income or becoming UK resident.

An accounting period ends on the earliest of the following events:

● 12 months from the beginning of the accounting period;

● the date on which the company draws up its accounts;

● the company begins or ceases to trade or ceases to be within the charge to corporation tax in respect of its trade or trades if more than one;

● the company begins or ceases to be UK resident;

● the company begins or ceases to be in administration; or

● the company goes into liquidation or winds up.

(*ICTA 1988, s 12.*)

Therefore, an accounting period will generally last for 12 months and will usually coincide with the period for which the company draws up accounts. If the statutory period of account exceeds 12 months, it is divided for corporation tax purposes into one or more accounting periods of 12 months, with a further accounting period covering the remainder of the period of account.

Each event will require the preparation of a separate company tax return.

Example 2.1—Commencement to trade

A Ltd incorporated on 1 January 2008. It completes form CT41G and commences trading on 1 April 2008. Form CT603 is issued on 1 April 2009. The company prepares accounts for the three months to 31 March 2008 and for the 12 months to 31 March 2009 and then to 31 March each year.

2.5 *Self-assessment*

A Ltd is required to prepare company tax returns from 1 January 2008 to 31 March 2008 and from 1 April 2008 to 31 March 2009. The latest filing date for the 31 March 2008 return will be 30 June 2009 being three months after receipt of the Form CT603. The latest filing date for the 31 March 2009 return will be 31 March 2010 being 12 months after the year end (see **2.9**).

Example 2.2—Change in accounting date

B Ltd has always prepared accounts to 30 September each year. In January 2008 it changes its accounting date to 31 December and prepares accounts for the 15 months to 31 December 2008.

B Ltd is required to prepare company tax returns from 1 October 2007 to 30 September 2008 and from 1 October 2008 to 31 December 2008. The filing date for both returns is 31 December 2009 being 12 months after the end of the period of accounts.

2.5   An accounting period of more or less than 12 months may result in profits being apportioned. As a general rule these should be apportioned on a time basis, according to the number of days in the accounting period (*ICTA 1988, s 834(4)*). Chargeable gains are apportioned to the period in which they occur (*TCGA 1992, s 8(3)*).

Example 2.3

	Days
A company prepares statutory accounts for the period 1 January 2007 to 31 March 2009. The company is trading throughout the whole period. Its total profits chargeable to corporation tax amount to £500,000	456

Its corporation tax accounting periods are:

	Days
First accounting period (12 months) from 1 January 2007 to 31 December 2007	365
Second accounting period (balance) from 1 January 2008 to 31 March 2008	91

The total profit is apportioned to accounting periods as follows:

	£
First accounting period profit is (£500,000 ÷ 456) × 365	400,219
Second accounting period profit is (£500,000 ÷ 456) × 91	99,781

(Working Together, Issue 18, August 2004—Company Tax Return Helpful Hints Example adapted).

2.6   Profits may be apportioned on a time basis if this gives more of an accurate result. This occurred in the case of *Marshall Hus & Partners Ltd v Bolton* (1980) 55 TC 539, [1981] STC 18. Marshall Hus & Partners Ltd was a property company that had not prepared accounts for six years. The time came for the company to fulfil its corporation tax requirements. In order to allocate its profits to the corporation tax accounting periods it averaged the profits over the entire period. The Inland Revenue objected because they had discovered that the first five accounting periods resulted in profits and the last in a substantial loss. The taxation legislation restricts the carry back of loss relief against profits of earlier periods: see **9.11**. The judges upheld the Inland Revenue's contention commenting that it was not obligatory for the Inland Revenue to divide and apportion profits where a 'more accurate and a fairer estimate of profit or loss' of the chargeable periods was available.

HMRC consider that transactions can only be matched with accounting periods where there are a few easily identifiable transactions (HMRC Company Taxation Manual 01405).

CT600

2.7   In practice, shortly after the commencement of the accounting period, HMRC will issue the company with a form CT 603 'Notice to deliver a corporation tax form'. HMRC will then issue the company with a company tax return CT600 (2008) Version 2.

Companies may also use the shorter version of the form CT600 (Short) (2008) Version 2 if this is sufficient to cover their activities (both forms are reproduced in the appendices). The shorter version omits overseas income, tonnage tax profits, intra-group activities and management expenses for companies with investment business. Additional or replacement copies may be obtained from the HMRC Orderline (telephone: 0845 300 6555 or fax: 0845 300 6777) or from the HMRC website (www.hmrc.gov.uk). HMRC also accept an HMRC approved substitute version.

If relevant to the company's activities the following supplementary pages must also be submitted together with the main return:

Supplementary pages

2.8

CT600A	Loans to participators by close companies	See Chapter 4
CT600B	Controlled foreign companies	See Chapter 13

CT600C	Group and Consortium	See Chapter 10
CT600D	Insurance	
CT600E	Charities and Community Amateur Sports Clubs (CASCs)	See Chapter 5
CT600F	Tonnage Tax	
CT600G	Corporate Venturing Scheme	See Chapter 12
CT600H	Cross-border royalties	See Chapter 3
CT600I	Supplementary charge in respect of ring fence trade	
CT600J	Disclosure of tax avoidance schemes	See Chapter 18

FILING DATE

2.9   The company tax return must be filed on the last day of whichever of the following periods is last to end:

- within 12 months of the end of the accounting period for which it is made;

- if the company's statutory accounting period is longer than 12 months but no longer than 18 months, 12 months from the beginning of the accounting period;

- if the company's statutory accounts are for a period longer than 18 months then 30 months from the beginning of that period;

- alternatively if the notice to deliver a return is given late then three months after the notice was served (*FA 1998, Sch 18, para 14*).

A company may amend its company tax return within 12 months of the filing date. Therefore if a company's accounting period is 31 December 2008, its filing date is 31 December 2009 and it is able to file an amendment to the return anytime up to 31 December 2010. If a company makes a return for a wrong period it can correct the position any time up to 12 months after the filing date on the assumption that the return had been made for the correct period (*FA 1998, Sch 18, para 15*).

HMRC also has the power to amend returns for errors and omissionsbut can only do so for up to nine months after the return was filed or nine months after an amendment was made if the correction follows an amendment. The company can in turn reject the correction within its amendment period or within three months of receipt of HMRC's amendment if later (*FA 1998, Sch 18, para 16*). With effect from 1 April 2009, an HMRC officer may also amend a return for anything else that he or she has reason to believe is incorrect, in the light of information available to him or her (*FA 2008, s 119(2)(b)*).

ONLINE FILING

2.10   Corporation tax returns can be filed online with HMRC by using the online facility at www.hmrc.gov.uk/businesses. The company tax return (CT600), supplementary pages A to J, the statutory accounts and computations can be filed with HMRC over the internet. Attachments should be sent in PDF format.

Taxpayers registering for the first time will be asked to enter their name and to select a password. After successful registration a username will be displayed on screen. The company will then receive confirmation by post of the company's User ID and Activation PIN(s) to the address that HMRC have on their database within seven days of registering. The User ID is required together with the password every time the company logs in. The service must be activated within 28 days of the Activation PIN letter date.

Taxpayers will need a computer with an internet connection. HMRC have given the following information on their frequently asked questions on their website. It is advisable to check this information for technological changes.

To use our Online Services, you will require access to a computer with an Internet connection

Operating system and browser requirements

Windows users:

- *Internet browsers: Internet Explorer 5.0 or above or Opera 7.0.*

Mac users:

- *Safari 2.0.4 and Opera 7.0.*

Please also note that your Internet browser must have JavaScript and cookies enabled and be capable of supporting 128-bit SSL.

Other operating systems and browsers

Browsers and versions, other than those listed above, such as Mozilla Firefox, may allow you to access the site and use the pages but might not display the site as designed or allow you to access all the functionality. To check for the latest version of your browser, please visit the supplier's website and follow any instructions provided.

(Frequently asked questions HMRC Website.)

2.11 *Self-assessment*

Any company with a CT Unique Taxpayer Reference can register and use corporation tax online filing. The Unique Taxpayer Reference (UTR) is made up of ten numbers and is shown on the company tax return, a notice to complete a company tax return or on the statement of account. It may also be on other documents from HMRC. Depending on the document or piece of correspondence, it may be printed next to the heading 'Tax Reference', 'UTR', or 'Official Use'.

Taxpayers may use HMRC's free online tax return—CT or any of the available third party products, which have successfully passed HMRC testing procedures.

Only the full company tax return may be filed online. The short return is a paper only option. The corporation tax software guides the user to the relevant sections of the full return. Questions are posed relating to the circumstances. It is important to understand the meaning of these questions and the consequences of the response. The software will perform the calculation. After successful submission the software will display an online message indicating that the return has been received and accepted. HMRC will also send an email confirming that the return has been received and accepted, if an email address has been given. Taxpayers have the facility to print out a copy of the return from the online return software.

An agent may submit an online return on behalf of a client and complete the declaration if the following are met:

- Authorisation is in place with a form 64–8 signed by a proper officer of the company.

- The agent must make a copy of the relevant information before it is sent.

- A proper officer of the company, (or other person authorised to make the return on behalf of the company) must confirm that the information is correct to the best of his knowledge and belief before the information is sent by the agent. The officer must approve and sign the copy approved as such.

This does not apply where the agent is a person authorised by the company to make the return on its behalf (*Income and Corporation Tax (Electronic Communications) Regulations 2003, SI 2003/282*).

PAYMENT

2.11   Electronically coded payslips are included within form CT603 notice to deliver a company tax return. Payment can be made electronically by BACS

(Bankers Automated Clearing Services) or CHAPS (Clearing House Automated Payments System) or by cheque to HMRC accounts office. It is important to use the payslip that corresponds to the relevant accounting period, otherwise the company's cheque may be misallocated.

A payment by cheque is deemed to be made on the day that the cheque is received by HMRC (*TMA 1970, s 70A*). *Finance Act 2007* includes provisions to enable HMRC to make regulations to treat the payment as being made when the cheque clears (*FA 2007, s 95 (1)*).

Interest is charged on any corporation tax paid late. Interest is earned on any overpaid corporation tax. The interest receivable calculations are based on the premise that the tax paid last is repaid first: see **3.17**. Interest on tax debts and repayment amounts is brought into account as a loan relationship debit or credit (*FA 1996, s 100(7), TMA 1970, s 90(2)*, HMRC Business Income Manual 45740 & Corporate Finance Manual CFM 5216).

FAILURE TO DELIVER A RETURN BY THE FILING DATE

Penalties for accounting periods commencing prior to 1 April 2008

2.12   These rules apply for returns for tax periods commencing before 1 April 2008 that are due to be filed before 1 April 2009. See **2.36** for details of the new provisions. Under the old penalty rules, failure to deliver a return on time incurs a flat rate penalty of £100 if the return is up to three months late and £200 in any other case. These penalties are increased to £500 and £1,000 where failure occurs for a third successive time (*FA 1998, Sch 18, para 17*). These penalties are not tax-related and will not reduce if the tax liability reduces. If an accounting period is longer than 12 months and HMRC has not been advised of the change, an automatic late filing penalty will be issued to meet the 12-month deadline. Companies should inform HMRC of any changes in accounting periods without delay.

If a company fails to deliver a return within 18 months of the end of an accounting period or by the later filing date then, in addition to the flat rate penalty, it will be liable to a tax-related penalty. The penalty is 10% of the unpaid tax if the return is delivered within two years after the end of the period for which the return is required or 20% of the unpaid tax in any other case (*FA 1998, Sch 18, para 18*).

There is no flat rate penalty where accounts are required under the *Companies Act* and the return is delivered no later than those accounts are required at Companies House (*FA 1998, Sch 18, para 19*). This would happen where a company extends its accounting period beyond 12 months.

Example 2.4

Renaldo Ltd, a small private company, prepares accounts to 31 March each year. However, the 2007 accounting period is extended to 30 September 2007. Renaldo Ltd prepared two corporation tax returns; the first to 31 March 2007 and the second to 30 September 2007. The two returns were submitted to HMRC on 30 April 2008. Provided Renaldo Ltd submitted the accounts to 30 September 2007 to Companies House by 30 June 2008 no penalty will ensue. If HMRC raise a penalty notice, the company should appeal under *FA 1998, Sch 18, para 19.*

HMRC's computer system (COTAX) automatically issues flat rate and tax-related penalty notices shortly after the date the penalty is incurred. Additionally, tax-related penalty determinations are automatically amended when the amount of tax payable recorded on COTAX is revised. A further flat rate penalty notice will be issued automatically when incurred after three months unless the initial flat rate penalty is under appeal (Working Together, Issue 13, June 2003).

A company is liable to a tax-related penalty if it makes a fraudulent or negligent return, which is incorrect. It is also liable to a tax-related penalty if it discovers that it has made an incorrect return, which was not made fraudulently or negligently, but which it does not correct without unreasonable delay (*FA 1988, Sch 18, para 20*). Such penalties are normally negotiated with HMRC: see **2.20**. These rules are replaced under the new penalty regime, see **2.36**. All tax related penalties carry interest. The rates are the same as for interest on unpaid tax: see **3.14** (*TMA 1970, s 103A*).

Determination assessment

2.13   HMRC have the power to make an estimation of the tax due for the accounting period, if no return is submitted in response to a notice requiring a return. The company has no right of appeal against such an estimation. If no return is due for the accounting period or the company can show that it has delivered a return for the period, then the determination has no effect (*FA 1998, Sch 18, para 36*). The determination replaces the company's self-assessment. See **2.32** for further details.

ENQUIRY

Time

Accounting periods ending prior to 31 March 2008

2.14   HMRC may by notice enquire into a company tax return any time within 12 months of the filing date, if the return was filed on or before the filing date. If the return was delivered late the enquiry time is extended to 12 months after the next 31 January, 30 April, 31 July or 31 October following the date the return was delivered. Similarly, if the company has made any amendments to the return, the enquiry time is extended to 12 months after the next 31 January, 30 April, 31 July or 31 October following the date the amendment was made (*FA 1998, Sch 18, para 24*). If the time limit has expired for enquiry into the main return but not the company amendments, then HMRC may only enquire into those amendments (*FA 1998, Sch 18, para 25*). If the time limit for a self-assessment enquiry has expired HMRC may make a discovery assessment (*FA 1998, Sch 18, para 41(1)*). See **2.32**.

The enquiry notice must be received by the company before the time limit. It is assumed that second-class post takes four working days to be delivered and first-class post takes two working days to be delivered. Working days do not include Saturdays, Sundays or Bank Holidays (Revenue Manuals EM1510). It would seem that notices or assessments received outside the statutory time limit may only be disputed by noting the post-mark on the envelope in which the notice was sent. Electronic filing is more efficient in this respect.

Accounting periods ended after 31 March 2008

2.15 For accounting periods ended after 31 March 2008, the time span for which HMRC may give notice of an enquiry into a single company or a company that is a member of a small group is shortened to 12 months from the date when the return was delivered to HMRC (*FA 2007, s 96(3) & (4)*)). A small group takes the Companies Act definition: see **6.20**. A company is required to indicate on the front of form CT600 if it is part of a group that is not small.

Procedure

2.16 Where fraud is not suspected, HMRC conducts its enquiries according to set practices, which are set out in its Codes of Practice ('COP'). COP14 Corporation tax self-assessment enquiries details the procedures regarding a corporation tax enquiry.

To begin an enquiry HMRC will issue notice, copied to an appointed agent, in the form of a letter that they intend to enquire into the company tax return (*FA 1998, Sch18, para, 24(1)*). Copies of these letters are reproduced in Working Together, Issue 12, February 2003.

The scope of the enquiry can extend to any item included in the return, any amount that affects the tax payable by the company for another accounting period and the tax liability of another company for any accounting period together with all claims and elections. The enquiry may also extend to the transfer pricing information. See Chapter 14 for a discussion on transfer pricing. If a return is made for the wrong period, HMRC may enquire into the period for which it should have been made (*FA 1998, Sch 18, para 26*).

HMRC expect and encourage the taxpayer's co-operation with the enquiry. They warn that if an offence has been committed and tax geared penalties result, they will take into account in calculating the amount of the penalty the extent to which the taxpayer has been helpful and has freely and fully volunteered any information about income or gains that were omitted or understated. Information on tax-geared penalties is given in IR 160 (enquiries under self- assessment) and is discussed below at **2.23**.

Overall the company is responsible for its affairs, even if it has appointed a professional adviser, who should be fully informed of the facts of the case. HMRC will deal with a professional adviser if one has been appointed. If matters are not progressing with the adviser with sufficient speed HMRC will advise the company and may then deal with the company direct.

In most cases enquiries take the form of an aspect enquiry; in other words just dealing with one or two issues on a claim or return. In-depth enquiries do occur with HMRC conducting a wide-ranging examination into some companies' tax affairs. In such an event HMRC will undoubtedly require to see the records from which the return was prepared. Thus the importance of keeping good accounting records (see **2.3**) manifests itself. Good accounting records are the company's only real defence in disputing HMRC claims. HMRC may ask to examine the records at the business premises or they may ask for them to be sent. With the withdrawal of the company statutory audit requirement and the influx of effective electronic systems into business life, the supporting evidence and vouchers are often ignored. The astute director/shareholder will ensure that he maintains good systems and company records.

In *Ferribly Construction (UK) Ltd v Revenue & Customs Commissioners* (2007) SpC 635, a construction company declared a profit on its self-assessment corporation tax return, which it later claimed should have been a loss. The company was unable to produce proper books and records to HMRC in support of the loss claim. The assessment therefore remained unchanged.

Whether or not a professional adviser can be sued by a client in the wake of a full-scale HMRC enquiry for not warning him to keep better records is a case in point. Companies must realise that maintaining good records is not just an administration function but also a statutory function. HMRC's enquiries can stretch to opening separate enquiries into the directors' personal tax affairs. Even if there is nothing untoward the inconvenience of the scenario can be very unpleasant for those involved.

Company documents – accounting periods ended prior to 1 April 2009

2.17   These rules are expected to continue to apply for accounting periods ending prior to 1 April 2009, from which time the new HMRC powers will be introduced (Budget 2008 BN97); see **2.46** et seq. HMRC may by notice require the company to produce documents and to supply information in connection with their enquiry. The company must be given at least 30 days to comply with the notice. The time limit must be specified on the notice. Copies of documents may be supplied, but HMRC may, by notice, inspect the original documents. HMRC have the right to take copies of, or make extracts from any document produced (*FA 1998, Sch 18, para 27*).

The company has the right of appeal to the Commissioners against the notice to supply the documents. The appeal must be given in writing and within 30 days after the notice was given to the company. The Commissioners' decision will be final.

Failure to comply with a notice to supply documents will result in a £50 penalty. If the failure continues after the penalty has been imposed there is a daily penalty of £30 under *TMA 1970, s 100* if imposed by an HMRC officer or a daily penalty of £150 if imposed by the Commissioners under *TMA 1970, s 100C* (*FA 1998, Sch 18, para 29*). Enquiries into the affairs of the directors and their companies.

2.18   In the case of many small and medium-sized companies the affairs of the company are closely linked with those of the directors. HMRC may consider enquiring into the directors' affairs when they enquire into the company's affairs (HMRC Enquiry Manual EM 8205). If the Revenue officer discovers or suspects an omission or understatement of income in the company directors' returns or the returns indicate a build-up of private capital inconsistent with known income, he will refer the matter to the Revenue company case owner. If the company case owner decides to enquire into the company's tax return and the directors' returns he will co-ordinate and take responsibility for all enquiries. The company case owner will take a risk-based approach to the enquiry and in so doing will work closely with the case owners responsible for the individual director's affairs (HMRC Enquiry Manual EM 8210). If the individual case owner of the director's affairs wishes to enquire into a director's affairs because of some known or suspected inaccuracy they will look to the company first of all to ensure that all matters and therefore all sources of income are brought into account (HMRC Enquiry Manual EM 8207). If enquiries are made into the directors', as well as the company's, affairs the directors must be issued with their own *TMA 1970, s 9(A)* letters from HMRC addressed to each individual director.

Enquiries into the directors' self-assessment returns

2.19   HMRC's opening enquiry letter into a director's return will refer to the matters into which they wish to enquire and will include a request for documents and/or information about the areas of the returns that are to be enquired into. If there is a concern about the probable close link between the company's and the directors' private finances, HMRC should mention this at the outset (HMRC Enquiry Manual EM 8211). A close link is understood to mean the director's use of company funds for private purposes, without any charge to taxation arising. HMRC will not be in a position to know for sure whether there is a linkage between the two unless both the company's and the director's private records are cohesively examined.

Directors' documents – accounting periods ended prior to 1 April 2009

2.20   A director's private papers, such as income statements and bank statements, are his own private property, under the existing rules that are expected to continue to apply for accounting periods ending prior to 1 April 2009. If HMRC is carrying out an enquiry into the company's affairs alone the case worker concerned cannot compel either the company or the director to provide this information. Corporation tax document requests under *FA 1998, Sch 18, para 27* do not grant these powers, but under the new rules HMRC may request any document (see **2.46**). Prior to that, HMRC may ask the director to provide them voluntarily with all his private account statements. Whether or not to adhere to this request depends upon each individual director and company concerned. The situation is not made easy because HMRC correspondence, as this is a company enquiry, is sent to the company or the professional agent. The company may have no knowledge of the director's personal affairs and the agent may not even act for the director concerned. When faced with such a problem, careful consideration must be given to all factors involved by the director, the agent and the company. If the director declines to give this information voluntarily to HMRC, HMRC may feel compelled to open an enquiry under *TMA 1970, s 9A* into the director's personal self-assessment tax return. Documents for accounting periods ending prior to 1 April 2009 will then be requested from the director under *TMA 1970, s 19A*. This will also enable HMRC to obtain information regarding *ICTA 1988, s 419* in respect of loans to directors and overdrawn loan accounts: see **4.14–4.22**. *TMA 1970, s 19A(2)* requires the director to submit this information within 30 days of the request.

If HMRC considers that a full enquiry into the director's return is not warranted they may issue a request to the director under *TMA 1970, s 20(3)* for the director to supply his private bank account statements to HMRC. HMRC may also make a request under *TMA 1970, s 20(3)* if the time limit for enquiring into the director's personal tax return has expired. For example, the enquiry window for self-assessment tax returns for the year ended 5 April 2007 will close on 31 January 2009.

If HMRC's concerns are justified the closure of the enquiry may result in a beneficial loan assessment under *ITEPA 2003, s 175* for the director and or an *ICTA 1988, s 419* liability for the company. In some cases the director's extraction of funds may be treated as employment income and, unless a PAYE direction transferring liability from the employer to the employee has been made, credit will be give in the income tax self-assessment for the PAYE that the company should have deducted.

In *Smith v Revenue and Customs Commissioners* SpC 680, HMRC enquiries into the company's affairs led to enquiries into the director's affairs, and to requests for documents under *TMA 1970, s 20*. No enquiry was opened into the director's personal tax returns. The Revenue officer raised an income tax assessment on the director without opening a self-assessment enquiry into his affairs and without all conditions being met. The assessment was allowed because the amount assessed was valid, despite the procedure being incorrect.

Course of enquiry

2.21   Normally the course of enquiry involves the company and/or the professional agent supplying information and documents to HMRC in response to their queries. There is a period of time over which this happens and replies to the Revenue should be given accurately and in good time. In any event, if any enquiry is in progress it should not hold up the submission of the next year's tax return even if best estimated entries are included when preparing the return.

In addition HMRC may call a meeting with the directors, company secretary or even the employees to discuss the company's business affairs. Many indeed will feel nervous and intimidated in such a situation. HMRC cannot compel those involved to attend a meeting. A professional adviser may attend as well as or instead of the company attendees. In all circumstances, whether or not a meeting takes place, HMRC must be provided with all the information necessary to answer their enquiries.

If a meeting takes place HMRC have formal procedures, which they must follow.

They require the company representatives to bring the necessary records either to answer HMRC's questions or to support their own queries. HMRC will make a written record of what is said at the meeting. The company may ask to see the notes.

HMRC may even go as far as requesting the company to sign a copy of their notes to signify agreement. HMRC cannot compel the company to do so. The company, of course, may comment on the notes if it wishes. The worth of attendance at a meeting from the taxpayer's perspective must be judged on its own merits in each and every case.

Corporation tax return amendment

2.22   HMRC may, by notice, amend the self-assessment calculation during the course of the enquiry if they consider it insufficient. The company has a 30-day time limit to lodge an appeal against the amendment (*FA 1998, Sch 18, para 30*). Similarly, the company may amend its return during the course of the enquiry. This will not restrict the scope of the enquiry, but it may be taken into account. The amendment will not take effect until the enquiry is finished (*FA 1998, Sch 18, para 31*). During the course of the enquiry, if the company considers that it may have additional tax to pay it can make an additional payment to reduce any interest charges that might arise. Overpayments are always repaid if incorrect. If, during the course of the enquiry, it is discovered that there is a period for which a return is required but for which none has been submitted, then such a return is required to be submitted within 30 days of the final determination (*FA 1998, Sch 18, para 35*).

COMPLETION OF ENQUIRY

2.23   The enquiry is complete when HMRC issues their closure notice to the company stating their conclusions (*FA 1998, Sch 18, para 32*). The closure notice must either state that in the officer's opinion no amendments are required as a result of the enquiry, or if amendments are required to amend the corporation tax return accordingly (*FA 1998, Sch 18, para 34* as amended by *FA 2008, s 119(6)*). The additional corporation tax payments will most likely include interest on overdue tax and may include a penalty.

Penalties – accounting periods ended prior to 1 April 2008

2.24   These rules apply to accounting periods ended prior to 1 April 2008. For the new rules, see **2.36**. The penalty can amount to up to 100% of the tax due under *FA 1998, Sch 18, para 20*. This is a situation whereby a company fraudulently or negligently delivers an incorrect company tax return to HMRC. It also covers the situation whereby a company, which discovering it had erroneously, as opposed to purposefully, delivered an incorrect company tax return to HMRC, failed to correct the error swiftly.

HMRC calculates the penalties and the agreed settlement as set out in IR 160 (enquiries under self-assessment). The procedure involves HMRC suggesting a pecuniary offer that the company should make to clear its corporation tax liabilities.

HMRC will calculate the amount of the offer based on tax, interest and penalty.

Tax and interest fall due under normal regulations and are non-negotiable. Penalties can amount to 100% of the tax underpaid or paid late and are negotiable.

HMRC commence their calculations with a 100% penalty. This can be reduced depending on how well or badly the company has co-operated with HMRC and its enquiries. Reductions are based on disclosure, co-operation and seriousness. The maximum reductions are shown in the chart below. In practice each situation will be viewed on its merits and the percentage reduction amended accordingly.

HMRC penalty reduction percentages

2.25

% reduction	Reason
20%	Full disclosure after HMRC enquiries commenced
30%	Full voluntary disclosure with no HMRC enquiry
40%	Co-operation
40%	Seriousness

Disclosure is distinguished by disclosure after HMRC enquiries commenced and a full voluntary disclosure prior to enquiry. Co-operation is determined by the speed with which questions are answered and information is truthfully and honestly supplied. Seriousness depends on the grievousness of the offence, be it slovenly accounting or a fraud.

Example 2.5

R Ltd failed to provide a company tax return for the year ended 31 December 2007.

The underpaid tax amounted to £20,000. Interest amounted to £2,000.

R Ltd assisted HMRC with its enquiries when contacted but was unable to produce all necessary documentation due to poor accounting.

HMRC thought that the company should be given the following reductions.

Disclosure	15%
Co-operation	30%
Seriousness	20%
Total	65%

With a 65% penalty reduction, a penalty of 35% will be payable.

	£
Corporation Tax	20,000
Interest	2,000
Penalties 35%	7,000
Total	29,000

2.26   The company may ask HMRC to reconsider the suggested offer, which HMRC may agree to or decline.

If the company agrees with HMRC's suggestion, formal documents recording the negotiated settlement and setting out the contractual terms will be prepared. These are in the form of letter from the company to HMRC offering to pay the agreed sum within a stated period and if satisfied an acceptance letter to the company from HMRC. A payslip will accompany the acceptance letter. If payment cannot be made straightaway the company may arrange to pay by instalments.

If the company refuses to accept the offer as laid down by HMRC, HMRC will prepare a closure notice and assess tax, interest and penalties as they consider fit.

If the company is dissatisfied with HMRC's offer it has a right of appeal.

Right of appeal

2.27   The company has the right of appeal against an amendment to the corporation tax return after the enquiry has finished (*FA 1998, Sch 18, para 34*).

The company's right of appeal can be exercised at any time during the course of the enquiry. An enquiry by default implies that a company is in the wrong. This may not necessarily be the case. It is the company's duty to prepare a complete and correct corporation tax self-assessment. If the company considers that it has done so and put all the information and explanations necessary to verify the company's tax return at HMRC's disposal with no avail it can apply to the Commissioners for the enquiry to be closed in a specified period (*FA 1998, Sch 18, para 33*). In practice, HMRC state in Code of Practice COP 14 that they would prefer that the company contacted them first to ascertain whether they can in fact close the enquiry or if they are seeking further information. Such an application by the company to the Commissioners is not an appeal against a decision. The procedures that the Commissioners must adopt before they are able to issue a direction to HMRC to close the enquiry are the same as appeal procedures.

In *Jade Palace Ltd v Revenue and Customs Commrs* SpC 540 the taxpayer was granted a closure notice within a set period. Correspondence between the taxpayer and HMRC was protracted. The taxpayer admitted that it was likely that additional tax was due. However, the legislation states that HMRC is only required to state their conclusions at the end of an enquiry and not that they must be satisfied as to the tax due before closing an enquiry.

Where enquiries into a company tax return and directors' returns are linked, the company and the individual directors can apply separately to the Commissioners for a direction to complete the enquiry into their own return. HMRC will not close either enquiry if they are linked and the corresponding director or company enquiry is incomplete (HMRC Enquiry Manual EM 8215).

During the course of the enquiry the company and HMRC may by written notice jointly refer matters to the Special Commissioners. No enquiry closure notice may be given during the course of the enquiry. The determination by the Special Commissioners is final and must be considered by HMRC in reaching conclusions on their enquiry (*FA 1998, Sch 18, paras 31A–31D*).

The company and HMRC have the right of appeal. If either party needs time to prepare they can ask the Commissioners to adjourn to a later date. HMRC will inform the company if they intend to take the case to appeal and give the company details of their intended proposals at least 14 days before the date of the hearing.

APPEALS PROCEDURES

Lodging an appeal

2.28 With effect from 1 April 2009 the appeal process is to change, see **2.31**. Until then, the following procedures apply. The company must lodge its appeal with the Commissioners within 30 days from the date that an assessment was issued (*FA 1998, Sch 18, para 48*). Normally cases are heard by the General Commissioners. If the appeal is more complex, HMRC or the company may request that the Special Commissioners hear it. The prime difference between the two types of Commissioners is that the General Commissioners work voluntarily and are usually involved in cases of fact whereas Special Commissioners are remunerated and are involved in cases of law. Hearings are held in public unless the company requests a private hearing.

The company must make its appeal in writing to HMRC at the address shown on the appeal decision. The appeal should indicate whether the case is to be heard by either the General or the Special Commissioners. Grounds for the appeal must also be included and the location for the hearing. The choice of location cannot be altered once made. No charges are involved. The company pays its own professional costs such as tax advisers' fees and legal fees. The General Commissioners have no power to award costs to either party once a decision has been given. Attendance and travelling costs cannot be claimed. Professional fees and costs of the appeal are not an allowable deduction for corporation tax purposes: see **5.20**—tax appeals.

On receipt of the appeal HMRC procedure is to try to resolve matters by mutual agreement (HMRC Code of Practice COP 14). If this fails they will pass the case to the Clerk to the Commissioners for a formal appeal hearing.

Preparing for a Commissioners hearing

2.29 In due course the company and its professional agent will receive details of the arrangements for the hearing. There is no compulsion for a company representative to attend the hearing, but it is expedient. The company may be represented by a director or company secretary or by its professional agent.

Prior to the hearing some preparatory work should be undertaken. HMRC advise that the company should assume that the tribunal is totally ignorant of the facts and nature of the hearing before them and that the company must provide them with all the necessary facts and information. Therefore, in preparation for the case, the company should consider the precise facts of the case, the evidence to support the company's case and the evidence against HMRC.

The company should also consider whether there are any witnesses and whether they and their representatives will be attending the hearing.

HMRC requires that the following documents should be brought to the hearing:

● a copy of the HMRC decision against which an appeal is lodged;

● copies of correspondence with, and any other papers received from, HMRC;

- notes of the date and content of any relevant telephone conversations with HMRC, and the names of the people spoken to; and

- any other relevant documents, eg accounts, invoices, receipts or bank statements.

At the hearing, the company will be invited to state its case first of all. HMRC will then state their case. The company can request a reverse order. Questions from all parties will follow and then the Commissioners adjourn to make their decision.

If either the company or HMRC disagrees with the decision they can ask for a review by the Commissioners. A review request must be made within 14 days from when the court's determination was sent to the company. The parties must be able to substantiate their claim.

Appeal to the High Court

2.30   A company dissatisfied with a reasonable claim may decide to take its case to the High Court. An appeal to the High Court must be made within 30 days of the date of the decision against the company. An appeal can only be made on a point of law. The High Court can award costs. An appeal against a General Commissioners' decision is made by firstly writing to the Clerk to the General Commissioners and identifying the point of law at issue. A £25 statutory fee must be enclosed. The Clerk to the General Commissioners will then prepare the case stated: a final draft of the case to be signed by the Commissioners and the company. The second stage in the appeal application process is for the company to send the case stated with form N161 (available from any county court office or downloadable from the court service website) known as the appellant's notice to HMRC's Solicitor's Office and any other party to the proceedings.

An appeal against a Special Commissioners' decision can be made by sending the appellants notice, together with a copy of the decision, to arrive within 56 days of the date of the decision. The case will then be heard at a fixed date by the High Court who can award costs (see Tribunals Service Tax Appeals Booklet April 2008 www.generalcommissioners.gov.uk).

The Tribunals, Courts and Enforcement Act 2007

2.31   The *Tribunals, Courts and Enforcement Act 2007* reforms all central government administrative tribunals including the tax appeal tribunals. It is anticipated that the tax chamber procedures will be introduced from April 2009; see www.financeandtaxtribunals.gov.uk – key dates for tribunal reform. There will be two tribunals, a First-tier Tribunal and an Upper Tribunal. The majority of tax appeals will appeal to the First-tier Tribunal at first instance and then to the Upper Tribunal on a point of law.

In preparation for the new tribunal system, HM Treasury have the power to review HMRC's appeals and administration processes (*FA 2008, s 124*).

DETERMINATIONS AND DISCOVERY ASSESSMENTS

2.32   If a company fails to submit a corporation tax return by the filing date, in response to a notice to deliver a corporation tax return, HMRC may at any time during the next five years, estimate the amount of corporation tax due in a determination assessment (*FA 1998, Sch 18 para 36*). *FA 2008, Sch 39, para 38* has reduced this period to three years, for periods expected to commence after 1 April 2009. Alternatively, if a return is filed for that period that is the subject of the notice to deliver but there is another accounting period ending during that return period, HMRC may issue a determination for that period within any time during the next five years (*FA 1998, Sch 18 para 37*). *FA 2008, Sch 39, para 39* has reduced this period to three years, for periods expected to commence after 1 April 2009. These determinations are treated as the company's self-assessment (*FA 1998, Sch 18 para 39*). If a self-assessment return is subsequently filed it will replace the determination, but the return must be filed no later than five years after HMRC were able to issue the determination assessment, or one year after the date of the determination assessment (*FA 1998, Sch 18, para 40*). *FA 2008, Sch 39, para 40* has reduced the five years to three years, for periods expected to commence after 1 April 2009. If a company has delivered a return, HMRC may make a discovery assessment or determination in cases where there is a loss of tax that was brought about carelessly or deliberately by the company or by a person acting on its behalf (*FA 1998, Sch 18 paras 42 & 43*). *FA 2008, Sch 39, para 41* has specified carelessly and deliberately, for periods expected to commence after 1 April 2009. Prior to this, the words fraud or negligent conduct are applied.

The time limit for cases of fraud and negligence are 21 years from the end of the accounting period to which it relates (*FA 1998, Sch 18, para 46(2)*). With effect from 1 April 2009, an assessment for a loss of tax brought about carelessly by the company or a related person may be made at any time not more than six years after the end of the accounting period to which it relates. In cases of loss of tax brought about deliberately by the company or a related person, a failure to comply with an assessment raised because it acted carelessly, or a failure to comply with a tax avoidance scheme obligation (see **Chapter 18**), the period is 20 years from the end of the accounting period, subject to any condition existing at the time, which allows a longer period (*FA 1998, Sch 18, para 46; FA 2008, Sch 39, para 42*).

If HMRC discovers that the amount assessed on a company tax return is insufficient or the relief has become excessive they may make a discovery assessment. They may also make a discovery assessment if there has been fraudulent or negligent conduct. A discovery assessment may be made at any time, even if the enquiry time had elapsed or they had completed their enquiries into the return, if they could not be reasonably expected, on the basis of the information made available to them, to be aware of the errors in the return. In *Revenue and Customs Commrs v Household Estate Agents Ltd* (2007) All ER(D) 175 (Jul) a company submitted a corporation tax return in accordance with prevailing practice. An employee benefit trust deduction was treated as an allowable deduction from profits, but following a later ruling was no longer held to be allowable. The company made no adjustment to its corporation tax computation. HMRC had opened enquiries into the following two returns and in the course of those enquiries enquired about payments into the trust. HMRC made a discovery assessment, which the company claimed was precluded by *FA 1998, Sch 18, para 45*. It was held that HMRC was not prevented from making a discovery assessment, because it would have been reasonable for the inspector if he had thought about it to initiate an enquiry, which could have been expected to reveal the full facts. It was further decided that the burden of proof that a taxpayer had not made a return in accordance with generally prevailing practice lay with the taxpayer and not the Revenue.

Information is regarded as being made available to HMRC if:

(i)   it is included in a company tax return or in the documents accompanying the return;

(ii) it is contained in a relevant claim made by the company or in any accounts, statements or documents accompanying any such claim; or

(iii) it is contained in any documents, accounts or information produced or provided by the company to HMRC for the purposes of an enquiry into a return or claim; or

(iv) it is information, the existence and relevance of which could reasonably be expected to be inferred by HMRC from the information supplied in circumstance (i), (ii) or (iii) above or is notified to HMRC (*FA 1998, Sch 18, para 44*).

It is therefore important to supply clear information to HMRC to support the return or the queries raised in order to avoid a discovery assessment.

Similar powers are afforded to HMRC in respect of a recovery of an excessive repayment (*FA 1998, Sch 18, para 53*). The normal time limit was six years, but this has been reduced to four years for periods expected to commence after 1 April 2009 (*FA 2008, Sch 39, para 44*).

FRAUD

2.33   HMRC conducts its investigations into cases of suspected fraud under Code of Practice COP 9 (2005)—Cases of Suspected Serious Fraud.

These procedures came into effect on 1 September 2005 and any cases that existed at that time are worked to a conclusion under the old Hansard procedures (Code of Practice COP 9). The procedure covers both direct and indirect taxes. The Hansard procedure implied that, if a taxpayer made a full statement and co-operated with the Revenue during their investigation, he could expect that case to be dealt with on a civil basis rather than a criminal basis. There was of course no guarantee. Under Code of Practice COP 9 (2005) HMRC has decided that a criminal prosecution regarding a particular matter will not follow the civil investigation.

Civil investigation fraud procedures

2.34   In cases of suspected serious tax fraud where HMRC opt for a civil rather than a criminal investigation, the company (and the directors) being investigated will be given one opportunity to secure maximum benefit by making a full disclosure of all tax irregularities. It is envisaged that a full declaration will speed the outcome and efficiency of the enquiry. Disclosure reports are expected to cover direct and indirect taxes.

If the company does not co-operate, HMRC will institute its own enquiry and penalties are likely to be higher. Under this code of practice HMRC will be investigating direct and indirect tax fraud. The same penalty reduction percentages apply as detailed in **2.25** above.

Prosecution for tax fraud

2.35   Under the new code if HMRC has made a decision to follow a civil investigation route then further criminal investigations for that offence will not follow. However, HMRC may still carry out criminal investigations into the company and its directors for other alleged offences. With effect from 1 December 2007, criminal investigations may be conducted under *s 114* of the *Police and Criminal Evidence Act 1984* (*PACE*) (*SI 2007/3175*). Under PACE, HMRC officers are able to apply for search warrants and be given powers of arrest (*FA 2007, s 82*). HMRC have staff authorised to use criminal investigation powers in criminal intelligence, internal governance, detection, risk and intelligence. See *HMRC Technical Note 30 November 2007 'HM Revenue and Customs – Criminal investigation powers and safeguards'.*

PENALTIES FOR ERRORS

New penalty regime effective after 1 April 2009

2.36   *Finance Act 2007* (*FA 2007, s 97, Sch 24* as amended by *FA 2008, Sch 40*). introduced a new penalty regime which comes into effect for returns or other documents for tax periods commencing on or after 1 April 2008 that are due to be filed on or after 1 April 2009 (*HMRC Brief 19/2008 2 April 2008*) (*SI/2008/568*)These rules not only apply to corporation tax but also to income tax, capital gains tax, construction industry deduction and VAT. See Revenue and Customs Brief no. 29/08 for HMRC learning package. HMRC have also introduced a new manual on this topic – Compliance Handbook Manual.

As regards corporation tax, HMRC will raise a penalty if the company or another person has either carelessly or deliberately supplied a document from the type listed below, containing an inaccuracy that leads to a tax understatement or a false or inflated allowable loss or a false or inflated claim to repayment of tax or to a payment of a corporation tax credit. Separate penalties are charged for each inaccuracy contained in the document.

(*FA 2007, Sch 24, paras 1 & 1A*).

The types of documents on which a penalty is payable are as follows:

- Company Tax Return (CT600 and/or supplementary pages) as required by *FA 1998, Sch 18, para 3*;

- any return, statement or declaration in connection with a claim for an allowance, deduction or relief;

- accounts in connection with ascertaining liability to tax; or

- any document which is likely to be relied upon by HMRC to determine, without further inquiry, a question about:

  — the company's tax liability;

  — the company's corporation tax payments or in connection with corporation tax;

  — any other payment made by the company including penalties; or

  — repayments or any other kind of payment or credit to the company.

Special returns subject to special penalties under *TMA 1970, s 98* are excluded: see **2.2** (*FA 2007, Sch 24, para 12*). Where the company or its officer (see **2.35**) has been convicted of an offence there is no liability to any further penalty (*FA 2007, Sch 24, para 21*).

Provided that the company takes reasonable care to avoid an inaccuracy in the supply of a document to HMRC, the company is not liable to a penalty in respect of any actions or omissions of its corporation tax agent (*FA 2007, Sch 24, para 18*).

The penalty rules imposed on companies that fail to notify HMRC that they are within the charge to corporation tax (see **2.2**) are contained in *FA 2008, Sch 41*. These rules mirror those of *FA 2007, Sch 24;* see **2.37**.

Circumstances in which a penalty is payable

2.37   If HMRC under-assesses the company's corporation tax liability and the company has failed to take reasonable steps to notify HMRC within a 30-day period commencing with the date of the under-assessment HMRC will raise a penalty. In deciding what is reasonable, HMRC will consider whether the company knew or should have known of the under-assessment and if so, what steps would have been reasonable to notify HMRC (*FA 2007, Sch 24, para 2*).

There are three degrees of inaccuracy on the part of the company, each with increasing degrees of seriousness on which a penalty may be charged: careless, deliberate but not concealed and deliberate and concealed. There is only one penalty if the error is attributable to another person. The penalty is based on a percentage of the potential lost revenue. Potential lost revenue is discussed at **2.38** onwards. The relevant percentages are:

Degree of inaccuracy	% penalty based on potential lost revenue
Careless,	30%
Deliberate but not concealed	70%
Deliberate and concealed	100%
Error attributable to another person	100%

A careless inaccuracy arises when the company fails to take reasonable care when supplying the document to HMRC. A deliberate but not concealed inaccuracy arises when the company wilfully supplies a document containing incorrect information but takes no steps to conceal the fact. A deliberate and concealed inaccuracy arises when the company again wilfully supplies false evidence, but this time takes steps to conceal the fact.

Even if the company delivered a document containing an inaccuracy to HMRC with neither a careless nor a deliberate intent but which later was discovered to contain an inaccuracy, the circumstance is treated as careless if the company has not taken reasonable steps to inform HMRC (*FA 2007, Sch 24, para 3*).

A penalty can be reduced if the company makes an unprompted error disclosure. A disclosure is unprompted if it is made at a time when the company has no reason to believe that HMRC has made or is about to discover it. In calculating the reduction, HMRC will consider the quality of the information provided, the assistance given to HMRC in calculating the additional liabilities, and the access given to the company's books and records. Companies are expected to take reasonable care in proportion to their circumstances when maintaining their books and records. They should seek assistance when dealing with unfamiliar transactions. HMRC may suspend a penalty that is invoked for failing to take reasonable care. See *HMRC Brief 19/2008 2 April 2008 'New Penalties for errors in returns and documents'*.

Potential lost revenue: normal rule

2.38   If tax is under-assessed because a company omits to submit a return, the penalty is 30 per cent of the potential lost revenue. The potential lost revenue is the additional tax due or payable as a result of correcting the inaccuracy in a document, including that attributable to a supply of false information or the withholding of information, or the assessment. The additional tax includes all tax due and any over-payments (*FA 2007, Sch 24, para 5*).

Although, inaccurate group relief claims and *s 419* tax can attract a penalty, they are ignored for the purposes of calculating the potential lost revenue (*FA 2007, Sch 24, para 5 (4)*).

Potential lost revenue: multiple errors

2.39   In the case of multiple inaccuracies in a document, careless inaccuracies are treated as being corrected first, followed by a deliberate but not concealed inaccuracy and followed by a deliberate and concealed inaccuracy. For the purposes of calculating potential lost revenue an overstatement of tax by the company is brought into consideration when calculating the penalty. The set off is first against understatements for which the taxpayer is not liable to a penalty and then against careless understatements, deliberate but not concealed understatements and then against deliberate and concealed understatements. No consideration is to be given to the increased tax revenue from another taxpayer as a result of the company's action (*FA 2007, Sch 24, para 6*).

Potential lost revenue: losses

2.40   If an inaccuracy results in a loss being incorrectly recorded the penalty is calculated according to the utilisation of the loss.

A penalty based on the potential lost revenue is also applied if a loss arises or if no loss would have arisen apart from the inaccuracy, and that loss has been used to reduce the amount of tax payable. If a different loss is recorded to the actual true loss the penalty is based on the potential lost revenue from the differential. The potential lost revenue is the amount of the additional tax due or payable as a result of correcting the inaccuracy or the assessment (*FA 2007, Sch 24, para 7(1)*). If the loss has been partially used to reduce the amount of tax payable and the balance remains unutilised, the penalty is the additional tax due or payable as a result of correcting the inaccuracy or the assessment for the loss used plus 10% of the part of the loss that has not been utilised (*FA 2007, Sch 24, para 7(2)*).

If a group makes an overall loss, so that even if an inaccuracy results in an understatement of profit in one group company the potential lost revenue is calculated as though there is an overall loss (*FA 2007, Sch 24, para 7(4)*).

The potential lost revenue will be reduced to nil if the company's circumstances are such that neither it nor any other company would be able to utilise the loss (*FA 2007, Sch 24, para 7(5)*).

Potential lost revenue: delayed tax

2.41   Where tax is declared late because of an inaccuracy, but a penalty based on lost revenue for Revenue Losses as in **2.39** does not apply, a penalty will still be calculated. This penalty is based on 5% of the delayed tax for each year of the delay. Part years are treated on a pro rata basis (*FA 2007, Sch 24, para 8*).

Reductions for disclosure

2.42   HMRC will give a penalty reduction for both prompted and unprompted disclosures. The reduction is based on the seriousness of the penalty and the quality of the disclosure.

For the purposes of these regulations, a company makes a disclosure to HMRC if that company:

- admits to HMRC that there is or may be an inaccuracy, a supply of false information or the withholding of information;

- takes active steps in giving HMRC reasonable help in quantifying the inaccuracy, a supply of false information or the withholding of information, or the under-assessment; and

- allows HMRC access to records for the purpose of ensuring that the inaccuracy, a supply of false information or the withholding of information, or under-assessment is fully corrected.

An unprompted disclosure can be made at any time when the person making it has no reason to believe that HMRC have discovered or are about to discover the inaccuracy or under-assessment. In all other cases the disclosure is unprompted. The quality of the disclosure depends on its timing, nature and extent.

The maximum reduced penalty that may be applied is as follows:

Penalty	Maximum reduced penalty for an Unprompted Disclosure	Maximum reduced penalty for a Prompted Disclosure
30%	0%	15%
70%	20%	35%
100%	30%	50%

(*FA 2007, Sch 24, para 9*)

HMRC have the discretion to reduce a penalty if they consider that special circumstances apply. The special circumstances do not include the company's ability to pay or the fact that a potential loss of revenue from one taxpayer is balanced by a potential over-payment by another. HMRC also have the discretion not to bring proceedings in relation to a penalty and to agree a compromise during any proceedings that should take place (*FA 2007, Sch 24, para 11*).

This penalty is reduced by any other penalty or surcharge applied to the same tax liability (*FA 2007, Sch 24, para 12*).

Procedures

2.43   HMRC will assess the penalty and notify the company. The notice will specify the tax period for which the penalty is assessed. The assessment will be treated and enforced in the same way as a corporation tax assessment. It may be also be combined with an actual corporation tax assessment (*FA 2007, Sch 24, para13(1) and (2)*).

The penalty assessment for a tax understatement must be made within 12 months of the period beginning with the end of the appeal period for the decision correcting the inaccuracy or if there is no penalty assessment the date on which the inaccuracy is corrected. The penalty assessment for a false or inflated loss must be made within 12 months of the period beginning with the end of the appeal period for the assessment of tax, which corrected the understatement (*FA 2007, Sch 24, para 13(3)* and *(4)*). An appeal period is a period during which an appeal could be brought or during which an appeal has been brought but has not been determined or withdrawn. The penalty is due for payment within 30 days of notification (*FA 2007, Sch 24, para 13(1A)*).

Suspension

2.44   HMRC may suspend a penalty for a careless inaccuracy leading to a tax understatement. The period of suspension must not exceed two years. HMRC must issue a notice specifying the part of the penalty to be suspended and stating the suspension conditions with which the company must comply. HMRC may suspend all or part of a penalty if they think that compliance with a condition of suspension would help the company to avoid the company becoming liable to further penalties (*FA 2007, Sch 24, para 14*). The conditions of the suspension may specify the action to be taken and a period within which it must be taken. If on the expiry of the extension period, HMRC is then satisfied that the conditions of the suspension have been complied with, the suspended penalty may be cancelled in whole or in part.

The company has the right of appeal to the First-tier Tribunal against the imposition, the amount, the denied suspension and the conditions of the penalty (*FA 2007, Sch 24, paras 15* and *16*). The tribunal may affirm or cancel the decision or recalculate the penalty (*FA 2007, Sch 24, para 17*).

Liability of company officers

2.45   In the case of a deliberate inaccuracy, which was attributable to an officer of the company, both the company and the officer are liable for the penalty (*FA 2007, Sch 24, para 19*). For this purpose an officer of the company includes a director, a shadow director (as defined in *CA 2006, s 251*) or a secretary (*FA 2007, Sch 24, para 19(3)*). There is no liability if the person concerned had already been convicted of an offence by reason of the inaccuracy (*FA 2007, Sch 24, para 21*).

HMRC powers to obtain information and documents

2.46   These rules come into effect on or after 1 April 2009 and it is anticipated that they will become fully operative after 1 April 2010 (Budget 2008 BN97).

HMRC have powers to:

- request supplementary information from the taxpayer and from third parties;

- inspect records;

- visit premises and to inspect records, assets and premises.

Supplementary information

2.47   The request for supplementary information to either the company or a third party must be made in writing (*FA 2008, Sch 36, paras 1* and *2*). A notice to a third party can only be given with the approval of the company or the First-tier Tribunal (*FA 2008, Sch 36, para 3*). A third party request must name the person to whom it relates unless this has been disapplied by a First-tier Tribunal. A copy of a third party notice must be given to the taxpayer unless the First-tier Tribunal disapplies this requirement (*FA 2008, Sch 36, para 4*). If there are reasonable grounds for believing that a company has not complied with the Taxes Acts, HMRC may request a notice approval from the First-tier Tribunal, even though the identity of the company is unknown to them (*FA 2008, Sch 36, para 5*). HMRC's notice may request the production of original or copy document. The notice must be complied with in full (*FA 2008, Sch 36, para 8*).

Inspect records

2.48   The Commissioners may authorise a person to access and inspect the operation of any computer and associated apparatus used in connection with a relevant required document at any reasonable time (*FA 2008, s 114(3)*).

Any person who obstructs the exercise of this power or does not provide assistance within a reasonable time is liable to a penalty of £300 (*FA 2008, s 114(6)*).

Powers to inspect businesses

2.49   Subject to at least 24 hours' notice being given, an HMRC officer may inspect the business premises and the business assets or the business documents that are on the premises at any time, if the inspection is required for checking the company's tax position (*FA 2008, Sch 36, para 10*). Business assets consist of any assets that a Revenue officer believes are owned, leased or used in connection with carrying on the business. Business documents include all business and statutory documents. Business premises consist of any premises that an officer believes are used for the purposes of carrying on a business and include any building or structure, and land or any means of transport.

Other powers

2.50   Revenue officers have powers to copy documents and to remove and retain a document for a reasonable time if it appears necessary to do so (*FA 2008, Sch 36, para 15*). HMRC are liable to pay the owner reasonable compensation should they cause any damage to the document (*FA 2008, Sch 36, para 16*). In addition HMRC have powers to mark documents and assets that have been inspected (*FA 2008, Sch 36, para 17*).

Restriction on powers

2.51   An information notice only requires a person to produce a document if it is in his possession or power (*FA 2008, Sch 36, para 18*). An information notice may not require a person to produce a document if the whole of the document originates more than six years before the date of the notice, unless the notice is given by, or with the agreement of, an authorised officer (*FA 2008, Sch 36, para 20*).

If a company has made a tax return under *FA 1998, Sch 18, para 3*, a notice may not be given for checking the company's corporation tax position. A notice may be given if an enquiry has commenced under *FA 1998, Sch 18, para 21* but has not yet been completed or if the Revenue and Customs officer has reason to suspect that there has been an under-assessment or excessive relief granted (*FA 2008, Sch 36, para 24*). Documents protected by legal privilege need not be supplied (*FA 2008, Sch 36, para 23*). Similarly, an auditor cannot be required to provide copies of his working papers (*FA 2008, Sch 36, para 24*) and a tax adviser cannot be required to supply copies of his client correspondence or working papers (*FA 2008, Sch 36, para 25*).

Right of appeal

2.52   A company has a right of appeal to the First-tier Tribunal against an information notice (*FA 2008, Sch 36, para 29*). There is no right of appeal if the document formed part of the statutory records or the First-tier Tribunal approved the information notice. Statutory records are documents that the company is required to keep under the Taxes Acts and CGT legislation. Records that do not relate to the business or need to be kept for VAT purposes become statutory records once the chargeable period to which they relate has ended and they need only be kept for the relevant statutory retention period (*FA 2008, Sch 36, para 62*).

Any person given a third party notice may also appeal to the First-tier Tribunal on the grounds that it would be unduly onerous to comply. There is no right of appeal if the notice relates to the company's statutory records or that of its parent or subsidiary (*FA 2008, Sch 36, para 35 (3)*), or if the First-tier Tribunal approved the giving of the notice (*FA 2008, Sch 36, para 30*). A company has a right of appeal if given a notice where the identity of the person is unknown on the grounds that it would be unduly onerous to comply with the notice or the requirement (*FA 2008, Sch 36, para 31*).

Form of the notice

2.53   Notice of appeal must be given in writing, within 30 days of the date when the information notice was given and to the Revenue and Customs officer who gave the notice. The appeal must state the grounds. The First-tier Tribunal's decision is final, and on receipt of the appeal it will either confirm, vary or set aside the information notice or a requirement in the information notice. Confirmations and variations must be complied with within the time limits set by the Tribunal, and if not set, within any reasonable time limit specified in writing by a Revenue and Customs officer following the Tribunal's decision (*FA 2008, Sch 36, para 32*).

Third party information notices given to any person to check the tax position of the parent undertaking and any subsidiary need only state this and the name of the parent, and not every subsidiary, which need only be sent to the parent (*FA 2008, Sch 36, para 35*). No consent is required from either the subsidiary or of the First-tier Tribunal, and no copy need be given to the subsidiary. The information notice restrictions in *FA 2008, Sch 36, para 21* (see **2.51**), in relation to the CTSA return and enquiry framework, apply as if the notice was a taxpayer notice given to a subsidiary. If a notice is given to the parent to check the tax position of a subsidiary whose identity is not known to the officer, the approval of the First-tier Tribunal is not required. The parent company cannot appeal against a requirement to produce documents which are part of the statutory records.

The definition of parent and subsidiary follows that of the *Companies Act 2006*.

An undertaking is a parent undertaking in relation to another undertaking if:

- it holds a majority of the voting rights of the other undertaking; or

- it is a member of the undertaking and has the right to appoint or remove a majority of its board of directors; or

- it has the right to exercise a dominant influence over the undertaking:

    — by virtue of provisions contained in the undertaking's articles; or

    — by virtue of a control contract; or

— it is a member of the undertaking and controls alone, pursuant to an agreement, with other shareholders or members, a majority of the voting in the undertaking.

(*CA 2006, s 1162.*)

Change of ownership of companies

2.54 A change of ownership of a company is determined under *ICTA 1988, s 769* (see **9.18**). In such circumstances there are no restrictions which restrict the giving of an information notice only during the course of an enquiry or where a Revenue and Customs officer has reason to suspect that there has been an under-assessment or excessive relief granted; see **2.51** (*FA 2008, Sch 36, para 36*).

Penalties

2.55 A penalty of £300 is invoked and followed by a daily penalty not exceeding £60 per day for:

● failure to comply with an information notice;

● deliberate obstruction of a Revenue officer in the course of an inspection;

● concealment or destruction of documents following and information notice or

● an informal information notice.

(*FA 2008, Sch 36, paras 39 and 40.*)

DESTRUCTION OF DOCUMENTS

2.56 A company must not conceal, destroy or dispose of a document which is the subject of an information notice addressed to that company. If the document has already been produced to the Revenue and Customs officer, the prohibition no longer applies unless the officer notified the person that the document must continue to be available for inspection. Copies of documents produced to a Revenue and Customs officer under *FA 2008, Sch 36, para 8(1)* may be destroyed six months thereafter, unless the officer previously notified the person that the document must continue to be available for inspection (*FA 2008, Sch 36, para 42*).

A company must not conceal, destroy or dispose of a document if an officer has informed the person within the previous six months that that document is likely to be the subject of an information notice (*FA 2008, Sch 36, para 43*).

REASONABLE EXCUSE

2.57 No penalty arises if there was a reasonable excuse for the failure or obstruction. Reasonable excuse is not defined, but it does not include an insufficiency of funds, unless this is outside the company's control, or reliance on the work of others, unless reasonable care to avoid failure or obstruction is taken (*FA 2008, Sch 36, para 45*). A company liable for a penalty will be assessed within 12 months of the relevant date being:

- the end of the period in which an appeal against the information notice could have been given;

- the date on which the appeal is determined or withdrawn if an appeal is given; or

- in any other case, the date on which the person became liable to the penalty.

(*FA 2008, Sch 36, para 46*)

RIGHT OF APPEAL

2.58 A company has a right of appeal to the First-tier Tribunal against a penalty notice and the amount of the penalty (*FA 2008, Sch 36, para 47*). The notice of appeal must be made in writing and must state the grounds. It must be made within 30 days of the day on which the notice was issued.

If a Revenue and Customs officer believes that a significant amount of tax is at stake through the company's failure to comply with a penalty notice, the officer may apply to the Upper Tribunal for an additional penalty within 12 months of the relevant date (*FA 2008, Sch 36, para 50*). The penalty is due for payment within 30 days of its notification (*FA 2008, Sch 36, para 51*).

OFFENCE

2.59 Any person found guilty of an offence is liable on summary conviction to a fine not exceeding the statutory maximum. On conviction or indictment he may be liable to imprisonment for a term not exceeding two years or a fine or both (*FA 2008, Sch 36, para 55*).

2.59 *Self-assessment*

A person is guilty of an offence if he is found to be concealing, destroying or otherwise disposing of documents required for an information notice which has been approved by a First-tier Tribunal is guilty of an offence. This is not the case if the person concerned acted after the document or copy has been produced to an officer unless an officer notified that the document should continue to be available. Nor is there an offence if the person acted six months after a copy document was produced to an officer, unless an officer previously requested the original document (*FA 2008, Sch 36, para 53*).

A person is also guilty of an offence if the person concealed, destroyed or otherwise disposed of a document after an officer has informed the person in writing that that document is likely to be the subject of an information notice and the officer intended to seek the First-tier Tribunal's approval. There is no offence if the person acts at least six months after the person was informed or a notice was given (*FA 2008, Sch 36, para 54*).

Chapter 3

Rates and payment of corporation tax

RATES OF CORPORATION TAX

Full rate

3.1 The corporation tax chargeable is calculated by applying the applicable corporation tax rate to the company's profits chargeable to corporation tax (PCTCT). The main rate of corporation tax for the financial year 2008 is 28% (*FA 2007, s 2*). The main rate of corporation tax for the financial year 2009 will remain at 28% (*FA 2008, s 6*). A 30% rate applies to 'ring fence profits'. Ring fence profits are a company's profits or gains from oil extraction and oil rights in the UK and the UK Continental shelf (*FA 2008, s6*).

Small companies rate

3.2 The small companies rate of corporation tax is 20% for the financial year 2007 and increases to 21% for the financial year 2008 (*FA 2008, s 7(1)*). It has been announced that the small companies rate will increase to 22% for the financial year 2009 (Budget 2007: BN04).

The 19% small companies rate and the 11/400 small companies fraction (see **3.4** below) will continue to apply to small companies with ring fence profits.

Starting rate and non-corporation distribution rate

3.3 Both the corporation tax starting rate and the non-corporate distribution rate were abolished with effect from 1 April 2006 (*FA 2006, ss 26(1)* and (*2*)). For further discussion of these topics see *Corporation Tax 2006/07* (from Tottel), Chapter 2.

Table of rates

3.4 The rates of corporation tax for the financial years 2008 and 2007 are:

	Financial Year 2008 Commencing 1 April 2008	Financial Year 2007 Commencing 1 April 2007
Full rate	28%	30%
Small companies' rate	21%	20%
Profit limit for small companies' rate	£300,000	£300,000
Profit limit for small companies' marginal relief	£1,500,000	£1,500,000
Marginal relief fraction for profits between £300,000 and £1,500,000	7/400	1/40

In addition, loans to participators attract *ICTA 1988, s 419* tax at 25% on the outstanding amount: see **4.14–4.22**.

Marginal rates of corporation tax

3.5 The small companies rate of corporation tax is applied to profits chargeable to corporation tax (PCTCT) if company profits for a financial year are £300,000 or less. Profits above £300,000 are chargeable at the full rate of corporation tax subject to the company's claim for marginal relief. This limit is proportionately reduced where the company has one or more associated companies (by dividing it by one plus the number of associated companies) and for accounting periods of less than 12 months (*ICTA 1988, s 13(3)*). (See **4.27–4.33**). Profits for this purpose are measured as PCTCT plus non-group FII. FII is the net dividend plus the 10/90 tax credit. A group for this purpose is the parent and any of the 51% subsidiaries (*ICTA 1988, s 13*).

A company may claim marginal relief by completing box 64 of the company tax return (*ICTA 1988, s 13(2)*).

Marginal relief is calculated as follows:

Fraction × (Upper relevant amount—profits) × (PCTCT ÷ profits)

Example 3.1

Apple Ltd's profits chargeable to corporation tax for the accounting period ended 31 March 2009 amount to £350,000. The company received a dividend of £9,000 from Pear Ltd a non-group company during the year. No dividends were paid during the year and there are no associated companies.

Corporation tax payable is calculated as follows:

	£
350,000 @ 28%	98,000
Less marginal relief:	
7/40 × (1,500,000–360,000) × (350,000÷360,000)	19,396
	78,604

FII = £(9,000 × 100/90)

Effective rates of corporation tax

3.6 For the financial years 2007 and 2008, in cases where no dividends are received corporation tax payable may be more simply calculated where marginal relief is involved by applying the following effective rates of corporation tax.

Corporation tax rates

	Financial year 2008		Financial year 2007	
	Rate of corporation tax	Maximum corporation tax payable	Rate of corporation tax	Maximum corporation tax payable
£	%	£	%	£
0–300,000	21	63,000	20	60,000
300,001–1,500,000	29.75	357,000	32.50	390,000
1,500,000	28	420,000	30	450,000

The effective rates for the financial year 2009 based on the Budget 2007 announcements will be:

	Financial year 2009	
	Rate of corporation tax	Maximum corporation tax payable
£	%	£
0–300,000	22	66,000
300,001–1,500,000	29.50	354,000
1,500,000	28	420,000

The eventual corporation tax payable is corporation tax chargeable less: marginal relief (if any) less CVS Investment Relief (see **12.31**), community investment tax relief (see **12.45**), double taxation relief (see **13.16**), ACT (see **16.10**) plus tax payable under *s 419* (see **4.16**), any supplementary charge in respect of ring-fence trades, sums chargeable in respect of controlled foreign companies (see **13.28**) less research and development tax credit (see **8.20**), together with any income tax deducted at source (*FA 1998, Sch 18, para 8*).

PAYMENT DATES

3.7   The corporation tax payment due date is nine months and one day following the end of the accounting period concerned (*TMA 1970, s 59D(1)*).

Small and medium-sized companies

3.8   A small or medium-sized company's corporation tax is due and payable nine months and one day after the end of the accounting period (*TMA 1970, s 59D*). Small and medium-sized companies are not required to pay corporation tax by quarterly instalments (see **3.10**).

Large companies

3.9   Large companies are charged to corporation tax at the 28% full rate. A company is large if its 'profits' plus franked investment income exceed the upper relevant amount, currently £1,500,000 for a year. Franked investment income (FII) is the company's UK dividends that it has received during the accounting period plus the corresponding tax credit. Dividends received from other group members are not included. Groups are discussed in Chapter 10. This limit is proportionately reduced where the company has one or more associated companies (by dividing it by one plus the number of associated companies) and for accounting periods of less than 12 months (*ICTA 1988, s 13(3)*). (see **4.27–4.33**). Hence a company with a large number of associates may be a 'large' company even though its profits are relatively small.

Quarterly instalments

3.10   Unlike small and medium-sized companies, 'large' companies are required to pay their corporation tax liabilities in up to four quarterly instalments, based on the company's estimated liability for that accounting period.

A company will not be required to pay by instalments in an accounting period where its PCTCT plus non-group FII (see **3.5**) for that period does not exceed £10m and it was not large for the previous year.

A company is not treated as large for an accounting period if its corporation tax liability does not exceed £10,000.

The £10m and the £10,000 limits mentioned above are reduced proportionately if the accounting period is less than 12 months. The limits are also reduced if the company has associated companies by dividing the limits by one plus the number of associated companies (see **4.33**) (*Corporation Tax (Instalment Payments) Regulations 1998, SI 1998/3175*).

Corporation tax is payable in four quarterly instalments, which are due:

Instalment	*Due*
First	Six months and 13 days after the start of the accounting period
Second	Three months after the first instalment
Third	Three months after the second instalment
Final	Three months and 14 days after the end of the accounting period.

Example 3.2

Twelve month accounting period ended 31 December 2009.

Instalment	*Due*
First	14 July 2009
Second	14 October 2009
Third	14 January 2010
Final	14 April 2010

3.11   If the accounting period is less than 12 months, the final instalment is due as normal three months and 14 days after the end of the accounting period. The earlier instalments only fall due if the payment date falls before the due date for the final instalment.

Example 3.3

Six month accounting period ended 30 June 2009.

Instalment	*Due*
First	14 July 2009
Final	14 October 2009

Calculation of tax due

3.12   A company, which considers that it is large, should calculate its quarterly payment at each due date. If it considers that it has paid too much tax for a quarter it may deduct the overpayment from the next quarter's liability.

The liability is calculated as follows:

3 × (Company's total liability ÷ Number of months in the accounting period)

Example 3.4

Wood Ltd's corporation tax liability for the year ended 31 December 2009 is £1,000,000.

Instalments are 3 × (1,000,000÷12) = £250,000

The liability for the year is payable as follows:

Instalment	Due	Amount
First	14 July 2009	£250,000
Second	14 October 2009	£250,000
Third	14 January 2010	£250,000
Final	14 April 2010	£250,000

3.13   Interest is charged on instalments paid late at the late instalment rate (see **3.14**).

If a company should have made quarterly instalment payments, regardless of whether or not it made such payments a cross should be placed in box 95. HMRC regards electronic payments as more efficient than payments by post. www.hmrc.gov.uk/howtopay gives more information on how to make electronic payments (Working Together, Issue 18, August 2004—Company Tax Return—Helpful Hints). See HMRC Company Taxation Manual CTM 92500 onwards for more information on quarterly instalments.

INTEREST

Late payment interest

3.14   If a company pays its corporation tax beyond the due date (nine months and one day after the end of the accounting period) it will be charged late payment interest under *TMA 1970, s 87A* on the corporation tax that it pays late. HMRC will not charge the company interest on interest paid late.

Late payment interest is calculated from the day after the normal due date until the effective date of payment. HMRC's computer is programmed to calculate the interest due. Situations not covered by the programmes are calculated manually by HMRC clerical staff.

The most current rates are:

Corporation tax interest on unpaid tax

From	*%*
6 January 2008	7.5
6 August 2007	8.5
6 September 2006	7.5
6 September 2005	6.5
6 September 2004	7.5
6 December 2003	6.5

REPAYMENTS

3.15 If a company has overpaid tax it may make a repayment claim. Normally a company is only able to ascertain whether it has made an overpayment when it prepares its corporation tax computation and company tax return. The repayment claim is made by placing a cross in the appropriate repayment claim box on the front of form CT600 and by completing the relevant repayment claim sections of CT600 or CT600 (Short). HMRC advise that a company will receive its repayment faster if it files online. The fastest and most secure repayment method is direct credit to the company bank account (by BACS). For this to take place the company must ensure that the 'Bank Details' section of the return is fully completed (page 12 of the main return and page 4 of the short return) (Working Together, Issue 18, August 2004—Company Tax Return—Helpful Hints).

If a company does not consider the overpayment to be worth claiming, it may indicate on the return by completing the CT600 boxes 139 or 140 that small overpayments are to be set against future liabilities instead of being repaid.

Income tax

3.16 A company may claim an income tax repayment. This can arise if the company has received income from which tax has been deducted at source. The claim must be made on the company tax return or on an amended return (*FA 1998, Sch 18, para 9*). Box 142 is the requisite box for completion (see **3.23** and Example 3.6 for an income tax calculation). Tax deduction vouchers are not required in support of the claim and will only be requested if the return is under enquiry.

Repayment interest

3.17   If a company overpays corporation tax it will be entitled to repayment interest. Repayment interest is calculated from the later of the day after the normal due date or the date the payment was made to the material date (*ICTA 1988, s 826*).

The material date is either the date when the repayment was issued or the HMRC allocation. HMRC assumes that the tax paid last is repaid first. If there are no loss carry-backs for an accounting period the material date is the normal corporation tax due date. If losses are carried back to an accounting period wholly within the previous 12 months the material date is the due date for the accounting period in which the tax was over paid (*ICTA 1988, s 826(2)*).

If the accounting period against which the losses are set does not fall wholly within the previous 12 months the material date becomes the due date of the accounting period in which the losses arise (*ICTA 1988, s 826(7A)*).

When a non-trading loan relationship deficit or double tax relief is carried back to an earlier period the material date is the due date for the accounting period in which the deficit or the double tax arose (*ICTA 1988, s 826(7C), (7BB)*).

The most current rates are:

Corporation tax repayment interest

From	*%*
6 January 2008	4%
6 August 2007	5%
6 September 2006	4%
6 September 2005	3%
6 September 2004	4%
6 December 2003	3%

Interest rate formulae

3.18   The interest rates charged are calculated using the formula given in the *Taxes (Interest Rate) Regulations 1989, SI 1989/1297, regs 3ZA* and *3ZB* (inserted by the *Taxes* (*Interest Rate*) (*Amendment No. 2*) *Regulations 1998, SI 1998/3176, reg 6*). This results in late payment interest being charged at approximately 2.5% above base rate and overpayment interest being credited at 1% less than base rate.

Late payment interest where there is a carry back of losses or a non-trading deficit

3.19 Companies that have incurred a trading loss or a non-trading deficit may elect to carry that loss back to be set against the total profits of the previous accounting period under *ICTA 1988, s 393A* and *FA 1996, s 83(2)(c)* respectively: see Chapter 9. In anticipation of so doing they may not pay the corporation tax due for the previous period. The company must be aware that the late payment interest will run from the normal due date to the due date of the later accounting period (*TMA 1970, s 87A(4A)*).

Example 3.5

Roquet Ltd anticipates a trading loss for the year ended 31 December 2008 of £200,000. For the accounting period ended 31 December 2007 it had a trading profit of £100,000. The company has no other source of income. On 1 October 2008 the directors consider that it is not worth paying the corporation tax due for the year ended 31 December 2007 because of the forthcoming loss.

Roquet Ltd will be charged interest on the corporation tax due on £100,000 for the period from 1 October 2008 until 1 October 2009.

QUARTERLY INSTALMENTS

Debit and credit interest

3.20 A large company that pays corporation tax by instalments will be charged interest on late quarterly instalment payments and will receive interest on quarterly instalment payments paid in advance (*Corporation Tax* (*Instalment Payments*) *Regulations 1998, SI 1998/3175, regs 7* and *8*). Interest paid is known as debit interest and interest received is known as credit interest. The interest rate formulae are similar to late payment interest but result in lower rates. Debit interest is approximately 1% above base rate and credit interest is approximately 0.25% below base rate.

3.20   *Rates and payment of corporation tax*

Debit interest is charged from the quarterly instalment due date until the earlier of the date of payment of the tax and the normal due date, being nine months and one day after the end of the accounting period (see **3.10**).

The most current rates are:

Debit interest charged on underpaid quarterly instalment payment

From	To	%
18 February 2008		6.25
17 December 2007	17 February 2008	6.50
16 July 2007	16 December 2007	6.75
21 May 2007	15 July 2007	6.50
22 January 2007	20 May 2007	6.25
20 November 2006	21 January 2007	6.00
14 August 2006	19 November 2006	5.75
15 August 2005	13 August 2006	5.5
16 August 2004	14 August 2005	5.75
21 June 2004	15 August 2004	5.5

Credit interest will accrue from the date on which the overpayment arises or from the due date for the first instalment payment, if later to the earlier of:

● the date the overpayment is removed by being utilised as payment for another quarter; and

● the normal due date, being nine months and one day after the end of the accounting period.

The most recent rates are:

Credit interest paid on overpaid quarterly instalment payments and on early payments of corporation tax not due by instalments

From	To	%
18 February 2008		5.00
17 December 2007	17 February 2008	5.25
16 July 2007	16 December 2007	5.50
21 May 2007	15 July 2007	5.25
22 January 2007	20 May 2007	5.00
20 November 2006	21 January 2007	4.75
14 August 2006	19 November 2006	4.5
15 August 2005	13 August 2006	4.25
16 August 2004	14 August 2005	4.5
21 June 2004	15 August 2004	4.25

GROUP PAYMENT ARRANGEMENTS

3.21   *FA 1998, s 36* allows one company in a group to attend to the administration of the corporation tax payments on behalf of the other group members if it enters into a group payment arrangement 'GPA' contract with HMRC. Details of the contract can be downloaded from HMRC's website: 'The Group Payment Arrangement Document and Schedule'.

In order to be eligible, group members must have a 51% group relationship and be up-to-date with their filing and payment obligations. A company can only be a member of one GPA. If any group member is liable to make quarterly instalment payments, the paying company should enter into the standard contract at least two months prior to the due date for the first payment. Payment of tax must be by electronic funds transfer.

A GPA also covers interest and penalties, and each individual company remains liable for its own corporation tax (see Application for a Group Payment Arrangement—Notes for Guidance and Working Together, Issue 20, February 2005).

QUARTERLY ACCOUNTING

CT61 procedures

3.22   Companies are required to make a return to the Collector of Taxes of income tax deducted and claimed in respect of certain interest and charges on income, through the completion of form CT61, obtainable from HMRC.

There are normally four quarterly CT61 return periods, plus a fifth where the company's accounting period does not coincide with one of the quarter ends (*ICTA 1988, Sch 16, para 2*). The return periods are to 30 March, 30 June, 30 September and 31 December. The company's first return will run from the start of its accounting period to the end of the relevant quarter. Subsequent returns will follow a quarterly cycle, and a fifth return (where appropriate) will cover the period from the end of the previous quarter to the end of the company's accounting period, if it does not coincide with the end of a normal return period. The completed CT61 return and any tax liability is due 14 days after the end of the return period.

Deduction of tax

3.23   Annual interest and other annual payments (e.g. copyright royalties) are generally paid under deduction of income tax (*ITA 2007, ss 874 and 914*). Companies are not required to deduct tax from interest, royalties, annuities and annual payments where the recipient is a company, which is chargeable to corporation tax in respect of that income (*ITA 2007, s 914*).

Companies also have the option to pay royalties overseas without deduction of tax at source (or at a reduced rate) without the approval of HMRC in advance, provided that there is a reasonable belief that the non-resident is entitled to relief from UK tax on those royalties under a double tax treaty (*ITTOIA 2005, s 758*).

Interest and royalty payments between associated companies in the UK and other EU states are not subject to deduction of income tax at source if the companies are at least 25% associates. HMRC must have issued an exemption notice in relation to interest payments, and a company making royalty payments must have a reasonable belief that the recipient company is entitled to the exemption (*ITTOIA 2005, ss 761, 762*).

The CT61 return allows for the offset of income tax due on relevant payments against tax deducted from the company's income. Where such payments exceed income, income tax is due only on the excess. Where income exceeds payments for a return period, income tax paid in an earlier return period may be repaid. At the end of an accounting period, if total income exceeds total interest and/or annual payments, the balance of tax suffered is offset against the company's corporation tax liability; any excess tax suffered is repaid (*ICTA 1988, Sch 16*). No repayment interest will be paid.

Example 3.6

S Ltd prepares accounts each year to 31 October. During the year ending 31 October 2009, it pays the following interest:

		£
21 December 2008	(net of tax @ 20%)	8,000
4 January 2009	(net of tax @ 20%)	5,600
9 August 2009	(net of tax @ 20%)	8,000
21 October 2009	(net of tax @ 20%)	12,000

All the interest is paid to individuals.

S Ltd will enter the following figures into its CT61 returns and account for tax as follows:

Return periods	Payments	Income tax paid
	£	£
1 November 2008 to 31 December 2008	8,000	2,000
1 January 2009 to 31 March 2009	5,600	1,400
1 April 2009 to 30 June 2009	(no return)	
1 July 2009 to 30 September 2009	8,000	2,000
1 October 2009 to 31 October 2009	12,000	3,000
Total income tax paid		£8,400

Chapter 4

Close companies and connected issues

INTRODUCTION

4.1   Ownership of a company is vested in its shareholders. A share is a bundle of rights; namely voting rights, dividend rights and a right to assets in a winding-up. Companies owned by a small number of individuals are in a position to control a company to their advantage. The corporation tax legislation looks through these relationships and modifies the corporation tax rules in particular in relation to:

- close companies;
- close investment holding companies; and
- associated companies.

CLOSE COMPANIES

Consequences

4.2   The close company provisions were included within corporation tax provisions when they were first introduced in 1965 and similar legislation was in existence before then.

The effect of the provisions (and if all the related conditions apply) is to widen the scope of a distribution to include shareholder and shareholder family member benefits (see Chapter 16 for distributions). The provisions regard some loans to shareholders as an extraction of profits and seek to tax the loan. Close investment holding companies are prevented from applying the lower rate of corporation tax on their profits.

Status

4.3   A close company is defined as:

'a "close company" is one which is under the control of five or fewer participators, or of participators who are directors ...' (*ICTA 1988, s 414(1)*).

Control

4.4   Control is the ability to exercise, or entitlement to acquire, direct or indirect control over the company's affairs, including the ownership of, or entitlement to acquire the greater part (over 50%) of the company's share capital; voting rights, distributable income or distributable assets (*ICTA 1988, s 416(2)*). If the rights and powers of two or more persons taken together amount to the greater part of the company's share capital etc, these two or more persons will control the company.

Rights and powers of a nominee, an associate and any company of which the person has control or he or she and or her associates (including nominees of associates but not associates of associates) have control are attributable to the person (*ICTA 1988, s 416(5), (6)*).

Exceptions

4.5   As with all definitions there are exceptions and a company with the following criteria is not close (or is open):

- a company not resident in the UK;

- a registered industrial and provident society or building society;

- a company controlled by or on behalf of the Crown;

- a UK resident company controlled by a non-resident company (unless the non-resident company would itself be close if resident in the UK);

- a company controlled by a non-close company or companies, where it cannot be treated as a close company except by including a non-close company as one of its five or fewer participators;

- a quoted company:

  — where 35% or more of the company's voting power is held by the 'public' (excluding shares entitled to a fixed rate of dividend); and

  — within the preceding 12 months those voting shares have been the subject of dealings on a recognised stock exchange unless the total voting power of the company's 'principal members' exceeds 85% (including shares entitled to a fixed rate of dividend) (*ICTA 1988, s 414(1)*).

A recognised stock exchange is any HMRC designated market of a UK or overseas recognised investment exchange (*FA 2007, s 109 Sch 26, para 1*).

Public

4.6   In this sense, the public excludes directors and their associates, any company controlled by them, any associated company, any fund for the benefit of past or present employees, directors or dependants of the company or associated companies, and the principal members (*ICTA 1988, s 415(5)*).

Principal member

4.7   A principal member is a person holding more than 5% of the company's voting power or where there are more than five such persons, one of the five possessing the greatest percentages. Where two or more persons hold equal percentages, so that the greatest percentages are held by more than five persons, a principal member is any one of that number (*ICTA 1988, s 415(6)*).

Director

4.8   A director includes any person who acts in that capacity whatever name is given to him. A director is also someone who gives directions upon which directors are accustomed to act or who is concerned in the management of the company's business and controls. A director is also someone who is able, either directly or indirectly, to control 20% or more of the company's ordinary share capital (*ICTA 1988, s 417(5)*).

Close company tests

4.9   In order to determine whether a company is close, HMRC apply five tests (HMRC Company Taxation Manual CTM 60102):

	Test	*Answer*	*Result*
1.	Is the company within one of the specific exceptions that exclude it from being a close company?	Yes	The company is not close.
		No	Consider further tests.

Test	Answer	Result
2. Who are the participators in the company and what powers or rights do they possess or are they entitled to acquire?		
3. What rights and powers of other persons are attributable to the participators?		
4. Having regard to the rights, etc, of each participator, and other persons' rights, etc, which are attributed to the participator, do:		
(i) five or fewer participators control the company, or	Yes	The company is close.
	No	Consider further tests.
(ii) participators who are directors control the company?	Yes	The company is close.
	No	Consider further tests
5. Would more than half the assets of the company be ultimately distributed to five or fewer participators, or to participators who are directors, in the event of the company being wound up?	Yes	The company is close
	No	The company is not close

The result as to which participators control the company should always be inferred from the minimum controlling holding. X, Y and Z may each own 33.33% of the company. Therefore control in applying the tests is given to X and Y or Y and Z or X and Z but never X, Y and Z (*ICTA 1988, s 416(3)*).

Participator

4.10   Test 2 requires the identity of the participator to be determined. The full definition of a participator is given as:

'A participator is any person having a share or interest in the capital or income of the company ... and includes:

(a)   any person who possesses or is entitled to acquire share capital or voting rights in the company;

65

(b)   any loan creditor of the company;

(c)   any person who possesses or is entitled to acquire a right to receive or participate in distributions of the company … or in any amounts payable by the company (in cash or kind) to loan creditors by way of premium or redemption;

(d)   any person who is entitled to secure that income or assets (whether present or future) of the company will be applied directly or indirectly for his benefit.' (*ICTA 1988, s 417(1)*.)

Generally speaking a participator is anyone who has a financial interest in a close company, ie who has invested into share capital or who has provided loan finance. A participator is 'entitled to acquire' or 'entitled to secure' if he has a contractual right to do so (see *R v CIR, ex p Newfields Developments Ltd* (2001) 73 TC 532, [2001] STC 901, [2001] 1 WLR 1111, [2001] 4 All ER 400 on this point).

The definition of a participator can be extended through a company structure (*ICTA 1988, s 419(7)*).

Example 4.1

In the following circumstances all companies are close:

Fact	Result
A is a shareholder of A Ltd.	A is a participator of A Ltd
A Ltd owns all the shares in B Ltd.	A is also a participator in B Ltd
If B Ltd makes a loan to A.	The loan is within ICTA 1988, s 419

Loan creditor

4.11   A loan creditor is also a participator and is defined as;

' "loan creditor" means a creditor in respect of any debt incurred by the company:

(a)   for any money borrowed or capital assets acquired by the company, or

(b)   for any right to receive income created in favour of the company, or

(c)   for consideration the value of which to the company was (at the time when the debt was incurred) substantially less than the amount of the debt (including any premium thereon), or in respect of any redeemable loan capital issued by the company.' (*ICTA 1988, s 417(7)*.)

Normal company trade creditors are not included in the definition. Any holder of redeemable capital is a loan creditor. Hire purchase arrangements are not regarded as part of loan capital. Arrangements where a person makes annual payments to a company in exchange for a capital sum at some future date treats the person as a participator.

Loans in the normal course of banking business do not bring about a loan creditor relationship (HMRC Company Taxation Manual CTM 60130).

Associate

4.12   An associate of a participator includes the following:

● any 'relative': spouses or civil partners, parents or remoter forebear, children or remoter issue, brothers or sisters (but not aunts, uncles, nephews and nieces). Separated spouses and half-brothers or sisters are associated, but divorced spouses and step-brothers or sisters are not;

● any business partner;

● the trustee(s) of any settlement in which the participator (or any living or dead 'relatives') is or was the settlor; and

● the trustee(s) of a settlement or personal representatives of an estate holding company shares in which the participator has an interest (where the participator is a company, any other company interested in those shares is also an associate) (*ICTA 1988, s 417(3), (4)*).

Benefits to participators

4.13   Benefits or services provided to close company participators, who are also directors or other employees, will be treated as remuneration and will be assessed to income tax, as calculated under the taxable benefit rules for employments (*ICTA 1988, s 418(3), (4)*). Payments to a non-working participator or the non-working associate of a participator cannot be classed as employment income and will be treated as a distribution to the participator. Hence the 'distributions' will not be an allowable expense of the company (*ICTA 1988, s 418(2)*).

Loans to participators

4.14   The company must self-assess tax liabilities in respect of any loans not in the ordinary course of business to participators or associates, which can result

67

in the requirement to make tax payments to HMRC equal to 25% of the outstanding loan or advance made during the accounting period. The tax need not be paid if the loan has been repaid, released or written off within nine months and one day following the end of the accounting period. Where the loan or advance is repaid, released or written off more than nine months after the end of an accounting period, the tax paid can be repaid nine months after the end of the accounting period in which the repayment, release, etc takes place.

Self-assessment disclosure

4.15   Loans to participators or their associates made during the accounting period must be disclosed on the corporation tax return. Supplementary page CT600A (2006) Version 2 (loans to participators by close companies) is used for this purpose and is reproduced in the Appendices. Details of the name of the participator or associate to whom the loan was made and the amount of the loan outstanding at the end of the accounting period for which the return has been made must be disclosed in Part 1.

If the loan has been repaid, released or written off within nine months and one day after the end of the accounting period, details of the name of the participator or associate whose loan has been repaid, released or written off, together with the amount and date repaid, released or written off, must be disclosed in Part 2.

The effect of completion of both Parts 1 and 2 will result in no liability to *s 419* tax at 25%. The practical implication is that HMRC will now have been informed of the amounts loaned to the participators and the associates and will be able to follow through the beneficial loan declarations on form P11D for directors, other employed participators and their associates. A benefit in kind may arise on a participator who is an employee or director in respect of direct loans. A benefit in kind may also arise on a participator who is an employee or a director in respect of direct loans made to their associates.

Relief is given if the loan is repaid, released or written off (*ICTA 1988, s 419(4)*). If the loan has been repaid, released or written off later than nine months and one day after the end of the accounting period, details of the name of the participator or associate whose loan has been repaid, released or written off, together with the amount and date repaid, released or written off must be disclosed in Part 3. It follows that if the loan has not been repaid, released or written off at all then neither Part 2 nor Part 3 can be completed. The effect of completion of Part 3 or non-completion of Parts 2 and 3 is that the *s 419* liability will be shown in Box A13. This amount should be shown in Box 79 on CT600 (the corporation tax self-assessment return for the year). Corporation tax software and online filing will automatically make these calculations but manual completion following the step-by-step instructions on form CT600A should arrive at this result. The tax at 25% of the outstanding loan then becomes payable with the main corporation tax. Any late payment falls within the normal interest provisions. Interest is charged on any outstanding liability from the due date until the earlier of the payment of the *s 419* tax and the date that the loan or part is repaid, released or written off (*TMA 1970, ss 87A(1), 109(3A)*). If the repayment, release or write-off of a loan takes place earlier then nine months and one day after the end of the accounting period in which the loan was made repayment interest will accrue from the later off nine months after the end of that accounting period and the date the tax was paid. If the loan is repaid, release or written-off more than nine months after the end of the accounting period in which the loan was made interest will accrue from the later of nine months after the end of the accounting period in which the loan was cleared and the date the tax was paid (*ICTA 1988, s 826(4)*). HMRC may make enquiries into the loan accounts as part of their corporation tax self-assessment enquiries.

Loans within s 419(1)

4.16   To be within *s 419(1)* the loan must have been made 'otherwise than in the ordinary course of a business carried on by it which includes the lending of money'. The principle of the lending of money was tested in *Brennan v Denby Investment Co Ltd* (2001) 73 TC 455, [2001] STC 536 and resulted in the comment that 'business requires some regularity of occurrence'. It would seem that without doubt a commercial lending bank's business includes lending money. HMRC state that they will look at the following characteristics to determine whether there is a money lending trade:

- Money lending advertisements aimed at the general public.

- Interest rate publication.

- Receipt of loan applications from the public.

- Commercial interest rate charge.

- *In situ* debt collection personnel and procedures.

- Legally enforceable written repayment term contracts.

- A reasonable number of existing loans (usually 200+) enabling inter alia loan set-off.

- Matched time period borrowing and lending.

If indeed there is a money lending business the loan to the participator must be made to the participator on the same commercial lending terms (HMRC Company Taxation Manual CTM 61520).

Loans to employee share schemes and employee benefit trusts are within *s 419*. *Section 419(1)* is applied at the time of the loan, if the trust is a shareholder or individual trustees are participators in the company. HMRC state that *ICTA 1988, s 419(5)* may apply when the trustees make payments to existing shareholders for their shares (HMRC Company Taxation Manual CTM 61525).

Loans to a tax transparent partnership, where a participator is a member are within s 419.

HMRC state that they will not apply *s 419* where money is lent to a partnership of which the company is a member where there is a genuine partnership with bona fide arrangements. However, HMRC may invoke *s 419(5)*. This section enables HMRC to assess a loan not made by the close company but by arrangements not in the ordinary course of business to *s 419(1)* (HMRC Company Taxation Manual CTM 61515). Payments by a company to a director in respect of the directors private business were held to be within *s 419* in *Grant (Andrew) Services Ltd v Watton (Inspector of Taxes) (aka HCB Ltd v HM Inspector of Taxes)* (1999) 71 TC 333, [1999] STC 330.

Loans not within s 419(1)

4.17   Not only are loans and advances that a company makes to its participators and/or their associates, other than in the ordinary course of business, within *s 419(1)*, but also:

- any debt due by the participator or associate to the company (*ICTA 1988, s 419(2)(a)*);

- any debt due to a third party, which has been assigned by the third party to the company (*ICTA 1988, s 419(2)(b)*); or

- the provision of goods or services in the ordinary course of trade or business to a participator on credit terms that exceed six months or are longer than normally given to the company's customers (*ICTA 1988, s 420(1)*).

As regards debts due to a third party, HMRC acknowledge that a debt can only be assigned by the third party. If the debtor (the person to whom the money is lent) and the close company of which he is a participator agree that the close company will pay the debt on his behalf, *ICTA 1988, s 419(2)(b)* cannot apply. However, a debt due from the participator to the close company may arise when the close company pays the debt to the third party on the participator's behalf, which will fall under *ICTA 1988, s 419(2)(a)*. Indeed, depending on the facts of the case, HMRC may treat the amount as remuneration or a distribution (HMRC Company Taxation Manual CTM 61535).

As regards the provision of goods or services, HMRC acknowledge that a credit period runs from the time that goods are delivered or services are performed until time of payment (*Grant (Andrew) Services Ltd v Watton* (1999) 71 TC 333, [1999] STC 330; HMRC Company Taxation Manual CTM 61535).

Section 419 does not apply to loans less than £15,000, where the borrower is a full-time working director or employee of the close company or of an associated company with no material interest in the company (*ICTA 1988, s 420(2)*). No material interest means 5% or less direct or indirect control (associates included) of the ordinary share capital or the assets in winding-up (*ITEPA 2003, s 68*). HMRC interpret full-time as not less than three-quarters of the normal working hours of the close company (HMRC Company Taxation Manual CTM 61540). As soon as the conditions of *s 420(2)* are no longer met, for example, by the borrower acquiring an interest of more than 5% then *s 419* will apply from that time. Spouses and civil partners, if employees of the company, have their own £15,000 limit.

Loan accounts

4.18   For accounts purposes if a loan is made to a participator the company will record the loan in its nominal ledger as a 'loan account'. Director loan accounts are a common feature of owner-managed companies, which are invariably close companies. HMRC will not concur to the netting off of one loan account against another unless there is a genuine joint loan, for example, as between spouses, where a joint nominal ledger loan account would be operated. A participator or director may have more than one nominal ledger loan account with the company, where loans carrying different terms are recorded. The fact that one loan account may be in debit and another in credit has no avail with HMRC. This is because HMRC treat all loan accounts as separate loans. If a genuine posting is made to clear the two loan accounts then this is treated as though the loan had been repaid under *ICTA 1988, s 419(4)*. The posting date is the repayment date (HMRC Company Taxation Manual CTM 61550).

Actual repayment by the participator or a third party takes place on the date that payment is made. A director's loan account may be cleared by a bonus payment. *ITEPA 2003, s18* onwards determines the date that the bonus is received by the director for income tax purposes. For *s 419* purposes the date of repayment is the date that the bonuses are voted or the date on which PAYE was operated if earlier (HMRC Company Taxation Manual CTM 61605).

The director/participator may wish to use a dividend payment to clear the loan account. In practice, the company's constitution should be examined for any matters that may affect dividend payments. A dividend may only be declared if there are sufficient net realised profits.

A dividend is paid when it is due and payable (*ICTA 1988, s 834(3)*) but for *s 419(4)* purposes *s 834(3)* does not apply and until the dividend is paid the debt remains outstanding to the company (HMRC Company Taxation Manual CTM 61605). 'A dividend is not paid and there is no distribution, unless and until the shareholder receives money or the distribution is otherwise unreservedly put at their disposal, perhaps by being credited to a loan account on which the shareholder has the power to draw' (HMRC Company Taxation Manual CTM 20095). Evidence of the payment or credit should be shown in the company's books of account. If a dividend is paid unlawfully and the shareholder knew or was in a position to know of this fact he or she is liable to return the distribution to the company (*CA 2006, s 847*)(*CA 1985, s 277*); (*It's a Wrap (UK) Ltd (in liquidation) v Gula* [2006] EWCA Civ 544).

HMRC acknowledge that in many small private companies the directors and shareholders are one and the same. A dividend is only paid when the money is placed unreservedly at the disposal of the directors/shareholders as part of their current accounts with the company. So, payment is not made until such a right to draw on the dividend exists (presumably) when the appropriate entries are made in the company's books.

If, as may happen with a small company, such entries are not made until the annual audit, and this takes place after the end of the accounting period in which the directors resolved that an interim dividend be paid, then the 'due and payable' date is in the later rather than the earlier accounting period.

A director may clear the account shortly before the year end by borrowing from an external third party shortly before the year end only to reinstate the loan at the beginning of the accounting period. HMRC will regard the company as submitting a negligent or fraudulent return under *FA 1998, Sch 18, para 20* or deliberately supplying a false document under the *Finance Act 2007* penalty regime, which can attract a tax-related penalty: see respectively **2.12, 2.36–2.37** (HMRC Enquiry Manual EM 8565).

Section 419 tax repayment

4.19   When the loan is actually repaid the company will be due the *s 419* tax that it has already paid. There is no facility for setting the repayable overpaid *s 419* tax against the corporation tax liability for the year in which the repayment is made. The company will need to complete an amended Part 3 CT600A for the accounting period in which the loan was made. If the loan is repaid in time to enable the amended CT600A to be completed and submitted within the 12-month enquiry period, this will act as an amended return and repayment will be issued. Alternatively, if submission is outside the enquiry period, the revised form will act as a separate claim under *TMA 1970, Sch 1A*.

Section 419 loan released

4.20 If the loan is released or written off, the same procedures apply to the company as for repayment but the individual participator will be treated as receiving a distribution net of the 10% tax credit (*ICTA 1988, s 421*). The *s 421* charge takes precedence over the employment income charge (HMRC Company Taxation Manual CTM 61630).

Circuitous and indirect loans

4.21 Circuitous and indirect loans are also caught by *s 419*. In particular, HMRC quote the situation whereby, for example, a close company makes a loan to an employee who is not a participator and that employee applies the loan in purchase of the shares from an existing shareholder. The existing shareholder is a 'deemed borrower' under *ICTA 1988, s 419(5)* and *s 419(1)* can apply (HMRC Company Taxation Manual CTM 61540).

This is because *s 419(5)* catches the situation where a close company makes a loan but no *s 419(1)* liability arises. A third party then makes a payment or transfers property to a participator or releases a participator's debt. HMRC give the following examples:

Example 4.2

Company D is a close company. Instead of making a loan directly to D, an individual participator, it makes it to an associated company, Company E. Company E then passes the loan to D. The loan by one company to the other is treated as if it had been made direct to D.

Example 4.3

Company T, a close company, makes a loan to A. A is an individual participator in Company W but not in Company T. Company W, acting in concert with Company T, then makes a loan to D, an individual participator in Company T. Company T and Company W have swapped loans to participators and are treated as if they had made loans to their own participators.

Such loans should be assessed to *s 419(1)* in the normal way except where the amounts form assessable income receipts for the individual concerned (HMRC Company Taxation Manual 61670 and 61680).

Anti-avoidance

4.22   *ICTA 1988, s 422* (extension of *s 419* to loans by companies controlled by close companies) is an anti-avoidance clause. A loan to a participator by a third party, directly or indirectly financed by the participator's close company, is within *s 419(1)* by virtue of *TA 1988, s 422*. In addition, a loan to a participator by a company controlled by a close company is within *s 419(1)*. A loan to a company that is acting in a fiduciary or representative capacity of a participator is also within *s 419 (ICTA 1988, s 419(6))*.

CLOSE INVESTMENT HOLDING COMPANIES

Consequences

4.23   Trading uncommercially or letting property to connected parties may mean that a close company becomes a close investment holding company.

The small company corporation tax rate can be utilised by a close company, but not by a 'close investment holding company', which will pay corporation tax at the full rate, regardless of profit levels *(ICTA 1988, s 13(1)(b))*.

Status

4.24   A close company will *not* be a close investment holding company if throughout the period it exists wholly or mainly for one or more of the following purposes:

- carrying on a trade on a commercial basis;
- making investments in land or estates or interests in land and in cases where the land is or is intended to be let to persons other than:
    - any person connected with the close company, or
    - any person who is the wife or husband of an individual connected with the relevant company, or is a relative, or the wife or husband of a relative, of such an individual or of the husband or wife of such an individual,
- the purpose of holding shares in and securities of, or making loans to, one or more companies each of which is a qualifying company or a company which:
    - is under the control of the relevant company or of a company that has control of the relevant company, and

— itself exists wholly or mainly for the purpose of holding shares in or securities of, or making loans to, one or more qualifying companies;

- the purpose of co-ordinating the administration of two or more qualifying companies;

- the purpose of a trade or trades carried on on a commercial basis by one or more qualifying companies or by a company that has control of the relevant company; and

- the purpose of the making, by one or more qualifying companies or by a company, which has control of the relevant company, of investments as mentioned in lands or estates as set out above (*ICTA 1988, s 13A(1), (2)*).

In general terms a 'qualifying company' is a trading company or a property investment company (*ICTA 1988, s 13A(3)*).

Letting of land to a connected person

4.25   Letting of land to a connected person may bring the company into the close investment holding company regime. Connection is defined here in *ICTA 1988, s 839(5), (6)*.

Connection to another company

'A company is connected with another company

(a)   if the same person has control of both, or a person has control of one and persons connected with him, or he and persons connected with him, have control of the other, or

(b)   if a group of two or more persons has control of each company, and the groups either consist of the same persons or could be regarded as consisting of the same persons by treating (in one or more cases) a member of either group as replaced by a person with whom he is connected.' (*ICTA 1988, s 839(5)*.)

Connection with another person

'A company is connected with another person if that person has control of it, or if that person and persons connected with him together have control of it.' (*ICTA 1988, s 839(6)*.)

Control is given the same meaning as at **4.4** (*ICTA 1988, s 416(2)*).

Letting of land

4.26   Land let to a relative may also bring the company within the close investment holding company regime.

A relative includes a brother, sister, ancestor or lineal descendant (*ICTA 1988, s 839(8)*). Lettings to a relative of the individual's spouse, or the spouse of a relative of the individual will affect the close investment holding company status.

Example 4.4

Facts

Joe is married to Mary. Joe owns 100% of Joe Ltd, a building and construction company in the South of England. Joe would like to provide Mary's mother Mrs K with a home where she could reside independently of Joe and Mary.

On 1 January 2008, Joe forms Mrs K Ltd, a 100% subsidiary of Joe Ltd. The subsidiary buys a plot of land with development value on which stands Plum Cottage, a Victorian property. Mrs K moves into the cottage and pays her landlord Mrs K Ltd a full market rent for the property. Mrs K maintains her independence and pays for the upkeep of Plum Cottage herself.

Comments

The facts appear to fall under *ICTA 1988, s 13A(2)(b)(ii)*.

This would bring the company within the close investment holding company regime. Corporation tax will be payable on profits at the full 30% rate.

Joe formed the company in order to buy a property suitable for his mother-in-law's occupation. The land on which the property stood had development value.

If the situation were reversed such that Joe bought land with development value (albeit through Mrs K Ltd) for use in his trade on which stood a vacant cottage, there may be an argument that the company had a trading 'purpose'. This would mean that the company might fall out of the close investment holding company regime. There is also the possibility that the company would pay corporation tax at the full rates because of the associated company rules.

ASSOCIATED COMPANIES

Consequences

4.27   Associated companies share the small companies rate band by dividing the lower relevant amount and the higher relevant amount equally between them. (See **3.5**, **3.9** and Example 4.7.)

A company is to be treated as an associated company of another at a given time if at that time one of the two has control of the other, or both are under the control of the same person or persons (*ICTA 1988, s 13(4)*).

Status

4.28   The same definition of control is used as for close companies (see **4.3** and **4.4**).

For these purposes not only are the rights of the person concerned taken into account but also the rights and powers of associates that can be attributed to that person (*ICTA 1988, s 416(6)*). Associates are as defined in **4.12**. HMRC expressly state that rights and powers of associates must not be attributed to the person concerned (HMRC Company Taxation Manual CTM 03750). However, rights and powers of the person's nominees must be attributed to the person (*ICTA 1988, s 416(5)*).

Associated companies share the £300,000 lower and £1,500,000 higher corporation tax profit limit bands between them. With the result that, if there are two associated companies, the small company rate band for each will only reach £150,000 and the full rate band will commence at £750,000.

STATUTORY EXCEPTIONS

Partners

4.29   Partners within the meaning of *ICTA 1988, ss 416(6)* and *417(3)(a)* (see **4.12**), with whom the company's shareholders or participators are within a business partnership, are only associated persons for small company rate purposes, if there are or have been tax planning arrangements in relation to the company, which will include its formation (*ICTA 1988, s 13(4A)–(4C)* inserted by *FA 2008, s 35*). Arrangements include any agreement, understanding, scheme, transaction or series of transactions (whether or not legally enforceable) other than any guarantee, security or change given to or taken by a bank.

This will be particularly relevant where a shareholder or participator is a member of a partnership, whose number of partners is unrestricted. The rights will only be attributed to other shareholders and participators in circumstances where tax planning arrangements exist and the small companies' rate reduces the corporation tax payable. These rules are effective from 1 April 2008; prior to that it was possible for a participator's business partners' interests to be attributed to him.

Non-trading companies

4.30   An associated company that has not carried on any trade or business during the accounting period in question is excluded from the count of associated companies (*ICTA 1988, s 13(4)*).

A trading company that ceased to trade and placed its surplus funds on a non-actively managed bank deposit account was regarded as dormant (*Jowett (Inspector of Taxes) v O'Neill and Brennan Construction Ltd* (1998) 70 TC 566, [1998] STC 482). A company that ceased trading but continued to receive rent from an established source that required little administration was also excluded from the count of associated companies (*HMRC v Salaried Persons Postal Loans Ltd* [2006] EWHC 763 (Ch), [2006] STC 1315).

A close company, which merely holds a bank deposit account, will fall into the definition of a close investment holding company and will be liable to corporation tax at the full rate, but can still be included in the count of associated companies.

A non-trading holding company is excluded from the count of associated companies provided that throughout the accounting period all the following conditions apply:

- Its only assets are its shares in its 51% subsidiaries.

- There is no deduction entitlement for charges or management expenses.

- It has no income of gains other than dividends, which it has distributed to its shareholders and which amount to franked investment income if distributed to a company (SP 5/94).

Rights of attribution

4.31   In practice the rights of attribution are an important consideration for close companies. By concession HMRC, in cases where there is no substantial commercial interdependence between companies, will only treat spouses, civil partners and minor children as relatives. HMRC interpret companies' interdependence in the commercial sense as reliance upon one another for trade or services etc. HMRC amongst other things will look at common administration or joint directorships, use of staff and facilities, purchasing and selling arrangements, co-operation on joint projects and inter-company loans and guarantees. HMRC interpret substantial in relative terms as not being insubstantial and as a guide anything more than 10% will be substantial (HMRC Company Taxation Manual CTM 03770).

Neither will HMRC attribute shares held by a trustee company to the party concerned if there is no other past or present connection with the trustee company (ESC C9).

In *R v CIR, ex p Newfields Developments Ltd* (2001) 73 TC 532, [2001] STC 901, [2001] 1 WLR 1111, [2001] 4 All ER 400 the Revenue's power to exercise attribution under *ICTA 1988, s 416(6)* was taken to the House of Lords.

The facts of this case are briefly as follows. Before his death, Mr W created a will trust in favour of his wife, Mrs W. The trustees of W's trust (Trustees A) owned shares in N Ltd for which the small companies rate of corporation tax was claimed. In his lifetime Mr W had also created a discretionary trust and had appointed separate trustees (Trustees B). Trustees B controlled a separate company L Ltd. The point of issue was whether N Ltd was associated with L Ltd.

The result of the House of Lords decision was as follows:

Mrs W was a participator. Her husband (a relative of hers) was the settlor of both the will trust and the discretionary trust. Therefore by reason of *ICTA 1988, s 417(3)(b)*, Mrs W was an associate of Trustees A and Trustees B. The rights and powers of both Trustees A and Trustees B could be attributed to her, even though she personally, owned no shares in the companies concerned. Therefore, indirectly, N Ltd and L Ltd were controlled by the same 'person' simply because of the rules of attribution and hence were associated companies.

In addition it was further decided that HMRC has neither discretion as to whether or not it should operate the rules of attribution nor indeed in deciding whether companies are associated.

In *Gascoignes Group Ltd v Inspector of Taxes* [2004] EWHC 640 (Ch), [2004] STC 844 the Revenue exercised the powers of attribution. In this case Mr D held 71% of the shares in G Ltd. Mr & Mrs G had created a settlement in favour of their three children. The settlement owned 99% of the shares in S Ltd. Mr D was a participator and therefore associated by reason of *ICTA 1988, s 417(3)(b)* with the trustees of the settlement. The rights and powers of the trustees must be attributed to him and hence he controls G Ltd and S Ltd and therefore these companies are associated companies for small companies rate purposes.

In HMRC Company Taxation Manual CTM 03750 HMRC acknowledge that attribution rights in some cases are limited by ESC C9. However, even if ESC C9 applies, rights will always be attributed to:

● spouse (civil partner) and minor children;

● business partners (but see **4.29**);

● trustee or trustees of a settlement where that person is the settlor, or the settlor's spouse or minor child.

The following examples are given:

Example 4.5

F Ltd and C Ltd have the following shareholders. Mr F and Mrs F are married to each other. Mr B and Mr C have no connection at all.

F Ltd	Shares	C Ltd	Shares
Mr F	60	Mrs F	75
Mr B	40	Mr C	25
Total issued shares	100	Total issued shares	100

Neither B nor C is an associate of Mr F or Mrs F. Mr F controls Company F. Mr F is a participator and under *ICTA 1988, s 416(6)* Mrs F's rights may be attributed to him. He therefore controls C Ltd. The two companies are associated whether or not there is substantial commercial interdependence between them because ESC C9 does not ignore the inter-spousal relationship.

Example 4.6

The situation is the same as **Example 4.5** except that Mrs C is Mr F's sister.

F Ltd	Shares	C Ltd	Shares
Mr F	60	Mrs C	75
Mr B	40	Mr C	25
Total issued shares	100	Total issued shares	100

Neither Mr B nor Mr C is an associate of Mr F. Mrs C is an associate of Mr F. Mrs C's rights may be attributed to Mr F. However, this will only occur if there is substantial commercial interdependence between F Ltd and C Ltd.

4.32 By concession, HMRC do not consider a company to be controlled by another (non-close) company if that control derives solely from preference shares or loans and that is the only connection (ESC C9). The loan in question must be a commercial loan. HMRC disregards fixed rate preference shares where the company takes no part in the management of the company and they have been subscribed for in the ordinary course of its business (HMRC Company Taxation Manual CTM 03810). In addition the fixed rate preference shares must be issued for new consideration, carry no conversion rights and have no rights to dividend other than the fixed dividend together with redemption rights at a reasonable commercial rate of return.

Company tax return

4.33 The corporation tax return form CT600 requires the number of associated companies to be entered in boxes 39, 40 and 41. This is necessary in order to determine the company's entitlement to small or marginal relief as appropriate, which must be the subject of a claim.

Example 4.7

Facts

The following companies are all wholly owned by Bill. They each make up accounts to 31 March each year.

A Ltd	B Ltd	C Ltd	D Ltd
£100,000	(£220,000)	£390,000	£20,000

Assessable profits and allowable losses for the year ended 31 March 2009 are shown.

Comments

The lower and upper relevant amounts of £300,000 and £1,500,000 are dividend by 4 resulting respectively in bands of £75,000 and £375,000.

The effective corporation tax paid by each company is as follows:

		Tax		*Tax*		*Tax*		*Tax*
	A Ltd		*B Ltd*		*C Ltd*		*D Ltd*	
	£		£		£		£	
Profits	100,000		Nil		390,000		20,000	
21%	75,000	15,750			75,000	15,750	20,000	4,200
29.75%	25,000	7,438			300,000	89,250		
28%					15,000	4,200		
Total corporation tax		23,188		Nil		109,250		4,200

Although B Ltd has made a trading loss it must still be included in the count of associated companies.

The company's total results are below £300,000, being £290,000, but it is not possible to make full use of the small companies rate. Bill may wish to consider restructuring the group to either put all activities into one company or to form a group. (See **Chapter 9** regarding losses and **Chapter 10** regarding group relief). Bill may also wish to consider reducing A Ltd's profits that fall within the marginal rate band.

Chapter 5

Income

RECEIPT OF INCOME AND BEING WITHIN THE CHARGE TO CORPORATION TAX

5.1   Commencing or ceasing to trade (**5.5**) or the receipt of income from any source is a question of fact. However, whether or not a company is within the charge to corporation tax can often in practice be more difficult to ascertain where the company is not in receipt of any income. *ICTA 1988, s 832(1)* states that a source of income is 'within the charge to corporation tax' if corporation tax would be chargeable on that income were there to be any from that source. *The Centaur Clothes Group Ltd v Walker* (2000) 72 TC 379, [2000] STC 324, [2000] 1 WLR 799, [2000] 2 All ER 589 was not carrying on a trade but had potential sources of income from an inter-company debt and an agency agreement. The company was held to be within the charge to corporation tax. The case overturned the established principle in *National Provident Institution v Brown* (1921) 8 TC 57, [1921] 2 AC 222 whereby a company had to be in receipt of a source of income to be within the charge to corporation tax. If a company is not carrying on any activity whatsoever, it is a dormant company. See **4.29** for further commentary.

HMRC regards a company as dormant if it does not receive any profits or income and holds no assets capable of producing assets of gains (HMRC Revenue Manual COTAX 'Dormancy'). The rule is relaxed if a company holds chargeable assets that are unlikely to produce any profits, income or gains in the near future. *FA 2004, s 55* requires companies to inform HMRC within three months of the beginning of the accounting period that it becomes within the charge to corporation tax. Coming within the charge to corporation tax marks the beginning of a new accounting period for corporation tax purposes (see **2.4**). Companies are required to follow the CT41G notification procedures detailed in **2.2**.

SOURCES OF INCOME

Computation of income and gains

5.2   Corporation tax is charged on income and chargeable gains but is not charged on dividends and distributions from UK resident companies.

Each source of income and each chargeable gain is computed separately, in accordance with income tax law and practice, but excluding provisions relating solely to individuals and subject to corporation tax provisions.

Thus the corporation tax computation and the corporation tax return bring together the company's total assessable income from trading and other sources, and chargeable gains. Deductions such as allowable losses and charges on income are taken into account in arriving at the company's profit chargeable to corporation tax (PCTCT).

An outline corporation tax computation is shown in **22.3**. The various sources of income reliefs are discussed as follows:

Source	Type of income	Chapter
Schedule A	Profits from rents and other income from property in the UK	12
Schedule D		
Case I	Profits from a trade	5
Case III	Interest	11
Case V	Income from foreign possessions	13
Case VI	Any income subject to tax but not taxed by any other Case or Schedule	5
Chargeable gains	Profits and losses arising from the disposal of capital assets	20
	Type of relief	
Management expenses	Expenses relating to investment business	12
Charges on income	Expenditure deducted from total income	9
Loss relief	Relief for excess of expenditure over income against other sources of income	9 and 10

TRADING INCOME

Accounting principles

5.3   Taxable profits must be computed in accordance with generally accepted accounting practice 'UK GAAP' (*FA 1998, s 42(1)*; *FA 2002, s 103 (5)*). See **Chapter 17** Accounting and Taxation for the interaction of accounting standards and taxation law. Accounting principles do not apply where they conflict with the tax legislation and case law. As a result, a company's PCTCT will usually differ from the profit shown in the company's profit and loss account or income statement.

Trading income

5.4   Trading and professional profits are computed according to the principles of Schedule D Cases I and II respectively (*ICTA 1988, s 18(1)(ii)*). A trade is defined as 'every trade, manufacture, adventure or concern in the nature of trade' (*ICTA 1988, s 83(1)*). There is no statutory definition of profession. It is normally understood to mean a high degree of skill or competence attributed to an individual, for which he or she has undergone specialised training. Therefore, professional income for incorporated firms of architects, engineers, lawyers etc would fall under the rules of Schedule D Case II. The rules for the two cases are virtually interchangeable and are referred to collectively as Schedule D Case I.

Trade

5.5   As to whether a trade is being carried on is a statement of fact. The badges of trade established by the Royal Commission on the Taxation of Profits and Income in 1955 look to the subject matter of the transaction, the period of ownership, the frequency of the transactions, the supplementary work, the circumstances or method of realisation and the motive. In other words, has the company acquired products or services over a short space of time that had no use to the company, which it enhanced in some way or to which it added its own identity, which it has then sold in a strategic manner in order to make a profit.

CASE LAW

5.6   There is a substantial body of case law relating to trading activities, which confirms the 'badges of trade' of which the following are a selection:

Subject matter of transaction. In the case of *Rutledge v CIR* (1929) 14 TC 490 the taxpayer bought and sold a large quantity of toilet rolls in an isolated transaction. The subject matter of the transaction determined that this was a trading transaction.

Period of ownership. In the case of *Marin v Lowry* (1926) 11 TC 297, [1927] AC 312 an agricultural machinery merchant with no previous connection with the linen trade bought a surplus of government stock of 44,000,000 yards of linen. Negotiations for sale to the linen manufacturers fell through. The taxpayer advertised the linen and eventually all was sold within a year to numerous purchasers. The goods were sold swiftly at a profit. It was held that this was an adventure in the nature of trade.

Frequency of transactions. In *Pickford v Quirke* (1927) 13 TC 251 the taxpayer was a member of four different syndicates involved in buying and selling cotton spinning mills. It was held that the repetition of this transaction implied a trading intention. In *Leach v Pogson* (1962) 40 TC 585, [1962] TR 289 the taxpayer founded a driving school which he later sold at a profit. He then founded 30 more driving schools. Once the schools were operational he transferred them to companies, partly for shares and partly for cash. Because of the frequency of the transactions the taxpayer was found to be trading.

Supplementary work. In *Cape Brandy Syndicate v CIR* (1921) 12 TC 358, [1921] 2 KB 403 three wine merchants all from different firms bought a quantity of South African brandy. Most of the brandy was shipped to the UK where it was blended with French brandy, re-casked and sold in numerous lots. It was held that the transactions amounted to a trade.

Circumstances or method of realisation. In *West v Phillips* (1958) 38 TC 203, [1958] TR 267 a retired builder owned 2,495 houses, of which 2,208 had been built as investments and 287 for eventual sale. After a period of time the taxpayer began to sell the houses. It was held that 287 houses were sold as trading stock but the sale of the remainder held for investment purposes not a trade.

Motive. In *Wisdom v Chamberlain* (1968) 45 TC 92, [1969] 1 WLR 275, [1969] 1 All ER 332 the taxpayer made a profit on the purchase and sale of silver bullion. The bullion was bought to protect his wealth against the devaluation of sterling. It was held that this was a trading activity because the silver had been purchased for the specific purpose of realising a profit.

Of recent importance is the decision in *Marson v Morton* (1986) 59 TC 381, [1986] STC 463, [1986] 1 WLR 1343. In this case factors that should be considered as to whether a particular transaction was a trading transaction were summarised as follows:

Factor to consider	*Comment*
Was the transaction a one-off transaction?	Frequency of transactions indicate a trade, but a one-off transaction may still constitute a trade depending on intention and other factors.
Was the transaction in some way related to a trade carried on by the taxpayer?	If related to the trade this will point to a trading transaction.

Was the transaction in a commodity of a kind which is normally the subject matter of trade?	If yes, then again this will point to a trading transaction.
Was the transaction carried out in a manner typical of a trade in a commodity of that nature?	If yes, then again this will point to a trading transaction.
How was the transaction financed?	If financed by borrowings, this often indicates that a trade is being carried on.
Was work done on the item before resale?	If yes it is more likely to be a trading transaction.
Was the item purchased broken down into several lots?	If so, there is an indication that a trading transaction has taken place.
What were the purchaser's intentions at the time of purchase? Was it intended to hold the asset as an investment?	If held as an investment, its resale is unlikely to be a trading transaction.
Did the asset purchased either provide enjoyment for the purchaser, or produce income?	. The production of income points to a trading transaction.

The issues can be transferred to professional income but here more than likely the central issue is whether professional skills are sold and marketed for remunerative gain.

All these indications point to whether a trade is being carried on. Overall the company's activities must be looked at as a whole. A company may carry on a trade and an investment business. Transactions for each must be kept separate as the rules for each are different. See **Chapter 11** for investment business.

5.7   On the premise that a trade is being carried on, the company must establish whether its receipt is from the trade and whether it is a capital or a revenue item. It is an established principle that trading income is received when it is recognised in the trader's accounts (HMRC Business Income Manual BIM 40070). See **Chapter 17** Accounting and Taxation.

SELF-ASSESSMENT OF TRADING INCOME

Company tax return

5.8   On the assumption that a company is carrying on a trade or profession, the company is required to declare its trading or professional turnover in box 1 of the company tax return. This information should be available from the company's accounts. Box 2 is for use by financial concerns such as banks, building societies and insurance companies.

Schedule D Case I and II profits

5.9   The company must then compute its assessable Schedule D Case I and II profits, to enable it to complete box 3 of the company tax return. The profit for each trade must be computed on separate computations and a calculation of the capital allowances claimed should also be provided.

The accounting profits form the basis of the taxable profits and so the starting point for computing the Schedule D Case I assessable profit is the reported profits.

It is necessary to review the computation of profits to ensure that it is compliant with tax law. It will be necessary to review the specific Schedule D Case I computational provisions on which trading profits for income tax and corporation tax are based, as discussed below. It will also be necessary to review the more recent legislation that has direct relevance to corporation tax. This will encompass intangible assets, research and development expenditure, loan relationships and transfer pricing. In this respect please see the respective following Chapters 7, 8, 11 and 13. Capital expenditure is not deductible for Schedule D Case I purposes.

CAPITAL V REVENUE

5.10   There is a body of case law, which established the revenue versus capital principles.

In general asset repair carried out during the course of trading activities is a revenue expense. Expenditure in order to put an asset into working order or the replacement of an entirety is not a revenue expense. In *Law Shipping Co Ltd v CIR* (1923) 12 TC 621, expenditure on repairs to a ship in order to make it seaworthy shortly after purchase was held to be capital expenditure. In contrast in *Odeon Associated Theatres Ltd v Jones* (1971) 48 TC 257, [1973] Ch 288, [1971] 1 WLR 442, [1972] 1 All ER 681 expenditure carried out on repairs to a useable cinema over a period of years was held to be revenue expenditure.

In *O'Grady v Bullcroft Main Collieries Ltd* (1932) 17 TC 93 a colliery company built a factory chimney at a cost of £3,067. After several years it became unsafe and was demolished. The company built another improved chimney near the site of the old one and claimed £287 of the cost as repairs. The whole of the cost was found to be capital expenditure because the new chimney was the replacement of an 'entirety'.

In *Samuel Jones & Co (Devondale) Ltd v CIR* (1951) 32 TC 513, [1951] TR 411 the company replaced a factory chimney and also incurred costs in respect of the removal of the old chimney. The expenditure was found to be an allowable revenue deduction because it was an integral part of the factory. The chimney was not an entirety as in the case of *O'Grady v Bullcroft Main Collieries Ltd.*

In *Brown v Burnley Football & Athletic Co Ltd* (1980) 53 TC 357, [1980] STC 424, [1980] 3 All ER 244 a stand at the football ground was found to be unsafe. It had been built in 1912 of wood and steel with a brick wall at the back. It was demolished and replaced with a new modern concrete stand. The new stand, with approximately the same capacity, was nearer the pitch but included office and other accommodation not provided by the old stand. The expenditure was held to be capital expenditure because the new stand was a replacement in its entirety.

Expenditure related in connection with enduring benefits to a trade is considered to be capital. In *Atherton v British Insulated & Helsby Cables Ltd* (1925) 10 TC 155, [1926] AC 205 a company set up a pension fund and made an initial lump sum contribution to enable the past service of existing staff to rank for pension. The expenditure was held to be capital. The principle was established that expenditure was normally capital if it was made not only once and for all but with a view to bringing into existence an asset or advantage for the enduring benefit of the trade.

In *Tucker v Granada Motorway Services Ltd* (1979) 53 TC 92, [1979] STC 393, [1979] 1 WLR 683, [1979] 2 All ER 801 the rent, which a company paid to the Ministry of Transport for a motorway service area, was calculated in part by reference to its gross takings. The gross takings included the duty on sales of tobacco. The lease was not assignable. In order to have the duty on sales of tobacco excluded from the gross takings, the company made a once and for all payment of £122,220 to the Ministry of Transport. The expenditure was held to be capital and therefore not deductible from profits. The expenditure related to an identifiable capital asset.

In *Beauchamp v F W Woolworth plc* (1989) 61 TC 542, [1989] STC 510, [1989] 3 WLR 1 a company entered into two loans, each for 50 million Swiss Francs, for five years but repayable earlier at the option of the company, subject to a payment of a graduated premium. The first loan was repaid six months early and the second on the due date, giving rise to losses of £11.4 million, due to currency exchange transactions.

It was held that the loss was incurred in relation to a capital transaction and was therefore not allowable as a revenue deduction. The company had increased its capital employed and thereby obtained an asset or advantage which endured for five years and as such was a capital asset. A loan is only a revenue transaction if it is part of the day-to-day incidence of carrying on the business, which was not the case in this situation. The loss was not deductible.

Often there is doubt as to whether an item of expenditure is capital or revenue. In the case of *Heather v P-E Consulting Group Ltd* (1972) 48 TC 293, [1973] Ch 189, [1973] 1 All ER 8 it was established that this is the court's decision. In this case a company undertook to pay 10% of its annual profits, subject to a minimum of £5,000 to a trust set up to enable its staff to acquire shares in the company and to prevent the company from coming under the control of outside shareholders. Accountancy evidence given at the time, which was accepted by the Commissioners, confirmed that the expenses were of a revenue nature. Although the Court of Appeal upheld the Commissioners' decision, it was made clear that whether the expenditure was capital or revenue was a matter of law for the court to decide and that accountancy evidence is not conclusive.

It was necessary to turn to the courts to establish whether the cost of airspace was capital or revenue. In *Rolfe v Wimpey Waste Management Ltd* (1989) 62 TC 399, [1989] STC 454 the company purchased several sites on which to tip waste under a contract with its customers. The company claimed that the purchases were revenue expenditure, on the grounds that it had acquired the land in order to use the airspace above it. The expenditure was held to relate to the land and was therefore capital.

Professional and other associated costs in connection with capital expenditure are also disallowed. See HMRC Business Income Manual BIM 35000 onwards for a discussion on the capital/revenue divide.

Waste disposal: restoration payments

5.11   A payment made in respect of site restoration as a condition of planning permission to use the site for the carrying out of waste disposal activities or to comply with any terms of any relevant agreement is an allowable trading expense except for capital expenditure which qualifies for capital allowances. Waste disposal activities are the collection, treatment, conversion and final depositing of waste materials or any of those activities (*ICTA 1988, s 91A*).

Relief for expenditure on waste disposal on the site is calculated according to the following formula:

$$(A - B) \times \frac{C}{C + D}$$

A   =   Total site preparation expenditure excluding expenditure already allowed and capital expenditure.

B   =   The total relief already given on the expenditure.

C = The volume of waste materials deposited on the site during the period in question.

D = The capacity at the end of the period of the site not used for the deposit of waste materials.

(ICTA 1988, s 91B)

Expenditure incurred before 6 April 1989 is excluded.

In the case of *Dispit Ltd v Revenue and Customs Comrs* SpC 579, it was decided that restoration expenditure was only an allowable expense from trading profits in the accounting period concerned up to the amount of the payments actually made.

SCHEDULE D CASE I COMPUTATIONAL PROVISIONS

5.12 As already mentioned, corporation tax is enshrined in income tax law and the reported profits.

The adjustments to the reported profit for taxation purposes follow four broad headings:

- Expenditure charged against profits in the accounts but not allowable as a deduction for tax purposes.

- Income that has not been included in profits in the accounts but that is taxable under Schedule D Case I.

- Income included in profits in the accounts but not taxable under Schedule D Case I.

- Expenditure that has not been charged against profits in the accounts but that is allowable under Schedule D Case I.

In particular it will be necessary to review the accounts for any capital items. Capital expenditure included within the profit and loss account for whatever reason is not an allowable deduction against profits for Schedule D Case I purposes.

EXPENDITURE CHARGED AGAINST PROFITS IN THE ACCOUNTS BUT NOT ALLOWABLE AS A DEDUCTION FOR TAX PURPOSES

Wholly and exclusively

5.13 Expenditure is only allowed as a deduction if it has been incurred 'wholly and exclusively' for the purposes of the trade or profession (*ICTA 1988,* *s 74(1)).* Company expenditure must be reviewed from this prerogative. Expenditure on preserving a trade from destruction was treated as incurred wholly and exclusively for the purposes of the trade (*McKnight v Sheppard* (1999) 71 TC 410, [1999] STC 669, [1999] 1 WLR 1133, [1999] 3 All ER 491).

In the normal business environment, the types of expenditure often under consideration include entertaining and remuneration. A summarised but not exhaustive list of other allowable and disallowable deductions is given in **5.20**.

Entertaining

5.14 Entertaining expenditure is disallowed by statute (*ICTA 1988, s 577*) except for staff entertainment. *Section 577* overrides the decision in *Bentleys, Stokes and Lowless v Beeson* (1952) 33 TC 491, [1952] WN 280, [1952] 2 All ER 82. Entertainment and gifts (excluding food and drink) that carry a conspicuous advertisement for the business, provided that the cost for the company is no more than £50 per donee in any one year, are also disallowed. Assets used for business entertainment do not qualify for capital allowances.

A number of relevant principles, based on VAT decisions involving business entertainment cases, indicate the like interpretation of *s 577*. Based on VAT decisions, the definition of business entertainment includes hospitality both free and subsidised (*Celtic Football and Athletic Club Ltd v Customs & Excise Commrs* [1983] STC 470). However, hospitality is not defined as business entertainment if it was given 'pursuant to a legal obligation in return for which it obtains proper and sufficient quid pro quo. The quid pro quo may be cash or it may be goods or services.' This also extends to a contractual obligation a company may have to provide hospitality (eg as part of a package).

Travel costs associated with business entertainment are not allowable expenses but exceptions exist such as employees travelling to meet a client.

ICTA 1988, s 577(10) allows the deduction of business entertainment expenses for the provision of items relevant to the trade and provided in the normal course of business, eg hospitality provided by restaurants and pubs (*Fleming v Associated Newspapers Ltd* (1972) 48 TC 382, [1973] AC 628, [1972] 2 All ER 574). Also, the cost of goods or services given away as an advertising promotion is allowable (*ICTA 1988, s 577(10)*).

Staff entertainment is allowable (*ICTA 1988, s 577(5)*) as long as it conforms to the wholly and exclusively for trade requirement and is not 'excessive'. Staff includes retired staff and partners. If an employee takes a client out for lunch *s 577(5)* does not apply and therefore the hospitality is not allowable. However, if the employee has an allowance, which is an expense of employment, such expenditure is allowable. The cost of subsistence for persons directly involved in the company's business or the conduct of the business are allowable expense.

Training costs for employees, which may include hospitality, are allowable. Hospitality is disallowed for persons not directly employed by the company who attend training courses paid by the company. The cost of sponsorship is not allowable in full if the company sponsoring receives other benefits for its sponsorship. Payments to specialist entertainment providers/organisers/ arrangers are disallowed (HMRC Business Income Manual BIM 45047).

Advertising and promotion costs will normally be allowed. A company incurring costs on room hire and entertaining potential customers in order to gain firm orders found that the entertaining costs were disallowed but the room hire cost was allowable (*Netlogic Consulting Ltd v HMRC*).

Remuneration

5.15 **Employees.** Provided the remuneration charged is 'wholly and exclusively' for the purposes of the trade it should be an allowable deduction (*Copeman v Flood (William) & Sons Ltd* (1940) 24 TC 53, [1941] KB 202; *LG Berry Investments Ltd v Attwooll* (1964) 41 TC 547, [1964] 1 WLR 693, [1964] 2 All ER 126). An employee will normally have an employment contract with the company, which together with *ITEPA 2003* will determine the time that payment is due to the employee. The existence of a contractual obligation for the company will bring about the allowable deduction, normally at the same time that the remuneration is 'earnings' for the employee. In order to qualify as a deduction from profits, remuneration charged must be paid to the employee within nine months of the year end (*FA 1989, s 43(1)*).

5.16 **Directors' remuneration.** A director is any person occupying the position of director by whatever name called (*CA 2006, s 250*; *CA 1985, s 741(1)*). A shadow director is any person in accordance with whose instructions directors are accustomed to act with the exception of a professional adviser (*CA 2006, s 251*; *CA 1985, s 741(2)*). A similar definition is used within *ITEPA 2003, s 67*.

The time that remuneration is due and payable to a director is not only determined by *ITEPA 2003* and the director's contract of employment but also by company law.

Directors are treated as having received earnings at the time when they become entitled to be paid them. However, an entitlement to payment is not necessarily the same as the date on which the employee acquires a right to be paid (HMRC Employment Income Manual EIM 42290).

The terms of a service agreement may be written, verbal or implied and may give entitlement to a regular salary or a contractual bonus or other sums. The director would then enjoy rights to earnings under the agreement. The time at which entitlement to earnings under a service agreement arises will be governed by the terms of the agreement.

5.16 *Income*

Under company law, a company may draft a special clause in its constitution regarding the directors' entitlement to directors' remuneration. Many companies have adopted Table A of the *Companies (Tables A–F) Regulations 1985.* Under *Companies Act 2006*, model articles are to be introduced from 1 October 2009 (*CA 2006, s 19*).

Regulation 82 states:

'Remuneration of Directors

The directors shall be entitled to such remuneration as the company may by ordinary resolution determine and unless the resolution provides otherwise the remuneration shall be deemed to accrue from day to day.'

The provision requires that directors' remuneration be voted in general meeting. This involves the members of the company passing a resolution that determines the amount payable to the directors. Under *Companies Act 2006*, a private company is not required to hold an AGM. The accounts must still be approved by the directors (*CA 2006, s 414*).

In small private companies a meeting may not take place, but the directors would have agreed the remuneration anyway, possibly because they are a single director or because the company operates in that way. Both *CA 1985, s 382B* and *CA 2006, s 356* require that a single member provides the company with a written record of the decision. In some cases, particularly where no other person other than the member is entitled to attend the meeting, this requirement can be overridden by the *Duomatic* principle.

In *Re Duomatic Ltd* [1969] 2 Ch 365, [1969] 1 All ER 161 the directors, who were also the only ordinary shareholders having a right to attend and vote at a general meeting, had drawn remuneration, which was subsequently shown in accounts, which they had as directors approved. That was challenged in the subsequent liquidation on the ground that it had never been sanctioned by a general meeting. The court held that although the directors did not take the formal step of constituting themselves a general meeting of the company and passing a formal resolution approving the payment of directors' salaries at the time of approving the accounts, they did apply their minds to the question, and accordingly, their consent should be regarded as tantamount to a resolution of a general meeting.

HMRC accept the *Duomatic* principle. If there is no such specific resolution, but the directors' remuneration is approved by the shareholders entitled to attend and vote at a general meeting, without a meeting actually taking place, this has the same effect as a resolution passed by the company in general meeting (HMRC Employment Income Manual EIM 42300).

Also, a resolution of the members approving the company's accounts will be a sufficient authorisation of directors' remuneration if the members are aware that by approving the accounts, they are also approving the directors' remuneration

(*Felix Hadley & Co v Hadley* (1897) 77 LT 131). The time at which entitlement to earnings arises is the time at which the resolution is passed, agreement reached or the accounts approved, unless specific provision otherwise is made at that time.

Although, these principles establish the time of payment to the individual they must be looked at carefully to establish whether they permit a deduction for corporation tax purposes. The time of passing a resolution is of particular importance if remuneration is unpaid and decided upon after the end of the accounting period.

In order to be acceptable for taxation purposes a company's accounts must be drawn up in accordance with GAAP. FRS 12 permits a provision if an entity has a present obligation as a result of a past event (see **17.16**). FRS 21 only permits adjustments to the accounts for events that occurred after the balance sheet date if they provided evidence of conditions that existed at the balance sheet date (see **17.11**). Unless a decision is made to vote additional remuneration or to pay a bonus before the year a corporation tax deduction appears to be prohibited (See *Taxation*, 20 April 2006, *Directors' remuneration—A not so simple question*, Tim Good).

Ideally a written service agreement between the company and the director should be put in place. In order to confirm the deductibility of payments when voted for corporation tax purposes, it is imperative that a formal decision be made before the end of the accounting period. A written record of any informal decision made by the members should be supplied to the company as soon as possible. Alternatively a separate written shareholder agreement outside of the memorandum and articles of association, granting an entitlement to remuneration for an accounting period but quantifying the amount after the end of accounting period, may be considered in order to satisfy the GAAP requirements.

Both employees and directors remuneration is normally paid under deduction of PAYE. See *Income Tax 2008/09* (from Tottel Publishing), Chapter 5. By concession if a professional partnership holds an office the income from that office may be taxed as fees rather than employment income (ESC A37 Revenue Manual EIM 02500). HMRC when notified will issue an NT coding, PAYE will not be due on these payments but the payments will still be liable to Class 1 NIC (Revenue Manual EIM 03002). The directorship should be a normal activity of the professional partnership, the fees are only a small part of the profits and under the partnership agreement the fees are pooled for division amongst the partners. The situation must be reviewed carefully by the director concerned. There is the possibility that the payment may fall within the personal services régime that can apply to a partnership as well as a company (see **5.17**).

A director or employee may of course provide services to a company in a separate business capacity, eg solicitor, accountant or consultant etc. If the services are provided to the company on the same basis as the director's or employee's other customers the payment to the director or employee would not be employment income and would not be subject to PAYE or NIC (Revenue Manual ESM1096).

Providing services through a company

Personal service company

5.17 Individuals who provide their services through a company may fall foul of the personal service company or managed service company legislation (*see Income Tax 2008/09* from Tottel Publishing). A deduction from corporation tax profits will be given if the deemed payment is treated as paid during that accounting period. Deemed payments are calculated for each income tax year ended 5 April.

Example 5.1

Mr Persona is an IT consultant who provides his services through Persona Services Ltd. It is understood that the personal services legislation applies. Persona Services Ltd prepares accounts to 28 February each year. Mr Persona's deemed payment for the year ended 5 April 2009 is £50,000. Relief for the deemed payment is given against profits for the year ended 28 February 20010.

Managed service company

5.18 A managed service company acts as an umbrella company in raising invoices on personal service individual's behalf, for which it charges a commission. Managed service companies must account for PAYE and NIC on the full amount invoiced to its clients for the individual's services, rather than the post-commission payment made to the individual (*FA 2007, s 25* and *Sch 3*). PAYE applies to full invoice payments from 6 April 2007 and NIC applies to full invoice payments from 6 August 2007 (*SI 2007/2070*).

Website development costs

5.19 Most businesses operate a website to promote their venture. The taxation treatment of website development costs incurred largely follows the UITF abstract 29 accounting treatment and SIC 32 Intangible Assets—Web Site Costs. The costs generally relate to planning, application and infrastructure development; design and content. As planning costs give rise to no future economic benefits these will be written off in the profit and loss account. If incurred wholly and exclusively for the purposes of the trade they will be allowable for corporation tax purposes. The remaining costs will be capitalised in intangible fixed assets if they provide an enduring benefit to the company. This will arise if the expenditure is separately identifiable and the technical and commercial viability of the website has been assessed with reasonable accuracy. The website must also generate sales or other revenues directly and the present value of the future cash flows generated will not be less than the amounts capitalised. Adequate resources must exist to enable the website to reach conclusion. If the costs satisfy the criteria of plant and machinery (see **6.7**) capital allowances will be available.

If the criteria are not satisfied the development costs are written off to the profit and loss account. Annual website maintenance costs are written off to the profit and loss account.

ALLOWABLE AND DISALLOWABLE DEDUCTIONS

5.20

Item	Explanation	References
General	Statutory rules on deductions under Schedule D Cases I and II are to be found in *ICTA 1988, ss 817, 74(1)*, which operate in a negative way by stating what cannot be deducted rather than what is allowed. The Courts' interpretation of the Taxes Acts is based on the principle that if an item of expenditure is an allowable deduction in line with ordinary accounting rules then it should be allowed under the Acts unless expressly prohibited. The business purposes must be the sole purpose for the transaction. Where there is a 'mixed' purpose, say providing additional amounts to employees, the amounts are assessed on the individual through the PAYE and benefits system. The deduction is not restricted in the company, unless it is totally disallowed by statute or because the payment is not 'wholly and exclusively' for the purposes of the trade. The following expenses are allowable where indicated unless capital or failing the wholly and exclusively test.	HMRC Business Income Manual BIM 42060 for prohibitions under *ICTA 1988, s 74(1), (2)* dealing with Schedule D Cases I and II. Specific rules for prohibitions including Schedule D Cases I and II are set out in HMRC Business Income Manual BIM 42070.

Item	Explanation	References
Accounts preparation	Fees in relation to the preparation of business accounts and other recurring accountancy and legal expenses arising from the preparation are normally allowable. Fee protection insurance charges to cover the risk of incurring additional costs are only allowable if the additional costs are of a revenue nature or if the costs covered would be allowable. The costs of an enquiry that reveals discrepancies resulting from fraud and negligence are not allowable.	HMRC Business Income Manual BIM 46450 HMRC Business Income Manual BIM 46452
Advertising	Ordinary current expenditure on advertising a company's goods or services is normally allowable.	HMRC Business Income Manual BIM 42550
Annuities and annual payments	An annuity or an annual payment is disallowed as a business deduction in accounts under *ICTA 1988, s 74(1)(m)*. In general terms an annual payment will be (a) paid under a legal obligation, (b) annually recurring and (c) pure income profit in the hands of the recipient but may be allowed as a charge on income (see **9.8, 9.15**).	HMRC Business Income Manual BIM 42601. *Gresham Life Assurance Society v Styles* (1890) 2 TC 633, (1890) 3 TC 185, [1892] AC 309.
Bad and doubtful debts Impairment losses	For accounting periods beginning on or after 1 January 2005, relief for bad debts is given as an impairment loss.	*(ICTA 1988, s88D)* See IAS 39 **17.9**

Item	Explanation	References
	Where a deduction for a bad or doubtful debt has been made and the company recovers the debt or an amount of its written-down value the amount recovered or the excess should be brought into the year of recovery.	HMRC Business Income Manual BIM 42730 *Bristow v Dickinson (William) & Co Ltd* (1946) 27 TC 157, [1946] KB 321, [1946] 1 All ER 448. (*ICTA 1988, s 94*).
	Companies can accept assets in satisfaction of trading debts. Where the market value of the asset at the date of acceptance of the asset is less than the amount of the outstanding debt the shortfall may be allowable as a deduction. However, the company must agree to account as a trading receipt any excess as a result of the disposal of the asset. The excess is excluded from CGT (*TCGA 1992, s 251(3)*).	HMRC Business Income Manual BIM 42735
Business archives	Costs incurred in maintaining historic business archives will generally be allowable expenses. Company expenditure on the provision of access to archives and on linked educational services is also usually allowable.	HMRC Business Income Manual BIM 42501
Capital	Capital payments are disallowed. A company's initial contribution to a staff pension fund was a capital payment because it was made not only once and for all, but with a view to bringing into existence an asset or an advantage for the enduring benefit of trade.	*Atherton v British Insulated and Helsby Cables Ltd* (1925) 10 TC 155, [1926] AC 205. HMRC Business Income Manual BIM 35320.

Item	Explanation	References
Car or motor cycle hire	Where the retail price of new vehicle (except an electric car or a car with low CO_2 emissions) exceeds £12,000 and is hired for the purposes of the trade the hire charge is reduced for tax purposes by using the formula $(12,000 + P) \div 2P$ where P is the retail price of the vehicle when new.	HMRC Business Income Manual BIM 47715–47720. *Lloyds UDT Finance Ltd v Britax International GmbH* (2002) 74 TC 662, [2002] STC 956, [2002] EWCA Civ 806 (*ICTA 1988, s 578A*).
	If the lease includes maintenance then costs should be excluded if separately identified in the lease agreement. The lease costs will include the 50% VAT charge if the company is VAT registered.	
Company administration	Costs a company occurs in ordinary annual expenditure on such matters as the keeping of the share register, the printing of annual accounts, and the holding of shareholders' AGMs are normally allowed as trading expenses. Also, the annual cost of a Stock Exchange quotation and the fees paid to newspapers for the inclusion of the company's shares in the newspaper's report of Stock Exchange prices and annual fees paid to trustees for debenture holders or mortgagees are treated as allowable expenses.	HMRC Business Income Manual, BIM 42510

Item	Explanation	References
Compensation and damages	Compensation and damages payments depend on the circumstances of the payment. A compensation payment may be reduced by the reimbursement of trading expenses allowable as a deduction. Compensation and damages payments require to be 'wholly and exclusively' for trade purposes and on 'revenue account'. Where compensation relates to normal trading activity and not an identifiable capital asset, it will be an allowable deduction. Compensation for termination of an agency was held to be a trading expense.	HMRC Business Income Manual BIM 42950 BIM 42955 BIM 42960 *Anglo-Persian Oil Co Ltd v Dale* (1931) 16 TC 253, [1932] 1 KB 124.
Computer software	Expenditure may either be capital or revenue expenditure. See **6.15**.	*CAA 2001, ss 71–73.*
Counselling services	Expenditure on employee counselling and other outplacement services, which fall within the earnings exemption of *ITEPA 2003*, is deductible in computing profits.	*ICTA 1988, ss 589A, 589B*
Crime	'No deduction shall be made for any expenditure incurred in making a payment, the making of which constitutes a criminal payment.'	HMRC Business Income Manual BIM 43100, BIM 43101, BIM 43105, BIM 43115 and BIM43160. *ICTA 1988, s 577A(1), (1)(a), (1)(b) & (2).*

Item	Explanation	References
Defalcations/ embezzlement	Funds misappropriated by a director then claimed as a remuneration payment on which PAYE was to be paid were held not to be an allowable deduction for corporation tax purposes. Losses are allowed as deductions but not misappropriations by a director. Defalcations made good are taxable.	*Bamford v ATA Advertising* (1972) 48 TC 359, [1972] 1 WLR 1261, [1972] 3 All ER 535; *Curtis v Oldfield (J & G) Ltd* (1925) 9 TC 319; *Gray v Penrhyn (Lord)* (1937) 21 TC 252, [1937] 3 All ER 468.
Dilapidations	Where the costs of repairs at the end of a lease, called dilapidations, would be the same if the repairs had been undertaken during the course of the lease period, and are not of a capital nature, then they should be allowable (*ICTA 1988, s 74(1)(d)*). At the expiry of the lease the lessee may agree to pay a sum, compensation in lieu of accrued repairs, to the lessor. This payment is allowable if it does not reflect capital costs.	HMRC Business Income Manua BIM 43250, BIM 43251, BIM 43255, BIM 43260, BIM 43265. *Hyett v Lennard* (1940) 23 TC 346, [1940] 2 KB 180, [1940] 3 All ER 133.
Employees' or directors' remuneration	Remuneration wholly and exclusively for the purposes of trade is deductible. See **5.15, 5.16**. Remuneration paid to connected parties, say to shareholder's family, must be on arm's-length terms.	*Stott and Ingham v Trehearne* (1924) 9 TC 69; *Earlspring Properties Ltd v Guest* (1995) 67 TC 259, [1995] STC 479; *Robinson v Scott Bader & Co Ltd* (1981) 54 TC 757, [1981] STC 436, [1981] 1 WLR 1135, [1981] 2 All ER 1116.
Employees seconded to charities and educational bodies	When an employee is seconded to a charity or an education body on a temporary basis, the expenditure attributable to the employment is deductible.	*ICTA 1988, s 86.* HMRC Business Income Manual BIM 47115, BIM 47120

Item	Explanation	References
Fee Protection Insurance	A premium for insuring against the costs incurred in the case of a tax enquiry are allowable, only to the extent that the costs insured against would themselves be allowable. If the premium covers the cost of accountancy fees incurred in negotiating additional liabilities resulting from negligent or fraudulent conduct, it is not deductible. Apportionment is not permitted.	HMRC Business Income Manual BIM 46452, BIM 46450
Fines	Fines are disallowed, as they are not incurred wholly and exclusively for the purpose of trade—as confirmed in case law. Penalties for breaches of trading regulations are disallowed. Legal costs in defending a business were allowable.	HMRC Business Income Manual BIM 42515. *CIR v Alexander von Glehn & Co Ltd* (1920) 12 TC 232, [1920] 2 KB 553; *McKnight v Sheppard* (1999) 71 TC 419, [1999] STC 669, [1999] 1 WLR 1133, [1999] 3 All ER 491.
Fine Parking	In situations where the employer pays a parking fine that is in fact the liability of the employee, the cost to the employer will be allowable in determining his trading profit and the employee will be chargeable on the emolument arising. Fines paid by the company on company cars are not a benefit for the employee but neither are they deductible for corporation tax. Fines resulting from civil actions arising out of trade may be allowed if not punitive.	HMRC Business Income Manual BIM 42515. *Golder v Great Boulder Proprietary Gold Mines Ltd* (1952) 33 TC 75, [1952] 1 All ER 360

Item	Explanation	References
Foreign Exchange	Foreign exchange gains and losses are dealt under the loan relationship provisions see Chapter 11.	HMRC Business Income Manual BIM 45875
Franchise payments	An appropriate part of the initial franchise fee will be considered a revenue payment if the items it represents are revenue items and are not separately charged for in the continuing fees. However, franchise fees are more likely to fall within the intangible assets regime see Chapter 7.	HMRC Business Income Manual BIM 57600–57620.
Gifts	Business gifts are not allowed as a deduction against profits (*ICTA 1988, s 577*). Included in 'gifts' are goods and	HMRC Business Income Manual BIM 45065, *ICTA 1988, s 577(9)*.
	services supplied below cost. An exception is gifts with a value of less than £50, containing the company's advertisement, and not related to food, drink or tobacco, will be allowed as a deduction. Free samples given to the public are not gifts are an allowable deduction. Gifts to charities are not disallowed. Sales promotion scheme gifts to customers are not disallowed provided the customer is obliged to do or give something in return.	BIM 45070 BIM 45070 BIM 45071, BIM 45032, BIM 45072, ESC B7 BIM 45085

Item	Explanation	References
Guarantee payments	Guarantee payments fall within loan relationships see Chapter 11. However, a payment under a loan guarantee is deductible only if the 'wholly and exclusively for the purpose of trade' concept is met at the time it was made and a capital advantage is not secured. Guarantees between grouped and/or associated companies may not fulfil these conditions. Payments under guarantee in respect of an associated company were held to be capital expenditure. An exhibition guarantee payment made in order to secure work was considered to be an allowable deduction.	HMRC Business Income Manual BIM 45301 *Milnes v J Beam Group Ltd* (1975) 50 TC 675, [1975] STC 487; *Garforth v Tankard Carpets Ltd* (1980) 53 TC 342, [1980] STC 251; *Redkite v Inspector of Taxes* [1996] STC (SCD) 501; BIM 45305 *Morley v Lawford & Co* (1928) 14 TC 229.
Hire Purchase	Revenue payments for the hire of an asset are deductible	HMRC Business Income Manual BIM 45351.
	but capital payments for the purchase of an asset are not. Payments under a hire purchase agreement are split between amounts for hire (allowable) and payments for the eventual purchase (capital). If ownership of the equipment passes to the purchaser at the time of signing the agreement and payment is via an extra charge then these payments are capital expenditure. Cost of repairs and renewal to hire purchase assets are allowable as a deduction. The accountancy treatment for hire-purchase contracts is governed by SSAP 21. (See **Chapter 17.**)	*Darngavil Coal Co Ltd v Francis* (1931) 7 TC 1. BIM 45351 BIM 45355 BIM 45360

Item	Explanation	References
Holding company formation expenses	This is treated as capital expenditure and is not deductible	*Kealy v O'Mara (Limerick) Ltd* [1942] 2 ITC 265; [1942] IR 616.
Incentive and reward schemes	Expenditure on performance related awards and incentive schemes, which satisfy all of the following conditions, may be allowable if (a) the award requires to be based on genuine performance achievement, (b) there is an obligation to provide the gift and (c) a formal scheme based on known rules is in place. Suggestion scheme awards are treated in a similar manner provided the award is reasonable.	HMRC Business Income Manual BIM 45080. BIM 47010 BIM 47015
In-house Professional fees	A company's in-house professional fees in relation to work involved with the company's capital assets are not allowed. Fees for the maintenance of a company's assets, facilities or trading rights are normally revenue expenses and allowable but fees in relation to rights or facilities of a capital nature are capital expenses.	HMRC Business Income Manual BIM 46410,
Insurance	Policies, which provide indemnity for loss or damage to fixed or intangible assets, current assets (trading stock or trade debts), are allowable if the business purpose requirement is satisfied (*ICTA 1988, s 74(1)(a)*), including policies which cover replacement 'new for old'. Insurance proceeds for stock lost are assessable as trading income.	HMRC Business Income Manual BIM 45501, BIM 45505, *Green v Gliksten (J) & Son Ltd* (1929) 14 TC 364, [1929] AC 381; BIM 45510, *Mallandain Investments Ltd v Shadbolt* (1940) 23 TC 367.

Item	Explanation	References
	Premiums for policies covering (a) fire at company's premises, (b) interruption or loss of use of income-producing assets, (c) interruption or cessation of the supply of raw materials, or (d) events causing loss of profits for a temporary period, are allowable deductions from trading profits.	BIM 45515
	An indemnity policy premium is allowable where it provides cover for professional negligence. However, damages paid as a result of professional negligence are not. Premiums paid to indemnify employees against legal action taken against them personally for actions in the course of the employment are allowable as a deduction in computing from the employer's trading profits. Insurance receipts in connection with the trade are taxed as trading receipts.	BIM 45520
Interest on director's property loan	Where interest is paid by a company on a loan (not overdraft) taken out by a director to purchase land or buildings occupied rent-free by the company and used for business purposes, it is considered that the company may obtain relief as a trading expense for the interest in the normal way and that the payments would not normally constitute either remuneration or a benefit of the director.	*ICTA 1988, s 74(1)(a)*. HMRC Business Income Manual BIM 45755

Item	Explanation	References
Key employee insurance	Premiums on policies in favour of the employer insuring against death or critical illness of key employees are generally allowable, and the proceeds of any such policies are treated as trading receipts. Keyman insurance proceeds were taxable as receipts of the trade. Premiums on policies taken out as a condition of loan finance are not deductible. See **11.23**. An insurance premiums covering the payment of compensation to employees is deductible. Life assurance receipts paid to a company in respect of insurance taken out at the request of a shareholder to guarantee the company's bank overdraft were held not to be receipts of the trade and were not taxable.	HMRC Business Income Manual BIM 45525, BIM 45530. *Keir & Cawder Ltd v CIR* (1958) 38 TC 23. *Greycon Ltd v Klaentschi* [2003] STC (SCD) 370. *CIR v Williams' Executor* (1944) 26 TC 23
Launch costs	A company may obtain relief for advertising and launch costs under the intangible assets regime (see Chapter 7).	HMRC Business Income Manual BIM 42551
Legal expenses	Legal expenses incurred in maintaining existing trading rights and assets are revenue expenses. The legal costs of defending an overseas branch's title to land in the foreign courts, which it used for the purposes of its trade was deductible from profits. Expenditure on defending a company from public ownership and thereby the prevention of the seizure of its business and assets was held to be an allowable business expense.	*Southern v Borax Consolidated* (1940) 23 TC 598, [1941] 1 KB 111, [1940] 4 All ER 412; *Morgan v Tate & Lyle Ltd* (1954) 35 TC 367, [1954] AC 21, [1954] 2 All ER 413.

Item	*Explanation*	*References*
Loan finance	See loan relationships Chapter 11.	
Losses	Losses arising in the normal course of trading are allowable. Losses arising from theft or misappropriation by directors are not allowable.	HMRC Business Income Manual BIM 45851, BIM 45855. *Curtis v Oldfield (J & G) Ltd* (1925) 9 TC 319; *Bamford v ATA Advertising Ltd* (1972) 48 TC 359, [1972] 1 WLR 1261, [1972] 3 All ER 535.
Management expenses	HMRC will accept reasonable management expenses allocations to group companies of expenses incurred by a group service company on their behalf. HMRC will investigate arrangements where expenditure is incurred by one company for the purposes of the trade of another that is outside the scope of UK tax. See **12.3.** However, expenses relating to the trade of one group company will not be allowable against the separate trade of another group member.	HMRC Business Income Manual BIM 42140, BIM 38230.
National Insurance Contributions	Secondary Class 1 NICs are deductible in computing profits, as are Class 1A NICs and Class 1B NICs.	*ICTA 1988, s 617(3)–(5).*
Onerous contract	Payment of a sum of money to remove a company from an onerous trading contract will usually be considered to be a trading expense. A payment by a company to secure release of an option over a trade investment was held to be a trading expense.	*Vodafone Cellular v Shaw* (1997) 69 TC 376, [1997] STC 734 (see HMRC Business Income Manual BIM 38220 for details); *Walker v Cater Securities Ltd* (1974) 49 TC 625, [1974] STC 390, [1974] 1 WLR 1363, [1974] 3 All ER 63.

Item	Explanation	References
Overseas taxes	Tax of an overseas country charged on the profits arising in that country will be available for tax credit relief in most cases. A deduction may in certain circumstances arise for taxes of a capital nature. Interest payable on overseas tax may be admitted as a Schedule D Case I deduction but not if it relates to a capital tax or overseas tax penalty. (See Chapter 13 generally regarding overseas taxes.)	HMRC Business Income Manual BIM 45901, BIM 45905. *Harrods (Buenos Aires) Ltd v Taylor-Gooby* (1964) 41 TC 450.
Patents and royalties	See Chapter 7 Intangible Assets.	
Payments in lieu of notice	Payments *in lieu* of notice on a cessation of trade were held to be an allowable deduction.	*O'Keefe v Southport Printers Ltd* (1984) 58 TC 88, [1984] STC 443.
Political expenses	No deductions are allowable for party political expenditure but propaganda costs to prevent the loss of business and protect assets may be allowable.	*Morgan v Tate and Lyle Ltd* (1954) 35 TC 367, [1955] AC 21, [1954] 2 All ER 413. HMRC Business Income Manual BIM 42528.
Premiums on leases	Payment of premiums for premises used for trading purposes is an allowable deduction under Schedule D Cases I, II where the lessor is liable under *ICTA 1988, ss 34, 35*. See **12.17**.	HMRC Business Income Manual BIM 46251, BIM 46255, BIM 46260, BIM 46265. *ICTA 1988, s 87*.
Pre-trading expenditure	Relief is given under *ICTA 1988, s 401* for allowable business expenditure incurred in the seven years prior to the commencement of a trade. Relief is given in the accounting period in which the trade commences, for revenue items, which satisfy the test under *ICTA 1988, s 74(1)(a)*.	HMRC Business Income Manual BIM 46351 BIM 46355.

Item	Explanation	References
Procurement fees	Procuring others to enter into a tax avoidance scheme was not considered to be a trade	*Ransom v Higgs* (1974) 50 TC 1, [1974] STC 539, [1974] 1 WLR 1594, [1974] 3 All ER 949.
Professional fees	Professional fees are not allowable if they are of a capital nature or excluded by statute. Costs of an unsuccessful planning application were held to be capital expenditure.	HMRC Business Income Manual BIM 46405 *ECC Quarries Ltd v Watkis* (1975) 51 TC 153, [1975] STC 578, [1975] 3 All ER 843; *Moore (A & G) & Co v Hare* (1941) 6 TC 572.
Professional negligence	Insurance policy premiums to cover professional negligence and employee indemnity risks are usually allowable as a deduction.	HMRC Business Income Manual BIM 45515, BIM 45520
Provisions	If a provision in the accounts satisfies the following requirements: (a) it has been estimated with reasonable accuracy, (b) it does not conflict with any statutory rules, (c) it relates to revenue and not capital expenditure and (d) agrees with UK GAAP and FRS 12 principles, it may be allowable. See **17.15**. Case law has disallowed provision in accounts held to be capital expenditure. A company's provisions calculation was held to be insufficiently accurate. To comply with FRS 12 it may be necessary to discount the provision to present value if it is material.	HMRC Business Income Manual BIM 46510 BIM 46555 *RTZ Oil & Gas Ltd v Ellis* (1987) 61 TC 132, [1987] STC 512, [1987] 1 WLR 1442 *Owen v Southern Railway of Peru Ltd* (1956) 36 TC 602, [1957] AC 334, [1956] 2 All ER 728. BIM 46525
Purchase of own shares	Fees in relation to raising equity finance including purchase of own shares are capital expenses and are not deductible.	HMRC Business Income Manual BIM 46425

Item	Explanation	References
Redundancy payments	To be allowed under Schedule D Cases I, II redundancy payments are required to be wholly and exclusively for employer's trade and the company does not acquire capital assets or rights (eg restrictive covenants). Redundancy payments in connection with the discontinuance of a trade are not allowable. Statutory redundancy payments are permitted under *ICTA 1988, ss 90, 579.*	HMRC Business Income Manual BIM 47200 , BIM 47205, BIM 47210 & BIM 47215 *ICTA 1988, ss 579, 580, 90.* *CIR v Anglo Brewing Co Ltd* (1925) 12 TC 803; *Hong Kong Commissioner of Inland Revenue v Cosmotron Manufacturing Co* (1997) 70 TC 292, [1997] STC 1134, [1997] 1 WLR 1288.
	Redundancy payments are allowed if the company has a contractual requirement to make the payments.	
Removal expenses	Reasonable employee removal costs due to an employee's change of residence at the employer's request are allowable. Usually where transactions are completed without delay, profits arising from the purchase and sale of the employee's earlier residence are taxed as a trading receipt and losses as an allowable deduction.	HMRC Business Income Manual BIM 42531
	Expenses incurred by a company moving to new premises is allowed in most cases.	BIM 42530
Renewal of short lease	Costs in relation to renewal of a short lease (less than 50 years to run) are revenue and allowable. Otherwise the amounts are capital.	HMRC Business Income Manual BIM 46420

Item	*Explanation*	*References*
Rent and rates	Costs associated with a company's premises including rent, rates, repairs, insurance will normally be allowed.	HMRC Business Income Manual BIM 46801, BIM 46810
Repairs and renewals	Repair costs are normally regarded as revenue expenditure. Repair by replacement of the whole asset is capital expenditure. Mere replacement of parts that are defective by the renewal of those parts is considered to be revenue expenditure Note concept of 'entirety' used by courts. Any repair expenditure resulting in an improvement or upgrade to an asset, is capital expenditure. See **5.10**.	HMRC Business Income Manual BIM 46900, BIM 46903, BIM 46904, BIM 46906 *Brown v Burnley Football & Athletic Co Ltd* (1980) 53 TC 357, [1980] STC 424, [1980] 3 All ER 244; *Transco plc v Dyall* [2002] STC (SCD) 199.
Restrictive covenants with employees	Where a business makes a restrictive covenant with an employee to protect its trade, if the employee were to leave, then, under *FA 1988, s 73(2)*, the employer may claim relief, only if the employee receives a payment as part of the agreement (which is taxable under *ITEPA 2003, s 225*).	HMRC Business Income Manual BIM 47005, BIM 35595, BIM 35510.
Security expenditure	Where a company needs to protect its employee from a special security threat because of the nature of the company's business then the revenue expenditure incurred in providing the required security measures are likely to be allowed if all the qualifying conditions are met under *ITTOIA 2005, s 81*.	HMRC Business Income Manual BIM 47301, BIM 47305, BIM 47310 & BIM 47315.

Item	Explanation	References
Sponsorship costs	Sponsorship costs are allowable in arriving at the profits of a company unless they are considered to be capital expenditure or the expenditure is not made wholly and exclusively for business purposes, in which case it is specifically disallowed. If sponsorship contains an element of hospitality this is disallowable under *ICTA 1988, s 577 or ITTOIA s 45*. Sums paid as sponsorship to support the personal hobbies and pastimes of a shareholders family were held not to be deductible from trading profits.	HMRC Business Income Manual BIM 42555, BIM 42560, BIM 42565. *Executive Network (Consultants) Ltd v O'Connor* [1996] STC (SCD) 29.
Subsidies, grants	Grants to a company under *Industrial Development Act 1982, s 7 or s 8* are trading receipts unless grant is specifically capital expenditure or as compensation for loss of capital assets.	*ICTA 1988, s 93. ITTOIA 2005, Sch 1, para 72.*
Subscriptions	Generally, charitable and political subscriptions are not allowable. Small local or trade charity subscriptions with a trade connection may be allowed. Subscriptions paid by a company to a professional body, which is assessed under Schedule D Case I, may be allowable.	HMRC Business Income Manual BIM 47400, BIM 47405, BIM47410, BIM47415, BIM 47420, BIM 47425, BIM 47430 and BIM47435
Take-overs costs	The acquirer's fees in relation to take-overs are normally capital and disallowable. The target's fees are capital if in relation to the structure, but revenue if in connection with protecting the trade.	HMRC Business Income Manual BIM 46460, BIM 38260.

Item	Explanation	References
Tax Appeals	The cost of a tax appeal, even if successful, is not deductible. Additional accountancy expenses incurred as a result of 'in-depth' examination by HMRC will be allowed if this results in no discrepancies. If there are discrepancies the costs are not allowable even if the investigation reveals no addition to profits. Costs of an appeal before the Special Commissioners was disallowed.	*Allen v Farquharson Bros & Co* (1932) 17 TC 59. HMRC Business Income Manual BIM 37840
Tied licensed premises	Receipts and expenses in respect of tied premises are accounted as trading receipts and expenses rather than under Schedule A. Improvements to tied premises are treated as capital.	*ICTA 1988, s 98.* *ITTOIA 2005, Sch 1, para 77.* *Usher's Wiltshire Brewery v Bruce* (1914) 6 TC 399, [1915] AC 433; *Mann Crossman & Paulin Ltd v Compton* (1947) 28 TC 410, [1947] 1 All ER 742. Business Income Manual BIM 51400, BIM 51420, BIM 51425, BIM 51430
Tied petrol stations	Exclusivity payments made to retailers by petroleum companies were allowed in computing the petroleum companies' profits. In the hands of the retailer they were held to be trading receipts rather than capital receipts.	*Bolam v Regent Oil Co Ltd* (1956) 37 TC 56, [1956] TR 403; *Tanfield Ltd v Carr* [1999] STC (SCD) 213.
Trade organisations	Company contributions to an industrial training board for its industry or trade are allowable.	HMRC Business Income Manual BIM 47605 *ICTA 1988, ss 79, 79A, 79B.*
Training, education and welfare	A company's expenditure on training, education and welfare are normally allowed.	HMRC Business Income Manual BIM 47080; BIM 47610.

Item	Explanation	References
Travel and subsistence	Reasonable expenses incurred by an employee on an occasional business journey (or overnight subsistence and accommodation when away from home on business) may be allowed. The allowable costs for hiring a car for business purposes are restricted under *ICTA 1988, s 578A*.	HMRC Business Income Manual BIM 47705
Unsuccessful applications	The expenses of unsuccessful applications for licences were held to be not allowable—the company accepted that expenses of successful applications are capital. Costs for variation of a licence were not an allowable deduction.	*Southwell v Savill Bros* (1901) 4 TC 430, [1901] 2 KB 349; *Pyrah v Annis & Co Ltd* (1956) 37 TC 163, [1957] 1 WLR 190, [1957] 1 All ER 196.
Valuations	The cost of valuations for accounts purposes or as required by the Companies Act are allowable. Valuations in connection with a company reconstruction are not allowable.	HMRC Business Income Manual BIM 42540.
VAT	VAT penalties and repayment supplements are not deductible.	HMRC Business Income Manual BIM 31610

APPROPRIATIONS OF PROFIT

5.21   Appropriations of profits, ie a distribution or dividend payment, are not deductible from profits. UK corporation tax payments themselves are not deductible and neither are payments from which tax has been deducted at source. Depreciation is disallowed but capital allowances are deductible as a trading expense (*CAA 2001, s 352*).

Only the depreciation charged in the profit and loss account must be added back in the corporation tax computation regardless of any other entry (*Revenue and Customs Comrs v William Grant & Sons Distillers Ltd Small (Inspector of Taxes) v Mars UK Ltd [2007* All ER (D) 459 (Mar). See also HMRC Business Income Manual BIM 33190.

5.22 Lease amortisation is given if a premium is paid on a short lease (less than 50 years) to a landlord assessable under Schedule A. The permitted deduction is the premium paid less 2% for every year of the lease except the first, spread over the duration of the lease. Capital expenditure is specifically disallowed. See **5.10**.

Income that has not been included in profits in the accounts but which is taxable under Schedule D Case I

5.23 If a company is operating GAAP correctly, there are unlikely to be any items not credited in the accounts, but circumstances vary between every company.

A transfer pricing adjustment increases taxable profits but never decreases chargeable profits. See **14.23**. Credits may arise under the intangible assets regime. See **7.17–7.20**.

Income credited in the accounts but not taxable under Schedule D Case I

5.24 In the main this will include items taxable under another schedule such as Rent—Schedule A, interest Schedule D Case III and sundry income Schedule D Case VI.

Expenditure that has not been charged against profits in the accounts but which is allowable under Schedule D Case I

5.25 If the company is operating GAAP there should not be too many expenses that fall into this category. As mentioned above capital allowances are not charged in the accounts but are allowed as a trading deduction.

EMPLOYEE INCENTIVES

5.26 Specific statutory deductions are given for the costs of setting up 'approved' employee share schemes known as SIP (share incentive plans), SAYE (savings-related share option schemes), CSOP (company share option plans) and APS (approved profit-share schemes) (*ICTA 1988, s 84A, Sch 4AA, para 7*), QUEST (qualifying employee share ownership trusts) (*ICTA 1988, s 85A*). This is on the proviso that the share schemes are approved within nine

117

months of the end of the accounting period in which they are charged and that the share ownership trust is executed within nine months of the end of the accounting period in which its expenditure is charged. If the criteria is not met in that accounting period the expenditure is carried forward to the next accounting period until it is met (*ICTA 1988, ss 84A(3ZA), 85A(3)*).

Normally a company's incidental running costs for an employee share scheme investing in 'qualifying shares', is a deduction under Schedule D. Shares that are not 'qualifying shares' under *FA 2003, Sch 23* do not qualify for relief (HMRC Business Income Manual BIM 44450). Relief under *FA 2003, Sch 23* is given under Schedule D Case I or Schedule A for trades and Schedule A businesses, *ICTA 1988, s 75* for companies with investment business and *ICTA 1988, s 76* for assurance companies. Qualifying shares must be fully paid-up, non redeemable ordinary shares (HMRC Business Income Manual BIM 44290). The employing company will qualify for a deduction for the costs of the shares except where the business is taken over by a successor company unless the companies are 51% members of the same group (*FA 2003, Sch 23, paras 16, 23*; HMRC Business Income Manual BIM 44295). Revenue-approved schemes and unapproved schemes, which satisfy the conditions previously mentioned, will be qualifying shares. It is also a requirement that the share options (or awards) are made by the employing company, which must be chargeable to corporation tax on the profits of its business.

In a group situation normally the employer will be able to claim the deduction. Under FRS 20 the reporting entity will typically measure the value of the services received in return for share-based payments by reference to the 'fair value' of the share-based payment. Intra group payments should represent arm's-length prices (Transfer-pricing and employee share plans—guidance for accounting periods beginning on or after 1 January 2005).

Relief is also given for the cost of providing employee share scheme shares (*FA 2003, Sch 23, para 8*). Full relief is given to a company offering EMI options by matching relief for the company with both the amount taxed on the employee and the amount on which income tax relief is given under the EMI scheme (*FA 2006, s 93*).

Shares acquired under EMI option before FA 2006

5.27   From 1 January 2003, an employer company receives corporation tax relief on an amount being the difference between the market value of the shares at the time the employee exercises an option and the price the employee pays. The relief is given in the accounting period in which the option is exercised and the shares acquired (*FA 2003, Sch 23, paras 15, 16*). The relief applies to enterprise management investment (EMI) scheme options, company share option plans (CSOP), unapproved share option plans and share acquisitions where the employee is subject to tax. The shares must be ordinary shares in a listed company, single company or holding company.

For share incentive plans (SIP) the company employer receives a corporation tax deduction for the market value of the shares in the accounting period in which they are awarded (*ITEPA 2003, s 488, Sch 2*).

Example 5.2

Longtemps Ltd granted its eligible employee Mr A EMI options over 1,000 shares, to be exercised at the current market price of £3 per share. Two years later when Mr A exercises the option the shares are worth £10 each.

As the option arrangement required Mr A to pay a price equal to the market value of the shares at the grant, there is no income tax on the exercise of this option. *ITEPA 2003, s 530* applies.

Longtemps Ltd can claim corporation tax deduction for the accounting period in which Mr A acquired ownership of the shares as follows:

	£
Value at exercise	10,000
Less amount paid	3,000
Corporation tax deduction (*FA 2003, Sch 23, para 8*)	7,000

Without the EMI share option arrangement, Mr A would normally be charged to income tax on £7,000 (*ITEPA 2003, s 476*). The company may still claim a deduction under *FA 2003, Sch 23, para 8*.

5.28   Relief for restricted shares has been introduced by *FA 2006, s 93 (2)*, which is treated as applying to the acquisition of shares from the exercise of EMI options on or after 1 September 2003, the date on which the restricted and convertible shares income tax legislation in *Finance Act 2003* came into force. Prior to *FA 2006* no relief was available.

Example 5.3—Pre FA 2006

B is granted EMI options over 1,000 shares, to be exercised at a discount of 50% to the current market value of £1, where the shares to be acquired are restricted. When B exercises his options, the unrestricted market value of the share is £5, but, because B has no voting rights for three years, the actual market value is only £3. As the options were granted at a discount *ITEPA 2003, s 531* rather than *s 530* applies.

The acquisition of shares is a chargeable event and the *ITEPA 2003, s 476* income tax charge on the employee is calculated as follows:

	£
Value at exercise	
Value of grant	1,000
Less consideration	nil
Amount paid for shares	500
Employee taxable amount	500
Corporation tax relief (*FA 2003, Sch 23, para 21(3)*)	500

Example 5.4—Post FA 2006

The employee has made an income tax saving being the difference between the exercise price and the amount paid for the shares. If an election were made under *ITEPA 2003, s 431* the unrestricted value can be taken as the exercise price, which will increase the potential savings. The same relief is now taken for corporation tax purposes.

	Income tax saved	Income tax saved with an election under ITEPA 2003, s 431
	£	£
Value at exercise	3,000	5,000
Value of grant		
Less consideration	—	—
Amount paid for shares	500	500
Income tax saved on	2,500	4,500
Corporation tax relief (*FA 2003, Sch 23, para 21(3)*)	2,500	4,500

5.29   These changes apply to the acquisition of shares from the exercise of EMI options on or after 1 September 2003, the date on which the restricted and convertible shares income tax legislation in *FA 2003* came into force.

Employee benefit trusts

5.30   An employee benefit trust (EBT) is a discretionary trust set up by an employer for the benefit of its employees and directors. EBTs can be resident in the UK or offshore, and can be subject to UK or foreign law. An 'offshore' EBT is only liable to UK income tax on its UK source income and is not liable to UK capital gains tax. An EBT is managed by trustees, who are usually appointed by the company. The trust fund will comprise of: (a) the initial amount settled by the employer to establish the trust, (b) subsequent contributions from the employer, and (c) sums paid to the trustees by third parties. The beneficiaries and life of the EBT will be defined in the trust deed (HMRC Business Income Manual BIM 44501 +). EBTs are used with employee share schemes, retirement benefit schemes, accident benefit schemes and healthcare trusts. EBTs set up with employee benefit schemes are called employee share ownership trusts (ESOT); they can also be known as employee share ownership plans (ESOP) trusts. ESOTs may be used by unquoted companies to provide a market for employees' shares (acquired through employee share schemes) that might otherwise not exist, maintain shareholder control and help with business planning and management buy-outs. Established case law has determined that where the trust is set up for the benefit of employees that the contributions meet the 'wholly and exclusively' test (*Heather v P-E Consulting Group Ltd* (1972) 48 TC 293, [1973] Ch 189, [1973] 1 All ER 8; *Rutter v Charles Sharpe & Co Ltd* (1979) 53 TC 163, [1979] STC 711, [1979] 1 WLR 1429; *Jeffs v Ringtons Ltd* (1985) 58 TC 680, [1985] STC 809, [1986] 1 WLR 266, [1986] 1 All ER 144; *E Bott Ltd v Price* (1986) 59 TC 437, [1987] STC 100). In *Mawsley Machinery Ltd v Robinson* [1998] SSCD 236 the 'wholly and exclusively' test was not met because the reason for the contributions was to facilitate a share purchase (HMRC Business Income Manual BIM 44155).

Providing healthcare benefits for employees is an allowable deduction in computing taxable profits of a company. However, there will be a liability to Class 1A NICs for the employer and income tax for the employee. General purpose EBTs can be set up for genuine business reasons and for use in avoidance, for example the payment of income tax by employees and Class 1A NICs by employers.

The timing of the employer's deduction and employee's liability to IT and employer's to NIC is governed by *FA 2003, Sch 24*.

If a close company settles assets in a discretionary trust for the benefit of shareholders in the company those deductions are disallowed and there may arise a lifetime IHT charge on the shareholders in proportion to their shareholdings. However, there are no IHT consequences if a close company makes a contribution to an EBT, which is allowed as a deduction in computing a company's taxable profits (*IHTA 1984, s 12*; HMRC Business Income Manual BIM 44550).There is no corporation tax deduction for amounts put into an EBT by an employer until the amount becomes taxable earnings of the employee. For this to occur the contributions must be paid to the employees within nine months of the end of the year in a form on which PAYE and NIC are charged. With effect from 21 March 2007, the employer can contribute to the EBT scheme by making payment direct to the Scheme Manager and to no other party. (*FA 2003,*

Sch 23, para 1) (FA 2007, s 34). Pension and accident benefit schemes are excluded. With effect from 2 December 2004, securities and options are included as benefits (*FA(No2) 2005, s 12, Sch 2*; *MacDonald v Dextra Accessories Ltd* [2005] UKHL 47, [2005] STC 1111).

PENSION CONTRIBUTIONS

5.31   Payments to a pension scheme are a revenue expense and will be deductible from profits in the year in which the premium is paid (*FA 2004, s 196 (2)(b)*), if the payment meets the wholly and exclusively for the purposes of the trade test. Under FRS 17 the amounts included in the profit and loss account will be based on actuarial assumptions and are unlikely to consist of the premiums paid for the year. Thus an adjustment will be required for corporation tax purposes that may also be reflected in the deferred tax account (see **17.32**).

Staff pension contributions are allowable unless there is an identifiable non-trade purpose. HMRC has highlighted the following circumstances where depending on the facts of the circumstances at the time there may be a non-trade purpose:

- contributions paid in respect of a controlling director or an employee who is a relative or close friend of the controlling director or proprietor of the business;
- contributions made as part of the arrangements for going out of business, in particular where there is no pre-existing contractual obligation to make such a contribution;
- contribution is required to be made pursuant to *Pensions Act 1995, s 75*;
- where following the issue of a notice by the Pensions Regulator, a person is required to pay a pension contribution;
- where a contribution is in respect of orphaned liabilities;
- contributions made as part of the bargain struck for the purposes of facilitating the sale of shares in a subsidiary;
- contributions made in connection with the pension deficit of another company's trade; and
- where the reputation of the payer's trade or the morale of its staff is not the sole purpose behind the contribution.

Contributions in respect of a controlling director or an employee who is a close friend or relative of the controlling director or proprietor of the business may be queried by HMRC. In establishing whether a payment is for the purposes of the trade they will examine the company's intentions in making the payment. If the level of the remuneration package is excessive for the value of the work undertaken by that individual for the employer, the contribution may be queried. The pension contribution will be viewed in the light of the overall remuneration package. HMRC acknowledge that employers may make increased pension contributions to remedy underfunding and will look at the full facts of the case. On the practical side it is well-worth ensuring that employment contracts are in place for directors of close companies. Such directors have the ability to withdraw available funds at will from the company, normally under the rationale that funds are available. Unless this can be proven at the outset by inclusion say in a contract any additional payment may be queried as being not wholly and exclusively for the purposes of the trade.

HMRC will accept that contributions in respect of a director of a close company, or an employee who is a close relative or friend of the director are paid wholly and exclusively for the purposes of the trade where the remuneration package paid is comparable with that paid to unconnected employees performing duties of similar value. The proportion of any amount not so expended will be disallowed (HMRC Business Income Manual BIM 46035).

An undertaking to provide a pension under an employee's contract of employment will be an allowable deduction from profits. HMRC regard a payment made for the purposes of going out of business or other non-business purposes as a non-allowable deduction but regard contributions made to preserve the reputation and morale of the staff as an allowable deduction (HMRC Business Income Manual BIM 46040).

Pension contributions in respect of other group company employees whose current employer can no longer contribute are generally deductible by the payer company. The matter may require further investigation if the current employer is in a position to contribute and the payer company's contribution has not been recharged to the current employer (HMRC Business Income Manual BIM 46065).

Pension scheme contributions paid in connection with the sale or transfer of the shares of a subsidiary may not necessarily be for the purposes of that company's trade. It is important for the company to be able to demonstrate that the pension contributions are unrelated to the sale of the company. Again, HMRC regard contributions made to preserve the reputation and morale of the staff as an allowable deduction (HMRC Business Income Manual BIM 46060).

Pension contribution spreading rules

5.32   Contributions paid by an employer to a registered pension scheme in respect of an individual are deductible for Schedule D Case I purposes if the company is carrying on a trade or are deductible as management expenses if the company has an investment activity (*FA 2004, s 196*). If the amount of the contribution for the current chargeable period (CCCP) exceeds 210% of the amount of the contributions paid in the previous chargeable period (CPCP) the payments made in the second period may have to be spread forward. In order to ascertain whether or not this is the case, the company must calculate its relevant excess contributions (REC). The REC is calculated by deducting 110% of the CPCP from the CCCP.

Example 5.5

Wishbone Ltd makes pension contributions of £250,000 in the year ended 31 December 2008. In the year ended 31 December 2009 it makes contributions of £775,000.

	£
CCCP	775,000
Less 110% × £250,000	275,000
REC	500,000

If the RECs are less than £500,000 there is no spreading. If the RECs are £500,000 or more but less than £1,000,000, one half of the RECs is spread into the following accounting period, in this case the year ended 31 December 2010. If the RECs are £1,000,000 or more but less than £2,000,000, one-third of the RECs is spread into each of the next two accounting periods. If the RECs are £2,000,000 or more, one-quarter of the RECs is spread into each of the next three accounting periods (*FA 2004, s 197*).

Example 5.6

Wishbone Ltd's pension contribution relief of £775,000 for the year ended 31 December 2009is spread as follows:

	£
Year ending 31 December 2008	500,000
Year ending 31 December 2009	275,000

Commencement of trade

5.33 The cost of setting up, a registered pension scheme, is capital expenditure and is not an allowable deduction (*Atherton v British Insulated and Helsby Cables Ltd* [1925] 10 TC 155 and *Rowntree and Co Ltd v Curtis* [1924] 8 TC 678).

Pension contributions arising from pension scheme obligations taken over on the purchase of a trade as part of the acquisition of the trade are treated as revenue expenditure (*FA 2004, s 196(2)*).

Cessation of trade

5.34   Payments by an employer, who has ceased trading, into a registered pension scheme to satisfy a liability falling due under *PA 1995, s 75*, or *Art 75* of the *Pensions* (*Northern Ireland*) *Order 1995* (*SI 1995/3213* (*NI22*)) are deductible against PCTCT for the final period of trading. The payment is treated as being made on the last day of trading (*FA 2004, s 199*). Thus it is not necessary for this income to be relieved under the provisions of *ICTA 1988, s105(1)*, (*3*). Under-funding contributions made because of a direction issued by the Pensions Regulator are normally allowable against profits (HMRC Business Income Manual BIM 46050).

CAPITAL ALLOWANCES COMPUTATION

5.35   A company may be able to claim capital allowances on its expenditure on plant and machinery, industrial and related buildings, agricultural land and buildings, mineral extraction and research and development allowances (*CAA 2001, s 1*) or an annual investment allowance (*FA 2008, s 74*) (see **6.47**) for expenditure incurred on or after 1 April 2008.

A company can also claim capital allowances on expenditure incurred prior to 1 April 2002 on patent rights and know-how. Capital allowances are discussed in Chapter 6 and the rates of capital allowances are shown in **6.18**.

Capital allowances are given by reference to accounting periods. Where an accounting period is less than 12 months, writing-down allowances are proportionately reduced. Where a trade starts part-way through an accounting period, capital allowances for plant and machinery, research and development etc are also proportionately restricted.

Trading and professional profits

5.36   On the assumption that all information is to hand the company can now calculate its trading and professional profits. If the result is positive this amount should be shown in box 3 of the company tax return. If the result is negative box 3 should be left blank.

VALUATION OF STOCK AND WORK IN PROGRESS

Statement of Standard Accounting Practice 9 (SSAP 9)

5.37 According to GAAP, stocks should be valued at the lower of cost and net realisable value (SSAP 9). Net realisable value is used where there is no reasonable expectation of sufficient future revenue to cover cost incurred, for example, as a result of deterioration, obsolescence or 'change in demand'. Ideally stocks should be considered item by item but this may be impractical and groups of items may be considered. Provisions may be made on a justifiable basis and in consideration of age, past and future movements and estimated scrap values, to reduce valuation from cost to net realisable value. Long-term contracts are valued on a pro-rata completion stage basis.

International Accounting Standard 2 (IAS 2) Inventories

5.38 IAS 2 adopts the same basic principle that inventories should be measured at the lower of cost and net realisable value. Net realisable value is the estimated selling price in the ordinary course of business less the estimated costs of completion and the estimated costs necessary to make the sale. See also **17.24**.

Lower of cost and net realisable value

5.39 *Companies Act2006, s 396 (SIs 2008/409* and *2008/410)* permits the addition of incidental costs of acquisition to the stock cost. The company may include production costs and interest on funds borrowed to finance the asset's production in the stock valuation. Interest should be separately disclosed in a note to the accounts.

Professional work in progress

5.40 Companies with professional work in progress will in particular need to consider the extent of the inclusion of 'production costs', ie staff remuneration and overheads etc in the light of Urgent Issues Task Force (UITF) Abstract 40, effective for accounting periods ended on or after 22 June 2005.

As a general rule, long-term contracts incomplete at the balance sheet date are valued in accordance with SSAP 9. Other work in progress is to be valued at cost plus attributable overheads, which are normally based on time costs.

UITF 40

5.41   A company, when applying GAAP (UK or International), may require to utilise SSAP 9 and Application Note G as interpreted by UITF 40. If the profits in the previous accounting period were calculated in accordance with GAAP but not as interpreted by UITF 40, this may result in a change of accounting approach from one period of account to the next in calculating the profits of a business for corporation tax purposes.

For corporation tax purposes, a company with a period of account ending on or after 22 June 2005 may opt to spread the adjustment over three accounting periods. The accounting periods in question are the accounting period in which the adjustment is made, followed by the two subsequent accounting periods.

The lesser of the following amounts are chargeable either:

- one-third of the amount of the original adjustment, or
- one-sixth of the profits of the business for that period.

In the fourth and fifth accounting periods, if the whole of the adjustment has not been charged to tax in the previous periods, an amount equal to whichever is the least of:

- the amount remaining untaxed,
- one-third of the amount of the original adjustment, and
- one-sixth of the profits of the business for that period,

is treated as arising and charged to tax (*FA 2006, Sch 15, para 10*).

In the sixth accounting period so much (if any) of the adjustment as has not previously been charged to tax is treated as arising and is charged to tax.

For these purposes 'the profits of the business' means the profits of the business as calculated for corporation tax purposes leaving without taking into consideration any other change of accounting basis under *FA 2002, Sch 22* (see **17.1**) or any capital allowances or balancing charges. Special rules apply to 'short' accounting periods of less than 12 months that arise in certain circumstances. The particular short periods are those arising because of a change of accounting date, a company entering administration (see **19.6**), or an insurance business transfer scheme under *ICTA 1988, s 12(7A), (7B)*. The amounts chargeable substitute the profits for the short period instead of the normal 12-month accounting period.

If the company ceases to be within the charge to corporation tax, or winding-up proceedings have commenced the whole of the untaxed amount is chargeable in that year. If the company ceases to trade, but remains within the charge to corporation tax, the spreading adjustment continues. The spreading relief is restricted to one-third of the adjustment for each year concerned amount with a final adjustment in year four if necessary (*FA 2006, Sch 15, para 12*).

Within 12 months of the company tax return filing date the company may elect for an additional amount to be treated as arising in that period and thereby disapply the spreading relief. The company may wish to do this if it has particular losses that it wishes to utilise. Spreading relief will continue to be available on any remaining balance (*FA 2006, Sch 15, para 13*).

The spreading relief occurs in any type of business where the adjustment is made. This includes; a trade or vocation, a Schedule A business or overseas property business. It also applies where the business is carried on by the company in partnership in accordance with the normal profit-sharing arrangements.

Example 5.7

Nimrod Ltd's trade is the provision of management consultancy advice. The company prepares accounts to 31 May each year. For the year ended 31 May 2006, the company calculated that its UITF taxable amounted to £90,000. Taxable profits exclusive of capital allowances were £120,000 for the year ended 31 May 2006. Taxable profits for the year ended 31 May 2007 are £132,000 and thereafter company estimates that its taxable profits will grow at the rate of 10% per annum over the next four years.

The adjustment is calculated as follows:

Year ending 31 May	*Profits*	*Calculation of taxable adjustment income*	*Adjustment income*
	£	£	£
(1) 2006	120,000	Lower of: $1/3 \times 90,000$ or $1/6 \times 120,000$	20,000
(2) 2007	132,000	Lower of: $1/3 \times 90,000$ or $1/6 \times 132,000$	22,000
(3) 2008	145,200	Lower of: $1/3 \times 90,000$ or $1/6 \times 145,200$	24,200
(4) 2009	159,720	Lower of: $[90,000 - (20,000 + 22,000 + 24,200)]$ or $1/3 \times 90,000$ or $1/6 \times 159,720$	23,800
		Total	90,000

Example 5.8

Nimrod Ltd elected to bring forward £45,000 of the £90,000 adjustment to the accounting period ended 31 May 2006.

The adjustment is calculated as follows:

Year ending 31 May	Profits	Calculation of taxable adjustment income	Adjustment income
	£	£	£
(1) 2006	120,000	Election to accelerate £45,000 of adjustment Income.	45,000
(2) 2007	132,000	Lower of: 1/3 × 45,000 or 1/6 × 132,000	15,000
(3) 2008	145,200	Lower of: 1/3 × 45,000 or 1/6 × 145,200	15,000
(4) 2009	159,720	Lower of: [90,000 – (45,000 + 15,000 + 15,000)] or 1/3 × 45,000 or 1/6 × 159,720	15,000
		Total	90,000

5.42 UITF 40 requires revenue to be recognised to the extent that a business has obtained the right to consideration through its performance. IAS 18 Revenue requires revenue to be recognised by reference to the stage of completion of the transaction at the balance sheet date. Revenue accrued is valued at the sales value. (For further narrative see HMRC Manual BIM 74201–74275, TAXGUIDE 8/06 www.icaew.co.uk and CCAB detailed guidance www.ccab.org.uk)).

Valuation of transfers to and from trading stock

5.43 Transfers from stock are valued at market value; see **17.24**. Case law has determined that the market value rule also applies where goods are acquired or appropriated into trading stock, other than in the course of a trade (*Sharkey v Wernher* (1955) 36 TC 275; [1956] AC 58; [1955] 3 All ER 493).*FA 2008, s 37, Sch 15* gives statutory effect to this rule.

Trading stock for this purpose is defined as any land or property, which is sold in the ordinary course of trade. Finished goods and work-in-progress are included (*FA 2008, Sch 15, para 5(2)*), but raw materials and services or bi-products produced are not (*FA 2008, Sch 15, para 5(3)*). If any stock is used for non-trade purposes, a taxable receipt is deemed to accrue to the company, equal to the market value of that stock at that time. Any actual receipt is then left out of account (*FA 2008, Sch 15, para 6(2)*).

Similarly, any item, which the company already owns that it transfers as a finished good or work-in-progress into stock, is to be valued at market value at the date of transfer (*FA 2008, Sch 15, paras 7–9*). If an item of stock has been acquired by other means than in the normal course of trade and the transfer pricing rules apply, the transfer pricing valuation will take precedence, which will normally agree with the market valuation (*FA 2008, Sch 15, para 10*).

SCHEDULE A INCOME

Income from UK land and buildings

5.44 Companies are charged to corporation tax on income arising from the letting of UK land and property under Schedule A (see **12.15–12.21**). Income from land and buildings is included in box 11 of the company tax return. Losses are recorded in box 26.

Furnished holiday lettings

5.45 Furnished holiday lettings are treated as a trade. For this to occur certain conditions apply. The property must be:

- available for holiday letting to the public on a commercial basis for 140 days or more, and
- let commercially for 70 days or more, and
- not occupied for more than 31 days by the same person in any period of seven months (*ICTA 1988, s 503*).

As the income is treated as a trade, loss relief is available but group relief is not available.

Example 5.9—Ilustrative Example

The following example is illustrative of a corporation tax computation.

Sebastian Ltd is a trading company with the following results. There are no associated companies:

Profit and loss account for the year to 31 March 2009

	£000	£000
Gross profit		900
Interest on bank deposit	70	
Schedule A	30	
Profit on sale of UK quoted shares	10	
		110

	£000	£000
		1,010
Less:		
Directors' remuneration	100	
Salaries	80	
Repairs	40	
Advertising and promotion	20	
Depreciation	100	
Miscellaneous expenses	50	
Goodwill amortisation	2	
		392
Profit before taxation		618
Miscellaneous expenses:		
Payment to various charities		10
Donation to political party		10
Staff entertaining		14
Christmas gifts:		
5,000 key rings with company name		5
Cigars		1
Other expenses (all allowable)		10
		50

The goodwill was acquired on 1 April 2003 (see Chapter 7)

Capital allowances for the year amount including the annual investment allowance amount to to £60,000 The chargeable gain on the sales of UK quoted shares is £5,000

Adjusted profits for the year ended 31 March 2009.

	£000	£000
Schedule D Case I:		
Net profit per accounts		618
Add:		
Depreciation	100	
Charitable donations	10	
Political donation	10	
Gifts—cigars	1	
		121
		739

	£000	£000
Less:		
Bank interest	70	
Profit on sale of shares	30	
Schedule A	10	
Capital allowances	60	170
Schedule D Case I		569

Corporation tax computation for the year ended 31 March 2009

	£000
Schedule D Case I	569
Schedule D Case III income	70
Chargeable gains	5
	644
Less:	
Charges on income:	
Payments to charity	10
PCTCT	634

Corporation tax payable

	£000
£634,000 at 28%	177,520
Less: 7/400 × (1,500,000 − 634,000)	15,155
Corporation tax liability	162,365

BODIES GRANTED EXEMPTION FROM CORPORATION TAX ON TRADING INCOME

Charities

5.46 Various exemptions are available to a company that meets the charitable status criteria provided by the Charities Commission (*ICTA 1988, s 505*). Trading income will be exempt from corporation tax in limited circumstances. Exemption applies if the profits from the trade are applied solely for the purposes of the charity. The trade must be exercised in the course of carrying out a primary purpose of a charity and the work in connection with the trade is mainly carried out by the beneficiaries of the charity (*ICTA 1988, s 505(1)(e)*), eg exhibition profits of a local history society. If a charity franchises its trading activities and receives royalty payments these will be exempt from tax (*ICTA 1988, s 505(1)C(ii)*).

Often a charity will form a trading subsidiary for the purpose of carrying out all its trading activities that do not meet the exceptions tests. Such a company's income will be taxable but it can arrange to gift aid it to the charity and obtain relief as a non-trading charge on income. The payment to the charity can be made up to nine months after the end of the accounting period (*ICTA 1988, s 339(7AA)*).

5.47 If the profits are not applied solely for the purposes of the charity, the profits are taxable. However, in respect of chargeable periods beginning on or after 22 March 2006, apportionment is available. Where a trade is exercised partly in the course of the actual carrying out of a primary purpose of the charity and partly otherwise, each part is treated as a separate trade. Expenses and receipts are to be apportioned on a reasonable basis (*FA 2006, s 56*).

The separate trade basis also applies where work in connection with the trade is carried out partly but not mainly by beneficiaries. Expenses and receipts are apportioned on a reasonable basis.

5.48 If a charity has activities unrelated to its primary purpose, it may operate these through a subsidiary company. A company that is owned by a single charity company by making a charge on income under *ICTA 1988, s 339* is able to gift aid its profits to its parent. With effect from 1 April 2006, this relief has been extended to companies that are owned by more than one charity (*FA 2006, s 57*). Previously such amounts were treated as distributions under *ICTA 1988, s 209(4)*.

Cash gifts to charities

5.49 There is no requirement for the company to deduct basic rate income tax for the payment (unlike payments by individuals). The charity in turn does not recover any tax from the receipt (*ICTA 1988, s 349(1B)*).

Benefits received

5.50 Close company payments will not qualify as gift aid payments if they are subject to conditions that the company is to receive a repayment to the company or a connected party is to receive benefits in excess of £250 in total. The actual benefits receivable is based on the formula:

Total donations in year	*De minimis limit of benefits*
£0–£100	25% of value of gift
£101–£1,000	£25
£1,000–£10,000	2.5% of value of gift

(*ICTA 1988, Sch 20.*)

Non-cash gift to charities

5.51   Companies may make gifts of trading stock or plant and machinery to a charity. There is no requirement to show the trading stock disposal in the corporation tax computation nor the plant and machinery disposal in the capital allowances computation (*ICTA 1988, s 83A*).

MUTUAL COMPANIES

Mutual trading

5.52   As a person cannot trade with themselves, a mutual trader is not liable to tax on any profits arising from their 'mutual' trade.

Mutual trading is a situation whereby an organisation is controlled by the people who use its services. Those in effect who contribute to an activity are its sole participators. Arrangements must be in place to ensure that any surplus ultimately finds its way back to the contributors, with no arrangements for it to go to anybody else. Rules that include a winding-up surplus to be gifted to charity will not support mutual trading. Donations to charity are permitted provided the gift is approved by all members.

In normal circumstances the *Companies Act* states that in the event of a winding up any surplus available to distribute to members will be distributed pro rata to shareholding.

The normal rules also provide that any such distribution will only be to the members on the register at that time.

For mutual trading purposes it will be necessary to amend the Articles of Association to state that on a winding up any surplus available for distribution will be returned to contributors in a reasonable proportion to their contribution to that surplus; and that any distribution will also need to include contributors who have left in the last five years.

MEMBERS' SPORTS CLUBS

5.53   Members' sports clubs would normally fall outside the scope of Schedule D Case I. This is because they are usually established by the members for their own social or recreational objects and any surplus is for distribution amongst the members. They are therefore not trading. Services provided commercially to non-members may constitute a trading activity within Schedule D Case I. Expenditure should be allocated on a reasonable basis, but costs specifically in relation to members are not deductible against the non-member related Schedule D Case I income. Other income received, such as interest or rents, will be taxed in the normal way.

COMMUNITY AMATEUR SPORTS CLUBS (CASCS)

CASC conditions

5.54   Reliefs are available to a community sports club that may register as a CASC provided certain conditions are satisfied. Namely, that it is open to the whole community, it is organised on an amateur basis and its main purpose is the provision of facilities for and the promotion of participation in one or more eligible sports (*FA 2002, Sch 18, para 1*).

A club is open to the whole community if membership of the club is open to all without discrimination. Club facilities must be available to members without discrimination, and any fees are set at a level that does not pose a significant obstacle to membership or use of the club's facilities (*FA 2002, Sch 18, para 2(1)*).

A club is organised on an amateur basis if it is non-profit making and it provides for members and guests only the ordinary benefits of an amateur sports club. The constitution must provide for any net assets on dissolution to be applied for approved sporting or charitable purposes (*FA 2002, Sch 18, para 3*).

CASC reliefs

5.55   The CASC may apply for exemption from corporation tax on the following income provided that it is applied for a qualifying purpose. The qualifying purpose being 'providing facilities for and promoting participation in one or more eligible sports' (*FA 2002, Sch 18, para 16(b)*).

- Trading income not exceeding £30,000 (*FA 2002, Sch 18, para 4*).

- Interest income and gift aid income (*FA 2002, Sch 18, para 5*).

- Rental income not exceeding £20,000 (*FA 2002, Sch 18, para 6*).

- Chargeable gains (*FA 2002, Sch 18, para 7*).

Where any income or gains are spent for non-qualifying purposes the tax exemption is reduced proportionately (*FA 2002, Sch 18, para 8*).

Donor reliefs

5.56   Gifts to a CASC will constitute a charity for gift aid and inheritance tax purposes.

CORPORATION TAX SELF-ASSESSMENT

5.57   Clubs and mutual companies are required to self-assess for corporation tax, unless they have agreed otherwise with HMRC. Following the removal of the nil starting rate of corporation tax with effect from 1 April 2006 HMRC announced that they would prevent the issue of notice to file returns to clubs where the annual corporation tax liability is not expected to exceed £100, and the club or unincorporated association is run exclusively for the benefit of its own members.

The club or unincorporated association will be treated as dormant, but will be subject to a review that will take place at least every five years.

This practice does not apply to privately owned clubs and unincorporated associations run as commercial enterprises, housing associations or registered social landlords as designated in the Housing Act 1986, trade associations, thrift funds, holiday clubs, friendly societies and any company which is a subsidiary of, or wholly owned by, a charity.

For each year of dormancy the body must have no anticipated allowable trading losses or chargeable assets likely to be disposed of or anticipated payments from which tax is deductible and payable to HMRC.

A flat owner property management company is also able to benefit from this practice if the company is not entitled to receive income from land and makes no distributions.

The company will be liable to income tax on any interest that it earns from holding service charges on trust received from tenants under *Landlord & Tenant Act 1987, s 42*. The company will be within income tax self-assessment and may be required to make a return to the relevant Trust Office. Income is chargeable at the special trust rates (40% for bank interest) except for the first £1,000 which remains chargeable at basic rates (20% for bank interest). Generally, where the income is below £1,000 and taxed at source, a return will not be required every year (Revenue Announcement 25 August 2006).

A CASC must give details of its income on supplementary pages CT600E (reproduced in the appendices), which also enables it to recover income tax on its gift aid receipts.

Chapter 6

Tangible fixed assets

ACCOUNTANCY TREATMENT

6.1   A company's fixed assets are disclosed in the balance sheet according to the *Companies Act 2006* and to Generally Accepted Accounting Principles (GAAP). The GAAP applied will either be FRSSE or FRS 15 (tangible fixed assets) when using UK GAAP or IAS 16 (property, plant & equipment). Investment properties are accounted for under the FRSSE SSAP 19 (accounting for investment properties) or IAS 40 (investment property). *Companies Act 2006* accounting rules are effective from 6 April 2008. See *the Small Companies and Groups (Accounts and Directors Report) Regulations 2008, SI 2008/409* and *the Large and Medium-sized Companies and Groups (Accounts and Reports) Regulations 2008, SI 2008/410.* These regulations replace *Companies Act 1985, Sch 4.*

FRS 15 defines tangible fixed assets as assets with physical substance that are held for use in the production or supply of goods or services for rental to others or for administrative purposes on a continuing basis in the activities of the reporting entity.

Tangible fixed assets are reported at cost less depreciation at a rate that reflects the economic consumption of the asset by the entity.

TAXATION TREATMENT

6.2   The taxation system maintains the capital/revenue divide for capital assets. Depreciation calculated for accounting purposes is not allowable deduction against income for taxation purposes. Instead, the taxation grants its own form of depreciation on qualifying assets through the capital allowance and annual investment allowance systems.

Capital allowances relate back to the *Income Tax Act 1945* and the *Finance Act 1945.* At that time the focus of the then Chancellor of the Exchequer, Sir John Anderson, was to create tax-breaks and incentives that would assist with the industrial regeneration of the UK economy. When calculating taxable business profits, there was a distinct divide between what was considered to be 'capital and revenue'. This principle was established in *In Re Robert Addie & Sons* CE 1875, 1 TC 1,12 SLR 274, *Coltness Iron Co v Black* HL 1881, 1 TC 287, 6 AC 315 *and Leeming v Jones* HL 1930, 15 TC 333, (1930) AC 415. Capital allowances permitted the deduction of capital expenditure from business profits over a period of years. The system has been amended by various governments to help UK industry develop.

With the technological advances in the economy and global energy and environmental concerns, the current Labour Government saw fit to remove industrial buildings allowances (IBAs) and its mirror relief agricultural buildings allowance (ABA) (ABAs are not covered in this book) over the period 1 April 2008 to 31 March 2011. The changes were announced in Budget 2007 and introduced in *Finance Act 2008*. Also substantial changes have been and are to be made to the plant and machinery capital allowances, together with the introduction of the annual investment allowance (AIA) and the payable tax credit. Reliefs continue to be available for innovative technologies (see **Chapter 8**) and for environmentally friendly and energy efficient installations.

HMRC have announced that the new capital allowances regime will be incorporated into both the paper and the online versions of the corporation tax return from October 2008.

Budget 2007 changes

6.3   The following table summarises the Budget 2007 changes and the legislation introduced to put them into effect. As with the changes to the corporation tax rates (see **3.1**), there is no change from the existing pre-budget 2007 regime for North Sea oil and gas ring fence activities (Budget 2007 BN02, BN06 and BN07).

Capital Allowance	Measure	Effective From	Legislation	Paragraph
Industrial Buildings Allowance				
Balancing adjustments	Withdrawal	21 March 2007	*FA 2007, s 36*	**6.80**

6.3 *Tangible fixed assets*

Capital Allowance	Measure	Effective From	Legislation	Paragraph
	Exceptions: ● pre-commencement contracts; ● qualifying enterprise zone expenditure.			
4% Writing Down Allowance (WDA)	Withdrawal over the period 2008–09 to 2010–11.	1 April 2008	*FA 2008, s 84*	**6.75**
Agricultural Buildings Allowance				
Balancing adjustment	Removal of the balancing adjustment option.	21 March 2007	*FA 2007, s 36*	
4% Writing Down Allowance (WDA)	Withdrawal over the period 2008–09 to 2010–11.	1 April 2008	*FA 2008, s 84*	
Plant and Machinery Capital Allowances				
First Year Allowance (FYA)	Available on low emission cars and gas refuelling stations. FYA for Small Enterprises discontinued from 1 April 2008.	1 April 2007	*FA 2007, s 37*	**6.27** **6.22**
25% Writing Down Allowance	Reduction from 25% to 20% effective from 2008–09.	1 April 2008	*FA 2008, s 80*	**6.35**
Annual Investment Allowance (AIA)	Applies to the first £50,000 of expenditure on plant and machinery in the general pool and introduced from 2008–09 and replaces the first year allowance.	1 April 2008	*FA 2008, s 74*	**6.46**

Capital Allowance	Measure	Effective From	Legislation	Paragraph
Long-life asset writing down allowance	Increased from 6% to 10% from 2008–09.	1 April 2008	*FA 2008, s 83*	**6.45**
Fixtures integral to a building	Reduced from 25% WDA to 10% WDA effective from 2008–09.	1 April 2008	*FA 2008, s 73*	**6.17**
'Energy-saving and environmen-tally beneficial plant and machinery	Allowance or a payable tax credit.	1 April 2008	*FA 2008, s 79*	**6.24** **6.25** **9.29**

See also HMRC Consultation July 2007—Business Tax Reform: Capital Allowances Changes.

QUALIFYING EXPENDITURE

Capital allowances claim

6.4   A company may claim capital allowances on its qualifying capital expenditure (*CAA 2001, s 1*). For corporation tax purposes, relief is given in an accounting period (*CAA 2001, s 6(1)(b)*).The reliefs given are a first year allowance (FYA), an annual investment allowance (AIA) (from 1 April 2008) a writing down allowance (WDA), an initial allowance (IA) (currently with-drawn)and a balancing allowance (BA). Capital allowance charges are referred to as balancing charges. The relief must be claimed (otherwise no relief is given) (*CAA 2001, s 3(1)*).

The allowances are claimed by including the amount of the claim in the respective boxes of the company tax return or an amended return. The company need not claim the full amount available. A company may choose either to make a reduced claim or not to claim at all if it wished to maximise a loss in a future accounting period (see Chapter 9). The claim is within the normal self-assessment corporation tax return time limits, being two years after the end of the accounting period concerned (see **2.9**) (*FA 1998, Sch 18, para 82*). The normal time limit is extended in such circumstances where there is an enquiry, amendment or appeal to 30 days after the respected closure notice, amendment or determination. HMRC has the power to extend the statutory time limits in exceptional circumstances but has stated that it will not extend the time limits in respect of the following:

- A change of mind.

- Hindsight showing that a different combination of claims might be advantageous: for example, the group relief available may be lower than the company expected it to be when it claimed capital allowances. The company may then want to claim further capital allowances. But that is not a circumstance beyond the company's control. It could have claimed sooner.

- Oversight or error, whether on the part of the company or its advisers.

- Absence or indisposition of an officer or employee of the company unless:

  — the absence or illness arose at a critical time, which delayed the making of the claim;

  — in the case of absence, there was good reason why the person was unavailable at the critical time; or

  — there was no other person who could have made the claim on behalf of the company within the normal time limit (HMRC Capital Allowances Manual CA 11140).

Capital allowances given in respect of a trade are deducted from trading income as an adjustment (see **5.21**). Balancing charges are added to trading income. Capital allowances in respect of non-trading activities are generally deducted primarily from the source of income to which they relate, eg Schedule A. If the accounting period is less than 12 months, the WDA and the AIA (but not the FYA) are time-apportioned accordingly. If the accounting period is longer than 12 months, the chargeable period for capital allowance purposes is divided into 12-month periods and the remaining balance.

Capital expenditure incurred—timing

6.5 For the purposes of claiming the allowances, capital expenditure is incurred on the date on which the obligation to pay becomes unconditional even if there is a later payment date (*CAA 2001, s 5(1)*). Delivery of the goods is normally the time when the obligation to pay becomes unconditional. Iif the contractual payment period is longer than four months the expenditure is treated as incurred on the payment due date (*CAA 2001, s 4(5)*).

For works under contract, expenditure is incurred upon the issue of a certificate of work to date. If a certificate is issued within one month of the end of the accounting period but the asset has become the company's property before the end of the accounting period, the expenditure is deemed to have been incurred on the last day of the accounting period concerned (*CAA 2001, s 5(4)*). However, expenditure incurred before a trade begins is treated as incurred on the first day of trading.

Expenditure still to be incurred under a hire purchase etc contract at the time when the asset is brought into use is treated as incurred on the date on which the asset is brought into use. Expenditure incurred on the purchase of an unused building or structure is deemed to be incurred on the date on which the purchase price becomes payable (HMRC Capital Allowances Manual CA 11800). If a company is not registered for VAT, any VAT paid on the cost of the asset is taken into account when calculating the allowances. If an additional VAT liability is incurred or an additional VAT rebate arises this is treated as taking place on the last day of the relevant VAT interval.

Sales between connected parties are deemed to be made at market value (*CAA 2001, s 567*). Parties under common control may elect for the asset to be transferred at the lower of tax written down value or market value (*CAA 2001, s 569*).

Assets on which capital allowances may be claimed

6.6   The types of capital expenditure that attract a capital allowance claim are:

Para		CAA 2001
6.04	Plant and machinery	Part 2
	The construction of industrial buildings, qualifying hotels, commercial buildings in enterprise zones	Part 3
	The construction of agricultural buildings and works	Part 4
	Flat conversion allowances	Part 4A
	Mineral extraction	Part 5
	Research and development	Part 6
	Know-how	Part 7
	Patents	Part 8
	Dredging	Part 9
	Assured tenancies	Part 10

This chapter discusses plant and machinery (**6.7–6.45**), the annual investment allowance (**6.46–6.54**), leasing (**6.55–6.64**), industrial buildings (**6.65–6.85**), business premises renovation allowances (**6.86–6.101**) and flat conversion allowances (**6.102–6.111**). Research and development is discussed in **Chap-**

ter **8**. Agricultural buildings allowance, mineral extraction and dredging are not discussed. Capital allowances are no longer available on know-how and patents. These are dealt with under the intangible assets regime (see **Chapter 7**) with effect from 1 April 2002. Capital allowances on assured tenancies are no longer available. Capital allowances may also be claimed on other types of expenditure such as agricultural buildings, mineral extraction, dredging etc but these types of expenditure are not covered in this text.

PLANT AND MACHINERY

Qualifying expenditure

6.7　　In order to be able to claim capital allowances for plant and machinery the company must incur qualifying expenditure on a qualifying activity (*CAA 2001, s 11(1)*). Qualifying expenditure is capital expenditure incurred on the provision of plant and machinery, wholly or partly for the purposes of the qualifying activity carried on by the company that incurs the expenditure. As a result of incurring the expenditure, the company 'owns' the asset (*CAA 2001, s 11(4)*).

A qualifying activity may consist of:

- a trade;

- an ordinary property business;

- a furnished holiday letting business;

- an overseas property business;

- a profession or vocation;

- mines, quarry or canal or other concern giving rise to profits from land charged to tax as a trade under Case I Schedule D in accordance with *ICTA 1988, s 55*;

- management of an investment company;

- special leasing business (*CAA 2001, s 15*).

Specific provisions relating to property businesses and investment companies are discussed in Chapter 12. This chapter deals with trades as well as the general allowance provisions.

6.8　　Capital allowances can only be claimed on the cost of the plant and machinery itself, not the additional costs of interest or commitment fees (*Ben-Odeco Ltd v Powlson* (1978) 52 TC 459, [1978] STC 460, [1978] 1 WLR 1093, [1978] 2 All ER 1111). HMRC only allow professional fees and preliminary fees to be included within the cost on an asset for capital allowance purposes if they relate directly to the acquisition, transport and installation of the plant and machinery (HMRC Capital Allowances Manual CA 20070).

Expenditure on buildings and structures

6.9   In general plant and machinery expenditure does not encompass expenditure on buildings and structures (*CAA 2001, s 21(1)*). Certain assets are not included in this general rule but, in order for a company to claim plant and machinery capital allowances, they still need to qualify as 'plant' in their own right.

A claim for plant and machinery capital allowances may be made for the following assets, which are not regarded as part of the fabric of the building:

● Thermal Insulation installed in industrial buildings.

● Fire safety (until 1 April 2008).

● Safety at designated sports grounds.

● Safety at regulated stands at sports grounds.

● Safety at other sports grounds.

● Personal security.

● Software and software rights

● Integral features see **6.17** (for expenditure incurred on or after 1 April 2008).

(*CAA 2001, s 23(2)*).

The following items in 'List C' are again not regarded as part of the fabric of the building:

1   Machinery (including devices for providing motive power) not within any other item in this list.

2   Gas and sewerage systems provided mainly:

(a)   to meet the particular requirements of the qualifying activity; or

(b)   to serve particular plant or machinery used for the purposes of the qualifying activity.

For expenditure incurred prior to 1 April 2008, electrical systems (including lighting systems) and cold water that meet the criteria above in (a) and (b).

3   *For expenditure incurred prior to 1 April 2008, space or water heating systems; powered systems of ventilation, air cooling or air purification; and any floor or ceiling comprised in such systems.*

4   Manufacturing or processing equipment; storage equipment (including cold rooms); display equipment; and counters, checkouts and similar equipment.

5   Cookers, washing machines, dishwashers, refrigerators and similar equipment; washbasins, sinks, baths, showers, sanitary ware and similar equipment; and furniture and furnishings.

6   Hoists. *For expenditure incurred before 1 April 2008, lifts, hoists, escalators and moving walkways.*

7   Sound insulation provided mainly to meet the particular requirements of the qualifying activity.

8   Computer, telecommunication and surveillance systems (including their wiring or other links).

9   Refrigeration or cooling equipment.

10   Fire alarm systems; sprinkler and other equipment for extinguishing or containing fires.

11   Burglar alarm systems.

12   Strong rooms in bank or building society premises; safes.

13   Partition walls, where moveable and intended to be moved in the course of the qualifying activity.

14   Decorative assets provided for the enjoyment of the public in hotel, restaurant or similar trades.

15   Advertising hoardings; signs, displays and similar assets.

16   Swimming pools (including diving boards, slides and structures on which such boards or slides are mounted).

17   Any glasshouse constructed so that the required environment (namely, air, heat, light, irrigation and temperature) for the growing of plants is provided automatically by means of devices forming an integral part of its structure.

18   Cold stores.

19   Caravans provided mainly for holiday lettings.

20   Buildings provided for testing aircraft engines run within the buildings.

21   Moveable buildings intended to be moved in the course of the qualifying activity.

22   The alteration of land for the purpose only of installing plant or machinery.

23   The provision of dry docks.

24   The provision of any jetty or similar structure provided mainly to carry plant or machinery.

25   The provision of pipelines or underground ducts or tunnels with a primary purpose of carrying utility conduits.

26   The provision of towers to support floodlights.

27   The provision of:

   (a)   any reservoir incorporated into a water treatment works; or

   (b)   any service reservoir of treated water for supply within any housing estate or other particular locality.

28   The provision of:

   (a)   silos provided for temporary storage; or

   (b)   storage tanks.

29   The provision of slurry pits or silage clamps.

30   The provision of fish tanks or fish ponds.

31   The provision of rails, sleepers and ballast for a railway or tramway.

32   The provision of structures and other assets for providing the setting for any ride at an amusement park or exhibition.

33   The provision of fixed zoo cages.

Items 1 to 16 do not include any asset whose principal purpose is to insulate or enclose the interior of a building or to provide an interior wall, floor or ceiling which, in each case, is intended to remain permanently in place.

The following assets are treated as part of the structure of the building and not plant and machinery (*CAA 2001, s 21(3)*). It is not possible to make a claim for plant and machinery capital allowances in their respect:

1   Walls, floors, ceilings, doors, gates, shutters, windows and stairs.

2   Mains services and systems, for water, electricity and gas.

3   Waste disposal systems.

4   Sewerage and drainage systems.

5   Shafts or other structures in which lifts, hoists, escalators and moving walkways are installed.

6   Fire safety systems.

The meaning of plant

6.10   Plant owes its meaning to the development of case law. Plant was first defined in the case of *Yarmouth v France* (1887) 19 QBD 647 as 'whatever apparatus is used by a businessman for carrying on his business—not his stock in trade which he buys or makes for sale but all goods and chattels, fixed or moveable, live or dead, which he keeps for permanent employment in his business'. In other words the assets that enable a business to be carried on. This was confirmed as the functional test in the case of *Benson v Yard Arm Club Ltd* (1979) 53 TC 67, [1979] STC 266, [1979] 1 WLR 347, [1979] 2 All ER 336. Capital allowances were refused on the cost of purchasing and adapting a floating restaurant on the grounds that this was the place where the business was carried on rather than the tools that enable it to be carried on. HMRC regard assets with a life of more than two years as falling within the definition of plant: *Hinton v Madden & Ireland Ltd* (1959) 38 TC 391, [1959] 1 WLR 875, [1959] 3 All ER 356 (HMRC Capital Allowances Manual CA 21100). Whether the setting in which the business is carried on is plant is a question of fact. Lighting that was part of the setting but performed no function was not held to be plant: *J Lyons and Co Ltd v Attorney-General* [1944] 1 All ER 477. Moveable office partitions in a shipping agents office, which were often moved to enable the trade to be carried on, were held to be plant; the partitions performed a function (*Jarrold v John Good & Sons Ltd* (1962) 40 TC 681, [1963] 1 WLR 214, [1963] 1 All ER 141). The law has now been changed on this issue: see item 13 List C at **6.9**. HMRC comment that only moveable partitions that possess mobility as a matter of commercial necessity qualify as plant (HMRC Capital Allowances Manual CA 21120). The function test was also met in *Leeds Permanent Building Society v Proctor* (1982) 56 TC 293, [1982] STC 821, [1982] 3 All ER 925 whereby decorative screens in a building society window were held to be plant. *CIR v Scottish & Newcastle Breweries Ltd* (1982) 55 TC 252, [1982] STC 296, [1982] 1 WLR 322, [1982] 2 All ER 230 was a landmark case in its time. Decorative assets in a pub and restaurant were allowed as plant because they provided atmosphere and ambience, within that trade; proving that assets must be judged within the context of the trade. The law has now been changed on this issue: see item 14 List C at **6.9** HMRC comment that decorative items only qualify as plant if:

- the trade involves the creation of atmosphere/ambience and in effect the sale of that ambience to its customers; and

- the items on which plant or machinery allowances are claimed were specially chosen to create the atmosphere that the taxpayer is trying to sell (HMRC Capital Allowances Manual CA 21130).

HMRC particularly give the example of a painting hanging in an accountant's office not qualifying as plant because selling atmosphere is not part of an accountant's business. The point of course is debatable.

Lighting

6.11   Lighting installed in a building in order to make that building useable was not considered to be plant; it is part of the building. Lighting installed into a useable building to enable a trade to be carried on more effectively was considered to be plant (*Cole Bros v Phillips* (1982) 55 TC 188, [1982] STC 307, [1982] 1 WLR 1450, [1982] 2 All ER 247).

Wimpy International Ltd v Warland (1988) 61 TC 51, [1989] STC 273 generally upheld the decision in *CIR v Scottish & Newcastle Breweries Ltd.* In particular the cost of lighting in a restaurant was allowed because it provided atmosphere and ambience. Since then case law has moved to the function test and whether the piece of equipment is used within the trade. The tests applied in this case which HMRC also apply are:

Questions

1   Is the item stock in trade?

2   Is the item the business premises or part of the business premises (the premises test)?

3   Is the item used for carrying on the business (the business use test)?

Response

If the answers to questions 1 and 2 are negative and the answer to question 3 is positive the item is plant (HMRC Capital Allowances Manuals CA 21010 and CA 21140).

In this case it was suggested in order to ascertain whether an asset was part of the premises the following four factors can be considered:

●   Does the item appear visually to retain a separate identity?

●   With what degree of permanence has it been attached to the building?

●   To what extent is the structure complete without it?

●   To what extent is it intended to be permanent or alternatively is it likely to be replaced within a short period?

HMRC accept that electrical installation is plant, if the installation is fully integrated, designed and adapted to meet the particular requirements of the trade, functions as apparatus of the trade and is essential for the functioning of the trade. If the installation fails to qualify as plant HMRC will adopt a piecemeal approach. The same general and then piecemeal approach is applied to cold water, sewerage and gas systems.

149

In particular, HMRC will accept that the following elements of an electrical installation are plant:

- the main switchboard, transformer and associated switchgear provided that a substantial part of the electrical installation—both the equipment and the ancillary wiring—qualifies as plant;

- a standby generator and the emergency lighting and power circuits it services;

- lighting in sales areas, if it is specifically designed to encourage the sale of goods on display;

- wiring, control panels and other equipment installed specifically to supply equipment that is plant or machinery.

Lighting in a sales area will qualify even if there is no other lighting. The public areas in banking businesses are treated as sales areas (HMRC Capital Allowances Manual CA 21180). HMRC also accept that central heating systems, hot water systems, air conditioning systems, alarm and sprinkler systems, ventilation systems, baths, wash basins and toilet suites qualify as plant. Flooring and ceilings are generally considered not to be plant (HMRC Capital Allowances Manuals CA 22070 and CA 22080).

Buildings alterations connected with installations of plant or machinery

6.12   Incidental capital expenditure on alterations to an existing building for the installation of plant and machinery for the purposes of the qualifying activity qualifies as plant (*CAA 2001, s 25*). A lift and its necessary wiring qualify as plant. Installation of a lift shaft in an existing building qualifies as plant. Installation of a lift shaft in a new building does not qualify as plant. Plant removal and re-erection costs qualify as plant if not allowable as a deduction from trading profits (HMRC Capital Allowances Manual CA 21190).

Demolition costs

6.13   Net demolition costs of plant and machinery that was last used for the purposes of a qualifying activity may either be added to the cost of the new plant if the plant is replaced, or added to other qualifying expenditure of the same chargeable period as the demolition if the plant is not replaced.

The net demolition costs are the costs of demolition less any money received for the remains of the asset or any insurance receipts (*CA 2001, s 26*).

Expenditure on required fire precautions

6.14   Expenditure incurred on fire safety equipment such as fire alarms and sprinkler systems by law by a person carrying on a qualifying activity will normally qualify as plant or revenue expenditure. Capital expenditure incurred prior to 1 April 2008, by a business on fire safety equipment in order to meet the requirements of a prohibition order, qualified as plant (*CAA 2001, s 29; FA 2008, s 72*).

Computer software

6.15   Computer software is within the intangible assets regime. An election may be made under *FA 2002, Sch 29, para 83* for it to be treated as plant for capital allowance purposes within *CAA 2001, s 71*. The election must be made within two years from the end of an accounting period in which the expenditure was incurred.

Thermal insulation of buildings

6.16   Thermal installation is qualifying expenditure for capital allowance purposes. Expenditure incurred prior to 1 April 2008 only qualified if it was incurred in connection with an industrial building. Post 1 April 2008 the expenditure will qualify for a 10% special rate allowance (see **6.41**) if it is incurred by a company on a building used in carrying on one of the qualifying activities within *CAA 2001, s 15* (see **6.7**) (*CAA2001, s 28(1)*), or on a building let by a property business or an overseas property business (*CAA 2001, s 28(2)*). A dwelling house does not qualify for an allowance (*CAA 2001, s 35*). If an energy savings deduction can be made under *CAA 2001, s 31ZA*, by which a landlord may claim a deduction for expenditure on acquiring and installing an energy-saving item in a dwelling-house or in a building containing the dwelling-house let by him in the course of his business (see **12.21**), no special rate allowance can be claimed (*CAA 2001, s 28(2B)(a)*).

Expenditure on integral features

6.17   A company incurring expenditure on or after 1 April 2008, on the provision or replacement of   integral features on a building or structure may claim a 10% annual writing down allowance if the company meets the following conditions:

● it carries on a qualifying activity;

151

- it uses the building for the purposes of the qualifying activity;

- it owns the plant and machinery as a result of incurring the expenditure.

(CAA 2001, s 33A(1) & (2).)

Integral features consist of:

- an electrical system (including a lighting system);

- a cold water system;

- a space or water heating system, a powered system of ventilation, air cooling or air purification, and any floor or ceiling comprised in such a system;

- a lift, an escalator or a moving walkway;

- external solar shading.

(CAA 2001, s 33A(5).)

Insulation expenditure is specifically excluded from the list. This is covered in *CAA2001, s 28* (see **6.16**). In practice some of these additions may also qualify as environmentally beneficial plant and machinery (see **6.24**) in which case the option is available to the company to claim one such allowance, but not both.

An integral feature is 'replaced' if, within 12 months from the time that the initial expenditure was incurred, more than 50% of its cost is spent on its replacement. It may be necessary to apportion the replacement expenditure between two accounting periods *(CAA 2001, s 33B(1–4)*. For practical purposes, if it is unknown whether a writing down allowance for the replacement of integral features can be made, the return may be filed and the allowance claimed at a later date *(CAA 2001, s 33B(5))*. A separate deduction for expenditure included in a writing down allowance claim cannot be made when computing the amount of profits chargeable to corporation tax under Case I or Case II of Schedule D *(ICTA 1988, s 74(1)(da))*.

Case law

6.18   There are a number of decided capital allowance cases, besides those mentioned above. A summary of which is given below:

Case	Asset	Held
Yarmouth v France (1887) 19 QBD 647	A horse	Plant

Case	Asset	Held
Benson v Yard Arm Club Ltd (1979) 53 TC 67, [1979] 1 WLR 347, [1979] 2 All ER 336	A floating restaurant	Not plant
J Lyons and Co Ltd v Attorney-General [1944] 1 All ER 477	Lighting—as part of the setting	Not plant
Jarrold v John Good & Sons Ltd (1962) 40 TC 681, [1963] 1 WLR 214, [1963] 1 All ER 141	Moveable office partitions	Plant
Leeds Permanent Building Society v Proctor (1982) 56 TC 293, [1982] STC 821, [1982] 3 All ER 925	Window screens—particular to the business	Plant
CIR v Scottish & Newcastle Breweries Ltd (1982) 55 TC 252, [1982] STC 296, [1982] 1 WLR 322, [1982] 2 All ER 230	Lighting and decor providing 'an atmosphere' necessary for the trade	Plant
Cole Bros v Phillips (1982) 55 TC 188, [1982] STC 307, [1982] 1 WLR 1450, [1982] 2 All ER 247	Certain electrical installations	Plant
	Others	Not plant
Wimpy International Ltd v Warland (1988) 61 TC 51, [1989] STC 273	Decorative items and certain specialist lighting	Plant
	Shop fronts	Not plant
Cooke v Beach Station Caravans Ltd (1974) 49 TC 514, [1974] STC 402, [1974] 1 WLR 1398, [1974] 3 All ER 159	Swimming pool used for a holiday caravan park	Plant
Hampton v Fortes Autogrill Ltd (1979) 53 TC 691, [1980] STC 80	False ceilings in a restaurant to conceal pipes and wires etc	Not plant

Case	Asset	Held
Grays v Seymours Garden Centre (*Horticulture*) (1995) 67 TC 401, [1995] STC 706	An unheated glass house—a planteria	Not plant
St John's (*Mountford*) *v Ward* (1974) 49 TC 524, [1975] STC 7	A pre-fabricated fixed school building	Not plant
Munby v Furlong (1977) 50 TC 491, [1976] 1 WLR 410, [1976] 1 All ER 753	A barrister's law books	Plant
Schofied v R & H Hall Ltd (1974) 49 TC 538, [1975] STC 353	Grain silos	Plant
Hinton v Maden & Ireland Ltd (1959) 38 TC 391, [1959] 1 WLR 875, [1959] 3 All ER 356	A shoe repairer's loose tools, knives and lasts—with an expected life of more than two years	Plant
Dixon v Fitch's Garages Ltd (1975) 50 TC 509, [1975] STC 480, [1976] 1 WLR 215, [1975] 3 All ER 455	A garage canopy to protect customers whilst vehicle refuelling	Not plant
Rose & Co (*Wallpapers & Paints*) *Ltd v Campbell* (1967) 44 TC 500, [1968] 1 WLR 346, [1968] 1 All ER 405	Wallpaper pattern books	Not plant

6.19   The expenditure is deemed to be incurred at cost on the first day of trading (*CAA 2001, s 12*). Expenditure is deemed to be incurred at the lesser of market value or cost at the date of a change of use if a change of use occurs (*CAA 2001, s 13*).

RATES OF ALLOWANCES

6.20   Current capital allowance rates for plant and machinery are:

Incurred by	Expenditure incurred	Allow-ance	Rate
All companies	Energy saving plant or machinery	FYA	100%

Incurred by	Expenditure incurred	Allow-ance	Rate
	Energy service providers		
	Low carbon dioxide emission cars not exceeding 110 gm CO_2/km (120 gm prior to 1 April 2008)		
	Equipment for refuelling vehicles with natural gas or hydrogen fuel		
	North Sea oil ring-fence plant and machinery		
SMEs	All other plant and machinery		
	expenditure incurred before 1 April 2008	FYA	40%
SEs	All other plant and machinery		
	expenditure incurred before 1 April 2008	FYA	50%
All companies	All plant and machinery	WDA	25%
	for accounting periods ending on or before 1 April 2008	WDA	
	for accounting periods ending after 1 April 2008		20%
	except:		
	long life assets		6%
	overseas leasing		10%
	special rate expenditure		10%
All companies	Annual Investment Allowance	Maxi-mum	£50,000

The FYA was distinguished either by the size of the company or by the type of expenditure. Subject to the necessary conditions, SMEs (Small and Medium-Sized Enterprises) and SEs (Small Enterprises) could claim FYAs on all their plant and machinery purchases, if the expenditure was incurred prior to 1 April 2008. Companies of any size may continue to claim FYAs generally on energy efficient technologies or oil technology if in that area of business.

FIRST YEAR ALLOWANCE

6.21   An FYA can only be claimed during the chargeable period in which the expenditure is incurred (*CAA 2001, s 52*). (See **6.5** above for the date thatexpenditure is incurred.) If that is also the period in which the qualifying activity is discontinued, no claim is allowed.

SMEs (small and medium-sized enterprises) and SEs (small enterprises)

6.22   SMEs and SEs were able to claim an FYA on qualifying expenditure incurred prior to 1 April 2008. The definition of SMEs and SEs for plant and machinery capital allowance purposes followed the *Companies Act 2006, s 382, s 383, s 465* and *s 466 definitions* (formerly *Companies Act 1985, s 247(3)* and *s 249(3)* definitions (as introduced by the *Companies Act 1985 (Accounts of Small and Medium-Sized Enterprises and Audit Exemption) (Amendment) Regulations 2004, SI 2004/16*). (See HMRC Capital Allowances Manual CA 23170 for definitions for the financial years ending before 30 January 2004). The limiting criteria are turnover, assets and the number of employees. A company means a company incorporated in the UK or a company with a place of business in the UK. To claim the FYA the company must be an SME or SE at the time the expenditure is incurred and not a member of a large group.

The definitions are as follows:

	Small company Not more than	Medium-sized company Not more than
Turnover	£5.6 million	£22.8 million
Balance sheet total	£2.8 million	£11.4 million
Number of employees	50	250

The balance sheet total is the aggregate of the company's assets as shown on the balance sheet before both current and long-term liabilities. The amounts are reduced proportionately for accounting periods of less than 12 months.

For the first year that a company satisfies two or more of the above mentioned requirements, it qualifies as an SME for that financial year. Once a company has qualified as an SME it will continue to be treated as such unless it fails to meet the requirements for two consecutive years. If a large company reduces in size to become an SME it will not be treated as such unless it has met the requirements for two successive years.

Groups

6.23   The definitions of a small and a medium-sized group are as follows:

	Small group		Medium-sized group	
	Not more than	Not more than	Not more than	Not more than
	Net	Gross	Net	Gross
Turnover	£5.6 million	£6.72 million	£22.8 million	£27.36 million
Balance sheet total	£2.8 million	£3.36 million	£11.4 million	£13.68 million
Number of employees	50		250	

The balance sheet total 'net' is the aggregate of the company's assets as shown on the balance sheet before both current and long-term liabilities, with inter-company balances 'netted' off.

The balance sheet total 'gross' is the aggregate of the company's assets as shown on the balance sheet before both current and long-term liabilities. Inter-company group balances are included.

A company may only claim an FYA if it is neither a parent undertaking nor a subsidiary undertaking of a large group (*CAA 2001, s 49(2)*). An undertaking is a corporate body, a partnership or an unincorporated association carrying on a trade of business with a view to profit. A parent undertaking is the body that exercises control either by votes or dominant influence (*CA 2006, ss 1162, 1161 formerly CA 1985, ss 259, 258*). The definition of a group includes an overseas parent.

If arrangements existed at the time the expenditure was incurred, which if they had come into effect before the expenditure was incurred would have made the company or its successor a member of a large group, the expenditure will not qualify for an FYA (*CAA 2001, s 49(4)*). Arrangements can be of any kind and need not be in writing or legally enforceable. A successor company is a company that carries on the trade or part of the trade of the predecessor under the rules of *ICTA 1988, s 343* (company reconstructions without a change of ownership). (See **Chapter 15**).

Example 6.1

Garcia plc is a large business. It wants to buy a new lathe but if it does it will not be entitled to FYAs because it is not an SME. Terry Ltd, an SME, buys the lathe for a qualifying activity of operating the lathe, thus obtaining FYA, with fixed supply and sale contracts with Garcia plc. The lathe is installed in Garcia plc's factory and operated by its workforce on a subcontract basis. The tax saving is shared by Garcia plc and Terry Ltd through the contract price.

Terry Ltd is not entitled to FYA's by reason of *CAA 2001, s 49(4)* (source HMRC Capital Allowances Manual CA 23110—Adapted).

A partnership of which a company is a member cannot claim an FYA (*CAA 2001, s 48(2)(b)*).

Environmentally beneficial plant and machinery

6.24   Particular plant and machinery that meets environment criteria qualifies for 100% FYA, which may be claimed by companies of any size. This machinery can be found by logging on to www.eca.gov.uk. The technologies that are included are:

- boilers (including oil-fired boilers);
- pipe insulation;
- combined heat and power (CHP);
- radiant and warm air heaters;
- compressed air equipment;
- solar thermal systems;
- heat pumps for space heating;
- thermal screens;
- lighting;
- variable speed drives (VSD);
- motors;
- refrigeration equipment (including display cabinets and compressors);
- automatic monitoring and targeting equipment;
- air-to-air energy recovery equipment;
- compact heat exchangers;
- heating, ventilation and air conditioning zone controls;
- vehicle wash waste reclaim units;
- efficient industrial cleaning; and

- waste management for mechanical seals.

It is necessary for the government to certify that the equipment meets the required standards or that the machinery is a product specified on the product list.

6.25   Certain water technologies and products also qualify for 100% FYA. These fall into classes of efficient taps, efficient toilets, flow controllers, leakage detection, meters and rainwater harvesting equipment (*SI 2003/2076*). With effect from 7 September 2006 efficient washing machines and small scale slurry and sludge dewatering equipment has been added (*SI 2006/2235*). Information regarding these products can be found on www.water-eca.gov.uk. See also the *Capital Allowances Energy Saving Plant and Machinery (Amendment) (Order) 2007 (SI 2007/2165)*. Component parts of an asset may meet the environmental criteria. If so, an FYA will be available in respect of these parts. A certificate issued to the buyer will indicate the cost of the environmental components, which should be used in calculating the FYA (*CAA 2001, ss 45H, 45J*). If the total expenditure incurred on the asset containing the qualifying component (or components) is less than the amount specified in the order for the component or components incorporated in that asset, the total expenditure qualifies for 100% FYA (HMRC Capital Allowances Manual CA 23135). If qualifying expenditure is incurred on an asset in stage payment, the payment is allocated pro-rata over the various payments.

If an environmental certificate is revoked, the company should withdraw the 100% FYA claim.

Both the expenditure on the energy saving plant and machinery (above) and the environmentally beneficial plant and machinery (see **6.24**) may qualify for a payable tax credit (see **9.29**).

Expenditure incurred by energy services provider

6.26   If a company energy service provider of any size supplies energy efficient plant and machinery, which is on the technology list of products list to his client he may be able to claim an FYA. The provider must make an election with this client. The plant must not be for use in a dwelling house and the service provider or another organisation with which it is connected must carry out all or substantially all of the operation and maintenance of the plant and machinery (*CAA 2001, s 180A*).

Expenditure on cars with low carbon dioxide emissions

6.27   Expenditure by any size of company on cars with low carbon dioxide emissions qualifies for an FYA if incurred between 17 April 2002 and 31 March

2013. The car must be unused and not second hand. It can either be an electric car or a car with CO_2 emissions of not more than 110 gm (120 gm for expenditure incurred before 1 April 2008) per km driven. Information regarding a car's carbon dioxide emissions figure can be found on the vehicle registration document (the 'V5') or on the Vehicle Certification Agency's website at www.vca.gov.uk. Neither the rules for cars costing more that £12,000 nor the car hire or leasing expenses restriction applies to these vehicles (*CAA 2001, s 45D*).

Expenditure on natural gas and hydrogen refuelling equipment

6.28   Expenditure incurred on natural gas, biogas (for expenditure incurred after 1 April 2008) and hydrogen refuelling equipment between 17 April 2002 and 31 March 2013 and installed in a refuelling station qualify for FYA. The stations can be private to the company or open to the public. Eligible expenditure includes storage tanks, compressors, controls and meters, gas connections, and filling equipment (*CAA 2001, s 45E*).

Expenditure on North Sea oil ring-fence plant and machinery

6.29   Extraction of gas or oil in the North Sea trades may claim a 100% FYA on equipment purchased for use in the 'ring-fence' trade. (A ring-fence trade is a trade subject to the supplementary charge). Long life assets qualify for 24% WDA (*CAA 2001, s 45G*).

Persons who are treated as owners of fixtures

6.30   If the plant and machinery purchased for the purposes of the trade becomes a fixture and the company holds a relevant interest in the land, the company will be able to claim the capital allowances. Where more than one party has an interest in the land the party entitled to claim is normally the party with the lowest interest (*CAA 2001, s 176*) (HMRC Capital Allowances Manual CA 26150).

Lessors and lessees of equipment fixtures used for a qualifying activity of the lessee may jointly elect for the fixture to be treated as belonging to the equipment lessor thus enabling the lessor to claim the capital allowances (*CAA 2001, s 177*). The election must be made within two years of the end of the accounting period for which it is to apply.

EXPENDITURE ON WHICH AN FYA MAY NOT BE CLAIMED

6.31   No FYA is available on the purchase of a car unless it is a low-emission car (see **6.27**). No FYA is available on a gifted asset. This is because to qualify for FYA the entity must incur the expenditure (*CAA 2001, s 52*). Similarly, an FYA is not available if a company buys an asset for one purpose and then uses the asset for another purpose. An FYA may not be claimed on the provision of plant and machinery for leasing, unless the expenditure is on qualifying energy saving plant and machinery, cars with low CO_2 emissions or natural gas or hydrogen refuelling equipment. HMRC take the view that the hire of machinery with an operative constitutes contract hire as in the non-tax case of *Baldwins Industrial Services plc v Barr Ltd* [2003] BLR 176. The expenditure is not within finance leasing and an FYA will be available (HMRC Capital Allowances Manual CA 23115). No capital allowances whatsoever are given on assets used for business entertainment (*CAA 2001, s 269*).

The general rule is that no FYA may be claimed on assets purchased from connected parties (*CAA 2001, s 217*). This rule does not apply where the asset is produced by the seller, unused and sold in the ordinary course of the seller's business (*CAA 2001, s 230*). Connection for these purposes is determined by *ICTA 1988, s 839* (see **4.25**). See **6.54** for common AIA provisions.

COMPUTATION OF CAPITAL ALLOWANCES

The pool

6.32   All qualifying expenditure is pooled in a multi-asset pool. Single asset pools are maintained for non low emission cars costing more than £12,000 (*CAA 2001, s 74*), and short life assets (*CAA 2001, s 86*). The writing down allowance on an expensive car is restricted to £3,000 per annum (pro-rata regulations are anticipated for accounting periods beginning on or after 1 April 2008). A separate asset class pool was maintained for expenditure incurred on long life assets (*CAA 2001, s 101*) prior to 1 April 2008. See **22.4** for an outline plant and machinery capital allowance computation.

Allowances

6.33   Four types of adjustment are made: first year allowance (FYA), annual investment allowance (AIA) (post 1 April 2008), writing down allowance (WDA) and a balancing adjustment (BA). An FYA or an AIA can only be claimed in year of purchase. There is no WDA in the accounting period in which an FYA is claimed (*CAA 2001, s 58(5)*). If an AIA is claimed, a WDA may also be claimed in that accounting period (*CAA 2001, s 58(4A); FA 2008, Sch 24, para 5*). WDAs are claimed annually on a reducing balance basis. The WDA is applied to the unrelieved pool of qualifying expenditure at the beginning of the year adjusted for disposals and additions ,but not additions on which FYA has been claimed. From 1 April 2008 the rate of WDA has been reduced from 25% to 20% (except for ring fence trades; see **3.1**) (*CAA 2001, s 56(1)*).

Disposal proceeds

6.34   When an asset is disposed of the disposal proceeds up to the amount of the original cost are deducted from the asset balance on the expenditure pool. If a positive balance remains after the deduction on a multi asset or long life asset pool the balance continues to be written off on a reducing balance basis, except in the final period of account when it becomes a balancing allowance that may be deducted from chargeable profits. If a negative balance remains on the pool after the deduction this forms a balancing charge, which must be added to the company's assessable profits. In the case of a single asset pool, a positive balance, after the deduction for sale proceeds, is allowed as a deduction from profits as a balance adjustment. A negative balance will become a taxable balancing charge (*CAA 2001, s 55*). If the assets concerned have not been the subject of a capital allowance claim it is not necessary to deduct the disposal proceeds from the pool. This is not the case if the asset was originally acquired from a connected person or by means of a series of transactions between connected persons and any one person has brought the disposal value into account (*CAA 2001, s 64*). The definition of connection follows *ICTA 1988, s 839* (*CAA 2001, s 575*) (see **4.25**). Expenditure on an asset that is partly used for a qualifying activity and partly for other purposes is put into a separate pool. The expenditure is apportioned on a just and reasonable basis and the allowances are reduced accordingly. If the market value of the asset in the pool exceeds that actual pool value by more than £1 million and there is a significant reduction in the value of the asset, the asset is deemed to have been disposed of at market value for the notional trade and reacquired for the purposes of the separate notional trade (*CAA 2001, s 208*).

Example 6.2

The written down value of Sebastian Ltd's plant, after deduction of capital allowances for the year to 31 March 2008, was £6,660.

In July 2008 the company sold an asset for £300 on which capital allowances had been claimed..

The capital allowance claim is as follows:

Capital allowances—plant and machinery:

	Pool £	Allowances £
WDV b/f	6,660	
Sales proceeds—July 2008	−300	
	6,360	
WDA @ 20%	−1,272	1,272
WDV c/f	5,088	

Allowances	1,272

An asset is disposed of if the person who incurred the qualifying expenditure on the plant and machinery:

- ceases to own the plant or machinery; or

- loses possession of the plant or machinery in circumstances where it is reasonable to assume that the loss is permanent.

The asset is also treated as being disposed of if the plant and machinery:

- has been in use for mineral exploration and access and the person abandons it at the site where it was in use for that purpose;

- ceases to exist as such (as a result of destruction, dismantling or otherwise);

- begins to be used wholly or partly for purposes other than those of the qualifying activity;

or if the qualifying activity is permanently discontinued (*CAA 2001, s 61(1)*).

WRITING DOWN ALLOWANCE FROM 1 APRIL 2008

Transitional rate

6.35 For accounting periods which begin before, but ending on or after, 1 April 2008 the rate is calculated according to the following formula:

6.36   *Tangible fixed assets*

$$x = \left(25 \times \frac{BRD}{CP}\right) + \left(20 \times \frac{ARD}{CP}\right)$$

x	rate of writing-down allowance rounded to two decimal places
BRD	number of days in the accounting period prior to 1 April 2008
ARD	number of days in the accounting period on and after the 1 April 2008
CP	number of days in the accounting period

(CAA 2001, s 56(9)–(11))(FA 2008, s 80.)

Example 6.3

The written down value of Transitio Ltd's plant, after deduction of capital allowances for the year to 30 September 2007, was £9,000.

The rate of writing down allowance for the year ended 30 September 2008, to be applied is:

$$x = \left(25 \times \frac{183}{366}\right) + \left(20 \times \frac{183}{366}\right) = 22.5\%$$

The capital allowance claim is as follows:

Capital allowances—plant and machinery:

	Pool £	Allowances £
WDV b/f	9,000	
WDA @ 22.5%	–2,025	2,025
WDV c/f	6,975	
ALLOWANCES		2,025

Short life assets

6.36   Assets that are continuously renewed, such as technology assets, may be placed in a separate short life pool. The company must make an irrevocable election for the asset to be treated as 'short life' within two years of the end of the chargeable period for which the expenditure was incurred (*CAA 2001, s 83(b)*). The asset then remains in the short life pool until the earlier of disposal or the fourth anniversary of the end of the chargeable period in which the asset was acquired. If the asset is disposed of, a balancing charge or a balancing allowance will arise. Alternatively, if unsold, the asset's net book value is transferred back to the main pool (*CAA 2001, s 86*).

For accounting periods which begin before, but end on or after, 1 April 2008, the balance of qualifying expenditure less any disposal receipts may be taken in full as the writing down allowance if this amount is equal or less than the annual small pool limit, introduced at £1,000 (*CAA 2001, s 56A*)(*FA 2008, s 81(3)*).

Long-life assets

6.37 Expenditure on any asset that is plant and machinery and whose expected life is 25 years or more, qualifies for a writing down allowance (*CAA 2001, s 91*). Expenditure incurred before 1 April 2008 was included in a separate pool to which a 6% writing down allowance applied. On 1 April 2008, the balance of this expenditure is to be transferred to the special rate pool, from which time a 10% rate applies. See **6.41** and **6.45**. All expenditure incurred on long life assets on or after 1 April 2008 is added to the special rate pool and now qualifies for a 10% rate. Expenditure on plant, machinery and fixtures in a house, hotel, shop or showroom will not qualify. Nor will expenditure on cars or where the total expenditure on long-life assets for the year is £100,000 or less (*CAA 2001, ss 93, 96, 98*)(*FA 2008, s 83*).

Reduced allowances

6.38 If the chargeable period is less than 12 months (ie if the accounting period is less that 12 months), the writing down allowance and the annual investment allowance are reduced proportionately (but not the first year allowance). A company may reduce or disclaim the allowances for any chargeable period. The tax written down value is carried forward to the next accounting period and will be written down accordingly (*CAA 2001, s 56*).

Assets purchased under hire-purchaser

6.39 The asset is treated as that of the hirer who may claim capital allowances (*CAA 2001, s 67*). The full contract cost is treated as expenditure incurred. The disposal value is the proceeds received, together with any unpaid capital instalments (*CAA 2001, s 68*).

6.40 A company may only claim capital allowances on plant and machinery if the assets belong to the company at some time (*CAA 2001, s 11(4)(b)*).

HMRC consider that, if there is a contractual relationship that states that 'a company may become the owner of the plant or machinery on the performance of the contract' and the purchasing company pays a deposit for plant that is not supplied, it will be able to claim capital allowances under *CAA 2001, s 67(1)(a)*. When the beneficial period ends the company must bring a disposal value into account (HMRC Capital Allowances Manual CA 23350 and Tax Bulletin, Issue 2, February 1992).

SPECIAL RATE EXPENDITURE AND THE SPECIAL RATE POOL

Special rate allowance

6.41   The special rate allowance is applied to the following types of expenditure from 1 April 2008:

● thermal insulation expenditure (see **6.16**);

● integral fixtures (see **6.17**);

● long-life asset (expenditure incurred before 1 April 2008) (see **6.37**);

● long-life asset expenditure incurred on or after 1 April 2008

(*CAA 2001, s 104A; FA 2008, Sch 26.*)

Where there is combined special rate and other expenditure, the amounts of expenditure are apportioned on a just and reasonable basis and only the special rate portion of that expenditure will qualify (*CAA 2001, s 104B; FA 2008, Sch 26, para (2)*).

The special rate expenditure must be allocated to a special rate pool or a single asset pool if it is expenditure of that type (see **6.32**) (*CAA 2001, s 104C*). A 10% rate of writing down allowance is applied to the balance of qualifying expenditure less disposal receipts. The rate is also applied to special rate expenditure that has been allocated to a single asset pool (*CAA 2001, s 104C*).

Disposal value of special rate assets

6.42   If a disposal results from a scheme or arrangement entered into to avoid tax and the actual disposal value is less than the notional written down value, the notional written down value is taken as the disposal value. This is the expenditure incurred less the special rate allowances which the company could have made for this expenditure (*CAA 2001, s 104E*).

Sale between connected persons

6.43 A special rate allowance cannot be claimed on sales and subsequent re-sales of integral features between connected parties, where the buyer incurred the original expenditure before 1 April 2008 or incurred expenditure after that date that was not qualifying. The expenditure will be qualifying if the original expenditure was qualifying expenditure or the buyer's expenditure would have been qualifying had it been incurred at the time the original expenditure was incurred (*FA 2008, Sch 26, para 15*). The definition of connection follows *ICTA 1988, s 839* (*CAA 2001,s 575*); (see **4.25**).

Intra-group transfers

6.44 Group members may elect to transfer integral features, between themselves, at written down value, where the expenditure was incurred before 1 April 2008. If the expenditure is expenditure of a type on which allowances can be claimed, it will be added to the purchasing company's main pool, and not to the special pool (*FA 2008, Sch 26, paras 16 an& 17*). The definition of a group is as for capital gains purposes, see **20.14** and **20.15**.

Existing long-life asset expenditure

6.45 Expenditure on long-life assets that was incurred before 1 April 2008 is to be added to the special rate pool and treated as if it were special rate expenditure. The annual writing down allowance increases from 6% to 10%. The rate for the transitional period covering 1 April 2008 is calculated according to the formula:

$$ x = \left(6 \times \frac{BRD}{CP} \right) + \left(10 \times \frac{ARD}{CP} \right) $$

x	Transitional % rate, rounded to two decimal places.
	Number of days in the accounting period:
BRD	- before the relevant date – 1 April 2008;
ARD	- after the relevant date –1 April 2008;
CP	- the complete period.

Any unrelieved qualifying expenditure in a single asset pool at 1 April 2008 is to be treated as if it were special rate expenditure carried forward in the single asset pool (*CAA 2001, s 104D*) (*FA 2008, Sch 26, para 2*).

Example 6.4

The written down value of Constance Ltd's long-life assets after deduction of capital allowances for the year to 30 September 2008, was £10,000. The company has no other assets on which allowances are claimed.

The rate of writing down allowance to be applied for the year ended 30 September 2008 is:

$$x = \left(6 \times \frac{183}{366}\right) + \left(10 \times \frac{183}{366}\right) = 8\%$$

The special rate allowance claim is as follows:

	Special rate pool £	Allowances £
Expenditure transferred from long-life pool	10,000	
WDA @ 8%	−800	800
WDV c/f	9,200	
Allowances		800

THE ANNUAL INVESTMENT ALLOWANCE 'AIA'

Introduction

6.46   The annual investment allowance 'AIA' replaces the plant and machinery first-year allowance. The maximum annual allowance is £50,000 for expenditure incurred on plant and machinery. Motor cars are not included (*CAA 2001, s 51A(5)*). The £50,000 allowance can be claimed for each 12 month accounting period beginning on or after 1 April 2008 (*FA 2008, Sch 24, para 23(3)*).

Qualifying expenditure retains the meaning adopted for capital allowances, being capital expenditure incurred on the provision of plant and machinery, wholly or partly for the purposes of the qualifying activity carried on by the company that incurs the expenditure. As a result of incurring the expenditure, the company 'owns' the asset (*CAA 2001, s 11(4) as modified by s 11(5) of CAA*) (see **6.5**). AIA is given for a chargeable period, which is the company's accounting period (*CAA 2001, s 6(1)*). If the accounting period is shorter or longer than a year, the maximum AIA is reduced or increased proportionately (*CAA 2001, s 51A(6)*). A company may claim all or part of an AIA (*CAA 2001, s 51A(7)*).

Although the annual investment allowance may be claimed by an individual, a partnership in which all the members are individuals, or a company, a mixed partnership of which the company is a member such as a limited liability partnership may not claim the allowance. Neither may the allowance be claimed by a trust (*CAA 2001, s 38A(3)*). A company is given the same meaning as in *ICTA 1988, s 832(1)* (see **1.4**).

Exclusions

6.47   Certain types of expenditure incurred are excluded from an AIA claim (*CAA 2001, s 38B*),

The expenditure is excluded if it is incurred:

* in an accounting period in which a qualifying activity is permanently discontinued;

* on the provision of a car (as defined below);

* wholly for the purposes of a ring fence trade (see **3.1**);

* in circumstances which are connected with a change in the nature or conduct of a trade or business carried on by a person other than the company incurring the expenditure, and the obtaining of an AIA is the main benefit, or one of the main benefits, which could reasonably be expected to arise from the making of the change;

* on plant not originally purchased for use in the qualifying activity;

* on plant purchased for long funding leasing and gifts.

A car is any mechanically propelled road vehicle that is not primarily used for the conveyance of goods or of a type that is not commonly used as a road vehicle (*CAA 2001, s 81*).

An AIA can also be claimed on pre-trading expenditure incurred on or after 1 April 2008 is included (*CAA 2001, s 38A-(3)*).

AIA CLAIMS

Single companies

6.48   Regardless of the number of activities that a company carries on, it may only claim a single AIA (*CAA 2001, s 51A(1)*).

Example 6.5

Northco Ltd carries on a manufacturing trade and also runs a property rental business. During the 12-month accounting period to 31 March 2009 the company incurred £120,000 on new plant and machinery for the manufacturing trade and £10,000 on plant used in the letting business.

The company decides to allocate its annual investment claim as follows:

Northco Ltd Annual Investment Allowance claim for the year ended 31 March 2009:

AIA	£
Expenditure incurred re	
Manufacturing trade	40,000
Rental business	10,000
Total claim	£50,000

Group companies

6.49   A group of companies is entitled to claim one AIA, which it may allocate to AIA expenditure as it thinks fit, between the companies that incurred the qualifying expenditure (*CAA 2001, s 51C(3)*).

In determining the existence of a group, the definition of a parent undertaking is applied according to the *Companies Act 2006, s 1162* (see **2.53**). Where the conditions are met, a company is treated as another company's parent undertaking for any financial year in which the other company's accounting period ends (*CAA 2001, s 51C (5)*). A financial year commences on 1 April and ends on 31 March.

Group companies and other companies under common control

6.50   Groups of companies and other companies under common control in any financial year are only entitled to one AIA, which they may allocate between them as they see fit (*CAA 2001, s 51D(3), 51E(3)*). Two or more groups of companies are under common control if they are controlled by the same person and are related to one another (*CAA 2001, s 51E(1)*).

A company is controlled by the same person if it is controlled by that person at the end of its chargeable period ending in that financial year (*CAA 2001, s 51F(1)*). Control has the meaning that a person has the power to determine that a company's affairs are conducted in accordance with his wishes (*CAA 2001, s 574(2)*).

Groups of companies and other companies are related to one another if during the financial year, they either share the same premises, or they derive more than 50 per cent of their respective turnovers from qualifying activities, within the same NACE common statistical classification (Nomenclature générale des activités Économiques dans les Communautés européennes). The NACE classification is the first level of the common statistical classification of economic activities in the European Union, established by Regulation (EC) No 1893/2006 of the European Parliament and the Council of 20 December 2006. The meaning of premises is not defined in the Act (*CAA 2001, s 51J*).

Example 6.6

Ashley Ltd has an accounting period ending on 30 April 2009. It had sole occupation of Ashley House, its business premises. On 1 July 2009, Burton Ltd with an accounting period ending on 31 December 2009, moved into Ashley House. Both companies occupied the premises until 31 December 2009. The companies are related during the financial year 2009.

Short chargeable periods

6.51   A company that has been a member of a group for a period of less than one year can only claim a proportionately reduced AIA (*CAA 2001, s 51A(6)*).

Example 6.7

Mr James controls Cuthbert Ltd, Damian Ltd and Eldridge Ltd. All companies have prepared accounts to 31 March 2009. Eldridge Ltd was formed on 1 July 2008. Each company incurs relevant AIA qualifying expenditure of £100,000, but the maximum allowance that could be allocated to Eldridge Ltd is 9/12 of £50,000 = £37,500.

Multiple accounting periods

6.52   If a company has more than one accounting period ending in a financial year, each accounting period must be examined separately in order to determine whether or not the related activities conditions are met (*CAA 2001, s 51L(2)*).

INTERACTION WITH CAPITAL ALLOWANCES

Allowance claims

6.53   A company may not claim an annual investment allowance and a first year allowance in respect of the same expenditure (*CAA 2001, s 52A*).

Example 6.8

Roderick Ltd incurs £100,000 on an item of plant or machinery that appears on the energy technology list, which qualifies for a 100 per cent allowance. Roderick Ltd may either claim energy-saving plant and machinery allowance on the full amount of expenditure incurred, or an AIA of up to £50,000, subject to the company's other expenditure on plant and machinery.

The qualifying expenditure is to be added to and the AIA is deducted from the pool of plant and machinery pool (*CAA 2001, s 58(4A)*) (*FA 2008, Sch 24, para 5*).

Example 6.9

Holbein Ltd is a single company. It incurs £200,000 on qualifying plant and machinery during the accounting period ended 31 March 2009. The value of its pool of qualifying capital expenditure brought forward at 1 April 2008 is £350,000. The adjustment to the pool is as follows:

	Pool of qualifying expenditure		£
1 April 2008	Written down value brought forward		350,000
	Add: qualifying expenditure	200,000	
	Less: AIA	(50,000)	
			150,000
			500,000
	WDA @ 20%		100,000
31 March 2009	Written down value carried forward		£400,000

Common provisions

6.54   There are aspects of the legislation common to first year allowances and the AIA.

- the allowances are to be reduced to a just and reasonable amount, if the expenditure has been incurred for non-business purposes (*CAA 2001, s 205*);

- the allowances are to be reduced if a subsidy is received (*CAA 2001, s 210*);

- no allowance is given for disposals to connected persons, for transactions entered into for avoidance reasons, and in sale and leaseback transactions (*CAA 2001, s 217*);

- any additional VAT liability related to the original expenditure on which an allowance has been claimed is deemed to be incurred at the same time as the expenditure, and will also qualify for the allowance (*CAA 2001, s 236*) (*FA 2008, Sch 24, para 6*).

Finance leasing accounting treatment

6.55   A finance lease is essentially a lending arrangement between two companies. The finance lessor company (the lender) retains ownership of the leased asset. The leased assets are not disclosed as fixed assets on the balance sheet but as a loan, which is normally the cost of the leased asset. The finance lessor's return is interest and loan repayment. Interest is recorded in the profit and loss account as income. Capital repayments reduce the amount of outstanding debt.

Although the finance lessee company (the borrower) does not own the asset it is recorded on the balance sheet as an asset under SSAP 21 (accounting for leases and hire purchase contracts) following the economic substance over form principle of FRS 5. Capital owed to the finance lessor is shown as a creditor. Interest payable is charged to the profit and loss account.

The finance lessee charges depreciation on the asset.

Finance leasing taxation treatment

6.56   Until 1 April 2006, the taxation legislation regarded the finance lessor as owner of the leased assets with entitlement to capital allowances. The lessor could only claim a 25% WDA. No FYA is available. Plant leased to companies not resident in the UK and whose activities are not charged exclusively to UK tax will only qualify for a 10% WDA during the designated period (*CAA 2001, s 105*). The designated period is ten years from the time that the plant and machinery is first brought into use. The equipment is placed in a separate pool.

FA 2006, Sch 8 introduced the concept of long funding leases, which applies with effect from 1 April 2006, or earlier if a written agreement was in place before 21 July 2005. A long funding lease is essentially a lease with a life of more than seven years. The effect being that the lessor company takes the finance element of the rentals arising under the lease as income. The less e company deducts the finance element of the rentals payable over the life of the lease as an expense and will be entitled to capital allowances if it so chooses (*FA 2006, s 81, Sch 8*). The Revenue's guidance is contained in its Business Leasing Manual.

Long funding leases

6.57   The lessor in a plant and machinery long funding lease arrangement is not entitled to capital allowances, but the lessee may be entitled to them (*CAA 2001, s 34A*). The lessee company must report the long-funding lease on its tax return (*CAA 2001, s 70H*).

In brief a 'long funding lease' is a funding lease (see **6.59**) which meets the following conditions:

- it is not a short lease (see **6.58**);

- it is not an excluded lease of background plant or machinery for a building (see **6.62**);

- it is not excluded because it is plant or machinery of a low percentage value leased with land (see **6.63**) (*CAA 2001, s 70G*).

With effect for leases entered into on or after 13 December 2007, if the lessee of any plant and machinery is also the lessor of a long funding lease, both leases are treated as non-funding (*FA 2008, Sch 20, para 8; CAA 2001, s 70H(1A)(1B)*).

Short lease

6.58   A short lease is any lease with a term of five years or less. If the lease term is more than five years but less than seven years the lease is a short lease if the following three conditions A, B and C are met:

Condition A

The lease is one which, under generally accepted accounting practice, falls (or would fall) to be treated as a finance lease.

Condition B

The residual value of the plant or machinery which is implied in the terms of the lease, is not more than 5% of the market value of the plant or machinery at the commencement of the term of the lease, as estimated at the inception of the lease.

Condition C

Under the terms of the lease the total rentals falling due in the 12 months beginning on the day following the commencement of the lease are no greater than 10% or less than the total rentals falling due in the following 12 months and the total rentals falling due in the final year or in any successive 12-month period after the second 12-month period are not greater than 10% of the total rentals falling due in the second12-month period.

If plant and machinery is the subject of a lease and finance leaseback arrangement, it is not a short lease.

(*CAA 2001, s 70I*).

A funding lease

6.59   A 'funding lease' is a plant or machinery lease (see *CAA 2001 s 70K*), which at its inception meets one or more of the following tests:

- the finance lease test—a lease which under GAAP falls to be a finance lease (*CAA 2001, s 70N*);

- the lease payments test—the present value of the minimum lease payments is equal to 80 % or more of the fair value of the assets. The present value is calculated by using the interest rate implicit in the lease (*CAA 2001, s 70O*); and

- the useful economic life test—the term of the lease is more than 65 % of the remaining useful economic life of the asset. The remaining useful economic life is the period beginning with the commencement of the term of the lease and ending when the asset is no longer used and no longer likely to be used by any person for any purpose as a fixed asset of the business (*CAA 2001, ss 70, 70P*).

The minimum lease payments are the minimum lease payments over the entire term of the lease after deducting minimum amounts such as VAT and any residual amount at fair value reasonably expected to be recovered by the lessor at the end of the lease (*CAA 2001, s 70YE*).

A non-funding lease

6.60   A non-funding lease is outside of the scope of the new regime and may be treated as belonging to the hirer (*CAA 2001, s 70J(3)*). A lease is not a funding lease if prior to the commencement of the term of the lease the relevant asset has been leased under one or more other leases, the aggregate terms of which exceed 65% of the remaining useful economic life of the asset at the commencement term of the lease, provided none of the earlier leases was itself a funding lease (*CAA 2001, s 70J(4)*).

A lease is not a long funding lease of the lessor if prior to 1 April 2006 the asset had been leased out under one or more leases for an aggregate period of at least 10 years and the lessor was also the lessor of the asset on the last day before 1 April 2006 (*CAA 2001, s 70J(6)*).

Anti–avoidance

6.61   This anti-avoidance provision aims to allocate all a lessor's receipts to income. Any receipt not already included in income, which the provision terms as a 'capital payment' will be included in the lessor''s accounts as lease income of the accounting period, in which the payment is made.

Where there is an unconditional obligation to make a 'capital payment', the lessor is treated as receiving lease income of the same amount in the accounting period, in which the obligation arises. A deduction may be claimed in the accounts, if it is expected that the amount will not actually be paid (*ICTA 1988, ss 785B and785E*) (*FA 2008, Sch 20, para 1*).

Background plant and machinery

6.62   Background plant and machinery contributes to the functionality of the building. Plant and machinery leased with a building is excluded from the funding lease regime and is of the following type (*CAA 2001, s 70R*):

(a)   heating and air-conditioning installations;

(b)   ceilings which are part of an air-conditioning system;

(c)   hot water installations;

(d)   electrical installations that provide power to a building, such as high and low voltage switchgear, all sub-mains distribution systems and standby generators;

(e) mechanisms, including automatic control systems, for opening and closing doors, windows and vents;

(f) escalators and passenger lifts;

(g) window cleaning installations;

(h) fittings such as fitted cupboards, blinds, curtains and associated mechanical equipment;

(i) demountable partitions;

(j) protective installations such as lightning protection, sprinkler and other equipment for containing or fighting fires, fire alarm systems and fire escapes; and

(k) building management systems.

The following types of plant or machinery are deemed to be background plant or machinery:

(a) lighting installations including all fixed light fittings and emergency lighting systems;

(b) telephone, audio-visual and data installations incidental to the occupation of the building;

(c) computer networking facilities incidental to the occupation of the building;

(d) sanitary appliances and other bathroom fittings including hand driers, counters, partitions, mirrors, shower and locker facilities;

(e) kitchen and catering facilities for producing and storing food and drink for the occupants of the building;

(f) fixed seating;

(g) signs;

(h) public address systems; and

(i) intruder alarm systems and other security equipment including surveillance equipment.

The following descriptions of plant or machinery are deemed not to be background plant or machinery:

(a) storing, moving or displaying goods to be sold in the course of a trade, whether wholesale or retail;

(b) manufacturing goods or materials;

(c) subjecting goods or materials to a process;

(d)   storing goods or materials—

   (i)   which are to be used in the manufacture of other goods or materials;

   (ii)   which are to be subjected, in the course of a trade, to a process;

   (iii) which, having been manufactured or produced or subjected in the course of a trade to a process, have not yet been delivered to any purchaser; or

   (iv)   on their arrival in the United Kingdom from a place outside the United Kingdom (*SI 2007/303*).

Plant and machinery leased with land: low percentage value

6.63   An exclusion applies to low percentage value plant and machinery leased with land where:

- the plant and machinery is affixed to the building or otherwise installed on the land;

- the plant and machinery is not background plant and machinery for any building situated in or on the land; and

- the plant or machinery is leased with the land under a mixed lease, the sole purpose of which is to secure a tax advantage.

In these circumstances, the lease is not a long funding lease if the AMV does not exceed both 5% of the market value of the land (including fixtures and fittings) and 10% of the aggregate value of the background plant and machinery (*CAA 2001, s 70U*). The AMV is the aggregate of the relevant plant and machinery and the market value of all other plant and machinery leased with the land.

Change of company ownership

6.64   It follows, that through the benefit of capital allowances, a lessor company's profits chargeable to corporation tax will be lower in the earlier years of the leasing contract than in the later years. Where there is a change of ownership of a single company, group company (see **10.5**), consortium company (see **10.6**) or changes in a company's partnership share of an interest in a business the available loss relief is restricted, with effect from 5 December 2005.

For corporation tax purposes an accounting period ends and a new accounting period commences on the date of the change. On the date of the exchange an adjustment is calculated which is treated as income for the accounting period prior to the change and as an expense of the accounting period post the change. If the expense adjustment in the second period results in a Schedule D Case I loss that loss is not available for set off under *ICTA 1988, s 393A(1)(b)* (see **9.11**).

For these purposes a company is considered to be a lessor company or carrying on a leasing business if at least half the accounting value of the plant is 'qualifying leased plant' or machinery or that at least half of the company's income in the period of 12 months ending with the date of the change derives from qualifying leased plant or machinery (*FA 2006, Sch 10, para 6*). Qualifying leased plant and machinery is plant and machinery bought wholly or partly for the purposes of the business, on which the company is entitled to plant and machinery capital allowances and which is leased at any time during the 12 months prior to the date of the change. Plant and machinery in let buildings owned by a property investment company does not fall into this category.

The accounting value of the leased plant and machinery is the company's leased plant and machinery at balance sheet net book value plus the net book value of any plant and machinery transferred to it by an associated company at the date of the change (*FA 2006, Sch 10, para 7*). An associated company is defined according to *ICTA 1988, s 416 (1)* (see **4.27**).

The adjustment that is to be made is calculated according to the formula:

PM – TWDV

PM	=	The amount of plant and machinery and the net investment in finance leases shown on the balance sheet at the date of the change for the company itself and its associates.
TWDV	=	The total of the tax written down value of the single asset pools, the class pools and the main pool at the start of the relevant accounting period following the date of the change.

If the result is negative it is assumed to be NIL.

(*FA 2006, Sch 10, paras 16–19*).

Example 6.10

Ludwig plc prepares accounts to 31 December each year. On I July 2008 the company is entirely taken over by Frank plc. At 30 June 2008 the balance sheet shows net investment in leased assets of £1,200 m. The same assets have a tax written down net book value of £640 m.

For corporation tax purposes Ludwig plc:

(i) has two accounting periods, the six months to 30 June 2008 and the 6 months to 31 December 2008.

(ii) the required adjustment is £(1,200 – 640)m = £560m

(iii) If the expense adjustment in the period to 31 December 2008 results in a loss, Ludwig will not be able to utilise that loss in an *ICTA 1988, s393A(1)(b)* claim.

These rules will continue to apply where there is a transfer of trade under *ICTA 1988, s 343 (FA 2007, Sch 6)*.

INDUSTRIAL BUILDINGS ALLOWANCES

Construction of an industrial building or structure

6.65   For many years a company was able to claim an industrial buildings allowance (IBA) if it had incurred expenditure on the construction of a building or structure. This allowance is being withdrawn over the period from 2008–09 until 2010–11.Until that time a transitional allowance may be claimed (see 6.75). IBAs are completely withdrawn for expenditure incurred on or after 1 April 2011 (*FA 2008, s 84*). In order to claim the allowance, the company must actually incur the expenditure. The expenditure cannot be covered directly or indirectly by a third party. In order to qualify the building or structure must be:

● in use for the purposes of a qualifying trade;

● a qualifying hotel;

● a qualifying sports pavilion; or

● a commercial building in a qualifying enterprise zone,

and the expenditure must be qualifying (*CAA 2001, s 271*).

As a result of incurring the expenditure the company must have the relevant interest in the building (*CAA 2001, s 286*).

HMRC acknowledge that there is no definition of a building within the industrial buildings legislation, and will treat anything with four walls and a roof as a building, provided it is of a reasonably substantial size. Something that is too small or insubstantial will be a structure (HMRC Capital Allowances Manual CA 31050). A structure is artificially erected or constructed and is distinct from the earth surrounding it (HMRC Capital Allowances Manual CA 31110) and roads, car parks which have a hard concrete or asphalt surface, concrete surfacing, tunnels and culverts, walls, bridges, aqueducts, dams, hard tennis courts and fences would qualify as such.

Qualifying trade

6.66   A list of qualifying trades is given in Table A of *CAA 2001, s 274(1)* and consists of the following:

1	Manufacturing	A trade consisting of the manufacturing of goods or materials.
2	Processing	A trade consisting of subjecting goods or materials to a process. This includes subject to *s 276(3)* maintaining or repairing goods or materials.
3	Storage	A trade consisting of storing goods or materials:

		(a)	which are to be used in the manufacture of other goods or materials,
		(b)	which are to be subjected in the course of a trade to a process,
		(c)	which having been manufactured or produced or subjected in the course of a trade to a process, have not yet been delivered to any purchaser, or
		(d)	on their arrival in the UK from a place outside the UK.

4	Agricultural contracting	

		(a)	Ploughing or cultivating land occupied by another person, or
		(b)	carrying out any other agricultural operation on land occupied by another person, or
		(c)	threshing the crops or vegetables of another person.

5	Working foreign plantations	A trade consisting of working land outside the UK used for:

		(a)	growing and harvesting of crops and vegetables;
		(b)	husbandry, or
		(c)	forestry.

6	Fishing	A trade consisting of catching or taking fish or shellfish.

7	Mineral extraction	A trade consisting of working a source of mineral deposits. Mineral deposits include any natural deposits capable of being lifted or extracted from the earth and for this purpose geothermal energy is to be treated as a natural deposit. 'Source of mineral deposits' includes a mine, an oil well and a source of geothermal energy.

Manufacturing

6.67 Manufacturing includes the making of articles and the assembly of component parts made elsewhere (HMRC Capital Allowances Manual CA 32210). Cold storage premises that contained ice-making machinery and plant were held to be an industrial building (*Ellerker v Union Cold Storage Co Ltd; Thomas Borthwick & Sons Ltd v Compton* (1938) 22 TC 195).

Goods and materials

6.68 Goods and materials are understood to be raw goods and materials. In *Girobank plc v Clarke* (1997) 70 TC 387, [1998] STC 182, [1998] 1 WLR 942, [1998] 4 All ER 312 the bank's processing of cheques and credit card slips was not a qualifying trade. Cheques and credit card slips are not within the definition of goods and services.

Similar decisions were made in *Buckingham v Securitas Properties Ltd* (1979) 53 TC 292, [1980] STC 166, [1980] 1 WLR 380 regarding coins or notes used as currency, in *Bourne v Norwich Crematorium Ltd* (1967) 44 TC 164, [1967] 1 WLR 691, [1967] 2 All ER 576 regarding human remains and in *Carr v Sayer & Sayer* (1992) 65 TC 15, [1992] STC 396 with respect to dogs and cats.

Subject to a process

6.69 In *Kilmarnock Equitable Co-Operative Society Ltd v CIR* (1966) 42 TC 675, [1966] TR 185 a building in which coal was screened and packed qualified as an industrial building. In *Vibroplant Ltd v Holland* (1981) 54 TC 658, [1982] 1 All ER 792 IBA was claimed on a building used to repair individual plant hire items when not being hired to customers. The activity was not considered to be a process because the items were treated individually. Repairing goods or materials is now treated as a process unless the person who repairs the goods or materials uses them in a non-qualifying trade (*CAA 2001, s 276(3)*).

Bestway (Holdings) Ltd v Luff (1998) 70 TC 512, [1998] STC 357 claimed IBA on its cash and carry wholesale store. The claim was refused because the checking, unpacking and labelling of goods was not considered to be a process and the goods were not retained for sufficient time to qualify for storage.

Storage

6.70   The trade of storage particularly refers to storage of goods for manufacture or process or goods manufactured or processed but not yet delivered to customers and includes imports (*CAA 2001, s 274*).

A company examined, selected and graded used tyre casings, which it sold on for remoulding. It used a building for storage of the items that were only delivered to customers in small batches. The building qualified as an industrial building (*Crusabridge Investments Ltd v Casings International Ltd* (1979) 54 TC 246).

The storage of goods on their arrival in the UK refers to their immediate storage. In *Copol Clothing Ltd v Hindmarsh* (1983) 57 TC 575, [1984] STC 33, [1984] 1 WLR 411 an IBA claim on a Manchester warehouse was refused because the building was the goods' ultimate place of storage. HMRC considers that a building will qualify for an IBA for storage of goods when they first enter the country if the following conditions are satisfied:

- the goods have been imported;

- the goods are being stored for the first time since their arrival in the UK; and

- the goods are still in transit—that is they have not yet arrived at their final destination in the UK (HMRC Capital Allowances Manual CA 32224).

In *Revenue and Customs Comrs v Maco Door & Window Hardware (UK) Ltd* [2006] EWHC 1832 (Ch) the company, a UK subsidiary of an Austrian company, claimed industrial buildings allowance on a warehouse. The warehouse was used to house goods such as door locks and door handles, which were manufactured by the Austrian company and stored in the warehouse while awaiting sale to wholesalers and to manufacturers of doors and windows in the UK. The company contended that it carried on a trade of storage. The court held that the company's trade was that of import and sale of doors and windows hardware. Storage was part of that trade. The industrial buildings allowance claim was refused.

Expenditure on which IBAs are available

6.71   IBAs are not given on the cost of land. Where repairs to an industrial building qualify as capital expenditure IBAs are given to that part as if it were a new construction at that time (*CAA 2001, s 272*). IBAs are given on the preparation of a site for building or for the installation of plant and machinery (if not allowed elsewhere).

Qualifying expenditure consists of the following:

- capital expenditure on the construction of a building;
- the purchase of an unused building without developer involvement;
- the purchase of an unused building from a developer;
- the purchase of a used building from a developer (*CAA 2001, s 292*).

IBAs are based on the cost of construction if the company erects the building (*CAA 2001, s 294*). HMRC regards the following expenditure as forming part of the cost of the building on which an IBA is available:

- expenditure on capital repairs (*CAA 2001, s 272(2), (3)*);
- demolition costs of the old building making way to erect a new building if these costs have not already been taken into account in calculating a balancing adjustment on the old building;
- professional fees relating to the design and construction of a building provided that the building is actually constructed (HMRC Capital Allowances Manual CA 31400).

Land preparation costs, including cutting, tunnelling or levelling land in readiness for the installation of plant and machinery, will qualify for an IBA if there are no other allowances available on that expenditure (*CAA 2001, s 273*).

HMRC does not consider that the following items of expenditure can be included within the cost of a building for IBA purposes:

- the cost of obtaining planning permission, except where included in the builder's quotation;
- capitalised interest;
- the cost of a public enquiry;
- the cost of land drainage and reclamation;
- landscaping;
- legal expenses;
- abortive expenditure.

These items do not qualify for IBA (HMRC Capital Allowances Manuals CA 31400 and CA 31410).

If the company decides to sell the building without bringing it into use the new purchaser can claim IBAs on the lower of purchase price and construction cost (*CAA 2001, s 295*). If the company buys an unused building from a property developer it can claim IBAs on the purchase price (*CAA 2001, s 296*).

If the company buys a used building from a developer, ie one on which IBAs have already been claimed, the company claims IBAs as the second user (*CAA 2001, s 297*). IBAs are not available on the cost of land (*CAA 2001, s 272(1)*). If the building is purchased with other assets the expenditure should be apportioned between the qualifying and non-qualifying assets on a just and reasonable basis (*CAA 2001, s 356*).

A dwelling house, a retail shop, or premises similar to a retail shop where retail trade or business (including repair work) is carried on, a showroom, a hotel or an office do not qualify for IBA (*CAA 2001, s 277(1)*). An office that forms part of the manufacturing process will qualify for IBA, such as a drawing office in the case of *CIR v Lambhill Ironworks Ltd* (1950) 31 TC 393. An 'industrial building' may have a non-industrial part such as an office. If the non-industrial part consists of 25% or less of the total cost of the building, allowances are given on the total cost of the building. If the non-industrial parts are more than 25% of the total cost, the allowances are only given on the industrial part. A drawing office in a factory qualifies as industrial usage. Staff welfare buildings in a qualifying trade will qualify for IBA (*CAA 2001, s 275*).

Hotels

6.72   A qualifying hotel has to be a permanent building, which is open during the year for at least four months during April to October. When the hotel is let during April to October:

- it must have ten or more letting bedrooms,

- the sleeping accommodation that it offers consists wholly or mainly of letting bedrooms, and

- the services provided for guests normally include the provision of breakfast and an evening meal, the making of beds and the cleaning of rooms (*CAA 2001, s 279(1)*).

Initial allowance

6.73   Initial allowances may no longer be claimed except on buildings in an enterprise zone where a 100% allowance is available. A list of enterprise zones can be found in HMRC Capital Allowances Manual CA 37600.

IBAs writing down allowance (WDA)

6.74   WDAs were, until the financial year beginning 1 April 2008, given at a rate of 4% per annum on a straight line basis on the assumption that the building had a tax life of 25 years (*CAA 2001, s 310*). The 4% allowance is now reduced by specified percentages during the transitional period from 1 April 2008 to 31 March 2011. Buildings in an enterprise zone continue to qualify for a straight line 25% WDA.

Transitional period

6.75   With the exception of qualifying enterprise zone expenditure, the writing down allowance claimed on an industrial building during the transitional period is reduced by the following formula:

If the whole of the accounting period falls within a financial year,

WDA × P

WDA	writing-down allowance subject to reduction
P	Specified percentage in relation to that year.

If the accounting periods spans financial years the transitional allowance is calculated by apportioning the writing-down allowance for each financial year in which the accounting period falls, and adding the amounts so calculated.

The apportioned writing-down allowance for a financial year in which part of a transitional chargeable period falls is:

$$\frac{DCPY}{DCP} \times WDA \times P$$

DCPY	number of days in the accounting period which fall in that year
DCP	number of days in the accounting period
WDA	writing-down allowance subject to reduction
P	Specified percentage in relation to that year

The specified percentage for the financial year is as follows:

Financial year beginning 1 April 2007 and earlier financial years	100%
Financial year beginning 1 April 2008	75%
Financial year beginning 1 April 2009	50%
Financial year beginning 1 April 2010	25%

Financial year beginning 1 April 2011 and later years   0%

(*FA 2008, s 85*).

Example 6.11

Sebastian Ltd's factory was built in December 1999 at a cost of £90,000. The company prepares accounts to 30 September each year. The annual writing down allowance available until 1 April 2008 was 4%. From 1 April 2008 the transitional annual available writing down allowance is calculated as follows:

£

Accounting Period ended 30 September 2008

Financial year beginning 1 April 2007

$\frac{366}{183}$ × £3,600 × 100%   1,800

Financial year beginning 1 April 2008

$\frac{366}{183}$ × £3,600 × 75%   1,350

Total allowances   £3,150

Accounting Period ended 30 September 2009

Financial year beginning 1 April 2008

$\frac{366}{183}$ × £3,600 × 75%   1,350

Financial year beginning 1 April 2009

$\frac{366}{183}$ × £3,600 × 50%   900

Total allowances   £2,250

Accounting Period ended 30 September 2010

Financial year beginning 1 April 2009

$\frac{366}{183}$ × £3,600 × 50%   900

Financial year beginning 1 April 2010

$\frac{366}{183}$ × £3,600 × 25%   450

Total allowances   £1,350

Accounting Period ended 30 September 2011

Financial year beginning 1 April 2010

$$\frac{366}{183} \times £3,600 \times 25\% \qquad\qquad\qquad\qquad 450$$

Financial year beginning 1 April 2011

$$\frac{366}{183} \times £3,600 \times 0\% \qquad\qquad\qquad\qquad 0$$

Total allowances $\qquad\qquad\qquad\qquad\qquad\qquad$ £450

Qualifying enterprise zone expenditure: transitional provision

6.76   Where a 100% initial allowance on enterprise zone expenditure has not or has only partially been claimed, a straight-line writing down allowance on cost is available until 1 April 2011.

For an accounting period which begins before, and ends on or after, 1 April 2011, the company's entitlement to a writing-down allowance is calculated according to the following formula:

$$\frac{DCPB}{DCP} \times WDA$$

DCPB   number of days in the accounting period before
                1 April 2011, the relevant date

DCP   number of days in the accounting period

WDA   writing-down allowance subject to reduction

(FA 2008, s 86.)

Example 6.12

Investico Ltd bought a factory in an enterprise zone on 1 May 2008 for £100,000, which qualified for a writing down allowance. The annual available writing down allowances are calculated as follows:

	£
Accounting Period ended 30 September 2008	
WDA available in full	25,000
Accounting Period ended 30 September 2009	
WDA available in full	25,000
Accounting Period ended 30 September 2010	
WDA available in full	25,000
Accounting Period ended 30 September 2011	
$\dfrac{183 \times £25,000}{366}$	12,500

Anti-avoidance

6.77   The buyer's writing down allowance is subject to reduction if:

- a purchase of a relevant interest is made from a connected party on or after 12 March 2008;

- both buyer and seller have different accounting periods;

- the purpose, or one of the main purposes, of the sale is for the buyer to obtain a tax advantage.

Parties are connected where one party has control of the other or both are under the same control (*CAA 2001, s 567*). Purchases made on or after 12 March 2008 in pursuance of a pre-commencement contract are not affected. A pre-commencement contract is an unconditional contract made up in writing before 12 March 2008 or if conditional, its conditions have been satisfied before 12 March 2008. In addition no terms remain to be agreed on or after 12 March 2008 and the contract is not varied in a significant way on or after that date (*FA 2008, s 87; CAA 2001, s 313A*).

Where restricted, the buyer's writing-down allowance is calculated as follows:

$$\frac{DI}{CP} \times WDA$$

where—

D1   number of days in the accounting period for which the buyer is entitled to the relevant interest

CP	number of days in the accounting period
WDA	writing-down allowance subject to reduction

Example 6.13

In pursuance of a tax advantage, Azron Ltd bought a building from Bulldozer Ltd on 12 March 2008. Both companies are owned and controlled by John Bulldog. The building qualifies an annual writing down allowance of £10,000. Azron Ltd prepares accounts to 31 March each year.

Azron Ltd's writing-down allowance for the accounting period ended 31 March 2008 is calculated as follows:

$$20 \times \frac{£3,660}{366} = £200$$

With effect from 12 March 2008 onwards, where the whole or part of a trade is transferred from one company to another, the sole purpose of which is to obtain a balancing allowance, no balancing allowance is due (*FA 2008, s 89; CAA 2001, s 343ZA*).6.78

6.78 For the allowance to be given, the building must be in use as an industrial building at the end of the chargeable period (*CAA 2001, s 309*).

If the building is not in industrial use at the end of the year, no WDA is given to the company. However, a notional WDA reduces the tax written down value of the building, because in effect its 25-year life is expiring. If the chargeable period is more or less than one year, the allowance is adjusted proportionately. No adjustment is made if the building was acquired during the chargeable period.

Temporary disuse

6.79 A period of temporary disuse is ignored (*CAA 2001, s 285*). Temporary disuse infers that the building is to be used for an industrial purpose, but there has been a short break in activities and industrial use is to be resumed.

The building must have been in use as an industrial building immediately before the period of temporary disuse. The legislation states no time limit for the temporary disuse unless the building was a qualifying hotel. A qualifying hotel, which becomes temporarily disused, is treated as a qualifying hotel for two years after the end of the chargeable period in which the temporary disuse begins but for no longer.

HMRC will accept that a building is temporarily disused if it is capable of being used at all. It need not be capable of being used for a qualifying trade, but if it is not capable of further use for any purpose it is not temporarily disused. If a company breaks its manufacturing pattern and moves into another qualifying trade, this is clearly a period of temporary disuse.

If the building is left to deteriorate or left empty prior to development or demolition, this is not a period of temporary disuse and any IBA claims will be rejected.

A claim made in good faith for a period of disuse may be made only to find that the disuse becomes permanent. Earlier claims will remain although no further claims can be made once it is known that the building has no further use (HMRC Capital Allowances Manual CA 32800).

Example 6.14

Marmaduke Ltd prepares accounts to 31 March each year. The company incurs expenditure on 1 June 2005 of £100,000, which qualifies for IBAs. The building is used throughout as an industrial building except for the period 1 June 2007 to 31 May 2008. The available industrial buildings allowances (assuming the 4% WDA rate continues) are as follows:

		£	Allowances
Year ending 31 March 2006			
Expenditure		100,000	
	WDA (4%)	4,000	4,000
		96,000	
Year ending 31 March 2007	WDA (4%)	4,000	4,000
		92,000	
Year ending 31 March 2008	Notional WDA (4%)	4,000	4,000
		88,000	
Year ending 31 March 2009	WDA (4%) x 75%	4,000	3,000
		84,000	

191

Disposal of an industrial building

Post-21 March 2007 regime

6.80   The available industrial buildings allowance has worked on the premise that a building has a 25-year tax life. Until 21 March 2007, if a building were sold before the 25-year life had expired a balancing event was deemed to occur and it was necessary to calculate a balancing adjustment on sale and to recalculate the industrial buildings allowance for the new purchaser. From 21 March 2007 balancing adjustments were withdrawn and instead the new purchaser takes over the balance of the expenditure known as the residue of qualifying expenditure (RQE).

Exceptions from the post-21 March 2007 regime

6.81   The pre-21 March 2007 regime is withdrawn except in respect of balancing events arising in the following two cases:

(i)   on qualifying enterprise zone expenditure or

(ii)   in pursuance of a relevant pre-commencement contract.

For details of qualifying enterprise zones see HMRC Capital Allowances Manual CA 37600.

For this purpose a relevant pre-commencement contract is a written contract drawn up before 21 March 2007. The contract is unconditional or its conditions have been satisfied before 21 March 2007 and no terms remain to be agreed on or after that date. In addition, the contract is not varied in a significant way on or after 21 March 2007. The balancing event in order to qualify for the pre-21 March 2007 treatment must take place before 1 April 2011 (*FA 2007, s 36*).

Pre-21 March 2007 regime

6.82   These rules apply to all sales prior to 21 March 2007 and to the exceptions detailed in **6.60** above. If a building is sold before the expiry of its 25-year life and it has been used as an industrial building throughout its life, the lesser of the sale proceeds and the cost for IBA purposes is deducted from the tax written down value that is known for these purposes as the 'residue before sale' to give rise to a balancing event. If the proceeds are less than the residue before sale a balancing allowance arises, which is deductible from profits. If the sale proceeds are more than the residue before sale a balancing charge arises that is added to profits chargeable to corporation tax. The balancing charge is restricted to the amount of the allowances actually given.

If a building is sold before the expiry of the 25-year life that has not been used throughout as an industrial building and it is sold for less than cost then the balancing allowance is the difference between the adjusted net cost of the building and the allowances actually given.

The adjusted net cost is calculated by the formula:

$(S - P) \times (I \div R)$

where:

S = original expenditure

P = sale proceeds

I = the period of industrial use

R = the total period of use

(*CAA 2001, s 323*)

If the building is sold for more than cost the balancing charge amounts to the allowances actually given (*CAA 2001, s 319(5)*).

The purchaser of the building is able to claim IBAs on the residue of qualifying expenditure for the remainder of the building's 25-year life according to the following formula:

$RQE \times (A \div B)$

where:

RQE = the amount of the residue of qualifying expenditure after sale

A = length of chargeable period

B = length of the period from the date of sale to the end of the building's tax life

(*CAA 2001, s 311*)

Example 6.15

Pre-21 March 2007 regime Herbert Ltd prepares accounts to 31 December each year. The company bought a new factory on 31 August 1997 for £100,000. On 1 January 2007, the company entered into a contract for the sale of the building to Maximillus Ltd. The contract was in writing and no changes were made until the eventual sale went through on 1 October 2007. Herbert Ltd and Maximillius Ltd have therefore entered into a pre-sale contract and the pre-21 March 2007 regime applies. The sale price is assumed to be (i) £90,000, (ii) £3,000, (iii) £120,000. Maximillius Ltd prepares accounts to 31 March each year.

Herbert Ltd

		(i)	(ii)	(iii)
		£	£	£
1 September 1997	Cost	100,000	100,000	100,000
Year ending 31 December 1997 to year ending 31 December 2006	WDA (4%) = £4,000 per annum for 10 years	(40,000)	(40,000)	(40,000)
	Residue before sale	60,000	60,000	60,000
1 October 2007	Proceeds	(90,000)	(3,000)	(120,000)
Year ending 31 December 2007	Balancing charge	(30,000)		(60,000)
	Balancing allowance		57,000	
	But restricted to allowances given			(40,000)

Maximillius Ltd

Maximillius Ltd obtains a transitional writing down allowance.

		(i)	(ii)	(iii)
		£	£	£
	Residue after sale (workings below)	90,000	3,000	100,000
Year ending 31 March 2008 (and transitional allowances available for a further three years)	WDA Residue × 1/15	6,000	200	6,667

At 31 August 2007 the building has a remaining life of 15 years.

Calculation of residue after sale

	(i)	(ii)	(iii)
	£	£	£
Residue before sale	60,000	60,000	60,000
+ balancing charge	30,000	0	40,000
– balancing allowance	0	(57,000)	0
Residue after sale	90,000	3,000	100,000

Example 6.16

Post-21 March 2007 regime

Herbert Ltd prepares accounts to 31 December each year. The company bought a new factory on 31 August 1997 for £100,000, which it sold to Maximillus Ltd on 1 October 2007. The sale price is assumed to be (i) £90,000, (ii) £3,000, (iii) £120,000. Maximillius Ltd prepares accounts to 31 March each year.

Herbert Ltd

		(i)	(ii)	(iii)
		£	£	£
1 September 1997	Cost	100,000	100,000	100,000
Year ending 31 December 1997 to year ending 31 December 2006	WDA (4%) = £4,000 per annum for 10 years	(40,000)	(40,000)	(40,000)
	Residue before sale	60,000	60,000	60,000

Neither a balancing charge nor a balancing allowance is calculated.

Maximillius Ltd

A full writing down allowance is available for the year ended 31 March 2008 and a transitional allowance for the next three years as follows:

		(i)	(ii)	(iii)
		£	£	£
	Residue after sale (understood to be the residue before sale)	60,000	60,000	60,000
Year ending 31 March 2008	WDA (4%)	4,000	4,000	4,000
Year ending 31 March 2009	WDA (4%) × 75%	3,000	3,000	3,000
Year ending 31 March 2010	WDA (4%) × 50%	2,000	2,000	2,000
Year ending 31 March 2011	WDA (4%) × 25%	1,000	1,000	1,000
Year ending 31 March 2012	WDA (4%) × 0%			

At 31 August 2007 the building has a remaining life of 15 years.

Fixtures qualifying for plant and machinery allowances

6.83   Although IBAs have been abolished, companies may still claim plant and machinery allowances on fixtures that were subject to a previous IBA. The maximum amount of claim is determined by the formula:

$$\frac{F \times R}{T}$$

F	Part of the consideration attributable to the fixture
T	Total consideration for that transfer
R	Residue of qualifying expenditure 'RQE' attributable to the relevant interest after sale on the assumption that all the RQE were sold

If the total consideration is less than the frozen RQE then the relief is restricted to the RQE (*CAA 2001, s 186; FA 2008, Sch 27, para 5*).

Example 6.17

Francis Ltd sold an industrial building on 1 January 2009, for £200,000. The residue of expenditure after sale amounted to £100,000, of which £20,000 was attributable to fixtures that qualified for plant and machinery allowances.

Francis Ltd may claim a plant and machinery allowance based on a calculated cost of:

$$\frac{20,000 \times 100,000}{200,000} = £10,000$$

Successions

6.84   Where the whole of a trade is transferred to another company under *ICTA 1988, s 343* without a change of ownership, the successor takes over the predecessor's assets at tax written down value for capital allowance purposes.

Enterprise zones

6.85   A balancing charge may still arise in respect of qualifying enterprise zone expenditure on a building on which a qualifying enterprise zone allowance has been claimed if the building is disposed of within seven years after first being brought into use (*FA 2008, Sch 27, para 31*).

Example

Jojohnson Ltd bought a building in an enterprise zone which was first used on 1 December 2010 and on which it claimed an initial allowance for the accounting period ended 31 March 2011. The relevant interest in the building is sold on 1 October 2016. Any balancing event that would have given rise to a balancing charge (and only a balancing charge) will result in a balancing charge being made.

BUSINESS PREMISES RENOVATION ALLOWANCES

Introduction

6.86   A company that incurs qualifying expenditure (**6.87**) on the conversion of a qualifying building (**6.89**) to qualifying business premises (**6.91**) or

197

incurs qualifying expenditure on the renovation of a qualifying building may be entitled to business premises renovation allowances if all conditions are satisfied (*CAA 2001, s 360A*). The company incurring the expenditure must have a relevant interest in the building. If that company acquires an interest after incurring the expenditure it will be treated as having the interest when the expenditure was incurred (*CAA 2001, s 360F*). The allowances are given as receipts or expenses of the trade or property income (*CAA 2001, s 360Z–s 360Z1*).

Qualifying expenditure

6.87   Qualifying expenditure is capital expenditure on the conversion or renovation of the qualifying building into qualifying business premises. Repair work to a qualifying building or repairs incidental to the conversion or renovation work is also included. The expenditure must be incurred before 11 April 2012 being the fifth anniversary of the appointed day. The appointed day has now been set as 11 April 2007 (*the Business Premises Renovation Allowances Regulations, SI 2007/945*).

Non-qualifying expenditure

6.88   Certain types of expenditure do not qualify for the business premises renovation allowance. This includes expenditure on:

- the acquisition of land or rights in or over land;
- the extension of a qualifying building (except to the extent required for the purpose of providing a means of getting to or from qualifying business premises);
- the development of land adjoining or adjacent to a qualifying building; or
- the provision of plant and machinery, unless it is or becomes a legally recognised fixture of the building within *CAA 2001, s 173(1)(a)*.

(*CAA 2001, s 360B(3)*)

Building repair expenditure not available for relief against the profits of a property business, or of a trade, profession or vocation, for tax purposes is treated as capital expenditure (*CAA 2001, s 360B(4)*).

A qualifying building

6.89   To be a qualifying building, the following conditions must be met at the date on which the conversion or renovation work begins. The building itself can be any building or structure, or part of a building or structure. The conditions are that the building:

- is situated in a designated disadvantaged area;

- was unused throughout the period of one year ending immediately before the date on which the conversion or renovation work began;

- had last been used:

  — for the purposes of a trade, profession or vocation; or

  — as an office or offices (whether or not for the purposes of a trade, profession or vocation);

- had not last been used as, or as part of, a dwelling; and

- in the case of part of a building or structure, on that date had not last been occupied; and

is used in common with any other part of the building or structure other than a part that was unused for a year before that date or which had last been used as a dwelling.

(*CAA 2001, s 360C*)

A disadvantaged area

6.90   A disadvantaged area is determined in accordance with Treasury regulations or in their absence in accordance with the designated disadvantaged areas for the purposes of the Stamp Duty disadvantaged areas relief (*FA 2003, Sch 6*), although this relief has now been withdrawn. See HMRC website Stamp Taxes section for the list of disadvantaged areas and the postcode search tool. If a building is partly situated in a disadvantaged area a just and reasonable apportionment of the expenditure will be made.

Qualifying business premises

6.91   Business premises can be any building or structure or part of a building or structure (*CAA 2001, s 360D(2)*), but must be a qualifying building (see **6.89**). The premises must be used or be available and suitable for letting for use for the purposes of a trade, profession or vocation, or as an office or offices. There is no requirement for any office to be used for the purposes of a trade, profession or vocation, therefore, a charitable organisation would qualify. Temporary periods of unsuitability are ignored if the building qualified in the immediate prior period (*CAA 2001, s 360D*). The premises must not be used, or be available for use as, or as part of, a 'dwelling'.

A dwelling

6.92 Premises that are in use or available for use as a dwelling will not qualify for business premises renovation allowance. There is no definition of 'dwelling' in *CAA 2001*.

A 'dwelling house' is defined in *CAA 2001, s 531* as having the same meaning as in the *Rent Act 1977*. HMRC confirm in Capital Allowances Manual CA 11520 that other references to a 'dwelling house' should be read in much the same way; namely for plant and machinery, industrial buildings and research and development. A dwelling house is defined as 'a building, or part of a building, which is a person's home. A person's second or holiday home is a dwelling house as is a flat that is used as a residence. A block of flats is not a dwelling house, although the individual flats within the block may be. University halls of residence, accommodation used for holiday letting, a hospital, a nursing home or a prison are not dwelling houses'.

It is for further consideration as to whether a 'dwelling' which is referred to for business premises renovation allowance purposes should not only include the separate unit of living accommodation but also any attached garden, yard, garage or other outbuildings, within the same occupancy.

Relevant interest

6.93 The relevant interest is the interest held by the company that incurred the qualifying expenditure or who incurs expenditure on conversion, if the person was entitled to more than one interest of which one was a reversionary interest, the reversionary interest becomes the relevant interest. If a leasehold and a reversionary interest are present, the leasehold interest merges with the freehold interest (*CAA 2001, ss 360E* and *360F*)

Initial allowances

6.94 The company incurring the expenditure on qualifying business premises may claim an initial allowance of up to 100% of that expenditure in the accounting period in which it is incurred provided it continues to own the relevant interest at the time of the claim. Part of the allowance may be disclaimed (*CAA 2001, ss 360G* and *360H*).

Writing down allowances

6.95 A company may claim a writing down allowance of 25% of the balance of unrelieved qualifying expenditure at the end of the chargeable period, if all the relevant conditions continue to apply, which are that:

- the company is entitled to the relevant interest in the qualifying building;

- the company has not granted a long lease (ie longer than 50 years) of the qualifying building out of the relevant interest in consideration of the payment of a capital sum; and

- the qualifying building constitutes qualifying business premises.

Part of the writing down allowance may be disclaimed (*CAA 2001, s 360I*). Any grant received is deducted from the qualifying expenditure for this purpose (*CAA 2001, s 360L*).

The writing down allowance is proportionately increased or reduced if the chargeable period is more or less than a year (*CAA 2001, s 360J*).

Balancing events

6.96 A balancing adjustment, ie a balancing charge or an allowance, is made on the company that incurred the expenditure when a balancing event takes place. There is no balancing adjustment if the balancing event occurs more than seven years after the time when the premises were first used, or suitable for letting for the purposes of a trade, profession or vocation or as an office or as offices (see **6.68**) (*CAA 2001, s 360M*).

A balancing event occurs in the following circumstances:

- the relevant interest in the qualifying building is sold; a long lease (ie a lease longer than 50 years) of the qualifying building is granted out of the relevant interest in consideration of the payment of a capital sum; if the relevant interest is a lease, the lease ends otherwise than on the person entitled to it acquiring the interest reversionary on it;

- the qualifying building is demolished or destroyed;

- the company is wound up;

- the qualifying building ceases to be qualifying business premises (without being demolished or destroyed).

- (*CAA 2001, s 360N*)

The proceeds from a balancing event are as follows:

Balancing events and proceeds:

Balancing event	Proceeds from event
1 The sale of the relevant interest.	The net proceeds of the sale.
2 The grant of a long lease out of the relevant interest.	If the capital sum paid in consideration of the grant is less than the commercial premium, the commercial premium (ie an arm's length premium).
	In any other case, the capital sum paid in consideration of the grant.
3 The coming to an end of a lease, where a person entitled to the lease and a person entitled to any superior interest are connected persons.	The market value of the relevant interest in the qualifying building at the time of the event.
4 The death of the person who incurred the qualifying expenditure.	The residue of qualifying expenditure immediately before the death.
5 The demolition or destruction of the qualifying building.	The net amount received for the remains of the qualifying building, together with: (a) any insurance money received in respect of the demolition or destruction; and (b) any other compensation of any description so received, so far as it consists of capital sums.
6 The qualifying building ceases to be qualifying business premises.	The market value of the relevant interest in the qualifying building at the time of the event.

(*CAA 2001, s 360O*)

Balancing adjustment

6.97   A balancing allowance is the difference between proceeds and the asset's tax written down value (termed as the residue) before disposal. A balancing charge arises if the proceeds are more than the tax written down value. A balancing allowance arises if the opposite occurs.

A balancing charge cannot exceed the total amount of capital allowances granted to the company making the disposal (*CAA 2001, s 360P*).

Writing off qualifying expenditure

6.98   Initial allowances are written off the qualifying expenditure at the time when the qualifying business premises are first used, or suitable for letting for use. Writing-down allowances are written off at the end of the chargeable period for which the allowance is made. A balancing event occurring at the end of the chargeable period will take into account all the allowances for the period (*CAA 2001, s 360R*).

Demolition costs

6.99   If the company, which is entitled to the allowances, also incurs the cost of demolition the net cost of the demolition (ie demolition costs less sale proceeds) is added to the residue of qualifying expenditure immediately before the demolition (*CAA 2001, s 360S*).

VAT

6.100   If an additional VAT liability accrues an additional allowance is given in the accrual chargeable period (*CAA 2001, s 360U*). An additional VAT rebate will not give rise to a balancing allowance but can give rise to a balancing charge (*CAA 2001, s 360X*). This occurs when the amount of the VAT rebate is more than the amount of the residue of qualifying expenditure or there is no residue (*CAA 2001, ss 360T–360Y*).

Termination of lease

6.101   Depending on the circumstances, the termination of a lease may be treated as a disposal or a continuation of the relevant interest.

The relevant interest continues in the following circumstances:

- If, with the consent of the lessor, the lessee of the qualifying building remains in possession of the qualifying building after the termination without a new lease being granted to him, the relevant interest continues as long as the lessee remains in possession.

- If, on the termination, a new lease is granted to a lessee as a result of the exercise of an option available to him under the terms of the first lease, the second lease is treated as a continuation of the first.

- If on the termination:

— another lease is granted to a different lessee; and

— in connection with the transaction that lessee pays a sum to the person who was the lessee under the first lease,

the two leases are to be treated as if they were the same lease, which had been assigned by the lessee under the first lease to the lessee under the second lease in consideration of the payment.

The relevant interest ceases in the following circumstance:

● If on the termination the lessor pays a sum to the lessee in respect of business premises comprised in the lease, the lease is treated as if it had come to an end by surrender in consideration of the payment.

(CAA 2001, s 360Z3).

FLAT CONVERSION ALLOWANCES

Relevant interest in a flat

6.102 Capital allowances are available in respect of expenditure incurred after 10 May 2001 on the conversion of parts of business premises into flats.

In order to qualify the person must not only have incurred the expenditure, but also have the relevant interest in the flat. The flat must be:

● a separate set of premises (whether or not on the same floor);

● form part of a building; and

● be divided horizontally from another part of the building.

(CAA 2001,s 393A).

The relevant interest is the interest the person had when the expenditure was incurred. If the person holds a reversionary interest the original interest will merge with the conversion *(CAA 2001, s 393F)*.

Expenditure qualifying for flat conversion allowances

6.103 The expenditure qualifying for flat conversion allowances is capital expenditure incurred on, or in connection with:

● the conversion of part of a qualifying building into a qualifying flat;

● the renovation of a flat in a qualifying building if the flat is, or will be, a qualifying flat;

or

- repairs to a qualifying building, to the extent that the repairs are incidental to expenditure on the conversion or the renovation.

In addition the expenditure must be made on a flat or part of a building that was unused or only used for storage through the year ending immediately before the date on which the conversion or renovation work began.

Expenditure qualifying for flat conversion allowances

6.104   The following types of expenditure do not qualify for the flat conversion allowance:

- the acquisition of land or rights in or over land;
- the extension of a qualifying building (except to the extent required for the purpose of providing a means of getting to or from a qualifying flat);
- the development of land adjoining or adjacent to a qualifying building; or
- the provision of furnishings or chattels.

Whether or not repair expenditure constitutes a capital or a revenue item is determined in accordance with the rules of Schedule A (*CAA 2001, s 393B*).

A qualifying building

6.105   In order to qualify for the flat conversion allowances the flat must form part of a qualifying building, ie a building which meets the following requirements:

- all or most of the ground floor of the building must be authorised for business use;
- it must appear that, when the building was constructed, the storeys above the ground floor were for use primarily as one or more dwelling;
- the building must not have more than four storeys above the ground floor; and
- the construction of the building must have been completed before 1 January 1980 (building extensions on or after 1 January 1980 will meet the conditions provided the extension was completed on or before 31 December 2000).

(*CAA 2001, s 393C*).

A qualifying flat

6.106   The flat itself must be a 'qualifying flat' and hence meet the following requirements:

- the flat must be in a qualifying building;

- the flat must be suitable for letting as a dwelling;

- the flat must be held for the purpose of short-term letting (ie a lease no longer than five years);

- it must be possible to gain access to the flat without using the part of the ground floor of the building that is authorised for business use in accordance with the Town and County planning requirements;

- the flat must not have more than four rooms (kitchens and bathrooms are ignored together with any closet, cloakroom or hallway not exceeding 5 square metres in area;

- the flat must not be a high-value flat;

- the flat must not be (or have been) created or renovated as part of a scheme involving the creation or renovation of one or more high-value flats; and

- the flat must not be let to a person connected with the person who incurred the expenditure on its conversion or renovation.

Periods of temporary unsuitability for letting are ignored provided they are immediately preceded by a qualifying period (*CAA 2001, ss 393C, 393D*).

High-value flats

6.107   A flat is considered to be a high-value flat if the flat would command an anticipated notional set market rent on the date the expenditure was incurred based on the following assumptions:

- the conversion or renovation has been completed;

- the flat is let furnished;

- the lease does not require the tenant to pay a premium or make any other payments to the landlord or a person connected with the landlord;

- the tenant is not connected with the person incurring the expenditure on the conversion or renovation of the flat; and

- the flat is let on a shorthold tenancy (applies to England or Wales or Scotland).

The following notional rents have been set:

Notional rent limits

Number of rooms in flat	Flats in Greater London Price per week £	Flats elsewhere Price per week
1 or 2	£350	£150
3	£425	£225
4	£480	£300

(*CA 2001, s 393E*)

Initial allowances

6.108   If all conditions apply an initial allowance of 100% of the qualifying expenditure is available to the person who incurred the expenditure. The allowance may be disclaimed in whole or in part. If the flat is sold before the first let the initial allowance will not be available and if already claimed will be withdrawn (*CAA 2001, s 393I*). The allowances are granted in the chargeable period in which the flat is first suitable for letting as a dwelling (*CAA 2001, s 393R*).

Writing down allowances

6.109   A company that has incurred qualifying expenditure during the chargeable period and owns the flat at the end of the chargeable period is entitled to a writing down allowance for that chargeable period. The company must have a relevant interest in the flat and not have granted a long lease (a lease with a duration of more than 50 years) out of the flat. The flat must remain a qualifying flat (*CAA 2001, s 393J*). The allowance is 25% on a reducing balance basis of the qualifying expenditure and is increased or decreased proportionately if the chargeable period is more than or less than one year. The allowance may be disclaimed in whole or in part.

Balancing events

6.110   A balancing event occurs on the following occasions:

- the relevant interest in the flat is sold;

- a long lease of the flat is granted out of the relevant interest in consideration of the payment of a capital sum;

- if the relevant interest is a lease, the lease ends otherwise than on the person entitled to it acquiring the interest reversionary on it;
- the person who incurred the qualifying expenditure dies;
- the flat is demolished or destroyed;
- the flat ceases to be a qualifying flat (without being demolished or destroyed).

(*CAA 2001, s 393N*)

Balancing adjustment

6.111   A balancing adjustment occurs when a balancing event takes place, being the difference between the disposal proceeds and the tax written down value of the flat. A balancing allowance occurs if the disposal proceeds are less than the tax written down value and a balancing charge occurs in the opposite situation. There is no balancing adjustment if the balancing event occurs more than seven years after the time when the flat was first suitable for letting as a dwelling. If more than one balancing event occurs, a balancing adjustment is made only on the first of them (*CAA 2001, s 393O*).

The proceeds from the balancing event are deemed to amount to the following:

BALANCING EVENTS AND PROCEEDS

	Balancing event	Proceeds from event
1.	The sale of the relevant interest.	The net proceeds of the sale.
2.	The grant of a long lease out of the relevant interest.	If the capital sum paid in consideration of the grant is less than the commercial premium (amount paid at arm's length rate), the commercial premium. In any other case, the capital sum paid in consideration of the grant
3.	The coming to an end of a lease, where a person entitled to the lease and a person entitled to any superior interest are connected persons	The market value of the relevant interest in the flat at the time of the event.
4.	The death of the person who incurred the qualifying expenditure.	The residue of qualifying expenditure immediately before the death.

5.	The demolition or destruction of the flat.	The net amount received for the remains of the flat, together with:
		(a) any insurance money received in respect of the demolition or destruction; and
		(b) any other compensation of any description so received, so far as it consists of capital sums

Demolition costs are added to the residue of expenditure immediately before demolition (*CAA 2001, s 393S*). The allowance is given as a Schedule A expense or as a trading expense depending on the business activities of the lessor.

Chapter 7

Intangible assets

SCOPE PRE AND POST 1 APRIL 2002

7.1 The intangible assets regime introduced with effect from 1 April 2002 provides companies with tax relief on their intangible assets including their intellectual property. The previous rules brought intangible asset disposal within the chargeable gains regime and taxed royalties and patent sales as income.

Existing assets

7.2 The pre 1 April 2002 rules have been in existence for many years and continue to apply to assets in existence on that date (*FA 2002, Sch 29, para 117*).

The legislation terms these assets as 'existing assets' (*FA 2002, Sch 29, para 118(3)*).

Chargeable intangible assets

7.3 The new intangible asset regime rules apply to assets, which are:

● intangible assets created by the company after 1 April 2002; or
● intangible assets that the company acquired after 1 April 2002, from a third party who was unrelated to the company at the time of the acquisition (*FA 2002, Sch 29, para 118(1)*).

The legislation terms these assets as 'chargeable intangible assets' (*FA 2002, Sch 29, para 137(1)(a)*).

The new intangible asset regime rules also apply to post 1 April 2002 chargeable intangible assets acquired from related third parties in the following circumstances:

- the asset at the time of sale was a chargeable intangible asset of the vendor company;

- if the asset is acquired from an intermediary who acquired the asset post 1 April 2002 from a third person, at the time of acquisition, the third person was neither a related party of the intermediary, nor of the company; or

- the asset was created after 1 April 2002 either by the person from whom it was acquired or by any other person (*FA 2002, Sch 29, para 118(2)*).

Transitional period

7.4   Therefore, the intangible asset regime does not apply to existing assets; namely those held by the company on 1 April 2002 or those acquired from a related party who held them on 1 April 2002. If an asset was internally generated, eg goodwill, and the business was in existence prior to 1 April 2002, the asset is treated as an existing asset prior to 1 April 2002. That being the case, the goodwill arising on incorporation of a sole trader or partnership business will remain as an existing asset and remain subject to capital gains on disposal if it was in existence prior to 1 April 2002. HMRC Corporate Intangibles Research and Development Manual CIRD 10145 gives a useful key to manual references applying to pre 1 April 2002 assets (grand-fathered assets). Internally generated goodwill is regarded as being created prior to 1 April 2002 if the business was carried on at any time by the company or by a related party (*FA 2002, Sch 29, para 121*).

Example 7.1

Ted commenced trading as a sole trader on 1 January 1987. Over recent years his business has expanded and he incorporates the business on 1 January 2009. He transfers the tangible fixed assets for £50,000 and the goodwill professionally valued at £20,000 to Ted Ltd, his newly formed company. Although Ted transfers the goodwill to the company after 1 April 2002, it was in existence prior to 1 April 2002 and is not within the intangible assets regime.

This example is continued in **7.10**, Example 7.3.

Example 7.2

Bill commenced trading as a sole trader on 1 January 2003. His business has expanded and he incorporates the business on 1 January 2009. He transfers the tangible fixed assets for £100,000 and the goodwill professionally valued at

£40,000 to Bill Ltd his newly formed company. Bill's goodwill was not in existence prior to 1 April 2002 and is therefore within the intangible assets regime.

This example is continued in **7.10**, Example 7.3.

MEANING OF AN INTANGIBLE ASSET

7.5   The legislation gives intangible assets their accountancy meaning and includes intellectual property within the meaning of an intangible asset.

Accountancy definition

7.6   FRS 10 (goodwill and intangible assets) defines intangible assets as:

'Non-financial fixed assets that do not have a physical substance but are identifiable and are controlled by the entity through custody or legal rights'.

Companies Act 2006, s 396; the Large and Medium-sized Companies and Groups (Accounts and Reports) Regulations 2008 (SI 2008/410) include intangible fixed assets under the following sub-headings:

- development costs;
- concessions, patents, licences, trade marks and similar rights and assets; and
- goodwill.

The assets may only be included in the balance sheet if they were acquired for valuable consideration or, with the exception of goodwill were created by the company itself.

For example, a company may include intangible assets under the following headings within intangible assets:

- patents, trade marks and other product rights;
- brand names;
- goodwill;
- publishing copyrights, rights and titles;
- newspaper titles;

- programmes, film rights and scores;

- databases;

- know-how agreements;

- development costs;

- betting office licences;

- trade value of retail outlets;

- exhibition rights and other similar intangible assets.

For taxation purposes intellectual property includes UK and overseas patents, trademarks, registered designs, copyright or design rights, plant breeders' rights, together with rights under *s 7* of the *Plant Varieties Act 1997* and the overseas equivalent. Assets owned outright and by licence are included, as are assets that are not protected by a legal right but which have an industrial, commercial or other economic value. Options or rights to acquire or dispose of an intangible asset are also included (*FA 2002, Sch 29, paras 2, 3*).

The intangible assets regime applies to goodwill and the accounting meaning is adopted (*FA 2002, Sch 29, para 4*), which defines goodwill as:

> 'The difference between the cost of an acquired entity and the aggregate of the fair values of that entity's identifiable assets and liabilities. Positive goodwill arises when the acquisition cost exceeds the aggregate fair values of the identifiable assets and liabilities. Negative goodwill arises when the aggregate fair values of the identifiable assets and liabilities of the entity exceed the acquisition cost'.

If a company has not drawn up accounts on this basis it will be treated as having done so for the purposes of corporation tax. Therefore HMRC will adjust accounts if they do not comply with GAAP and in particular FRS 10 (goodwill and intangible assets) (*FA 2002, Sch 29, para 5*).

For further discussion of the constituent parts of goodwill see HMRC Manual CG68050–68098, Tax Bulletin 83 and *Balloon Promotions Ltd v HMRC* (2006) SpC 524.

Excluded assets

7.7   Assets entirely excluded from the intangible assets regime comprise rights over land or tangible moveable property, oil licences, financial assets, shares in a company, trust and partnership rights and powers and assets neither held for a business nor a commercial purpose (*FA 2002, Sch 29, paras 72–77*).

The FRS 13 definition of financial assets FRS 13 (derivatives and other financial instruments: disclosure) is adopted namely:

> 'cash, a contractual right to receive cash or another financial asset from another entity, a contractual right to exchange financial instruments with another entity under conditions that are potentially favourable or an equity instrument of another entity.' (*FA 2002, Sch 29, para 75(2)*)

Assets excluded in certain situations

7.8   Apart from royalties all assets owned by a life assurance business and a mutual trade association are excluded from the definition of intangibles. Expenditure on films, sound recording and computer software expenditure (when accounted for with the hardware) is also excluded apart from expenditure on royalties (*FA 2002, Sch 29, para 76*). If the computer software is bought separately, the company may elect for the software to be removed from the intangible assets regime (*FA 2002, Sch 29, para 83*).

The valuation of the intangible assets if need be is made on a just and reasonable basis.

Royalties and licences granted over existing assets from related parties are themselves treated as existing assets for accounting periods ending on or after 5 December 2005 (*FA 2006, s 77*).

Research and development expenditure

7.9   Research and development expenditure has its own taxation regime (see Chapter 8). The proceeds from the sale of research and development are included within the intangible assets regime (*FA 2002, Sch 29, para 82*).

CORPORATION TAX TREATMENT

Debits and credits

7.10   With effect from 1 April 2002, gains and losses relating to intangible assets bought or made for continuous use in a business are taxed generally as revenue items (*FA 2002, Sch 29, para 1*).

Expenditure within the legislation is known as 'debits' and income as 'credits'.

The treatment of the debits and credits in calculating the taxable profits will depend on whether the assets are held for the purposes of a trade, a property business or if the company is non-trading.

Debits and credits in respect of assets held for the purposes of a trade are treated as receipts and expenses of that particular trade and are brought into the Schedule D Case I computation. Likewise, debits and credits held for a property business are treated as income and expenses of that property business. A property business includes normal Schedule A lettings, furnished holiday lets and an overseas property business.

Expenditure and the reversal of an earlier gain are deductible from profits as it is written off in the accounts. Depreciation is allowed on an accounting basis or on a Revenue fixed rate basis (*FA 2002, Sch 29, para 7(1)*).

HMRC will look to consistency with UK group accounting policies to determine whether the individual company's accounting treatment may be adopted for taxation purposes (*FA 2002, Sch 29, para 6*).

Example 7.3

Example continued from Examples 7.1 and 7.2.

Assuming the same facts as Examples 7.1 and 7.2, Bill Ltd but not Ted Ltd will be able to write off the cost of the goodwill on incorporation in its books. Assuming Bill decides a 10% deprecation rate, the annual write off is £4,000(10% × £40,000).

This example is continued in Example 7.5.

Annual payments and patent royalties

7.11   Irrespective of when the intangible assets were acquired, the related annual payments and patent royalties are no longer deducted from total income as a charge on income. Instead they are deducted as a 'debit' on an accruals basis (*FA 2002, Sch 29, para 8(3)*).

If the royalty is payable to a related party and the payment is not made within 12 months after the end of the accounting period it cannot be allowed as a deduction for that period (*FA 2002, Sch 29, para 94*). See **7.27** regarding related parties.

Depreciation

7.12   The company may select its own depreciation policy or it may adopt the legislation policy. If using the legislation policy, it must make a written irrevocable election to HMRC no later than two years after the end of the accounting period in which the asset is created or acquired. The asset is then depreciated at 4% per annum on a straight-line basis apportioned for accounting periods less than 12 months (*FA 2002, Sch 29, paras 10, 11*).

Non-trading debits and credits

7.13   Non-trading debits and credits are netted off against each other. A net gain is assessable under Schedule D Case VI. A net loss is relieved in the following way:

● By claim within two years of the end of the accounting period to which the loss relates to set the loss against the company's total profits for that accounting period.

● By claim within two years of the end of the accounting period to which the loss relates to surrender by group relief under *ICTA 1988, s 403*.

● Any unutilised loss is carried forward to the next accounting period as if it were a non-trading debit of that period (*FA 2002, Sch 29, para 35*).

PRESCRIBED DEBIT AND CREDIT ADJUSTMENTS

7.14   There are certain prescribed pro rata debit and credit adjustments. These are summarised in the following paragraphs.

Impairment review

7.15   The acquisition of an asset may be part of FRS 7 (fair values *in acquisition accounting*) impairment review because the acquisition cost is more than fair value. This could happen if a subsidiary was acquired in stages and deferred values are obtained. The accounting loss pro rata the tax and accounting cost is an allowable deduction from profits. The following formula is used to calculate the deductible debit in the year of acquisition:

Accounting loss × (Tax cost ÷ Accounting cost)

where:

Accounting loss	=	the amount of the loss recognised for accounting purposes
Tax cost	=	the amount of expenditure on the asset that is recognised for tax purposes
Accounting cost	=	the amount capitalised in respect of expenditure on the asset

In subsequent periods of account the following adjustment is made:

Accounting loss × (Tax value ÷ Accounting value)

where:

Accounting loss	=	the amount of the loss recognised for accounting purposes
Tax value	=	the tax written down value of the asset immediately before the amortisation charge is made or, as the case may be, the impairment loss is recognised for accounting purposes
Accounting value	=	the value of the asset recognised for accounting purposes immediately before the amortisation charge or, as the case may be, the impairment review (*FA 2002, Sch 29, para 9*).

Reversal of a previous accounting gain

7.16   If an accounting loss is recognised, where the tax value and the accounting value of the asset differ, the amount of the loss is adjusted in accordance with the following formula:

Accounting loss × (Previous credit ÷ Accounting gain)

where:

Accounting loss	=	the amount of the loss recognised for accounting purposes
Accounting gain	=	the amount of the gain that is (in whole or in part) reversed

217

| Previous credit | = | the amount of the credit previously brought into account for tax purposes in respect of the gain (*FA 2002, Sch 29, para 12*). |

This could occur on a change in an accounting policy during an accounting period.

Income taxable

7.17   Receipts, revaluations, negative goodwill credits and reversals of any previous debits are all taxable as income on an accounting basis as they accrue (*FA 2002, Sch 29, para 13*). Apart from assets for which an election has been made for the 4% fixed rate depreciation, accounting adjustments brought about by a revaluation of intangible assets or the restoration of past losses are adjusted by the following formula:

Accounting adjustment × (Tax value ÷ Accounting value)

where:

Accounting adjustment	=	the amount of the increase in the accounting value of the asset
Tax value	=	the tax written down value of the asset immediately before the revaluation
Accounting value	=	the value of the asset by reference to which the revaluation is carried out (*FA 2002, Sch 29, para 15*).

Any gain recognised in calculating negative goodwill is apportioned to the intangible assets on a just and reasonable basis and included in income accordingly (*FA 2002, Sch 29, para 16*).

Accounting gain reversals of previous losses recognised in the company's accounts is adjusted as follows:

Accounting gain × (Tax debit ÷ Accounting loss)

where:

Accounting gain	=	the amount of the gain recognised for accounting purposes
Accounting loss	=	the amount of the loss that is (in whole or in part) reversed
Tax debit	=	the amount of the tax debit previously brought into account in respect of the loss (*FA 2002, Sch 29, para 17*).

Realisation of intangible fixed assets

7.18   Amounts arising from asset sale (proceeds less incidental costs of realisation) or balance sheet writing off are compared to the asset's tax written down value and the resultant net debit or credit is included in calculating profits chargeable to corporation tax. Abortive expenditure costs are allowed as a deduction (*FA 2002, Sch 29, para 26*).

In the case of a part realisation, the tax written down value is apportioned by the following formula:

Reduction in accounting value ÷ Previous accounting value

where:

Reduction in accounting value	=	the difference between the accounting value immediately before the realisation compared with that immediately after the realisation.
Previous accounting value	=	the accounting value immediately before the realisation (*FA 2002, Sch 29, para 22*).

Cost is substituted for tax written down value if the asset has not been depreciated. Where there is no balance sheet valuation for the asset, possibly because it was created by the company, the full sale proceeds are brought into the profit and loss account as income.

Where the asset has been written down on an accounting basis, the tax written down value is calculated as follows:

Tax cost − Debits + Credits

where:

Tax cost	=	the cost of the asset recognised for tax purposes
Debits	=	the total amount of the depreciation debits previously brought into account for tax purposes
Credits	=	the total amount of any credits previously brought into account for tax purposes in respect of a revaluation (*FA 2002, Sch 29, para 15*).

The comparable adjustment for assets that have been written down on the fixed basis is as follows:

Tax cost − Debits

where:

Tax cost	=	the cost of the asset recognised for tax purposes
Debits	=	the total amount of the depreciation debits previously brought into account for tax purposes on the fixed rate basis (*FA 2002, Sch 29, para 28*).

Part realisation of an asset

7.19   If there has been a partial sale of an intangible asset, the tax written down value of the asset immediately after the part realisation is calculated as follows:

Previous tax value × (New accounting value ÷ Previous accounting value)

where:

Previous tax value	=	the tax written down value of the asset immediately before the part realisation
New accounting value	=	the accounting value of the asset immediately after the part realisation
Previous accounting value	=	the accounting value immediately before the part realisation (*FA 2002, Sch 29, para 29*).

An asset may cease to be a chargeable asset during its lifetime in which case there is a deemed disposal for the company (*FA 2002, Sch 29, para 108*).

SALE OF AN INTANGIBLE ASSET

Sale proceeds

7.20   Sale proceeds arising from a sale of intangible assets are credited to the profit and loss account. Disposal costs are allowed as a deductible debit. Relief is also given for abortive costs of sale (*FA 2002, Sch 29, para 26*).

Roll-over and reinvestment relief

7.21   When a company sells an intangible asset it may, provided all conditions are met, be able to claim reinvestment relief. The effect being that it will avoid the credit (sale proceeds less incidental costs of sale) to its profits.

The conditions imposed are first that the asset disposed of must have been within the intangible assets regime throughout its ownership. Where the asset was within the intangible assets regime at the time of sale and for a substantial period of the ownership (but not the whole), it will be treated as a separate asset for the time that it so qualified. Sales proceeds are apportioned on a just and reasonable basis. Secondly, the sale proceeds must be greater than the original cost of the original asset or adjusted cost where there has been a part realisation.

The new assets acquired must be immediately chargeable intangible assets for the company as soon as they are acquired (as recognised for accounting purposes). The expenditure must be capitalised. The time limits for incurring the expenditure are 12 months before the sale of the old asset and three years thereafter (*FA 2002, Sch 29, para 39*).

Any claims to HMRC must be in writing, must specify the old assets, identify the expenditure on new assets and must state the amount of the relief claimed (*FA 2002, Sch 29, para 40*). A company may make a provisional claim for relief if it has sold an intangible asset and intends to replace it with new intangible assets. The provisional claim continues until the earlier of its being withdrawn, replaced by a new claim or the expiry of four years after the end of the accounting period in which the realisation took place. Adjustments are then accordingly made to the corporation tax returns or are assessed regardless of time limits (*FA 2002, Sch 29, para 43*).

The effect of the claim is to reduce the realisation proceeds and the tax cost of the new asset by the same amount.

The amount is calculated as follows:

- If the new expenditure on other assets is equal to or greater than the proceeds of realisation of the old asset, the amount available for relief is the amount by which the proceeds of realisation exceed the tax cost of the old asset.

- If the amount of the new expenditure on other assets is less than the proceeds of realisation of the old asset, the amount available for relief is the amount (if any) by which the new expenditure on other assets exceeds the tax cost of the old asset.

- If the new expenditure does not exceed the tax cost of the old asset no relief is given (*FA 2002, Sch 29, para 41*).

Example 7.4

P Ltd makes up accounts to 31 December each year. The following accounting transactions take place:

Year ended		Sale pro- ceeds	Cost	Profit and loss account		Net book value
		£000	£000	£000		£000
31 December 2008	Bought copyright with an estimated life of five years		50	10 debit	Annual depreciation	40

221

31 December 2009	Sold	70		30 credit	Profit on sale	Nil
	Bought copyright with an estimated life of five years		75	15 debit	Annual depreciation	60

For corporation tax purposes the company wishes to claim reinvestment relief on the first disposal. In order to do this it must first analyse the gain arising.

Year ended	Total gain	Arising from depreciation	Gain available for reinvestment	Actual new chargeable intangible asset purchased	Tax cost of new asset purchased
	£000	£000	£000	£000	£000
31 December 2009	30	10	20	75	55

The corporation tax deductions on these transactions are as follows:

Year ended 31 December		Purchase and sale transactions	Reinvestment relief	Opening tax value	Adjustment to profits for corporation tax	Closing tax value
		£000	£000	£000	£000	£000
2008	Bought			50	10 Debit	40
2009	Sold	70	20		10 Credit	Nil
	Bought	75	20	55	11 Debit	44

7.22 On a part realisation the adjusted cost is calculated as follows:

Reduction in accounting value ÷ Previous accounting value

where:

Reduction in accounting value = the difference between the accounting value immediately before the part realisation compared with that immediately after the part realisation

Previous accounting value = the accounting value immediately before the part realisation

A company may wish to sell and reacquire the same asset. In which case this is treated as an independent disposal on which reinvestment relief is available. Deemed realisations are not recognised for reinvestment relief.

GROUPS

Meaning of a group

7.23 Group for intangible assets purposes adopts the capital gains tax definition: see **20.14**.

A group member must be an effective 51% subsidiary of the principal company, but the principal company cannot be a 75% subsidiary of another group and a company cannot be a member of more than one group.

Four criteria are applied to determine to which group a company belongs in the following order: voting rights, profits available for distribution, assets on a winding-up and percentage of directly and indirectly owned ordinary shares (*FA 2002, Sch 29, para 50*).

The group remains intact until the principal company becomes a member of another group, in which case other companies join the group. The four criteria above must be applied to determine the group members.

Intra-group asset transfers

7.24 Intra-group transfers of assets have no tax effect except for tax-exempt friendly societies and dual resident investing companies. The transferee company adopts the asset as if it were its own.

Reinvestment relief is also available to group members but not in respect of intra-group asset transfers. Neither is it available to a dual resident investing company. Both companies involved are required to claim (*FA 2002, Sch 29, para 56*).

Purchase by a company of the controlling interest in a non-group company that subsequently becomes a member of the group is treated for reinvestment purposes as a purchase of the underlying assets on which relief is available. Expenditure incurred by a company on its new purchase is treated as the lesser of the tax written down value of the underlying assets immediately before acquisition and the consideration paid for the controlling interest. If the relief applies the tax value of the underlying intangible assets is reduced by the amount of the relief (*FA 2002, Sch 29, para 57*).

Leaving a group

7.25   When a company leaves a group, having acquired a chargeable intangible asset by intra-group transfer within the past six years, there is a de-grouping charge on the transferee based on market value at the date of transfer. A debit or credit adjustment is made in the accounting period in which the company leaves the group (*FA 2002, Sch 29, para 58*).

There is no de-grouping charge where two companies who have made intra-group transfers of assets within the time limits leave the group at the same time. There is no de-grouping charge if the entire group becomes a member of another group. If the transferee ceases to qualify as a member of the new group within six years of transfer, it is treated as having sold and reacquired the asset at the time of transfer. Any adjustment is included in the corporation tax computation for the period in which the company leaves the group. Group de-grouping charges can, by joint election between transferor and transferee company, be passed to the transferor company to form part of its income. It will be treated as a non-trading gain. The transferor company must be resident in the UK or be deemed to be carrying on a trade in the UK through a branch or agency. (The company must not be a friendly society or a dual resident holding company.) Unpaid tax may be recovered from any group members or controlling directors of non-UK resident companies carrying on a trade in the UK, if not paid by the relevant company. Inter company roll-over and de-grouping charge payments are left out of account for corporation tax purposes provided they do not exceed the amount of relief (*FA 2002, Sch 29, para 71*). There is no de-grouping charge on a demerger carried out for bona fide commercial reasons.

Reconstructions

7.26   In general reconstructions avoid a tax charge. In order to ensure this effect a clearance procedure is available (*FA 2002, Sch 29, para 88*).

In a scheme of reconstruction where the whole or part of a business is transferred for shares or loan stock by a company, provided the company received no part of the consideration there is no tax charge. Although the consideration must be in shares apportionment is possible. The reconstruction must be made for bona fide commercial reasons and must not be part of a scheme of avoidance. (The company must not be friendly society or a dual resident holding company) (*FA 2002, Sch 29, para 84*).

There is no tax charge on transfers of UK trades and companies resident in EU states follow the same lines provided the consideration is in securities issued by the transferor to the transferee. The intangible asset is transferred to the transferee company complete with its tax history (*FA 2002, Sch 29, para 85*).

Where intangible assets are transferred from a UK company's overseas branch to a non-UK resident company the gain may be deferred, the trade must be transferred in exchange for securities. If the securities are later sold a taxable credit must be brought into account by the transferor equal to the deferred gain. Also, if at any time within six years after the transfer the transferee disposes of the relevant assets taxable credit must be brought into account by the transferor equal to the deferred gain (*FA 2002, Sch 29, para 86*). Relief for any foreign tax is available if there is no deferral of the gain (*FA 2002, Sch 29, para 87(2)*).

Where an existing intangible asset (see **7.2**) is transferred under a reconstruction to which *TCGA 1992, s 139 or s 140A* applies the asset remains an existing asset in the hands of the transferee (*FA 2002, Sch 29, para 84*).

Related parties

7.27 Transfers of intangible assets between related parties take place at market value (*FA 2002, Sch 29, para 92*) subject to the transfer pricing provisions.

Example 7.5

Continued from Example 7.3.

Continuing with the same facts as Example 7.2 and Example 7.3, Bill had his goodwill upon incorporation professionally valued so there is no question of its value being adjusted.

However, if Bill had opted for a *TCGA 1992, s 165* hold-over claim (see *Capital Gains Tax 2008/09* from Tottel) the amount held over will be deductible from the deemed market value of the goodwill for the purposes of calculating the annual write off (*FA 2002, Sch 29, para 92(4C)*).

Thus supposing Bill's hold-over relief amounted to £10,000, the annual write off will be £3,000 (10 % × (40,000–10,000)).

7.28 Part realisation roll-over relief is not available to a related party. Royalty payments to a related party not paid within 12 months of the accounting period in which they are accrued and not brought in as a credit by the recipient company are not allowed as a deduction for the payee.

7.28 *Intangible assets*

A related party relationship exists where:

Case 1

A company has control or a major interest in another company

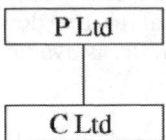

Case 2

Companies are under the control of the same person.

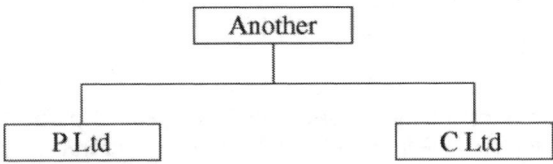

Case 3

C Ltd is a close company of which P is a participator or an associate of a participator (*ICTA 1988, s 417*; close company definitions apply: see **4.10**, **4.12**).

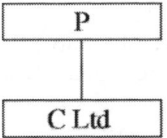

Case 4

P Ltd and C Ltd are companies in the same group.

Control means that a person is able to secure that the company's affairs are conducted in accordance with their wishes either by shareholdings, voting power or by powers conferred by the Articles of Association. A major interest exists if two persons have control of a company and each of them has at least 40% of the total shareholding (*FA 2002, Sch 29, para 96*). Rights and powers owned singly and jointly are taken into account namely: rights and powers that he is entitled to acquire at a future date or will, at a future date, become entitled to acquire and others rights and powers that can be exercised on his behalf, under his direction or for his benefit. Rights and powers of a person connected with him are also taken into account, but not persons connected to a connected person (*FA 2002, Sch 29, para 97*). Loan security arrangements are not taken into account. Rights and powers of a person as a member of a partnership are only taken into account if the person has a major interest (40%) in the partnership (*FA 2002, Sch 29, para 99*).

Connected persons

7.29   Connected persons include spouses and civil partners, relatives and relatives of their spouses. Relatives are siblings, grandparents and grandchildren. (Great-grandparents and great-grandchildren etc are also included). The trustee of a settlement is connected with the settlor, a person connected with the settlor and any company connected with the settlement. The company must be a close company (or only not a close company because it is non-UK resident) of which the trustees are participators (*FA 2002, Sch 29, para 101*). (A company is a body corporate or unincorporated association (*ICTA 1988, s 832*) see **1.4**.)

Grants

7.30   Regional development grants and certain Northern Ireland grants are not taxable credits for the purposes of computing corporation tax. All other grants received are taxable credits (*FA 2002, Sch 29, para 102*).

Finance lessors

7.31   Finance lessors are within the intangible assets regime for assets leased under finance leases to other companies. However, neither fixed rate depreciation nor reinvestment relief is available (*FA 2002, Sch 29, para 104* and the *Corporation Tax (Finance Leasing of Intangible Assets) Regulations 2002, SI 2002/1967*).

INTERNATIONAL ASPECTS

Company ceasing to be UK resident

7.32   There is a deemed disposal of a chargeable intangible asset at market value when a company ceases to be UK resident (*FA 2002, Sch 29, para 108*). A

UK holding company and a 75% subsidiary may jointly elect for the gain to be postponed on assets used for the purposes of the trade of the branch or agency where market value exceeds cost. The gain being the excess market value over cost is chargeable as a non-trading taxable credit on the UK holding company if the now non-resident subsidiary company disposes of the asset within six years of becoming non-resident. The gain is also chargeable on the holding company if it ceases to be UK resident or the non-resident company is no longer a subsidiary.

Controlled foreign companies

7.33   Gains relating to controlled foreign companies are brought into the assumed profits computation (see **13.27–13.44**) for *ICTA 1988, s 747* for apportionment purposes as taxable credits (*FA 2002, Sch 29, para 116*).

Chapter 8

Research and development

INTRODUCTION

8.1   Relief is available for capital research and development (R&D) through the capital allowance rules and for revenue R&D through the tax relief for expenditure on research and development (*FA 2000, Sch 20* and *FA 2002, Sch 12*). Similar relief is available for expenditure on vaccine research (*FA 2002, Sch 13*).

CAPITAL EXPENDITURE

Capital allowances

8.2   Capital allowances on research and development allowances may be claimed by any size of company but only if the company carries on a trade. If the company does not already carry on a trade it must set up and commence a trade connected with the R&D after incurring the expenditure (*CAA 2001, s 439(1)*). The company need not carry on the research itself; a third party may carry on the research on the company's behalf. The R&D must be related to the trade that is being carried on, known as 'the relevant trade'. R&D capital allowances can neither be claimed against investment income nor against professional and vocational income. Capital R&D expenditure qualifies for 100% initial allowance for capital allowance purposes. R&D is also available on oil and gas exploration. Thus the company is able to write off the full cost in the accounting period in which it is incurred (*CAA 2001, s 437*).

Meaning of research and development

8.3   For the purposes of claiming 100% capital allowances on R&D, the definition of R&D follows the accounting definition given in UK GAAP SSAP 13 (accounting for research and development) or IAS 38 (intangible assets) as appropriate (*ICTA 1988, s 837A*).

8.4 *Research and development*

The SSAP 13 definition

- Pure (or basic) research: experimental or theoretical work undertaken primarily to acquire new scientific or technical knowledge for its own sake rather than directed towards any specific aim or application.

- Applied research: original or critical investigation undertaken in order to gain new scientific or technical knowledge and directed towards a specific practical aim or objective.

- Development: use of scientific or technical knowledge in order to produce new or substantially improved materials, devices, products or services, to install new processes or systems prior to the commencement of commercial production or commercial applications, or to improving substantially those already produced or installed.

The IAS 38 Definition

- Research is original and planned investigation undertaken with the prospect of gaining new scientific or technical knowledge and understanding.

- Development is the application of research findings or other knowledge to a plan or design for the production of new or substantially improved materials, devices, products, processes, systems or services before the start of commercial production or use.

8.4   Allowances are given for pure and applied research in order to gain new or scientific knowledge. Oil and gas exploration is included. The trade related R&D may be of a sort that may lead to or facilitate an extension of the company's trade. It may also be of a medical nature, which has a special relation to the welfare of workers employed in that trade (*CAA 2001, s 439(5)*). If the research is carried on by a third party on the company's behalf, the company must retain responsibility for the research and the expenditure must be undertaken directly.

Example 8.1

S Ltd had a part share in a petroleum exploration licence. It arranged for G Ltd to provide the funds and the equipment to conduct operations. In return S Ltd gave G Ltd the rights to the ownership of all the petroleum won and saved to which it was entitled. G Ltd claimed that the expenditure incurred under that agreement qualified as R&D capital expenditure because it was incurred on scientific research directly undertaken on its behalf.

G Ltd is not entitled to the R&D capital allowance because the research was not directly undertaken by or on behalf of G Ltd. The facts are those of *Gaspet Ltd v Ellis* (1987) 60 TC 91, [1987] STC 362, [1987] 1 WLR 769.

8.5   Medical research undertaken for the benefit of the community as a whole may qualify for R&D allowance if it may lead to or facilitate an extension of the trade. For example, medical research undertaken by a drug company for the purpose of its trade may qualify because it is related to its trade of manufacturing drugs (HMRC Capital Allowances Manual CA 60400). With effect from 1 April 2000 R&D expenditure has been expanded to include payments made to clinical trial volunteers for taking part in such tests for companies that are not SMEs. The start date for SME companies has yet to be announced (*FA 2006, s 28* and *Sch 2*).

Qualifying expenditure

8.6   Relief may be claimed on providing facilities to carry out the research (*CAA 2001, s 438*). Land does not qualify for relief, nor does the cost of a dwelling that is more than 25% of the cost of the building (*CAA 2001, s 438(4)*). Expenditure on the acquisition of rights in research and development or rights arising out of research and development does not qualify for R&D (*CAA 2001, s 438(2)*).

Example 8.2

Novotech plc is engaged in a qualifying research project and incurs the following expenditure:

- A building for £2.5m excluding the cost of the land. The cost of the building is apportioned between research laboratories £2m and living accommodation £500,000.

- A car for each researcher who is required to travel about the country carrying out research activities.

- The patent rights to a patented invention that Novotech considers may be of assistance with the current project.

The building, including the living accommodation, will qualify for R&D. This is because the living accommodation is less than 25% of the cost of the whole building. The motor cars qualify as expenditure on research and development. The cost of acquiring the patent rights does not qualify for R&D because it is expenditure incurred in acquiring rights arising out of R&D.

Allowances

8.7   A 100% capital allowance may be claimed on the expenditure during the accounting period in which the expenditure is incurred. A reduced claim may be made (*CAA 2001, s 441(3)*) but there is no facility to claim further allowances (such as writing down allowances) in subsequent accounting periods.

If ownership of the asset changes hands or if it destroyed, a disposal value must be included within the company's corporation tax computation. On sale it will be the net proceeds of sale or market value in other cases. If the asset is demolished or destroyed any insurance or compensation monies received are taken as the disposal value. In the accounting period of disposal a balancing charge will be included being the smaller of the difference between the disposal value and the balance of unclaimed expenditure and the R&D allowance claimed (*CAA 2001, s 442*). There is no facility in the legislation for claiming a balancing allowance.

The balancing charge and R&D allowance are treated accordingly as receipts and expenses of the trade (*CAA 2001, s 450*).

Example 8.3

In the year of acquisition of a £2.5m research building, Novotech plc makes a claim for £1m R&D. Some years later it sells the building for £5m. The balancing charge is the smaller of:

- the difference between the disposal value and the balance of unclaimed expenditure:

$$£5m - £(2.5m - 1m) = £3.5m$$

and

- the R&D allowance claimed:

$$£1m$$

The balancing charge is £1m, the R&D claim made.

8.8 If the company ceases to use the asset for the R&D purpose this is not a disposal for R&D purposes. The R&D allowance is eventually recouped when the asset is sold. On a change of use the asset may qualify for plant and machinery allowances or industrial buildings allowance (see Chapter 6). The R&D allowance is not clawed back at this stage. It is only clawed back on the eventual sale of the asset.

Disposal value

8.9 If an R&D asset on which an R&D allowance has been claimed is demolished and the demolition costs exceed the disposal value, (which in many cases may be nil), the excess demolition costs may qualify for R&D allowance. They will only qualify if the asset has not begun to be used for any purpose other than research and development (*CAA 2001, s 445*). The excess is not to be treated as expenditure on any property that replaces the demolished asset.

Any additional VAT liability incurred on the R&D asset qualifies for R&D allowances provided that the company, which incurred the original expenditure on the asset, still owns it and the asset has not been demolished or destroyed. Any additional VAT rebate is treated as a disposal value provided that the company that incurred the original expenditure on the asset still owns it and the asset has not been demolished or destroyed. If there is no unclaimed R&D allowance, the VAT rebate is treated as a balancing charge. If there is unclaimed R&D allowance and the additional VAT rebate is less than the unclaimed R& D allowance, the additional VAT rebate is deducted from the unclaimed R&D allowance and the result treated as the unclaimed R&D allowance for future disposal events. If the additional VAT rebate is more than the unclaimed R&D allowance the difference is treated as a balancing charge (*CAA 2001, ss 448, 449*). (See also HMRC Capital Allowances Manual CA 60750.)

REVENUE EXPENDITURE

Revenue deductions

8.10   The tax relief for expenditure on research and development provisions may be claimed by all companies. In general the small company rules are contained in *FA 2000, Sch 20* and the large company rules in *FA 2002, Sch 12*. The relief only applies to companies and for this purpose the company definition given in *ICTA 1988, s 832(1)* applies being 'any body corporate or unincorporated association but does not include a partnership, a local authority or a local authority association'. The company must also be within the charge to corporation tax (HMRC Corporate Intangibles Research and Development Manual CIRD 81200).

Companies qualify for an enhanced deduction if expenditure incurred is more than £10,000 in an accounting period. The enhanced deduction is included within the adjusted trading profits. Companies claim the enhanced relief by completing boxes 99 to 102 as appropriate. The following paragraphs provide a summary of the detailed rules.

Meaning of research and development expenditure

8.11   The same GAAP definitions are used as in 8.3. In addition the research must be within the DTI guidelines. HMRC recommends that the DTI guideline

233

tests be applied before the SSAP 13 and IAS 38 tests. Essentially a project will qualify as an R&D project if it is carried on in a field of science or technology and is undertaken with an aim to extend knowledge to which the relief applies (HMRC Corporate Intangibles Research and Development Manual CIRD 81300). The DTI guidelines are reproduced in HMRC Corporate Intangibles Research and Development Manual CIRD 81900. Paragraph 19 of the DTI guidelines defines the meaning of a project:

> 'A project consists of a number of activities conducted to a method or plans in order to achieve an advance in science or technology. It is important to get the boundaries of the project correct. It should encompass all the activities that collectively serve to resolve the scientific or technological uncertainty associated with achieving the advance, so it could include a number of different sub-projects. A project may itself be part of a larger commercial project, but that does not make the parts of the commercial project that do not address scientific or technological uncertainty into R&D.'

Therefore, in practice, every research activity should be broken down into its separate parts to ascertain whether or not it will qualify as R&D.

Relevant research and development

8.12   Relief can only be claimed on relevant R&D. Relevant R&D is defined in *FA 2000, Sch 20, para 4* (which essentially deals with small companies) to mean that it is R&D related to a trade carried on by the company, or from which it is intended that a trade to be carried on by the company will be derived. The same meaning is adopted in *FA 2002, Sch 12, para 4(4)* and *FA 2002, Sch 12, para 9(3)*, which deal with all company and SME research respectively.

The R&D expenditure may relate to a trade already carried on by the company or the expenditure may lead to or facilitate an extension of that trade and if medical research it has a special relation to the welfare of workers employed in that trade (*FA 2000, Sch 20, para 4*).

Staffing costs include salaries and wages for all employees actively engaged in the research, together with employer's NIC and employer's pension fund contributions relevant to them. Benefits are not included in staff costs with effect from 1 April 2004. Costs for employees only partly engaged in research are apportioned appropriately (*FA 2000, Sch 20, para 5*). (Employees in this context includes directors). Secretarial and administrative costs are excluded.

Qualifying R&D expenditure

8.13   Qualifying R&D expenditure for both the small and the large company schemes is similar but not identical. It can be summarised as follows:

The expenditure:

- must not be capital;

- is attributable to relevant R&D directly undertaken by the company or on its behalf;

- is incurred on staffing costs for directors or employees or on software or consumable items or on qualifying expenditure on externally provided workers or is qualifying expenditure on subcontracted R&D, and from 1 April 2006 on clinical trials;

- is not incurred by the company in carrying on contracted-out activities;

- is not subsidised (SME scheme only);

- any intellectual property created as a result of the R&D will be vested in total or in part in the company (SME scheme only); and

- if the expenditure is incurred in carrying on activities contracted out to the company, they are contracted out by:

    — a large company; or

    — a person otherwise than in the course of a trade, profession or vocation the profits of which are chargeable to tax under Case I or II of Schedule D.

(FA 2000, Sch 20, para 3; FA 2002, Sch 12, para 4).

Staffing costs for directors or employees include salary, benefits, secondary Class I contributions, UK staff pension fund and from 1 August 2008 compulsory contributions under the social security legislation of an EEA State other than the UK or Switzerland *(FA 2000, Sch 20, para 5)(SI 2008/1930).*

Intellectual property

8.14 Intellectual property includes:

- any industrial information or technique likely to assist in:

    — the manufacture or processing of goods or materials; or

    — the working of a mine, oil well or other source of mineral deposits or the winning of access thereto; or

    — the carrying out of any agricultural, forestry or fishing operations;

- any patent, trademark, registered design, copyright, design right or plant breeder's right or overseas equivalent *(FA 2000, Sch 20, para 7).*

The intellectual property if vested should be vested at the time when the intellectual property is created.

Subsidised expenditure

8.15   Subsidised expenditure is any expenditure for which a grant or assistance is directly or indirectly received.

Externally provided workers

8.16   Externally provided workers are those engaged on the project who are not employed by the company but are under the company's supervision. The external workers' services must be supplied to the company through a staff provider. Self-employed consultants are not externally provided workers, although their costs may form part of subcontracted R&D (HMRC Corporate Intangibles Research and Development Manual CIRD 84100).

Where the staff provider and the company are not connected, 65% of the staff provision payment cost is treated as qualifying expenditure on externally provided workers.

If external workers are provided by a connected person, and the whole of the fee is included in the relevant provider's GAAP accounts for a period ending not more than 12 months after the end of the accounting period in which the company claiming the R&D allowance makes the payment, then the company may claim R&D tax credit on the lower of:

• the qualifying payment for staff that it makes to the staff provider, and

• the amount that the staff provider includes as relevant expenditure in its accounts (*FA 2000, Sch 20, para 8C*).

If the staff provided and the company are not connected they may jointly elect in writing, within two years of the end of the accounting period in which the contract arrangement is entered into, for the connected persons treatment to apply. This election must apply to all staff under the same arrangement (*FA 2000, Sch 20, paras 8A–8E and FA 2002, Sch 12, para 17(d)*).

Subcontracted research and development

8.17   An SME can claim relief on the payments that it makes to subcontractors. The treatment is similar to the externally provided workers treatment. If the parties are not connected, only 65% of the costs are deductible by the company.

If the contractor is a connected person, and the whole of the amount that is paid to the subcontractor is included in the subcontractor's GAAP accounts for a period ending not more than 12 months after the end of the accounting period in which the company claiming the R&D allowance makes the payment, then the company may claim R&D tax credit on the lower of:

- the payment that it makes to the subcontractor, and

- the amount that the subcontractor includes as relevant expenditure in his or her accounts.

If the subcontractor and the company are not connected they may jointly elect, in writing, within two years of the end of the accounting period in which the subcontract arrangement is entered into, for the connected persons treatment to apply (*FA 2000, Sch 20, paras 9–12*).

A large company's R&D expenditure that it subcontracts to other parties is generally not allowable (see HMRC Corporate Intangibles Research and Development Manual CIRD 84200) although it can have work subcontracted out to it (see **8.6**).

DEFINITION OF AN SME

8.18 An SME is defined in accordance with the European recommendation as detailed in *FA 2000, Sch 20, para 2* as amended by *FA 2007, s 50*. The criteria for enlarging an SME was introduced with effect from 1 August 2008 (*SI 2008/1878*).

Definition of a Micro, Small and Medium-sized company – from 1 August 2008.

	Medium	*Small*	*Micro*
If the company has fewer than	500 employees	50 employees	10 employees
And			
either an annual turnover not exceeding	€100m	€10m	€2m
or			
A balance sheet total not exceeding	€86m	€10m	€2m

Definition of a Micro, Small and Medium-sized company – prior to 1 August 2008.

	Medium	Small	Micro
If the company has fewer than	250 employees	50 employees	10 employees
And			
either an annual turnover not exceeding	€50m	€10m	€2m
Or			
A balance sheet total not exceeding	€43m	€10m	€2m

(2003/361/EC)

BASIS OF DEFINITION OF AN SME

8.19   The staff head count is based on the number of full-time person years attributable to people who have worked within or for the concern during the year in question. Part-time, seasonal and temporary workers are included on a pro-rata basis.

'Employees' includes actual employees, persons seconded to the enterprise, owner-managers and partners (other than sleeping partners). Apprentices or students engaged in vocational training with an apprenticeship or vocational training contract, or any periods of maternity or parental leave are excluded.

Turnover is taken per the accounts (net of VAT). The balance sheet total is the gross amount of assets shown in the accounts. Results are converted from sterling to euros to ascertain whether the tests are met.

The EC defines the enterprise as either autonomous, linked or partner. Autonomous means that there are no partner or linked enterprises. A linked enterprise is an enterprise whereby one company is able to exercise control directly or indirectly over the other. A partner enterprise exists where the enterprises are not linked but where one enterprise is able to exercise control either directly or indirectly over the affairs of the other. If a company has partner or linked enterprise relationships the results are aggregated. (See Flow Chart HMRC Corporate Intangibles Research and Development Manual CIRD 92850).

The conditions are relaxed for public investment corporations, and venture capital companies, 'business angels', provided the total investment of those business angels in the same enterprise is less than €1.25m, universities or non-profit research centres, institutional investors, including regional development funds and autonomous local authorities with an annual budget of less than €10m and fewer than 5,000 inhabitants.

A company may change its status from SME to large company. This will only take place if the conditions are satisfied for two consecutive years.

SMALL OR MEDIUM-SIZED COMPANY

Tax relief for expenditure on research and development

8.20 A small or medium-sized company (SME) will qualify for an enhanced deduction from trading profits of 175% of its qualifying R&D expenditure if this expenditure amounts to £10,000 or more during a 12-month accounting period. For expenditure incurred prior to 1 August 2008, the rate was 150% (*FA 2008, Sch 8, para 1*)(*SI 2008/1933*).The amount is reduced proportionately if the accounting period is less than 12 months (*FA 2000, Sch 20, para 1*). (The £10,000 limit was introduced for accounting periods ending on or after 27 September 2003. Previously the limit was £25,000). Qualifying expenditure is expenditure that would be allowable as a deduction in computing the taxable profits of a trade carried on by the company, or would have been allowable if the trade were being carried on at the time that the expenditure was incurred. Pre-trading expenditure is not treated as incurred on the first day of trading (*ICTA 1988, s 401*) but when it is actually incurred.

Relief

8.21 175% relief can be obtained by the company if it is carrying on an R&D trade during that accounting period. An adjustment is included in the Schedule D Case I computation under the heading 'Deductible expenditure not included in the accounts' (*FA 2000, Sch 20, para 13*).

If the company has not yet started the trade it may elect to treat 175% of the expenditure as a trading loss of the accounting period in which the expenditure was incurred. The relief for pre-trading expenditure (*ICTA 1988, s 401*) is ignored. The election must be made in writing within two years of the accounting period to which the loss relates (*FA 2000, Sch 20, para 14*). However, this deemed trading loss may not be set off against profits of a preceding accounting period (where *ICTA 1988, s 393A(1)(b)* applies) where the company is also entitled to a deemed trading loss for that earlier period.

Alternatively, the company may surrender the loss for a cash payment of 14% of the loss for the chargeable period (*FA 2008, Sch 8, para 1*). For expenditure incurred prior to 1 August 2008 (*SI 2008/1933*), the rate was 16%.The cash payment cannot exceed the total of the company's PAYE and NIC liabilities for the period. Employee child tax credits, working tax credit, statutory sick pay and statutory maternity pay are ignored in these calculations (*FA 2000, Sch 20, para 17*). The relief claimed is included in box 89 of the company tax return. Trading losses carried forward are restricted accordingly. The time limit for making the claim is two years from the end of the relevant accounting period.

The relief is only available to SMEs. If the SME is owned by a consortium no R&D relief may be surrendered to any group company that is not an SME (*FA 2000, Sch 20, para 22*).

Cap on R&D aid

8.22   The maximum R&D relief or R&D tax credit that an SME may claim is restricted to €7.5m (£6m approximately) R&D Aid (*FA 2008, s 29*). R&D aid is calculated according to the following formula:

$$A = (TC + R + (P \times CT)) - (N \times CT)$$

A   Total R&D aid,

TC   Total tax credits paid to the claimant in respect of expenditure attributable to that project and claims made, but not paid or applied unless refused by HMRC

R   Actual reduction in tax liability in respect of expenditure attributable to that project for all accounting periods concerned and for all companies concerned if a group or consortia exists and group relief has been claimed

P   Potential relief, being the aggregate of all relief other than a tax credit, for which the claimant has made a claim or election, unless refused by HMRC

CT   The main rate of corporation tax at the time when the total R&D aid is calculated

N   Notional relief that the company could have claimed if it were a large company throughout the accounting period

These rules come into effect from 1 August 2008 (SI 2008/1928). There is no restriction on expenditure incurred prior to this date (*FA 2008, Sch 10*).

Example 8.4

The Wonderco Ltd was an SME that made up accounts to 31 March each year. It incurred expenditure that qualified for R&D. The company wishes to know the amount of R&D relief available for the year ended 31 March 2012.

The company has received the following R&D relief:

Year ended 31 March 2009	R&D reduction in tax liability	£4m
Year ended 31 March 2010	R&D Tax credit	£1m
Year ended 31 March 2011	R&D reduction in tax liability	£3m

The main rate of corporation tax for the year ended 31 March 2012 is assumed to be 25%. If the company were to have been a large company it could have qualified for relief of £4m for the years ended 31 March 2009 and 2011. There were no claims outstanding.

The company's total R&D aid is calculated as follows:

$$Aid = £(1 + 7 + (0 \times CT)) - (4 \times 25)m$$

$$= £7m$$

There is no R&D relief for the year ended 31 March 2012.

LARGE COMPANY

Tax relief for expenditure on research and development

8.23   A large company will qualify for an enhanced deduction from trading profits of 130% of its qualifying R&D expenditure if this expenditure amounts to £10,000 or more during a 12-month accounting period. For expenditure incurred prior to 1 April 2008, the rate was 125%..

The amount is reduced proportionately if the accounting period is less than 12 months (*FA 2002, Sch 12, para 1*). (The £10,000 limit was introduced for accounting periods beginning on or after 9 April 2003. Previously the limit was £25,000). Qualifying expenditure is expenditure that would be allowable as a deduction in computing the taxable profits of a trade carried on by the company, or it would have been allowable if the trade were being carried on at the time that the expenditure was incurred. Pre-trading expenditure is not treated as incurred on the first day of trading (*ICTA 1988, s 401*) but when it is actually incurred.

Qualifying R&D expenditure

8.24   Large company R&D not only includes direct research and development expenditure (as discussed in **8.10** onwards) but also subcontracted R&D and contributions to independent R&D (*FA 2002, Sch 12, para 3*).

Subcontracted research and development

8.25 Subcontracted R&D may qualify for relief if it is subcontracted to an individual, or a partnership made up of individuals. It may also qualify for relief if it is subcontracted to a qualifying body. A qualifying body is a charity, a higher education institution, a scientific research organisation or a health service body.

The research carried out must be relevant revenue research directly undertaken on the company's behalf. In addition if the work is subcontracted out to the company it must be subcontracted by a large company or by a person in the course of that person's trade (*FA 2002, Sch 12, para 5*).

Contributions to independent research and development

8.26 Contributions to independent relevant R&D qualify for relief if the expenditure known as 'the funded R&D' is incurred in making payments to an individual, or a partnership made up of individuals or a qualifying body (as defined in **8.25**). The company must not be connected with an individual or any individual in the partnership when the payment is made. In addition the funded R&D must not be contracted out to the qualifying body, the individual or the partnership concerned by another person (*FA 2002, Sch 12, para 6*).

Work subcontracted to small or medium-sized enterprise

8.27 An SME can make a claim under *FA 2002* large company rules, for subcontract work that it carries out. The revenue expenditure concerned must consist of expenditure on staffing costs, software or consumable stores or externally provided workers.

It can also claim R&D on relevant research work that it subcontracts to others. The work must be contracted to an individual, a partnership made up of individuals or a qualifying body consisting of a charity, a higher education institution, a scientific research organisation or a health service body (*FA 2002, Sch 12, paras 9, 10*).

If the company claims under the large scheme rules the reliefs detailed above in **8.23** will be available.

Location

8.28 There is no statutory provision restricting the location of the R&D work carried out. In fact, the ECJ has ruled that *art 49* of the EC Treaty precluded legislation of a Member State, which restricted the benefit of a tax credit for research to research carried out in that member state (*Laboratoire Fournier SA v Direction des Verifications Nationales et Internationales* Case C-39/04 [2006] STC 538, [2005] ECRI-2057).

Time limits for enhanced deduction

8.29   The time limit for claiming an enhanced deduction (see **8.20** and **8.23**) is two years from the end of the accounting period (*FA 2006, s 29 and Sch 3*).

The transitional rules that expired on 31 Match 2008, allowed claims made up to six years after the end of the relevant accounting period. If such a claim were made the normal two-year time limit remains for all other corporation tax claims, such as loss relief (see **9.11**) or group relief (see **10.5**).

Going concern

8.30   Research and development relief may not be claimed by a company that is not a going concern. If a company ceases to be a going concern after having made the claim, the claim becomes invalid (*FA 2000, Sch 20, para 18A*). This provision was introduced by *FA 2008, s 22, Sch 9, para 1* with effect from 1 August 2008 (*SI 2008/1929*).

A company is a going concern for this purpose if its latest published accounts were prepared on a going concern basis, and nothing in those accounts indicates that they were only prepared on that basis because of an expectation that the company would receive R&D relief or R&D tax credits. 'Publication' is interpreted in accordance with the Companies Act in that the accounts are circulated in a way that invites members of the public or a class of members of the public to read them (*CA 2006, s 436(2)*).

Tax relief for expenditure on vaccine research

8.31   Similar rules also allow for companies to deduct an additional 40% of R&D expenditure on vaccines and medicines, from taxable profits (an additional 50% for expenditure incurred prior to 21 July 2008, or to claim a 16% tax credit if the company is an SME and has a surrenderable loss (*FA 2002, Sch 13*). No relief may be claimed by companies that are not a going concern (*FA 2008, Sch 9 para 2; FA 2002, Sch 13 para 18A*). Large companies submitting a claim on or after 1 August 2008 must include a declaration that the availability of the relief has increased the amount, scope or speed of the company's R & D or the company's expenditure on R & D (*FA 2008, s 30*) (*SI 2008/1925*).

SPECIALIST HMRC UNITS FOR R&D TAX CREDIT CLAIMS

8.32 The Large Business Service and the seven specialist research and development (R&D) tax credit units deal with claims from small and medium enterprises under *FA 2000, Sch 20* as well as claims by large companies under *FA 2002, Sch 12* and claims to vaccine research relief under *FA 2002, Sch 13*. These units should be approached if there are any queries.

The DTI has published a brochure of case studies setting out the experiences of 14 companies that have claimed the relief. The brochure is available from the DTI publications orderline via email from publications@dti.gsi.gov.uk or by calling 0845 015 0010, and for downloading from the R&D pages of the DTI.

Companies and agents should send corporation tax returns with R&D tax credit claims to the specialist unit dealing with the postcode for the location of the main R&D activity of the company, apart from companies dealt with by the Large Business Service and companies dealt with by the specialist pharmaceutical units in Manchester.

Contact details for the new units are as below:

Cambridge R&D Unit Eastbrook,
Shaftsbury Road,
Cambridge CB2 2DJ.
Tel 01223 442534

Croydon R&D Unit,
Southern House.
Wellesley Grove,
Croydon,
Surrey CR9 1WW.
Tel 020 8633 4307

Leicester R&D Unit,
Saxon House,
1 Causeway Lane,
Leicester LE1 4AA.
Tel 0116 2535400

Maidstone R&D Unit,
Medvale House,
Mote Road,
Maidstone,
Kent M15 6AE.
Tel 01622 760403

Manchester R&D Unit,
6th floor Albert Bridge House,
1 Bridge Street,
Manchester M60 9AF.
Tel 0161 288 6118

Southampton R&D Unit,
8th Floor Queens Keep,
1 to 4 Cumberland Place,
Southampton SO15 2UN.
Tel 02380 204253

Cardiff R&D Unit (Wales, Scotland and Northern Ireland) 14 West,
Phase 2 Ty Glas,
Llanishen,
Cardiff CF14 5FP.
Tel 029 2032 7003/7026

Companies whose main R&D activities are located in one of the following postcodes should send their corporation tax returns containing R&D tax credit or relief claims to the appropriate office listed below.

Postcode	Office	Postcode	Office	Postcode	Office
AB	Cardiff	HD	Manchester	RG	Southampton
AL	Cambridge	HG	Manchester	RH	Maidstone
B	Leicester	HP	Croydon	RM	Maidstone
BA	Cardiff	HR	Cardiff	S	Leicester
BB	Manchester	HS	Cardiff	SA	Cardiff
BD	Manchester	HU	Leicester	SE	Maidstone
BH	Southampton	HX	Manchester	SG	Cambridge
BL	Manchester	IG	Cambridge	SK	Manchester
BN	Maidstone	IP	Cambridge	SL	Croydon
BR	Croydon	IV	Cardiff	SM	Croydon
BS	Cardiff	KA	Cardiff	SN	Southampton
BT	Cardiff	KT	Croydon	SO	Southampton
CA	Manchester	KW	Cardiff	SP	Southampton
CB	Cambridge	KY	Cardiff	SR	Manchester
CF	Cardiff	L	Manchester	SS	Maidstone
CH	Manchester	LA	Manchester	ST	Leicester
CM	Maidstone	LD	Cardiff	SW	Croydon

Postcode	Office	Postcode	Office	Postcode	Office
CO	Maidstone	LE	Leicester	SY	Cardiff
CR	Croydon	LL	Cardiff	TA	Cardiff
CT	Maidstone	LN	Cambridge	TD	Cardiff
CV	Leicester	LS	Manchester	TF	Leicester
CW	Manchester	LU	Cambridge	TN	Maidstone
DA	Maidstone	M	Manchester	TQ	Cardiff
DD	Cardiff	ME	Maidstone	TR	Cardiff
DE	Leicester	MK	Cambridge	TS	Manchester
DG	Cardiff	ML	Cardiff	TW	Croydon
DH	Manchester	N	Cambridge	UB	Croydon
DL	Manchester	NE	Manchester	W	Croydon
DN	Leicester	NG	Leicester	WA	Manchester
DT	Southampton	NN	Cambridge	WC	Cardiff
DY	Leicester	NP	Cardiff	WD	Cambridge
E	Maidstone	NR	Cambridge	WF	Manchester
EC	Maidstone	NW	Croydon	WN	Manchester
EH	Cardiff	OL	Manchester	WR	Cardiff
EN	Cambridge	OX	Southampton	WS	Leicester
EX	Cardiff	PA	Cardiff	WV	Leicester
FK	Cardiff	PE	Cambridge	YO	Leicester
FY	Manchester	PH	Cardiff	ZE	Cardiff
G	Cardiff	PL	Cardiff		
GL	Cardiff	PO	Southampton		
GU	Southampton	PR	Manchester		
HA	Cambridge				

RELIEF FOR EXPENDITURE ON REMEDIATION OF CONTAMINATED LAND

Introduction

8.33 Providing all conditions apply, a company may be able to obtain relief for expenditure incurred after 11 May 2001 on the remediation of contaminated land. 150% of the expenditure is relievable against the profits of a Schedule A rental business or against the Schedule D1 profits of a trade (see **8.45**).

Legislation is contained in *FA 2001, s 70, Sch 22 and Sch 23*. There is no entitlement to relief for artificial arrangements (*FA 2001, Sch 22, para 29*).

Land

8.34   In order to qualify for the relief the land must be in the UK and acquired by a company for the purposes of a trade carried on by the company. At the time of acquisition all or part of the land must have been in a contaminated state and the company incurs remedial capital expenditure in respect of the land. The company may elect by notice in writing for this expenditure to be allowed as a deduction against PCTCT. The election must state the accounting period in which the relief is to be claimed and should be given within the normal time limit ie within two years after the end of the accounting period concerned. Expenditure is incurred if it is recognised in the accounts drawn up under GAAP.

Expenditure incurred before trading commences is treated as being incurred on the first day of trading (*FA 2001, Sch 22, para 1*).

Land in the UK means any estate, interest or rights in or over land that is situated in Great Britain and Northern Ireland (*FA 2001, Sch 22, para 31*). Land includes buildings on the land. An enforceable option to purchase land, and an enforceable agreement or contract for a lease, fall within this definition (HMRC Corporate Intangibles Research & Development Manual CIRD 60130).

Qualifying land remediation expenditure

8.35   In order to qualify there are various conditions applying to the expenditure incurred:

- either all or part of the land must be in a contaminated state;

- the expenditure must be incurred on relevant land remediation directly undertaken by the company or on its behalf;

- the expenditure must be incurred
  - on employee costs; or
  - on materials;
  - or is qualifying expenditure on subcontracted land remediation;

- the expenditure would not have been incurred had the land not been in a contaminated state; and

- the expenditure is not subsidised.

(*FA 2001, Sch 22, para 2*).

Contaminated state

8.36   The land is considered to be in a contaminated state if substances in or under the land either cause actual or possible harm or are likely to cause pollution of controlled waters. A nuclear site is not land in a contaminated state (*FA 2001, Sch 22, para 3*).

A substance is any natural or artificial substance, either in solid or liquid form or in the form of a gas or vapour. A substance is matter that has uniform properties. Asbestos is a substance but life forms are not (*FA 2001, Sch 22, para 31 (1)*). Harm means harm to the health of living organisms, interference with the ecological systems of which any living organisms form part, offence to the senses of human beings, or damage to property (*FA 2001, Sch 22, para 31 (1)*). See HMRC Corporate Intangibles Research and Development Manual CIRD 60135.

Relevant land remediation

8.37   Land remediation activities may involve 'the doing of any works (including preparatory activities), the carrying out of any operations or the taking of any steps' in relation to the land itself, the controlled waters affected by the land and any land adjoining or adjacent to the contaminated land. Such work will include the total or partial prevention or the putting right of the effects, of the harm to the land or the pollution of the controlled waters (*FA 2001, Sch 22, para 4*).

Employee costs

8.38   Only the employee costs of directors or employees directly and actively engaged in the relevant land remediation can be attributed to the relevant land remediation. Administration and support services are not included. Employee costs consist of all salaries and benefits to the company's directors or employees, employer's Class 1 NI contributions and company pension fund contributions.

Employee costs of those not working full-time on the land remediation are calculated pro-rata except for two circumstances. If a director or employee spends less than 20% of his total working time on land remediation work, none of the employee costs relating to him are treated as attributable to relevant land remediation. If a director or employee spends more than 80% of his total working time on land remediation work, the whole of the employee costs relating to him are treated as attributable to relevant land remediation (*FA 2001, Sch 22, para 5*).

Expenditure on materials

8.39   Expenditure on materials is attributable to relevant land remediation if the materials are employed directly in that relevant land remediation (*FA 2001, Sch 22, para 6*).

Expenditure incurred because of contamination

8.40   If expenditure incurred on the land is increased only because the land is in a contaminated state, that increased amount is relevant land remediation expenditure (*FA 2001, Sch 22, para 7*).

Subsidised expenditure

8.41   Company land remediation expenditure is treated as subsidised if a grant or subsidy is obtained or it is met by another person. Any receipt not allocated to a particular payment will be allocated on a just and reasonable basis (*FA 2001, Sch 22, para 8*).

Treatment of expenditure where company and subcontractor are connected persons

8.42   The company may incur subcontracted expenditure on land remediation. If the company and the subcontractor are connected persons, the amounts brought into account in accordance with normal accounting practice up to the subcontractor's relevant expenditure is treated as relevant expenditure (*FA 2001, Sch 22, para 10*). Connection is determined under *ICTA 1988, s 839* (see **4.25**).

A person has a relevant connection to a company, where the company's land is in a contaminated state wholly or partly as a result of anything done, or not done, at any time by that person, if:

- the person was connected to the company at that time;
- the person was connected to the company at the time when the land was acquired; or
- the person was connected to the company at any time when the land remediation is, or was, undertaken by the company.

(*FA 2001, Sch 22, para 31(4)*)

Treatment of subcontractor payment in other cases

8.43   Where the company is not connected to the subcontractor the whole of the amount of the subcontractor payment is treated as qualifying expenditure on subcontracted land remediation (*FA 2001, Sch 22, para 11*).

Entitlement to relief

8.44   A company will qualify for land remediation relief if it has incurred qualifying land remediation expenditure on UK land that it acquired in a contaminated state for the purposes of a Schedule A business or a trade that it carries on. The land remediation relief is given in the accounting period in which the qualifying land remediation expenditure is deductible for Schedule A or trading purposes. The claim should be included on form CT600 Box 104.

However, a company is not entitled to land remediation relief if the land is in a contaminated state, wholly or partly as a result of any thing done or omitted to be done at any time by the company or a person with a relevant connection to the company (*FA 2001, Sch 22, para 12*).

Deduction in computing profits of Schedule A business or trade

8.45   Where all conditions are satisfied the company may make a claim for 150% of the qualifying remediation expenditure to be deducted against the Schedule A income or the business profits (*FA 2001, Sch 22, para 13*).

Entitlement to land remediation tax credit

8.46   If the company incurs a Schedule A or a trading loss in the same business or trade for which the contaminated land was acquired it may claim a land remediation tax credit if it has a 'qualifying land remediation loss' in an accounting period.

The 'qualifying land remediation loss' is the lower of:

- 150% of the related qualifying land remediation expenditure; and
- the unrelieved Schedule A loss or trading loss.

The 'unrelieved' Schedule A loss or trading loss is the loss for the accounting period as reduced by the amount of any Schedule A loss (*ICTA 1988, s 392A*) or trading loss (*ICTA 1988, s 393A(1)(a)*) claim that could be made in that accounting period and any other relief claimed by the company in respect of the loss for that accounting period. This will include losses relieved against profits of an earlier accounting period (*ICTA 1988, s 393A(1)(b)*) and losses surrendered to group or consortium members (*ICTA 1988, s 403(1)*).

Schedule A losses (*ICTA 1988, s 392A(2)*) or trading losses (*ICTA 1988, s 393(1)*) brought forward from an earlier accounting period and any trading losses carried back from a later accounting period (*ICTA 1988, s 393A(1)(b)*) are ignored for this purpose.

The corresponding loss carried forward is reduced accordingly (*FA 2001, Sch 22, para 17*).

Example 8.5

Arthur plc incurs land remediation expenditure of £80,000 in the accounting period ended 30 September 2008. The expenditure is deductible against Schedule D Case I profits and the company claims land remediation relief of £40,000.

The company's results for the year are as follows:

	£
Schedule D Case I loss	(140,000)
Schedule D Case III	40,000

The company makes a claim to surrender the full amount of its qualifying land remediation loss in exchange for a payment of land remediation tax credit. It makes no other loss relief or group relief claims for the period.

The 'qualifying land remediation loss' is the lower of:

	£
150% of the qualifying land remediation expenditure (£80,000 × 150%) and	120,000
The company's unrelieved trading loss for the accounting period (£140,000 less £40,000)	100,000
Qualifying land remediation loss	100,000
The tax credit payable (£100,000 × 16%)	16,000
Trading loss available to carry forward to future accounting periods (£140,000 less £100,000)	40,000

Amount of land remediation tax credit

8.47   The company's entitlement to land remediation tax credit is 16% of the qualifying land remediation loss for the period (*FA 2001, Sch 22, para 15*). This is not income for taxation purposes (*FA 2001, Sch 22, para 18*). The credit is claimed on the form CT600 box 144.

Payment in respect of land remediation tax credit

8.48   HMRC may use the credit to settle any outstanding corporation tax liability (*FA 2001, Sch 22, para 16*).

The credit may be applied in discharging any liability of the company's to pay corporation tax, and to the extent that it is so applied the HMRC's obligation under *subpara (1)* is discharged. If a return is under enquiry the tax credit will not be repaid until the enquiry is complete, although HMRC have discretionary powers to pay a provisional amount.

HMRC are not required to pay a tax credit for an accounting period if the company has no outstanding PAYE and NIC liabilities for the same accounting period.

Certain qualifying land remediation expenditure excluded for purposes of capital gains

8.49   Qualifying land remediation expenditure that has been used in a tax credit claim is excluded expenditure for capital gains tax purposes (*FA 2001, Sch 22, para 19*). Capital expenditure on qualifying land remediation allowed as a deduction in computing the profits (losses) of a trade or Schedule A business, is not an allowable deduction for capital gains purposes (*TCGA 1992, s 39*).

Penalties

8.50   The company is liable to a penalty where it fraudulently or negligently makes an incorrect claim for a land remediation tax credit or discovers that the claim although neither made fraudulently nor negligently is incorrect and does not remedy the error without unreasonable delay. The penalty is an amount not exceeding the excess land remediation tax credit (*FA 1998, Sch 18, para 83L*).

If a land remediation tax credit is paid to a company and it is discovered that the payment is excessive, HMRC may make a 'discovery' assessment to recover the overpayment as if it were unpaid tax for that accounting period (*FA1998, Sch 18, para 52(2),(5)*). Excessive interest on tax overpaid may be recovered in the same way (*ICTA 1988, s 826*).

Chapter 9

Single company trading losses

SCHEDULE D CASE I TRADING LOSSES

Computation

9.1   The vagaries of business life will mean that a company can make a loss on its trading ventures just as easily as it can make a profit. A 'trade loss' as it is termed in the legislation is computed in exactly the same way as a trading income, which is the profit of the trade (*ICTA 1988, ss 393(7), (8), 393A(9)(a)*). When a company incurs a trading loss it must prepare its corporation tax computation in the normal way to send to HMRC together with form CT600 and the statutory accounts. If a trading loss is incurred during the accounting period the chargeable profits are recorded as 'nil'. This is achieved by leaving box 3 (trading and professional profits) of the company tax return CT600 blank. The legislation allows the company to claim relief for the loss against its other income (**9.11–9.16**) or to carry forward the loss against future profits of the same trade (**9.2–9.10**). A company that incurs expenditure on or after 1 April 2008 on the new technologies may surrender its loss and claim a repayable tax credit. For details see **9.29–9.43**).

CARRY FORWARD OF TRADING LOSS AGAINST FUTURE TRADING PROFITS

Loss claim

9.2   Unless a trading loss is utilised in other ways it will automatically be carried forward to set against profits of the same trade in the next and subsequent accounting periods. The loss can only be used if there are available profits and once used it cannot be used again. There is no facility to disclaim the whole or even part of the loss, which must be matched consecutively year on year to available profits until depleted (*ICTA 1988, s 393(1)*). If a market gardening or farming business makes a loss for five consecutive years, the next year's loss can only be carried forward against future profits of the same trade (*ICTA 1988, s 397*).

The loss relief is only available if the trade continues to be carried on, when the loss is to be relieved *(ICTA 1988, ss 393(1), 393A(1))*. What is more, the trade has to be the same trade. Commercial dictum dictates that business shifts from unprofitable to profitable sources. As business life moves swiftly it is often difficult to determine whether a new activity is in fact an extension of the existing trade or a new trade. The former situation will permit the loss relief but the latter will deny it. Case law has determined the following.

Case law

9.3   Gordon & Blair Ltd traded as brewers. The company's activities consisted of brewing and selling beer to third parties. After a period of time Gordon & Blair Ltd stopped brewing beer and engaged another company to brew to its specification. Gordon & Blair Ltd continued to sell the beer. It was held that the brewing trade had ceased and a new trade of beer selling had commenced. The effect being that the brewing trade's losses could not be set against the beer sales profits *(Gordon & Blair Ltd v CIR* (1962) 40 TC 358).

Bolands Ltd, an Irish company, traded in Ireland as millers and bakers. The company owned two mills and it used about half of the flour it produced in its own bakeries. The company hit dire times. The company made losses and closed the mills. A year later it reopened one of the mills mainly to supply the bakeries. It was held that a single trade was carried on throughout. Therefore it was able to utilise its trading losses *(Bolands Ltd v Davis* (1925) I ITC 91, (1925) 4 ATC 532).

In contrast J G Ingram & Sons Ltd manufactured and sold surgical goods. At that time the company used rubber in its manufacturing process. The company suffered large losses. A receiver was appointed, the plant sold and the factory closed. The company continued to sell surgical goods under its own brand that were made by an associated company. A year later a change of ownership took place and the company recommenced manufacturing but used plastic rather than rubber in its production process. The sale of surgical goods continued. The company claimed that it carried on the continuing trade of the sale of surgical goods. The courts disagreed and deemed that a new trade commenced with the production of plastic surgical goods *(JG Ingram & Sons Ltd v Callaghan* (1968) 45 TC 151).

More recently in *Kawthar Consulting Ltd v HMRC*, the *JG Ingram* argument was used. Kawthar Ltd's trade was the provision of computers and monitors. Unfortunately the company's client went into liquidation and Kawthar Ltd suffered large losses. Two to three years later, the company won a lucrative contract for the supply of compliance software. The company regarded itself as an IT company and set the earlier trading losses against the current profits under

ICTA 1988, s 393(1). The Special Commissioners decided that the company's trade of dealing in computers had ceased and a new trade of providing IT consultancy services had begun. The result being that Kawthar Ltd was unable to utilise its brought forward trading losses against its current profits (*Kawthar Consulting Ltd v HMRC* [2005] SWTI 1237, [2005] STC (SCD) 524).

Corporation tax self-assessment

9.4   As *s 393(1)* loss relief is automatic, the legislation requires no formal claim. (A formal claim was required for accounting periods ended before 1 October 1993).

In order to satisfy the corporation tax self-assessment filing requirement the company, when completing form CT600, is required to state the amount of the loss to be relieved in box 4 of the return. Only the amount to actually be set against profits should be entered on the return. A separate loss calculation should be supplied with the company tax return to explain how the loss has been utilised. In particular, if more than one trade is being carried on, the computation should clearly show how the trading losses are utilised against each particular trade's income. As soon as the trade ceases it will no longer be possible to carry forward the loss.

The company in its corporation tax self-assessment submission must distinguish between an existing trade and a new or different trade when claiming loss relief.

This is where the practical difficulty lies.

From the earlier case law examples, it seems that, if a company changes its activities during the course of its existence, it must be able to demonstrate that these activities are sufficiently uninterrupted and interrelated to constitute a continuing trade.

Losses and HMRC enquiries

9.5   The fact that a company incurs a loss during the year rather than a profit has no effect on HMRC's powers of enquiry. They remain the same (see **Chapter 2**). A brought forward trading loss shown on a corporation tax computation cannot be enquired into under *FA 1998, Sch 18, para 25* if the time limit of two years after the end of the accounting period in which the loss was incurred has expired. If HMRC wished to enquire into earlier losses it would have to open a discovery enquiry under *FA 1998, Sch 18, para 43*. A discovery enquiry can only be opened if HMRC suspects fraud or negligence on the part of the company, its representative or anyone who was in partnership with the company at the relevant time. Alternatively an enquiry may be opened into the use of a trading loss where there is a reconstruction (*ICTA 1988, s 343(3)*) or a change of ownership (*ICTA 1988, s 768*). *Section 343* permits losses to be transferred from one company to another company with substantially the same ownership, this is discussed in **15.24–15.25**. *Section 768* prevents loss utilisation where there is a change of ownership. (See **9.17**). HMRC have also stated that they will enquire into the use of a trading loss carried forward in a later accounting period where there is a dispute about whether a trade has continued or whether it has ceased and a new trade commenced (HMRC Company Taxation Manual CTM 04150).

Within the charge to corporation tax

9.6   In order to be granted loss relief, not only must the company be carrying on the same trade, but it must also be within the charge to corporation tax (*ICTA 1988, ss 393(10), 393A(9)(c)*). These clauses are most likely to affect companies who become resident in the UK after having been resident abroad.

When a company becomes UK resident it falls within the charge to corporation tax, if it has a source of income. If the company carries on the same trade when it becomes UK resident as it carried on before it became UK resident its loss relief capacity is restricted. The now resident, UK resident company will not be given relief for its trading losses incurred whilst non-UK resident against profits earned when it becomes UK resident. On the other hand a non-UK resident company that is carrying on a trade in the UK through a permanent establishment is within the charge to corporation tax (*ICTA 1988, s 11(1)*). A permanent establishment may consist of a branch or agency. Therefore the branch or agency will obtain relief for any UK losses it incurs against the UK income that it earns. If the accounts and records are kept in a foreign currency, the loss should be converted to sterling using the same exchange rate as used for the conversion of profits entered in box 3.

CORPORATION TAX COMPUTATION

9.7   The following example details the presentation of a corporation tax computation in circumstances where there are trading losses brought forward to set against future trading income from the same traded under *ICTA 1988, s 393(1)*.

Example 9.1

The Abracadabra Trading Company Ltd has the following results for the year ended 31 March 2009.

	£000
Schedule D Case I profits	200
Schedule A	1,600
Schedule D Case III	400
Chargeable gains	300
Gift aid payment	300
Loss brought forward under *ICTA 1988, s 393(1)*	5,000

The company calculates its profits chargeable to corporation tax and its trading loss carried forward as follows:

Corporation tax computation for the year ended 31 March 2009

	£000
Schedule D Case I	200
Less: Loss brought forward under *ICTA 1988, s 393(1)*	(200)
	0
Schedule A income	1,600
Schedule D Case III income	400
Chargeable gains	300
Total profits	2,300
Less: Non-trade charge on income	(300)
Profits Chargeable to Corporation Tax	2,000

Loss utilisation

	£000
Loss brought forward	5,000
Used against trading income of the year	(200)
Loss carried forward *ICTA 1988, s 393(1)*	4,800

Charges on income

9.8   *ICTA 1988, ss 393(9), 393A(8)* allow excess trade charges to be added to a trading loss carried forward. With the introduction of the intangible assets regime on 1 April 2002 very few items will qualify from this time as 'trade charges'. From 25 July 2002 the definition of charges is restricted to:

- annuities or other annual payments,

- qualifying donations to charity,

- amounts allowed as charges on income, namely gifts of shares etc to charity).

Any amount that is deductible in computing profits cannot be allowed as a charge on income (*ICTA 1988, s 338A (2)*).

If trade charges were to be added to a loss claim the following format would be adopted.

Example 9.2

A company has a trading loss brought forward for its accounting period ended 30 June 2002 of £5,000. In that year it has excess trade charges of £10,000. The company has no other income. The trading loss carried forward to the accounting period ended 30 June 2003 is therefore £15,000.

Relief for trading losses against interest and dividends

9.9   *ICTA 1988, s 393*(8) allows the inclusion of interest and dividends as trading income that would be included as trading income but for the fact that tax has been deducted at source. Dividends from UK companies are excluded. In practice this section will only be applied where investment forms part of the trade. The treatment was refused in *Bank Line Ltd v CIR* (1974) 49 TC 307, [1974] STC 342 and *Nuclear Electric plc v Bradley* (1996) 68 TC 670, [1996] STC 405 (HMRC Company Taxation Manual CTM 04250).

Companies entering into partnership

9.10   The business may determine that the company forms links with other companies in order to further its trading activities. Groups are discussed in Chapter 10. A company may be engaged in a certain trading activity and whilst carrying on this trade enters into partnership with another company or individual. Of concern to the company is whether and how it may utilise its trading losses. HMRC have confirmed that the company can relieve trading losses it incurred before it entered into partnership against profits earned whilst in partnership, provided the same trade is carried on. It can also relieve losses under *ICTA 1988, s 393(1)* against its share of the partnership trading income (HMRC Company Taxation Manual CTM 04200).

Set the loss against other profits in the same accounting period and then accounting periods falling within the previous 12 months

9.11   Rather than carry forward the trading loss to set against future trading profits the company may, by claim, offset the loss against its other profits.

Example 9.3

A Ltd's results for the year ending 31 March 2009 show:

	£		£
Trading loss	(10,000)	Chargeable gains	7,200
Schedule A	3,000	Trade charges	(2,000)
Schedule D Case III	4,000	Non-trade charges	(1,000)

The loss may be relieved as follows.

	£
Schedule A	3,000
Schedule D Case III	4,000
Chargeable gains	7,200
	14,200
Deduct trading loss	(10,000)
	4,200
Deduct trade charges	(2,000)
Non-trade charges	(1,000)
Profits chargeable to CT	1,200
CT payable at 20%	240

9.12   The profits that are eligible are the total profits for the same accounting period as the loss followed by the total profits of the previous 12-month chargeable period, provided the trade was being carried on in that chargeable period, in the same accounting period and then accounting periods falling within the previous 12 months. The relief must be taken in that order and the relief for the same chargeable period must be taken in full up to the amount of the chargeable profits. It is not possible to make a partial claim. Only after this relief is taken can the balance of the loss be set against the total profits of the accounting period ended within the previous 12 months.

Example 9.4

A company made a trading loss of £35,000 in the accounting period 1 January 2009 to 31 December 2009. Other corporation tax profits of the period amounted to £20,000. The company continues to trade. The corporation tax profits of earlier accounting periods were as follows.

	£
1 July 2008 to 31 December 2008	10,000
1 July 2007 to 30 June 2008	20,000

The trade in which the loss was incurred was carried on throughout the whole of the period from 1 July 2007 to 31 December 2009. The company claims relief under *ICTA 1988, s 393A(1)(b)* to extend the relief to the 'preceding period', the 12-month period, which ends on 31 December 2008.

Relief is given as follows:

Against profits of the accounting period	£
1 January 2009 to 31 December 2009	20,000
1 July 2008 to 31 December 2008	10,000
1 July 2007 to 30 June 2008	5,000
Total amount of profits relieved	35,000

Example 9.5

The facts are the same as the previous example, except that the trading loss for the period from 1 January 2009 to 31 December 2009 was £45,000.

Relief is given as follows:

Against profits of the accounting period	£
1 January 2009 to 31 December 2009	20,000
1 July 2008 to 31 December 2008	10,000
1 July 2007 to 30 June 2008	10,000
Total amount of profits relieved	40,000

The set-off for the accounting period ended 30 June 2008 is limited to the proportion (183/366 × £20,000 = £10,000) of the profits of the period that fall into the 12 months ending on 31 December 2008. The unused balance of the loss for accounting period ending 31 December 2009 (£5,000) is available for carry forward under *ICTA 1988, s 393(1)* (HMRC Company Taxation Manual CTM 04540 adapted).

Profits for the accounting period ended 30 June 2008have been apportioned on a time basis. There is always the possibility to apportion the profits on an actual basis if this gives a more accurate result. For this see the discussion on *Marshall Hus & Partners Ltd v Bolton* (1980) 55 TC 539, [1981] STC 18 in **2.6**.

9.13   It is not compulsory to take *s 393A(1)* relief. The relief can be ignored and the loss can be carried forward in an automatic *s 393(1)* set-off. If *s 393A(1)* is claimed current year relief must always be taken before prior year relief.

Where there are losses arising in consecutive accounting periods and relief is claimed under *ICTA 1988, s 393A(1)* for each accounting period the order of set-off is:

(i)   loss of the first accounting period against total profits of the same accounting period;

(ii) loss of the first accounting period against the preceding 12 months' profits;

(iii) loss of the second accounting period against total profits of the same accounting period;

(iv) loss of the second accounting period against profits of the preceding 12 months, which in effect amounts to the 'first accounting period'.

This can often result in insufficient profits against which to make a carry back election for the second accounting period.

Example 9.6

A company commenced trading on 1 January 2008 and prepares six monthly accounts for its first two years of trading. It makes trading losses of £25,000 in its six-month accounting period ended 30 June 2009 and £40,000 in its six-month accounting period ended 31 December 2009. The corporation tax profits of the preceding periods were as follows.

	£
Accounting period 6 months to 31 December 2008	20,000
Accounting period 6 months to 30 June 2008	10,000

Relief for the £25,000 loss for the period ended 30 June 2009 is given before relief for the £40,000 loss for the year ended 31 December 2009. Relief is given as follows:

Loss for the period to 30 June 2009

	Profit	*Loss*	*Net*
	£	£	£
Against profits of the accounting period:			
• 6 months to 31 December 2008	20,000	20,000	—
• 6 months to 30 June 2008	10,000	5,000	5,000
Total	30,000	25,000	5,000

Loss for the period to 31 December 2009

The profits against which the loss can now be set against are reduced as follows after the 30 June 2008 loss relief.

	Profit	*Loss*	*Net*
	£	£	£
Against profits of the accounting period:			
• 6 months to 31 December 2009	—	40,000	(40,000)
• 6 months to 30 June 2009	—	25,000	(25,000)
Total	—	65,000	(65,000)

This loss cannot be carried back. This is because all of the profits for accounting periods in the 12 months immediately preceding the accounting period ended 31 December 2009 (that is the 12 months to 30 June 2009) have already been covered by loss relief from the earlier period. The company would have preferred to claim relief for the period ended 31 December 2009 first. If it had been able to do this, relief for the period ended 31 December 2009 would have been given against the profits of the period ended 31 December 2008. The loss for the period ended 30 June 2009 could then have gone against the whole of the £10,000 profits for the period ended 30 June 2008. But the legislation does not allow this.

(HMRC Company Taxation Manual CTM 04550 adapted).

9.14 The loss can only be set against the total profits of the accounting period ended in the previous 12 months if and only if the trade in question was carried on at some time in that accounting period on a commercial basis. It is not necessary for the trade to have been carried on for the whole of the preceding 12-month period. If the trade was carried on at some time during the previous 12 months the loss will still be relievable against total profits of that period (HMRC Company Taxation Manual CTM 04510).

Again the facts of each case must be reviewed carefully to ascertain whether or not a trade is being carried on, on a commercial basis. The loss up to the full amount of the total profits must be utilised or if less the full amount of the loss. The balance of any unused loss is available to carry forward under *ICTA 1988, s 393(1)*.

A claim must be made within two years of the end of the accounting period in which the loss is incurred. The claim can be made by completing box 122 of the company tax return and by giving full details of the loss and the trade to which it refers (*ICTA 1988, s 393A*).

Charges on income

9.15   Charges on income are now in the main restricted to donations and gifts to charities (*ICTA 1988, s 338A*) (see **9.8**). As such payments are not related to a company's trading activity they are termed as 'non-trade charges' (*ICTA 1988, s 393A(1)(b)*); loss carry back is given before non-trade charges for the year. Excess non-trade charges can only be relieved against current year profits.

Example 9.7

Wizard Ltd prepares accounts to 30 June each year. The company has recently changed its accounting date from 31 December.

Wizard Ltd's results both actual and forecast are as follows:

	Year ended 31 December 2007	Six months ended 30 June 2008	Year ended 30 June 2009	Year ended 30 June 2009
	£000	£000	£000	£000
Schedule D Case I profit/(loss)	35	20	(120)	90
Schedule A	5	3	6	4
Chargeable gain	10	0	8	0
Gift aid payments	(3)	(2)	0	0

ICTA 1988, s 393A(1)(a) claim for the year ended 30 June 2009

	Year ended 30 June 2009 £000
Schedule A	6
Chargeable gain	8
	14
Less: loss claim	(14)
Profits chargeable to corporation tax	0

ICTA 1988, s 393A(1)(b) for the previous 12 months

	Year ended 31 December 2007	Six months ended 30 June 2008
	£000	£000
Schedule D Case I profit	35	20
Schedule A	5	3
Chargeable gain	10	0
	50	23
Less: loss claim	(25)	(23)
	25	0
Non-trade charges	(3)	0
Profits chargeable to corporation tax	(3)	0

The non-trade charges are lost for the six months ended 30 June 2008 as set-off is after loss relief.

ICTA 1988, s 393(1) loss carried forward against future trading profits

	Year ended 30 June 2010
	£000
Schedule D Case I profit/(loss)	90
Less: loss claim	(58)
	32
Schedule A	4
Chargeable gain	0
Profits chargeable to corporation tax	36

Loss utilisation

	£000
Trading loss for the year ended 30 June 2009	120
Less: *ICTA 1988, s 393A(1)(a)* claim for the current year	(14)
	106
Less: *ICTA 1988, s 393A(1)(b)* claim for the previous 12 months:	
• Six months to 30 June 2008	(23)
• Six months to 31 December 2007	(25)
Loss carried forward (*ICTA 1988, s 393(1)*)	58
12 months to 30 June 2010	(58)
Total	0

Example 9.8—Losses carried forward and back with trade charges

B Ltd has carried on the same trade for many years. The results for the years ended 30 September 2006, 2007 and 2008 are shown below.

Year ended 30 September	2006	2007	2008
	£000	£000	£000
Trading profit/(loss)	(20)	20	(17)
Schedule D Case III	5	3	5
Chargeable gains	5.6	4.7	4
Trade charges	(3)	(9)	(5)
Non-trade charges	—	(1)	—

The losses may be relieved as follows.

Year ended 30 September	2006	2007	2008
	£000	£000	£000
Schedule D Case I		20	
Deduct loss brought forward		(12.4)	
		7.6	
Schedule D Case III	5	3	5
Chargeable gains	5.6	4.7	4
	10.6	15.3	9
Trading losses of same period	(10.6)		(9)
Deduct trade charges		(9)	
		6.3	
Deduct trading loss carried back from year ended 30 September 2008		(6.3)	
Profits chargeable to CT	—	—	—
Non-trade charges unrelieved		1	

Loss memorandum

Year ended 30 September	2006	2007	2008
	£000	£000	£000
Trading loss	20		17

Trade charges	3	9	5
Non-trade charges		1	
	23	10	22
Losses used in current year	(10.6)		(9)
Charges used in current year		(9)	
Carried back to year ended 30 September 2007			(6.3)
Losses/charges carried forward	12.4	—	6.7
Non-trade charges unrelieved		1	

RELIEF FOR A TRADING LOSS AGAINST TOTAL PROFITS OF THE PRECEDING ACCOUNTING PERIODS WHEN A COMPANY CEASES TO TRADE

Cessation of trade

9.16   When a company ceases trading it is most likely to cease at or during its normal accounting period rather than on the last day of the accounting period. The legislation recognises this and allows the loss of the last 12 months of trading to be utilised in a carry back claim. The loss will most likely include the loss of the last trading period of less than 12 months and a proportionate part of a loss that falls into the preceding accounting period. In addition the loss carry back period of *ICTA 1988, s 393A(1)* is extended from a 12-month period to a three-year-period by *ICTA 1988 s 393A(2A)*, provided the trade was being carried on at that time. Losses are set off against profits of the preceding accounting period before earlier accounting periods.

Example 9.9

Hardwood ceased trading on 30 June 2009. It had the following results:

Accounting period ended	Months	Tradeprofit £	Tradeloss £
30 June 2009	6		30,000
31 December 2008	12		40,000
31 December 2007	12		3,000
31 December 2006	12	20,000	
31 December 2005	12	50,000	
31 December 2004	12	2,000	

9.16 *Single company trading losses*

ICTA 1988, s 393A(2A) and *(2B)* claims are made as follows:

	£
Loss arising in the accounting period falling wholly in the 12-month period prior to cessation—6 months to 30 June 2009	30,000
Proportion of the loss arising in the accounting period falling partly in the 12-month period prior to cessation—6 months to 31 December 2008: (183/365) × 40,000	20,000
Total	50,000

The £20,000 loss for the period to 31 December 2008 is utilised before the £30,000 loss for the later period to 30 June 2009.

The losses are relieved as follows:

Accounting period ended	Months	Trade profit	Loss utilised	Profit accessed	ICTA 1988, s 393(2A), (2B)	ICTA 1988, s 393A(1)
		£	£	£	£	£
30 June 2009	6				(30,000)	
31 December 2008	12				(20,000)	(20,000)
31 December 2007	12					(3,000)
31 December 2006	12	20,000	(3,000)	Nil	17,000	3,000
			(17,000)			
31 December 2005	12	50,000	(3,000)	17,000	3,000	
			(30,000)		30,000	
31 December 2004	12	2,000		2,000		
Total		72,000	(53,000)	19,000	Nil	(20,000)

It is not possible to utilise the £20,000 loss remaining for the year ended 31 December 2008, as there are no profits in the year ended 31 December 2007 against which it can be set.

LOSS RELIEF RESTRICTION

Changes in situation

9.17   Loss relief carry forward and carry back is denied where:

- in a three-year period there is both a change in the ownership of a company and a major change in the nature or conduct of the trade, or

- at any time after the scale of the company's activity becomes negligible and before any significant revival of the trade takes place there is a change in ownership of the company (*ICTA 1988, ss 768, 768A*).

Change of ownership of a company

9.18   A change of ownership of the company arises if a single person or a group of persons acquire more than half the ordinary share capital of the company. Holdings of 5% or less are ignored unless the acquisition is in respect of an existing holding (*ICTA 1988, s 769*). Any two points in a three-year period may be compared. Connected persons holdings are included. The *ICTA 1988, s 839* definition is used (see **4.25**), but unsolicited gifts of shares and legacies are not included. If the company is a 75% subsidiary, changes in ownership are ignored if it remains a 75% subsidiary of the same ultimate parent but a change in ownership of a holding company will extend to the subsidiary (*ICTA 1988, s 769*).

Major change in the conduct or nature of trade

9.19   What constitutes a major change in the nature or conduct of the trade is largely a question of fact but *ICTA 1988, s 768(4)* includes the following:

- a major change in the type of property dealt in, or services or facilities provided, in the trade; or

- a major change in customers, outlets or markets of the trade.

The effect of the change is to restrict the loss relief both before and after the change, with the activity before and the activity after the change being treated as two separate accounting periods. Balancing adjustments will be calculated for capital allowance purposes.

Examples of HMRC's view of what would and would not constitute a major change in the conduct or nature of trade are given in SP 10/91.

These are:

Examples where a major change would be regarded as occurring:

(i)   A company operating a dealership in cars switches to operating a dealership in tractors (a major change in the type of property dealt in).

(ii) A company owning a public house switches to operating a discotheque in the same, but converted, premises (a major change in the services or facilities provided).

(iii) A company fattening pigs for their owners switches to buying pigs for fattening and resale (a major change in the nature of the trade, being a change from providing a service to being a primary producer).

Examples where a change would not in itself be regarded as a major change:

(i)   A company manufacturing kitchen fitments in three obsolescent factories moves production to one new factory (increasing efficiency).

(ii) A company manufacturing kitchen utensils replaces enamel by plastic, or a company manufacturing time pieces replaces mechanical by electrical components (keeping pace with developing technology).

(iii) A company operating a dealership in one make of car switches to operating a dealership in another make of car satisfying the same market (not a major change in the type of property dealt in).

(iv) A company manufacturing both filament and fluorescent lamps (of which filament lamps form the greater part of the output) concentrates solely on filament lamps (a rationalisation of product range without a major change in the type of property dealt in).

Schedule D Case V

9.20   Losses from an overseas business assessed under Schedule D Case V may only be carried forward and set off against profits from the same trade (*ICTA 1988, s 393*). They cannot be set against other profits of the accounting period of the loss or the previous 12 months (*ICTA 1988, s 393A(3)*). Profits arising from an overseas branch are included within the Schedule D Case I assessment.

Government investment written off

9.21   It has been part of the government's policy to invest in certain companies. Where the government writes off the debt, the company's losses that are carried forward are reduced accordingly. The losses affected are:

- *ICTA 1998, s 393(1)*—loss carried forward against future trading profits from the same trade;

- *ICTA 1988, s 75(3)*—excess management expenses or charges on income;

- *CAA 2001, s 260(1), (2)*—special leasing allowances; and

- *TCGA 1992, s 8*—capital losses.

Where a claim is made to set the loss against current profits under *ICTA 1988, s 393A* (trading loss set against profits of the same or earlier accounting period), *CAA 2001, s 260(3)* (special leasing allowance to be set against current profits) or *ICTA 1988, s 402* (group relief), it will not be disturbed (*ICTA 1988, s 400*).

SELF-ASSESSMENT

Loss claims and elections

9.22   If a company makes a loss claim it must quantify the amount of the loss at the time (*FA 1998, Sch 18, para 54*). Normally, this is included on the corporation tax computation and on the company tax return CT600 boxes 122–138. There is a general time limit of six years from the end of the accounting period to which the claim relates (*FA 1998, Sch 18, para 55*). This is overridden if the legislation gives a shorter time limit. In particular a loss claim under *ICTA 1988, s 393A(1)* must be made within two years of the end of the accounting period in which the loss arises. Normally, the loss is claimed on the company tax return CT600 and corporation tax computation for the year of the loss and this fulfils the claim requirement. If for any reason CT600 is delayed a separate quantified loss claim should be submitted to HMRC. Any errors in a claim or election can be corrected within the claim time limits (*FA 1998, Sch 18, para 56*).

The legislation differentiates between:

- claims affecting a single accounting period (*FA 1998, Sch 18, para 57*);

- claims or elections involving more than one accounting period (*FA 1998, Sch 18, para 58*);

- all other claims and elections (*FA 1998, Sch 18, para 59*).

Claims affecting a single accounting period

9.23   As stated above claims are usually included within the company tax return. If the company does not include the claim with the company tax return but submits it at another date, although still within the company tax return filing date period, the claim will be treated as an amendment to the return (*FA 1998, Sch 18, para 15*). The amendment should be made formally by letter; and more importantly the relief sought must be given a brief description and the amount of the claim must be quantified (HMRC Company Taxation Manual CTM 90625). If the 12-month period after the year end amendment period has expired, a claim can be made under *TMA 1970, Sch 1A*.

Claims or elections involving more than one accounting period

9.24   In this scenario a company makes a claim for an accounting period, which effects more than one accounting period. This will occur where a company claims to carry back a trading loss under *ICTA 1988, s 393A(1)* against its profits of the previous 12 months. The claim is made for the accounting period but it affects the previous accounting period. If the claim is made within the amendment period for the first accounting period, which contains the profits against which the losses are to be set, it will be treated as an amendment to the return. If the amendment period is past it is treated as an amendment under *TMA 1970, Sch 1A*. Depending on the circumstances the corporation tax repayment will either reduce the current year liability or be repaid direct to the company.

All other claims and elections

9.25   The corporation tax self-assessment enquiry period only runs to 12 months after the end of the filing date of the return. Some claims and elections may be submitted after this. This would mean that HMRC would be unable to enquire into the claim or election. Hence such elections fall under *TMA 1970, Sch 1A*. HMRC has similar powers of enquiry but they are extended to one year and the quarter day after the claim is filed (*TMA 1970, Sch 1A, para 5*). HMRC can amend obvious errors within 12 months of the claim being made (*TMA 1970, Sch 1A, para 3(a)*) and the company may amend the claim at any time within 12 months of the claim, provided that it is not under enquiry.

HMRC AMENDMENTS TO TAX RETURNS AND CLAIMS AND ELECTIONS

9.26   HMRC acknowledge that it has the following powers to amend returns:

- Amendment of a company tax return under *FA 1998, Sch 18, para 34(2)(a)*.

- Discovery assessment made under *FA 1998, Sch 18, para 41*.

- An assessment to recover excess group relief under *FA 1998, Sch 18, para 76* (HMRC Company Taxation Manual CTM 90650)

In turn the company may make, revoke or vary certain claims (*FA 1998, Sch 18, para 61*) outside the normal time limit. The extended time limit is one year from the end of the accounting period in which the HMRC adjustment was made (*FA 1998, Sch 18, para 62(1)*).

Certain liabilities can be reduced by the claim. These are:

- the increased liability resulting from the amendment or assessment;

- any other tax liability for the accounting period to which the amendment or assessment relates; or

- any other tax liability for any subsequent accounting period, which ends not later than one year from the end of the relevant accounting period (*FA 1998, Sch 18, para 62(3)*).

However, the claim cannot reduce the eventual liability by more than the additional assessment (*FA 1998, Sch 18, para 64*).

Where the claim affects another person's tax liability, the company must obtain the other person's consent (*FA 1998, Sch 18, para 62(3)*).

In situations of fraud and neglect a company can make additional claims but only those that can be given effect in HMRC's assessment. The claims must be made before the assessment is raised (*FA 1998, Sch 18, para 65(1)*, (*2*); HMRC Company Taxation Manual CTM 90665).

Assessments under appeal

9.27   If an HMRC amendment to a company tax return or an HMRC assessment is under appeal, claims cannot be made through the *FA 1998, Sch 18, para 54* etc claims procedures. Any claims that the company wishes to make must be made through an application to the Commissioners presiding over the appeal for a determination of the amount that is to be repaid, pending the final determination of the liability. The application is heard in the same way as an appeal (see **2.23–2.25**) (*TMA 1970, s 59DA(4)*, (*5*)) (HMRC Company Taxation Manual CTM 92110).

REPAYMENTS

Repayment interest

9.28   A loss carry back under *ICTA 1988, s 393A* (or a non-trading deficit under *FA 1996, s 83(2)(c)*) may bring about a corporation tax repayment for an earlier period. Repayment interest runs from the due date for the accounting period for which the loss is incurred (*ICTA 1988, s 826(7A), (7C)*).

The repayment interest will be calculated from the normal due date for the accounting period in which the loss or deficit is incurred (see **3.17**).

Example 9.10

Lettice Ltd made a Schedule D Case I trading loss in the accounting period ended 31 March 2009 of £100,000. It has no other income in the year and elects to carry the loss back against its total profits for the year ended 31 March 2008 of £90,000. Corporation tax of £17,100 was paid on 1 January 2009, the due date. The repayment interest is calculated from 1 January 2009.

If the loss is carried back further than 12 months repayment interest is calculated with reference to the period for which the loss was incurred.

Entitlement to first-year tax credits

9.29   If a company incurs relevant first year expenditure (**9.31**) on or after 1 April 2008, it may claim a first-year tax credit for an accounting period in which it has a surrenderable loss (**9.30**), unless it is an excluded company (**9.32**) for that accounting period.

Surrenderable loss

9.30   A company has a surrenderable loss for an accounting period if in that period:

- a first-year allowance is made to the company in respect of relevant first-year expenditure (see **9.31**) incurred for the purposes of a qualifying activity the profits of which are chargeable to corporation tax; and

- the company incurs a loss in carrying on that qualifying activity.

The amount of the surrenderable loss is equal to the lower of:

- the unrelieved loss; and

- the first-year allowance made in respect of the relevant first-year expenditure in the chargeable period in question.

Any first year tax credit claimed reduces the amount of the loss carried forward (*FA 2008, Sch 25, para 19*).

Relevant first-year expenditure

9.31   Relevant first-year expenditure is any expenditure, which is incurred in the period commencing on 1 April 2008 and ending on 31 March 2013 and is either expenditure on:

- energy-saving plant or machinery (*CAA 2001, s 45A*) (see **6.25**); or

- environmentally beneficial plant or machinery (*CAA 2001, s 45H*) (see **6.24**).

Additional expenditure attributable to a VAT liability may be included (*CAA 2001, s 236*). Expenditure incurred before a qualifying period commenced cannot be included (*FA 2008, Sch 25, para 3*).

Excluded company

9.32   A company is an excluded company if it is disregarded for corporation tax purposes being a co-operative housing association (*ICTA 1988, s 488*) or a self-build society (*ICTA 1988, s 489*). The company is also excluded if it is a charity (*ICTA 1988, s 505*) (see **5.46**) or a scientific research association under (*ICTA 1988, s 508; FA 2008, Sch 25, para 1(4)*).

Amount of first-year tax credit

9.33   If a company has a surrenderable loss for the accounting period it is entitled to claim a first year tax credit of an amount equal to the lower of:

- 19% of the amount of the surrenderable loss for the accounting period; or

- the upper limit (*FA 2008, Sch 25, para 2(1)*).

The upper limit is the greater of:

- the total amount of the company's PAYE and NICs liabilities for payment periods ending in the accounting period; and

- £250,000 (*FA 2008, Sch 25, para 2(2)*).

A company may claim the whole or part of the amount that it is entitled to claim.

Total amount of company's PAYE and NICs liabilities

9.34   The total amount of the company's PAYE and NICs liabilities for payment periods ending in the accounting period is:

- PAYE due to HMRC for the period disregarding child tax credit and working tax credit deductions; and

- Class 1 national insurance contributions due to HMRC for that period, disregarding statutory sick pay, statutory maternity pay, child tax credit or working tax credit deductions.

A payment period is a period, which ends on the fifth day of a month and for which the company is liable to account for income tax and national insurance contributions to HMRC (*FA 2008, Sch 25, para 17*).

UNRELIEVED LOSS

Trade or a furnished holiday lettings business

9.35 For a qualifying activity that is a trade or a furnished holiday lettings business, the unrelieved loss is calculated as follows:

Trading loss for the period

less

any relief:

- available under *ICTA 198,8 s 393A(1)(a)*, against profits of same accounting period (see **9.11**);

- obtained under *ICTA 1988, ss 393A(1)(b)* or *393B(3)*, against profits of previous accounting period (see **9.11**);

- available under *ICTA 1988, s 403(1)*, group relief (see **10.7**);

- surrendered under a tax credit provision, of:

    - *FA 2000, Sch 20* (research and development), (see **8.21**);

    - *FA 2001, Sch 22* (remediation of contaminated land), (see **8.33**);

    - *FA 2002, Sch 13* (expenditure on vaccine research), (see **8.31**); and

    - *FA 2006, Sch 5(d)* (film tax credits); and

- set off against the loss under *ICTA 1988, s 400*, government investment write off (see **9.21**) (*FA 2008, Sch 25, para 11(2)*).

No account is to be taken of any loss:

- brought forward from an earlier accounting period under *ICTA, 1988 s 393(1)*, (see **9.2**);

- carried back from a later accounting period under *ICTA, 1988 s 393A(1)(b)* or *ICTA s 393B(3)* (see **9.11**); or
- incurred on a leasing contract (*ICTA 1988, s 395*).

(*FA 2008, Sch 25, para 11(3)*)

Example 9.11

On 1 June 2008 Radius Ltd invests in a solar powered energy system that qualifies for a first year allowance of £100,000. The company has traded at a loss, but its prospects have now improved. Radius Ltd is not a member of a group. It has PAYE and NIC liabilities for the year of £18,000. It surrenders its loss for the year ended 31 March 2009 and claims a tax credit. Its results are as follows:

Year ended 31 March 2009

	£
Schedule D 1 Loss	(500,000)
Schedule A	80,000
Schedule D III	5,000
First Year Allowance	100,000

There is no income for the year ended 31 March 2008.

The surrenderable loss for the year ended 31 March 2009 is calculated as follows:

	£	£
Loss for the year		500,000
Less relief against profits of the same accounting period		
Schedule A	80,000	
Schedule D III	5,000	85,000
Maximum surrenderable Loss		415,000
Restricted to first year allowance	100,000	
The tax credit is restricted to the lower of: 19% of the first year allowance and the upper limit which is the greater of		
(i) the total of the PAYE and NIC liabilities for the year – £18,000		
(ii) £250,000		
The company claims a tax credit of	19,000	
Loss restriction		100,000
Loss carried forward		315,000

Lettings business other than a furnished holiday lettings business

9.36   For a qualifying activity that is a lettings business other than a furnished holiday lettings business, the unrelieved loss is calculated as follows:

Loss from lettings for the period

less any relief:

- available under *ICTA 1988, s 392A(1)*, Schedule A losses (see **12.23**);
- available under *ICTA 1988, s 403(1)*, group relief (see **10.7**);
- surrendered under a tax credit provision, of *FA 2001, Sch 22* (remediation of contaminated land) (see **8.33**);
- set off against the loss under *ICTA 1988, s 400*, government investment write-off (see **9.21**).

(*FA 2008, Sch 25, para 12(2)*)

No account is to be taken of any loss brought forward from an earlier accounting period under *ICTA 1988, s 392A(2)*, Schedule A losses (see **12.23**).

(*FA 2008, Sch 25, para 12(3)*)

Overseas property business or a furnished holiday lettings business

9.37   For a qualifying activity that is an overseas property business trade or a furnished holiday lettings business, the unrelieved loss is calculated as follows:

Loss from lettings for the period

less any relief:

- set off against the loss under *ICTA 1988, s 400* government investment write-off (see **9.21**).

(*FA 2008, Sch 25, para 13(2)*)

No account is to be taken of any loss brought forward from an earlier accounting period under *ICTA 198,8 s 392B(1)*, losses from an overseas property business.

278

Management of investments

9.38   For a qualifying activity that is the management of investments, the unrelieved loss is calculated as follows:

Excess management expenses for the period

less any relief:

- available under *ICTA 1988, s 403(1)*, group relief (see **10.7**).

- set off against the loss under *ICTA 1988, s 400*, government write-off (see **9.21**).

(*FA 2008, Sch 25, para 15(2)*)

No account is to be taken of any loss brought forward from an earlier accounting period under *ICTA 1988, s 75(9)*, management expenses (see **12.12**) (*FA 2008, Sch 25, para 15(3)*).

Payment in respect of first-year tax credit

9.39   A first-year tax credit may either be repaid to the company, or together with any repayment interest (see **3.17**) be used to discharge any of the company's corporation tax liabilities (*FA 2008, Sch 25, para 18 (1)–(3)*). If the return is under enquiry, HMRC are under no obligation to make a repayment until the enquiry is complete. However, they may make a repayment of an amount that they consider to be appropriate (*FA 2008, Sch 25, para 18(4)–(5)*). HMRC are precluded from making a repayment if any PAYE or Class 1 NIC is outstanding (*FA 2008, Sch 25, para 17(6)*). A payment in respect of a first-year tax credit is not chargeable to corporation tax (*FA 2008, Sch 25, para 23*).

CLAWBACK OF FIRST-YEAR TAX CREDIT

Circumstances in which first-year tax credit clawed back

9.40   If a company disposes of an item on which a first-year tax credit is paid before the end of the clawback period, the loss is restored and the first-year tax credit is treated as if it never should have been paid (*FA 2008, Sch 25, para 24*). The clawback period begins when the relevant first-year expenditure on the item is incurred, and ends four years after the end of the accounting period for which the tax credit was paid (*FA 2008, Sch 25, para 25 (10)*).

A company disposes of an item of tax-relieved plant or machinery if the circumstances for a disposal of plant and machinery are met (see **6.34**) or the business is in new ownership. The disposal value of the item is the actual amount received, but this is replaced by market value if the disposal is made to a connected person for less than its market value, or the business is in new ownership (*FA 2008, Sch 25, para 25*). Broadly, this is one where there has been a transfer of a business and, for the purposes of making allowances and charges under the *Capital Allowances Act 2001*, anything done to or by the transferor is treated as having been done to or by the transferee.

Amount of restored loss

9.41   The amount of the restored loss is determined by the formula:

(LS – OERPM) – (OE – DV) – ARL

If the result is less than nil, the amount of the restored loss is nil.

LS   Amount of the loss surrendered in the accounting period for which the first-year tax credit was paid.

OERPM   Amount (or the aggregate of the amounts) of the original expenditure on the retained tax-relieved plant and machinery after the item is disposed of.

OE   Aggregate of the amount of the original expenditure on the item disposed of, and the amounts of the original expenditure on any items of tax-relieved plant and machinery, which the company has previously disposed of.

DV   Aggregate of the disposal value of the item disposed of, and the disposal values of any items of tax-relieved plant and machinery which the company has previously disposed of.

ARL   Amount of the restored loss (or the aggregate of the amounts of prior restored losses)

(*FA 2008, Sch 25, para 26*)

Example 9.12

For the accounting period ended 31 December 2008, Nonsuch Ltd incurred expenditure of £60,000 on plant that qualified as relevant first year expenditure. It surrendered a loss of £60,000 and obtained a tax credit. During the accounting period ended 31 December 2010 it sells part of the plant for £15,000. The original cost of the plant unsold was £10,000. There have been no other disposals or tax credit claims.

Nonsuch Ltd's restored loss is calculated as follows:

(LS – OERPM) – (OE – DV) – ARL

£(60,000 – 10,000) – (50,000 – 15,000) – 0 = £15,000

Clawback of first-year tax credits

9.42   If after submitting the corporation tax return the company becomes aware that the first- year tax credit has been included incorrectly in the tax return and the return is now incorrect; it must notify HMRC and give details of the amendment required. The notice must be given within three months beginning with the day on which the company became aware that a claw back was required (see **9.40**) (*FA 2008, Sch 25, para 27*).

Tax credit claim

9.43   The tax credit claim must be included in the corporation tax return.

The following details must be given:

- the plant or machinery on which the claim is made;
- the relevant first-year expenditure incurred; and
- the date on which that expenditure was incurred (*FA 1998, s 83ZA(1–2)*).

It must also provide a certificate for energy-saving plant and machinery (*CAA 2001, s 45B*) and environmentally beneficial plant and machinery (*CAA 2001, s 45 I*).

A claim is ignored if arrangements are entered into wholly or mainly for a disqualifying purpose whose main object is to obtain a first-year tax credit to which the company would not otherwise be entitled, or of a greater amount than that to which it would otherwise be entitled (*FA 2008, Sch 25, para 28*.

The company will be liable to a penalty if it fraudulently or negligently makes a claim for a first-year tax credit which is incorrect, or discovers that a claim for a first-year tax credit made by it (neither fraudulently nor negligently) is incorrect, and does not remedy the error without unreasonable delay.

9.43 *Single company trading losses*

The maximum penalty is the excess first-year tax credit claimed for the accounting period, which is the difference between the company's tax credit entitlement and the amount of the first year tax credit claimed for the period (*FA1998, s 83ZA (4)–(5); FA 2008, Sch 25, para 29*).

Chapter 10

Groups

BUSINESS STRUCTURE

10.1   As a business grows its affairs develop and the company may consider whether a simple single company structure remains appropriate for its activities or whether it should consider other forms of organisation.

From a taxation perspective the single company offers many advantages. The absence of associated companies means that the small companies rate is not unduly dissipated (see **3.5**). Capital gains and losses can be set against one another without the *TCGA 1992, s 179* restrictions (see **20.32**). Possibly more importantly all the company's activities fall within one company. The merged activities may form one trade, whereas if the trades are split amongst group members they become separate trades in themselves. Retaining activities in one company also avoids the practicalities of preparing group relief claims and company tax returns for each separate entity.

However, taxation does not rule a commercial world and separate business structures may be required. The company may consider buying or forming another company (see **15.1**). Ownership of another company's shares by a company may bring about a group situation. The rapid changes in projects and deals may mean that a business structure is only required for a short amount of time and an acquisition or a new formation may not be the best structure for a deal. Before entering into a group arrangement the company may well be advised to consider a partnership or a joint venture, which it may find simpler to operate.

Corporate partners' share of profits and losses are assessed to corporation tax on the basis of a separate trade being carried on by each partner (*ICTA 1988, s 114*). The company's share of the partnership losses are available to the company to set against its other income for the same or previous year, if the partnership and its trade existed at that time, or to carry forward against its share of future partnership trading income. The partnership can prepare accounts in any format they wish, although they must be in accordance with GAAP. If a corporate partner exercises a dominant influence the (*CA 2006, s 1162; formerly CA 1985, s 258(2)(c)*) and the FRS 2 (accounting for subsidiary undertakings) must be considered. Most notably each corporate partner will have joint and several liability. With this in mind the business partners may decide upon a limited liability partnership (LLP) as introduced by the *Limited Liability Partnership Act 2000* with effect from 6 April 2001.

A joint venture between the business partners may be a simpler structure. No special legal form is required and the business activities are included within the accounts of the venturer thus easing the loss utilisation.

Companies committed to growth may form or acquire new companies and create a group structure. Specific taxation provisions and compliance issues affect groups of companies.

ACCOUNTING AND TAXATION REQUIREMENTS

Accounting

10.2   For company law, a group consists of parent and subsidiary undertakings (*CA 2006, s 474; formerly CA 1985, s 262*). For these purposes an undertaking can be a body corporate, a partnership or an unincorporated association carrying on a business with a view to profit (*CA 2006, s 1161; formerly CA 1985, s 259(1)*). Groups of companies must prepare consolidated accounts unless they are exempted by the small group exemptions (*CA 2006, s 399; formerly CA 1985, s 227*). Each company within the group must prepare its own individual company accounts (*CA 2006, s 394; formerly CA 1985, s 226*).

Taxation

10.3   For corporation tax purposes each company within a group must submit its corporation tax computation, its company tax return and statutory accounts to HMRC (see **2.1**). Group accounts may be submitted as supporting information. Corporation tax is calculated in respect of each individual company's profits. Hence, there is no requirement to prepare a group company tax return. The group situation is brought into account when calculating the individual company's liability and when granting reliefs. Companies must prepare the supplementary form CT600C where group relief and eligible unused foreign tax is claimed or surrendered.

RELIEFS AVAILABLE TO GROUPS

10.4   The taxation legislation recognises that a group is one large trading or business entity made up of several components. Although each group company makes its own self-assessment return in its own name and is responsible for its own corporation tax liability, the taxation legislation permits a certain amount of loss sharing amongst group members. Groups have the opportunity to transfer losses to other group members to be relieved against that group member's profits and to transfer assets within the group without a charge to chargeable gain arising and to surrender eligible unused foreign tax (see Chapter 13). There are different definitions of a group applying to revenue losses, capital losses and consortium situations. These definitions are particular to the taxation legislation and will not always concur with the *Companies Act*.

GROUP RELIEF

Definition of a group

10.5   Various conditions must be satisfied before losses can be transferred in this way between group members. The first condition is that a group actually exists.

A group exists if one company is a 75% subsidiary of the other company and both companies are 75% subsidiaries of a third company. Shares held by share dealing companies as stock in trade are ignored (*ICTA 1988, s 413(3), (5)*). A 75% subsidiary is a company whose ordinary share capital is owned directly or indirectly by another company. 'Own' in this context means possessing the beneficial ownership (*ICTA 1988, s 838*).

Example 10.1

A Ltd owns 100% of the ordinary share capital of B Ltd.

B Ltd owns 80% of the ordinary share capital of C Ltd.

A Ltd, B Ltd and C Ltd are a group.

A Ltd owns 100% of B Ltd and effectively 80% of C Ltd (100 × 80).

Example 10.2

A Ltd owns 75% of the ordinary share capital of B Ltd.

B Ltd owns 80% of the ordinary share capital of C Ltd.

A Ltd and B Ltd are a group as A Ltd owns 75% of B Ltd.

A Ltd and C Ltd are not a group because A Ltd only effectively owns 60% of C Ltd (75 × 80).

B Ltd and C Ltd are a separate group.

Definition of a consortium

10.6   A company is owned by a consortium if 75% or more of the ordinary share capital of the company is beneficially owned by companies of which none owns less than 5%. The consortium member's share is measured by the lowest of the members' percentage interests in shares, profits or assets. Where these have varied over the year the weighted average is taken (SP/C 6). A 90% trading company subsidiary of a company which is itself a 75% owned consortium company is also included (*ICTA 1988, s 413(7)*). With effect from 1 April 2000 overseas companies are included within the count of group companies (*FA 2000, Sch 27, para 4*). The UK branch of a non-resident subsidiary may also claim or surrender group relief.

Example 10.3

P Ltd has an issued share capital of 1,000 ordinary shares, which are within the following beneficial ownership:

Q Ltd	200
R Ltd	100
S Ltd	100
T Ltd	100
U Ltd	100
V Ltd	100
X Ltd	50
Total	750

The remaining shares are held by individual shareholders.

P Ltd is owned by a consortium because 75% of the ordinary share capital is beneficially owned by companies of which none owns less than 5%.

Example 10.4

Z Ltd has an issued share capital of 1000 ordinary shares, which are within the following beneficial ownership:

Q Ltd	200
R Ltd	100
S Ltd	100
T Ltd	100
U Ltd	100
V Ltd	50
X Ltd	50
Total	700

The remaining shares are held by individual shareholders.

Z Ltd is not owned by a consortium because 75% of the ordinary share capital is not beneficially owned by companies of which none owns less than 5%.

Group relief

10.7   Group relief is the surrender of and claim of group and consortium members' trading losses (*ICTA 1988, s 402*).

Surrenderable losses are those incurred for the current year and include:

- trading losses,

- excess capital allowances,

- non-trading loan relationship deficits,

- charges on income,

- Schedule A losses,

- management expenses, and

- a non-trading loss on intangible fixed assets (*ICTA 1988, s 403*).

Trading losses, excess capital allowances and non-trading loan relationship deficits may be set off against the claimant company's profits even though the surrendering company has other profits for the same accounting period against which they can be set.

Excess charges on income, Schedule A losses, excess management expenses and a non-trading loss on an intangible fixed asset are only available for surrender if in total they exceed the surrendering company's gross profits for that period. If a surrender is made, the order of set-off is deemed to be:

   (i)   charges on income,

  (ii)   Schedule A losses,

 (iii)   management expenses, and

 (iv)   a non-trading loss on an intangible fixed asset (*ICTA 1988, s 403*)

The surrendering company's gross profits are its profits for that period before deducting any trading losses, excess capital allowances, non-trade loan relationships deficits, charges, Schedule A losses or management expenses, without any deduction for losses etc from other accounting periods (*ICTA 1988, s 403ZE*).

All Schedule D Case I losses are available for group relief. Schedule D Case V losses may not be group relieved nor may losses from trades not carried out on a commercial basis. Farming and market gardening losses within the *ICTA 1988, s 397* restriction may not be group relieved. (There is a profit requirement every five years in order to be able to set these losses against the company's other income) (*ICTA 1988, s 403ZA*). Excess capital allowances are allowances that are required to be set in the first instance against a specified class of income, eg special leasing (*ICTA 1988, s 403ZB*). A non-trading loan relationship deficit is discussed in **11.17**. Charges are the actual charges paid by the company during the period. A Schedule A loss must be a commercial loss and must not include any loss brought forward from a previous period. Management expenses means the annual amount deductible by the company for the accounting period, but does not include amounts brought forward from earlier periods. See **7.13** for a non-trading loss on an intangible fixed asset (*ICTA 1988, s 403ZD*).

A claimant company must use its own trading losses brought forward before it makes a group relief claim (*ICTA 1988, s 393(1)*).

Example 10.5

Omega Ltd owns 75% of the shares and voting rights of Epsilon Ltd and Zeta Ltd. All companies prepare accounts to 31 March each year. The results for the year ended 31 March 2009 are as follows:

	Omega Ltd	Epsilon Ltd	Zeta Ltd
	£	£	£
Schedule D Case I	400,000	90,000	−380,000
Schedule A	30,000	14,000	23,000
Schedule D Case III	6,000	1,000	2,000
Chargeable gain	40,000	—	10,000
Gift aid payment	1,000	—	—

Zeta Ltd is not expected to make a trading profit in the near future. Both Omega Ltd and Epsilon Ltd's future trading results are uncertain.

		Small companies rate
Upper limit	(1,500,000/3)	500,000
Lower limit	(300,000/3)	100,000

The position for each company prior to group relief is as follows:

	Omega Ltd	Epsilon Ltd	Zeta Ltd
	£	£	£
Schedule D Case I	400,000	90,000	—
Schedule A	30,000	14,000	23,000
Schedule D Case III	6,000	1,000	2,000
Chargeable gain	40,000	—	10,000
Gift aid payment	(1,000)	—	—
PCTCT	475,000	105,000	35,000
Marginal rate	29.75%	29.75%	21%

Omega Ltd should receive the maximum relief, in order to bring profits down to the lower limits for the small companies rate.

	Omega Ltd	Epsilon Ltd	Zeta Ltd
	£	£	£
PCTCT	475,000	105,000	35,000
Less: *s 402* relief	375,000	5,000	
PCTCT	100,000	100,000	35,000
Corporation tax at 21%	21,000	21,000	7,350

Utilisation of loss

		£
Loss		380,000
(i)	Omega Ltd	375,000
(ii)	Epsilon Ltd	5,000
(iii)	Zeta Ltd	0
		380,000

Zeta Ltd will have trading losses in the next accounting period, which it can carry back against this year's profits. Both Omega Ltd and Epsilon Ltd's future profits are uncertain.

Example 10.6

A Ltd (a group member) has the following results.

	Year ending 31 December 2007	Year ending 31 December 2008
	£	£
Case I (loss) brought forward	(500)	—
Case I income/(loss)	1,000	(1,000)
Case III income	500	500

For the accounting period ended 31 December 2007:

- The loss brought forward must be relieved in priority to group relief. The maximum amount of group relief claimable will be £1,000.

- If relief for this period is claimed for so much of the trading loss of the following period as cannot be relieved in that period, ie £500, such relief would be displaced by a group relief claim, and would then be available for carrying forward.

For the accounting period ending 31 December 2008:

No group relief is obtainable, whether or not the trading loss is carried back.

AVAILABILITY OF GROUP RELIEF

UK losses

10.8   The next issue, assuming that losses as detailed in **10.7** have been incurred, is whether group relief is available.

A group relief loss claim for the items within the ambit of UK corporation tax may be made where:

- the surrendering company and the claimant company are both members of the same group,

- the surrendering company is resident in the UK or is not so resident but carries on a trade there through a permanent establishment, and

- the claimant company is resident in the UK or is not so resident but carries on a trade there through a permanent establishment (*ICTA 1988, s 402(2); FA 2006, Sch 1, para 1*).

UK group members and UK branches may, inter alia, claim and surrender losses, so may UK resident consortia.

Overseas losses

10.9   Following the decision in *Marks & Spencer v David Halsey* C-446/03 [2006] STC 237 with effect for accounting periods beginning on or after 1 April 2006, a 'qualifying overseas loss' may be surrendered for group relief (*ICTA 1988, s 403A, Sch 18A*).

For this to occur, the surrendering company must be chargeable to tax under the laws of any European Economic Area (EEA) territory and it must be:

- a 75% subsidiary of a UK resident claimant company, or

- both the surrendering company and the claimant company are 75% subsidiaries of a third company that is UK resident.

The company will be chargeable to tax in an EEA territory if it is resident in the territory or if it carries on a trade in any EEA territory through a permanent establishment (*ICTA 1988, s 402(2A), (2B); FA 2006, Sch 1, para 1*).

The following countries are members of the EEA:

Austria	Finland	Ireland	Malta	Slovenia
Belgium	France	Italy	Netherlands	Spain
Cyprus	Germany	Latvia	Norway	Sweden
Czech Republic	Greece	Liechtenstein	Poland	UK
Denmark	Hungary	Lithuania	Portugal	
Estonia	Iceland	Luxembourg	Slovakia	

Comments in the *Marks & Spencer* case pointed to the fact that the UK was unfairly discriminating against overseas subsidiaries.

Marks & Spencer ECJ ruling

As Community law now stands, *Arts 43* and *48* of the EC Treaty do not preclude provisions of a member state, which generally prevent a resident parent company from deducting from its taxable profits losses incurred in another member state by a subsidiary established in that member state although they allow it to deduct losses incurred by a resident subsidiary. However, it is contrary to *Arts 43* and *48* to prevent the resident parent company from doing so where the non-resident subsidiary has exhausted the possibilities available in its state of residence of having the losses taken into account for the accounting period concerned by the claim for relief and also for previous accounting periods and where there are no possibilities for those losses to be taken into account in its state of residence for future periods either by the subsidiary itself or by a third party, in particular where the subsidiary has been sold to that third party.

Relief in respect of overseas losses of non-resident companies

10.10   An overseas loss of a non-resident company is available for surrender by way of group relief by a non-resident company if the 75% relationship is met.

The loss must meet the following conditions in relation to the EEA territory:

(a)   The equivalence condition: The loss must be of a kind that would be available for relief by a UK company.

(b)   The EEA tax loss condition:

   For EEA resident companies:

   • the loss is calculated under the laws of the EEA territory, and

   • the loss is not attributed to a UK permanent establishment of the company.

   For non-EEA resident companies:

   • the company carries on a trade through a permanent establishment in the EEA territory,

   • the loss is calculated under the laws of the EEA territory, and

   • the activities are not exempt under a double tax treaty, as these would be ignored.

(c)   The qualifying loss condition:

   • The loss cannot be given qualifying relief for any period ('the current period') or any past or future period, and

- the loss has not been given any other qualifying relief under the law of any territory outside the United Kingdom (other than the EEA territory concerned).

(d) The precedence condition: The loss cannot be relieved in any other grouping (*ICTA 1988, s 403F; FA 2006, Sch 1, para 4(1)*).

The relevant accounting period concerned is the accounting period the company would have if it were UK resident (*ICTA 1988, Sch 18, para 1A; FA 2006, Sch 1, para 6(4)*). The loss will not qualify for relief if it arose from artificial arrangements (*ICTA 1988, s 403G; FA 2006, Sch 1, para 4(2)*). The qualifying loss condition must be satisfied at or up to the time when the company makes the group relief claim (*Marks and Spencer plc v Halsey (Inspector of Taxes) (CA) 2007*).

Application of UK rules to non-resident company

10.11 The corporation tax computation must be recalculated using the applicable UK tax rules. The calculated loss cannot exceed the non-resident company actual loss and if the result is a profit, no relief is available (*ICTA 1988, Sch 18A, para 11; FA 2006, Sch 1, para 7*).

On preparing the computation it is necessary to assume that the company is UK resident and that its trade is carried on wholly or partly in the UK. Rental income and income from land is calculated on the assumption that the land is based in the UK and on Schedule A principles. The accounting period on which the computation is based is assumed to begin at the beginning of the loss period. If plant and machinery is purchased it is assumed that capital allowances are available (*ICTA 1988, Sch 18A, para 15; FA 2006, Sch 1, para 7*).

Arrangement for transfer of a company to another group or consortium

10.12 If a company has made arrangements that could result in it leaving the group, it will not be able to partake in the group relief claims by surrender of claim with other group companies (*ICTA 1988, s 410*). Its ineligibility for group relief will only last for the period in which the arrangements exist (*Shepherd v Law Land plc (1990) 63 TC 692, [1990] STC 795*).

Also all rights over shares are deemed to have been exercised at the earliest possible date. If rights differ over the ownership period the lowest common denominator is applied to the holdings to ascertain whether group relief is available (*ICTA 1988, Sch 18, para 5*).

Group relief claim

10.13   A group relief claim can be made for a corresponding accounting period. Often group member accounting periods are not co-terminous and the available profits and losses must be apportioned. The amount that may be surrendered is the smaller of:

- the unused part of the surrenderable amount for the overlapping period, and

- the unrelieved part of the claimant company's total profits for the overlapping period.

The overlapping period is the period common to both companies (*ICTA 1988, s 403A*).

Example 10.7

Mu Ltd owns 90% of the ordinary share capital of Nu Ltd.

Mu Ltd has prepared annual accounts to 30 June 2009.

Profits for the year amount to £48,000.

Nu Ltd has prepared annual accounts to 31 December 2009.

The trading loss for the year amounts to £56,000.

Although Mu Ltd and Nu Ltd are a group for group relief purposes, they can only claim and surrender losses pro rata to their common accounting periods.

Nu Ltd's maximum loss surrender

(1 January 2009 to 30 June 2009) ÷ (1 January 2009 to 31 December 2009) = 6/12

£56,000 × 6/12 = £28,000

The remaining £28,000 loss is available for relief against Nu Ltd's other income for the year.

Mu Ltd's maximum profits against which loss may be surrendered

(1 January 2009 to 30 June 2009)÷(1 January 2009 to 31 December 2009) = 6/12

£48,000 × 6/12 = £24,000

Only £24,000 of Nu Ltd's £56,000 trading loss can be group relieved against Mu Ltd's profits. The remaining £32,000 is available for relief against Nu Ltd's other income.

Consortium relief claim

10.14   Not only does the overlapping period restriction apply to consortium companies but also the claim is restricted to the members' interests in the consortium. The members' interest in the overlapping period for this purpose is the lower of the percentage of:

- ordinary share capital,

- profits available for distribution, and

- assets on a winding up.

If the percentages fluctuate over the period, the average is taken (*ICTA 1988, s 403C*).

Example 10.8

Delta Ltd is a consortium company, which is owned 60% by Alpha Ltd, 20% by Beta Ltd and 20% by Gamma Ltd. All companies prepare accounts to 31 December each year. In the accounting period ended 31 December 2008 Delta's trading loss amounts to £75,000. The maximum loss claim is as follows:

		£
Total loss		75,000
Alpha Ltd	60%	45,000
Beta Ltd	20%	15,000
Gamma Ltd	20%	15,000
		75,000

Loss relief will be given provided each company has sufficient profits.

In the accounting period ended 31 December 2009, Delta Ltd makes a profit of £80,000. Alpha Ltd makes a loss of £120,000, Beta Ltd makes a loss of £30,000 and Gamma Ltd makes a profit of £60,000.

10.14 *Groups*

The maximum surrenderable losses are calculated as follows:

		£	£
Delta Ltd	Profit		80,000
	Losses surrendered:		
Alpha Ltd	Loss made	(120,000)	
	Maximum surrender is 60% of £80,000	48,000	(48,000)
	Not available for surrender	(72,000)	
Beta Ltd	Loss made	(30,000)	
	Maximum surrender is 20% of £80,000	16,000	(16,000)
	Not available for surrender	(14,000)	
Gamma Ltd	Not applicable		
	PCTCT		16,000

Example 10.9

A Ltd owns 100% of the share capital of B Ltd.

B Ltd owns 40% of the share capital of D Ltd.

C Ltd owns 60% of the share capital of D Ltd.

D Ltd owns 100% of the share capital of E Ltd.

D Ltd owns 100% of the share capital of F Ltd.

This can be shown as follows.

A	
100%	
B	C
40%	60%
D	
100%	100%
E	F

There are two groups:

- A and B, and
- D, E and F.

D is owned by a consortium of B and C. All companies have the same accounting periods. None of the companies has any losses brought forward.

The companies have the following results for the year ended 31 July 2009:

A Ltd	£100,000	profit
B Ltd	(£30,000)	loss
C Ltd	Nil	
D Ltd	(£20,000)	loss
E Ltd	£10,000	profit
F Ltd	(£3,000)	loss

E Ltd claims group relief (in priority to consortium relief) as follows:

	£	£
Profit		10,000
Deduct:		
Group relief: loss surrendered by F Ltd	3,000	
Group relief: loss surrendered by D Ltd	7,000	
		(10,000)
		—

A Ltd can claim group relief first and then consortium relief as follows:

	£	£
Profit		100,000
Deduct:		
Group relief: loss surrendered by B Ltd	30,000	
Consortium relief: loss surrendered by D Ltd	5,200	
(£20,000 – £7,000) × 40%		
		(35,200)
		64,800

Group relief claimant company

10.15   The claimant company sets the relief against its total profits for the year to reduce its overall corporation tax liability. The claimant company is not required to pay the surrendering company for utilisation of the loss. There is no tax effect if a payment is made (up to the amount of the loss) (*ICTA 1988,* *s 402(6)*). If a payment is not made this may be viewed as a depreciatory transaction (*TCGA 1992, s 176*). HMRC have stated that they will not seek an adjustment (IR letter, 3 February 1981).

Company tax return

10.16 Details of the group relief claim are included on Company Tax Return Form—Supplementary Pages Group and Consortium CT600C. Both the claimant and the surrendering company must each complete their respective CT600C forms, which formalise the claim. The claimant company includes the amount of group relief and consortium relief claimed in box 36 of the main Company Tax Return CT600. The claim must be made within the normal self-assessment time limits, ie two years after the end of the chargeable period for which the claim is made. A claim made out of time can be refused (*Farmer v Bankers Trust International Ltd* (1990) 64 TC 1, [1990] STC 564).

Alternatively, 'an authorised group company', normally the holding company, may request HMRC in writing to grant it the power to furnish group relief claims and surrender notices on behalf of the other group and consortium companies. The application should include:

- the name and the tax office reference of the authorised company,

- the names and the tax office references of the authorising companies,

- details relating to the authorised company and each of the authorising companies that are sufficient to demonstrate that the company concerned is a member of the group of companies or, as the case may be, a consortium company, and

- a statement by the authorised company and the authorising companies that they agree to be covered by the arrangements and to be bound by claims, surrenders and withdrawals made under the arrangements.

The application must be accompanied by:

- a specimen copy of group relief claim and surrender statement that the authorised company proposes to use for the purpose of making and withdrawing surrenders and claims on behalf of itself and the authorising companies; or

- in the case of a company that is a consortium company, an agreement, signed by each member of the consortium and the consortium company, consenting to the authorised company acting on their behalf in relation to the arrangements.

The application must be signed on behalf of each of the companies concerned by an officer of the company, normally the company secretary and be sent to the tax office dealing with the tax affairs of the authorised company (*FA 1998, Sch 18, para 77; SI 1999/2975*).

Repayments of corporation tax

10.17 Groups of companies with an *ICTA 1988, s 402* group relationship are able to jointly elect for repayment due to one company to be surrendered to another company in payment of its corporation tax liability. The facility is aimed at reducing the group's exposure to interest on overdue tax. The companies involved must have the same accounting period and must be members of the same group throughout the accounting period (*FA 1989, s 102*). Any inter-company tax payment up to the amount of the tax is ignored. There is no prescribed format for the election. A letter to HMRC will suffice with details of the company and tax district reference numbers. Each company should appoint an authorised person to sign the form on its behalf.

The joint notice is not given in the return form CT600, but must be made separately. The surrendering company should use the 'repayment' section of the return form to claim its refund and show how much is to be surrendered by completing boxes 145 to 148 accordingly. A copy of the joint notice should be enclosed with the return. (See HMRC Company Taxation Manual CTM 92440 for further details).

Refunds of quarterly instalments

10.18 The intra-group arrangement is also available for quarterly instalments (see **3.10**) (intra-group surrender: legislation *SI 1998/3175, reg 9*, as amended by *SI 1999/1929, reg 3*). A refund of tax that is paid under the instalment arrangements can be surrendered to fellow group members at the date of payment. Again the aim is to reduce the group's exposure to interest by netting off the debit and credit interest to eliminate the differential interest that it would otherwise suffer arising from underpaid and overpaid instalment tax.

The amended version only applies when a tax refund is due to be made to the surrendering company. The refund may be due either under *reg 6* or *TMA 1970, s 59D(2)*. HMRC explain the effects as follows: the result is that:

- payments made during the quarterly instalment payment period may retrospectively be allocated between group members to mitigate the interest position of the group, beyond that limited circumstance,

- *reg 9* only applies in relation to CT paid on account of the surrendering company's own liability,

- a group is unable to make a global payment in the name of a dormant company or one that will have no CT liability, and then reallocate it between group members retrospectively.

Under *reg 9* the surrendering company must give notice to HMRC, at the time when the joint surrender notice is given, specifying the payment(s) out of which the refund is to be treated as made (*FA 1989, s 102* or *reg 9(5C)*). The surrendering company then has 30 days in which to bring its specification into line with the amount of the repayment due. If it fails to do so within that time, the repayment can be made as if no notice of surrender had been given (*FA 1989, s 102* and *reg 9(5D)*, *(5E)*) (HMRC Company Taxation Manual CTM 92740).

Example 10.10

Red Ltd and Blue Ltd are within the same group and they both qualify under the special rules of *FA 1989, s 102*.

Both companies have 31 December year ends and each company makes the following quarterly payments:

	Red Ltd	Blue Ltd
	£	£
14 July 2009	500,000	500,000
14 October 2009	500,000	500,000
14 January 2009	250,000	500,000
14 April 2010	150,000	500,000
Total paid	1,400,000	2,000,000

The actual corporation tax liability for the year is as follows:

	Red Ltd	Blue Ltd
	£	£
Corporation tax liability year ending 31 March 2009	10,000	3,500,000

Red Ltd makes a repayment claim for £1,390,000 under *reg 6* because it is now known that no instalment tax was due.

Blue Ltd should have paid quarterly instalments of £875,000.

So Blue Ltd's cumulative underpayment of instalments is:

	Instalments due	Instalments paid	Shortfall
	£	£	£
14 July 2009	875,000	500,000	375,000
14 October 2009	875,000	500,000	375,000
14 January 2010	875,000	500,000	375,000
14 April 2010	875,000	500,000	375,000
	3,500,000	2,000,000	1,500,000

Red Ltd makes a repayment claim for the overpaid instalments.

Red Ltd and Blue Ltd give joint notice of surrender, so that the instalment tax paid by Red Ltd is treated as paid by Blue Ltd with Red Ltd's payment dates.

Red Ltd is treated as if the overpaid tax had been repaid to it on those dates.

The claim results in Red Ltd not making any quarterly payments. Its corporation tax of £10,000 is now due by 1 January 2010. Blue Ltd has to make a further instalment payment as soon as possible of £100,000, which is calculated as follows:

	£
Corporation tax due year ending 31 March 2008	3,500,000
Quarterly instalments paid by Blue Ltd	(2,000,000)
Quarterly instalments paid by Red Ltd	(1,400,000)
Net amount due	100,000

10.19   *SI 1998/3175, reg 10* empowers HMRC, at any time after the filing date, to require a company to furnish such information as may reasonably be required about:

- the computation of any instalment payment,

- the reasons it omitted to make quarterly instalment payments, and

- a *reg 6* repayment claim.

The time allowed for providing the information must not be less than 30 days and must be shown on the notice.

Regulation 11 empowers HMRC to require the company to produce 'books, documents and other records in its possession or power' for the purposes of *reg* 10. HMRC accept photostat copies as long as the originals are available for inspection. These powers are not part of the enquiry procedures.

Group income

10.20   A UK company is not required to deduct tax at source from intra-group interest and royalty payments where the other company is UK resident or if not UK resident operates from a permanent establishment (*FA 2001, s 85; FA 2002, s 96*).

Chapter 11

Corporate finance

COMPANY FINANCE

Equity v loan finance

11.1 Companies raise finance by borrowing, issuing shares and exploiting their assets. A debt has a legal right to repayment whereas shares have no such rights. Various controls are exercised on a company's activities through the *Financial Services and Markets Act 2000*, the *Companies Act 2006* and the Stock Exchange.

For taxation purposes the basic premise is that equity finance, which relates to the issue of shares, will have no direct effect on the company's corporation tax liability. UK distributions received are not taxable on a company. On eventual disposal the profit on sale to the vendor will be assessable as a capital gain.

Loan finance does have an effect on the company's corporation tax liability. Lenders are rewarded by an interest payment. Lenders look to some form of asset security or guarantee regarding the loan repayment. Interest payments are deductible against a company's corporation tax liability and interest receipts are taxable.

The loan relationship provisions

11.2 The provisions of *Finance Act 1996, ss 80–105* and *Schs 8–15* introduced the 'loan relationship' rules governing corporate debt, principally aimed at aligning the taxation treatment of loan finance with the accounting treatment. With the ever increasing sophistication of the financial markets the original rules have been amended by subsequent *Finance Acts*; notably *FA 2002* (generally for accounting periods beginning on or after 1 October 2002), *FA 2004, F (No 2) A 2005* (generally for accounting periods beginning on or after 1 January 2005) and *FA 2006* for accounting periods ended on or after 22 March 2006.

Finance Act 2002 brought exchange gains and losses on loan relationships denominated in a foreign currency into the calculation of the overall profit or loss on the loan relationship. In general the *FA 1996* loan relationships legislation also applies to exchange gains and losses.

303

The loan relationship rules aim to treat capital and revenue receipts in a like manner and show no distinction between realised and unrealised amounts. Gains and losses are calculated according to the basis adopted in the accounts and are termed 'credits' and 'debits'. A different treatment is applied to trading and non-trading debits and credits. Trading debits and credits are included in the Schedule D Case I computation. Non-trading debits and credits are included within Schedule D Case III.

The loan relationship rules apply to both trading and non-trading companies, unincorporated associations subject to corporation tax, UK branches of overseas companies and controlled foreign companies. The rules apply to companies that are members of a partnership but not to individuals. Non-resident companies come within the loan relationship rules if they trade in the UK through a branch or agency, and the loan relationship is held for trading purposes by that branch or agency

LOAN RELATIONSHIP

Meaning

11.3 The first issue that a company will want to address is whether the debt arrangement that it has entered into constitutes a loan relationship. In most situations this will be the case. A loan relationship exists where:

- the company stands in the position of a creditor or debtor as respects any money debt; and
- that debt is one arising from a transaction for the lending of money;

and references to a loan relationship and to a company's being a party to a loan relationship shall be construed accordingly (*FA 1996, s 81(1)*).

For a company to be within the loan relationship provisions it must have a money debt.

MONEY DEBT

Legislative definitions

11.4 The legislation initially defined a money debt as a debt which falls to be settled by the payment of money or by the transfer of a right to settlement under a debt which is itself a money debt. When originally enacted it was understood that a money debt was one that was settled by the payment of money or the transfer of another money debt. *Finance Act 2006* amended the meaning of debt in response to anti-avoidance schemes that arranged to repay debt with a share issue on the basis that the transaction would fall out of the loan relationship provisions. In respect of loan relationships to which a company is party on 22 March 2006, *FA 2006, Sch 6, para 10(2)* added that a money debt could be settled by the issue or transfer of shares in any company (*FA 1996, s 81(2)*). In circumstances that are divorced from loan relationships the disposal of a shareholding would bring about a chargeable gain or an allowable loss. Therefore, on 22 March 2006 the holding enters the loan relationship regime at fair value and a chargeable gain or an allowable loss is deemed to arise. The gain or loss is held over until the company ceases to be a party to the loan relationship. Therefore at this time there will not only be a loan relationship adjustment but also a chargeable gain or an allowable loss brought into charge (*FA 2006, Sch 6, para 10(6)*).

Existence of a loan relationship

11.5 A company has a loan relationship where the following two conditions are satisfied:

- it is a creditor or a debtor for a money debt, and
- that money debt has arisen from a transaction for the lending of money (*FA 1996, s 81(1)*).

A normal trade debt is not a loan relationship.

If an instrument has been created that represents the rights under the debt then this will be within the loan relationship rules (FA 1996, s 81(3)). The following types of debt have always been included within loan relationships: overdrafts, mortgages, advances, gilts, bank loans and deposits, building society shares and deposits, debentures, certificates of deposit, company securities and eurobonds, government stock, discounts, premiums, bills of exchange and promissory notes. For corporation tax a qualifying corporate bond is a loan relationship. A qualifying corporate bond is a security, which at all time has represented a normal commercial loan and which is only redeemable in sterling (*TCGA 1992, s 117*). A convertible loan note is not a qualifying corporate bond (*Weston v Garnett* [2005] EWCA Civ 742, [2005] STC 1134). A loan note or security that contains a currency conversion option on issue is not a qualifying corporate bond, even if the option were to lapse in the meantime (*Harding v Revenue and Customs Comrs* [2008] EWHC 99 (Ch)).

Money debts included within the loan relationship rules

11.6 A money debt is not necessarily a loan relationship. Certain money debts were brought within the loan relationship rules with effect from 1 October

2002. These include interest on late payment for goods and services, interest on judgment debts, late payment interest on completion and late payment of tax. Only the interest and exchange gains and losses are treated as loan relationships and included as debits or credits. Interest imputed under transfer pricing (see **14.20–14.21**) is also included within loan relationships (*FA 1996, s 100*). Whether the interest is trading or non-trading depends on whether it is receivable or payable for the purposes of the trade. Interest receivable from or payable to HMRC is always non-trading (*FA 1996, s 100(7)*).

Interest in excess of a reasonable commercial return, which is treated as a distribution by virtue of *ICTA 1988, s 209(2)(d)* (see **16.7**), is not a loan relationship (*FA 1996, Sch 9, para 1*). *FA 1996, Sch 9, para 1* ensures that interest that is characterised as a distribution under *ICTA 1988, s 209(2)(d)* or (*e*) cannot be a debit or credit.

With effect from 16 March 2005 discounts on money debts are also loan relationships, but discounts that are treated as distributions under *ICTA 1988, s 209(2)(e)* are not. With effect from 16 March 2005, shares are treated as loan relationships (see **11.7**).

Shares treated as loan relationships

11.7   From 16 March 2005 onwards certain shares are treated as loan relationships which include:

- **Shares subject to outstanding third-party obligations**. The investing company holds a share in another company, the investee company that is subject to third party obligations and is an interest like investment. In other words another person must meet the calls on the shares and that its fair value increase represents a return at commercial rate of interest with no deviations. In that case the investing company must treat the share as a creditor loan relationship. The distributions received are neither treated as a dividend nor a repayment of capital. The investing company must bring the debits and credits into account on an accounting fair value basis (*FA 1996, s 91A*).

- **Non-qualifying shares**. A non-qualifying share is a share held by an investing company in another company, the investee company, which is neither a holding in a unit trust or offshore fund (see *FA 2005, Sch 10, para 4*) nor a (*s 91A*) share subject to outstanding third party obligations. In addition the share is not a dealer share (*ICTA 1988, s 95*) but it satisfied one of three conditions:

  1   Its fair value increase represents a return at a commercial rate of interest with no deviations.

2   The share is redeemable such that its return equates with a return on invested money, eg redeemable preference shares.

3   The share and one or more derivative contracts are together designed to produce a return based on a commercial rate of interest.

In that case the investing company must treat the share as a creditor loan relationship. The distributions received are neither treated as a dividend nor a repayment of capital. The investing company must bring the debits and credits into account on an accounting fair value basis.

Where condition 1 above applies no debits or transactions are to be brought into account which prevent the value of the share increasing at a rate of return representing a commercial rate of interest.

If condition 3 applies debits and credits are to be brought into account in respect of any associated transaction as if it were a derivative contract.

The (*ss 91A, 91B*) shares were deemed to be sold and reacquired when entering the loan relationship regime. The gain was subject to capital gains on 1 January 2005 (*FA 2004, Sch 10, para 9*).

Non-loan relationships

11.8   From the above it may be difficult to judge what arrangement can be considered not to be a loan relationship. However, the following are accepted as not being loan relationships (for the time being); namely trade debts arising from the purchase of goods and services are not within the loan relationship regime. Finance leases, HP agreements, court settlements and loan guarantees also fall outside the definition (HMRC Corporate Finance Manuals CFM 51150 and CFM 51160). A contingency cannot be a loan relationship as it does not derive from the lending of money (*FA 1996, s 81(1)*).

Accounting treatment

11.9   For accounting periods beginning on or after 1 January 2005 UK GAAP or IAS as appropriate, subject only to specific statutory override is the accepted accounting treatment. IAS 39 (financial instruments: recognition and measurement) and IAS 32 (financial instruments: presentation and disclosure) have direct significance in this context. Their counterparts in UK GAAP are FRS 25 (financial statement of authorised funds) and FRS 26 (financial instruments: measurement). Listed companies not applying IAS for single company accounts were required to adopt FRS25 and FRS 26 for accounting periods beginning on or after 1 January 2005. For other companies, the presentation part of FRS 25 was mandatory for accounting periods ended on or after 1 January 2005, and for companies that use fair value accounting, adoption of the remainder of FRS 25 and of FRS 26 was mandatory for accounting periods beginning on or after 1 January 2006. There are proposals for all companies apart from those using the FRSSE (financial reporting standard for smaller entities) to use FRS 26 for accounting periods beginning on or after 1 January 2007.

Companies that apply the FRSSE continue to apply UK GAAP as it applied to accounting periods beginning on or after 1 January 2005. The FRSSE adopts certain elements of FRS 4 (capital instruments); namely the balance sheet recognition, the allocation of borrowing costs to the relevant periods at a constant rate of return on the carrying amount and the allocation of dividends on an accruals basis unless payment is remote.

The taxation legislation requires that GAAP be applied, specifying that, if a company does not use GAAP for this purpose, it will be treated as having done so (*FA 1996, s 85A*). Prior to this the two authorised methods of accounting applied; either the authorised accruals basis or the mark to market basis (*FA 1996, ss 85, 86*). More often the authorised accruals was used, which simply applied an accrual basis of accounting, ie transactions are allocated to the accounting period in which they accrue rather than the accounting period in which they fall due or are paid or received and operated a bad debt system. The mark to market basis brought amounts into account in each period at fair value; ie the amount the company would expect to receive or pay (according to the relationship) to an independent third party for the transfer of rights or the release of liabilities. With the introduction of IAS the authorised accruals basis and the mark to market basis have been rooted into IAS 39 as the amortised cost basis and the fair value basis respectively.

CORPORATION TAX TREATMENT

Trading and non-trading loan relationships

11.10   It is necessary to distinguish between a trading and a non-trading loan relationship. Essentially, if a company owes funds or is due funds for the purposes of its trade, then it is within a trading loan relationship (*FA 1996, s 80(2)*). For lenders the test is tighter and they will only be within a trading loan relationship if it entered into the loan 'in the course of activities forming an integral part of its trade' (*FA 1996, s 103(2)*). In practice only companies within the financial sector such as insurance companies, banks and finance trades lend funds as an integral part of their trade.

Group finance companies may be an exception.

Money lending was not deemed to be the integral part of the trade of an electrical energy producer and supplier. It was not the normal activity of an energy producer or supplier. Hence, interest earned on money set aside by to meet future liabilities was deemed to relate to a non-trading loan relationship (*Nuclear Electric plc v Bradley* (1996) 68 TC 670).

TRADING LOAN RELATIONSHIPS

Schedule D Case I

11.11 The appropriate accounting method will result in all credits and debits arising from profits, gains and losses, both capital and revenue, interest, charges and expenses together with exchange gains and losses relating to the company's loan relationships being brought into the corporation tax computation. Credits and debits resulting from a trading loan relationship are included as trading receipts or expenses within the Schedule D Case I computation (*FA 1996, s 82*). The loan relationship legislation overrides *ICTA 1988, s 74* (see **5.13**) (*FA 1996, s 82(7)*). Accounting matching procedures that result in the derecognition of matched income are ignored for corporation tax purposes (*FA 2006, Sch 6, para 6*). Any subsequent profits or losses arising are assessable or relievable accordingly under the rules of Schedule D Case I. This is not the case for non-trading loan relationships, which have special computational rules (See **11.16, 11.17**).

Example 11.1

Aurora Ltd is a small trading company that requires additional finance for the purposes of its trade. The bank grants an additional £1m 6% fixed interest loan facility on 1 January 2008. The company is charged legal fees and other professional costs in relation to obtaining the loan of £5,000. The company applies the FRSSE. Accounts are prepared to 31 December each year.

The loan is a trading loan relationship as it has been taken out for trading purposes. As the company apples the FRSSE, the finance costs of borrowings are allocated to the accounting periods over the term of the borrowings at a constant rate on the carrying amount. The amounts charged will form the allowable debits and no adjustment to profits is required when preparing the corporation tax computation. The expenses will be allowable by reason of *FA 1996, s 84(3)*: see **11.23**.

Example 11.2

Q plc acquires shares in a new subsidiary for £10m. It pays the vendor company £8m in cash, and issues loan notes for the remaining £2m. Subsequently, Q plc finds out facts about the financial position of its new subsidiary that had not come to light in the due diligence process. Discussions with the vendor company follow, as a result of which it is agreed that the purchase price should be reduced by £1m. Accordingly, £1m of the loan notes issued by Q plc are cancelled. It accounts for the transaction as:

| Cr | Cost of investment | £1 million |
| Dr | Creditors (loan notes) | £1 million |

For tax purposes, the loan notes are loan relationships since, although there has been no lending of money, an instrument has been issued representing security for the creditor's rights under the £2m money debt. The cancellation of £1m of the notes does not, however, give rise to a tax charge under the loan relationships rules. Although a credit appears in the company's books, there is no amount that has been recognised in determining the company's profit or loss for the period. Nothing therefore falls within *FA 1996, s 85A(1)* (HMRC Corporate Finance Manual CFM 5203a).

UNALLOWABLE PURPOSE

Non-business or non-commercial

11.12   Relief is denied for debits arising from an unallowable purpose.

An unallowable purpose is any non-business or non- business or commercial or any purpose that consists of securing a tax advantage (*FA 1996, Sch 9, para 13(2)*).

Example 11.3

The CASH Bank plc grants the Village Tennis Club a loan to finance the construction of a new club house.

For corporation tax purposes the allowable and non-allowable interest expense is apportioned pro rata to the club's taxable income from non-members and non-taxable income from members.

Example 11.4

Chekov is the UK branch of Zagrev, a non-UK resident Russian holding company. The company uses British banks to fund its global activities. A £12m loan is raised from the CASH Bank plc to fund Zagrev's activities in Guatemala. Chekov has no involvement in these activities but agrees to pay the interest.

The interest charged is deemed to be 'an unallowable purpose' for Chekov, and hence is disallowable (*FA 1996, Sch 9, para 13(3)*) (HMRC Corporate Finance Manual CFM 6214).

A tax avoidance purpose

11.13   A tax avoidance purpose is any purpose that consists in securing a tax advantage either for the company or for any other person (*FA 1996, Sch 9, para 13(5)*). A tax avoidance purpose becomes an unallowable purpose when it is the main purpose or one of the main reasons that the company became a party to the relationship or entered into a related transaction. The usage of funds to secure or finance a tax avoidance scheme will amount to an unallowable purpose (*FA 1996, Sch 9, para 13(5)*).

Whether a tax avoidance purpose is the main, or one of the main, purposes is a question of fact, which depends on all the circumstances of the particular case.

Example 11.5

A company borrows £50m from a finance company at arm's length. The company becomes insolvent and disposes of all its assets. This leaves it with an outstanding debt of £40m. The company is not liquidated and interest continues to accrue on the debt. The finance company either omits to accrue the interest receivable or it accrues the interest and then writes it off as a bad debt. The company accrues the interest and makes a deficit on which group relief claims are made. The company has no activity which is within the charge to corporation tax (*FA 1996, Sch 9, para 13(3)*). The purpose of the loan relationship is therefore specifically excluded from being a business or commercial purpose and it is an unallowable purpose. In addition, although the loan relationship was originally bona fide, its continued existence is not commercial. The relating debits to the loan relationship are disallowed.

The only purpose of the loan relationship in the current accounting period is to generate group relief thereby securing a tax advantage for another group company (*FA 1996, Sch 9, para 13(5)*) (HMRC Corporate Finance Manual CFM 6215a).

Write off of loans for an unallowable purpose

11.14   Write off of loans for an unallowable purpose will also not qualify for relief. For example, an interest-free loan made by a company, whose business consists of manufacturing kitchen tables, which had lent the money to a yacht club supported by one of the directors of the company for the purpose of providing financial support to the yacht club. If the company borrowed to make the loan to the yacht club, the interest will also be disallowed.

If the purpose of the loan included a commercial or other business purpose such as advertising, then this would be taken into account in arriving at the amount attributable to the unallowable purpose on a just and reasonable basis (*FA 1996, Sch 9, para 13(1)*) (HMRC Corporate Finance Manual CFM 6224).

HMRC advice

11.15   If taxpayers or their advisers seek advice from HMRC as to whether a proposed course of action would be deemed to be an unallowable purpose under *FA 1996, Sch 9, para 13* they will be referred by HMRC to the Economic Secretary's Finance Bill 1996 Report Stage comments at HMRC Corporate Finance Manual CFM 6216a, particularly the penultimate paragraph.

The comments are as follows:

> 'The Government are aware of concerns that have been raised by my hon. Friends and by others regarding the particular anti-avoidance provisions in paragraph 13. This paragraph was amended significantly in Standing Committee but, because of the concerns that my hon. Friends and others have raised, I take the opportunity to allay some of the fears that have been expressed about the anti-avoidance rules. Paragraph 13 of the schedule disallows tax deductions to the extent that tax avoidance is the main motive behind a loan relationship. We have been told of concerns that this could be interpreted as preventing companies from getting tax relief for legitimate financing arrangements. I am happy to offer a reassurance that this is not the intention of the legislation. The paragraph denies tax deductions on loans that are for the purpose of activities outside the charge to corporation tax. Among other things, this will ensure that United Kingdom branches of overseas companies do not get tax relief for borrowings that are for overseas activities outside the United Kingdom tax net. We have been asked whether financing—which, for example, is to acquire shares in companies, whether in the United Kingdom or overseas, or is to pay dividends—would be affected by the paragraph. In general terms, the answer is no, but the paragraph might bite if the financing were structured in an artificial way. It has been suggested that structuring a company's legitimate activities to attract a tax relief could bring financing within this paragraph— some have gone so far as to suggest that the paragraph might deny any tax deduction for borrowing costs. These suggestions are clearly

a nonsense. A large part of what the new rules are about is ensuring that companies get tax relief for the cost of their borrowing. One specific point has been put to me by my hon. Friend the Member for Gloucester—that is, borrowing by a finance leasing company to acquire assets where this is more tax efficient than the lessee investing in the asset direct. Again, I am happy to offer a reassurance. Where a company is choosing between different ways of arranging its commercial affairs, it is acceptable for it to choose the course that gives a favourable tax outcome. Where paragraph 13 will come into play is where tax avoidance is the object, or one of the main objects, of the exercise. Companies that enter into schemes with the primary aim of avoiding tax will inevitably be aware of that. The transactions we are aiming at are not ones which companies stumble into inadvertently. As one top tax adviser said recently, companies will know when they are into serious tax avoidance; apart from anything else, they are likely to be paying fat fees for clever tax advice and there will commonly be wads of documentation. The last thing I want to do, however, is set out a list of so-called acceptable or unacceptable activities. Borrowing for commercial purposes can be structured in a highly artificial way in order to avoid tax. If we said that borrowing for certain types of activity would always be okay, tax advisers would quickly take advantage and devise artificial financial arrangements simply to avoid tax. Provided that companies are funding commercial activities or investments in a commercial way, they should have nothing to fear. If they opt for artificial, tax-driven arrangements, they may find themselves caught. It is clear that a balance must be struck between meeting the concerns that have been raised and weakening the provision in those instances where it needs to apply, but I can assure my hon. Friends that we shall keep the matter under review.'

(Hansard, 28 March 1996, Finance Bill Report Stage, Columns 1192- 1193.)

The Economic Secretary's comments are the extent of the guidance HMRC are able to give in accordance with Code of Practice 10 (information and advice) and regard the application of Para 13 as a matter of careful judgment (HMRC Corporate Finance Manual CFM 6228).

NON-TRADING LOAN RELATIONSHIPS

Schedule D Case III

11.16   A company is party to a non-trading loan relationship, if it is party to the relationship not for the purposes of the trade. For many companies their only non-trading income will be bank interest received from an investment of surplus funds. Schedule A business or an overseas property business is not a trade for these purposes. Interest paid by banks and building societies is paid gross, as is interest on loans for fixed periods of less than a year. Income tax is deducted at source from other interest at the lower rate of 20%, unless (from 1 April 2001) the recipient is a company chargeable to corporation tax in respect of the income. Before 1 April 2001, groups could elect to make intra-group payments gross.

Non-trading loan relationship debits and credits are aggregated to result in a Schedule D Case III surplus or deficit. A surplus will be assessable as Schedule D Case III income.

Example 11.6

On 1 January 2009 Aurora Ltd bought £20,000 nominal gilt-edged stock at £95 per £100 nominal stock. The investment was not for the purposes of trade. The securities are redeemable on 31 December 2013 at par. Interest at 3% is payable annually on 31 December.

As the investment has no relationship to the trade this amounts to a non-trading loan relationship and the interest and the discount is assessable under Schedule D Case III.

Again the accounting treatment will be adopted and the assessable amounts are as follows:

Year ended	31 December 2009	31 December 2010	31 December 2011	31 December 2012	31 December 2013
	£	£	£	£	£
Interest received	600	600	600	600	600
Discount	100	100	100	100	100
Schedule D Case III	700	700	700	700	700

RELIEF FOR NON-TRADING DEFICITS

Manner of non-trading deficit relief

11.17   Relief is given as follows for all or part of the deficit to be;

(a)   by claim in a group relief claim (*ICTA 1988, s 403*); or

(b)   by claim:

    (i)   set against any profits of the company for the deficit period (*FA 1996, s 83(2)(a)*); or

    (ii)   carried back and set against profits of the accounting periods for the previous 12 months that are chargeable under Schedule D Case III as profits or gains from loan relationships (*FA 1996, s 83(2)(c)*); or

(c)   any remaining amount will be carried forward and set against non-trading profits in succeeding accounting periods (*FA 1996, s 83(2), Sch 8, para 3*).

A claim under *ICTA 1988, s 403* can be made at any time up to the first anniversary of the filing date of the return (*FA 1998, Sch 18, para 74*). A claim under *FA 1996, s 83(3A)* must be made within two years of the end of the accounting period in which the deficit arose (*FA 1996, s 83(6)*).

Example 11.7—Single company—No deficits in previous years

Aurora Ltd's results in years to come are shown below. Aurora Ltd has a non-trading deficit for the year ended 31 December 2012 of £10,000. There are no group companies.

Year ended	31 December 2009	31 December 2010	31 December 2011	31 December 2012	31 December 2013
	£	£	£	£	£
Schedule D Case I	10,000	20,000	30,000	500	900
Schedule D Case III	1,000	1,000	5,000	200	300
PCTCT	11,000	21,000	35,000	700	1,200

Relief is obtained as follows:

	£	£
Total loss		10,000
Set against any profits of the company for the deficit period	700	
Carried back and set against profits of the accounting periods for the previous 12 months that are chargeable under Schedule D Case III as profits or gains from loan relationships	5,000	

Carried back and set against profits of the accounting periods for the previous 12 months that are chargeable under Schedule D Case III as profits or gains from loan relationships	5,000
Carried forward and set against non-trading profits in succeeding accounting periods (*FA 1996, s 83(2)*)	300

Loss utilised	6,000
Balance available to carry forward	4,000

Example 11.8—Group company—No deficit in previous years

Horatio Ltd has the following results for the years ended 30 June 2007, 2008 and 2009.

Year ended	30 June 2007	30 June 2008	30 June 2009
	£	£	£
Schedule D Case I	5,000	15,000	40,000
Schedule D Case III surplus	10,000	10,000	
Schedule D Case III deficit			(5,000)

Horatio Ltd has the option of utilising the £5,000 deficit in:

(i)   a group relief claim (*ICTA 1988, s 403*), or

(ii)   against profits for the year ending 30 June 2008 (*FA 1996, s 83(2)*), or

(iii)   against the Schedule D Case III surplus for the year ending 30 June 2008, or

(iv)   carry forward against non-trading profits in succeeding periods (*FA 1996, s 83(3A)*).

Example 11.9—Single company partial loss claim for current year

Nelson Ltd has the following results for the year ended 31 March 2009 and makes a partial claim to set its non-trading deficit against profits of the same period.

	£
Schedule D Case I	78,000
Schedule D Case V (foreign tax paid £8,400)	40,000
Non-trading deficit	152,000

Nelson Ltd's partial loss claim is as follows:

	Schedule D Case 1	Schedule D Case V	Total	Schedule D Case III deficit utilisation memorandum
	£	£	£	£
Income	78,000	40,000	118,000	(152,000)
Partial deficit claim (*FA 1996, s 83(2)(a)*).	(78,000)	(10,000)	(88,000)	88,000
PCTCT	0	30,000	30,000	
Corporation tax @ 28%			8,400	
Tax credit relief			8,400	
Corporation tax payable			nil	
Deficit available				64,000

to: (i) carry back under *FA 1996, s 83(2)(c)* or (iii) carry forward *FA 1996, s 83(3A)*.

Current year order of non-trading deficit relief set-off

11.18   If the deficit is set against profits of the period the order of set-off is as follows:

(i)   after relief for trading losses carried forward, but before relief for:

(ii)   Sch A losses set against profits for the same period (*ICTA 1988, s 392A(1)*),

(iii) trading losses set against profits for the same period, or carried back from a later period (*ICTA 1988, s 393A(1)*),

(iv)   a non-trading deficit carried back from a later period (*FA 1996, s 83(2)(c)*) (*FA 1996, Sch 8, para 1*).

Carry back previous year order of non-trading deficit relief set-off

11.19   If the deficit is carried back to the previous 12-month accounting period the order of set-off is as follows:

after any amounts claimed that relate to:

  (i)   losses or deficits from any period before the deficit period—or treated as coming from an earlier period,

 (ii)   charges for trade purposes under *ICTA 1988, s 338* before 24 July 2002,

(iii)   trading losses set against profits of the same or preceding year under *ICTA 1988, s 393A*,

(iv)   deficits of the claim period.

If the company is a company with investment business (or an investment company for accounting periods beginning before 31 March 2004), the following are given prior relief:

●   capital allowances,

●   management expenses under *ICTA 1988, s 75*,

●   business charges under *ICTA 1988, s 338*, paid before 16 March 2005 (*FA 1996, Sch 8, para 3*).

Example 11.10—Group company with deficit in previous year

If Horatio Ltd's results for the years ended 30 June 2007, 2008 and 2009 (see Example 11.8) had been as follows:

Year ended	30 June 2007	30 June 2008	30 June 2009
	£	£	£
Schedule D Case I	—	15,000	40,000
Schedule D Case III surplus		10,000	
Schedule D Case III deficit	(8,000)		(5,000)

Horatio Ltd can still use the £5,000 deficit for the year ended 30 June 2009 in a group relief claim or against other profits but can only relieve £2,000 of the deficit in 2008 as the brought forward deficit has priority.

Example 11.11—Single company with deficit in previous years

Kiora Ltd is a single company, prepares accounts to 31 March each year and has the following actual and forecast results:

Year ended	31 March 2008	31 March 2009	31 March 2009
	£000	£000	£000
Schedule D Case I loss brought forward	(90)		
Schedule D Case I	400	200	500
Schedule A	50	50	20
Chargeable gain	100	100	2
Schedule D Case III:			
Interest accrued (credits)	(10)	(8)	(20)
Interest accrued (debits)		400	400
Net debits		392	380

Schedule D Case III debits can be relieved as follows:

Year ended	31 March 2008	31 March 2009	31 March 2010
	£000	£000	£000
Schedule D Case I	400	200	500
Loss: *ICTA 1988, s 393(1)* brought forward	(90)		
Schedule D Case I (post loss relief)	310	200	500

Year ended	31 March 2008	31 March 2009	31 March 2010
	£000	£000	£000
Schedule D Case III	10	—	—
Schedule A	50	50	20
Chargeable gain	100	100	2
Total non-trading profits	160	150	22
Total profits	470	350	522
Set-off against current profits of whatever description (*FA 1996, s 83(2)(a)*)		(350)	(380)

Year ended	31 March 2008	31 March 2009	31 March 2010
	£000	£000	£000
Set-off against Schedule D Case III income of the previous 12 months (*FA 1996, s 83(2)(a)*)	(10)		
Carry forward to set against future non-trading profits (*FA 1996, s 83(3A)*)			(22)
Total relief	(10)	(350)	(402)
PCTCT	460	0	120
Non-trading deficit memorandum			
Net deficit		392	380
Current year relief		(350)	(380)
Prior year relief		(10)	
Future year relief		(22)	
Balance carried		10	0

Carry forward of non-trading deficit relief

11.20   If no other claim is made the deficit will be carried forward by default under *FA 1996, s 83(3A)*. The deficit may be set against the company's non-trading profits for the following years, which will include Schedule D Case V income, chargeable gains, Schedule A income and Schedule D Case III income.

Disclaimer of carry forward non-trading deficit relief

11.21   Within two years of the end of the accounting period in which the brought-forward non-trading deficit would otherwise be utilised the company may claim that a specified amount of this deficit is not to be set against the non-trading profits of the following period. This would, for example, facilitate a double taxation relief claim against Schedule D Case V income. Any unused relief is carried forward to the following period and set against the non-trading profits of that period or disclaimed accordingly (*FA 1996, Sch 8, para 4(3)*).

Example 11.12—Single company partial claim for deficit brought forward

Josephine Ltd only carries on overseas activities for which the company receives an overseas dividend of £90,000 for the year ended 30 September 2009. The overseas tax credit is £16,800. Many years ago Josephine Ltd incurred a

Schedule D Case III deficit. The balance brought forward under *FA 1996, s 83(3A)* at 30 September 2008 is £100,000.

Josephine Ltd claims under *FA 1996, Sch 8, para 4(3)* that only part of the deficit be set against the current year's income with the following result:

	Year ending 30 June 2009
	£
Schedule D Case V	90,000
Schedule D Case III part deficit	(30,000)
PCTCT	60,000
Corporation tax @ 28%	16,800
Tax credit	16,800

The balance of deficit available to carry forward is £70,000.

Pre-trading expenditure

11.22   Any interest that a company incurs before trading commences is classified as a non-trading debit (*FA 1996, s 84(4)*). The company may elect within two years of the end of the accounting period in which the debit arose under the provisions of *ICTA 1988, s 401(1AB)* that it is not to be brought in as a non-trading debit. A trading company may wish to do this as non-trading deficits carried forward can only be set against future non-trading income, which may not accrue to the company. If the company commences to trade within seven years of that period and the debit would have been allowable if incurred in a period since trading commenced, then the company may treat the debit as a trading expense of that later year.

TRADING AND NON-TRADING LOAN RELATIONSHIPS

Costs of obtaining loan finance

11.23   HMRC consider that the following expenses directly incurred in the following activities are an allowable debit for both trading and non-trading loan relationships under *FA 1996, s 84(3)*.

	Expense	Examples
FA 1996, s 84(3)		
(a)	Bringing a loan relationship into existence	Arrangement fees with banks. Fee or commission for a loan guarantee. DTI fees for investing surplus cash in a liquidation.
(b)	Entering into, or giving effect to, a related transaction	Broker's fees on purchase or sale of existing securities. Legal fees on the transfer of a security
(c)	Making a payment under a loan relationship or related transaction	Cost of making interest payments. Early redemption penalties.
(d)	Pursuing payments due under a loan relationship or related transaction	Solicitor's fees incurred in pursuing a debt defaulter.
FA 1996, s 84(4)	Attempting to bring a loan relationship into existence	This covers abortive expenditure. As long as the expense would have been allowable had the company raised the loan, it is still allowable even if the loan never exists.

Key person insurance premiums, other insurance policies or general investment advice, are not considered to be directly incurred (HMRC Corporate Finance Manual CFM 5210).

Costs of finance included in the accounts as required by GAAP

11.24 Under GAAP, when accounting for the incidental costs of purchase of shares in a subsidiary the costs of the loan finance to buy the shares are normally spread over more than one accounting period. Where this takes place relief will be granted in each respective accounting period. However, where the shares are held as a fixed asset and it is within GAAP to capitalise the costs, relief will be given by adjusting the corporation tax computation (*FA 1996, Sch 9, para 14*) (HMRC Corporate Finance Manual CFM 5230b).

Interest and loan expenses on fixed capital assets, which have been capitalised according to GAAP, should be relieved against profits chargeable to tax by adjusting the corporation tax computation. This treatment is mandatory. Where capitalised interest on loans of this type is not included in the tax computation, the company must amend its self-assessment. HMRC will keep a record of the relief given, to check that the company makes an adjustment when amortisation of the asset is taken to profit and loss account, or when the asset is sold, and the interest then appears in the profit and loss account (*FA 1996, Sch 9, para 14*) (HMRC Corporate Finance Manual CFM 5230). This treatment does not apply where interest is charged to work-in-progress. This is because interest has been charged in the profit and loss account albeit there has been a rise in the value of work-in-progress (HMRC Corporate Finance Manual CFM 5230a).

CONNECTED PERSONS

Meaning of connection

11.25   Special rules apply for connected parties. A connection exists in the following circumstances:

Circumstances for a connection

'... there is a connection between the company and:

(a)   in the case of a debtor relationship of the company, a person standing in the position of a creditor as respects the debt in question; or

(b)   in the case of a creditor relationship of the company, a person standing in the position of debtor as regards that debt.' (*FA 1996, s 87(1)*)

The person standing in the position of a creditor is the lender.

The person standing in the position of the debtor is the borrower.

Connection in these circumstances means:

'... there is a connection between a company and another person for an accounting period if ...

(a)   the other person is a company and there is a time in that period when one of the companies has had control of the other; or

(b)   the other person is a company and there is a time in that period when both companies have been under the control of the same person.' (*FA 1996, s 87(3)*)

Although an individual or a partnership cannot be a party to a loan relationship, in a loan relationship series he or she may be considered to indirectly stand in the position of debtor or creditor and so bring about a loan relationship (*FA 1996, s 87(5)*) (HMRC Corporate Finance Manual CFM 5416).

Control prior to 1 October 2002

11.26   For accounting periods ending prior to 1 October 2002 the definition of control was that given by *ICTA 1988, s 416(2)–(6)* (see **4.4**). In essence, companies were connected if a person (through his or her associates) has control over the company's affairs and possessed or was entitled to acquire the greater part of the share capital, voting, dividend or assets on winding up, within the two previous accounting periods. A two-year time limit was given for the conditions to apply ending at the beginning of the accounting period in question. Again for accounting periods ended prior to 1 October 2002, a close company was connected with its participator (see **4.10**) or its participator's associate (see **4.12**) during the accounting period or the previous two years. Thus close company shareholders and directors were connected with their companies. This is no longer so post 1 October 2002 (*FA 1996, s 87(3)*).

Control post 1 October 2002

11.27   The definition was amended to the other meaning of control akin to *ICTA 1988, s 840* and the two-year time limit was withdrawn.

Meaning of control

Control in relation to a company means the power of a person to secure:

(a)   by means of the holding of shares or the possession of voting power in or relation to the company or any other company; or

(b)   by virtue of any powers conferred by the articles of association or other document regulating the company or any other company, that the affairs of the company are conducted in accordance with his wishes (*FA 1996, s 87A(1)*).

Shares held as trading stock are not included (*FA 1996, s 87A(2)*) and in general creditor relationships that result from activities forming an integral part of the trade carried on by that company during the accounting period are exempted.

Example 11.13

Mr Link controls Right Ltd and Left Ltd. If Right Ltd lent money directly to Left Ltd there would a connection under *FA 1996, s 87(3)(b)* because both companies are under the control of the same person.

Example 11.14

Right Ltd lends money to Ms Wong, who then lends it to Mr Wight who in turn lends it to Left Ltd. Right Ltd and Left Ltd are connected, because they are controlled by Mr Link, but neither company is connected with Ms Wong, nor Mr Wight. As a result of *FA 1996, s 87(5)*, Left Ltd stands indirectly in the position of debtor in relation to Right Ltd's loan relationship in this series of loans. Note that there are no consequences for Ms Wong.

Example 11.15

Norman Ltd controls Saxon Ltd. If Norman Ltd lent money directly to Saxon Ltd there would be a connection under *FA 1996, s 87(3)(a)* because one company is controlled by the other.

Angle Ltd is not connected to either Norman Ltd or Saxon Ltd. Norman Ltd lends £50,000 to

Angle Ltd. There is no connection between Norman Ltd and Angle Ltd, so *FA 1996, s 87(3)* does not apply to the loan relationship.

Angle Ltd then lends £50,000 to Saxon Ltd on identical terms. There is no connection between Angle Ltd and Saxon Ltd, so *FA 1996, s 87(3)* does not apply to the loan relationship.

However, in relation to Norman's loan relationship, Saxon Ltd stands indirectly in the position of debtor through a series of loan relationships. Therefore there is a connection, under *FA 1996, s 87(5)*, for the creditor loan relationship between Norman Ltd indirectly to Saxon Ltd, and conversely the debtor loan relationship between Saxon Ltd indirectly from Norman.

CONSEQUENCES OF CONNECTION

Amortised cost basis of accounting

11.28 Where a loan relationship debtor and creditor are connected certain rules are applied to the accounting treatment.

Regardless of the accounting method used in the company's accounts, the debits and credits brought into account must be determined according to the amortised cost basis of accounting (*FA 1996, s 87(2)*).

11.29 *Corporate finance*

The amortised cost of a financial asset or a financial liability is the amount at which the asset or liability is measured at initial recognition (usually its cost) less any repayments of principal, less any reduction for impairment or uncollectibility, and in addition or less the cumulative amortisation of the difference between that initial amount and the maturity amount (*FA 1996, s 103(1)*).

HMRC comment that the amortised cost basis of accounting is broadly equivalent to the authorised accruals basis that applied in periods of account beginning before 1 January 2005. If a company does not adopt IAS 39 or FRS 26—for example, where a small company continues to use the FRSSE—and the company previously accounted for loan relationships on an authorised accruals basis, the *FA 2004* changes to the loan relationships legislation should not bring about any change in the basis on which its debt assets and liabilities are taxed (HMRC Corporate Finance Manuals CFM 5151, CFM 16025).

The amortisation is calculated using the effective interest rate. The effective interest rate is the internal rate of return (IRR), ie the rate at which the net present value of the instrument is nil.

Example 11.16

A £200,000 bond will pay £210,000 on maturity in a year's time.

The IRR is $£200,000 \times (1 + r)^1 = £210,000$

$$
\begin{aligned}
r &= [(210{,}000 - 200{,}000) \div 200{,}000] \\
&= 0.05 \\
&= 5\%
\end{aligned}
$$

The future value of £200,000 @ 5% = $£200,000 \times (1 + 0.05)^1 = £210,000$

The present value of £210,000 = $£210,000 \times \{1 \div (1 + 0.5)^1\} = £200,000$

The present value £200,000 less the initial investment £200,000 equals the net present value which is nil.

Therefore the effective rate of return is 5%.

11.29 More complex calculations may be made by using the financial IRR (internal rate of return) function in Microsoft Excel (HMRC Corporate Finance Manual CFM 16025a).

Any resultant deficit or surplus in carrying value resulting from the change to amortised cost basis of accounting must be accounted for accordingly as a debit or credit (*FA 1996, s 87(2A), (2B) and (2C)*).

If the creditor company is connected to the debtor in exempt circumstances, ie in the course of its trade, it is not required to apply the amortised cost basis of accounting (or, for periods beginning before 1 January 2005, the accruals basis of accounting) or to follow the other provisions that apply to connected persons. The debtor company must apply the connected persons rules (*FA 1996, s 88(5)*).

Example 11.17

The CASH Bank plc issues listed security bonds worth £10m, which it places with its security trader subsidiary company Rowbowthams plc. Rowbothams plc is to place the bonds with unconnected investors.

The market is slow and Rowbothams plc holds the bonds for three months whilst it finds buyers. The bonds are part of its trading stock. It applies GAAP when preparing its accounts. The parties are connected under *FA 1996, s 87*. Without the *FA 1996, s 88* exemption Rowbothams plc would have to account for the bonds using the amortised cost basis of accounting. However, this is an ordinary commercial arrangement, with Rowbothams plc buying and selling the bonds as part of its trade. By applying *FA 1996, s 88*, Rowbothams plc can continue to account for the debt as trading stock. The CASH Bank plc is not exempted by *s 88* and will therefore use the amortised cost basis when accounting for the securities (HMRC Corporate Finance Manual CFM 5421c).

Unpaid interest

11.30   There is no debit for accrued unpaid interest for the debtor relationship company, unless the creditor relationship company has a corresponding credit. If the accrued unpaid interest is not paid within 12 months of the end of the accounting period, relief will only be given when that interest is eventually paid (*FA 1996, Sch 9, para 2*).

Discounted securities

11.31   Where the parties have a connection, relief on securities issued at a discount is deferred until redemption rather than being allowed as a debit over the life of the loan (*FA 1996, Sch 9, paras 17, 18*).

Creditor relationships and benefit derived by connected persons

11.32   Benefit directly or indirectly received by a company that is connected with a company that has a third-party creditor loan relationship as a result of the loan relationship is treated as a credit using fair value accounting of the creditor company if the actual return that the creditor company receives is below a commercial rate of interest. This applies to loan relationships to which the companies are parties to on or after 22 March 2006 (*FA 2006, Sch 6, para 16*).

Bad debt relief and impairment losses generally

11.33   The loan relationship rules in general grant relief for bad debts. For accounting periods commencing on or after 1 January 2005 impairment losses are accounted for using the IAS 39 or FRS 26 principles. The exception is a change in the rules relating to the acquisition of impaired debt (see **11.34**). The standards prescribe rules for identifying and measuring impairment losses at the year end. If the company correctly applies the relevant standard, to arrive at a debit for impairment losses (or a credit for reversal of impairment losses), the debit will be allowable (or the credit taxable) in accordance with the normal computational provisions of *FA 1996, s 85B*.

In periods of account beginning before 1 January 2005, the authorised accruals basis of accounting required the company to assume that every amount under a creditor loan relationship was payable in full, unless a departure from that assumption was specifically permitted. Departure from the assumption ('bad debt relief') was allowed only where a debt was bad or doubtful. Bad debt relief was granted by *FA 1996, Sch 9, para 5* to companies applying the authorised accruals accounting method. Bad debt relief was automatically given to companies applying the mark to market basis of accounting.

Connected parties and bad debt relief and impairment losses

11.34   Special rules apply to bad debt relief and impairment losses for connected parties. The general rule is that bad debt or impairment loss relief is denied if the companies to the loan relationship are connected (*FA 1996, Sch 9, para 6*).

For accounting periods commencing before 1 January 2005 connected companies had to use the accruals basis of accounting but were denied bad debt relief. For accounting periods commencing on or after 1 January 2005 connected companies are prevented from receiving debits for impairment losses.

For accounting periods only commencing before 1 January 2005 bad debt relief was not denied if the bad debt relief was given before the companies were connected or if the creditor acquired impaired debt in certain circumstances. Normally this was at an arm's-length price and there was no connection during the period four years before and 12 months after it acquired the debt (*FA 1996, Sch 9, para 6B(1)–(7)*).

Impairment loss relief is not denied if the connection only arises because the debt is exchanged for equity, provided that the companies were not connected when the creditor company acquired possession of or entitlement to the shares (*FA 1996, Sch 9, para 6(4)*). Neither is it denied if the creditor company goes into insolvent liquidation (*FA 1996, Sch 9, para 6A*).

The corresponding creditor company is not required to include a credit for the loss or bad debt relief reversal (*FA 1996, Sch 9, para 6(3A)*), whether or not the companies are still connected when the reversal takes place.

If any rights or liabilities (known as related transactions) are acquired at a non-arms length price they are accounted for as though they were a transaction between independent persons (*FA 1996, Sch 9, para 11*).

GROUPS AND CONSORTIA

11.35   Group companies are connected under the loan relationship rules. Loan relationship intra-group transfers are tax neutral (*FA 2006, Sch 9, para 12*).

Consortia companies may not be connected under *FA 1996, s 87*, but consortium members are in a position to obtain not only consortium relief but also bad debt or impairment relief. Therefore there are restrictions on the available amount of bad debt relief where there has been a claim to group relief and vice versa.

The effect of the restriction is to reduce the impairment relief by the amount of the group relief claimed, with the result that overall impairment and group relief claimed will not exceed the greater of the bad debts claimed or the group relief (*FA 1996, Sch 9, para 5A*).

The rules apply to each consortium member and all group loans are taken into account.

Example 11.18

Winston Ltd is a consortium company with £1,000 issued ordinary shares.

Its ownership is as follows:

	No of shares
A Ltd	400
B Ltd	400
C Ltd	200

All companies prepare accounts to 31 December.

Winston Ltd incurs a loss of £40,000 for the year ended 31 December 2009, which is used in a group relief claim by the consortium members.

On 1 January 2009 C Ltd made a £50,000 loan to Winston Ltd. At 31 December 2009 it seems unlikely that Winston Ltd will be able to repay C Ltd's loan. C Ltd writes off £25,000 as bad. *FA 1996, Sch 9, para 5A(5)* will restrict C Ltd's impairment loss by the amount of the group relief claim, ie £16,000. Therefore only £9,000 (25,000 – 16,000) may be claimed. The group relief claim remains intact and the £16,000 restricted amount is carried forward, to be considered for future group and impairment loss claims.

The group's total group relief for the year ended 31 December 2010 is £20,000 and the group's impairment loss for the year ended 31 December 2011 is £50,000.

The position may be summarised as follows:

Cumulative position

Year ending	Brought forward	Impair- ment loss	Group relief	Impair- ment loss	Group relief claim allowed	Total relief
	£	£	£	£	£	£
31 December 2008		25,000	16,000	9,000		25,000
31 December 20089	9,000		20,000		11,000	11,000
31 December 2010	11,000	50,000		39,000		39,000
Total		75,000	36,000			75,000

Therefore the total relief is the greater of the bad debt or the group relief claim, ie £75,000.

LOAN RELATIONSHIPS, DERIVATIVES AND FOREIGN EXCHANGE GAINS AND LOSSES (FOREX)

11.36   *FA 2002* brought derivatives and FOREX within the same loan relationship treatment regime. (*FA 2002, s 79, Sch 23; FA 2002, s 83, Schs 26, 27, 28*).

Therefore 'credits' and 'debits' are brought into the corporation tax computation following the accepted accounting principles. All relevant capital and revenue profits, gains and losses must be included together with charges and expenses. Trading and non-trading surpluses are included within the respective Schedule D Case I or Schedule D Case III computations. Non-trading deficits are aggregated with other non-trade debits and credits and included within the Case III profit or non-trade deficit for the year (*FA 1996, s 84A*).

A company may match its foreign currency non-monetary assets with its foreign currency borrowings to provide a commercial hedge. The tax treatment will follow the accounts treatment and the gain or loss on foreign currency liabilities or on currency contracts will be deferred until accounted for or until a disposal (*FA 2002, Sch 26, para 16*).

Loan Relationships and Derivative Contracts (*Disregard and Bringing into Account of Profits and Losses*) (*Amendment*) *Regulations, SI 2005/2012* came into force on 11 August 2005. Changes in fair value of some derivative contracts are to be disregarded for tax purposes when they are recognised in the accounts and in some cases to be brought back on maturity or disposal. An election from the old to the proposed new rules should be made by 31 December 2005. FRS 26 was brought into line with IAS 39 with effect from 1 January 2006.

For accounting periods beginning or or after 1 January 2008, if a company uses a liability or a derivative to hedge its net investment in a foreign operation, such as shares in an overseas subsidiary, it may elect to value the shareholding for this purpose at the value of the net assets underlying the shares, rather than being restricted to the cost of the shares. It may also make an election, to review the extent to which liabilities or derivatives are matched with shares during the course of an accounting period (*SI 2007/3431*).

Finance (*No 2*) *Act 2005, s 40* brought loan relationships within the transfer pricing regime with effect from 4 March 2005. (See Chapter 14).

Repos

11.37 A repo represents a quasi-loan. In simple terms, a repo transaction takes place when the owner of securities sells them to a buyer and later purchases them from the same buyer at a higher price. The difference is treated as interest. Repos are effectively taxed on the substance of the transaction: *DCC Holdings* (*UK*) *Ltd v Revenue & Customs* SpC 611. Where more than one party is involved in a repo the interest is treated as being received by the end seller: *Revenue and Customs Comrs v Bank of Ireland Britain Holdings Ltd* [2008] EWCA Civ 58. New legislation came into force on 1 October 2007. These rules replace *ICTA 1988, ss 731–738* and bring repos within the loan relationship regime. A company as borrower has a debtor rep if the following conditions A to E are met:

(A)   under an arrangement the company either singly or as a member of a partnership receives money or another asset 'the advance' from another person 'the lender'.

(B)   The company's accounts for the period record the transaction as a financial liability in accordance with GAAP.

(C)   Under the terms of the arrangement the company sells securities at any time to the lender.

(D)   The arrangement makes provision conferring a right or imposing an obligation on the company to buy those of similar securities at any subsequent time.

(E)   In accordance with GAAP the subsequent purchase of those or similar securities would clear the financial liability shown as an advance in the company's accounts.

(*FA 2007, Sch 13, para 2*)

A debtor quasi-repo

11.38   A debtor quasi-repo is said to exist where there is no debtor repo as such but conditions A to E exist.

(A)   under an arrangement thecompany either singly or as a member of a partnership receives money or another asset 'the advance'.

(B)   The company's accounts for the period record the transaction as a financial liability in accordance with GAAP.

(C)   Under the terms of the arrangement the company sells securities at any time to the lender.

(D)   The arrangement makes provision conferring a right or imposing an obligation on the company to buy those of similar securities at any subsequent time or makes provision conferring such a right or imposing such an obligation on any other person and makes arrangements for the receipt of money or other asset from the company under that arrangement for the purpose of enabling the other person to make the subsequent purchase, or for the discharge of any liability to the company under that arrangement for that purpose by way of set-off or otherwise.

(E) In accordance with GAAP the subsequent purchase of those or other securities by the company or the receipt of the asset from the borrower or the discharge of the liability to the company under the arrangement or other arrangement would clear the financial liability shown as an advance in the company's accounts.

(*FA 2007, Sch 13, para 3*)

Charge to and relief from corporation tax

11.39 A company with a repo or quasi-repo arrangement that recognises income therefrom in its profit and loss account in accordance with GAAP is to be charged to corporation tax on the income arising on the securities during the period they are subject to the repo agreement (*FA 2007, Sch 13, para 4*). Likewise, the seller should obtain relief for the costs of obtaining the finance included in the accounts (*FA 2007, Sch 13, para 5*). Any subsequent acquisition of the securities by the borrower is disregarded for the purposes of chargeable gains subject to corporation tax (*FA 2007, Sch 13, para 6*).

Creditor repo

11.40 A company as lender has a creditor repo if the following conditions A to E are met:

(A) under an arrangement another person. the borrower company either singly or as a member of a partnership receives money or another asset 'the advance' from the lender company.

(B) The lender company's accounts for the period in which the advance is made record a financial asset in respect of the advance.

(C) Under the arrangement the borrower sells securities at any time to the lender company.

(D) The arrangement makes provision conferring a right or imposing an obligation on the lender company to sell those or similar securities at any subsequent time.

(E) In accordance with GAAP the subsequent sale of those or similar securities would clear the financial asset shown as an advance in the lender company's accounts.

(*FA 2007, Sch 13, para 7*)

Creditor quasi-repo

11.41   A company as lender has a creditor quasi-repo if the following conditions A to E are met:

(A)   under an arrangement another person. the borrower company either singly or as a member of a partnership receives money or another asset, 'the advance' from the lender company.

(B)   The lender company's accounts for the period in which the advance is made record a financial asset in respect of the advance.

(C)   Under the arrangement (or other arrangement) a person sells securities at any time to the lender company or any other person.

(D)   The arrangement makes provision conferring a right or imposing an obligation on the lender company to sell those or similar securities at any subsequent time or makes provision conferring such a right or imposing such an obligation on any other person and makes arrangements for the receipt of money, securities or other asset from the lender company under that arrangement for that purpose by way of set-off or otherwise.

(E)   In accordance with GAAP the subsequent sale of those or similar securities by the lender company or the receipt of the asset from the lender company or the discharge of the liability to the lender under the arrangement or other arrangement would clear the financial asset shown as an advance in the lender company's accounts.

(*FA 2007, Sch 13, para 8*)

Charge to and relief from corporation tax for creditor and quasi-creditor repos

11.42   A company with a creditor repo or quasi-creditor repo arrangement that recognises income therefrom in its profit and loss account in accordance with GAAP is to be charged to corporation tax on the income arising on the securities during the period they are subject to the repo agreement (*FA 2007, Sch 13, para 9*).

However, the lender company will be charged corporation tax on any financial return eg interest from the creditor or quasi creditor repo if this return is recognised in the accounts in accordance with GAAP (*FA 2007, Sch 13, para 10*). Any subsequent sale of the securities by the lender is disregarded for the purposes of chargeable gains subject to corporation tax (*FA 2007, Sch 13, para11 (5)*).

If the situation changes and it becomes apparent that the lender will not sell those securities or similar securities under the arrangement or the accounting condition ceases to be met the securities resume treatment as a chargeable asset for capital gains tax purposes (subject to corporation tax) with the lender acquiring the securities for market value at that time.

Anti-avoidance

11.43   Any arrangement the main purpose of which is to obtain a tax advantage that does not fall into the creditor repo or quasi-creditor repo criteria but is designed to produce interest on a money investment will be treated according to the foregoing rules for corporation tax purposes (*FA 2007, Sch 13, para 12*).

COMPANY TAX RETURN

11.44   Companies provide details of their non-trade deficits on loan relationships in boxes 20 and 28 of the company tax return. All other details are supplied by means of the corporation tax computation and the accounts.

Chapter 12

Investment business

INTRODUCTION

12.1   Prior to 1 April 2004, a company with purely investment business was classed as an investment company and thus obtained relief for management expenses. Post 1 April 2004, all companies are able to claim management expenses in respect of their investment business.

Close investment holding companies retain their separate status. A company is a 'close investment holding company' (CIHC), unless it exists wholly or mainly as a trading company, an investment company letting land and property other than to connected persons or a trading group member. A CIHC's profits will be subject to the main rate of corporation tax (30%), irrespective of income levels (see **4.23–4.26**).

CORPORATION TAX COMPUTATION

12.2   A company's investment income will typically include Schedule A and income from non-trading loan relationships. As stated in **12.1** all companies may now claim a deduction for management expenses if they have investment business.

Example 12.1

XYZ Ltd draws up accounts to 31 March each year. Results for the year ended 31 March 2009 show the following:

	£000
Rents receivable	197
Interest receivable accrued (gross)	5
Chargeable gains	48
Management expenses	
attributable to property	25

	£000
attributable to management	40
Capital allowances	
attributable to property	5
attributable to management	1
Charitable charges on income	10

The company has unrelieved management expenses brought forward from previous accounting periods of £42,000.

XYZ Ltd corporation tax computations for the year ending 31 March 2009

	£000	£000
Schedule A		197
Less		
Capital allowances	5	
Management expenses	25	
		30
		167
Schedule D Case III		5
Chargeable gains		48
		220
Less		
Management expenses unrelieved brought forward for year		
Unrelieved brought forward	42	
For year	40	
Capital allowances	1	
		83
		137
Less charges		10
PCTCT		127

MANAGEMENT EXPENSES

Definitions

12.3   The definition of an investment company is:

'an investment company means any company whose business consists wholly or mainly of making investments and the principal part of whose income is derived from those investments ... but includes any savings bank or other bank for savings except ... a trustee savings bank' (*ICTA 1988, s 130*).

With effect from 1 April 2004, the definition regarding investment activities was extended to include a company with investment business:

'A company with investment business means any company whose business consists wholly or partly in the making of investments' (*ICTA 1988, s 130*).

The importance of the criteria being the relief for management expenses (*ICTA 1988, s 130*). As each type of income is assessed to corporation tax according to its source rules it may occur that an investment company could be put at a disadvantage if say it only had bank interest or dividend income (see HMRC Company Taxation Manuals CTM 08040 and CTM 08050 for a discussion of investment business).

Management expenses

12.4   A deduction for management expenses for an accounting period is allowed against the total profits of the accounting period (*ICTA 1988, s 75(1)*). Management expenses include all those expenses that are not otherwise deductible in computing profits, but do not include capital expenditure (*ICTA 1988, s 75(2)*). Capital allowances may be claimed on capital expenditure (*ICTA 1988, s 75(7)*).

The type of expense that can be included in 'management expenses' is as the name describes being:

'the expenses are in respect of so much of the company's business as consists in the making of investments and the investments concerned are not held by the company for an unallowable purpose during the accounting period' (*ICTA 1988, s 75(4)(a)*).

The description is specific and unlike the *ICTA 1988, s 74* 'wholly and exclusively' trading company criteria. Expenses of management cannot just amount to general administration costs.

Running costs in connection with managing the company's investment business, including reasonable directors' remuneration, staff salaries and pension contributions are chargeable as management expenses (*LG Berry Investments Ltd v Attwooll* (1964) 41 TC 547). The same timing rules for remuneration payments apply as for Schedule D Case I (see **5.16**) (*FA 1989, s 44*). Company secretarial costs such as maintaining the share register, printing annual accounts and holding an AGM are regarded as expenses of management. Entertaining expenditure and expenditure involving crime is specifically prohibited (*ICTA 1988, ss 577, 577A*). No relief is given if the expenses are incurred for an unallowable purpose. An unallowable purpose occurs when the company holds investments neither for a business nor a commercial purpose or the company is not within the charge to corporation tax. (See **12.7** below).

Management expenses are deductible from investment income of both UK resident companies and non-resident companies with a permanent establishment in the UK from where the income is derived (*ICTA 1988, s 75(6)*).

Management expenses are charged on an accruals basis provided the accounts follow GAAP (*ICTA 1988, s 75A*). Prior to 1 April 2004, the management expenses had to be 'disbursed', ie paid but not necessarily within the accounting period for which they were properly charged. This rule no longer applies. Credits for management expenses first reduce the management expenses for the year and are then brought into charge as Schedule D Case VI income (*ICTA 1988, s 75B*). In practice, company expenditure may relate to a number of activities in which case it should be allocated between them on a just and reasonable basis. For accounting periods beginning on or after 20 June 2007, there is no deduction for management expenses incurred directly or indirectly to secure a tax advantage (*FA 2007, s 28*).

Management activities

12.5   Management expenses cannot be claimed unless the company is chargeable to corporation tax. This would, for example, exclude a mutual trading company, as its profits are not chargeable to corporation tax (see **5.52**). In order for a company to be chargeable to corporation tax it must have an activity, otherwise it would be totally dormant. On the assumption that the company had no other business, activities that would bring a company with investment business within the charge to corporation tax would be the holding of shares in another non-dormant company (*ICTA 1988, s 12(4)*) or the disposal of an asset resulting in a chargeable gain or allowable loss (*TCGA 1992, s 8(3)*). The management expenses claim for the year is made by completing box 24. A claim for management expenses carried forward is included in box 136, with the maximum available for group relief surrender in box 137.

Group companies

12.6   Group companies often recharge expenses to other group members such as administration charges. Provided the allocation is done on a reasonable basis this will result in each group member deducting its share of administration costs from its relevant trade or activity. See **5.20**. (HMRC Business Income Manual BIM 42140).

Unallowable purpose

12.7   Expenses in connection with investments held for a non-business or non-commercial purpose or in connection with activities not within the charge to corporation tax are not chargeable as management expenses. Such activities will include:

- investments held by a company for social or recreational purposes;

- provision of services and facilities by a members' club to its members;

- UK branch expenses of a non-resident company in respect of activities not connected with the UK branch;

- mutual trading activities (these fall outside the scope of Schedule D Case I).

However, a company that merely receives dividends from UK companies within *ICTA 1988, s 208* will still be classed as an investment company or a company with investment business. As will any company whose capital gains are covered by the substantial shareholding exemption or collective investment scheme gains exempt under *TCGA 1992, s 100(1)* (HMRC Company Taxation Manual CTM 08230).

Capital expenditure

12.8   From 1 April 2004 capital expenditure is specifically excluded as a deduction for management expenses purposes (*ICTA 1988, s 75(3)*). HMRC's view is that expenditure incurred on appraising the purchase or sale of an investment up to the decision point is revenue and expenditure following the decision to acquire or dispose of an investment is capital (HMRC Company Taxation Manual CTM 08260). Success fees that are only payable when the deal goes through must by their very nature be capital and therefore excluded from management expenses. It is necessary to examine the facts of each case and to apply *the same criteria to abortive expenditure*. The costs associated with purchase and sale are not regarded as management expenses. Brokerage and stamp duties were not allowed as management expenses (*Capital and National Trust Ltd v Golder* (1949) 31 TC 265, [1949] 2 All ER 956 and *Sun Life Assurance Society v Davidson* (1957) 37 TC 330).

Cost of asset valuations for accounts purposes (*SI 2008/409* and *SI2008/410*)) are considered to be management expenses but valuations related to the acquisition and disposal of assets are not (HMRC Company Taxation Manual CTM 08420).

Capital expenditure on assets used for the purpose of management qualifies for capital allowances. The capital allowances are a management expense. Balancing charges are income of the investment business. See **12.4**. (*CAA 2001, ss 18, 253*).

Insurance premiums

12.9   Premiums paid on assets used in the management of the company are considered to be management expenses but not premiums paid on the insurance of the investments. This is because the view is taken that the expenses incurred must relate to management and not to general administration (HMRC Company Taxation Manual CTM 08320). Depending on the circumstances such premiums may be classed as capital expenditure.

Companies ceasing to trade

12.10   Practical considerations may arise when a company ceased to trade. The holding of a static bank account when trading ceased classifies a company as 'dormant' (*Jowett v O'Neill & Brennan Construction Ltd* (1998) 70 TC 566). In such circumstances it would be necessary for the company to show that it intends to continue with an investment activity if it wishes to claim management expenses for that period. The same criteria will apply to a company that is in liquidation. It will be necessary to show that it is 'making investments'.

Pensions paid to former employees by a company that ceases to trade and becomes an investment company or a company with investment business are not expenses of management if the former employees at no time were employees of the company after it ceased to trade. This is because the pension payments relate to the former trade and not to the investment activity (HMRC Company Taxation Manual CTM 08350).

Self-assessment

12.11   The corporation tax computation for a company with investment business would normally show income and gains from the investment activity in full, rather than adjusted profits. Appeals may be heard by the General Commissioners. Appeals in respect of expenditure incurred prior to 1 April 2004 could only he heard by the Special Commissioners.

Management expenses set-off

12.12 Management expenses are deducted from the company's profits chargeable to corporation tax before charges and before loss relief claimed under *ICTA 1988, s 393A* (*ICTA 1988, s 75(1)*). Excess management expenses are carried forward to be used in the subsequent accounting period as management expenses of that period (*ICTA 1988, s 75(9)*). A company may group relieve management expenses for the chargeable period against group income.

A company may only surrender management expenses that exceed the gross profits for the accounting period (*ICTA 1988, ss 402, 403(1)*). The order of set-off being charges on income, Schedule A losses and management expenses or a non-trading loss on intangible fixed assets in that order. (See **10.7**).

Example 12.2

Kappa Ltd owns 90% of the ordinary share capital of Lamda Ltd. Kappa Ltd is the group investment holding company.

Both companies prepare accounts to 31 December each year.

Results for the year ended 31 December 2008 are as follows:

	Kappa Ltd	*Lamda Ltd*
	£000	£000
Schedule D Case I		50
Schedule A	10	20
Schedule D Case III	40	30
Charges		2

Kappa Ltd's corporation tax liability after management expenses and management expenses for group relief are as follows:

	£000
Management expenses	
(*ICTA 1988, s 75(1)*) for the year	100
(*ICTA 1988, s 75(3)*) brought forward	5
	105

	£000
Management expenses	
Excess management expenses for group relief	
Management expenses	
(*ICTA 1988, s 75(1)*) for the year	100
Schedule A	10
Schedule D Case III	40
	50
Excess management expenses	50
Group relief	50
	0
Excess management expenses brought forward and carry forward	5

Lamda Ltd corporation tax computation after group relief is as follows:

	£000
Schedule D Case I	50
Schedule A	20
Schedule D Case III	30
	100
Charges	2
Total profits	98
Group relief (management expenses)	50
PCTCT	48

Restriction on management expenses

12.13   Management expenses are restricted where there is a change of owner-ship and after the change there is a significant increase in the company's capital. Alternatively, within a period of six years beginning three years before the change, there is a major change in the nature or conduct of the business, or the change in ownership occurs after the scale of activities has become small or negligible and before any considerable revival of the business (*ICTA 1988, s 768B*).

A change of ownership occurs where:

 (i)   a single person acquires more than half the ordinary share capital of the company or

(ii)   two or more persons each acquire a holding of 5% or more of the ordinary share capital of the company, and those holdings together amount to more than half the ordinary share capital of the company or

(iii) two or more persons each acquire a holding of the ordinary share capital of a company, and those holdings together amount to more than half the ordinary share capital of the company. Holdings of less than 5% are disregarded unless it is in addition to an existing holding and the two holdings together amount to 5% or more of the ordinary share capital (*ICTA 1988, s 769*).

The 5% threshold means there is no need to examine small shareholdings, particularly those of public companies.

Note, it is possible for more than half of a company's shares to change hands and yet not trigger a change of ownership if the shares are purchased by a number of unconnected persons, each of whom acquires a holding of less than 5%.

A major change in the nature or conduct of the business includes a major change in the nature of the investments held, even if that change was the result of a gradual process which began before the period of six years within which the change has to take place (*ICTA 1988, s 768B(3)*).

INVESTMENT IN PROPERTY

12.14   If a company invests in property it will show the property as a fixed asset on the balance sheet and will record letting income as Schedule A income. Property disposals will attract a capital gain. Letting income will be assessable under Schedule A rules.

A company could be a property dealer or developer in which case the property cost is shown in trading stock on the balance sheet. The company earns its income from the sale of properties and the business is assessed as a trade under Schedule D Case I.

Transactions between property dealing companies and their non-dealing associates are brought into charge on the associate as either Schedule D Case I income or Schedule D Case VI income (*ICTA 1988, s 774*).

SCHEDULE A INCOME

Income from UK land and buildings

12.15   Companies are charged to corporation tax on income arising from the letting of UK land and property. The income is treated as a single 'Schedule A business' (*ICTA 1988, s 15(1)*).

The types of income assessable include receipts from:

- payments for a licence to occupy, use or exercise a right over land;
- rent charges, ground annuals, feu duties and other annual payments in respect of land;
- income from furnished lettings, including furnished holiday lettings; and
- income from caravans or houseboats where their use is confined to one location in the UK.

Schedule A income is included in box 11 of form CT600.

Computation of profit

12.16   Schedule A business profits are computed in accordance with GAAP. Capital allowances are available on plant used in the letting business, eg a motor vehicle used in connection with site visits, and are deductible as a Schedule A business expense.

Capital allowances are not available for plant let for use in a dwelling house (*CAA 2001, s 35*). Relief is given for furnished lettings by allowing 10% of rental income (net of the landlord's outlay on council tax and water rates if any) as a wear and tear deduction. Alternatively, relief can be claimed on a renewals basis for capital items replaced in a let property. Interest is excluded from a Schedule A computation and dealt with as a non-trading 'debit' under the loan relationship rules.

Lease premiums

12.17   Where a lease is granted for a duration of 50 years or less (a 'short' lease) any premium paid is treated partly as a disposal for capital gains and partly as income. The income portion is treated as rental income in the year in which the lease is granted. The income portion is calculated as the amount of the premium less 2% for each complete year of the lease except the first (*ICTA 1988, s 34*). Where the company is the tenant and pays a lease premium, the income portion is an allowable Schedule D Case I deduction, spread over the life of the lease (*ICTA 1988, s 87*).

Example 12.3

Horatio Ltd granted a 21-year lease to Eustace Ltd on 1 January 2009 with a £50,000 premium and £60,000 annual rent. Horatio Ltd prepares accounts to 31 December each year. The rental business receipts for the year ended

31 December 2009 are as follows:

Schedule A	£000
Premium receivable	50
Less: (2% of £50,000) × 20 years	20
	30
Plus: rent for the year ended 31 December 2008	60
Schedule A rental business	90

Eustace Ltd leases the property for business purposes and claims the following Schedule D Case I deduction in its accounting period ending 31 December 2009:

	£000
Rental costs	60
Amount of premium treated as additional rent: £30,000 ÷ 21 = £1,428	1
Total Schedule D Case I deduction for rent	61

(*ICTA 1988, s 70(2)*).

Reverse premiums

12.18   Where a landlord pays a sum to induce a tenant to take a lease (a reverse premium) then (unless it reduces expenditure qualifying for capital allowances) it is generally treated as Schedule D Case I income of the tenant corresponding with the treatment of the rental payments. However, certain benefits (eg the grant of a rent-free period) are not taxable under these rules (*FA 1999, s 54, Sch 6*).

If the landlord is a property development company the payment will be a deduction against Schedule D Case I profits. If the landlord is a property investment company the payment will be treated as a capital payment that enhances the value of the underlying asset. The premium will not be deductible from rental income (See HMRC Business Income Manual BIM 41060).

Repair expenditure

12.19   Property repair expenditure is an allowable deduction. If the repair takes the asset beyond its condition prior to the repair this will be deemed a capital expense and hence disallowable. Repair expenditure of the subsidiary parts of an asset is classed as revenue expenditure (HMRC Property Income Manual PIM 2020).

Legal fees

12.20   Legal fees of a revenue nature wholly and exclusively in connection with the rental business are deductible.

The expenses incurred in connection with the first letting or subletting of a property for more than one year are capital expenditure and therefore not allowable. The expenses may include, legal expenses, lease preparation costs, agent's and surveyor's fees and commission. If the lease is for less than one year the expenses are deductible.

Legal and professional costs incurred in respect of the renewal of a lease for less than 50 years are allowable. Legal costs in relation to the payment of a premium on the renewal of a lease are not deductible.

Legal expenses in connection with letting arrangements that closely follows the terms of previous arrangements are considered to be a revenue expense and will not be disallowable except for the legal or other costs that relate to the payment of a premium on the renewal of a lease.

Legal costs in connection with a change of use of the premises in between lets will be treated as a capital expense and hence disallowable.

HMRC have identified the following legal and professional costs as allowable:

- costs of obtaining a valuation for insurance purposes,
- the normal accountancy expenses incurred in preparing rental business,
- subscriptions to associations representing the interests of landlords,
- the cost of arbitration to determine the rent of a holding,
- the cost of evicting an unsatisfactory tenant in order to relet the property.

The following costs are disallowable:

- legal costs incurred in acquiring, or adding to, a property,
- costs in connection with negotiations under the *Town and Country Planning Acts*,
- fees pursuing debts of a capital nature, for example, the proceeds due on the sale of the property.

Normal accountancy costs are deductible, including, by concession, agreeing the taxation liabilities. However, legal costs in connection with acquisition of a property or costs in connection with negotiations under the *Town and Country Planning Acts* are not deductible. Legal fees on drawing up a new lease are allowable if the lease is for less than one year. If more than one year, it is not allowable because the expense is capital (HMRC Property Income Manual PIM 2205).

Corporation tax deduction for expenditure on energy-saving items

12.21 To complement the 'Landlords Energy Saving Allowance' (or 'LESA') for income tax purposes, *FA 2007, s 17(ICTA 1988, ss 31ZA(5) and 31ZC)* allows companies which operate a residential property letting business either in the UK or overseas, to deduct the cost of acquiring and installing certain energy-saving items in the residential properties which they let, from the rental business profits assessable to corporation tax. The relief is introduced with effect from 8 July 2008.

There is a maximum amount of allowable expenditure of £1,500 for each property (or 'dwelling house'). Any contributions received from persons not entitled to a deduction reduce the amount of the deduction. A property for this purpose means a separate dwelling ie a separate unit; therefore the £1,500 limit will be applied to each flat in a block of separate apartments rather than the entire building. The deduction is only available for expenditure incurred before 1 April 2015. See **6.92** for a discussion on 'dwelling' and 'dwelling house'.

The qualifying expenditure in question is capital expenditure, which does not qualify for capital allowances or the annual investment allowance, but is incurred 'wholly and exclusively' for the purposes of the letting business and is of an energy saving nature. The qualifying expenditure is expenditure on hot water system insulation, draught proofing, cavity wall insulation, solid wall insulation, floor insulation and loft insulation.

If a landlord incurs qualifying expenditure that benefits more than one property then this should be apportioned amongst the relevant properties on a just and reasonable basis *(ICTA 1988, s 31ZA)*. No deduction for the cost of the energy saving item is permitted if it is installed in the property during the course of construction. The landlord must have a legal title to the property. If the energy-saving item is installed whilst the landlord is in the course of acquiring a legal title or changing that legal title no deduction is permitted. No deduction is permitted in respect of property used in a furnished holiday letting business (see **5.44**). The expenditure only qualifies as pre-trading expenditure under *ICTA 1988, s 401* if it is incurred in no more than six months before the residential letting business commenced. In addition the acquisition and the installation expenditure must have been incurred solely for the purposes of the dwelling-house (*ICTA 1988, s 31ZB*).

In practice, more than one party can have a legal interest in the property and any apportionment of the relief or the expenditure should be made on a just and reasonable basis.. The company has the right of appeal should there be a dispute (*ICTA 1988, s 31ZC*)(*SI 2008/1520*)(*SI 2008/1521*).

Treatment as Schedule D Case I

12.22   Where rent is received from the letting of surplus accommodation on a short-term basis, this by concession is taxable under Schedule D Case I, and no adjustment is required in the computations (HMRC Tax Bulletin, Issue 10).

Moderate rental income from the temporary letting of part of the trader's business premises may be treated as Schedule D Case I income. This treatment only applies to the letting of accommodation and not to the letting of land.

The letting income from properties held as trading stock is Schedule A rental income. Expenses must be apportioned on a reasonable basis. Property development is a trade. Any property held awaiting sale will be included in trading stock. If that property were to be let for a short time the costs of letting would be deducted from the letting receipts and the net profit would be part of the rental business income assessable to Schedule A. If there is an excess of expenditure over income that excess is deducted from the property dealing or development trade (HMRC Property Income Manual PIM 4300).

Rents and premiums received from tied premises are Schedule D Case I income and not Schedule A income. The same applies to the taxable amount of any premium received. Any expenditure on the tied premises will be deducted in the computation of the trading profits and should similarly be excluded from the rental business (*ICTA 1988, s 98*). If other services are provided that go beyond those normally provided by a landlord they may constitute a separate trade and not a rental business. Expenses normally provided by a landlord are:

- the cleaning of stairs and passages in multi-unit premises,
- the provision of hot water and heating,
- supervision involving rent collection and arranging new tenancies,
- arranging for repairs to the property.

The facts of each case must be examined on their merits to see if a separate trade is being carried out (HMRC Property Income Manual PIM 4300).

Travelling expenses to and between properties when incurred wholly and exclusively for the rental business are deductible (HMRC Property Income Manual PIM 2210).

SCHEDULE A LOSSES

12.23   Losses incurred in an accounting period in a Schedule A business which is carried on commercially is set against the company's total profits for the same accounting period. If there are insufficient profits, against which to set the loss, it is carried forward to the next accounting period and treated as a loss of that period to be set against total profits. Excess losses are carried forward in this way until the Schedule A business ceases. When the Schedule A business ceases the remaining loss will be carried forward and treated as management expenses under *ICTA 1988, s 75 (ICTA 1988, s 392A)*.

Where there is a change of company ownership, as described in **12.13**, the losses arising before the change of ownership cannot be carried forward to be set against profits arising after the change of ownership. If the change of ownership occurs during an accounting period losses pre and post the change are apportioned according to the length of the accounting bases or if this is unjust, on a just and reasonable basis (*ICTA 1988, s 768D*).

Schedule A losses are included in CT600 boxes 127 and 128.

INVESTMENT IN OTHER LIMITED COMPANIES

12.24   An investment in another limited company will bring about share ownership for the company. The subsequent disposal of the shares will bring about a capital gain. Income will take the form of dividend receipts. UK dividends have in effect already borne corporation tax (see **1.1**). Overseas dividends may bring an entitlement to a tax credit (see **13.16–13.24**). There are important reliefs for share disposals:

- losses on shares in unquoted trading companies,
- substantial shareholding exemption,
- corporate venturing scheme relief.

Capital losses

12.25   An investment company may claim relief against income for capital losses arising on the disposal of shares in unquoted qualifying trading companies, which had been subscribed for by the investment company. The loss incurred, which is calculated under normal CGT rules, may be set-off against income (before management expenses and charges) of the same and (if not wholly relieved) preceding accounting periods (*ICTA 1988, s 573*). A loss claim may also be made where an asset has proven to be of negligible value (*TCGA 1992, s 24*). A computation must be prepared by taking the negligible value of the asset as its sale proceeds.

Loss relief for allowable capital losses is available to an investment company (irrespective of whether it is a close investment-holding company), which has subscribed for shares in a qualifying trading company (*ICTA 1988, s 573*). The relief must be claimed, in writing, within two years after the end of the accounting period in which the loss was incurred.

The investment company obtains relief for its capital loss by set-off against its income chargeable to corporation tax. The loss relief is set against income of the accounting period in which the loss is incurred and income of previous accounting periods ending within the 12 months immediately preceding the accounting period in which the loss was incurred. Where an accounting period falls partly within and partly outside the 12-month period, only a proportion of its income can be relieved.

The loss relief against income is given before deduction of charges on income and expenses of management. Where loss relief is given under these provisions, the loss is ignored for the purpose of corporation tax on chargeable gains.

The main conditions to be satisfied in order to qualify for this relief against income are as follows:

● The company subscribing for shares and incurring the capital loss must, generally, have been an investment company for the whole of the previous six years.

● The shares subscribed for must be share capital of a qualifying trading company as defined in *ICTA 1988, s 576(4)*.

● The investment company must not control the trading company, the two companies must not be under common control, and the two companies cannot be members of the same group.

For this purpose the distinction between an investment company and a trading company is maintained. An investment company has the same meaning as *ICTA 1988, s 130* (see **12.3**) but does not include the holding company of a trading group. A trading company is defined as a company whose business consists wholly or mainly of the carrying on of a trade or trades (*ICTA 1988, s 576*).

Substantial shareholdings exemption

The relief

12.26 Provided all relevant conditions are met, the gain on the disposal of shares or an interest in shares held by a company in another company will not be a chargeable gain. However, if a loss were to arise on the disposal of the shares, this loss will not be an allowable loss and hence not available for set-off against other gains. The company has the benefit of no tax payable on the gain but all loss relief is 'lost'.

The exemption does not apply where disposal is deemed to be a no gain/no loss transfer for capital gains under *TCGA 1992, s 171* (see **20.16**).

Substantial shareholding

12.27 Essentially the investing company must hold at least 10% of the investee company's share capital and be entitled to at least 10% of the profits and assets available for distribution to equity holders by the investee company. The investing company must have held the shares for a continuous period of at least 12 months ending not more than one year before the disposal (*TCGA 1992, Sch 7AC*).

Group member holdings can be aggregated in order to calculate whether the 10% holding criteria is met (*TCGA 1992, Sch 7AC, para 26*). The capital gains tax group definition is used (see **20.14**) using a 51% relationship rather than a 75% relationship.

Even if shares are vested in a liquidator the company continues to be treated as the beneficial owner of the assets (*TCGA 1992, Sch 7AC, para 16*). The shares must have been held for at least 12 months ending not more than one year before disposal. If some of the shares have been sold during the 12-month period the remainder of the holding will continue to qualify (*TCGA 1992, Sch 7AC, para 7*). The period of ownership also looks back through the no gain/no loss transfers and share reorganisations so that this time of ownership is also brought into consideration (*TCGA 1992, Sch 7AC, paras 10, 14*). However, for deemed sales and reacquisitions, the time of ownership commences with the reacquisition of the holding (*TCGA 1992, Sch 7AC, para 11*). Repurchase agreement arrangements treat the time of ownership as that commencing with the original owner (*TCGA 1992, Sch 7AC, para 12*). Similarly, stock lending arrangements have no effect on the original ownership time span (*TCGA 1992, Sch 7AC, para 13*). A demerger that has a reorganisation treatment (*TCGA 1992, s 192*) is also looked through when calculating the period of ownership (*TCGA 1992, Sch 7AC, para 15*). In addition, if the 10% shareholding exemption applies as described above, the exemption will also be extended to an option or conversion right connected with the shares (*TCGA 1992, Sch 7AC, para 2*).

Conditions affecting the investing company

12.28 The investing company must have been a sole trading company or a member of a trading group throughout the 12-month period and immediately after the disposal (*TCGA 1992, Sch 7AC, para 18*). The relief also applies in a group situation where the company holding the shares does not qualify, but assuming an intra-group transfer under *TCGA 1992, s 171* another company would qualify. Where there is a deferral of the completion date on disposal the investing company must qualify at the time of completion (*TCGA 1992, Sch 7AC, para 18*).

Conditions affecting the investee company

12.29 The investee company must have been a trading company or the holding company or a trading group during the 12-month period and also be a trading company immediately after the disposal of the shares (*TCGA 1992, Sch 7AC, para 19*). From 19 July 2006 the responsibility for determining whether a company, in which shares (or interests in shares or assets related to shares) were held and since disposed of, was a qualifying company, lay with the investor company concerned (Tax Bulletin 84, August 2006). With effect from 1 June 2007 HMRC have reinstated the Code of Practice 10 procedure with regard to the substantial shareholdings exemption. Companies requiring information and guidance on this aspect of tax law should write in the first instance to the tax office dealing with their affairs (HMRC Brief 41/2007 1 June 2007).

As for the investor, where there is a contract for sale with delayed completion the investee company must quantify at the time of sale (*TCGA 1992, Sch 7AC, para 19*).

Trading activities

12.30 HMRC use the same: meaning of 'trading company' as for taper relief. See HMRC Tax Bulletin 53.

A 'trading company' is defined as a company which is either 'a company existing wholly for the purpose of carrying on one or more trades' or a company that would fall within that definition 'apart from any purposes capable of having no substantial effect on the extent of the company's activities'.

In this context 'wholly' to means solely, ie the company had no purpose other than to trade. Wholly for a trading purpose is considered according to the requirements of the company's trade. The generation of investment income does not necessarily mean that a company is not trading. For example, the company may set aside funds short-term for the expansion of the business or a cyclical business may hold large funds from time to time that it needs to settle its trading debts. A company's purpose is understood to mean its actual or its intended activities; this will mean examining the directors intentions.

Trading activities for these purposes will include activities carried on by a company:

- in the course of, or for the purposes of, a trade it is carrying on;

- for the purposes of a trade it is preparing to carry on;

- with a view to it acquiring or starting to carry on a trade;

- with a view to it acquiring a significant interest in the share capital of a trading company, or the holding company of a trading group or subgroup (subject to the restrictions outlined below).

The company's view to acquire or start a trade or its view to acquire a shareholding must materialise as soon as is reasonably practical in the circumstances. 'Significant' for these purposes only refers to ordinary share capital and the company to be acquired must not already be a member of the same group (*TCGA 1992, Sch 7AC, para 20*).

Holding funds for a longer term may prove to be insubstantial.

Any non-trading activities should be insubstantial. This is normally understood to be 20% of all the activities or less (*TCGA 1992, Sch 7, para 20*). HMRC applies the same criteria as the test for taper relief (see Tax Bulletin 53); namely the proportion of turnover, assets and management time derived from or employed in the non-trading activity. HMRC have stated that these are not pass/fail tests and are not the only indicator of whether a company is a trading company. In general HMRC attach less importance to the assets measure than to turnover or management time. HMRC will examine the situation over a period of time.

A holding company of a trading group is 'a company whose business (disregarding any trade carried on by it) consists wholly or mainly of the holding of shares in one or more companies which are its 51% subsidiaries'. HMRC interpret 'wholly or mainly', in this context, as more than half of whatever measure is reasonable in the circumstances of the case. Intra-group activities are disregarded for the purpose of the financial tests.

Trading activities also include a qualifying interest in a joint venture company (*TCGA 1992, Sch 7AC, para 20*).

Example 12.4

Atlantic Ltd is a trading company, with two wholly-owned subsidiary companies, India Ltd and China Ltd.

On 1 July 2007, Atlantic Ltd acquired 25% of the ordinary share capital of Pacific Ltd.

On 1 September 2007 Pacific Ltd is taken over by Adriatic Ltd.

Atlantic Ltd received an exchange of shares under the no gain/no loss treatment (*TCGA 1992, s 135* applied *TCGA 1992, s 127*). As a result Atlantic Ltd now owns 20% of Adriatic Ltd.

On 1 March 2007 Atlantic Ltd transfers its holding in Adriatic Ltd on a no gain/no loss basis so that *TCGA 1992, s 171* applies to its 100% subsidiary India Ltd.

On 1 July 2008 India Ltd sells the holding to a third party.

The holding was bought on 1 July 2007 and sold on 1 July 2008. It is necessary to look back through the period of ownership to ascertain whether the substantial shareholdings exemption applies (*TCGA 1992, Sch 7AC, para 10*). The holding throughout has remained within the group. India Ltd is treated as owning the shares for 12 months prior to disposal and so the substantial shareholding example applies.

Corporate venturing scheme

12.31   The corporate venturing scheme rules are contained in *FA 2000, Sch 15*.

The rules offer companies relief for investment in qualifying shares in other companies during the period from 1 April 2000 until 1 April 2010. The companies involved can be of any size, but more usually between a larger company and a smaller one in the same line of business; thus providing the smaller company with another form of finance.

The larger company may invest in the smaller company. The connection provides an alternative or supplementary source of finance for the investee firm and a useful business outlet for the investor company. The investor company may take an interest in the investee by offering its skills and financial advice but must not have a major interest in the company.

Tax reliefs

12.32   There are three types of relief available:

- **Investment relief**. Relief against corporation tax of up 20% of the amount subscribed for the full-risk ordinary shares held for three years.

- **Deferral relief**. Any gain on the sale of shares can be rolled into the cost of new shares acquired under the scheme.

- **Loss relief**. Any loss on the sale of the shares can be relieved against income or chargeable gains.

The investing company

12.33   The investing company's interest in the investee company must not be more than 30% and it must not be in a position to control the company (*FA 2000, Sch 15, paras 5–8*). Connected company interests are taken into account together with directors' and the directors' relatives' interests. A relative is taken to mean a spouse, civil partner, parent and grandparent, child and grandchild etc. No reciprocal arrangements must exist regarding the investment (*FA 2000, Sch 15, para 6*). The investing company must be a trading company or the holding company of a trading group and financial activities are precluded. If the investment does not qualify for some reason the relief will be withdrawn.

The issuing company

12.34   The issuing company must be an unquoted trading company or the holding company of a trading group, when the shares are issued (AIM and PLUS market shares are unquoted for this purpose). The company can be preparing to carry on a trade. It must not have made any arrangements to become a quoted company.

The company must have gross assets of no more than £7m immediately before, and £8m immediately after the issue (if the issuing company is the parent company of a group, this test is applied to the group as a whole). For shares issued before 6 April 2006, the limits are £15m before and £16m after.

With effect from 6 April 2007 if the issuing company is a single company, there must be less than 50 full-time or equivalent employees when the shares are issued (*FA 2000, Sch 15, para 22A*). The equivalent number of full-time employees is found by taking the actual number of full-time employees and adding to this the fractional apportionment for each additional employee (*FA 2007, Sch 16*).

Throughout the qualification period the issuing company must not be a member of a group of companies, unless it is the parent company of the group, and must not be under the control of another company. With effect from 6 April 2007, if the issuing company is a parent company, there must be less than 50 full-time or equivalent employees (as calculated above) for that company and for each of its qualifying subsidiaries when the shares are issued (*FA 2000, Sch 15, para 22A*) (*FA 2007, Sch 16*).

At least 20% of the issuing company's ordinary share capital must be held by individuals other than directors or employees (or their relatives) of an investing company, or any company connected with it (*FA 2000, Sch 15, para 18*).

The investment

12.35   The investment must be in cash and the shares must be fully paid-up at the time they are issued. There can be no arrangement in force to protect investors from normal commercial investment risk.

The investing company must use at least 80% of the funds it receives from issuing the shares for the purposes of a qualifying trade, or for research and development intended to lead to or benefit a qualifying trade. The funds must be used no later than the end of the period of 12 months starting with the issue of the share or the 12 months following the commencement of the trade if later. The remaining 20% of the funds must be used within the following 12 months (*FA 2000, Sch 15, para 36*). With effect from 6 April 2007, the total investment in the company's relevant investments is restricted to £2 million. The company's relevant investments include investments made in any company that is or has at any time during the year in question been a subsidiary of the issuing company regardless of whether it was a subsidiary at the time when the investment was made. Relevant investments are investments included on a *FA 2000, Sch 15 para 42* compliance statement, which confirms that the scheme conditions are met (*FA 2007, Sch 16*).

Trading activities

12.36   In order to qualify for the relief, the company must be carrying on a qualifying trade during the qualification period. The qualification period commences with the issue of the shares and ends immediately before the third anniversary of the issue date. If the money raised wholly or mainly for the purposes of the trade had not been used for that trade by the issuing company or its qualifying 90% subsidiary, the qualification period ends on the third anniversary of the trading date.

A qualifying 90% subsidiary of the issuing company is any company in which the issuing company owns not less than 90% of the issued share capital, not less than 90% of the voting power, has entitlement to not less than 90% of the assets in a winding-up and has entitlement to not less than 90% of the profits on a distribution. In addition no other person has control according to the meaning in *ICTA 1988, s 840* (see **14.4**) and no arrangements are in existence so that any of the aforementioned conditions would cease to be effective (*FA 2000, Sch 15, para 23A*).

Qualifying trade

12.37   The following activities are excluded from a 'qualifying trade'

- dealing in land, commodities or futures or in shares, securities or other financial instruments;

- dealing in goods otherwise than in the course of an ordinary trade of wholesale or retail distribution;

- banking, insurance, money-lending, debt-factoring, hire-purchase financing or other financial activities;

- leasing (including letting ships on charter or other assets on hire) or receiving royalties or other licence fees;

- providing legal or accountancy services;

- property development;

- farming or market gardening;

- holding, managing or occupying woodlands, any other forestry activities or timber production;

- operating or managing hotels or comparable establishments or managing property used as a hotel or comparable establishment; and

- operating or managing nursing homes or residential care homes, or managing property used as a nursing home or residential care home. (*FA 2000, Sch 15, para 26*).

Obtaining clearance

12.38   The investee company can obtain clearance before the shares are issued (*FA 2000, Sch 15, para 89*). If the issue goes ahead the issuing company should complete form CVs 1 confirming it has met all the necessary conditions with which it must comply. The company must submit the form to HMRC and if satisfied HMRC will authorise the issuing company to provide the investing company with a compliance certificate to enable it to claim investment relief (and, where applicable, deferral relief). The compliance certificate can only be issued after the issuing company has been carrying on the trade (or, where appropriate, research and development) for which the funds were raised for at least four months.

Obtaining relief

12.39 The investing company claims investment relief against its corporation tax liability by completing the corporate venturing scheme CT600G supplementary pages and including the relief claimed in box 71 of the main return. Loss relief is included in CT600 box 22.

The necessary conditions must be complied with for three years or else the relief is withdrawn. The relief is only available during the accounting period for which the investment is made. The relief is given against corporation tax after marginal relief but before any double taxation relief.

Example 12.5

If during an accounting period, an investing company subscribes £30,000 for 3,000 shares in company A and £90,000 for 6,000 shares in company B, then the maximum investment relief available is £24,000 (20% of £30,000 + £90,000).

If the investing company's corporation tax liability for the accounting period is £18,000 before taking account of any investment relief, then only three-quarters of the available investment relief can be used.

So, the amount attributable to the shares in A is:

$$£30,000 \times £18,000/£120,000 = £4,500$$

The amount attributable to the shares in B is:

$$£90,000 \times £18,000/£120,000 = £13,500$$

It would also be possible for the investing company to claim investment relief only in respect of the shares in company B, so all the investment relief would be attributable to those shares. But, this would prevent shares in company A from qualifying for CVS loss relief and deferral relief, because there would be no investment relief attributable to the shares in company A immediately before any future disposal.

359

12.40   If value, other than insignificant value, is received from the investee company, relief is withdrawn accordingly, being 20% of the value received. Receiving value could amount to acquiring an asset at undervalue, money lending etc. The provision of goods and services at market rates during the course of trade is not understood to be receipt of value (*FA 2000, Sch 15, para 47*).

An insignificant amount is £1,000 or if more, the amount is insignificant in relation to the amount subscribed for the shares (*FA 2000, Sch 15, para 47(7)*) (HMRC Venture Capital Manual VCM 50630).

Deferral relief

12.41   The reinvesting company may claim deferral relief on its disposal of qualifying shares, if investment relief was attributable to the shares immediately before the disposal and, if the investing company holds the shares continuously from the time they were issued until the disposal. The new company in which the investee company invests must comply with the investment relief conditions. The gain must be reinvested in the other qualifying company at any time beginning four years before the deferred gain arose.

The gain is deferred until the shares in the other company are disposed of, or an event occurs (such as, a receipt of value or certain share reorganisations), which causes any of the investment relief attributable to the shares to be withdrawn.

The investing company claims deferral relief on the corporate venturing scheme supplementary pages. It may do so after it has received the second investment's compliance certificate. The amount of the deferral must be shown on the claim.

If the investment relief is withdrawn for any reason, this does not affect the deferral relief.

Relief for losses

12.42   A loss on disposal can be set against a chargeable gain, or carried forward to set against future chargeable gains, in the normal way. Alternatively, the investing company may claim that the loss be set against its income for the accounting period in which the disposal was made, with any excess carried back to periods ending in the 12 months before that period.

The loss must have arisen from an arm's-length disposal and not arise from a scheme or arrangement. The shares must have been held continuously by the company since issue. The amount of the loss is reduced by the amount of any investment relief retained (*FA 2000, Sch 15, paras 67–71*).

Example 12.6

An investing company subscribes £100,000 for 100,000 shares (obtaining investment relief of £20,000).

It retains the shares for four years before disposing of them all for £55,000.

The allowable loss is calculated as follows:

Disposal proceeds £55,000 – £80,000 (consideration given for shares less investment relief given and not withdrawn).

So the allowable loss is £25,000.

Any unutilised loss cannot be carried forward as a trading loss but may be carried forward as a capital loss.

Other reliefs

12.43 The investing company will hold the shares in the investee company as an investment. Corporate venture scheme holdings will not qualify for group relief, but if all necessary conditions apply, they may qualify for consortium relief (see **10.14**). For further information see HMRC Guidance, The Corporate Venturing Scheme: www.hmrc.gov.uk/guidance/cvs.

INVESTMENT IN COMPANY OR GOVERNMENT LOAN STOCK

12.44 Loan stock investments are within the loan relationships regime (see Chapter 11).

COMMUNITY INVESTMENT TAX RELIEF

Eligibility for tax relief

12.45 Companies that make investments in an accredited community development finance institution (CDFI) may obtain community investment tax relief (*FA 2002, Sch 16, para 1*). The investor company itself cannot be a CDFI (*FA 2002, Sch 16, para 16*). There must be no tax avoidance purposes (*FA 2002,*

Sch 16, para 18). The investment may take the form of a secured or unsecured loan subscription to a securities or share issue but not in the form of an overdraft (*FA 2002, Sch 16, para 2*).

The relief is given over a five year period, which commences on the day that the investment is made (*FA 2002, Sch 16, para 1*).

The relief

12.46   The company must claim on box 72 of form CT600 for its corporation tax liability to be reduced by the smaller of 5% of the invested amount and the amount which reduces the investor's corporation tax liability to zero. The claim can be made for the accounting period in which the investment is made and in each of the following four accounting periods (*FA 2002, Sch 16, para 20*). The company must have received a tax relief certificate relating to the investment from the CDFI.

Accreditation

12.47   The company must apply for accreditation as a community development finance institution to provide finance, or business advice for SMEs in disadvantaged communities (*SI 2003/96* and *SI 2008/383*). SMEs in disadvantaged communities include both SMEs located in disadvantaged areas, and SMEs owned or operated by, or designed to serve, members of disadvantaged groups (*FA 2002, Sch 16, para 4*).

No claim can be made unless the company is an accredited CDFI (*FA 2002, Sch 16, para 24*). If the investor company itself becomes a CDFI no claim is possible (*FA 2002, Sch 16, para 25*). When granted a period of accreditation will last for three years (*FA 2002, Sch 16, para 7*).

Conditions to be satisfied in relation to loans

12.48   There are conditions related to loans. First the CDFI either receives the full amount of the loan on the investment date or the draw down period must commence no later than 18 months after the investment date. Secondly, the loan must not carry any present or future rights for conversion to shares or securities redeemable within the five-year period beginning with the day the investment is made. Thirdly, the loan must not be repayable during the first two years; no more than 25% of the loan outstanding at the end of the first two years can be repaid in the third year; no more than 50% of the loan capital can be repaid before the end of the fourth year and no more than 75% of the loan capital can be repaid before the end of the loan period. Other normal commercial conditions may be imposed (*FA 2002, Sch 16, para 9*).

Conditions to be satisfied in relation to securities

12.49   Any securities issued must be subscribed for wholly in cash and be fully paid for on the investment date. The securities must not carry any present or future right to be redeemed within the five year period, or any present or future right to be converted into or exchanged for a loan which is, or securities, shares or other rights which are, redeemable within that period (*FA 2002, Sch 16, para 10*).

Conditions to be satisfied in relation to shares

12.50   Shares must be subscribed for wholly in cash, and be fully paid up on the investment date (*FA 2002, Sch 16, para 10*). Shares are not fully paid up for the purposes of *para 10(b)* if there is any undertaking to pay cash to the CDFI at a future date in connection with the acquisition of the shares.

The shares must not carry any present or future right to be redeemed during the five year period, or any present or future right to be converted into or exchanged for a loan which is, or securities, shares or other rights which are, redeemable within that period (*FA 2002, Sch 16, para 11*).

Tax relief certificates

12.51   Tax relief certificates may be issued by the CDFI in respect of retail investments made in the CDFI in that period with an aggregate value exceeding £10m, and in any other case, in respect of investments made in the CDFI in that period with an aggregate value exceeding £20m (*FA 2002, Sch 16, para 12*). The investment consists of the amount of the loan or the investment in shares. There is a £3,000 penalty for any tax relief certificates issued fraudulently or negligently.

There can be no risk exclusion other than normal commercial risks (*FA 2002, Sch 16, para 13*). At any time during the five year period the investor or a connected party must not control the CDFI. When considering control, all future rights and powers are attributed to the investor and the investor must be the sole beneficial owner of the investment or loan repayment entitlement when it is made (*FA 2002, Sch 16, para 14*).

Investment

12.52   As regards securities or shares, the invested amount for a tax year or accounting period is the amount subscribed by the investor for the securities or shares. The shares must have been held by the investor throughout the accounting period (*FA 2002, Sch 16, para 23*).

The amount of a loan investment is determined according to its average capital balance. The average capital is the mean of the daily balances of capital outstanding during the period. The investment is as follows:

- for the tax year or accounting period in which the investment date falls, the average capital balance for the first year of the five year period;

- for the tax year or accounting period in which the first anniversary of the investment date falls, the average capital balance for the second year of the five year period;

- for any subsequent tax year or accounting period:

    — the average capital balance for the period of one year beginning with the anniversary of the investment date falling in the tax year or accounting period concerned; or

    — if less, the average capital balance for the period of six months beginning 18 months after the investment date.(*FA 2002, Sch 16 para 21*).

The loan must be outstanding at the end of the accounting period concerned (*FA 2002, Sch 16, para 22*).

Where more than one investment is made the relief is attributed pro-rata (*FA 2002, Sch 16, para 26*).

Withdrawal of relief

12.53   If the relief is withdrawn or reduced for any reason a Schedule D Case VI assessment will be made on the company for the accounting period for which the relief was obtained (*FA 2002, Sch 16, para 27*). An assessment may be made at any time not more than six years after the end of the accounting period for which the relief was obtained, but if a loss of tax is brought about deliberately by the company or a related person, the period is extended to 20 years (*FA 2008, Sch 39, para 48*).

In the case of a loan the relief is withdrawn if the investor disposes of the loan within the five year period other than through the dissolving or winding up the CDFI or the CDFI loses its accreditation. A full or partial loan repayment is not treated as a disposal (*FA 2002, Sch 16, para 28*).

In the case of share or securities the relief is withdrawn if the investor disposes of the whole or any part of the investment within the five year period other than through the dissolving or winding up the CDFI, or the CDFI loses its accreditation, or the repayment, redemption or repurchase of securities or shares included in the investment (*FA 2002, Sch 16, para 29*).

In addition, the disposal must be at arm's length or for full consideration.

Repayments of loan capital

12.54 The relief is withdrawn if loan capital is repaid and the average capital balance of the loan for the period of six months beginning 18 months after the investment date is less than the prescribed percentage being 75% for the third year, 50% for the fourth year and 25% for the final year. The relief is not withdrawn if the amount does not exceed £1,000.

The average capital is the mean of the daily balances of capital outstanding during the period disregarding any non-standard repayment.

A repayment is non-standard if it is made at the choice or discretion of the CDFI and not as a direct or indirect consequence of a contractual obligation (*FA 2002, Sch 16, para 30*). The same situation applies if value is received in repayment of a loan (*FA 2002, Sch 16, para 31*).

Excessive returns to an investor

12.55 Relief is withdrawn or pro rata partially withdrawn, if the investor receives excess value from the company during the first three years of the period of six years beginning one year before the investment date (the period of restriction). Amounts of less than £1,000 are ignored.

Relief is also withdrawn if the aggregate amount of value received by the investor before the beginning of the fifth year of the period of restriction (as mentioned above) is more than 25% of the invested capital or 50% before the final year and 75% during the final year. Amounts of less than £1,000 are ignored (*FA 2002, Sch 16, para 32*).

Value received

12.56 An investor received value from a CDFI at any time when the CDFI:

(a) repays, redeems or repurchases any securities or shares included in the investment;

(b) releases or waives any liability of the investor to the CDFI or discharges, or undertakes to discharge, any liability of the investor to a third person:

    (i) A CDFI shall be treated as having released or waived a liability if the liability is not discharged within 12 months of the time when it ought to have been discharged.

(c) makes a loan or advance to the investor, which has not been repaid in full before the investment is made:

    (i) A loan is treated as made by the CDFI to the investor if there is a debt incurred by the investor to the CDFI (other than an ordinary trade debt) or a debt due from the investor to a third person which has been assigned to the CDFI.

(d) provides a benefit or facility for:

    (i) the investor or any associates of the investor; or

    (ii) if the investor is a company, directors or employees of the investor or any of their associates.

(e) disposes of an asset to the investor for no consideration or for a consideration which is or the value of which is less than the market value of the asset;

(f) acquires an asset from the investor for a consideration which is or the value of which is more than the market value of the asset; or

(g) makes a payment to the investor other than the following:

    (i) any payment by any person for any goods, services or facilities provided by the investor (in the course of his trade or otherwise) which is reasonable in relation to the market value of those goods, services or facilities;

    (ii) the payment by any person of any interest, which represents no more than a reasonable commercial return on money, lent to that person;

    (iii) the payment by any company of any dividend or other distribution which does not exceed a normal return on any investment in shares in or securities of that company;

    (iv) any payment for the acquisition of an asset, which does not exceed its market value;

    (v) the payment by any person, as rent for any property occupied by the person, of an amount not exceeding a reasonable and commercial rent for the property; and

    (vi) a payment in discharge of a trade debt for goods or services supplied in the ordinary course of a trade or business with credit terms of not more than six months and not longer than that normally given to customers of the person carrying on the trade or business (*FA 2002, Sch 16, para 35*).

Reconstructions

12.57   If there is a restructuring by the CDFI the new investment is treated as made and not when the original investment was made (*FA 2002, Sch 16, para 40*). A share exchange is treated as a disposal of shares and the relief may be lost (*FA 2002, Sch 16, para 41*).

If the relief is to be withdrawn, the investor company must inform HMRC within the period of 12 months beginning with the end of the accounting period in which the event occurred (*FA 2002, Sch 16, para 42*). An investor must notify HMRC of value received by any person no later than 60 days beginning when the investor comes to know of that event if this is later than the period of 12 months beginning with the end of the accounting period.

Chapter 13

Overseas matters

INTRODUCTION

13.1 Companies may be resident in the UK with overseas income or vice versa. Alternatively, they may invest abroad, in which case they will be able to receive tax relief on their income or their investment may fall within the controlled foreign companies regime.

COMPANY RESIDENCE

13.2 A company is resident in the UK if it is incorporated in the UK (*FA 1988, s 66*).

If a company is not incorporated in the UK if will be resident in the UK if it is centrally managed and controlled in the UK. The case of *De Beers Consolidated Mines Ltd v Howe* (1906) 5 TC 198, [1906] AC 455 involved a company that was registered in South Africa where it worked diamond mines. The company's head office and shareholders' general meetings were held in South Africa, but the directors' meetings took place in both South Africa and the UK. The majority of directors lived in the UK. The company claimed that it was not resident in the UK. It was held that the company was resident in the UK because the majority of the directors who had the overall control were situated in London.

The place where the management and control is exercised from then on has been interpreted as the place where the effective management decisions are taken and not necessarily where it was constitutionally managed. In *Wood v Holden (Inspector of Taxes)* [2006] EWCA Civ 26, [2006] 2 BCLC 210 although a company's board meetings took place in London, the authority given by those board meetings was usurped by the overseas parent and the company was held to be non-UK resident. Thus it is necessary for the courts to apply two tests; first the *situs* of the management and control of its own constitutional organs and secondly where that control is usurped. These tests were applied in the later case of *News Datacom Ltd v Atkinson (Insp of Taxes; News Data Security Prod-*

368

ucts Ltd v Atkinson (Insp of Taxes)) SpC 561 where there was no usurpation and the company was deemed to be non UK resident on its facts.

Double tax treaty

13.3   If a double tax treaty is in place between the UK and the overseas territory it should be consulted in order to verify the company's deemed place of residence.

A company may be 'treaty non-resident'; in other words, solely resident in the other country. A discussion is given in HMRC International Manual INTM 120070.

If residence is or could be awarded to the treaty partner, the company becomes treaty non-resident. A treaty non-resident company is not resident for UK tax purposes (*FA 1994, s 249*).

A double tax treaty ensures that companies that carry on business in more than one country are only taxed once on their income. A reciprocal provision to the effect that the profits of a non-resident company, which carries on a trade, profession or business that is controlled or managed outside the UK are only subject to UK tax if those profits are attributable to a permanent establishment in the UK is often included. In relation to income arising on or after 12 March 2008, the inclusion of such a clause does not prevent the company's other income from being chargeable to UK tax (*FA 2008, s 59*)(*ICTA 1988, s 815ZA*).

UK RESIDENT COMPANY WITH OVERSEAS INCOME

13.4   A company resident in the UK is chargeable to corporation tax on all its profits wherever the income arises and wherever the assets on which the gain on whose disposal the gain was calculated were situated and whether or not received or transmitted to the UK. Trading income of a UK trade earned abroad will be assessed within the Schedule D Case I computation.

NON-UK RESIDENT COMPANY CARRYING ON A TRADE IN THE UK

Circumstances in which chargeable to UK corporation tax

13.5   A non-resident company is chargeable to corporation tax, if, and only if, it carries on a trade in the UK through a permanent establishment in which case the following becomes chargeable:

- any trading income arising directly or indirectly through or from the permanent establishment;

- any income from property or rights used by, or held by or for, the permanent establishment;

- chargeable gains accruing on the disposal of assets situated in the UK used for the purposes of the trade of the use of the permanent establishment (*ICTA 1988, s 11*; *TCGA 1992, s 10*).

Meaning of 'permanent establishment'

13.6 Non-resident companies are assessed to UK corporation tax (subject to treaty override: see **13.2**), if they have a permanent establishment in the UK. Prior to 1 January 2003 non-resident companies were assessed to UK corporation tax if they had a branch or agency in the UK. A permanent establishment may of course be a branch or agency, but the precise change of wording was introduced to bring the UK legislation in line with various internationally recognised characteristics commonly used in the UK's double tax agreements.

FA 2003, s 148 states that a company has a permanent establishment in a territory if, and only if, it has a fixed place of business there through which the business of the company is wholly or partly carried on, or an agent acting on behalf of the company has and habitually exercises there authority to do business on behalf of the company.

A fixed place of business

13.7 A fixed place of business can be a place of management, a branch, an office, a factory, a workshop, an installation or structure for the exploration of natural resources, a mine, an oil or gas well, a quarry or any other place of extraction of natural resources or a building site or construction or installation project (*FA 2003, s 148(1), (2)*).

Circumstances in which there is no permanent establishment

13.8 A company is not regarded as having a permanent establishment if it carries on business there through an independent agent acting in the ordinary course of the agency business. A company is regarded as having a permanent establishment if it maintains a fixed place of business for the purpose of carrying on activities that have not yet commenced. Neither will the company be regarded as having a permanent establishment if an agent carries on preparatory or auxiliary activities in relation to the business of the company as a whole.

The legislation provides examples of preparatory or auxiliary activities, of a company as a whole, which will not be considered sufficient business activities to constitute the existence of a permanent establishment. The list is not exhaustive but includes:

- the use of facilities for the purpose of storage, display or delivery of goods or merchandise belonging to the company;

- the maintenance of a stock of goods or merchandise belonging to the company for the purpose of storage, display or delivery;

- the maintenance of a stock of goods or merchandise belonging to the company for the purpose of processing by another person (*FA 2003, s 148(4), (5)*).

NON-RESIDENT COMPANY BECOMING LIABLE TO UK CORPORATION TAX

Assessment, collection and recovery of corporation tax

13.9 When an overseas company commences trading in the UK it should notify HMRC that it is within the charge to corporation tax. This will be the commencement of an accounting period (*ICTA 1988, s 337*). When it becomes chargeable to UK corporation tax, it is chargeable to corporation tax, subject to any exceptions provided for by the *Corporation Tax Acts*, on all profits, wherever arising, that are attributable to its permanent establishment in the UK (*ICTA 1988, s 11AA*).

UK permanent establishments compute their taxable profits on the same principles as UK resident companies. Only where the UK has a tax treaty with the permanent establishment's home country and there is a conflict between the treaty and the UK corporation tax domestic law the effect of the treaty will be to modify or prevent the application of UK corporation tax principles (*FA 2003, s 149*). *ICTA 1988, s 788(3)* specifies that relevant treaty provisions take precedence over domestic legislation.

ICTA 1988, s 11AA(2) adopts the wording of Article 7(2) of the OECD model tax convention and states that the permanent establishment's taxable profits are the profits that it would have made if it were a distinct and separate enterprise, engaged in the same or similar activities under the same or similar conditions, dealing wholly independently with the rest of the non-resident company of which it is a part.

When calculating the profits it is assumed that the permanent establishment has the same credit rating as the non-resident company of which it is a part and has such equity capital and loan capital as it could reasonably be expected to have in regard to its circumstance (*ICTA 1988, s 11AA(2), (3)*).

A deduction is given for expenses, wherever they are incurred, if they are incurred for the purposes of the permanent establishment and if they would be deductible if incurred by a company resident in the UK (*ICTA 1988, s 11AA(4)*).

A non-resident company pays corporation tax at the full rate. No claim can be made for the small companies rate (*ICTA 1988, s 13(1)*).

Responsibility for UK corporation tax

13.10   The UK representative of the overseas company is responsible for the permanent establishment's corporation tax affairs (*FA 2003, s 150*). The company in turn is bound by the acts or omissions of the UK representative. However, a non-resident company is not bound by mistakes in information provided by its UK representative in pursuance of an obligation imposed on the representative by this section, unless the mistake is the result of an act or omission of the company itself, or to which the company consented or in which it connived. Therefore, the UK representative of a non-resident company can only be prosecuted for a criminal offence if it committed the offence itself, or consented to or connived in its commission (*FA 2003, s 150*).

NON-UK RESIDENT COMPANY NOT CARRYING ON A TRADE IN THE UK BUT WITH OTHER UK INCOME

Liability to income tax

13.11   A non-resident company not carrying on a trade in the UK through a branch or agency is chargeable to income tax at the basic rate on any other UK income. Therefore a UK property investment business operated by a non-resident company will be subject to income tax at the basic rate on its profits. The profits are computed according to income tax rules (see *Income Tax 2008/09* from Tottel).

Where tax is deducted at source from such income the tax payable is limited to the tax deducted at source. This includes savings and dividend income (*FA 2003, s 151*).

UK COMPANY BECOMING NON-UK RESIDENT

HMRC notification and outstanding liabilities

13.12   When a company ceases to be chargeable to corporation tax, for example, by becoming non-UK resident it must comply with *FA 1988, s 130* requirements. It must notify HMRC of the date that it intends to become non-resident, provide a statement of all amounts owing and provide details of the arrangements it will make for payment. HMRC will require a payment guarantor to be provided and the arrangements must be approved by HMRC or otherwise they are void. (Treasury consent is not required for companies ceasing to be UK resident from 15 March 1988 onwards). If a company becomes non-resident without HMRC approval, it and its directors together with controlling company directors may be liable to a penalty based on its outstanding liabilities (*ICTA 1988, s 131*). Outstanding amounts of tax may be recovered from the company directors or directors of other companies in the group (*ICTA 1988, s 132*).

The company's UK departure will be the cessation of an accounting period (*ICTA 1988, s 337*). Therefore balancing adjustments must be calculated for capital allowance purposes.

It is unlawful without Treasury consent for a UK resident company to cause or permit a non-UK resident company over which it has control to create or issue any shares or debentures. It is also unlawful without Treasury consent for a resident company to dispose of any shares or debentures in a non-resident company that it controls (*ICTA 1988, s 765*). These are criminal offences. A £10,000 fine can be levied and those involved may be sentenced to two years imprisonment (*ICTA 1988, s 766*).

Deemed disposal of chargeable assets

13.13   Also the company will be deemed to have disposed of all its chargeable assets at market value thus creating a chargeable gain under *TCGA 1992, s 185*. A charge under *TCGA 1992, s 185* will also arise where a company becomes treaty non-resident. Roll-over relief is not available. If the chargeable assets are assets used in a trade that the company carries on, say through a branch or agency in the UK, there is no chargeable gain and therefore roll-over relief would be available. Following the case of *Hughes de Lasteyrie du Saillant v Minisère de l'Économie, des Finances et de l'Industrie* Case C-902/02, the European Commission has invited member states to improve the coordination of their national exit tax rules on accrued capital gains (EC 19 December 2006). No changes have been made to the UK legislation as yet.

Postponement of exit charge

13.14   Postponement of the exit charge may occur if:

- the assets are situated outside the UK and are used in or for the purposes of a trade carried on outside the UK ('foreign assets'),

- the company is a 75% subsidiary (by ordinary shares) of a UK resident company (the 'principal company') and

- both companies make an election within two years of the company becoming non-resident.

The postponed gain becomes a chargeable gain of the principal company in whole or in part if:

- the asset is disposed of within six years of the company becoming non-resident; and

- the company ceases to be a 75% subsidiary:

    — by disposal of ordinary shares;

    — for any other reason; or

    — by the principal company ceasing to be UK resident.

HMRC do not consider that the issue of new shares by the principal company to a third party will bring the gain into charge (*TCGA 1992, s 187*).

The capital gains charge under *TCGA 1992, s 185* also applies to companies who become treaty non-resident.

DUAL RESIDENT COMPANY

Restrictions

13.15 The transfer of the central management and control of a non-UK resident company to the UK will result in the company being UK resident. In practical terms the foreign jurisdiction may determine that the company remains resident abroad because of incorporation or because of trading activities. Hence, the company becomes a dual resident company. In such situations the relevant double tax treaty, if any, should be examined.

A dual resident investment company (ie a non-trading company) cannot claim or surrender group relief for the chargeable period (*ICTA 1988, s 404*). Neither can it make intra-group asset transfers on a no gain/no loss basis (*TCGA 1992, s 171*). Group roll-over relief is unavailable (*TCGA 1992, s 175(2)*).

The carry forward of trading losses on a succession to a trade without a change of ownership is also prohibited, together with the transfer of assets at written-down value for capital allowance purposes (*ICTA 1988, s 343(2)*).

Double tax relief

13.16   The double tax treaty between the UK and the country concerned may exempt the income in question from corporation tax. It should be examined in every case. (Double tax agreements can be viewed in HMRC Double Taxation Relief Manual DT 2140 onwards).

Credit relief for overseas corporate taxes paid is available against UK corporation tax payable. A claim should be made according to the terms of the double taxation agreement (*ICTA 1988, s 793A*).

Where there is no entitlement to relief under a double taxation agreement, unilateral relief (*ICTA 1988, ss 790, 793*) together with relief for withholding tax may be claimed. The general rule is that income is calculated according to UK principles (*George Wimpey International Ltd v Rolfe* [1989] STC 609) and the credit cannot exceed the calculated UK corporation tax.

OVERSEAS DIVIDENDS

Underlying tax

13.17   The only credit available for overseas dividends is withholding tax unless the UK company owns more than 10% of the overseas company's equity, in which case relief for underlying tax is available (*ICTA 1988, s 790*). Underlying tax is the tax on profits out of which the dividend is paid whereas withholding tax is tax deducted at source from the dividend payment.

Example 13.1

England Ltd, a UK resident company, receives a dividend of £9,000 net of 10% withholding tax, from Overseas Ltd, a foreign company in respect of the accounting period ended 31 March2009.

Extracts from Overseas Ltd's profit and loss account (converted to sterling) show the following:

	£
Profit before tax	450,000
Provision for corporation tax	90,000
Distributable profits	360,000

Corporation tax paid £140,000.

Computation of underlying tax

	£
Distributable profits	360,000
Foreign tax paid	140,000
	500,000

The effective rate of underlying tax is 28%.

Relief for underlying tax on a dividend received from outside the UK is restricted where the reclaim only emanates from an avoidance scheme (*ICTA 1988, s 801A*).

Relevant profits for calculating underlying tax

13.18   The distributable profits for these purposes are the profits shown in the company's accounts drawn up in accordance with the law of the company's home state. No provision is permitted for reserves, impairment losses or contingencies other than required by the company's home state law. The home state is the country or territory of incorporation or formation (*ICTA 1988, s 799(5)–(7)*. The company must take all reasonable steps to reduce the amount of foreign tax paid (*ICTA 1988, s 795A*).

If a company pays tax in another country on the aggregated profits of itself and other companies as if they were a single entity, for the purposes of calculating credit relief the relevant profits of these companies are regarded as a single aggregate figure in respect of a single company and the foreign tax paid by the responsible company as if it were paid by that single company. For the purposes of calculating the underlying tax only the profits of companies that are resident as a matter of fact in the country concerned may be included in the calculations of relevant profits and foreign tax for the deemed single entity (*ICTA 1988, s 803A*). Therefore dividend resolutions for such a group or companies specifying the profits from which the dividends are paid are inappropriate. HMRC will accept dividend resolutions from or Board Resolutions of the paying company specifying the accounting period from which the dividend is paid (HMRC International Manual INTM164130).

Credit relief: 'mixer cap'

Limit

13.19   The credit relief given is limited to the lower of the overseas tax paid or the UK corporation tax. The following formula is used:

$$(D + U) \times M\%$$

where

D = the dividend,

U = the amount of underlying tax paid overseas, and

M = the UK Corporation tax rate when the dividend was paid (*ICTA 1988, s 799(1A)*).

The formula looks back through the paying company to the source of the dividends.

Example 13.2

England Ltd receives two dividends from Overseas Ltd of £9,000 each arising in its accounting period ended 31 March 2009. The dividends are paid out of the foreign company's profits for the years ended 31 December 2008 and 31 December 2009 with respective underlying rates of tax of 28% and 50%. Each net dividend plus withholding tax amounts to £10,000.

Schedule D Case V income

	£	£
Dividend 1: £10,000 + £2,800 underlying tax	12,800	
Dividend 2: £10,000 + £5,000 underlying tax	15,000	
	27,800	
UK corporation tax: £27,800 at 28%		7,784
Less credit		
Dividend 1	2,800	
Dividend 2 (restricted to £15,000 at 28%)	4,200	
		7,000
Corporation tax payable		784

If a company's accounting straddles 1 April 2008, its rate of corporation tax will be based on the number of days falling into the financial years 2007 and 2008, with the respective rates of 30% and 28% being adjusted accordingly. Dividend income is also apportioned on the same time basis. (See **2.5**). Therefore credit relief may be restricted for dividends received before 1 April 2008. The Government intends to address this issue in Finance Act 2009.

Unrelieved tax credits

Carry back and carry forward

13.20 Unrelieved tax credits on Schedule D Case V dividends known as eligible unrelieved foreign tax (EUFT) may be eligible for relief by:

- carry back to the three previous accounting periods,

- carry forward to the next accounting period, or

- through the mixer cap (*ICTA 1988, s 806D*).

Eligible unrelieved tax credits are those that have not been restricted, eg by *ICTA 1988, s 801A* (see **13.16**), and is the difference between the credits allowed and the foreign tax suffered up to a maximum of 45%. The EUFT that may be relieved is calculated by the following formula:

$(D + U) \times 45\%$

where

D	=	the dividend (excluding lower level dividends),
U	=	the amount of underlying tax paid overseas not attributable to any lower level dividends, and
45%	=	maximum relief (*ICTA 1988, s 806B*).

Example 13.3

England Ltd's EUFT on its second dividend receipt amounts to:

	£
$(D + U) \times 45\% = (10{,}000 + 5{,}000) \times 45\%$	6,750
Less foreign tax relievable	4,500
Eligible EUFT	2,250

13.21 EUFT may be relieved by carry back to accounting periods beginning no more than three years before the current period. The later years are relieved before the earlier years but after relief for the current period (*ICTA 1988, s 806E*). Alternatively EUFT can be carried forward to the next accounting period (*ICTA 1988, s 806D*). Credit relief is given for underlying tax before withholding tax in all cases (*ICTA 1988, s 806F*).

The EUFT may be carried forward to the next accounting period or back to previous accounting periods.

The order of carry back is:

1   the accounting periods beginning not more than three years before the accounting period in which the relievable tax arises;

2   later accounting periods are relieved in priority to earlier accounting periods, but

3   after current tax is offset in the following order:

    (i)   aggregated foreign tax in respect of the single dividend for that period (so far as it does not consist of relievable tax arising in another accounting period), and

    (ii)   relievable tax arising in any accounting period before that in which this relievable tax arises.

However the amount of credit given must not exceed the corporation tax liability on that single dividend, ie it cannot produce EUFT (*ICTA 1988, s 806E*).

Credit is given for underlying tax before withholding tax. Current year set off is given priority to other years (*ICTA 1988, s 806F*).

Claims must be made within six years from the end of the chargeable period for which the income is chargeable to corporation tax (*ICTA 1988, s 806*). Claims are made in writing or by completion of boxes 73, 74 and 75 of the company tax return.

Credit relief and eligible unrelieved foreign tax: the 'mixer cap'

13.22   In calculating credit relief it is necessary to look back to the source of the dividends. In the case of a group this will mean looking back to dividends paid by the subsidiary companies.

Example 13.4

There are four companies:

UK Ltd	UK resident company
Foreign Land BV	foreign company (non-UK resident)
Faraway SA	foreign company (non-UK resident)
Furtheraway SA	foreign company (non-UK resident)

Faraway SA pays corporate taxes of £25,000 and a £75,000 dividend to Foreign Land BV.

Furtheraway SA pays corporate taxes of £35,000 and a £65,000 dividend to Foreign Land BV.

Foreign Land BV pays a £140,000 dividend to UK Ltd and corporate taxes of £60,000

The mixer cap formula with a 28% corporation tax rate and an upper EUFT rate of 45% is applied to each dividend paid which in effect contributes to the final dividend payable to the UK company.

Dividend	Tax	$(D + U) \times 28\%$	Credit
	£000		£000
Faraway SA	25	$(75 + 25) \times 28\% = 28$	25
Furtheraway S	35	$(65 + 35) \times 28\% = 28$	28
Foreign Land BV	60	$(140 + 60) \times 28\% = 56$	56

The mixer cap gives a UK foreign tax credit of £56 but this is restricted to £53 (25 + 28).

13.23 Similarly, the eligible unrelieved foreign tax is calculated at each level but dividend and tax relating to lower levels are excluded (*ICTA 1988, s 806B*). Negative results are treated as zero.

Example 13.5

Dividend	Tax		Total EUFT
	£000		£000
Faraway SA	25	$(75 + 25) \times 45\% = 45$	
Furtheraway S	35	$(65 + 35) \times 45\% = 45$	
Foreign Land BV	60	$[(140 - 75 - 65) + (56 - 25 - 28)] \times 45\% = 1.35$	1.35

The total EUFT is £1,350.

Onshore pooling

13.24   For credit relief purposes all Schedule D Case V qualifying foreign dividends (QFDs) may be pooled. The pooling does not apply where the dividends are treated as trading income or to dividends from controlled foreign companies following an acceptable distribution policy (ADP) or where an eligible unrelieved foreign tax credit arises.

The credit is calculated by subtotalling the following:

● Qualifying dividends paid by a related company.

● Qualifying dividends paid by an unrelated company.

● Underlying tax on related qualifying foreign dividends.

● Other taxes on both related and unrelated qualifying foreign dividends.

A related company is a subsidiary or one in which the holding is greater than 10%.

Credit relief is given as if each total were the only single dividend and single amount of tax paid respectively. A related company exists where the UK company owns 10% of the voting power.

Example 13.6

UK company receives the following dividends from overseas companies, all of whom are in different countries:

Company	Holding	Dividend	Underlying tax	Withholding tax	Qualifying foreign dividend	Comment
P	100%	55	45	Nil	No:	EUFT will arise
Q	100%	80	20	8	Yes	Related QFD
R	90%	90	10		Yes	Related QFD
S	100%	CFC: ADP dividend 95, underly-ing tax 5	5		No	No: ADP dividend
T	1%	200	n/a	30	Yes	Unre-lated QFD
U	1%	50	n/a	10	Yes	Unre-lated QFD

These are subtotalled as follows:

	Underlying tax	Withholding tax
Qualifying dividends paid by a related company		
Q	20	8
R	10	
Qualifying dividends paid by an unrelated company		
T		30
U		10
Total	30	48

The £30 underlying tax is treated as though it arose from a single dividend and full credit relief is given for the £48 withholding tax.

Dividends received from controlled foreign companies (CFCs)

13.25   CFCs are overseas companies controlled by UK persons. A CFC follows an acceptable dividend policy (ADP) if it distributes 90% of its net chargeable profits as a dividend. Acceptable distribution policy dividends are not 'mixed' with dividends from other companies but are treated as being received direct by the UK holding company, with the result that the foreign tax set-off is restricted to the tax actually paid.

The rule does not apply to a dividend paid by a non-resident company that is exempt from the CFC rules because it passes the exempt activity or motive tests.

Groups

13.26   Group companies may surrender their EUFT to other group companies (but not consortium companies) (*ICTA 1988, s 806H*; *SI 2001/1163*). The definition of a group is as used for group relief: see **10.5**.

The companies must be members of the same group throughout the surrendering company's accounting period in which the surrenderable EUFT arises.

A company can only surrender current year surplus EUFT following its own current and previous year actual and available utilisation.

A company can claim all or part of the amount of any available EUFT from the surrendering company, which will then be treated as the claimant company's own EUFT for all purposes.

Where there are non-coterminous accounting periods the surrendering company's accounting period is followed. The dividend to which the EUFT belongs is treated as arising in the claimant company's accounting periods in which the last day of the surrendering company's accounting period falls.

The time limit for claim and surrender is the same as for all claims to utilise EUFT. The normal time limits relating to the amending of a company's tax return do not apply to making or withdrawing a claim for EUFT (*SI 2001/1163, reg 9*).

Supplementary pages CT600C of the company tax return provides a section to surrender and claim EUFT within a group.

Anti-avoidance

13.27   Anti-avoidance regulations are contained in *ICTA 1988 ss 804ZA-ZC*. These operate where there is a scheme or arrangement designed to increase the relief for foreign tax. With effect from 6 December 2006 the UK is included within the meaning of foreign tax (*FA 2007, s 35*). HMRC have the power to issue a notice to a company to adjust the corporation tax return to remove the effects of the scheme. There is no formal clearance procedure.

CONTROLLED FOREIGN COMPANIES

Meaning

13.28   A company resident outside the UK, that is controlled by UK residents and which pays less than three quarters of the tax in its country of residence, which it would have paid on its income had it been resident in the UK is known as a controlled foreign company (*ICTA 1988, s 747(1)*). This being the case, the CFC's income may be apportioned to the UK resident owners.

Developments in controlled foreign companies legislation

13.29   The controlled foreign companies legislation was brought to the European Courts with the case of *Cadbury Schweppes plc and Another v Inland Revenue Commissioners* (Case-196/04). The company concerned was an international group with a UK parent company. The group included two subsidiaries in Ireland who were established at the International Financial Services Centre in Ireland whose business was the financing of subsidiaries in the group. The two Irish subsidiaries were subject to a 10% rate of corporation tax and HMRC assessed the profits under the CFC legislation. Cadbury Schweppes plc appealed on the grounds that the legislation was contrary to *Arts 43* and *48* of the EC Treaty. *Article 43* prevents restrictions on the freedom of establishment of nationals of Member States in another Member State. *Article 48* provides that companies shall be treated in the same way as individuals.

The court ruled that *Arts 43* and *48* precluded the inclusion of the profits of a controlled foreign company, which had been subject to a lower rate of tax, in the tax base of a resident company, unless the inclusion related only to wholly artificial arrangements intended to escape the national tax normally payable. The inclusion was not to be applied where despite the existence of tax motives the controlled company was actually established in the host Member State and carried on economic activities there.

The ECJ decided that the rules were compatible with European Law provided they were not applied to companies carrying on genuine economic activities in other EU member states. However, as a result several changes were made to the UK's CFC legislation (*FA 2007, s 48, Sch 15*). In particular the 'exempt activities test' was extended (**13.38**), the public quotation condition (**13.39**) was removed and a formal claim procedure was introduced to enable a CFC company to be able to demonstrate that it is carrying on economic activities in the country concerned (**13.45–13.46**). These changes have effect for accounting periods beginning on or after 6 December 2006. If an accounting period straddles 6 December 2006, for CFC purposes there are deemed to be two accounting periods: the first to 5 December 2006 and the second to the end of the accounting period in question.

Residence

13.30   For these purposes the company is resident in the country where its place of management is situated. A company may be resident in two countries. In order to decide the country of residence it is taken to be the country which has the greatest amount of assets at the accounting year end. The assets are valued at market value (*ICTA 1988, s 749*).

A company may make an irrevocable election for a CFC to be treated as resident in a certain territory. The election must be made within 12 months of the end of the first accounting period to which it is to apply (*ICTA 1988, s 749A*).

If HMRC deems a country of residence it must give notice to all persons with an interest in the CFC. A person has an interest in a company if he can secure that the assets or income can be applied directly or indirectly for his benefit or if either alone or with others he has control of the company.

A UK company that becomes treaty non-resident after 1 April 2002 (see **13.2**) remains UK resident for controlled foreign company purposes (*ICTA 1988, s 747*). (This does not apply to companies that migrated before 1 April 2002.)

Self-assessment requirements

13.31 Under self-assessment companies are required to make their own assessment of any liability. Form CT600B is used. The information that is required is:

- a calculation of the profits chargeable to tax on a UK corporation tax basis (exclusive of capital gains);

- an apportionment of the profits among those with an interest in the company; and

- corporation tax self-assessment where 25% or more of the profits are allocated.

Associates are included when considering the 25% threshold but are not included in the calculation of corporation tax due.

For accounting periods commencing before 16 March 2005, the self-assessment the accounts are prepared in accordance with the accountancy rules of the country concerned. If no accounts are required they are drawn up along *Companies Act* principles (*ICTA 1988, s 747A*). Profits computed in a foreign currency are converted to sterling at the rate for the last day of the accounting period (*ICTA 1988, s 748(4), (5)*). For accounting periods commencing on or after 16 March 2005, the accounts are drawn up in accordance with GAAP (*FA 2005, s 24*).

Apportionment

13.32 Apportionment can be made to the following persons who have an interest in the company (*ICTA 1988, s 752*):

- members of the company who are entitled to acquire voting rights and to participate in distributions,

- loan creditors entitled to a premium on redemption,

- persons who are able to secure that income or assets are applied directly or indirectly for their benefit,

- those who alone or with others control the company (*ICTA 1988, s 749B*).

Distributions

13.33 Distributions follow the meaning of *ICTA 1988, s 209*: see **16.2–16.8**, with the exception of close company distributions (*ICTA 1988, s 749*).

Calculation of the profits chargeable

13.34 Each year the company should calculate its chargeable profit irrespective of HMRC direction or whether an apportionment is required (*ICTA 1988, Sch 24, para 1*).

The profits chargeable to corporation tax are calculated in the normal way with the following added criteria:

- The company is assumed to be UK resident from the beginning of the first accounting period for which a direction is given. The company then continues to be notionally UK resident for subsequent accounting periods until it ceases to be controlled by UK residents (*ICTA 1988, Sch 24, para 2*).

- The company is assumed to be an open company (ie not a close company) (*ICTA 1988, Sch 24, para 3*).

- The company assumed to make full use of any claims or reliefs against corporation tax (*ICTA 1988, Sch 24, para 4*).

- Group relief is denied. If the company is a member of a group and relief has already been given, it is added back to the chargeable profits (*ICTA 1988, Sch 24, para 5*).

- If a CFC transfers a trade to a UK company the *ICTA 1988, s 343* succession treatment for losses carried forward from the CFC predecessor company to the UK successor company will apply (see **15.12–15.22**). The same does not apply to a transfer of trade from another company to a CFC company (*ICTA 1988, Sch 24, para 8*).

- Losses incurred within six years before the first year in which a direction or apportionment is made on a non-UK resident CFC may be treated as incurred within the first year. A claim must be made within 20 months of the CFC's first accounting period (*ICTA 1988, Sch 24, para 9*).

- Notional capital allowances are given in calculating the tax due (*ICTA 1988, Sch 24, para 10*).

- Unremittable income is ignored in the calculation until it is remitted to the UK (*ICTA 1988, Sch 24, para 12*).

Chargeable profits for an accounting period include income which accrues during that accounting period to the trustees of a settlement in relation to which the company is a settlor or a beneficiary. Any distributions made by the company to the trustees are excluded from that income. Income from any settlement can only be included once. Where there is more than one settlor or beneficiary in relation to the settlement, the income is to be apportioned between the company and the other settlors or beneficiaries, on a just and reasonable basis (*FA 2008, s 64(2)*).

(*ICTA 1988, s 747(6)*).

Control

13.35   A person has control of a company if he or she has the power to secure that the affairs of the company are conducted in accordance with his or her wishes. This is brought about by the ownership of the greater part of the share capital or voting rights or by powers granted by any document regulating the affairs of the company.

There are additional rules for determining whether two or more persons taken together control a company. A UK resident and a non-UK resident may control a company together if the UK person has interests, rights and powers representing at least 40% of the holdings, rights and powers by which the company is controlled and the non-UK person has interests, rights and powers representing at least 40% but not more than 55% of such holdings, rights and powers. Attribution of connected persons' rights and powers applies (*ICTA 1988, s 755D*).

With effect from 12 March 2008, a person also controls a company if he or she possesses, or is entitled to acquire, such rights as would:

- if the whole of the income of the company were distributed, entitle the person to receive the greater part of the amount so distributed;

- if the whole of the company's share capital were disposed of, entitle the person to receive the greater part of the proceeds of the disposal; or

- in the event of the winding-up of the company or in any other circumstances, entitle the person to receive the greater part of the assets of the company which would then be available for distribution.

(*FA 2008, s 64(3); ICTA 1988, s 755D*)

Exclusion from profit apportionment

13.36   No apportionment of profits is required for an accounting period in which:

- the CFC pursues an acceptable distribution policy or

- the CFC is engaged in exempt activities throughout the period or

- the CFC has a public quotation or

- the chargeable profits are £50,000 or less or

- the CFC is situated in one of the exempt territories (*ICTA 1988, s 748*).

For accounting periods ending before 6 December 2006, the public quotation condition was still in force. This was abolished for subsequent accounting periods (*FA 2007, Sch 15, para 8*).

Acceptable distribution policy

13.37 An acceptable distribution policy is in place if the company pays a dividend equal to or greater than 90% of its net chargeable profits within 18 months of the end of its accounting period to UK resident persons (*ICTA 1988, Sch 25, paras 1–4A*).

For income accruing after 12 March 2008, the company must satisfy a further condition. The distributed profits must include:

- any income accruing during the relevant accounting period to the trustees of a settlement in relation to which the company is a settlor or a beneficiary; and

- any other income which accrues during that period to a partnership of which the company is a partner apportioned between the company and the other partners on a just and reasonable basis.

A partnership can be any entity established under the law of another territory of a similar character to a partnership, with the respective owners being treated as partners (*FA 2008, s 64(4); ICTA 1988, Sch 25, paras (4A)–(4D)*).

Exempt activities test

13.38 The exempt activities test is met if the company satisfies the following requirements throughout the accounting period:

- it has a 'business establishment' in its territory of residence (see **13.6**);

- its business affairs are 'effectively managed' in its territory of residence; and

- its main business at no time consists of certain defined activities; namely investment business, import and exports and trading with connected or associated persons (*ICTA 1988, Sch 25, paras 5–12A*).

The affairs of the business will not be considered to be effectively managed unless there are sufficient individuals working for the company in the territory who have the competence and authority to undertake all or substantially all the company's business. Individuals are regarded as working for a company in the other territory if they are employed by the CFC or their working activities are controlled in another way by the CFC (*FA 2007, Sch 15, para 7*).

A company may be exempt from the charge if the holding company carries out an exempt activity. A holding company's gross income accruing after 12 March 2008 includes any income to which it is entitled and any income accruing to a trustee of a trust of which it is a settlor or beneficiary (*FA 2008, s 64(5); ICTA 1988, Sch 25, para 6*).

Public quotation condition

13.39   The public quotation condition which existed for accounting periods ended before 6 December 2006 (see **13.36**) was met if the public held at least 35% of the company's voting rights and the shares were dealt with on a recognised stock exchange. The condition was not met if at any time the principal members owned more than 85% of the voting power. A principal member is a member holding 5% or more of the voting power (*ICTA 1988, Sch 25, paras 13–15*).

De minimis exclusion

13.40   The de minimis test excludes a company's chargeable profits of £50,000 or less in a 12-month accounting period from the apportionment requirements (*SI 1998/3081, reg 5*).

Motive test

13.41   Transactions that result in a minimal reduction in UK tax and for which the main purpose was not to achieve a reduction in tax by diversifying profits away from the UK will satisfy the motive test and will not be included in the apportionment calculation (*ICTA 1988, Sch 25, paras 16–19*).

Territorial exclusion from exemption

13.42　No apportionment is required if the company is situated in one of the excluded countries. See *Pt I* or *II* of the *Excluded Countries Regulations 1998, SI 1998/3081, regs 4, 5.*

Creditable tax and reliefs

13.43　A company can claim set-off of:

- trading losses,
- charges on income,
- non-trading deficits on loan relationships,
- management expenses,
- certain capital allowances, and
- group relief (*ICTA 1988, Sch 26, para 1*).

Tax suffered but unrelieved in any other way may be offset in the capital gains computation if the shares are later sold (*ICTA 1988, Sch 26, para 1(5)*).

Dividends from controlled foreign companies

13.44　Dividends paid by CFCs to UK companies are assessable as Schedule D Case V income. If the dividend is paid out of apportioned profits the apportioned tax paid is treated as underlying tax in respect of the dividend received (*ICTA 1988, Sch 26, para 4*).

Genuine economic activities

13.45　For CFC purposes a genuine economic activity is considered to be carried on if the following three conditions are satisfied throughout the accounting period concerned:

- the controlled foreign company must have a business establishment in the EEA territory;
- there are individuals who are employed by and work for the controlled foreign company in that territory; and

- UK resident company has a relevant interest in the controlled foreign company.

HMRC will remove those profits representing the net economic value attributable to the persons and work undertaken by that EEA business establishment. Net economic value does no include any value which derives directly or indirectly from the reduction or elimination of any liability of any person to any tax or duty imposed under the law of any territory.

A 'business establishment' means premises which are to be occupied with a reasonable degree of permanence and from which the company's business is wholly or mainly carried on (*ICTA 1988, Sch 25, para 7*).

Formal claim procedure

13.46   A company that carries on a genuine activity in another EEA state may make a formal claim to HMRC for some or all of its profits to be exempted from the controlled foreign companies legislation. The claim can be made for an accounting period in which an apportionment would be due.

The application must be made at any time before the normal self-assessment filing date (see **2.9**) and may be amended or withdrawn at any time before it is agreed by HMRC. If HMRC has agreed the application and the company has delivered its tax return, the company has 30 days beginning with the day on which the application is granted to amend that application. If refused, the company has the right of appeal (*ICTA 1988, s 751A* (inserted by *FA 2007, Sch 15, para 5*)).

HMRC have indicated that the information to be included in applications under *s 751A* is as follows:

1. Name of controlled foreign company (CFC).

2. United Kingdom Company's interest in the CFC's share and loan capital (by virtue of *s 749B*).

3. Tax district and reference number of United Kingdom interest holders where known.

4. Territory of residence of the CFC and details of branches including those in the United Kingdom.

5. Place, and for new companies, date of incorporation of the CFC.

6. Confirmation that no other exemption is available to the CFC under the legislation at *s 748*.

7. The other EEA state(s) where the CFC has a business establishment and individuals working for the CFC in the state(s).

8. A copy of the most recent accounts of the CFC (or where these have not yet been drawn up, management accounts or financial projections).

9. Actual or expected equity at the beginning and end of the CFC's accounting period.

10. Details of all investments held by the CFC and actual or projected income from these during the accounting period for which the application is made.

11. Details of all direct or indirect transactions between group affiliates and in particular between the United Kingdom and the CFC. This will include interest on loans (direct or indirect), royalties, payments for services, purchase or sale of goods etc.

12. Full details (including address) of the CFC's business establishment(s), the number of hours, days etc. occupied on the company's business, the size of premises, whether premises are shared, in particular with group affiliates, the amount of rent paid by the CFC etc.

13. Full details of staff working for the CFC in business establishment(s) in EEA states, including details of duties, experience, position of authority and salary.

14. Details of any outsourced business activity.

15. Full details of the business activity undertaken by the CFC. Where there is more than one business activity, details of where each activity is carried out and which individuals in each territory as detailed above at 13 are involved in carrying out each business activity.

16. Details of sources of funding for the CFC's activities, in particular sources of equity and intra-group borrowing.

17. A computation of the CFC's chargeable profits and creditable tax for the relevant accounting period.

18. The computation of how the specified amount was arrived at and the reasons why it is considered that this amount is a part of the CFC's chargeable profits that represents the net economic value created directly by the work of individuals working for the CFC in another EEA state where the CFC has a business establishment. Include details of the work directly carried out by individuals and how the net economic value to relevant interest holders or other members of the group was arrived at.

19. Provide a computation of the amount by which the creditable tax of the CFC for the relevant accounting period should be reduced and an explanation of why you consider this to be the correct amount on a just and reasonable basis.

Applications, or potential applications under the new rules, should be sent to:

CFC Team,
International CT,
HMRC03C/01,
100 Parliament Street,
London SW1A 2BQ.
For Attn: Mary Sharp, Team Leader
Telephone 020 7147 2656

Note: In considering applications HMRC may request further information and documentation in relation to the application, though it is thought that the above information should be sufficient in most cases (HMRC Draft Guidance 6 December 2006—*Changes to Controlled Foreign Companies Rules*).

Chapter 14

Transfer pricing

INTRODUCTION

14.1 The transfer pricing modus operandi dictates that transactions between connected parties should be treated for tax purposes as if the same transactions had taken place between unconnected parties. The 'arm's-length principle' should apply. Modern business these days is transacted globally with many business partners and associates. Groups are able to pick the country or regime that best suits their business in order to minimise their corporation tax liabilities. To prevent any unfairness taxation legislation requires that the 'arm's-length principle' be applied to all relevant transactions. The UK transfer pricing rules are included in *ICTA 1988, s 770A, Sch 28AA*. It is more than likely that other countries will have their own comparable domestic legislation. For countries that have a double taxation treaty it is included in the OECD Model Tax Convention on Income and on Capital (OECD Model Treaty), art 9.

For periods beginning 1 April 2004 inter-company UK trading is brought within the ambit of transfer pricing.

THE UK TRANSFER PRICING RULES

14.2 The rules apply for accounting periods ending on or after 1 July 1999. The transfer pricing rules cover:

- the purchase and sale of goods,

- the provision of management and other services,

- rents and hire charges,

- transfers of intangible property, such as trademarks, patents and know-how,

- sharing of expertise, business contacts, supply systems, etc,

- provision of finance, and other financial arrangements, and

● interest.

The legislation aims to mitigate the loss of tax arising from non-arm's-length pricing; irrespective of a tax motive.

Application of transfer pricing

14.3   Transfer pricing rules apply for accounting periods ending on or after 1 July 1999 if there is a provision by means of a transaction or a series of transactions between any two companies under common control where:

● one of the affected persons was directly or indirectly participating in the management, control or capital of the other, or

● the same person or persons was or were directly or indirectly participating in the management, control or capital of each of the affected persons.

The controlling person may be an individual.

The provision made is different to an arm's-length provision that would be made between independent parties and gives one of the two affected parties a UK taxation benefit (*ICTA 1988, Sch 28AA, para 1*). An adjustment must be made to the taxable profits of the person or persons enjoying the tax advantage.

These rules also apply to securities issued by one company to another for accounting periods beginning after 31 March 2004 (*ICTA 1988, Sch 28AA, paras 1A, 1B*).

Control

14.4   Control is defined by *ICTA 1988, s 840* as the power to secure that the company's affairs are conducted in accordance with a person's wishes. The powers so recognised are voting power, power given by the Articles of Association and the actual ability of a person to direct the affairs of the company in the absence of the visible signs of such rights.

Indirect participation examines the following issues.

A person participates indirectly in another entity if:

● he would be participating directly had certain rights and powers been attributed to him, or

● he is one of the major participants in the other entity.

395

The rights and powers that can be attributed are those:

- which the potential participant is entitled to acquire at a future date,

- exercisable by other persons on behalf of the potential participant or under his direction or for his benefit and

- of connected persons.

A person is a major participant in a company or partnership if the participant and another person together have a 40% interest therein thus creating a joint venture (*ICTA 1988, Sch 28AA, para 4(7)*).

Transfer pricing only applies to transactions between at least one of the joint venture parties and the joint venture itself and not between the two joint venturers unless they are under common control.

Corporation tax self-assessment

14.5   Transfer pricing is within the self-assessment regime. It closely follows the OECD Model Treaty, Art 9. From 1 April 2004 transactions between UK entities are included within the transfer pricing rules (previously only transactions between foreign entities and UK entities were included). Also from 1 April 2004 small and medium-sized enterprises and dormant companies are excluded from the legislation.

Companies are required to include the adjustment to profits within their own self-assessment.

The transaction

14.6   The basic pricing rule follows the OECD Model Tax Convention (*ICTA 1988, Sch 28AA, para 2*). The meaning of transactions is extremely wide and includes binding and unbinding arrangements, understandings and mutual practices. A series of transactions is considered to be a sequence in any order that is in connection with a single arrangement (*ICTA 1988, Sch 28AA, para 3*). In comparing the actual provision with the arm's-length provision it is necessary to look at all of the terms and conditions of the transactions in question and to adjust them to arm's-length terms if necessary.

A third party can be involved in a series of transactions. Interest payments to third parties under finance arrangements guaranteed by related companies.

A potential advantage arises from a non-arm's-length price, if, as a result, taxable profits are reduced, or losses together with expenses of management or group relief are increased. The transfer pricing adjustment may only increase profits or reduce losses (*ICTA 1988, Sch 28AA, para 5*).

SMALL AND MEDIUM-SIZED ENTERPRISES

Exemption

14.7   In this context SMEs are defined according to the European Commission Recommendation 2003/361/EC. They are exempt from the basic transfer pricing except in the following circumstances:

- where the company irrevocably elects to disapply the provision in relation to a chargeable period or

- where the company enters into transactions with a company resident in a territory with which the UK does not have a tax treaty containing a suitable non-discrimination clause (*ICTA 1988, Sch 28AA, para 5B*).

- Alternatively, HMRC may issue the company with a transfer pricing notice for that chargeable period (*ICTA 1988, Sch 28AA, para 5C(1)*).

If an SME carries on activities with overseas associates it must indicate on the front of the return if it qualifies for an SME exemption. This will not be possible if the company transacts business in a country with which the UK does not have a tax treaty with a suitable non discrimination clause. See **14.12**.

Definition

14.8   The SME definition follows that given by the European Commission Recommendation (2003/361/EC). The definition and the User Guide can be viewed on http://ec.europa.eu.int/comm/enterprise/enterprise_policy/sme_definition/index_en.htm

The definition not only applies to companies but to any entity engaged in an economic activity, irrespective of its legal form and includes entities subject to income tax as well as corporation tax.

An entity qualifies as either small or medium if it meets the staff headcount ceiling for that class and either one or both of the following financial limits.

	Maximum number of staff	And less than one of the following limits:	
		Annual turnover	Balance sheet total
Small enterprise	50	£10 million	£10 million
Medium enterprise	250	£50 million	£43 million

This test is made and determined solely by reference to the period for which a return is being made.

Staff includes employees, persons seconded to work for a business, owner managers and partners; proportioned accordingly to the amount of time that they work.

Turnover and balance sheet totals are net of VAT and otherwise have their ordinary meaning for accounting purposes. Balance sheet total means total gross assets without any deduction for liabilities.

Conversion to sterling should be made at the average exchange rate for the period of account whose profit is being computed or the exchange rate on the date the account was drawn up if this produces a fairer result.

As with any of the thresholds, companies close to the limit should not rely on changes to the exchange rate but should plan in advance to meet the requirements (if any) which changing designation requires.

If the entity is a member or a group or has an associated entity the limits are applied to the whole group. For this purpose the company is said to have linked or partnership enterprises (HMRC International Manual INTM 432112).

Linked enterprises

14.9   A linked enterprise is an enterprise which has the right either directly or indirectly to control the affairs of another enterprise. Control can be by shareholding, voting rights or contractual rights.

In order to ascertain which is the dominant linked company the following is taken into consideration:

- majority of the shareholders or members' voting rights in another enterprise;

- the right to appoint or remove a majority of the members of the administrative, management or supervisory body of another enterprise;

- the right to exercise a dominant influence over another enterprise pursuant to a contract entered into with that enterprise or to a provision in its memorandum or articles of association.

The data for all linked companies and partnership companies must be aggregated to ascertain whether the SME limits have been exceeded.

Partnership enterprises

14.10   A partnership enterprise is one that holds 25% or more of the capital or voting rights of another company but is not a linked company. Where linked enterprises jointly hold rights these must be aggregated to see if the 25% threshold has been passed.

Excluded holdings

14.11   Holdings and investments by the following are ignored for the purposes of aggregation: public investment corporations, venture capital companies, individuals or groups of individuals with a regular venture capital investment activity who invest equity capital in unquoted businesses ('business angels'), provided the total investment of those business angels in the same enterprise is less than €1,250,000; universities or non-profit research centres; institutional investors, including regional development funds; autonomous local authorities with an annual budget of less than €10m and fewer than 5,000 inhabitants.

The rights of a person in office as a liquidator or administrator are not to be taken into account when considering partnership or linked enterprises (HMRC International Manual INTM 432112). Dormant companies are excluded (*ICTA 1988, Sch 28AA, para 5A*) but there is the possibility that the party to the transaction may remain within transfer pricing (HMRC International Manual INTM 432114).

Appropriate non-discrimination clause

14.12   With effect from 1 April 2004, small and medium-sized companies may be exempted from the transfer pricing rules. The exemption does not apply where a business has transactions with or provisions that include a related business in a territory with which the UK does not have a double tax treaty with an appropriate non-discrimination article. Such transactions remain subject to the transfer pricing rules.

An appropriate non-discrimination article is one that ensures that the nationals of a contracting state may not be less favourably treated in the other contracting state than nationals of that latter state in the same circumstances (in particular with respect to residence).

HMRC regards the following double taxation treaties as containing an appropriate non-discrimination article as at 1 April 2004 (except where stated otherwise).

Argentina	Luxembourg
Australia	Macedonia
Austria	Malaysia
Azerbaijan	Malta
Bangladesh	Mauritius
Barbados	Mexico
Belarus	Mongolia
Belgium	Morocco
Bolivia	Myanmar
Bosnia-Herzegovina	Namibia
Botswana	Netherlands
Bulgaria	New Zealand
Canada	Nigeria
Chile (wef 21/12/2004)	Norway
China	Oman
Croatia	Pakistan
Cyprus	Papua New Guinea
Czech Republic	Philippines
Denmark	Poland
Egypt	Portugal
Estonia	Reunion
Falkland Islands	Romania
Fiji	Russian Federation
Finland	Serbia and Montenegro
France	Singapore
Gambia	Slovak Republic
Georgia	Slovenia
Germany	South Africa
Ghana	Spain

Greece	Sri Lanka
Guyana	Sudan
Hungary	Swaziland
Iceland	Sweden
India	Switzerland
Indonesia	Taiwan
Ireland	Tajikistan
Israel	Thailand
Italy	Trinidad & Tobago
Ivory Coast	Tunisia
Jamaica	Turkey
Japan	Turkmenistan
Jordan	Uganda
Kazakhstan	Ukraine
Kenya	USA
Korea	Uzbekistan
Kuwait	Venezuela
Latvia	Vietnam
Lesotho	Zambia
Lithuania	Zimbabwe

The Treasury has the power to make regulations adding to the list of territories that qualify even if the double taxation treaty in question does not contain an appropriate non-discrimination article, or to exclude territories even if the treaty in question does contain such an article (HMRC International Manual INTM 432112).

Election to remain subject to transfer pricing rules

14.13   There may be occasions where a business wishes to apply transfer pricing rules even though it would qualify for exemption. A business can elect that the exemption will not apply. An election can be made for a specified chargeable period and will cover all transactions or provisions made in that period. It will be irrevocable.

A pre-existing dormant company

14.14   A dormant company that was dormant for an accounting period ending on 31 March 2004, or for the whole of the three months prior to 1 April 2004, is exempt from transfer pricing for accounting periods commencing on or after

1 April 2004 as long as it remains dormant. If it engages in any business activity it will lose its exemption (*ICTA 1988, Sch 28AA, para 5A*).

Compensating relief

14.15   Where transactions take place between two UK taxpayers and a transfer pricing adjustment is made to the corporation tax return of one taxpayer, the other party may claim compensating relief in its corporation tax return in order to prevent profits being taxed twice (*ICTA 1988, Sch 28AA, para 6*). The claimant company is required to indicate on the front of CT600 if a compensating adjustment has been claimed.

This may bring about other adjustments if the effects are worked through, for example, to the double tax credit if double taxation is involved (*ICTA 1988, Sch 28AA, para 7*).

Balancing payments

14.16   If the claimant company makes a payment to the tax advantage company up to the amount of the compensating relief this is without any tax effect (*ICTA 1988, Sch 28AA, para 7A*).

Transfer pricing does not apply to FOREX or to financial instrument legislation.

Other provisions deal with transactions not at arm's length in these cases (*ICTA 1988, Sch 28AA, para 8*) but transfer pricing rules apply to sales of oil and gas produced by a company in which the buyer and linked companies have an interest of 20% or more (*ICTA 1988, Sch 28AA, para 9*).

Appeal hearings

14.17   Appeal hearings are heard by the Special Commissioners (*ICTA 1988, Sch 28AA, para 12*).

Capital allowances and chargeable gains

14.18   The transfer pricing rules do not apply to capital allowances (including balancing charges), chargeable gains or allowable capital losses (*ICTA 1988, Sch 28AA, para 13*).

Matching loans and derivatives

14.19   A corporate group structure may assist with the external borrowing facilities for the individual group members. Further advantage may be taken of the group structure by one group member taking out a foreign currency loan to match a non-monetary asset acquired by another group member. The loan may then be further lent to the asset acquiring company interest-free. In addition, the company may enter into a forward exchange contract to cover the forward exchange risk. From 1 April 2004 no transfer pricing adjustment is required for foreign exchange gains and losses on 'matching' loans (*ICTA 1988, Sch 28AA, para 8*). However, from 22 March 2006 artificial losses created by contrived arrangements were disallowed (*Loan Relationships and Derivative Contracts (Disregard and Bringing into Account of Profits and Losses) Regulations 2006, SI 2006/843, reg 5* and *Loan Relationships and Derivative Contracts (Disregard and Bringing into Account of Profits and Losses) (Amendment) Regulations 2006, SI 2006/936, reg 5*).

Interest-free loans

14.20   Under the transfer pricing regulations an interest-free loan between related parties will attract a tax charge on the lender (*ICTA 1988, Sch 28AA, para 1*) and a compensating adjustment for the ultimate borrower (*ICTA 1988, Sch 28AA, para 6*). The borrowing capacity of a UK company is assessed in isolation without regard to the borrowing capacity of the whole group. This also applies where a guarantee is made by a fellow group company. Any adjustment will be met by a compensating adjustment (HMRC International Manual INTM 561000).The foreign exchange element of these adjustments is ignored for transfer pricing purposes (*ICTA 1988, Sch 28AA, para 8*).

Where asset backed matching loans are involved, the company with the debtor loan relationship would normally follow SSAP 20 and take the foreign exchange gains and losses on both the asset and the matching loan to reserves. The company with the creditor loan relationship will record foreign exchange gains and losses on the loan to the group company and the loan from a third party (external to the group) in its loans in its profit and loss account.

Foreign exchange gains and losses of the debtor loan relationship company are excluded from taxable income for corporation tax purposes, where they can be matched against gains and losses from an asset (*FA 1996, s 84A(3)(b)*). *Loan Relationships and Derivative Contracts (Disregard and Bringing into Account of Profits and Losses) Regulations 2004, SI 2004/3256, reg 3*, from 1 January 2005 to 22 March 2006, will apply to disregard such exchange differences. Where an arm's length adjustment is required, only the arm's-length element will become chargeable. If the company would not have been able to borrow at all in an arm's-length situation no amount of the foreign exchange gain or loss will be taxable.

Foreign exchange gains and losses of the creditor loan relationship are brought to account immediately through the profit and loss account (*FA 1996, s 84A(1)*).

Loans on which interest is charged

14.21   If interest is charged on an intra-group loan the tax treatment for the company with the debtor loan relationship is exactly the same. This is because the effect of the matching rules is to disregard the foreign exchange gain or loss arising.

The company with a non-arm's-length creditor loan relationship that receives a less than arm's-length amount of interest is in the same position as if no interest had been charged on the loan.

If the amount of interest receivable on the loan is more than an arm's-length amount the non-arm's-length amount of the foreign exchange gain or loss is disregarded. If a group company acts as guarantor it can make a compensating adjustment claim (*ICTA 1988, Sch 28AA, para 6D*).

Otherwise the result is that the creditor does not have a symmetrical position as far as its foreign exchange gains and losses on its lending and borrowing are concerned.

Currency contracts

14.22   In general the foreign exchange gains and losses on 'matching' currency contracts are also disregarded for transfer pricing purposes (*ICTA 1988, Sch 28AA, para 8*).

However, transfer pricing rules will apply to premium receipts and to non-arm's-length interest payments. Arrangements to assign, terminate or vary a currency contract may also fall within the transfer pricing conditions. *FA 2002, Sch 26, para 27* applies to tax the amount of the gain that would have been taxed had an arm's-length rate applied.

SELF-ASSESSMENT

14.23   There are no supplementary pages to a tax return, which relate to transfer pricing; businesses make computational adjustments in their returns in cases where transactions as recorded in their accounts are not at arm's length. A business (as in **14.13**) wishing to make an election to remain subject to transfer pricing rules should do so as part of its computation of taxable income in its return.

Companies are required to make tax returns in accordance with the arm's-length principle. If a company submits a fraudulent or negligent return (see Chapter 2) a tax-related penalty may be charged (*ICTA 1988, Sch 18, para 20*). The maximum penalty is the tax lost. A Revenue officer authorised by HMRC has the power to determine a penalty at any amount he considers appropriate (*TMA 1970, s 100(1)*).

Such a penalty can ensue if a company fails to comply with the transfer pricing requirements. This is the case if the company had been negligent.

Negligence must be judged on its own facts and merits, with the guiding principle being that a company will not have been negligent if it has done what 'a reasonable person would do'. Where a company can show that it has made an honest and reasonable attempt to comply with the legislation, there will be no penalty even if there is an adjustment. Indeed, the onus will be on HMRC in this area, as it is more generally, to show that there has been fraudulent or negligent conduct by the taxpayer before any penalty can be charged.

There is, therefore, an obligation on taxpayers to do what a reasonable person would to ensure that their returns are made in accordance with the arm's-length principle. This would involve, but not be limited to:

● using their commercial knowledge and judgment to make arrangements and set prices, which conform to the arm's-length standard (or to make computational adjustments in their returns where they do not);

● being able to show (for example, by means of good quality documenta-tion) that they made an honest and reasonable attempt to comply with the arm's-length standard and with the legislation; and

● seeking professional help where they know they need it.

Taxpayers should document what they do to the extent necessary to enable them to sustain the arm's-length nature of their arrangements and prices in any discussions with HMRC. The documentation will include the following:

● the relevant commercial or financial relations falling within the scope of the new legislation;

● the nature and terms (including prices) of relevant transactions (including transactions which form a series, and any relevant offsetting transac-tions). Transactions which are clearly in one family (eg regular purchases made by a distributor throughout a return period of the same or similar products for resale) may be aggregated, provided any significant changes during the period in the nature or terms of the transactions are recorded;

- the method or methods by which the nature and terms of relevant transactions were arrived at, including any study of comparables and any functional analysis undertaken;

- how that method has resulted in arm's-length terms etc or, where it has not, what computational adjustment is required and how it has been calculated. This will usually include an analysis of market data or other information on third party comparables;

- the terms of relevant commercial arrangements with both third party and affiliated customers. These will include commercial agreements (eg service or distribution contracts, loan agreements), and any budgets, forecasts or other papers containing information relied on in arriving at arm's-length terms etc or in calculating any adjustment made in order to satisfy the requirements of the new transfer pricing legislation.

In order to be adequate the documentation must show that the company had good grounds for believing their arrangements and prices were in accordance with the arm's-length principle.

HMRC have provided the following examples for illustration purposes.

Example 14.1

A company, whose business is to provide services to other group members, charges out its services at cost plus 5%. 5% accords with a policy in place throughout the group, and is documented in correspondence involving members of the main Board, the Finance Directorate, and the Tax Department; and in a group agreement. It is established in discussion with HMRC that the arm's-length range for the services in question is 10%–15%. The company cannot show from its records that it even considered whether its own 5% rate complied with the arm's-length principle. HMRC would view any tax lost as a result of the undercharge as having been lost through negligence, and would wish to consider a penalty.

Example 14.2

As Example 14.1, except that in the correspondence it is asserted several times that the group's policy is to comply with the arm's-length standard, and that 5% is an arm's-length price. However, the company is unable to bring forward any convincing evidence in support of its assertions, while HMRC is able to show that an arm's-length price would be in the 10%–15% range. HMRC would wish to consider a penalty.

Example 14.3

As Example 14.1, except that the company charges out at cost plus 8%, and can show that at the time the rate was set it had run a check of available industry data, and had found what it considered to be a comparable uncontrolled price supporting the 8% rate. In discussion with HMRC, the company agrees that the comparable it used was flawed, and that the weight of evidence points towards a price in the 10%–15% range. HMRC accept that the company had made an honest and reasonable attempt to comply with the arm's-length principle. There is an adjustment but no penalty.

Example 14.4

A company, whose business is to provide services to other group members, charges at cost plus 5%. As in Example 14.1, 5% accords with a policy in place throughout the group, and is documented in correspondence and a group agreement. The company includes an adjustment in its computation, bringing the effective rate of charge-out up to 8%. It did so after searching available industry data for possible comparable uncontrolled prices, this search being made at the time the tax computation was being prepared. As with Example 14.3, the company sees this information as supporting its opinion that 8% accorded with the arm's-length principle, but it later agrees that the price should have fallen in the 10%–15% range. Once again, HMRC accept that the company had made an honest and reasonable attempt to comply with the arm's-length principle, and there is an adjustment but no penalty.

14.24   The factors which the Board takes into account when considering abatement are described in leaflet IR 160 (see **2.20**). These will apply to penalties arising from transfer pricing adjustments.

When considering the abatement in relation to the size and gravity of the failure HMRC will take into account the absolute size of the adjustment; the size of the adjustment relative to the turnover and profitability of the business against which the adjustment is being made; and where this is possible, the size of the adjustment in relation to the volume and value of the related party transactions giving rise to the adjustment (Tax Bulletins, Issues 37 October 1998 and 38 December 1998).

Record keeping

14.25   The record keeping in **14.23** above was suggested in 1998. Under self-assessment, the requirement is for companies to keep records to support its transfer pricing policy, its arm's-length justification policy and the adjustments made to the corporation tax return. The records kept will vary to each country and to each particular company's circumstances. General guidance is given in Chapter V of the OECD Transfer Pricing Guidelines.

The self-assessment penalties will ensue upon the company if the company were unable to supply supporting records. As a transitional measure, businesses were relieved from penalty exposure for failure to provide 'arm's-length' evidence for the two years ended 31 March 2006.

As regards evidence to support an arm's-length policy HMRC have now suggested the following:

- Associated businesses should be identified and the form of association.

- Description of business activity in which transactions took place.

- Details of contractual relationship and understanding between the parties involved.

- Description and justification for method used to establish the arm's length result.

- Evidence need not be provided where companies do not fall within the UK transfer pricing rules.

- Useful to provide supporting information regarding the company's general strategy.

- English translations of documentation should also be given.

The European Commission has adopted a proposal for a Code of Conduct to standardise the documentation that multinationals must provide to tax authorities on their pricing of cross-border intra-group transactions. The documentation would consist of two main parts namely a 'blueprint' master file of the transfer pricing system together with business information and standardised documents for intra-group transactions.

It is expected that Member States would implement the Code by legislating for it in national law or through administrative guidelines. Until then companies must comply with the national documentation requirement IP/05/1403 and MEMO/05/414.

Enquiries

14.26 An enquiry would follow normal HMRC enquiry procedures. Details are to be found in HMRC International Manual 434020 onwards. In particular, HMRC would seek evidence to support the arm's-length policy. Additional guidance as to the conduct of the enquiry is given in HMRC Guidance Notes

10 July 2008 – Guidance for the conduct of transfer pricing enquiries. Here, HMRC explains that cases are normally to be settled within 18 months and possibly 36 months for more complex cases. Although aimed at transfer pricing, similar procedures will be adopted in determining the attribution of a profit to a permanent establishment. All enquiries will commence with a risk assessment, which is based on the quantum risk, the behaviour risk and the transaction risk of the matters that are being enquired into. Following the risk assessment HMRC may decide to investigate further and develop a business case, whereupon a thorough enquiry into the nature of the transactions, their treatment and the supporting information will take place. HMRC will specify the transactions that are subject to the enquiry.

Example 14.5

A UK company is engaged to provide research and development (R&D) activities on behalf of its overseas affiliate. The group employs a cost-plus pricing method under which the overseas affiliate pays the UK company a sum consisting of the UK company's costs plus a mark-up of 10%. This is characterised in the UK company's transfer pricing documentation as a 'contract research arrangement'.

HMRC's criteria and the areas for enquiry are as follows:

	Criterion	*Area of enquiry*
1.	The transactions subject to the enquiry.	The provision of research and development facilities by the UK company to the overseas affiliate
2.	The aspect(s) of the transaction and its pricing to be tested	HMRC will test whether cost-plus is an appropriate method to set the pricing between the UK company and its overseas affiliate.
3.	The criteria by which the transaction is to be tested	HMRC will consider whether the actual functions carried out by the UK company are consistent with their respective characterisations as low-risk research provider and research contractor.
4.	What HMRC needs to understand in order to achieve this.	• How decisions are made concerning the identification and prioritisation of research projects, who makes these decisions and where the people making them are located.

- The process for reviewing and assessing R&D projects. Who is involved in this and where are they located.
- The ownership of any value, including the intellectual property, arising from the R&D.
- Whether the UK company uses the intellectual property it created in its wider range.

Thin capitalisation

14.27 Where a UK group member company borrows more from an internal or external lender than it would do if it were not part of a group, it is said to be thinly capitalised. Interest payments are deductible from taxable profits but dividend payments are not so deductible. Companies who structure their investments in subsidiaries by means of inordinate large loans may also fall within the thin capitalisation rules.

The result is that the admissible interest deduction from assessable profits is restricted to an arm's-length amount. All parts of the borrowing arrangement will be examined to ascertain if thin capitalisation is involved including guarantees and the like.

Thin capitalisation falls within the transfer pricing regime (*ICTA 1988, Sch 28AA*). Until 1 April 2004 it was dealt with by treating the amount as a dividend (*ICTA 1988, s 209(2)(da)*). *ICTA 1988, s 209(2)(da)* only applied where there was a 75% overseas relationship (together with effective 51% subsidiaries) between borrower and lender, whereas transfer pricing applies to all UK and overseas relationships with no 75% demarcation.

Payments of interest abroad

14.28 Subject to any existing double taxation agreement, payments of annual interest to an overseas lender are made net of withholding tax. The rate of withholding tax is linked to the basic rate of income tax (HMRC International Manual INTM 542010) (*ICTA 1988, s 349(2)*). Assessments can be raised to recover any outstanding withholding tax together with any accrued interest (*ICTA 1988, Sch 16*; *TMA 1970, s 87*).

Advance pricing agreement (APA)

14.29   A company with more complex affairs can enter into an APA with HMRC (*FA 1999, s 85*). APAs are written agreements between a taxpayer and HMRC, which determine a method for resolving intricate transfer pricing issues in advance of a return being made. If the terms of the arrangement are complied with, the company can be assured that HMRC will accept those transfer issues covered by the agreement.

The matters that can be covered include the determination of:

- the arm's-length provision for the purposes of *ICTA 1988, Sch 28AA, s 770A*;

- the profits attributable to a branch or agency through which a trade is carried on in the UK; and

- the amount of any income arising outside the UK and attributable to the overseas branch of a UK company.

HMRC recommend bilateral agreements rather than unilateral agreements. The APA will be operative for a specified number of years from the date of entry into force as set out in the agreement. The term is normally for a minimum of three, and a maximum of five, years. The formal submission of an APA request should normally be made no later than six months before the start of the first chargeable period to be covered by the APA. The APA process will typically comprise four stages: expression of interest, formal submission of application for clarification, evaluation, and agreement. In essence, when agreed if prices are set in accordance with the APA they will satisfy the transfer pricing regulations. SP 3/99 gives further details.

Advance thin capitalisation agreements (ATCA)

14.30   The UK thin capitalisation rules are aimed at insuring that investors do not finance their UK sub-groups with large sums of debt that give rise to excessive interest deductions, but maintain an arm's-length standard by reference to the amount and the terms of their debt (see **14.27**).

Transactions with countries with a double taxation treaty may be agreed in advance with HMRC in accordance with the treaty (HMRC International Manual INTM 574000). For transactions with countries with which there is no double tax treaty, the company may enter into an advance thin capitalisation agreement (ATCA) under the APA legislation (*FA 1999, s 85*). (HMRC Statement of Practice 04/07).

Chapter 15

Reconstructions and amalgamations

BUYING AND SELLING A COMPANY

Buying a company

15.1   Purchase of another company's share capital requires careful consideration. Depending upon the percentage acquired, the new acquisition will be a subsidiary or an investment for the acquiree. All taxation aspects of the transaction must be considered, not only corporation tax but also VAT and stamp duty land tax (for VAT: see *VAT 2008/09* from Tottel).

Asset purchase

15.2   Alternatively the company may wish to consider an asset purchase. In this case the acquired company is absorbed into the existing company rather than being maintained as a separate corporate unit. Apart from the normal funding and synergy issues the acquiring company will need to consider a variety of issues affecting the taxation impact of the transaction.

The purchased tangible and intangible assets will be included within the company's fixed assets as shown on the balance sheet. In particular, the excess of the purchase price of the assets acquired over the price paid: namely the goodwill will also be shown on the balance sheet. This in turn will form an intangible asset for which an annual tax-deductible write down is available (see **7.10**).

The company will also be able to utilise the newly acquired asset in a roll-over relief claim for fixed assets (see **20.6**) and intangible assets (see **7.21**). The assets are also established at a high base cost for capital gains tax purposes, because the gain to date is assessed on the predecessor company.

The acquisition of stock will be a deduction from trading profits. Importantly the purchaser avoids taking over any of the vendor's liabilities.

For capital allowances purposes the assets in question are disposed of by the vendor; balancing charges and allowances arising and acquired by the successor. If the companies are connected within the definition given by *ICTA 1988, s 839* then *ICTA 1988, s 343* may apply as described later in this chapter. If *s 343* does not apply both companies may elect for the assets to be transferred at tax written-down value. If this occurs during an accounting period the allowances are proportioned pro-rata (*CAA 2001, ss 266, 569*).

Whether or not connected, the purchaser and the vendor may wish to make use of the provisions of *CAA 2001, s 198*, which allows the parties to jointly elect that sale proceeds relating to a building inclusive of fixtures be allocated agreed by the parties. The value must not be more than cost (*CAA 2001, s 198*).

Acquisition finance costs

15.3   Regardless of a share or asset purchase, the company will invariably require the use of borrowed funds to finance the acquisition. Any interest or finance costs charged in acquiring a company are non-trading debits within the loan relationship regime. They are not costs in connection with the trade (see **11.23** for relief for costs of obtaining loan finance).

Selling a company

15.4   The 'reversed' considerations to acquiring a company must be considered when selling a company. If the assets are to be sold a chargeable gain may arise within the company. The company may be cash-rich, which then presents a problem for cash extraction. If the company is owned by individual investors they will need to consider their own capital gains position if the company is to be wound up or sold (see *Capital Gains Tax 2008/09*from Tottel). In practical terms the sale may be negotiated to make use of the *s 343* relief as described in **15.12** onwards.

If shares are to be sold and another company owns the company it may be able to make use of the substantial shareholdings exemption, see **12.26–12.30**. If a company cannot make use of the substantial shareholdings exemption in order to reduce the chargeable gain on sale the investor company may wish to consider the payment of a pre-sale dividend by the investee company. This in effect reduces the sale price but results in tax-free funds being received by the investor company; hence the company's sale price must be renegotiated accordingly. Under the *Companies Act* a pre-sale dividend is permitted financial assistance for the company's purchase of its own shares (*CA 2006, s 681 (2)(a)*; formerly *CA 2005, s 153 (3)(a)*). In this respect it is necessary to consider the capital gains anti-avoidance provisions (see **20.24–20.31** re value shifting).

COMPANY RECONSTRUCTIONS AND AMALGAMATIONS

Introduction

15.5   The development of a limited company's trading activity may mean that it has to change its structure. Shares in a corporate structure can be bought or sold or created or cancelled. Shares may be owned by individuals or large corporations alike. A change in a company's capital structure may be a necessity to enable it to carry on its future activities. Such changes will have taxation consequences. This may involve the formation of a new company and the transfer of the predecessor's assets to the new company. The result being that the ownership of the business remains in the same hands, but is earned through a different corporate structure. The shareholders receive a share for share exchange.

Companies Act

15.6   The *Companies Act* permits reconstructions and amalgamations subject to certain conditions. The requirements are detailed in *Companies Act 2006, ss 895–941*; formerly *Companies Act 1985, ss 425–427A* and in *Insolvency Act 1986, s 110*.

The court will sanction an arrangement with the members (or creditors) of the company provided this is voted on with 75% agreeing to the scheme at the company meeting (*CA 2006, ss 899, 907*; *CA 1985, s 425*). *Companies Act 2006, s 922*,gives the courts the power to order a scheme. *Insolvency Act 1986, s 110* permits a liquidator to transfer the company's business or property to another company. The liquidator will receive shares for the distribution. Any dissenting member may require the liquidator to purchase his shares.

CAPITAL GAINS TAX

Reorganisation of share capital

15.7   In effect the action that the company takes is to transfer the company's assets to another company in exchange for shares. A reorganisation of share capital whereby the shareholder receives new shares in exactly the same proportion as the old shares is tax neutral. No charge to CGT arises. The new shares are deemed to have been acquired at exactly the same time as the old shares (*TCGA 1992, ss 126–131*).

Any cash received is treated either as a capital distribution or as a part disposal (*TCGA 1992, ss 122, 128*). Consideration given for the new holding is treated as being given for the original holding but is indexed from the time that it is given rather than from the time that the original shareholding was acquired.

Company reconstructions

15.8   The no gain/no loss treatment contained in *TCGA 1992, ss 127–131*, will also apply to a company reconstruction in the following situation. The situation is such that a company issues shares or debentures to a person in exchange for shares or debentures that person owns in another company and:

● as a result of the exchange, the successor company holds or will hold more than 25% of the ordinary share capital of the original company, or

● the successor company issues shares or debentures as a result of a general offer made conditional upon the successor company acquiring control over the original company to the members of the successor company or any class of them, or

● the successor company holds or will hold as a result of the exchange the greater part of the voting power of the original company (*TCGA 1992, s 135*).

Further rules apply if the shares in the successor company are cancelled. The shareholders will benefit from the no gain/no loss treatment provided the following conditions are satisfied. Conditions one and two must be met together with either condition three or condition four.

Condition 1. The successor must only issue ordinary shares to the original company's ordinary shareholders (*TCGA 1992, Sch 5AA, para 2*) and not to any other party.

Condition 2. The original ordinary shareholders in the same class all obtain the same proportional entitlement to ordinary shares in the new company. There is no requirement that all the shareholders of the old company become shareholders in the new company but the shares must be issued to the same persons (*TCGA 1992, Sch 5AA, para 3*).

Condition 3. There must be continuity of the business. The whole of the business must be carried on by one successor company or by two or more successor companies of which the original company may be one (*TGCA 1992, Sch 5AA, para 4*).

Condition 4. The scheme is carried out in pursuance of a compromise arrangement under *CA 1985, s 425* or foreign equivalent and no part of the business is transferred to any other person (*TCGA 1992, Sch 5AA, para 5*).

Bona fide commercial arrangements

15.9   The conditions only apply if the scheme is made for bona fide commercial arrangements where the main purpose is not the avoidance of capital gains tax. This restriction does not apply to holders of less than 5% of the shares. If the conditions are not met or there is found to be an anti-avoidance purpose, HMRC can collect the tax from any of the shareholders concerned (*TCGA 1992, s 137*). A tax avoidance purpose was found in *Snell v HMRC Comrs* SpC 532, [2006] STC (SCD) 296. On advice received from an adviser, a taxpayer became non-resident to avoid a capital gains tax liability. The Special Commissioners decided that as the taxpayer had full knowledge and understanding of the proposed course of action it arose from a tax avoidance purpose.

The company may apply for a clearance to HMRC that the proposed reconstruction or reorganisation is for bona fide commercial purposes. The full facts of the transaction should be given to HMRC who have 30 days to reply. If HMRC does not issue a clearance notice to the company, the company may refer its case to the Special Commissioners (*TCGA 1992, s 138*). See **18.5** for further details regarding clearance procedures.

Reconstruction involving transfer of business

15.10   Where the whole or part of a business is transferred to another company for no consideration apart from taking over the liabilities, the asset transfer apart from the trading stock is deemed to take place for such consideration that provides neither gain nor loss (*TCGA 1992, s 139*). More often than not the consideration in such circumstances is a share exchange for the shareholders concerned.

Again for this section to apply the transfer must be made for bona fide commercial purposes. Similar provisions relate to intangible assets (*FA 2002, Sch 29, para 84*). A clearance procedure is also available (*FA 2002, Sch 29, para 88*). Where an existing intangible asset (see **7.2**) is transferred under a reconstruction to which *TCGA 1992 s 139* or *s 140A* applies the asset remains as an existing asset in the hands of the transferee (*FA 2002, Sch 29, para 127*).

This situation whereby some or all of a company's assets or liabilities are transferred from one company to a successor company is commonly known as 'a hive down'. The successor company is often newly formed. Such a transaction is used to facilitate a company sale; so that only the chosen activities and assets and liabilities are taken over. The transaction may also facilitate a division in a group's activities.

Company reconstruction example

Example 15.1

A scheme of reconstruction can be used to break up an existing business into separate undertakings. This can involve the liquidation of the original company. See Chapter 19 for liquidations.

Facts

The issued share capital of Union Ltd is of one class of share and is held as follows:

Shareholders	£1 Ordinary Shares
	£
Jack	50,000
Jill	50,000
	£100,000

The company has two businesses; it rents holiday homes in the UK and arranges tours of Great Britain, mainly for overseas visitors.

Original structure

It is proposed to separate the two businesses. There are four possible solutions that will satisfy the conditions of *TCGA 1992 Sch 5AA* (see **15.8**). Solutions 1 and 2 both involve the liquidation of Union Ltd.

Reconstruction Solution 1

Union Ltd enters into a scheme under *Insolvency Act 1986, s 110*. The original shares in Union Ltd are organised into A shares and B shares. The holdings are now as follows:

Shareholders	Total		£1 A Ordinary Shares	£1 B Ordinary Shares
	£	£	£	£
Jack		50,000	25,000	25,000
Jill	50,000	25,000	25,000	
	100,000	50,000	50,000	

The assets and liabilities of the holiday home rental business are allocated to the A shares. The assets and liabilities of the tours of Great Britain business are allocated to the B shares.

Union Ltd is placed in liquidation. The liquidator transfers the holiday home rental business to a new company, Country Homes Ltd (a successor company). Country Homes Ltd issues ordinary shares to the holders of the A shares in proportion to their respective holdings. The tours of Great Britain business is transferred to a new company Roving Ltd (a successor company) which issues ordinary shares to the holders of the B shares in proportion to their respective holdings.

Structure post Reconstruction 1

Example 15.2

Reconstruction Solution 2

The same facts apply as in *Reconstruction Solution 1* except that the new A shares are issued to Jack and the new B shares are issued to Jill. The new shareholdings are as follows:

Shareholders	*Total*	*£1 A Ordinary Shares*	*£1 B Ordinary Shares*
	£	£	£
Jack	50,000	50,000	—
Jill	50,000	—	50,000
	100,000	50,000	50,000

The assets and liabilities of the holiday home rental business are allocated to the A shares. The assets and liabilities of the tours of Great Britain business are allocated to the B shares.

Union Ltd is placed in liquidation. The liquidator transfers the holiday home rental business to a new company, Country Homes Ltd (a successor company). Country Homes Ltd issues ordinary shares to the holders of the A shares in proportion to their respective holdings. The tours of Great Britain business is transferred to a new company Roving Ltd (a successor company) which issues ordinary shares to the holders of the B shares in proportion to their respective holdings.

Structure post Reconstruction 2

Example 15.3

Reconstruction Solution 3

The same facts apply as in Reconstruction Solution 2 except that it is not necessary to liquidate Union Ltd.

Instead, Union Ltd declares a dividend on the B shares, which it pays by transferring the assets and liabilities of the touring business to Roving Ltd. Roving Ltd then issues Jill with ordinary shares. The B shares in Union Ltd are now worthless. Jack now owns all the shares in Union Ltd which holds the holiday home business.

Structure post Reconstruction 3

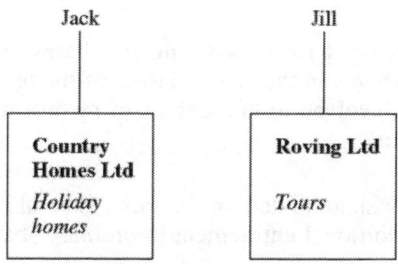

Example 15.4

Reconstruction Solution 4

Solution 4 takes place under the demerger rules. See **16.14** Example 16.3 (ii). There is no requirement to liquidate Union Ltd. The original shareholdings in Union Ltd are:

Shareholders	*£1 Ordinary Shares*
	£
Jack	50,000
Jill	50,000
	100,000

A new company Roving Ltd is formed with Jack and Jill each owning 50% of the issued ordinary share capital. The tours of Great Britain business is transferred to Roving Ltd. The holiday home letting business continues to be operated by Union Ltd

Structure post Reconstruction 4

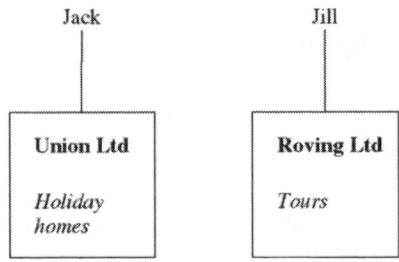

In all four solutions, the conditions of *TCGA 1992, Sch 5AA* (see **15.8**) are met:

Reconstruction—Conditions satisfied

Condition 1	*(TCGA 1992,*
The successor companies have issued ordinary shares to the	*Sch 5AA,*
holders of ordinary shares in the share classes of the original	*para 2)*
company, which are involved in the scheme of reconstruction	
and to no other person.	

Condition 2	*(TCGA 1992,*
The original ordinary shareholders in the same class all	*Sch 5AA,*
obtain the same proportional entitlement to ordinary shares in	*para 3)*
the new company.	

Condition 3 (*TCGA 1992,*
If the activities of the successor companies are taken together *Sch 5AA,*
they carry on the whole of the business of the original *para 4*)
company.

The result is that the disposal of Jack and Jill's holdings in Union Ltd in solutions 1 & 2 and the disposal of Jill's holding in solution 3 and the acquisition of the respective new holdings results in a no gain/no loss transaction (*TCGA 1992, s 136*). In solution 4 there is no disposal of the original holding.

The liquidator's transfer of the two businesses to Holiday Homes Ltd and Roving Ltd in solutions 1 and 2 is a no gain/no loss disposal (*TCGA 1992, s 139*).

In practice, these steps would not be taken in isolation of other factors; in particular the stamp duty costs and company procedural matters must be considered. In addition, if the trades have accumulated loss the utilisation of these losses will be hampered if there is cessation of the relevant trades concerned.

Solutions 1 and 2 will involve a cessation of Union Ltd's trade. Solution 1 offers the protection of *ICTA 1988, s 343* (see **15.11** and **15.12**) but not solution 1, because the same ownership structure pre and post reconstruction is not retained.

Solutions 3 and 4 involve the cessation of the touring trade. *Section 343* protection will be given to Roving Ltd in solution 4 but not in solution 3 because the same ownership structure pre and post reconstruction is not retained. Union Ltd's holiday home trade continues.

Groups

15.11 If the reconstruction involves a group relationship (see **20.14** for a definition of a group), company assets can be transferred between group members without a charge to capital gains arising (*TCGA 1992, s 171*). However, if the company subsequently leaves the group a capital gains tax charge will crystallise. The capital gain is based on the market value of the asset at the date of transfer. The gain is deemed to arise at the end of the accounting period in which the company leaves the group (*TCGA 1992, s 179*).

This provision does not apply to inter-group asset transfers between associated companies who cease to be group members at the same time (*TCGA 1992, s 179(2)*). The companies must have been associated at the time that the asset transfer was made (*Johnston Publishing (North) Ltd v Revenue and Customs*

Comrs [2007] All ER (D) 240 (Mar). The companies must remain associated after they leave the group. For this purpose 'associated companies' are defined as companies that would themselves form a group (*TCGA 1992, s 179(10)*).

TRADING LOSSES

Company reconstruction without a change of ownership

15.12   The utilisation of trading losses is restricted where a trade ceases and where there is a change of ownership of the company (*ICTA 1988, ss 768, 768A*) as discussed in **9.17–9.19**. Where there is a company reconstruction without a change of ownership and a continuing trade, the losses incurred by the previous company will be available to set against profits earned by the new company provided the same ownership and charging conditions apply pre and post transfer (*ICTA 1988, s 343*). Loss relief is given automatically without claim. It is necessary for the same trade to continue.

There is also a restriction on management expenses and Schedule A losses. See **12.13**. The restrictions placed on an intangible assets unused non-trading loss are similar to trading losses (*ICTA 1988, s 768C*).

Ownership

15.13   Ownership of the trade is the beneficial ownership obtained by owner-ship of the share capital. The ownership condition is met if, at any time within two years after the transfer of trade, the beneficial ownership was held by the same person or persons as at any time within the 12 months prior to the transfer of trade (*ICTA 1988, s 343(1)(a)*). No minimum period of ownership is required, but in practice HMRC may query short periods of ownership.

Charge to corporation tax

15.14   The charging condition is met if the trade has been carried on by companies within the charge to corporation tax within the prescribed period of ownership (*ICTA 1988, s 343(1)(b)*). The situation not only applies to UK resident companies but also to non-resident companies chargeable to corpora-tion tax in respect of a trade carried on by a UK branch or agent. The relief applies to a 'trade' and will also apply if part of a trade is transferred (*ICTA 1988, s 343(8)*).

Relief

15.15   Normally, when a company ceases to trade, its corporation tax liability is computed as though this was a discontinuance (*ICTA 1988, s 337*). This is not the case under *s 343*.

Essentially the trade is not treated as discontinued and a new one commenced. Capital allowances continue uninterrupted with balancing charges falling on the successor company (*ICTA 1988, s 343(2)*). The loss carried forward by the successor is reduced by any excess of liabilities taken over (*ICTA 1988, s 343(4)*).

It should be noted that the relief only applies to trading losses. Schedule A losses; the remaining Schedule D losses, management expenses, non-trading loan relationship deficits, etc are not included.

Beneficial ownership

15.16   Ownership of the ordinary share capital for these purposes is the beneficial ownership. Ordinary share capital is defined in *ICTA 1988, s 832* and means all the issued share capital of the company, by whatever name it is called, other than capital whose holders have only a right to a dividend at a fixed rate, but have no other right to share in the profits.

A beneficial owner is not necessarily the person in whose name the ordinary shares are registered. A person who holds shares as a nominee is not a beneficial owner (*ICTA 1988, s 344(3)(a)*). Beneficial ownership is established by looking through to the ultimate owners.

15.17   The ownership of a trade is established whenever the *s 343* and *s 344* trade ownership tests are met. Ownership can fall to the holders of the ordinary share capital of the company carrying it on under *ICTA 1988, s 344(2)(a)*, or to the parent of the company carrying on the trade under *ICTA 1988, s 344(2)(b)*. Ultimately, the holders of the ordinary share capital of the parent under *ICTA 1988, s 344(2)(b)* may be the beneficial owners of the company. Finally, as will apply in most owner-manager controlled companies, the person or persons who by voting power, or by powers given in the Articles of Association or other document regulating the company, can direct or control the affairs of a company, which directly or indirectly owns the ordinary share capital of the company carrying on the trade (*ICTA 1988, s 344(2)*). HMRC will look to the person who can control the company 'by other means', which seems to imply that they may accept an arrangement not formalised by a written document (HMRC Company Taxation Manual CTM 06020).

15.18 *Reconstructions and amalgamations*

A 75% parent and subsidiary ownership relationship is required for *ICTA 1988, s 344(2)(b)* above, under *ICTA 1988, s 344(3)(b)*. Relatives are treated as a single person and include spouses, civil partners (with effect from 5 December 2005), siblings, children and grandchildren etc, and parents and grandparents etc.

Example 15.5

Matthew, Mark and Luke each own 33.33% outright of the ordinary share capital of the publishing company W Ltd. H Ltd takes over the publishing trade from W Ltd. Matthew, Mark, Luke and John each own 25% of H Ltd.

Common ownership of the trade is achieved because the same group of persons owns not less than 75% of both companies.

Example 15.6

Sleekstyles Ltd manufactured hairdressing products but is now dormant. On 1 January 2009 Sleekstyles Ltd trade was taken over by Crazystyles Ltd. The percentage ownership of the ordinary shares of both companies is as follows:

	Sleekstyles Ltd	*Crazystyles Ltd*
	%	%
William	60	40
Nathan	20	40
Roger	10	8
Susan	5	7
Clementine	3	3
Nadia	2	2
Total	100	100

William and Nathan formalised their relationship by entering into civil partnership on 5 December 2006. Roger and Susan became engaged to be married on 1 January 2008. Clementine and Nadia are senior employees. William and Nathan's shares are aggregated. Common ownership of the trade is achieved because the same group of persons owns not less than 75% of both companies.

15.18 For the relief to be given, beneficial ownership of the shares must be in place.

In *Wood Preservation Ltd v Prior* (1969) 45 TC 112, [1969] 1 All ER 364, the carry forward of loss relief was denied because Wood Preservation Ltd's trade was transferred after its parent company lost beneficial ownership of Wood's shares. HMRC explain that beneficial ownership passes from vendor to purchaser where an unconditional sale document is signed. If the contract is subject to a condition the beneficial ownership does not pass until the condition is satisfied. Equally a legal owner of shares can lose the beneficial ownership if that person entered into an unconditional contract to sell the shares in advance of signing a contract. An oral agreement can be an unconditional contract (HMRC Company Taxation Manual CTM 06030). Therefore a potential vendor should be particularly vigilant with respect to the point in time at which beneficial ownership is transferred.

Transfer of trade

15.19 HMRC has identified the following four practical situations where either a trade or part of a trade is transferred between companies. Firstly, a succession to an entire trade, arising under *ICTA 1988, s 343(1)*, where a company ceases to carry on a trade and another company begins to carry it on. Secondly, a transfer of the activities of a trade under *ICTA 1988, s 343(8)*, where a company ceases to carry on a trade and another begins to carry on the activities of that trade as part of its trade. Thirdly, a transfer of the activities of part of a trade, where a company ceases to carry on part of a trade and another company begins to carry on the activities of that part as its trade, again under *ICTA 1988, s 343(8)*. Finally, also under *ICTA 1988, s 343(8)*, where a company ceases to carry on part of a trade and another company begins to carry on the activities of that part as part of its trade (HMRC Company Taxation Manual CTM 06060).

Succession

15.20 In practical terms sufficient of the predecessor's trading activities must be transferred to the new company. For example, if, as in the case of Example 15.6, Sleekstyles Ltd transferred its factory, its manufacturing operations and its employees to Crazystyles Ltd without its book debts or its sales distribution unit, this may be a sufficient trading activity transfer to qualify as a succession. In *Malayam Plantations Ltd v Clark* (1935) 19 TC 314 the acquisition of a rubber plantation and its employees without the book debts or the selling organisation was considered to be a 'succession'. The fact that one company actually succeeds to the trade of another company within the same ownership will bring about the relief as in *Wadsworth Morton Ltd v Jenkinson* (1966) 43 TC 479, [1967] 1 WLR 79, [1966] 3 All ER 702.

Activities of a trade

15.21 The relief is also given if the predecessor's trade is added to the successor's trade in an identifiable form. For example, two shoe- manufacturing companies supplied shoes wholesale to their parent company for retail sale. The parent company wound up the subsidiaries. It took over the factories and the staff, and manufactured the shoes itself. The parent company was denied use of the subsidiaries' losses because although the manufacturing activities continued the wholesale activities failed to continue. The trade was not carried on in the same identifiable form as before the transfer (*Laycock v Freeman Hardy and Willis Ltd* (1938) 22 TC 288, [1939] 2 KB 1, [1938] 4 All ER 609). In *Rolls Royce Motors Ltd v Bamford* (1976) 51 TC 319, [1976] STC 152, it was held that the successor trade was different to that of the predecessor and *s 343* loss relief was denied.

A jeans and casual clothing company made trading losses. A company with which it was associated marketed its merchandise. The marketing company bought the manufacturing company and carried on its trade. The trading losses were available for relief after transfer because the trade continued, although the profits were not earned separately (*Falmer Jeans Ltd v Rodin* (1990) 63 TC 55, [1990] STC 270).

The identifiable form test was also met in *Briton Ferry Steel Co Ltd v Barry* (1939) 23 TC 414, [1940] 1 KB 463, [1939] 4 All ER 541.

Activities of part of a trade

15.22   There is no definition of part of a trade within the legislation. HMRC regard part of a trade as being a free-standing apparatus and making profits or losses in its own right. A part of a trade does not have to amount to anything as distinctive as a branch or a division (HMRC Company Taxation Manual CTM 06060).

LATER EVENTS

15.23   When a trade is transferred between two companies but the full ownership test is never met, although within two years there is a transfer to a company that does meet the ownership test, then *s 343* still applies and it is still possible to transfer losses to the third company (*ICTA 1988, s 343(7)*).

PRACTICAL EFFECTS OF SECTION 343 RELIEF

Trading losses carried forward

15.24   If all conditions apply, the successor is able to utilise the remaining predecessor's loss in an *ICTA 1988, s 393(1)* claim against future income from the same trade (*ICTA 1988, s 343(4)*). The remaining loss is the loss that the predecessor has not utilised less the relevant liabilities restriction. The relevant liabilities restriction is the difference between the retained relevant liabilities, the retained relevant assets and the consideration (*ICTA 1988, s 343(4)*.

The relevant liabilities are taken at their actual value immediately before the predecessor ceased to trade. Relevant liabilities exclude share capital, share premium, reserves or relevant loan stock and any liabilities transferred to the successor. Inter-group debts are included in relevant liabilities (*ICTA 1988, s 344(6)*). Relevant loan stock can be secured or unsecured but not that arising from a person carrying on the trade of money lending (*ICTA 1988, s 344(11), (12)*).

Relevant assets are the assets that the company owned immediately before it ceased to trade (*ICTA 1988, s 344(5)(a)*) and are valued at market value (*ICTA 1988, s 344(7)*).

The consideration is the amount given by the predecessor to the successor of the trade. Liabilities assumed by the successor are not included within the consideration (*ICTA 1988, s 344(5)(b)*). However, if a liability is transferred to the successor and the creditor agrees to accept less than the full amount due in settlement of the outstanding debt, the shortfall is treated as a liability for the purposes of the restriction.

If losses exceed the net relevant liabilities there is no restriction. Any losses disallowed are not available to the predecessor company (*ICTA 1988, s 343(4)*). Where part of a trade is transferred, a just apportionment of receipts, expenses, assets or liabilities is to be made for this purpose (*ICTA 1988, s 343(9)*). The restriction only applies to trading losses and not to capital allowances and balancing charges.

The release of a trading debt will be a taxable receipt of the trade (*ICTA 1988, s 94*).

Example 15.7

Alfonso Ltd took over the trade and assets of Bertino Ltd on 1 January 2009. *Section 343* relief applies. Bertino Ltd's unutilised trading losses amount to £150,000. Neither cash nor trade creditors are included in the sale. The balance sheet at 31 December 2008 directly before transfer is shown below. The business is assumed to be sold by Alfonso Ltd to Bertino Ltd for:

(i) £10,000, and

(ii) £100,000.

Bertino Ltd: Balance sheet at 31 December 2008

	£000	£000
Fixed assets		
Plant and machinery		60
Current assets		
Stock	20	
Debtors	10	
Cash	5	
	35	
Current liabilities		
Trade creditors	30	
		5
		65
Shareholders' funds		
Share capital		50
Profit and loss account		15
		65

The restriction is calculated as follows:

(i)   Sale proceeds: £10,000

	£000
Trade creditors	30
Less cash	(5)
	25
Less sale consideration	(10)
Loss relief restriction	15

The losses that are available for relief are £150,000 – 15,000 = £145,000

(ii)   Sale proceeds: £100,000

	£000
Trade creditors	30
Less cash	(5)
	25
Less sale consideration	(100)
Loss relief restriction	(75)

As the sale consideration exceeds the value of the liabilities and assets not taken over there is no loss restriction.

If only £50,000 of the plant were taken over, the restriction would be calculated as follows:

Sale proceeds	£10,000	£100,000
	£000	£000
Trade creditors	30	30
Less plant retained	(10)	(10)
Less cash	(5)	(5)
	15	15
Less sale consideration	(10)	(100)
Loss relief restriction	5	(75)

If the company is sold for £10,000, the losses that are available for relief are:

$$£150,000 - £10,000 = £140,000$$

If the company is sold for £100,000, there is no loss restriction as the sale consideration continues to exceed the value of the liabilities and assets not taken over.

Capital allowances

15.25   For capital allowances purposes where a company is sold to a successor such that the original company's trade ceases (*ICTA 1988, s 337(1)*), the assets are deemed to be sold to the new company at market value. Therefore, balancing charges and allowances will ensue for the predecessor (*CAA 2001, s 559*).

If the conditions of *s 343* apply the assets are transferred from predecessor to successor at tax written-down value. If the transfer is made during the accounting period the writing-down allowances are reduced proportionately. When the assets are eventually sold any balancing charge or allowances will fall upon the party carrying on the trade at the time, ie the successor as if he had always owned the assets (*ICTA 1988, s 343(2)*).

European Mergers Tax Directive

15.26   The European Mergers Tax Directive was introduced to remove the tax obstacles that hinder cross-border business restructuring operations within

Europe. As a result, reconstructions that involve a company resident in another member state should receive the same treatment as those that only involve UK resident companies. See *SI 2007/3186 Corporation Tax* (*Implementation of the Mergers Directive*) *Regulations 2007* and *Directives 90/434EEC 1990* and *2005/19/EC*.

Chapter 16

Distributions

INTRODUCTION

16.1   A dividend is a shareholder's expected reward for an investment in a limited company. Under company law, a company may declare and distribute a dividend out of its realised profits. The dividend is then payable to the shareholders pro rata to their shareholdings(*CA 2006, Pt 23*).

For corporation tax purposes, the distribution rules apply whenever cash or assets are passed to the members of the company. For taxation purposes, a dividend is a distribution of profits falling within *ICTA 1988, s 209(2)(a)*. If the payment relates to the member's services to the company it is not a distribution but a payment for services performed for the company. The payment will be chargeable upon the member as employment income under the rules of *ITEPA 2003* and any payments so made should be relievable by the company for corporation tax purposes.

However, a distribution can take a variety of forms and includes capital (other than a repayment of capital) or assets. For a company shareholder a distribution constitutes franked investment income (if non group) and dividend income for an individual assessable under *ITTOIA 2005, s 384* (see *Income Tax 2008/09* from Tottel).

MEANING

16.2   Distribution for corporation tax purposes does not have the same meaning as the company law meaning of distribution of share capital in a winding up. The former deals with allocating profits and the latter with apportioning a company's assets (*ICTA 1988, s 209(1)*).

PAYMENTS CLASSED AS A DISTRIBUTION

16.3   Particular payments are classed as distributions. These include not only dividends but also bonus securities or redeemable shares, transfers of assets and of liabilities between a company and its members, payments of interest or other distributions to the extent that they exceed a commercial rate, payments of interest or other distributions on certain securities, a bonus issue on or following a repayment of share capital and any other distributions out of assets of the company in respect of shares in the company.

Dividend

16.4   In general a dividend paid by a company including a capital dividend is a distribution (*ICTA 1988, s 209(2)(a)*). Exceptions are stock dividends and dividends paid by building societies and industrial provident societies. If a company transfers an asset to a member, the amount of the distribution is the market value of the asset less the market value of any new consideration given by the member (*ICTA 1988, s 209(4)–(6)*).

A distribution of shares by a close company to its members when they are worth more is not a distribution but can be a transfer of value between members (*IHTA 1984, s 94*). A dividend waiver may constitute a settlement if there is an element of bounty in the arrangement (*ITTOIA 2005, ss 619–648*).

Distribution of assets

16.5   If a distribution of a company's asset is made to members at an undervalue, the difference between that and the market value of the asset is treated as a distribution (*ICTA 1988, s 209(4)*). If the person to whom the asset is passed is also a director then it is a matter of fact whether he or she receives the asset as shareholder or as employee. If received as an employee the amount will be assessed as employment income (*ICTA 1988, s 209(2)(b), (4)*). There is no distribution if the payer and the recipient are both UK companies and one is a subsidiary of the other or both are subsidiaries of a third company (*ICTA 1988, s 209(5)*). Again there is no distribution between two independent companies, neither of which is a 51% subsidiary of a non-resident company where the companies are not under common control. The *ICTA 1988, s 416* definition of control is used here (*ICTA 1988, s 209(6)*). If an asset is transferred from one company to another, any material difference between the market value and the consideration given should be treated as a distribution within *ICTA 1988, s 209(4)* or *ICTA 1988, s 209(2)(b)* as appropriate unless *ICTA 1988, s 209(5)* or *ICTA 1988, s 209(6)* applies.

Unless the payments are intra company for *ICTA 1988, s 209(5), (6)* purposes other payments or asset transfers may be classed as distributions (*ICTA 1988, s 209(2)(b)*).

A repayment of share capital is not a distribution.

Bonus issue subsequent to a repayment

16.6   A bonus issue subsequent to a repayment of share capital (other than fully paid preference shares) is deemed to be a distribution of the nominal value of the shares so issued and is added to the purchase price of the shares (*ICTA 1988, s 210*). This does not apply to a bonus issue of non-redeemable share capital by a non-close listed company, which takes place more than ten years after the repayment of capital (*ICTA 1988, s 211*).

The distribution is calculated as follows:

the nominal amount of the bonus issue up to the amount of the capital repaid,

minus

the new consideration received,

minus

any amounts in respect of the same repayment of capital, already treated as distributions under *ICTA 1988, s 210(1)*.

Example 16.1

A Ltd repays £200,000 of its share capital.

It then issues:

* 100,000 fully paid £1 ordinary shares at 30p per share, and later

* 500,000 fully paid £1 preference shares for no new consideration.

The issue of ordinary shares results in a distribution of:

$$100,000 \times (£1 - £0.30) = £70,000.$$

The second (bonus) issue is of shares with par value of £500,000 (500,000 × £1).

This distribution is restricted to a maximum of the repayment of share capital less the earlier distribution. The amount of this distribution is, therefore:

$$£200,000 - £70,000 = £130,000.$$

Interest and other situations

16.7   Interest payments in excess of a normal commercial rate of return may be treated as a dividend.

Distributions in a winding up are not income distributions and are subject to capital gains tax. A distribution has an extended meaning for close companies (*ICTA 1988, s 418*) (see **4.13**).

There is a general anti-avoidance provision where two companies enter into reciprocal arrangements. Each company makes payments to the other company's members. In this instance the payments are classed as distributions (*ICTA 1988, s 254(8)*).

NON-QUALIFYING DISTRIBUTION

16.8   Non-qualifying distributions are bonus issues of redeemable shares or securities. They can be issued directly or issued from bonus redeemable shares or securities received from another company (*ICTA 1988, s 209(2)(c)*).

The amount of the non-qualifying distribution for the purposes of *ICTA 1988, s 209(2)(c)* for redeemable share capital is the excess of the nominal amount of the share capital together with any premium payable on redemption, in a winding up or in any other circumstances over any new consideration received.

Individual shareholders receive a 10% credit and may be charged at the 32.5% upper rate. The company must notify HMRC on form CT2 within 14 days after the end of the quarter in which the non-qualifying distribution is made (*ICTA 1988, s 234(5)*).

SMALL COMPANY DIVIDEND PAYMENTS

16.9   Small private company owner managers generally take their reward from their companies in the form of dividends and or remuneration. Remuneration is deductible for corporation tax purposes. Dividend payments are not tax deductible.

If there are no special clauses regarding dividend payments in the Articles of Association Table A *1985 Regulations* will preside. Table A draws a distinction between interim and final dividends. Under *Companies Act 2006*, model articles are expected to be introduced on 1 October 2009 (*ss 30–36* concern dividends and other distributions) (*CA 2006, s 19*).

Final dividends may be declared by the company in general meeting but no dividend shall exceed the amount recommended by the directors (*Art 102 Table A 1985 Regulations*). Interim dividends may be paid by directors from time to time (*Art 103 Table A 1985 Regulations*). Directors may only pay interim dividends if it appears to them that they are justified by the profits of the company available for distribution.

The timing of the dividend payment may have a marked impact on the directors' personal taxation situation. A dividend is not paid until the shareholder receives the funds direct or the dividend amount is unreservedly put at his or her disposal, for example by a credit to a loan account from which the shareholder has the power to draw.

Final dividends are normally due and payable on the date of the resolution unless a future date is set for payment. Interim dividends are not an enforceable debt and can be varied or rescinded prior to payment. Interim dividends are due when paid or when the funds are placed at the disposal of the director/shareholders as part of their current accounts with the company. HMRC state that 'payment is not made until such a right to draw on the dividend exists (presumably) when the appropriate entries are made in the company's books. If, as may happen with a small company, such entries are not made until the annual audit, and this takes place after the end of the accounting period in which the directors resolved that an interim dividend be paid, then the "due and payable" date is in the later rather than the earlier accounting period' (HMRC Company Taxation Manual CTM 20095).

For taxation purposes an 'illegal dividend' will be treated in the same way as a legal dividend. However, there is the possibility that if the directors were to pay an interim dividend during an accounting period and it is not possible to demonstrate that the interim dividend payment was paid out of available profits (or alternatively as a repayment of loans due from the company) that HMRC could attack that nature of the payment classing it as remuneration and assess the company for PAYE and NIC. If a shareholder knew or was in a position to know that a dividend was illegal at the time of payment it is refundable to the company. See **4.18**. Companies must therefore be meticulous in their statutory record keeping as regards interim dividend payments.

A final dividend can only be waived before payment. An interim dividend must be waived before entitlement to payment because payment and entitlement take place at the same time. If waiver takes place afterwards it is not an effective waiver but merely a transfer of income.

With effect for accounting periods commencing on or after 1 January 2005 a company may not recognise a dividend in its accounts unless it is a liability at the balance sheet date (FRS21 and IAS10). See also ICAEW Technical Release Tech 57/05.

SURPLUS ACT

16.10   Post 6 April 1999 there is no liability to corporation tax if a company makes a distribution payment. Prior to 6 April 1999 if a company made a dividend payment it had to account for advance corporation tax (ACT). ACT was calculated as 1/4 of the dividend paid. The ACT paid was, as its name describes, an advance payment of corporation tax. The advance payment could be set against the mainstream liability up to a 20% limit. Any surplus was carried forward for relief in the next year. The problem for companies post 6 April 1999 is to obtain relief for its pre-6 April 1999 surplus ACT against its post-6 April 1999 mainstream corporation tax. It can only do this if it takes account of its 'shadow' or notional ACT.

The company is required to follow this procedure:

1   Calculate the ACT that it would have paid on its distributions.

2   Calculate the maximum ACT set-off.

3   Calculate the remaining offset capacity after the notional ACT has been used.

This can be used to set off the surplus ACT.

Example 16.2

Lotus Ltd's profits chargeable to corporation tax for the year ended 31 March 2009 amount to £300,000. The company paid a dividend of £35,000 during the year. Surplus ACT brought forward at 1 April 2008 amounts to £90,000. The position is as follows:

	£
Maximum ACT set-off £300,000 × 20%	60,000
Less shadow ACT £35,000 × 20/80	8,750
Surplus ACT set-off	51,250
Surplus ACT brought forward	90,000
Less set-off accounting period ended 31 March 2008	51,250
Surplus ACT carried forward	38,750
The final corporation tax liability is:	
Corporation tax	63,000
Less surplus ACT set-off	51,250
Final tax liability	11,750

16.11 If a company wishes to make large payments to shareholders it may choose to do so in the form of share capital rather than as a distribution. However, from 6 April 1999 non-qualifying distributions are included with qualifying distributions for the purposes of calculating shadow ACT (*FA 1998, s 32*; *Corporation Tax (Treatment of Unrelieved Surplus Advance Corporation Tax) Regulations 1999, SI 1999/358*).

EXEMPTIONS FROM THE DISTRIBUTION RULES

16.12 Certain transactions are relieved or exempted from the overall distribution rules. These include:

- Demergers by *ICTA 1988, s 213* and *TCGA 1992, s 192*.

- Purchase by a company of its own shares (*ICTA 1988, s 219*).

- Distributions in a winding up by ESC C16.

DEMERGERS

16.13 It may be seen as beneficial for a subsidiary company to leave a group. For this to happen the ownership of the subsidiary's shares passes out of the control of the ultimate holding company to another company or group. This transfer of capital will not be treated as a distribution provided certain conditions apply. Both the distributing and the subsidiary company, whose share are transferred, must be trading companies or holding companies of a trading group at the time of the distribution (*ICTA 1988, s 213*). Both companies must be resident in the UK at the time of the distribution.

16.14 *ICTA 1988, s 213* facilitates three types of transaction where subject to additional conditions such a transaction is treated as an exempt distribution. SP 13/80 provides additional interpretation and guidance. Exempt distributions may consist of:

(i) A distribution by a company of its shares in one or more 75% subsidiaries.

(ii) A transfer of a company's trade to one or more companies in consideration for the issue of shares in the transferor company.

(iii) A distribution of shares in a 75% subsidiary or subsidiaries to one or more companies which issue their shares to the members of the distributing company.

Example 16.3—(i) A distribution by a company of its shares in one or more 75% subsidiaries (ICTA 1988, s 213(3)(a))

This results in a direct demerger.

In this situation B Ltd, a group company, leaves the group, but its ultimate ownership remains with A and B.

Before the demerger:

- A and B owned A Ltd, and
- A Ltd owned B Ltd and C Ltd.

After the demerger:

- A and B own A Ltd and B Ltd, and
- A Ltd owns C Ltd.

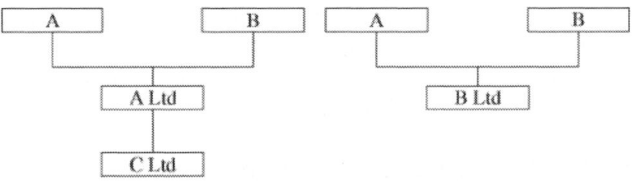

In particular, in this situation, the B Ltd shares that are distributed by A Ltd to A and B, must be non-redeemable and must be the whole or substantially the whole of the ordinary shares and voting rights that A Ltd holds in B Ltd (*ICTA 1988, s 213(6)(a)*). 'Whole' is interpreted as around 90% or more (SP 13/80).

Example 16.4—(ii) A distribution of a company's trade or shares in one or more 75% subsidiary companies in consideration for the issue of shares in the transferor company (ICTA 1988, s 213(3)(b))

This is known as an indirect demerger.

A & B Ltd carries on a trade or trades and the desired effect is for another company to carry on some of its activities. A new company, B Ltd, is formed to which part of the trade is transferred. A & B Ltd remains in active existence.

Before the demerger:

- A and B owned A & B Ltd, which is involved in trade A and trade B.

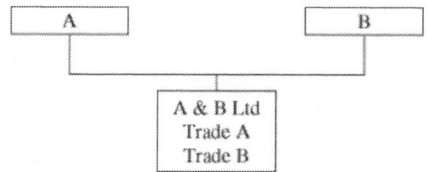

After the demerger:

- A and B own A & B Ltd, which is involved in trade A, and

- A and B own B Ltd, which is involved in trade B.

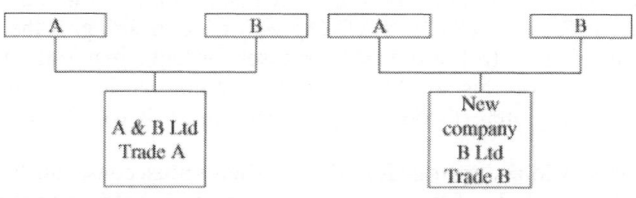

Example 16.5—(iii) A distribution of shares in a 75% subsidiary or subsidiaries to one or more companies, which issue their shares to the members of the distributing company

B Ltd, a subsidiary company, leaves the group to be within the ownership of a newly formed company but remains within A and B's ultimate ownership.

Before the demerger:

- A and B owned A Ltd, and

- A Ltd owned B Ltd and C Ltd.

After the demerger:

- A and B own A Ltd and the new company D Ltd,

- A Ltd owns B Ltd, and

16.15   *Distributions*

- D Ltd owns C Ltd.

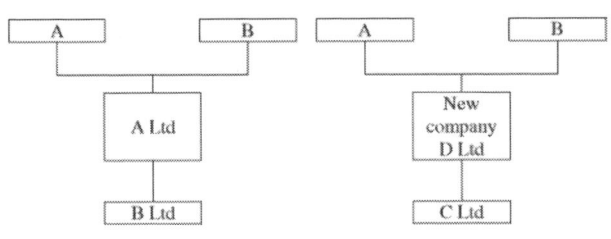

16.15   In the cases above, the transferor, ie A & B Ltd in Example 16.4 and A Ltd in Example 16.5, must not retain any material interest in the transferred trade (*ICTA 1988, s 213(8)(a)*). HMRC give a wide meaning. If the transferor company retained control of the trade or assets or had a material influence on the profit destination this would amount to retaining an interest in the trade. Otherwise a minor interest would amount to around 10% (SP 13/80).

If shares in a subsidiary are transferred those shares must constitute the whole or substantially the whole of the distributing company's holding of the ordinary share capital of the subsidiary and must confer the whole or substantially the whole of the distributing company's voting rights in the subsidiary (*ICTA 1988, s 213(8)(b)*).

The only or main activity of the transferee company or each transferee company after the distribution must be the carrying on of the trade or the holding of the shares transferred to it (*ICTA 1988, s 213(8)(c)*).

The shares issued by the transferee company or each transferee company must not be redeemable, must constitute the whole or substantially the whole of its issued ordinary share capital and must confer the whole or substantially the whole of the voting rights in that company (*ICTA 1988, s 213(8)(d)*).

After (but not 'for ever after' SP13/80) the distribution the distributing company must be either a trading company or the holding company of a trading group unless the transfer relates to two or more subsidiaries and the transferor is dissolved and has no other assets available for distribution or it is itself a 75% subsidiary (*ICTA 1988, s 213(6)(b), (8)(d)*). ESC C11 permits the company to retain funds to meet the costs of liquidation and to repay a negligible amount of share capital remaining. Negligible is interpreted as meaning £5,000 or less.

There are certain conditions if the distributing company is itself a 75% subsidiary of another company. The group to which the distributing company belongs must be a trading group (*ICTA 1988, s 213(12)(a)*). The distribution by the subsidiary must be followed by one or more of the Example 16.3 or Example 16.4 distributions (*ICTA 1988, s 213(12)*).

Shareholders effectively enter into a share for share exchange. The trade or business remains with the companies.

Reliefs

16.16   The share transfer is an exempt distribution and is not taxable on the individual shareholders (*ICTA 1988, s 213*).

The direct demerger is not treated as a capital distribution under *TCGA 1992, s 122* but instead is treated as a paper for paper reconstruction under *TCGA 1992, ss 126–130*. Thus the capital gains base cost is apportioned to the shares in the transferee company and in the distributing company in proportion to their values at the time of the distribution. There is no charge if the company leaves the group provided the company has not made a chargeable payment within five years of making the exempt distribution. A chargeable payment is a payment that is neither for money's worth nor for commercial purposes but will possibly be part of a tax avoidance scheme (*ICTA 1988, s 214; TCGA 1992, s 192*). In the case of an indirect demerger, capital gains relief is obtained in practice under *TCGA 1992, s 136* because the demerger is often a reconstruction (see HMRC Capital Gains Tax Manuals CG 52720/1 and CG 33920A for HMRC's comments).

General conditions

16.17   All companies involved in the transactions must be UK resident at the time of the distribution (*ICTA 1988, s 213(4)*). The distributing company and any company whose shares are distributed must be a trading company or a member of a trading group (*ICTA 1988, s 213(5)*). The distribution must be made wholly or mainly for the benefit of some or all of the trading activities formerly carried on by a single company or group and after the distribution carried on by two or more companies or groups (*ICTA 1988, s 213(10)*). The distribution must not form part of a scheme or arrangement for:

● the avoidance of tax;

- the making of a chargeable payment;

- the transfer of control of a relevant company to persons other than members of the distributing company;

- the cessation of a trade or its sale after the distribution (*ICTA 1988, s 213(11)*).

Clearance procedure

16.18 A clearance procedure is available under *ICTA 1988, s 215* for the distributing company and also for any person considering making a chargeable payment within five years of an exempt distribution. A chargeable payment is any payment not made for money's worth. This will be treated as a company distribution if made during the five-year period of an exempt distribution. Individuals receiving a chargeable payment will be charged to income tax in full. Companies receiving a chargeable payment will be charged to corporation tax under Schedule D Case VI on the full amount of the receipt (*ICTA 1988, s 214(1A), (1B)*). A return of exempt distributions must be provided to HMRC within 30 days of making the distribution (*ICTA 1988, s 216*). See **18.5** for further details regarding clearance procedures.

PURCHASE OF OWN SHARES

Effects of the legislation

16.19 The Companies Act permits a company to purchase and redeem their own share capital. In absence of any relieving legislation a distribution will arise under *ICTA 1988*, s 209(2)(b) on the difference between the subscribed capital and the purchase or redemption proceeds.

Relief is given under *ICTA 1988, s 219* for payments made by an unquoted trading company or the unquoted holding company of a trading group on the purchase or redemption of their own shares. A quoted company is 'a company whose shares are listed in the official list of the Stock Exchange' (*ICTA 1988, s 229(1)*). Shares dealt in by the unlisted securities market or the alternative investment market are unquoted for these purposes (HMRC Corporation Tax Manual CTM 17507).

Payments on purchase and redemption to quoted companies remain within the distribution legislation. The excess of the payment above the refund of share capital is treated as a distribution. If certain conditions are complied with there is no distribution treatment. Instead the disposal receives the capital gains treatment in the hands of the vendor shareholder.

Conditions—purpose

16.20   The purpose of the transaction must be to benefit the company's trade or any of its 75% subsidiary's trade. It must not form part of a scheme or arrangement to enable a shareholder to participate in company profits without receiving a dividend, or any other form of tax avoidance (*ICTA 1988, s 219(1)(a)*). HMRC will review the circumstances of each case. The case of *Allum v Marsh* SpC 446; [2005] STC (SCD) 191 was subject to such a review. The facts are as follows: Mr and Mrs A owned 99% and their son 1% of the ordinary shares in A Ltd an unquoted trading company. Mr and Mrs A and their son were all directors. The company owned a property from which the business was carried out and there was a large loan due to the directors. The company approved a contract for the sale of the property and when the sale had been completed it voted to purchase Mr and Mrs A's shares in A Ltd. Mr and Mrs A resigned as company directors. A new company secretary was appointed and the board voted to make voluntary payments to Mr and Mrs A in appreciation for their services to the company. Their shareholdings were duly purchased by the company. The next year the company's activities became small and negligible and the company could not find suitable premises from which to carry out its activities. Mr and Mrs A were assessed to a distribution on the basis that the exemption under *ICTA 1988, s 219(1)(a)* did not apply because the purchase of the shares was not made wholly or mainly for benefiting the company's trade. The voluntary payments were assessed as emoluments. Therefore it is necessary to demonstrate that the purchase takes place for the benefit of the trade.

Alternatively, the whole of the payment (apart from any sum applied in paying capital gains tax charged on the redemption, repayment or purchase) may be applied by the recipient in discharging a liability of his for inheritance tax charged on a death and is so applied within the period of two years after the death (*ICTA 1988, s 219*).

Conditions—shareholder residence

16.21   The vendor shareholder must be resident and ordinarily resident in the UK in the year of assessment in which the purchase is made. If the shares are held through a nominee, the nominee must also be so resident and ordinarily resident (*ICTA 1988, s 220(1)*).

The shares must have been owned by the vendor throughout the period of five years ending with the date of the purchase (*ICTA 1988, s 220(5)*). For an individual a spouse's period of ownership is also taken into consideration (*ICTA 1988, s 220(6)*).

Shareholder's interest in the company

16.22   Immediately after purchase the shareholder's interest or the combined interests with associates must be substantially reduced (*ICTA 1988,* *s 221(1),(2)).* By this it is meant first that the total nominal value of the shares owned by him immediately after the purchase, expressed as a fraction of the issued share capital of the company at that time, does not exceed 75% of the corresponding fraction immediately before the purchase (*ICTA 1988, s 221(4)*). Second, if the share of profits available for distribution immediately after purchase exceeds 75% of the corresponding fraction immediately before the purchase, the shareholding will not be treated as substantially reduced (*ICTA 1988, s 221(5)*).

In a group situation other group members' and associates' interests are also taken into account (*ICTA 1988, s 222(4)*). Group for these purposes is a 51% relationship (*ICTA 1988, s 222(7)*).

After the purchase the ex-shareholders must not be connected with the company making the purchase or with any company that is a member of the same group as that company (*ICTA 1988, s 223(1)*).

Clearance procedure

16.23 An advance clearance procedure is available under *ICTA 1988, s 225*. The full procedure is set out in SP 2/82. 60 days after making the payments the company must make a return to HMRC giving details of the payment and the circumstances (*ICTA 1988, s 226*).

Associated persons

16.24 Associated persons include spouses who are living together and children under the age of 18 together with their respective associates. With effect from 5 December 2005, civil partners are also associated persons. Two or more companies are connected if they are both under the same control. Trustees are connected with the settlor, the beneficiaries and the respective associates.

A personal representative is associated with the beneficiaries. A person connected with a company is an associate of the company and of any company controlled by it, and the company and any company controlled by it are his associates. Trustees are associated with the settlor or an associate of his or the beneficiaries if any one of the beneficiaries has an interest of more than 5%. Personal representatives are associated with beneficiaries if the beneficiary has an interest of more than 5% in the estate.

Also, if one person is accustomed to act on the directions of another in relation to the affairs of a company, then in relation to that company the two persons are associates of one another. Exempt approved pension schemes and employee trusts are not included in these arrangements (*ICTA 1988, s 227(8)*).

Connected persons

16.25   A person is connected with a company if he directly or indirectly possesses or is entitled to acquire more than 30% of the issued ordinary share capital, 30% of the combined loan capital and issued share capital, 30% of the voting power or 30% of the assets available for distribution on a winding up.

An interest in loan capital, acquired during the normal course of a money lending business, is disregarded, if the person takes no part in the management or conduct of the company.

DISTRIBUTIONS IN A WINDING UP BY ESC C16

Striking off a defunct company

16.26   If the registrar of companies believes that a company is not carrying on a business he may strike it off. The procedure involves the registrar writing to the company. If a reply is not received within a month a second letter is sent within 14 days, this time by registered post. If no reply is received within one month, the registrar may publish a notice in the London Gazette and will send a notice to the company stating that within three months from the date of the notice the company will be struck off the registrar and dissolved (*CA 2006, s 1001* – now applicable from 1 October 2009; formerly *CA 1985, s 652*).

Request for striking off by a private company

16.27   A private company may voluntarily request that the registrar strike it off. In practice the company completes a Companies House form 652a, which it sends to the registrar of companies, together with a cheque for £10. The form must be signed by all or a majority of the directors. The directors must confirm that in the previous three months it has not carried on any business, or changed its name, disposed of any of its assets or engaged in any other activities apart from making the application, settling its affairs or meeting a statutory requirement. The company must, of course, not be involved in any other insolvency proceedings (*CA 2006, s 1003* – now applicable from 1 October 2009; formerly *CA 1985, s 652A*). The registrar then publishes a notice in the London Gazette. Within seven days of sending the form to the Registrar, all members, creditors, Crown departments, employees and any directors who have not signed the form should be sent full information as to the company assets and liabilities and should have a copy of the letter that was sent to the Registrar of Companies. Creditors should be invited to petition for the winding up of the company as an alternative. In most cases, creditors would not wish to take up this option, as to do so would involve them in material court costs which they could not substantially recover. If no objections are received, three months after the date of the notice, a further notice will be placed in the London Gazette and the company will be removed (See form BVC 17 on the Bona Vacantia website www.bonavacantia.gov.uk).

ESC C16

16.28   As a *CA 2006, s 1000*or *s 1003* (formerly *CA 1985, s 652* or *s 652A*) method of striking off is not a formal winding up, HMRC regards any distribution of assets as an income distribution within *s 209*. By concession HMRC will treat the distribution as a capital distribution provided certain criteria are complied with; namely that the shareholders accept personal liability for the company's unpaid taxation liabilities. HMRC will require written signed statements from the company and its shareholders.

The company must provide assurances that it:

- does not intend to trade or carry on business in future;
- intends to collect its debts, pay off its creditors and distribute any balance of its assets to its shareholders (or has already done so); and
- intends to seek or accept striking off and dissolution.

The company and its shareholders agree that:

- they will supply such information as is necessary to determine and will pay any corporation tax liability on income or capital gains; and
- the shareholders will pay any capital gains tax liability (or corporation tax in the case of a corporate shareholder) in respect of any amount distributed to them in cash or otherwise as if the distributions had been made during a winding up (ESC 16).

This method of winding up is widely used by small private companies. Assuming all other conditions apply, the capital gains tax treatment enables the shareholders to take advantage of business asset taper relief. As the capital gains tax treatment is only a concession, HMRC could refuse to apply it if they perceived a tax avoidance motive.

Treatment of assets and liabilities

16.29   Before a company is dissolved, the members should ensure that its assets are transferred out of its ownership. If this is not done, any assets owned at the date of dissolution will pass to the Crown and become *bona vacantia*. Assets held in trust by the company for another do not pass to the Crown (*CA 2006, s 1012* – now applicable from 1 October 2009; formerly *CA 2005, s 654*).

The company should request well in advance and whilst the company is still in existence for any corporation tax repayments to be made to the shareholders or directors. Otherwise with a closed bank account the company will not be able to receive the repayment and with a company no longer in existence it will not be possible to give alternative payment instructions to HMRC with the result that the corporation tax repayment will also be *bona vacantia*.

The company's liabilities are extinguished on dissolution unless the debt is secured on the company's property by a mortgage or charge. The creditor's remedy for unsecured debts is to restore the company to the Register, and then bring legal proceedings against the restored company. The time limit for which a company can be restored to the Register is six years in the case of *CA 2006, s 1000* – now applicable from 1 October 2009 or *s 1003* now applicable from 1 October 2009 (formerly *CA 2005, s 652* or *652A*) strike off.

Bona vacantia

16.30   *Bona vacantia* or 'vacant goods' is ownerless property, which passes to the Crown. The collection of the assets of dissolved companies in England and Wales is dealt with by the Treasury Solicitor as nominee for the Crown. The Treasury Solicitor has published guidelines in respect of companies registered under the *Companies Acts 1929* to *1985* at: www.bonavacantia.gov.uk.

Unauthorised distribution

16.31   If there is an unauthorised return of the share capital to the members, the company has a right to recover that money from its members. That right of recovery from the members is a 'right' for the purposes of *CA 2006, s 1012* – now applicable from 1 October 2009 (formerly *CA 1985, s 654*), which would pass to the Crown as *bona vacantia* when the company is dissolved. If there was an unauthorised distribution of share capital to the members prior to dissolution, therefore, the Crown would be entitled to recover that distribution from the members. The only legal way to avoid this 'right' passing to the Crown as *bona vacantia* is to put the company into formal liquidation prior to dissolution, or to legally reduce the amount of the share capital legally prior to the company dissolution (Form BVC 17 www.bonavacantia.gov.uk).

Permitted distributions

16.32   It has been recognised that it would be unreasonable for the Treasury Solicitor to expect that a company is put into formal liquidation when that would be uneconomic, especially bearing in mind that HMRC ESC C16 permits a distribution for tax purposes without the company having to incur the costs of a formal liquidation. It has, therefore, been agreed with HM Treasury that if:

- a company has been struck off under either *CA 2006, s 1000* or *1003* – now applicable from 1 October 2009; and

- the shareholders have taken advantage of ESC C16; and

- the amount of the distribution is less than £4,000,

as a concession the Treasury Solicitor will waive the Crown's right to any funds, which were distributed to the former members prior to dissolution. (£4,000 is considered to be the average cost of putting a company into liquidation.) (Form BVC 17 www.bonavacantia.gov.uk).

Example 16.6

Beat Ltd is a private company, which has made trading losses for the past few years.

The directors plan to sell the company's assets, settle the company debts, distribute the balance and apply for the company to be struck off. HMRC has agreed to the application of ESC C16.

The shareholders funds are:

	£
Issued Ordinary Shares	1,000
Share Premium	50
Retained Profits	250
	1,300

The company distributes £1,300 to the former members. The Treasury solicitor will not attempt to recover any of that distribution from the members.

Example 16.7

Deadbeat Ltd is a private company, which has made trading losses for the past few years.

The directors plan to sell the company's assets, settle the company debts, distribute the balance and apply for the company to be struck off under *CA 2006, s 1003* – now applicable from 1 October 2009; formerly *CA 1985, s 652A*. HMRC has agreed to the application of ESC C16. The shareholders funds are:

	£
Issued Ordinary Shares	2,000
Share Premium	50
Retained Profits	3,250
	5,300

If the company distributes £5,300 to the former members, the Treasury solicitor will attempt to recover the distribution from the members. In order to avoid this, the company could:

- pay an unauthorised distribution of less than £4,000. £1,300 or assets will be sacrificed but the overall cost may be less than a formal liquidation;

- abandon a *s 1003* – now applicable from 1 October 2009 (*s 652A*) approach and appoint a liquidator under a formal winding-up; and

- consider a redemption or purchase of own shares out of capital (*CA 2006, s 709* – now applicable from 1 October 2009; formerly *CA 1985, s 171*).

Chapter 17

Accounting and taxation

GENERALLY ACCEPTED ACCOUNTING STANDARDS

17.1   For accounting periods beginning from 1 January 2005, either UK GAAP or international accounting standards (IAS) as set out in EC Regulation 1606/2002 may be used (*FA 2004, s 50*). UK GAAP will be applied in cases of inter-group transactions where one group member to the transaction obtains a tax advantage by the use of UK GAAP whilst the other group member to the transaction uses IAS (*FA 2004, s 51*).

Those companies whose securities are traded on an EU regulated market are required to prepare their consolidated accounts in accordance with IAS for accounting periods ended on or after 1 January 2005.

A change in accounting practice following UK accounting principles from 1 January 2005, a change from UK GAAP to IAS, may bring about a prior period adjustment. Positive adjustments are taxed as receipts and negative adjustments are allowed as expenses. For accounting periods beginning on or after 1 January 2005, these prior period adjustments are treated as arising on the first day of the first period of account for which the new basis is adopted. For accounting periods beginning before 1 January 2005, the prior period adjustment was treated as taking place on the last day of the first period of account for which the new basis was adopted (*FA 2005, s 81*; *FA 2002, s 64, Sch 22*).

Companies qualifying as small under the *Companies Act* definition (see **6.20–6.21**) may opt to apply the financial reporting standard for smaller entities (FRSSE). The FRSSE replaces all other accounting standards and UITF abstracts. A smaller companies IAS has been proposed.

ACCOUNTING POLICIES

17.2   A company's accounts prepared in accordance with GAAP form the basis for the company's corporation tax computation (see **1.8–1.10**). This rule applies to trading profits, a letting business, an overseas property business, loan relationships, derivatives, intangible property, management expenses and leases.

Taxation law has no authority to impose compliance with the *Companies Act* or to impose any requirements as to audit disclosure upon the company (*FA 1998, s 42(2)*). Accounts prepared according to GAAP and in accordance with the *Companies Act* form the basis of the corporation tax computation. The profits are then normally adjusted further because the laws of taxation take precedence over accounting principles (see Chapter 5).

As regards the accounts basis, HMRC employ revenue accountants with wide auditing and accounting experience to whom they refer all their accountancy queries (see Tax Bulletin, Issue 58, April 2002). If HMRC open an enquiry into a company's corporation tax return, the Revenue accountants may also enquire into the accounting policies which the company has adopted (see 'TAXline', February 2003 and Working Together, Issue 13, June 2003).

17.3   A synopsis of the current UK and international standards is given on the accompanying pages, together with notes on the interaction of accounting and taxation principles where appropriate. The UK accounting standards are published by the Accounting Standards Board (ASB) and are based on overriding principles rather than detailed prescription.

17.4   UITF assists the ASB where unsatisfactory or conflicting interpretations have developed (or seem likely to develop) about a requirement of an accounting standard or the *Companies Act*. The UITF seeks to arrive at a consensus on the accounting treatment within the ASB framework that should be adopted. UITF consensuses are published in the form of UITF Abstracts. Compliance with UITF Abstracts is necessary (other than in exceptional circumstances) in accounts that claim to give a true and fair view. International accounting standards are published by the International Accounting Standards Board. Overall there is a general convergence between UK GAAP and IAS.

UK GAAP

17.5

	Financial Reporting Standards	*Commentary*
FRSSE (2008)	Financial reporting standard for smaller entities (FRSSE 2008)***	**17.8**
FRSSE (2007)	Financial reporting standard for smaller entities (FRSSE 2007)**	**17.8**
FRS 29	(IFRS 7) Financial instruments: disclosures**	

17.5 *Accounting and taxation*

	Financial Reporting Standards	*Commentary*
FRS 28	Corresponding amounts*	
FRSSE (2005)	Financial reporting standard for smaller entities*	**17.8**
FRS 27	Life assurance+	
FRS 26	(IAS 39) Financial instruments: measurement*	**17.9**
FRS 25	(IAS 32) Financial instruments: disclosure and presentation*	
FRS 24	(IAS 29) Financial reporting in hyperinflationary economies*	
FRS 23	(IAS 21) The effects of changes in foreign exchange rates*	**17.10**
FRS 22	(IAS 33) Earnings per share*	
FRS 21	(IAS 10) Events after the balance sheet date*	**17.11**
FRS 20	(IFRS 2) Share-based payment*	
FRSSE (2002)	*Financial reporting standard for smaller entities* (FRSSE 2005)	
FRS 19	Deferred tax	**17.30**
FRS 18	Accounting policies	**17.12**
FRS 17	Retirement benefits	**17.21**
FRS 16	Current tax	**17.28**
FRS 15	Tangible fixed assets	**17.13,17.14**
FRS 14	*Earnings per share* (FRS 22)	
FRS 13	Derivatives and other financial instruments: disclosures	
FRS 12	Provisions, contingent liabilities and contingent assets	**17.15,17.16**
FRS 11	Impairment of fixed assets and goodwill	
FRS 10	Goodwill and intangible assets	**17.17**
FRS 9	Associates and joint ventures	
FRS 8	Related party disclosures	
FRS 7	Fair values in acquisition accounting	
FRS 6	Acquisitions and mergers	
FRS 5	Reporting the substance of transactions	**17.18**
FRS 4	Capital instruments	
FRS 3	Reporting financial performance	**17.19, 17.20**
FRS 2	Accounting for subsidiary undertakings	
FRS 1	Cash flow statements	
	Statements of Standard Accounting Practice	
SSAP 25	Segmental reporting	
SSAP 24	Accounting for pension costs	**17.21**

	Financial Reporting Standards	*Commentary*
SSAP 21	Accounting for lease and hire purchase contracts	**17.22**
SSAP 20	*Foreign currency translation* (FRS 23)	
SSAP 19	Accounting for investment properties	**17.23**
SSAP 17	*Accounting for post balance sheet events* (FRS 21)	**17.11**
SSAP 13	Accounting for research and development	**17.17**
SSAP 9	Stocks and long-term contracts	**17.24**
SSAP 4	Accounting for government grants	**17.25**
SSAP 5	Accounting for value added tax	

Notes

Bracketed references show the identical IFRS.

* Effective for accounting periods beginning on or after 1 January 2005—see standard for extent of application.

** Effective for accounting periods beginning on or after 1 January 2007—see standard for extent of application.

*** Effective for accounting periods beginning on or after 6 April 2008—see standard for extent of application.

\+ Effective for accounting periods ending on or after 23 December 2005—see standard for extent of application.

Superseded standards are italicised. Replacement standard is shown in brackets.

INTERNATIONAL GAAP

17.6

	International Financial Reporting Standards	*Commentary*
IFRS 1	First-time adoption of international financial reporting standards	**17.26**
IFRS 2	Share-based payments	
IFRS 3	Business combinations	
IFRS 4	Insurance contracts	
IFRS 5	Non-current assets held for sale and discontinued operations	
IFRS 6	Exploration for and evaluation of mineral assets	
IFRS 7	Financial instruments disclosures	

17.6 *Accounting and taxation*

	International Financial Reporting Standards	Commentary
IFRS 8	Operating segments	
	International Accounting Standards	
IAS 1	Presentation of financial statements	**17.19**
IAS 2	Inventories	**17.24**
IAS 7	Cash flow statements	
IAS 8	Accounting policies, changes in accounting estimates and errors	**17.20**
IAS 10	Events after the balance sheet date	**17.11**
IAS 11	Construction contracts	**17.24**
IAS 12	Income taxes	**17.29, 17.39**
IAS 14	Segment reporting	
IAS 16	Property, plant and equipment	**17.13**
IAS 17	Leases	**17.22**
IAS 18	Revenue	
IAS 19	Employee benefits	**17.21**
IAS 20	Accounting for government grants and disclosure of government assistance	**17.25**
IAS 21	The effects of changes in foreign exchange rates	**17.10**
IAS 23	Borrowing costs	**17.14**
IAS 24	Related party disclosure	
IAS 26	Accounting and reporting by retirement benefit plans	
IAS 27	Consolidated and separate financial statements	
IAS 28	Investments in associates	
IAS 29	Financial reporting in hyperinflationary economies	
IAS 31	Interests in joint ventures	
IAS 32	Financial instruments: presentation	
IAS 33	Earnings per share	
IAS 34	Interim financial reporting	
IAS 36	Impairment of assets	**17.17**
IAS 37	Provisions, contingent liabilities and contingent assets	**17.15**
IAS 38	Intangible assets	**17.17**
IAS 39	Financial instruments: recognition and measurement	**17.9**
IAS 40	Investment property	**17.23**
IAS 41	Agriculture	

INTERACTION OF ACCOUNTING AND TAXATION PRINCIPLES

17.7   Accounting standards deal with accounting treatments. Certain aspects of the accounting treatment may have a direct impact for taxation purposes.

FRSSE

17.8   The FRSSE consolidates and modifies the relevant accounting requirements and disclosures from the other accounting standards and UITF Abstracts for smaller entities and was originally introduced in November 1997. Companies who qualify as 'small' under the *Companies Act* may apply the standard (see **6.20–6.21**). In April 2008 the FRSSE (2008) was introduced to reflect changes in the *Companies Act* and other legislation and accounting standards. A company complying with the FRSSE complies with GAAP.

In February 2007, the International Accounting Standards Board (IASB) published an Exposure Draft (ED) of its proposed International Financial Reporting Standard for Small and Medium-sized Entities (IFRS for SMEs). The IASB is seeking comments to 11 questions to be submitted no later than 1 October 2007.

FRS 26 Financial instruments: measurement and IAS 39 Financial instruments: recognition and measurement

17.9   IAS 39 and FRS 26 require assets and liabilities to be measured at fair value (see **11.9**). Fair value is the amount for which an asset could be exchanged between knowledgeable, willing parties in an arm's-length transaction. An impairment loss of a financial asset should be recognised only when it is incurred. An impairment loss is the amount by which the carrying amount of an asset exceeds its recoverable amount. The Standard provides additional guidance about how to evaluate impairment that is inherent in a group of loans, receivables or held-to-maturity investments that cannot be identified with any individual financial asset in the group. The guidelines state that if an asset is found to be individually impaired it should not be included in a group of assets that are collectively assessed for impairment. A collective assessment of impairment should be based on credit risk, the debtors' ability to pay together with contractual cash flows and historical loss experience. Historical loss rates should be adjusted to reflect current economic conditions. The impairment review procedures should ensure that the loss is not recognised on the initial recognition of an asset (IAS 39 Introduction).

FRS 23 The effects of changes in foreign exchange rates and IAS 21 Currency accounting

17.10 Under IAS 21 and FRS 23 income and expenditure of foreign operations (including branches) are translated at actual or average rates (not at closing or average rates).

FA 1993, s 92D requires that foreign currency be converted at the average exchange rate for the current accounting period of the appropriate spot rate of exchange for the transaction in question.

For accounting periods beginning on or after 1 January 2005, accounts for taxation purposes must be prepared in sterling (*FA 1993, s 92*). If a UK resident company prepares accounts in a currency other than sterling, for corporation tax purposes the accounts must be computed for GAAP in sterling (*FA 1993, s 92A*). If a UK resident company prepares accounts in a currency other than sterling, but then uses another non-sterling currency as its functional currency, that functional currency is used for preparing accounts according to GAAP. The resulting profits or loss are then converted to sterling (*FA 1993, s 92B*). Similar rules apply if a UK resident company prepares accounts in a currency other than sterling and neither *s 92A* nor *s 92B* applies, or if a non-resident company prepares its accounts in a non-sterling currency. The accounts currency is used for preparing accounts according to GAAP. The resulting profits or loss are then converted to sterling (*FA 1993, s 92C*).

FRS 21 (IAS 10) Events after the balance sheet date and SSAP 17 Accounting for post balance sheet events

17.11 FRS 21 specifies the accounting treatment to be adopted (including the disclosures to be provided) by entities for events occurring between the balance sheet date and the date when the financial statements are authorised for issue. It replaces SSAP 17 Accounting for post balance sheet events.

FRS 21 sets out the recognition and measurement requirements for two types of event after the balance sheet date:

- **Adjusting events**. Those events that provide evidence of conditions that existed at the balance sheet date for which the entity shall adjust the amounts recognised in its financial statements or recognise items that were not previously recognised (adjusting events). For example, the settlement of a court case that confirms the entity had a present obligation at the balance sheet date.

- **Non-adjusting events**. Those events that are indicative of conditions that arose after the balance sheet date for which the entity does not adjust the amounts recognised in its financial statements. For example, a decline in market value of investments between the balance sheet date and the date when the financial statements are authorised for issue.

Dividends declared after the balance sheet date should no longer be reported as liabilities. The FRS removes the requirement to report dividends proposed after the balance sheet date in the profit and loss account and instead requires disclosures in the notes to the financial statements.

The FRS sets out other disclosure requirements. These include:

- the disclosure of the date when the financial statements were authorised for issue;

- the disclosure of information received about conditions that existed at the balance sheet date; and

- if non-adjusting events after the balance sheet date are material and non-disclosure could influence the economic decisions of users, the entity should disclose the nature of the event and an estimate of its financial effect, or a statement that such an estimate cannot be made.

The FRS also requires that an entity shall not prepare its financial statements on a going concern basis if management determines after the balance sheet date that it intends to liquidate the entity or to cease trading or that it has no realistic alternative but to do so (see Chapter 19).

When SSAP 17 (Accounting for post balance sheet events) applied HMRC found that companies paid insufficient or no attention to adjusting post balance sheet events as regards stock obsolescence provisions, impairment provisions (where the debts are recovered in full) and provisions for claims against an entity that were settled for less in the post balance sheet period (Working Together, Issue 11, June 2003).

FRS 18 Accounting policies

17.12 HMRC have commented that in some cases work completed before the year end has been invoiced after the year end but not correctly accounted for (FRS 18, para 26; Working Together, Issue 11, June 2003).

FRS 15 Tangible fixed assets and IAS 16 Property, plant and equipment

17.13 For taxation purposes the distinction between capital and revenue expenditure is maintained. Revenue deductions will follow the timing of recognition in the accounts. FRS 15 provides principles for measurement, valuation and depreciation of fixed assets that are not recognised for taxation purposes (HMRC Business Income Manual BIM 31060).

FRS 15 permits renewals accounting (FRS 15, para 97) on infrastructure assets only in specified circumstances; that is, where the infrastructure is treated as a single system, is maintained by continuing replacement of parts according to a projected asset management plan (AMP) calculated by a qualified and independent person. The system or network has to be in a mature or steady state. Under renewals accounting, the estimated level of expenditure required to maintain the operating capacity (over the AMP period) is treated as depreciation and is charged to the profit and loss account. Actual maintenance expenditure is capitalised. There is no direct link between the actual expenditure in any one year and the amount charged to the profit and loss account. Renewals accounting provides a mechanism to smooth the profile of maintenance expenditure (HMRC Business Income Manual BIM 31065).

FRS 15 renewals accounting is not specifically permitted under IAS 16. If a company adopts IAS 16 there may be a change of accounting policy adjustment (*FA 2002, s 64*; HMRC International Accounting Standards—the UK Tax Implications, July 2006).

FRS 15 Tangible fixed assets and IAS 23 Borrowing costs

17.14   IAS 23 and FRS 15 permit the capitalisation of borrowing costs. UK tax law departs from FRS 15 by allowing relief for capitalised borrowing costs as if they were a profit and loss account item but only where they relate to a fixed asset or project (*FA 1996, Sch 9, para 14*). The same approach will continue where IAS 23 is followed (HMRC International Accounting Standards—the UK Tax Implications, July 2006).

FRS 12 Provisions, contingent liabilities and contingent assets and IAS 37 Provisions, contingent liabilities and contingent assets

17.15   There is no significant difference between IAS 37 and FRS 12, which is followed for tax purposes (subject to adjustment where the expenditure is capital for tax purposes or otherwise disallowable).

Under FRS 12 provisions must satisfy the definition of liabilities: 'obligations of an entity to transfer economic benefits as a result of past transactions or events'. Mere anticipation of future expenditure, however probable and no matter how detailed the estimates, is not enough, in the absence of an obligation at the balance sheet date. Provisions are defined by FRS 12 as 'liabilities of uncertain timing or amount' (HMRC Business Income Manual BIM 46515).

Under FRS 12 a provision should be recognised when:

- an entity has a present obligation (legal or constructive) as a result of a past event;

- it is probable that a transfer of economic benefits will be required to settle the obligation; and

- a reliable estimate can be made of the amount of the obligation.

If these conditions are not met, no provision should be recognised.

FRS 12 does not apply to trade creditors, accruals, adjustments to the carrying value of assets, insurance company provisions arising from contracts with policy holders, provisions that are specifically addressed by other accounting standards, such as losses on long-term contracts (SSAP 9), provisions relating to leases (SSAP 21) other than operating leases that have become onerous and pension costs (SSAP 24).

Trade creditors are understood to be liabilities to pay for formally invoiced received goods or services. Accruals are understood to be liabilities to pay for received goods or services, not yet formally invoiced.

HMRC have commented that because of the changes brought about by FRS 12 (effective for accounting periods ending on or after 23 March 1999), the following provisions are no longer allowable for tax purposes:

- provisions for 'future operating losses' that is, losses that will or may arise from obligations entered into subsequent to the balance sheet date;

- restructuring provisions until the business has a 'detailed formal plan' for restructuring and has created a 'valid expectation' in those affected that it will carry it out;

- provisions where the only event that might require them is an unpublished decision of the directors;

- provisions for future expenditure required by legislation where the business could avoid the obligation by changing its method of operation, for example, by stopping doing whatever is affected by the legislation;

- provisions for future repairs of plant and machinery owned by the business (HMRC Business Income Manual BIM 46535).

HMRC have commented that the following provisions will be allowable:

- in the period of sale for the cost of work under a warranty which a trader gives on the sale of merchandise (or under consumer protection legislation);

- for commission refundable by an insurance intermediary on the lapse of a policy where the commission is recognised as income at the inception of the policy;

- by builders for rectification work, including retentions up to the level that these have been recognised as income within accounts (HMRC Business Income Manual BIM 46545).

FRS 12 Provisions, contingent liabilities and contingent assets

17.16 If HMRC wish to challenge a provision they will firstly ascertain whether it accords with GAAP and then possibly look into the accuracy of the provision. Under FRS 12 a provision should only be recognised if a company has a present obligation as a result of a past event, it is probable that a transfer of economic benefits will be required to settle the obligation, and reliable estimate can be made of the amount. HMRC comment that when enquiring into company accounting matters they have found problems with refurbishment expenditure, onerous contracts and the debtor's ability to pay when applying this standard.

Major refurbishment expenditure should only be provided for if it is in excess of normal repairs and maintenance expenditure. For example, if the lining of a furnace needs to be replaced every five years and at the balance sheet date has been in use for three years, there is no present obligation to make a provision. Similarly, no annual provision is required in the accounts of an airline that is required to overhaul its aircraft once in every three years, the cost being expended when incurred (FRS 12, para 19 and example 11).

In contrast, provisions should be made for onerous contracts, but only those that are truly onerous. When providing for onerous leases, for example, the expected rental income or surrender or sale of the lease should be taken into account (FRS 12, para 73). If the facts show that there is no real likelihood of having to pay, for example where the creditor company has already been wound up and the liquidator has decided not to pursue the debt, then practically speaking, no provision is required (FRS 12, para 23). Finally, provisions have been made to 'smooth profits' rather than to comply with FRS 12, para 14 (Working Together, Issue 13, June 2003).

With effect from 2 January 2007, producers of electrical and electronic equipment are responsible for financing waste management costs. These costs will include the costs of collection, treatment, reuse, recovery and environmentally sound disposal (*SI 2005/3289*). UITF Abstract 45 (IFIRC Interpretation 6)

Liabilities arising from Participating in a Specific Market—Waste Electrical and Electronic Equipment implements FRS 12 and IAS 17 principles in providing for these costs.

FRS 10 Goodwill and intangibles; SSAP 13 Accounting for research and development; IAS 38 Intangible assets and IAS 36 Impairment

17.17   IAS 38 does not permit goodwill amortisation. Under IFRS 1 a company has the option of keeping goodwill at the amortised cost at the date of the opening comparative balance sheet in a company's first IAS accounts, and only impairing from that basis figure. *FA 2002, Sch 29, paras 116A, 116B* ensure that any write up on the transition from UK GAAP to IAS will be a taxable credit for *Sch 29*, and *para 116F* ensures that any such credit is limited to the net amount of relief already given. Any impairment from written up cost will be deductible.

IAS 38 requires the capitalisation of development expenditure in R&D. *FA 2004, s 53* nevertheless permits a revenue deduction.

IAS 38 requires website costs, when capitalised, to be treated as an intangible asset.

Where website costs have been the subject of capital allowance claims, but are reclassified as intangible fixed assets under IAS 38, *FA 2002, Sch 29, para 73A* disapplies the intangibles rules so that capital allowances may continue. If intangible asset costs have been written off to the profit and loss account and are then brought into the balance sheet under IAS 38 as an asset there will be an intangibles credit and possibly an adjustment under *FA 2002, s 64*. Rules for the transition from UK GAAP to IAS are within *FA 2002, Sch 29, paras 116A–116H*. See **5.19** and **6.15**.

FRS 5 Reporting the substance of transactions

17.18   In general, the reporting of revenue in accounts is followed for tax purposes. There is no general standard for revenue recognition in UK GAAP, but the recently added Application Note G to FRS 5 goes some way to dealing with certain aspects of IAS 18. In March 2005 the UITF of the ASB issued UITF Abstract 40 (Revenue recognition and service contracts) to provide further guidance on Note G. *FA 2005, Sch 15* permits a spreading adjustment (see **5.41**).

FRS 3 Reporting financial performance and IAS 1 Presentation of financial statements

17.19 UK tax law uses the balance on a profit and loss account as the starting point for Schedule D Case I basis computations (including Schedule A, overseas property, Schedule D Case V trades; *FA 1998, s 42* non-trading income from loan relationships, derivative contracts and intangibles). Amounts are recognised when they are included in the profit and loss account or in the statement of recognised gains and losses or the IAS equivalent statement of changes in equity or other statement used for calculating the company's profit (*FA 1996, s 85B*; HMRC International Accounting Standards—the UK Tax Implications, July 2006).

FRS 3 Reporting financial performance and IAS 8 Accounting policies, changes in accounting estimates and errors

17.20 Prior period accounting adjustments are brought into the Schedule D Case I computation, in the year of change (*FA 2002, s 64, Sch 22*). A change in valuation from a realisation basis to a market to market basis (possibly occurring in a financial trade) may be spread over six years (*FA 2002, Sch 22, paras 8, 9*). Where amounts have been allowed as a deduction on an old basis they will not be allowed again on a new basis (*FA 2002, Sch 22, para 6*).

FA 2002, s 64 does not apply to fundamental errors. In such cases prior periods must be restated. This is effected by an amendment to the corporation tax return (see **2.9**).

SSAP 24 Accounting for pension costs; FRS 17 Retirement benefits; and IAS 19 Employee benefits

17.21 The accounts figures for contributions to and changes in value of pension schemes are irrelevant for tax purposes. Relief is given on a paid (and sometimes deferred basis). For pension scheme contributions see **5.31– 5.32**. See **5.26– 5.30** for non-pension employee benefits (HMRC International Accounting Standards—the UK Tax Implications, July 2006).

SSAP 21 Accounting for lease and hire purchase contracts and IAS 17 Leases

17.22 UK tax law is not entirely consistent with SSAP 21 (see **6.38**). IAS 17 is drawn up along similar lines to SSAP 21.

SSAP 19 Accounting for investment properties and IAS 40 Investment property

17.23　The accounts treatment of investment properties is generally irrelevant for tax, as the capital gains rules apply. There may be cases where a property developer uses land for investment purposes before sale, and in such cases IAS 40 may apply. If the company adopts the fair value basis, a transitional adjustment may arise falling within *FA 2002, s 64*.

Where a company elects to treat an interest in a property held, which it holds as a lessee under an operating lease, as an investment property it is required to account for it as a finance lease. Where this happens the tax rules applying to finance leases will apply (HMRC International Accounting Standards—the UK Tax Implications, July 2006).

SSAP 9 Stocks and long-term contracts; IAS 2 Inventories; and IAS 11 Construction contracts

17.24　SSAP 9 is followed for tax purposes. If a trade ceases, the stock is valued at market value. If the stock is transferred to an unconnected party for the purposes of their trade, stock is valued at the consideration given. If stock is sold to a connected party, it is valued at an arm's-length value (*ICTA 1988, s 100*). If stock is taken for a participator's own use, it is valued at selling price (*Sharkey v Wernher* (1955) 36 TC 275, [1956] AC 58, [1955] 3 All ER 493). See **5.43**.

HMRC comment that they have found problems with aspects of SSAP 9.

In particular they have found that where companies have made stock provisions they have not been supported by the facts of the case. Long-term contracts are not always identified and accounted for as such (SSAP 9, para 22). Companies have sometimes valued stock and work in progress at net realisable value on the theoretical basis that it would have to be sold as an emergency sale in its current condition, rather than being sold in the normal course of business (SSAP 9, Appendix 1, paras 19, 20; Working Together, Issue 11, June 2003).

HMRC comment that they see no difference between SSAP 9, IAS 2 and IAS 11 except that they do not recognise the IAS 2 LIFO (last in first out) stock valuation method (HMRC International Accounting Standards—the UK Tax Implications, July 2006).

SSAP 4 Accounting for government grants and IAS 20 Government grants

17.25　For both taxation and accounting purposes grants are treated as income (HMRC International Accounting Standards—the UK Tax Implications, July 2006).

IFRS 1 First time adoption of international financial reporting standards

17.26 Differences between the previous GAAP and the current IFRS treatment are recognised in the opening comparative balance sheet thus enabling any adjustments to be made under *FA 2002, s 64*.

ACCOUNTING FOR TAX

17.27 Tax is represented in the accounts in both the profit and loss account and the balance sheet. The two types of tax to be shown are current year tax and deferred tax.

FRS 16 Current tax

17.28 Current tax is the estimated tax charge payable based on the taxable profits for the company for the year. Current tax is measured using the tax rates and laws applicable at the balance sheet date.

Dividends received from UK companies are reported as the net amount received. Dividends received from other countries are reported gross only to the extent that they have suffered a withholding tax. Interest received or receivable is shown gross of withholding tax.

Current tax for the period must be recognised in the profit and loss account except to the extent that it relates to gains or losses that have been recognised directly in the statement of total recognised gains and losses. Such tax should also be recognised in the statement of total recognised gains and losses (STRGL).

The profits per the accounts are usually different from the profits chargeable to corporation tax. This is because the nature of the accounts is to attain a profit that incorporates all the expenses and income that have been charged and received as true business expenses and income and incurred during the accounting period, irrelevant of whether payment has actually been made or not. Taxable profits on the other hand have disallowable expenses and income, which must be added back or removed from the profit. In instances where there are timing differences between the accounting profits and the taxable profits an adjustment is made for deferred tax (see **17.31**).

For accounts purposes, the current year's tax provision is disclosed as a current liability, together with a disclosure note. The format of the note is as follows:

Illustration of profit and loss account disclosure

	£000	£000
UK Corporation tax		
Current tax on income for the period	a	
Adjustments in respect of prior periods	b	
	C	
Double taxation relief	(d)	
		E
Foreign tax		
Current tax on income for the period	f	
Adjustments in respect of prior periods	g	
		H
Tax on profit in ordinary activities		I

If an item of tax relates to an item in the statement of total recognised gains and losses, where the tax is also recognised there, then it should not be recognised in the profit and loss account per FRS 16. This includes gains on disposals of fixed assets previously revalued and differences on foreign currencies. The format for the STRGL as per FRS 3 is set out below:

Statement of total recognised gains and losses for the year

	£000
Profit for the financial year (per the profit and loss account)	X
Items taken directly to reserves:	
Unrealised surplus on revaluation of fixed assets	X
Surplus/deficit on revaluation of investment principles	X
Foreign currency exchange differences	X
Total recognised gains and losses for the year	X
Prior period adjustments	(x)
Total gains and losses recognised since last annual report	X

IAS 12 Income taxes

17.29   IAS 12 is drawn up along similar lines with the following notable differences. IAS 12 requires current tax to be shown separately on the face of the balance sheet. FRS 16 has no such requirement. IAS 12 also requires items to be charged to equity if they relate to equity. FRS 16 does not have this requirement. IAS 12 also requires disclosure of the tax expense relating to discontinued operations. FRS 16 does not require this. IAS 12 has no requirement as to the presentation of outgoing or incoming dividends.

FRS 19 Deferred tax

FRS 19's objective

17.30 Deferred tax is sometimes considered more of an accounting issue as opposed to a tax issue. This is largely due to the nature of deferred tax and what it intends to cover. Income and expenditure are often recognised in the accounts at different times to when they are necessarily taxable or relievable. FRS 19 prescribes timing different accounts adjustments to enable the accounts to show a true and fair view.

The overall objective of FRS 19 is to require 'full provision to be made for deferred tax assets and liabilities arising from timing differences between the recognition of gains and losses in the financial statements and their recognition in a tax computation' (FRS 19 Summary).

Deferred tax should be recognised as a liability or asset if the transactions or events that give the entity an obligation to pay more tax in future or a right to pay less tax in future have occurred by the balance sheet date.

Deferred tax should be recognised on most types of timing difference, including those attributable to:

- accelerated capital allowances;
- accruals for pension costs and other post retirement benefits that will be deductible for tax purposes only when paid;
- elimination of unrealised intra-group profits on consolidation;
- unrelieved tax losses;
- other sources of short-term timing differences.

FRS 19 prohibits the recognition of deferred tax on timing differences arising when:

- a fixed asset is revalued without there being any commitment to sell the asset;
- the gain on sale of an asset is rolled over into replacement assets;
- the remittance of a subsidiary, associate or joint venture's earnings would cause tax to be payable, but no commitment has been made to the remittance of the earnings.

As an exception to the general requirement not to recognise deferred tax on revaluation gains and losses, the FRS requires deferred tax to be recognised when assets are continuously revalued to fair value, with changes in fair value being recognised in the profit and loss account.

There is also the requirement that deferred tax assets are to be recognised to the extent that they are regarded as more likely than not that they will be recovered.

Calculation of deferred tax

Fixed assets

17.31   FRS 19 deals with the depreciation, disposal and revaluation aspects of fixed assets.

The depreciation charge within the accounts is likely to differ to the capital allowances granted for tax purposes. The difference is usually removed when the asset is sold, however, whilst the asset is still owned by the company, the difference in depreciation of the asset can result in timing differences and thus the asset will have a differing value to that of the accounts and as recognised in the accounts. Thus, an adjustment will be made to reflect the timing differences within the accounts. When the asset is sold, an adjustment will be made in the tax computation reversing the excess capital allowances previously given.

The timing differences for accelerated capital allowances for an asset bought in 2006 for £5,000 with a depreciation charge of 25% straight line and sold at the end of 2008 can be shown thus:

Year	2006	2007	2008
	£	£	£
Depreciation charge	1,250	1,250	1,250
Capital allowances	2,000	750	563
Timing differences	750	(750)	(687)

The cumulative timing difference at 31 December 2008 is (£687). The cumulative timing difference at 31 December 2007 is nil being £750 at 31 December 2006 and £(750) at 31 December 2007.

Deferred tax should not be recognised on timing differences arising where fixed assets are revalued or sold unless by the balance sheet date the reporting entity has entered into a binding agreement to sell the revalued asset and has recognised the gains and losses expected to arise on sale. There is an exception to this rule, however, in that if the asset is to be replaced and roll-over relief is obtained or expected to be obtained then no deferred tax should be recognised. Even if the gain from the sale of the asset is to be rolled over for use in replacement assets, as long as no roll-over relief is obtained or expected to be obtained then an adjustment for deferred tax should be made.

Pension costs

17.32   Another element of deferred tax where an adjustment may need to be made is with pension liabilities. The FRS describes the use of deferred tax here as when the liabilities are 'accrued in the financial statements but are allowed for tax purposes only when paid or contributed at a later date'. Pension costs are only allowable in a tax computation for the period in which they are paid. Thus, where they have not been paid in the accounts, but are shown in the profit and loss account in the accounts, then an adjustment for the deferred tax will be made as it relates to a timing difference between expenses in an accounting period and in a tax period.

Tax losses

17.33   Timing differences may occur with unrelieved tax losses leading to a tax reduction or refund. If, however, they are used against future profits a deferred tax asset may arise as per FRS 19 a timing difference can arise if a tax loss is not relieved against past or present taxable profits but can be carried forward to reduce future taxable profits.

Unremitted earnings of subsidiaries, associates and joint ventures

17.34   As regards the unremitted earnings of subsidiaries, associates and joint ventures FRS 19 states that tax that could be payable (taking account of any double taxation relief) on any future remittance of the past earnings of a subsidiary, associate or joint venture should be provided for in certain circumstances. These are only to the extent that, at the balance sheet date, dividends have been accrued as receivable or a binding agreement to distribute the past earnings in the future has been entered into by the subsidiary, associate or joint venture. This again refers to timing differences between the accounting and tax periods, as all earnings by the parent or related company are either accrued or past profits.

Full provision liability method

17.35   FRS 19 adopts the full provision liability method as opposed to the partial provision deferral method. Full provision rationale records the tax effect of all gains and losses in the accounts in full. Partial provision provides for tax liabilities that are expected to arise.

The deferral method provides for deferred tax at the rate of taxation in use when the differences occur. No adjustment is made if the rates subsequently change. If the timing differences reverse, the tax is calculated again at the rate in force when the differences first arose. The liability method provides for deferred tax at the rate that is expected to apply when the timing differences reverse. This method is considered to more accurately reflect the amount of tax that is expected to be paid.

Discounting

17.36 FRS 19 permits but does not require a company to discount its deferred tax assets and liabilities to reflect the time value of money. The discount period being the number of years between the balance sheet dates and the date on which it is estimated that the underlying timing differences will reverse (FRS 19, para 47). The discount rates prescribed are the post-tax yields to maturity that could be obtained at the balance sheet date on government bonds with maturity dates and in currencies similar to those of the deferred tax assets or liabilities (FRS 19, para 52).

Recognition of deferred tax assets

17.37 Deferred tax assets should be recognised to the extent that they are regarded as recoverable. This judgment should be made from all available evidence (FRS 19, para 23). Deferred tax should only be recognised if it is likely that the company has sufficient taxable profit to cover any future reversal of the underlying timing differences. In making this assessment the company should also consider its tax planning opportunities.

Accounts presentation

17.38 FRS 19 requires that deferred tax be recognised in the profit and loss account for the period, except to the extent that it is attributable to a gain or loss that is or has been recognised directly in the statement of total recognised gains and losses.

Within the profit and loss account the charge for the period should be included under the heading *Tax on profit or loss on ordinary activities*. The deferred tax balance will be shown separately in the balance sheet within either *Provisions for liabilities and charges* if the balance is a net deferred tax liability or within *Debtor*s should the balance be a net deferred tax asset.

The deferred tax debit and credit balance should only be offset within the debtor and creditors if they relate to taxes levied by the same tax authority and arise in the same taxable entry or in a group of taxable entries where the tax losses of one entity can reduce the taxable profits of another meaning that the liabilities have to match in time period and transaction and so be offset without confusion in the accounts.

The accounts must also show within the balance sheet the total deferred tax balance showing the amount recognised for each significant type of timing difference separately showing the impact of discounting on, and the discounted amount of, the deferred tax balance and the movement between the opening and closing net deferred tax balance analysing separately:

- the amount charged or credited in the profit and loss account for the period;

- the amount charged or credited directly in the statement of total recognised gains and losses for the period; and

- movements arising from the acquisition or disposal of businesses.

The deferred tax will also need to be shown in a disclosure note showing the different elements as per the example below.

Example 17.1

Taxation on profit on ordinary activities

(a) Analysis of charge in the period

	£000	£000
Current tax		
UK corporation tax on profits of the period	40	
Adjustments in respect of previous periods	10	
Total current tax		50
Deferred tax		
Origination and reversal of timing differences	27	
Adjustments in respect of previous periods		
Total deferred tax		27
Total tax charge		77

(b) Factors affecting the tax charge for the period

The difference between the tax charge based on applying the UK corporation tax rates to the reported profit before taxation to the actual current tax charge is reconciled below.

	£000
Profit on ordinary activities before taxation	536
Profit on ordinary activities before taxation multiplied by the standard rate of corporation tax in the UK of 28%	150
Effects of:	
Expenses not deductible for tax purposes	30
Capital allowances (more than) less than depreciation	(60)
Utilisation of tax losses	(80)
Current tax charge for the period	40

(c) Factors that may affect future tax charges

Based on current capital investment plans, the company expects to be able to continue to claim capital allowances in excess of depreciation in future years but at a slightly lower level than in the current year. The company has tax losses that have not been recognised due to the uncertainty over their availability. If they become available they will reduce the future tax charge.

Provisions for deferred tax

(a) Deferred tax liability/(asset) provided in the accounts comprises:

	£000
Accelerated capital allowances	140
Tax losses	(60)
Other short-term timing differences	(1)
	(79)

(b) Deferred tax liability/(asset) not provided in the accounts comprises:

	£000
Chargeable gains subject to roll-over relief	70
Tax losses	(20)
Other short-term timing differences	(1)
	49

The potential deferred tax asset has not been recognised in the accounts because it is unlikely that the losses will be utilised in the foreseeable future.

(c) Analysis of movement in the period

	£000
Deferred tax asset at 1 April 2008	(106)
Deferred tax charge in the profit and loss account	27
Deferred tax asset at 31 March 2009	(79)

Deferred tax has been calculated at 28% (2008– 30%) being the prevailing rate of UK corporation tax rate at 31 March 2009.

As can be seen FRS 19 provides in-depth analysis to assist account users in comprehending the effects of the overall tax charge. There are significant differences between FRS 19 and IAS 12 that are summarised below.

IAS 12 Income tax

17.39 IAS 12 (Income tax) deals with deferred taxation. It is drawn up on similar lines except that provisions are required in the following circumstances:

- on a revaluation of a non-monetary asset whether or not it is intended that the asset will be sold and whether or not roll-over relief could be claimed;

- on a sale of assets where the gain has been or might be rolled over into replacement assets;

- where adjustments recognise assets and liabilities at their fair values on the acquisition of a business;

- on the unremitted earnings of subsidiaries, associates and joint ventures;

- on exchange differences on consolidation of non-monetary assets;

- on unrealised intra-group profits eliminated on consolidation, provision is required on the temporary difference rather than on the timing difference of the profit that has been taxed but not recognised in the consolidated financial statements.

Chapter 18

Avoidance

INTRODUCTION

Tax mitigation, tax avoidance and tax evasion

18.1   Tax mitigation, tax avoidance and tax evasion are often referred to in common parlance. Their understanding over the years has been developed by case law principles. Tax mitigation is understood to mean making full use of the tax relieving provisions as intended by the legislation. Tax avoidance is understood to mean legally utilising the tax regime to one's own advantage, but not necessarily with the intention with which it was drafted, in order to minimise the amount of tax payable. Tax evasion in contrast is the deceit to purposefully evade the payment of taxes by misrepresentation or other dishonest means. Tax evasion is a crime punishable by penalties and fines and/or imprisonment for the taxpayer and adviser.

Case law

18.2   The UK has a developed economy and a sophisticated taxation system. The law is constantly updated to meet the changing times and the nation's needs. Legal drafting of taxation statutes over the years unknowingly created situations whereby taxpayers used legislation to their advantage rather than the purpose for which the legislation was introduced in the first place. Taxpayers were able to make use of the form of the legislation rather than its substance. This was confirmed in *Duke of Westminster v CIR* (1935) 19 TC 490 where Lord Tomlin commented 'every man is entitled if he can to order his affairs so that the tax attaching under the appropriate Acts is less than it otherwise be'. Such a comment shows no distinction between tax avoidance and tax mitigation and overall the courts from that time seemed to have shown a neutral approach.

However, times moved on. Tax legislation and economies became more complex and the courts showed hostility to contrived tax avoidance schemes. In 1981 the case of *WT Ramsay Ltd v CIR* (1981) TC 101, [1981] STC 174 reached the House of Lords. The case involved a series of transactions whose purpose was to avoid tax. The judgment went against the taxpayer and was based on reviewing all the transactions as a whole. Looking behind these transactions, it was found that there was no commercial justification for them whatsoever. This approach was upheld in *Furniss v Dawson* (1984) 55 TC 324, [1984] STC 153 and *Craven v White* (1988) 62 TC 1, [1988] STC 476.

In the meantime the case of *New Zealand Commr of Inland Revenue v Challenge Corpn Ltd* [1986] STC 548 recognised the distinction between tax avoidance and tax mitigation. Lord Templeman stated that tax mitigation occurs 'where the taxpayer obtains a tax advantage by reducing his income or incurring expenditure in circumstances in which the taxing statute affords a reduction in tax liability'. Tax avoidance occurs 'when the taxpayer reduces his liability to tax without involving him in the loss or expenditure which entitles him to that reduction. The taxpayer engaged in tax avoidance does not reduce his income or suffer a loss or incur expenditure but nevertheless obtains a reduction in his liability to tax as if he had'.

The view was supported by Lord Nolan in *CIR v Willoughby* (1997) 70 TC 57, [1997] STC 995. Lord Nolan described tax mitigation as 'the acceptance of an offer of freedom of tax which Parliament had deliberately made' and tax avoidance as 'a course of action designed to conflict with or defeat the evident intention of Parliament'.

The tax avoidance motive was challenged in *Ensign Tankers (Leasing) Ltd v Stokes* (1992) 64 TC 617, [1992] STC 226 and in *Pigott v Staines Investments Ltd* (1995) 68 TC 342, [1995] STC 114. Both cases were decided in favour of the taxpayer. The first because, although a taxpayer invested in a project for its tax saving advantages, the project's activities involved a true trading motive. The second failed because the courts looking into the facts considered that a normal commercial transaction could not be treated as an abnormal transaction.

The *Ramsay* approach continues to be applied by the courts. In *Mason v Barclays Mercantile Business Finance Ltd* [2004] UKHL 51, (2004) 76 TC 446, [2005] STC 1, [2005] 1 All ER 97 the company entered into a normal trading transaction, this was associated with an abnormal transaction but the facts turned in favour of the taxpayer. In *Inland Revenue Commissioners v Scottish Provident Institution* [2004] UKHL 52, (2004) 76 TC 538, [2005] STC 15, when a complicated set of transactions was treated as a composite transaction with no commercial purpose, the taxpayer lost. The taxpayer lost again in *EDI Services Ltd v HMRC* (2005) SpC 515 when paying employee bonuses in gold coins to avoid Class 1 NIC showed a tax avoidance intention.

Tax evasion remains a crime. HMRC is responsible for investigating suspected criminal activity across the whole range of its responsibilities throughout the UK, including investigating tax fraud and tax credit fraud involving organised crime. Its investigatory powers have been extended by the *Police and Criminal Evidence Act 1984, s 114* (*FA 2007, s 82*).

In order to investigate tax crime, HMRC currently has powers to apply for production orders for search warrants and to make arrests. HMRC have sought to extend these powers to include the power to take fingerprints, to charge or bail suspects and to search persons as well as premises. HMRC also has more specialised powers used to protect frontiers, powers under the *Proceeds of Crime Act 2002* and various surveillance powers.

UK ANTI-AVOIDANCE LEGISLATION

UK approach to anti-avoidance

18.3   Once known, a 'tax avoidance' scheme or method is swiftly removed by legislation. This of course begs the question that if a type of transaction has been entered into previously by other parties and not removed by legislation, is that transaction being indirectly approved as genuine mitigation?

The UK has no general anti-avoidance rule (GAAR). Instead, there are anti-avoidance clauses within the legislation and since 18 March 2004 there has been formal disclosure of tax avoidance schemes.

EXISTING CORPORATION TAX AVOIDANCE LEGISLATION

Income and Corporation Taxes Act 1988

18.4   The main corporation tax avoidance legislation is contained in *ICTA 1988, Pt XVII*. *Chapter I* refers to tax advantages from certain transactions in securities. It will be invoked if the transaction in securities was entered into to gain a tax advantage and not as a bona fide commercial transaction. This could result in a Schedule D Case VI assessment. *Chapters II* and *III* deal with income tax. *Chapter IV* deals with controlled foreign companies, which is discussed in this book (see **13.28–13.46**). *Chapter V* applies to collective investment schemes.

Chapter VI deals with miscellaneous matters. The sections applicable to corporation tax and where they are discussed in this book are detailed as follows:

ICTA 1988	Section	Commentary
ss 765–767	Migration of companies	**13.12**
ss 767A-769	Change in ownership	**15.12**
ss 770A-774	Transactions between associated persons	**14.1–14.29,12.14**

Clearances

18.5   HMRC offer a statutory and a non-statutory clearance service. HMRC aim to respond to a request within 28 days of application. A non-statutory clearance is written confirmation of HMRC's view of tax law. A statutory clearance is provided for by statute and covers the areas listed below:

:•   *ICTA 1988, s 215* (demergers);

•   *ICTA 1988, s 225* (purchase of own shares);

•   *ICTA 1988, s 707* (transactions in securities);

•   *TCGA 1992, s 138(1)* (share exchanges);

•   *TCGA 1992, s 139* (reconstructions involving the transfer of a business);

•   *TCGA 1992, s 140B* (transfer of a UK trade between EU member states);

•   *TCGA 1992, s 140D* (transfer of non-UK trade between EU member states); and

•   *FA 2002, Sch 29, para 88* (intangible fixed assets).

The application should be sent to:

Clearance & Counteraction Team
Anti-Avoidance Group
First Floor
22 Kingsway
London
WC2B 6NR
Tel: 020 7438 7474
Fax: 020 7438 4409
Email: reconstructions@hmrc.gsi.gov.uk

FA 1988, s 130(2)(a) (company migrations)

Hazel Ford
International CT & VAT
03/64/01, 3rd Floor
100 Parliament Street
London SW1A 2BQ
Tel: 020 7147 2689
Fax: 020 7147 2649

Upon making the clearance application, full facts must be given to HMRC of the applicant, the transaction, the commercial background and the legal points. HMRC have provided a checklist for non-statutory clearances, which may be pre- or post-transaction. See HMRC Clearance service for businesses – how to get certainty on significant business tax issues.

DISCLOSURE OF TAX AVOIDANCE SCHEMES

HMRC strategy

18.6 *FA 2004, ss 307–319* introduced procedures for the disclosure of tax avoidance schemes with effect from 18 March 2004. HMRC are determined to crack down on those who use the system to their advantage. Their strategy in this matter is as follows:

- To discourage taxpayers from using schemes. This includes a critical appraisal of all new legislation to reduce the potential for tax avoidance as well as publicising successes in closing down avoidance schemes.

- To identify as early as possible schemes that are being used.

- To challenge avoidance schemes by contesting returns and, where necessary, pursuing the matter through the courts.

- To produce legislative changes that will close down avoidance schemes where litigation is not appropriate or where the amount of tax at stake is particularly large.

On tax avoidance schemes Dawn Primarolo has commented:

'HMRC has not prosecuted any accountancy firm for selling aggressive tax avoidance schemes; selling an avoidance scheme would not normally involve activity that amounts to a criminal offence' (*House of Lords Hansard col 1428 W 28 June 2005*).

However, with the proposed introduction of extended criminal investigatory powers (see **18.2**) practitioners and taxpayers must remain ever vigilant.

When first introduced in 2004, the disclosure rules only applied to employment and financial products. This has resulted in a number of tax avoidance methods being legislated against in *FA 2006, s 76, Sch 6*.

From 1 August 2006 the disclosure rules have been widened to include corporation tax together with income tax, capital gains tax and stamp duty land tax. The *Tax Avoidance Schemes (Prescribed Descriptions of Arrangements) Regulations 2006, SI 2006/1543* came into force on 1 August 2006 to replace the *Tax Avoidance Schemes (Prescribed Descriptions of Arrangements) Regulations 2004, SI 2004/1863* regarding notification to HMRC of any tax avoidance scheme (*FA 2004, ss 306–319*). The *Tax Avoidance Schemes (Information)*

Regulations 2004, SI 2004/1864 (as amended by *SI 2004/2613, SI 2005/1869* and *SI 2006/1544*) and the *Tax Avoidance Schemes* (*Promoters and Prescribed Circumstances*) *Regulations 2004, SI 2004/1865* (as amended by *SI 2004/2613*) are still currently in force.

NOTIFICATION

18.7   A notifiable arrangement is anything which obtains a tax advantage. Persons who are responsible for the design of such arrangements or who make the arrangement notifiable for implementation by other persons could be promoters.

A promoter is required to notify HMRC of the scheme within five days of it becoming available. Form AAG 1 (notification of scheme by promoter) is used for this purpose. The user may be required to notify HMRC if the promoter is based outside the UK, an adviser has legal privilege or there is no promoter. Form AAG 2 (notification of scheme by user where the promoter is off-shore) is available for use. HMRC will then issue the promoter with an eight digit scheme reference number (SRN) which the promoter must pass to those clients to whom he provides services in connection with the scheme. A person who designs and implements a hallmarked scheme (own scheme) must disclose the scheme within 30 days of implementation. Form AAG 3 (notification of scheme by user in other circumstances) (eg where legal privilege applies or the scheme is devised for use 'in-house') is used for these purposes. Form AAG 5 (continuation sheets) are also available. (See HMRC Disclosure of Tax Avoidance Schemes, June 2006 for further guidance.) The company client must include the SRN details HMRC on the corporation tax return for the accounting period in which the advantage is being obtained. A co-promoter is not required to disclose a scheme to HMRC if another promoter has disclosed the scheme, or a scheme substantially the same, to HMRC (*FA 2004, ss 308–313*).

DISCLOSABLE ARRANGEMENTS

Pre 1 August 2006

18.8   Prior to 1 August 2006 disclosure of anti-avoidance measures was determined according to a series of filters. These included the premium test, the confidentiality test and the off-market test. If the promoter charged a fee for his advice aligned to the tax savings advantage from the scheme, disclosure was required. If the promoter's advice was provided on a confidential basis, so that the promoter could obtain it to maintain the premium fee potential, disclosure was required. If the 'off-market' test involved the promoter charging a small fee for the arrangement but a much larger fee for the financial product that he sold as part of the tax avoidance arrangement, disclosure was required.

From 1 August 2006

18.9   From 1 August 2006 a scheme is disclosable if it meets any one of a series of hallmark tests. 'Disclosable' is defined by HMRC as 'the requirement to provide prescribed information to HMRC'. Hallmarks is defined as the descriptions prescribed, for the purpose of *FA 2004, s 306(1)(a), (b)*, and the *Tax Avoidance Schemes (Prescribed Descriptions of Arrangements) Regulations 2006*.

Hallmarked tests

18.10   HMRC have devised a series of tests to determine whether a hall-marked scheme exists, which when applied to corporation tax are as follows:

Test	Question	Consequence for a positive answer	Consequence for a negative answer
		Positive	*Negative*
1	Are there arrangements (including any scheme, transaction or series of transactions), or proposals for arrangements, that enable, or might be expected to enable, any person to obtain an advantage in relation to income tax, corporation tax or capital gains tax?	Yes: apply test 2	No: not a hallmarked scheme
2	Are those arrangements or proposals such that the main benefit, or one of the main benefits that might be expected to arise from them, is the obtaining of that advantage?	Yes: apply test 3	No: not a hallmarked scheme benefit, or one of the main benefits that might be expected to arise from them, is the obtaining of that advantage?

Test	Question	Consequence for a positive answer	Consequence for a negative answer
3	Is there a promoter of the arrangements or are they devised for use 'in-house'?	Yes, a promoter: apply test 4. Yes, in-house: apply test 5	
4	Do any of the hallmarks for arrangements where there is a promoter apply?	Yes: a hall-marked scheme	No: not a hallmarked scheme
5	Is the tax advantage intended to be obtained by a business that is not a small or medium enterprise?	Yes: apply test 6	No: not a hallmarked scheme
6	Do any of the in-house hallmarks apply?	Yes: a hall-marked scheme	No: not a hallmarked scheme

Hallmarks

18.11   The hallmarks for arrangements where there is a promoter are as follows:

1   Confidentiality from other promoters.

2   Confidentiality from HMRC.

3   Premium fee.

4   Off-market terms.

5   Standardised tax products.

6   Loss schemes.

7   Leasing arrangements.

The hallmarks for in-house arrangements are:

2   Confidentiality from HMRC.

3   Premium fee.

7   Leasing arrangements.

The small business definition is the same as is used for research and development (see **8.18**).

The confidentiality, premium fee and off-market terms hallmarks follow through from the pre-1 August 2006 filters mentioned in **18.10**. The confidentiality from HMRC hallmark has been added and applies to a promoter who would wish to keep matters confidential from HMRC, for example, to secure future fee income.

A standardised tax product hallmark exists where there is a promoter of a mass-marketed product that needs little or no alteration to suit a client's situation. Enterprise investment schemes (EIS), venture capital trust schemes (VCTs) and corporate venturing schemes (CVS) arrangements are specifically excluded; as are approved employee share schemes and regulated pension schemes. The hallmark for a loss scheme is the existence of a promoter and is intended to capture various loss creation schemes used by wealthy individuals. The leasing arrangement applies to promoted and in-house arrangements. In-house arrangements do not apply if the party intended to benefit from the arrangement is an SME. The hallmark applies to certain high value sale and leaseback arrangements which involve a party outside the charge to corporation tax and a removal of risk from the lessor.

Clearances

18.12   There are special rules to avoid the duplication of information where the arrangement includes transactions for which a statutory clearance exists (*SI 2004/1864, para 5*).

They apply for the purposes of:

- Purchase of own shares by an unquoted company (*ICTA 1988, s 215*) (see **16.19–16.25**);

- Company demergers (*ICTA 1988, s 225*) (see **16.13–16.18**);

- Transfer of business (*ICTA 1988, s 444*);

- Transactions in securities (*ICTA 1988, s 707*);

- Reconstruction of company or trade (TCGA 1992, *ss 138, 139, 140B* or *140D*) (see **15.7–15.10**).

Where statutory clearance is available then the promoter or user may apply for clearance at the same time as making the disclosure. If there is no clearance request the promoter must make the disclosure not later than five working days following the day on which reasonable intention to make a clearance application ceased or the normal 'relevant date' if this is later.

Where a transaction occurs prior to the submission of a clearance application then the disclosure must be made within five working days of any transaction that is part of the scheme occurring.

HMRC have confirmed that clearance applications will be considered in the usual way and clearance will not be refused merely on the grounds that some part of the proposed transaction involves a disclosable scheme.

Disclosures made in this way should be sent with the clearance application.

CORPORATION TAX SELF-ASSESSMENT

CT600 completion

18.13   Companies who use a tax avoidance scheme are required to put an 'X' in the box so named on the first page of CT600 and to complete the disclosure of tax avoidance schemes supplementary pages form CT600J. The scheme number is required in box J and the accounting periods that benefit in JA.

Penalties

18.14   Failure to notify incurs the following penalties:

Taxpayer failing to disclose a scheme	Initial penalty maximum	£5,000
	Daily penalty	£600 per day
Promoters failing to give registration number to client	Initial penalty maximum	£5,000
Taxpayer failing to disclose scheme registration numbers on returns	Initial penalty	£100
	Second failure penalty	£500
	Third and subsequent failure penalty	£1,000

Subject to right of appeal, the Special Commissioners will determine the initial penalties for both the promoters and the taxpayers.

INTERNATIONAL TAX AVOIDANCE

International agreements

18.15   The UK is also extending its network of international tax avoidance intelligence (*ICTA 1988, s 815C*). In May 2005, exchange of information agreements were entered into between Jersey, Guernsey and the Isle of Man (*SI 2005/1261*; *SI 2005/1262*; *SI 2005/1263*). In June 2005, exchange of information agreements were entered into between the Virgin Islands, Aruba, Montserrat and Netherlands Antilles (*SI 2005/1457*; *SI 2005/1458*; *SI 2005/1459*; *SI 2005/1460*).

The EU entered into a co-operation agreement with Switzerland on 14 February 2006 (*SI 2006/307*). On 10 September 2007 the Joint International Tax Shelter Information Centre (JITSIC) opened its London office. The centre aims to curb tax avoidance shelters and those who promote and invest in them. The other JITSIC office is in Washington DC.

Effects of disclosure of tax avoidance schemes

18.16 In response to the required disclosure of tax avoidance schemes in 2004, counter legislation has been introduced in successive *Finance Acts*; particularly in relation to financial arrangements. The measures are contained in *F (No 2) A 2005, Sch 7, FA 2006, Sch 6* and *FA 2007, Sch 5*. As the UK has no GAAR, legislation tends to be more specific and transaction based as with the capital loss targeted anti-avoidance rules. It is anticipated that future legislation will continue along these lines. Over 1,450 direct tax schemes (income tax, corporation tax, capital gains tax and stamp duty land tax) and over 800 VAT schemes had been reported under the disclosure of tax schemes regime for the period to 31 March 2007 *Hansard 13 June 2007, vol 461, no 104, col 1124 W.*

CAPITAL LOSSES

Restrictions on allowable losses

18.17 A capital loss is a valuable tool for a company, as it can be carried forward indefinitely and set against future capital gains (see **20.5**). Improper utilisation of capital losses was targeted in *FA 2006* and *FA 2007*. With effect from 5 December 2005, a company's allowable losses exclude losses generated as part of a company tax avoidance scheme (*FA 2006, s 69*; *TCGA 1992, s 8(2)*). From 6 December 2006, these rules were extended to any person in situations where a taxpayer's capital loss will not be an allowable capital loss if it accrues in disqualifying circumstances. A loss accrues in disqualifying circumstances if it accrues directly or indirectly in consequence of or in connection with any arrangements of which the main purpose is to secure a tax advantage. The rationale is that capital loss relief should only be available in circumstances where there has been a true commercial disposal of an asset accompanied by a genuine commercial loss because of economic conditions existing at that time.

Losses created by schemes that result in a tax loss greater than the actual loss or leave the economic ownership of the asset virtually intact are not allowed (*TCGA 1992, s16A*).

Targeted anti-avoidance rules

18.18   With effect from 5 December 2005 three targeted anti-avoidance rules (TAARs) were introduced. The legislation is aimed at the buying of capital losses and gains (*TCGA 1992, ss 184A and 184B*) and the conversion of an income stream into a capital gain or a capital gain matched by an income stream thus covering the gain with an allowable loss (*TCGA 1992, s 184G*) and the artificial generation of capital losses (*TCGA 1992, s 184H*).

Measures to counter bed and breakfast arrangements existed up to 5 December 2005 (*TCGA 1992, s 106*). This prevented companies selling and buying shareholdings within a short space of time in order to utilise a capital loss. The current anti-avoidance rule supersedes the bed and breakfast rule.

Restrictions on buying losses: tax avoidance schemes (TCGA 1992, s 184A)

18.19   The restriction of pre-entry loss rules within *TCGA 1992, Sch 7A* remains (see **20.34**) but *TCGA 1992, s 184A* has precedence (*TCGA 1992, s 184F(3)*). The pre-entry gains legislation of *TCGA 1992, Sch 7AA* ceases to have effect (*TCGA 1992, s 184F(4)*). The *TCGA 1992, Sch 7A* rules are aimed at a group acquiring another company with latent losses. *TCGA 1992, s 184A* focuses on a company with latent losses changing its ownership. The rule only applies where there is an arrangement to avoid tax.

Situations where the restriction is applied

18.20   A group company is able to set its capital loss against the capital gain of another group company. However, this will be denied in the following circumstances:

- where there is a direct or indirect change of ownership of a company,

- where a loss accrues to the company or any other company on the disposal of an asset acquired prior to the change in ownership (a pre-change asset),

- where the main purpose of the change of ownership is to secure a tax advantage, and

- where the advantage involves the deduction of a qualifying loss from any chargeable gains, whether or not any other transactions or events are involved.

The resulting loss is not deductible from gains arising on assets belonging to the new owners.

Arrangements include any agreement, understanding, scheme, transaction or series of transactions whether or not they are legally enforceable. It is irrelevant as to whether the loss accrues before or after the change of ownership. It is irrelevant whether there are any chargeable gains at the time against which it can be utilised or whether the tax advantage accrues to the company to whom the loss has accrued or to any other company.

A qualifying change of ownership occurs at any time that:

- a company joins a group of companies,

- the company ceases to be a member of a group of companies,

- the company becomes subject to different control (TCGA 1992, s 184C).

A group is determined by *TCGA 1992, s 170* (see **20.14**) (*TCGA 1992, s 184C*).

Group off-set of losses is only available if both the companies in question were members of the same group immediately before the disposal and have remained members until immediately after the disposal (*FA 2006, s70(12)*).

A tax advantage means relief or increased relief from corporation tax or repayment or increased repayment of corporation tax. It also means the avoidance or reduction of a charge to corporation tax or an assessment to corporation tax or the avoidance or a possible assessment to corporation tax (*TCGA 1992, s 184D*).

Example 18.1

Sam Arkwright and Bill Weatherspoon each own 50% of Solo Ltd a single company with substantial capital losses. Solo Ltd owns Nevercourt, a property that it is in negotiations to sell. Solo Ltd issues ordinary shares that amount to 30% of the nominal value of the ordinary share capital to Alfonso Roderigo (an unconnected third party). Mr Roderigo's shares only have dividend rights. Sam Arkwright and Bill Weatherspoon then sell the original shares in Solo Ltd to the Multi Group plc. Although in economic terms Solo Ltd has joined the Multi Group plc it has not joined the Multi Group plc's capital gains group because Multi Group plc owns less that 75% of the issued share capital. Multi Group plc intends to transfer all of its assets that have not yet risen in value, but that it expects to rise in value to Solo Ltd in the expectation that any resulting chargeable gains could be covered by the purchased losses. The issue of shares in Solo Ltd to Alfonso Roderigo is clearly intended to prevent Solo Ltd joining the Multi Group plc when the original shareholders sell their shares. This prevents *TCGA 1992, Sch 7A* from applying.

Solo Ltd has neither left nor joined a chargeable gains group but it has become subject to a different control. There has, therefore, been a qualifying change of ownership as defined by *TCGA 1992, s 184C*. Solo Ltd has accrued losses on pre-change assets. The change of ownership has occurred in connection with arrangements, the main purpose of which is to secure a tax advantage for the Multi Group plc. *TCGA 1992, s 184A* applies and Solo Ltd's losses are qualifying losses and are not to be deducted from any gains arising to the company, except those accruing to Solo Ltd on a disposal of pre-change assets. If Nevercourt, the property owned by Solo Ltd at the time of the change of ownership is then sold giving rise to a chargeable gain, this gain can be covered by the losses.

Restrictions on buying gains: tax avoidance schemes (TCGA 1992, s 184B)

18.21   The same criteria apply to a change of company ownership and the realisation of a chargeable gain to be relieved by capital losses, which accrued prior to the change in ownership.

Disposal of pre-change assets

18.22   If a company has disposed of a pre-change asset but still retains an interest in the asset, that interest will remain as a pre-change asset.

The capital gain on the following disposals may be deferred:

- Reconstructions involving transfers of business (*TCGA 1992, s 139*).

- Postponement of charge on transfer of assets to non-resident companies (*TCGA 1992, s 140*).

- Transfer of a UK trade (*TCGA 1992, s 140A*).

- Merger leaving assets within UK tax charge (*TCGA 1992, s 140E*).

- Replacement of business assets (*TCGA 1992, ss 152, 153*).

- Postponement of charge on deemed disposal under *s 187* (*TCGA 1992, s 185*).

Any gain or loss accruing as a result of any subsequent event will be treated as accruing on a pre-change asset (*TCGA 1992, s 184E*).

Pre-change securities are pooled. Any disposal is matched first for these purposes; pre-change securities are pooled separately from post-change securities. A disposal of securities after the change is to be matched first against the post-change pool, then against the pre-change pool and then in accordance with the usual share identification rules (*TCGA 1992, s 184F*).

Avoidance involving losses: schemes converting income to capital (TCGA 1992, s 184G)

18.23   This situation arises where a company receives a receipt directly or indirectly on the disposal of an asset in connection with any arrangements. A chargeable gain accrues to the company on the asset disposal but capital losses accrue on other assets before or after the first asset's disposal as part of the arrangements. The arrangements enable a capital receipt to be accounted for instead of an income receipt, which would indeed have happened had the arrangements not been in place. The main purpose of the arrangement is to obtain a capital loss deduction from the capital gain irrespective of any other purpose.

Avoidance involving losses: schemes securing a deduction (TCGA 1992, s 184H)

18.24   This situation arises where a chargeable gain accrues to a company directly or indirectly in consequence of or in connection with any arrangements and losses accrued on any disposal of any asset before or after the first asset's disposal as part of the arrangements. Also as part of the arrangements the company or a connected company incurs expenditure which is allowable as a deduction in computing total profits but is not allowable in computing its chargeable gains. The main purpose of the arrangement is to obtain a deduction for the expenditure in computing profits and a capital loss deduction from the relevant gain irrespective of any other purpose.

Arm's-length arrangements, arrangements in respect of land, unconnected party arrangements and certain sale and leaseback arrangements are excluded.

HMRC notice

18.25   If HMRC consider that the purpose of these arrangements is to secure a tax advantage they may give the company a notice under *TCGA 1992, s 184G* or *184H*. If all conditions are satisfied no loss accruing to the relevant company may be deducted from the relevant gain.

If a company submits its tax return within a 90-day period after the receipt of the notice, it may disregard the notice in preparing the return and within the 90-day period amend the return in order to comply with the notice.

If the company has already submitted its company tax return, HMRC can only give the company a notice in respect of these anti-avoidance schemes if a notice of enquiry has also been given to the company in respect of the return for the same period.

HMRC may give the company a notice after any enquiries into the return have been completed if two conditions are satisfied. First, that at the time the enquiries into the return were completed HMRC could not have been reasonably expected on the basis of information made available to them before or at that time or to an officer of theirs before that time to have been aware that the circumstances necessitated the issue of a notice. The second condition is that the company or any other person was requested to produce or provide information during an enquiry into the return for that period and if the request had been duly complied with HMRC could have been reasonably expected to give a notice in relation to that period.

HUSBAND AND WIFE COMPANIES

18.26   Spouses or civil partners, who jointly own and manage a private company, each have a personal allowance and the various tax brackets to apply to any income withdrawn from the company. In some circumstances HMRC regard all the income to fall to the income-producing spouse by means of a settlement where the other spouse is seen as taking no part in the function of the business and possessing a holding that only reflects an income right. This situation was tested in the case of *Jones v Garnett* (*Inspector of Taxes*) [2005] UKHL 35, [2005] EWCA 1553 and a settlement was found not to exist. However, each case must be reviewed on its merits. See *Income Tax 2008/09* (from Tottel).

Limitation period

18.27   Claims for corporation tax overpayments cannot normally be made for accounting periods ending more than six years before the claim. However, under the *Limitation Act 1980, s 30(1)(c)* and corresponding legislation for Northern Ireland and Scotland there is an extension if a common law action is brought for restitution under a mistake of law. For these purposes the limitation period does not begin to run until the plaintiff has discovered the mistake (*LA 1980, s 30(1)(c)*). For direct tax and hence corporation tax purposes, this extension was disapplied for actions brought on or after 8 September 2003 (*FA 2004, ss 320, 321*). Following the decision of the Deutsche Morgan Grenfell case the extension was also disapplied for actions brought before 8 September 2003 (*FA 2007, s106*).

The legislation came about because in March 2001 the European Court of Justice in the case of Hoechst AG (CaseC-410/98) decided that there was a right of compensation regarding payments of ACT made on dividend payments to a German parent company where a group income election was not available. (See **16.10** for further narrative on ACT. In brief by making a group income election UK group members had the facility to ignore ACT on intra-group dividends. This facility was not available to non-UK group members.)

In October 2000, the claimants, Deutsche Morgan Grenfell brought an claim for the recovery of interest payments and ACT from HMRC based on this decision for ACT paid in 1993, 1995 and 1996 *Deutsche Morgan Grenfell Group plc v Inland Revenue Commissioners* [2006] UKHL 49. HMRC argued that the limitation period ran from the date that the ACT was paid. This would have meant that the 1993 ACT was time barred. The claimants relied on the interpretation of *LA 1980, s 30(1)(c)* stating that the period should begin when they were aware of their mistake, ie March 2001 the date of the *Hoechst* decision and not when the payments were made. The House of Lords decided in the company's favour.

The Deutsche Morgan Grenfell claim was brought in October 2000. The amended legislation applies to any direct tax action involving mistake of law brought before 8 September 2003, except where a claimant is subject to a final judgment given by the courts before 6 December 2006 as to the application of *s 32(1)(c)* in relation to such relief, or to a Group Litigation Order (GLO) which has a binding judgment.

The new legislation is relevant only for actions brought before 8 September 2003 since *FA 2004* introduced similar provision for actions brought on or after 8 September 2003. The *FA 2004* legislation is currently subject to judicial challenge in the UK.

DISCLOSURE OF TAX AVOIDANCE SCHEMES

Doubt as to notifiability

18.28   With effect from 16 August 2007, if HMRC consider that a proposal is to be treated as notifiable or that arrangements are to be treated as notifiable under the disclosure regulations (see **18.9** and **18.10**) they may apply to the Special Commissioners for an order that the scheme be treated as notifiable. The application must specify the proposal or arrangements and the name of the promoter, If the Special Commissioners are satisfied that HMRC have taken all reasonable steps to established whether the scheme is notifiable and they have reasonable grounds for suspecting that the proposal or arrangement is notifiable they will issue the order. Reasonable grounds may include not taking action under *FA 2004, ss 313A* or *313B*. Grounds for the suspicion are that the arrangements fall within the regulations (see **18.10**), or the promoter attempts to avoid or delay in providing information or documents in connection with the proposed arrangements under *FA 2004, ss 313A* or *313B* (*FA 2004, s 306A*). Alternatively, the promoter may have failed to comply with a requirement under *FA 2004, ss 313A* or *313B* in relation to another proposal or arrangement. If the promoter fails to comply, he will incur a penalty of £5,000 and a further daily penalty of an amount yet to be announced (£5,000 has been proposed) if the failure continues after the penalty has been introduced (*TMA 1970, s 98C (2A)*).

Again if HMRC consider that a promoter has provided insufficient information they may apply to the Special Commissioners for an order requiring the promoter to provide specified information or documents relating to the notifiable arrangements. If the Special Commissioners are satisfied that HMRC have reasonable grounds for suspecting that the information or documents form part of the prescribed information or will support the prescribed information they will issue the order (*FA 2004, s 308A*).

Pre-disclosure enquiry

18.29 If HMRC consider that a person is the promoter of a notifiable proposal or arrangement, they may issue a written notice requiring the promoter to state whether in his opinion the arrangements are notifiable, and if not to give reasons. It is not sufficient for the promoter to refer to professional advice. The reasons must show by reference to the regulations why the promoter considers that the scheme is non-notifiable. The promoter must comply with HMRC's request during the time limit prescribed (*FA 2004, s 313A*). If the promoter fails to comply, he will incur a penalty of £5,000 and a further £600 daily penalty if the failure continues after the penalty has been introduced (*TMA 1970, s 98C*).

If the Special Commissioners issue the promoter with a notice to supply this information, the promoter has ten days from the day of issue to comply with this request. The *Tax Avoidance Schemes (Information) (Amendment) Regulations 2007 (SI 2007/2153)*.

Reasons for non-disclosure

18.30 If HMRC are not satisfied with the promoter's statement of reasons, they may apply to the Special Commissioners for an order requiring the promoter to provide specified information or documents in support of the scheme, with which the promoter must comply within the specified time (*FA 2004, s 313 B*). If the promoter fails to comply, he will incur a penalty of £5,000 and a further £600 daily penalty (proposed to increase to £5,000) if the failure continues after the penalty has been introduced (*TMA 1970, s 98C*).

Order to disclose

18.31   HMRC may apply to the Special Commissioners or the First-tier Tribunal for an order that any scheme is to be treated as notifiable. The application must specify the proposal or arrangements and the name of the promoter (*FA 2004, s 314A*). If the promoter fails to comply, he will incur a penalty of £5,000 and a further daily penalty of an amount yet to be announced (£5,000 has been proposed) if the failure continues after the penalty has been introduced (*TMA 1970, s 98C(2B)*).

Courts procedure

18.32   The courts adopt normal procedures when dealing with these cases (see **2.28** and **2.31**).

Chapter 19

Liquidations

INSOLVENCY

Insolvent company

19.1   If a company becomes insolvent the only option may be to 'wind up' or liquidate the company. A solvent company may also be put into liquidation.

If a company becomes insolvent there are various courses or mixtures of courses of action that it can take. Firstly, the company can enter into a 'voluntary arrangement' with its creditors. Secondly, a secured creditor, with either a fixed or floating charge, such as the bank, may appoint a receiver who then assumes control of the company's business, who then becomes an administrative receiver. Thirdly, the court may make an administration order. An administrator will then take control of the company. An administrator has similar powers to a receiver. Finally, a compulsory liquidation may take place with the company being wound up by a court order under the *Insolvency Act 1986, s 73* or a voluntary liquidation may take place following a resolution passed at a general meeting of the company.

Solvent company

19.2   A solvent company may be put into liquidation when there is no further use for the company, say in a group reconstruction or when the share-holders or directors of a family company want to extract their capital. When such a course is contemplated the company directors, or a majority of them, must make a statutory declaration of solvency to the Registrar of Companies to the effect that the company will be able to pay or provide for all of its debts (including interest) within 12 months. Within five weeks of that declaration the directors must pass a resolution to wind up the company. A members' voluntary winding-up starts on the day the resolution to wind up the company is passed.

ADMINISTRATION PROCEEDINGS

Administration order

19.3   An administration order is a court order placing a company that is, or is likely to become, insolvent under the control of an administrator following an application by the company, its directors or a creditor. The purpose of the order is to preserve the company's business, allow a reorganisation or ensure the most advantageous realisation of its assets whilst protecting it from action of its creditors.

Receivers and administrators

19.4   A receiver takes his appointment from a secured creditor. Sometimes this is through a court order on behalf of the creditor. The receiver is assigned to take control of the secured assets on behalf of the creditor and to sell them if need be to pay off the creditors. If the receiver succeeds in this work, the directors continue with their responsibilities. If the receiver is unable to discharge the secured debt it normally follows that the company is put into liquidation. Prior to 15 September 2003, a receiver normally assumed control of the company's business as an administrative receiver with statutory powers. An administrative receiver is an insolvency practitioner. Administrative receivership was abolished for floating charges created on and after 15 September 2003 with certain exceptions (such as financial market transactions and public private partnerships). Under the *Enterprise Act 2002* lenders appoint administrators in situations that would previously have been dealt with by administrative receivership. From 15 September 2003 an administrative receiver in post must vacate office on the appointment of an administrator (HMRC Insolvency Manual INS 1203).

The administrator may be appointed by the court, the creditors or the directors to manage the affairs, business and property of company. Essentially, the administrator seeks to rescue the company and if possible seek better results for the creditors. Eventually he may realise property in order to make a distribution.

Effect of appointment

19.5   The appointment does not affect the corporate existence of the company. The directors and officers retain their respective positions and are not relieved of their duties and liabilities although the administrator has effective control of the company.

Corporation tax in administration

19.6   For companies entering administration on or after 15 September 2003, a new accounting period begins where the company enters into administration (*ICTA 1988, s 12(7ZA)*) and an accounting period ends where it ceases to be in administration (*ICTA 1988, s 12(3)(da)*). Within this time the accounting period may run to the next 12 months or to the original accounting date if so required. If the company is to be dissolved at the end of the administration period, the corporation tax will be charged on the company's profits for the final year based on current rates available at the time (*ICTA 1988, s 342A*). If the company receives any interest on overdue tax in the final accounting period, provided that it does not exceed £2,000, it will not be subject to corporation tax.

When a company enters into administration it does not cease to be the beneficial owner of its assets. Therefore the reconstruction procedure described in **15.5–15.10** will still apply.

Whether the company may claim group relief is a debatable point. As the administrator or receiver is effectively controlling the company, the company's shareholders cannot secure that the affairs of the company are conducted in accordance with their wishes (*ICTA 1988, s 840*). Therefore it could cease to be grouped with parent and subsidiaries for group relief (*ICTA 1988, s 410(1)(b)(ii)*). If the company arranges to dispose of a subsidiary it may lose entitlement to group relief (*ICTA 1988, s 410*).

Effect of cessation of trade

19.7   A company may continue to trade during its administration or liquidation period. However, such an event is unlikely. The date of cessation of trade marks the end of an accounting period (*ICTA 1988, s 12(3)*).

A cessation of trade has various corporation tax implications. Trading stock, if sold to an unconnected UK trade, is valued at sales price. In other circumstances, such as a sale to a connected party or an overseas trader it is valued at market value. The company should provide for all known bad debts and impairment losses. If trading ceases and a debt proves to be irrecoverable it can only be relieved against post-cessation receipts. Similarly, all known expenses should be provided for.

The permanent cessation will give rise to a balancing charge or balancing allowance in the final period (*CAA 2001, s 65*). Disposal proceeds will be the sale price if sold to an unconnected third party or market value in any other case. The connected parties may elect in writing within two years of the end of the accounting period in which the trade ceased to substitute the higher of the sales price or the actual cost price. The purchaser will use the same stock valuation (*ICTA 1988, s 100(1C)*). Trading losses in the final period accounting period can be utilised in a group relief claim (see **10.7**) or carried back in a terminal loss claim (see **9.16**).

When a company ceases to trade its unrelieved trading losses are not available to shelter other income received in the period. It may still offset its non-trading deficits against its non-trading credits.

Unrelieved trading losses may be set against post cessation receipt income (*ICTA 1988, s 105*). In addition any balancing charge arising from the disposal of a building that is temporarily out of use may be relieved by the unutilised losses (*CAA 2001, s 354*).

LIQUIDATION PROCEEDINGS

Winding-up

19.8   The winding-up of a company may take place voluntarily by company resolution or by order of the court (*IA 1986, s 73*). Following the winding-up order or resolution a liquidator is appointed to 'wind up' the affairs of the company; namely to realise the assets and settle outstanding liabilities. The liquidator will then apply to have the company dissolved and removed from the Register at Companies House. The company will then cease to exist. In a member's voluntary winding-up the company is dissolved three months after the date on which the Registrar of Companies is advised that the winding-up is complete.

Liquidator

19.9   A liquidator can be appointed by the creditors, the members or the court, depending on the type of liquidation. The liquidator is assigned to realise all company assets within his control and to apply the proceeds in payment of the company's debts in order of priority. If any surplus funds remain, the liquidator will repay the members the amounts paid up on their shares. If any further surplus remains he will distribute the surplus amongst the members according to their entitlement.

Commencement

19.10   A winding-up commences on the date that the resolution is passed for a voluntary members' or creditors' winding-up or the date of the winding-up petition in any other case (HMRC Insolvency Manual INS 1520). On hearing a petition the court will make an order for the winding-up of the company if all necessary conditions have been followed and the court is satisfied that the company is unable to pay its debts. If the winding-up follows a company administration the date the company went into administration is the date of the liquidation (HMRC Insolvency Manual INS 1612).

Corporation tax

19.11 The date of the winding-up order marks the end of one accounting period and the beginning of the next. Thereafter the accounting periods run to the 12-month anniversary of the winding-up (*ICTA 1988, s 12(7)*). The profits during the winding-up remain chargeable to corporation tax on the company and not on the liquidator (*ICTA 1988, s 344(2)*). If the company receives any interest on overdue tax in the final accounting period, provided that it does not exceed £2,000 it will not be subject to corporation tax (*ICTA 1988, s 342(3A)*).

The liquidator will provide HMRC with a provisional date for completion of the winding-up. The corporation tax will be charged on the company's profits for the final year based on current rates available at the time (*ICTA 1988, s 342(2)(a)*).

If it transpires that the provisional date is incorrect an accounting period is deemed to end on that date and a new one commences (*ICTA 1988, s 342(6)*).

Effect of winding-up order

19.12 When a company has entered into liquidation it loses the beneficial interest in its assets (*Ayerst v C & K (Construction) Ltd* (1975) 50 TC 651, [1975] STC 345, [1976] AC 167, [1975] 2 All ER 537). Hence group relief both for groups and consortiums is no longer available (*ICTA 1988, s 410(1)(b)(ii)*) and reconstruction hive down utilising *ICTA 1988, s 343* (see Chapter 15) is also prohibited. The company remains a group member for capital gains purposes (*TCGA 1992, s 170(11)*); therefore the liquidator may transfer assets to group members with *TCGA 1992, s 171* continuing to apply (see **20.16**).

No distributions of profits may be made to shareholders in respect of their share capital (*ICTA 1988, s 209(1)*). The close company distribution rules of *ICTA 1988, s 418* continue to apply. However, distributions of assets may still be made (*ICTA 1988, s 209(4), (5), (6)*) (see **16.5**).

Loans to participators

19.13 Loans to participators may either be called in, in order to pay out the shareholders or alternatively they will be written off. The normal procedures will follow as described in **4.16–4.22**.

ESC C16

19.14   Where a company has ceased business it may ask the Registrar of Companies to strike it off under *CA 2006, s 1003: CA 1985, s 652A* or wait for the Registrar of Companies to strike off the company (see **16.26–16.28** and HMRC Company Taxation Manual CTM 36220).

Taxation liabilities of office holders

19.15   Although a receiver deals with all preferential claims, the corporation tax arising during receivership remains the responsibility of the company and will be dealt with by any subsequent liquidator either as an unsecured claim or to the extent that the income and gains arose after the commencement of winding-up as a liquidation expense.

When appointed a liquidator or an administrator becomes the proper officer of the company dealing with its corporation tax affairs (*TMA 1970, s 108(3)*).

Corporation tax arising prior to appointment is an unsecured claim; post appointment it is an administration or liquidation expense and strictly must be paid ahead of the liquidator's remuneration (*Re Mesco Properties Ltd* (1979) 54 TC 238, [1979] STC 788, [1980] 1 WLR 96, [1980] 1 All ER 117).

Subsidiary company in liquidation

19.16   The substantial shareholding exemption (*TCGA 1992, Sch 7AC(3)*) prevents a capital gain and a capital loss accruing where more than 10% of the shares of a trading company are owned by another UK company (see **12.26– 12.30**) if the shares are held throughout a 12-month period beginning not more than two years before the date of disposal. In other circumstances the holding company may be able to make a negligible asset claim under *TCGA 1992, s 24*.

During the liquidation period it is unlikely that the company will be carrying on a trade. Therefore the liquidator's costs will not be relievable. They may form part of the incidental costs of disposal of certain assets, but apart from that no relief will be given.

A close company in liquidation may be treated as a close investment holding company (CIC) (see **4.23–4.26**). Where a close company commences liquidation, *ICTA 1988, s 13A(4)* provides that it is not to be treated as a CIC in the accounting period immediately following the commencement of winding-up if it was not a CIC in the accounting period immediately before liquidation commenced. In any subsequent accounting period a close company in liquidation will be excluded from being a CIC only if it then meets the usual conditions of *ICTA 1988, s 13A(2)* (see **4.24**). HMRC have commented that it may happen that there is a very short gap between the end of a period in which the company was not a CIC and the commencement of winding-up, so that strictly the company will not have the benefit of *s 13A(4)*. This may cause difficulties in some cases and an undertaking has been given to review the position where a company has not been able to avoid a short gap and would suffer significantly if not given the protection of *s 13(4)* (HMRC Company Taxation Manual CTM 60780).

From a practical perspective HMRC should be contacted to ascertain whether any enquiries are to be made. Any distributions to shareholders during the liquidation period are capital distributions and do not fall within *ICTA 1988, s 209(1)*.

Chapter 20

Capital gains

INTRODUCTION

Chargeable gains for companies

20.1   Companies are not liable to capital gains tax, but instead pay corporation tax on chargeable gains, at the same rate as trading profits and other
income. Gains arising on the disposal of assets are chargeable to capital gains
tax except where exemptions apply (*TCGA 1992, s 1*). From a company's
perspective disposals that are most likely to fall within the capital gains net are
disposals of land and property held on capital account and share holdings. The
disposal of loan stock comes within the loan relationship rules (see Chapter 11)
and the disposal of intangible assets comes within the intangible asset rules (see
Chapter 7).

Capital gains are broadly computed in accordance with normal CGT principles
(*see Capital Gains Tax 2008/09* from Tottel) but there is no taper relief (before
removal) or annual exemption. A company's chargeable gains are adjusted for
post-March 1982 indexation allowances. The reform of CGT for individuals,
trustees and personal representatives, which froze indexation relief at April
1998 and introduced taper relief provisions, did not extend to the capital gains
of companies. Gains on the disposal of a company's chargeable assets are
included in box 16 of the corporation tax self-assessment return.

There are a number of relieving provisions that are discussed as follows:

Roll-over relief	**20.6–20.13, 20.21**
Intra-group asset transfers	**20.14–20.17**
Losses on shares in unquoted trading companies	**12.25**
Substantial shareholdings exemption	**12.26–12.30**
Corporate venturing schemes	**12.31–12.43**
CGT on reconstructions	**15.7–15.10**

20.2 *Capital gains*

Special computational provisions apply to:

Transfers of assets to trading stock	**20.18–20.19**
Transfers of assets from trading stock	**20.20**
Companies leaving a group	**20.22**

There are also many anti-avoidance provisions which are discussed as follows:

Value shifting	**20.24–20.31**
Depreciatory transactions	**20.32**
Dividend stripping	**20.33**
Pre-entry gains and losses	**20.34**
The targeted anti-avoidance rules (TAARs)	**18.18–18.25**

BASIC CAPITAL GAINS COMPUTATION

20.2   The gross sale proceeds less the allowable items of expenditure and indexation results in the chargeable gain. Allowable items include the purchase cost and the costs of acquisition and disposal (*TCGA 1992, s 38*). Indexation based on purchase and acquisition costs is still available to companies from the date of purchase or 31 March 1982 if later, until date of sale.

When preparing the capital gains computation the incidental costs of sale are deducted from sale proceeds and may include such items as valuation fees, auctioneers' or estate agency fees, costs of advertising or legal costs. These costs do not qualify for the indexation allowance. Allowable expenditure includes the original cost of the asset, any enhancement expenditure and the incidental costs of sale. All this expenditure qualifies for indexation allowance.

Enhancement expenditure

20.3   Enhancement expenditure is capital expenditure, which adds to, improves or enhances the value of the asset. Expenditure deductible on revenue account such as repairs, maintenance and insurance are excluded since such costs only maintain the value of an asset. Conversely, capital expenditure that has not qualified as a deduction on revenue account may qualify as a deduction for capital gains purposes, so long as it enhances the value of the underlying asset.

Indexation

20.4 Indexation allowance is calculated by multiplying the relevant allowable expenditure by the indexation factor. The indexation factor is computed by expressing the following fraction as a decimal (to three decimal places) (*TCGA 1992, s 54*).

$$(RD - RI) \div RI$$

Where RD is the retail prices index (RPI) for the month of disposal and RI is the RPI for the later of:

- March 1982; or

- the month in which the expenditure was incurred. (See Appendix 1 for Retail Price Indices)

If there should be a decrease in RPI between the base month and the month of disposal, the indexation allowance is nil. If expenditure is incurred on two or more dates, separate indexation calculations are required for each. No indexation is available if proceeds less costs results in a loss before indexation is calculated (*TCGA 1992, s 53(2A)*). Neither can indexation allowance be deducted so as to turn a gain before indexation into a loss. Instead, the gain is reduced to nil (*TCGA 1992, s 53(1)(b)*).

Capital losses

20.5 The company's chargeable gains for the accounting period are reduced by allowable losses of the same period, and any unrelieved allowable capital losses brought forward from previous accounting periods. Capital losses may only be set against capital gains of the current year or carried forward to set against future capital gains.

Unused capital losses are carried forward for offset against capital gains of subsequent accounting periods. There are no provisions allowing for the carry back of capital losses, the surrender of capital losses between group companies, or the offset of capital losses against trading or other income (except for losses of investment companies on shares in qualifying unquoted trading companies, or losses of trading companies on shares within the Corporate Venturing Scheme: see **12.31–12.41**).

Allowable capital losses including losses brought forward are recorded in box 17 of the company tax return.

Example 20.1

The West End Trading Co Ltd prepares accounts to 31 March each year. The company disposes of an office block on 3 December 2009 for £40m. The incidental costs of sale are £1m. The block was purchased in January 2003 for £15.5m. Costs of acquisition amounted to £0.5m. In January 2004 a new frontage at a cost of £2m was added to the building that was deemed to be capital expenditure. The chargeable gain to be included within the corporation tax computation for the year ended 31 March 2010 is calculated as follows:

		£000	£000
December 2009	Gross sale proceeds		40,000
	Less: Incidental costs of sale		1,000
	Net sale proceeds		39,000
	Less: Relevant allowable expenditure:		
January 2003	Acquisition cost	15,500	
January 2003	Incidental costs of acquisition	500	
January 2004	Enhancement expenditure	2,000	
			18,000
	Unindexed gain		21,000
	Less: Indexation allowance		
	Cost 16,000 × 0.233	3,728	
	Enhancement 2,000 × 0.202	404	
			4,132
	Chargeable gain		16,868

Workings: calculation of indexation factor

RPI	December 2009	*220.0
RPI	January 2003	178.40
RPI	January 2004	183.10

Factor			
Cost	(RPI December 2009—RPI January 2003) ÷ RPI January 2003		0.233
Enhance-ment	(RPI December 2009—RPI January 2004) ÷ RPI January 2004		0.202
* assumed			

RELIEVING PROVISIONS

Roll-over relief

20.6   Assets sold in excess of cost may bring about a chargeable gain, assessable upon the company. If the assets are of a certain class and if new assets have been purchased to replace them the gain may qualify for roll-over relief under *TCGA 1992, s 152*. This will enable the gain to be deferred within the cost of the new asset.

The assets that can qualify for relief are listed under *TCGA 1992, s 155*.

The relevant classes of assets are as follows:

Class 1 Assets within heads A and B are given below.

Head A

   (i)   Any building or part of a building and any permanent or semi-permanent structure in the nature of a building, occupied (as well as used) only for the purposes of the trade.

   (ii) Any land occupied (as well as used) only for the purposes of the trade. Head A has effect subject to *s 156*.

Head B

Fixed plant or machinery which does not form part of a building or of a permanent or semi-permanent structure in the nature of a building.

Class 2

Ships, aircraft and hovercraft ('hovercraft' having the same meaning as in the *Hovercraft Act 1968*).

Class 3

Satellites, space stations and spacecraft (including launch vehicles).

Class 4

Goodwill. (But not applicable after 1 April 2002).

Class 4

Goodwill no longer qualifies after 1 April 2002 as it is included within the intangible assets regime. See **Chapter 7** for intangible assets.

Conditions affecting the old assets and the new assets

20.7   The old assets must have been used solely for the purposes of the trade throughout the period of ownership. The consideration received must be used in acquiring new assets or an interest therein. Upon acquisition the new assets must also be used solely for the purposes of the trade. The new assets must not be acquired for the purposes of realising a gain, ie as an investment (*TCGA 1992, s 152(5)*).

The trading company can then claim that the consideration on the sale of the old assets is reduced up to the amount reinvested that produces neither a gain nor a loss on disposal. The acquisition cost of the new asset is reduced by the same amount. The relief is given after indexation.

The new assets must be acquired during the period commencing 12 months before and ending three years after the disposal of, or of the interest in, the old assets. A provisional claim may be made if the company enters into an unconditional contract for purchase.

Apportionment takes place if the old asset is not used throughout the period of ownership for the purposes of the trade or if only part of an asset is used for the purposes of a trade. Periods before 31 March 1982 are ignored in calculating the period of ownership.

Assets only partly replaced

20.8   If only part of the asset is replaced it follows that the gain on disposal of the old asset is limited to the amount of consideration reinvested with the balance of the gain being rolled over (*TCGA 1992, s 153*).

New assets which are depreciating assets

20.9   If the new assets are depreciating assets the chargeable gain is not deducted from the cost of the new asset but is held over and becomes chargeable at the earliest of the following events:

- the new asset is disposed of;
- the asset is no longer used for the purposes of the trade; or
- 10 years have elapsed since the acquisition of the new asset.

A depreciating asset is any asset that will become a wasting asset within 10 years of acquisition. A wasting asset is an asset with a predictable life of 50 years or less (*TCGA 1992, s 44*). Fixed plant and machinery installed in a building with a life of more than 60 years to run will not be a depreciating asset. A leasehold building with less than 60 years to run will be a depreciating asset (Tax Bulletin, Issue 7, May 1993).

Land and buildings and roll-over relief

20.10 Land and buildings are treated as separate assets for roll-over relief purposes. HMRC wish to see separate computations to support a claim together with an appropriate apportionment of costs (HMRC Capital Gains Tax Manual CG 60990). No roll-over relief is available for land held or property dealt with in the course of trade by a property dealing or development company other than land and buildings that it used for the purposes of the trade. Lessors of tied premises are treated as occupying and using the premises for the purposes of their trade (*TCGA 1992, s 156(4)*).

New assets not purchased

20.11 By concession proceeds used from the disposal of old assets may be used to enhance the value of qualifying assets already held. The other assets must only have been used for the purposes of the company's trade and on completion of the work undertaken the assets are immediately taken back for use in the trade (ESC D22).

Similarly, by concession if proceeds from the sale of old assets are used to acquire a further interest in another asset that is already being used for the purposes of the trade that new interest is treated as a new asset if it is taken into use for the purposes of the trade (ESC D25).

New asset not brought immediately into trading use

20.12 If a new asset on acquisition is not taken immediately into use for the purposes of the trade, roll-over relief will still be available in the following circumstances:

- the owner proposes to incur capital expenditure for the purposes of enhancing its value;

- any work arising from such capital expenditure begins as soon as possible after acquisition and is completed within a reasonable time;

- on completion of the work the asset is taken into use for the purpose of the trade and for no other purpose; and

- the asset is neither let nor used for any non-trading purpose in the period between acquisition and taking into use for trade purposes (ESC D24).

Assets owned personally but used for the purposes of the trade of a personal company

20.13   If an individual exercises no less than 5% of the voting rights of a company, which uses an asset owned by that individual for the purposes of its trade, that individual will be entitled to roll-over relief if all other conditions apply (*TCGA 1992, s 157*).

INTRA-GROUP ASSET TRANSFER

Group structure

20.14   For chargeable gains purposes, a group consists of a company (known as the principal company) and all its 75% subsidiaries together with each subsidiary's 75% subsidiary company. Each subsidiary must be an effective 51% subsidiary of the principal company. A principal company must not be a 75% subsidiary of another company. The principal company can be UK or overseas resident and the inclusion of a non-resident subsidiary does not disturb the group relationship.

Example 20.2

A Ltd owns 75% of the ordinary share capital of B Ltd.

B Ltd owns 80% of the ordinary share capital of C Ltd.

A Ltd and B Ltd are a group, as A Ltd owns 75% of B Ltd.

A Ltd and C Ltd are a group because A Ltd effectively owns 60% of C Ltd (75 × 80).

20.15   A company can only be a member of one group. Where the conditions qualify so that a company would be a member of two or more groups the group that it is deemed to be a member of is determined establishing its links to the principal company and if the group conditions are not met the links should be established with the next group (*TCGA 1992, s 170*).

Example 20.3

A Ltd owns 75% of the ordinary share capital of B Ltd.

B Ltd owns 80% of the ordinary share capital of C Ltd.

C Ltd owns 75% of the ordinary share capital of D Ltd.

D Ltd owns 75% of the ordinary share capital of E Ltd.

A Ltd and B Ltd are a group.

A Ltd and C Ltd are a group.

A Ltd and D Ltd are not a group because A Ltd effectively owns 45% of D Ltd $(75 \times 80 \times 75)$.

D Ltd and E Ltd are a group.

Relief

20.16   For chargeable gains purposes intra-group transfers of assets are always deemed to be made at a price that results in neither gain nor loss for the transferee company (*TCGA 1992, s 171*) (*Innocent v Whaddon Estates Ltd* (1981) 55 TC 476, [1982] STC 115).

The relief is automatically applied and given without claim, but does not apply where a transfer arises in the satisfaction of a debt, a disposal of redeemable shares on redemption, a disposal by or to an investment trust, Venture Capital Trust (VCT) or qualifying friendly society; or a disposal to a dual resident investing company. On a company reconstruction where *TCGA 1992, s 135* applies (see **15.8**), *s 135* takes preference so *s 171* does not apply.

Although a non-UK company can be a member of the group, it cannot take part in the asset transfer unless it trades in the UK through a permanent branch or agency. The asset must be in the UK and be used for the branch or agency trade.

When a company eventually disposes of the asset to a third party the company selling adopts the original base cost of the asset to the group plus indexation for the capital gains computation.

Election to treat a disposal as if made by another group member

20.17   In order to fully utilise the group's capital losses, a group company may treat a disposal of an asset outside the group as though it were made by another group member. This will enable the asset to be placed in the company that has the capital losses. Both companies must make a joint election for the deemed transfer to apply, within two years of the end of the chargeable period in which the transfer takes place (*TCGA 1992, s 171A*).

Special computational provisions

Transfers of assets to trading stock

20.18   Where one group member acquires a capital asset, from another member, that it appropriates to trading stock, the intra-group asset transfer will be at no gain/no loss, but as soon as the asset is transferred to stock a chargeable gain arises on the transferee. The transferee adopts the transferor's asset base cost and indexation. Alternatively, the transferee can elect under *TCGA 1992, s 161(3)* to treat the asset as acquired at market value less the capital gain arising. The gain will, therefore, be taken as part of the trading profit on the asset.

Example 20.4

O Ltd transfers a fixed asset to its holding company N Ltd. N Ltd appropriates the asset to its trading stock. The indexed cost of the asset was £12,500 to O Ltd and the market value on transfer is £20,000. N Ltd eventually sells the asset to a third party for £30,000.

Without a *TCGA 1992, s 161(3)* election the position is as follows:

N Ltd	£
Market value	20,000
Indexed cost	12,500
Capital gain	7,500
Sale proceeds	30,000
Deemed cost	20,000
Trading profit	10,000

With a *TCGA 1992, s 161(3)* election the position is as follows:

N Ltd	£
Sales proceeds	30,000
Indexed cost	12,500
Trading profit	17,500

20.19   There is the potential here to turn a capital loss into a trading loss. The loss will only be allowed if there is a true trading intention (*Coates v Arndale Properties Ltd* (1984) 59 TC 516, [1984] STC 637, [1984] 1 WLR 1328, [1985] 1 All ER 15).

Transfers of assets from trading stock

20.20   Where a group company transfers an asset that it holds as trading stock to another group company that holds it as an asset it is deemed to be transferred at market value in the transferor's books giving rise to a trading profit. When the transferee company sells the asset outside the group it adopts the market value of the asset when it was transferred from the transferor company as base cost on which is based indexation allowance, etc.

Example 20.5

N Ltd transfers a chargeable asset from its trading stock to its subsidiary company O Ltd. O Ltd will hold the asset as an investment. The cost of the asset was £10,000 and the market value on transfer is £30,000. O Ltd then sells the asset to a third party for £40,000. The indexation from the time of transfer is £500.

N Ltd	£	£
Market value		30,000
Cost		10,000
Trading profit		20,000
O Ltd		
Sale proceeds		40,000
Deemed cost	30,000	
Indexation	500	
		30,500
Capital gain		9,500

Replacement of business asset by members of a group

20.21   *TCGA 1992, s 152* roll-over relief is extended to group situations. For this purpose all group assets and trades are treated as one. The new assets must be purchased outside the group (*TCGA 1992, s 175*). See **6.51** *et seq.*

Companies leaving the group

20.22 If a company leaves a group within six years of an inter-group transfer a chargeable gain arises on retained assets acquired, on a no gain/no loss basis, from other group members within the previous six years (*TCGA 1992, s 179*). The chargeable gain is calculated on the basis that the company leaving the group sold and repurchased the asset at market value on the day that it was acquired from the other group member (*TCGA 1992, s 179(3)*) but the gain is charged in the accounting period in which the company leaves the group.

The company and the other group member from whom the asset was acquired may jointly elect that the capital gain on leaving the group be treated as that of the other company (*TCGA 1992, s 179A*). If qualifying, the asset will be available for roll-over relief (*TCGA 1992, s 179B*).

Example 20.6

In 1989 N Ltd acquired a freehold property for £280,000. In 2002 when the market value was £500,000 and the indexation to date was £20,000 N Ltd transferred the freehold property to P Ltd a fellow group member. P Ltd leaves the group on 1 January 2009. Both companies prepare accounts to 30 June each year.

The *s 179* gain for the year ended 30 June 2009 is calculated as follows:

P Ltd	£
Market value	500,000
Indexed cost	300,000
Capital gain	200,000

If P Ltd purchases another qualifying asset P Ltd will be able to make a roll-over relief claim under *TCGA 1992, s 152*.

If N Ltd and P Ltd could jointly elect for the gain to fall in N Ltd only, N Ltd will be able to make a roll-over relief claim, which must be against its acquisition of a qualifying asset.

20.23 HMRC have confirmed that a degrouping charge will not be imposed on assets transferred to the parent of a two-company group, which disposes of its single subsidiary (HMRC Capital Gains Tax Manual CG 45450).

ANTI-AVOIDANCE

Value shifting

20.24   The shareholders own a company through its share structure. A share or security is a chargeable asset for capital gains purposes (*TCGA 1992, s 21*). Transactions that affect the value of these shares could fall within the capital gains rules for value shifting found in *TCGA 1992, ss 29–34* or the depreciatory transaction rules found in *TCGA 1992, ss 176–181*.

General application

20.25   If a shareholder exercises his control over the company, so that value passes out of that person's or the shares of a connected party a disposal is deemed to have taken place at market value (*TCGA 1992, s 29(2)*). Similarly, a loss on disposal arising in this situation will not be an allowable loss (*TCGA 1992, s 29(3)*). Similar rules apply for intangible assets *TCGA 1992, s 33A*. The value shifting rules are applicable to all companies.

Free benefits

20.26   A disposal at market value is also deemed to take place where a scheme or arrangement materially reduces the value of an asset and gives rise to a tax-free benefit on the person making the disposal or on a connected party (*TCGA 1992, s 30(1)*). (These rules do not apply to disposals between husband and wife or between civil partners (*TCGA 1992, s 58(1)*), disposals by personal representatives to legatees (*TCGA 1992, s 62(4)*).

A benefit arises when a person becomes entitled to any money or money's worth, when the value of an asset increases or when a liability is reduced or cancelled (*TCGA 1992, s 30(3)*). It follows that post an HMRC value shifting uplift there is a complementary asset value uplift for future chargeable gains purposes.

These rules do not apply to group asset transfers groups (*TCGA 1992, s 171(1)*) (see **20.16**) and companies ceasing to be a member of a group (*TCGA 1992, ss 178* and *179*) (see **20.22**).

Again these rules do not apply if it is shown that avoidance of tax was not the main purpose or one of the main purposes of the scheme or arrangements in question (*TCGA 1992, s 30(2)*).

Distributions within a group followed by a disposal of shares

20.27   *TCGA 1992, s 31* is particularly drawn up to deal with situations where an intra-group dividend payment and an intra-group asset transfer is followed by the disposal of the subsidiary.

In normal circumstances before the sale of a subsidiary takes place, the payment of a dividend by the subsidiary to the holding company out of profits that have already suffered tax is not a depreciatory dividend for the purposes of *TCGA 1992, s 31*. It is recognised that such a transaction avoids a double taxation charge.

The legislation, however, applies where a company has profits that in some way it has engineered which have not been charged to tax. A revaluation of assets or the transfer of an asset on a no gain no loss basis under *TCGA 1992, s 171* may create such profits (*TCGA 1992, ss 31A, 32*).

Profits are chargeable in this circumstance if they satisfy the three conditions of *TCGA 1992, s 31*.

First, there must be a transaction that gives rise to distributable commercial profits, but which does not give rise to taxable profits. Such transactions are:

- an intra-group disposal at no gain/no loss under *TCGA 1992, s 171(1)*;

- an intra-group exchange of shares or debentures, or a reconstruction or amalgamation, which is treated as a reorganisation of share capital by *TCGA 1992, s 135(3)*; or

- a revaluation of an asset.

In practice, an asset revaluation will not give rise to distributable profits as a dividend may only be paid out of realised profits (*CA 2006 s 830; formerly CA 1985, s 263*). However, this matter may require consideration when dealing with overseas groups (*TCGA 1992, s 31(6)*)

Secondly, there must be no real disposal of the asset other than a no gain/no loss disposal under *TCGA 1992, s 171(1)* and there has been no deemed disposal under *TCGA 1992, s 178* or *179* (*TCGA 1992, s 31(7)*).

Thirdly, immediately after the disposal the asset must be owned by a third party who remains outside the group (*TCGA 1992, s 31(8)*).

HMRC will investigate the following type of transactions:

Intra-group 'depreciatory' dividends:

- before the disposal the subsidiary paid a dividend out of reserves which were created by the intra-group transfer of an asset at a commercial (book) gain, and the transferred asset left the group at the same time as the shares in the subsidiary,

Intra-group asset transfers:

- before the disposal there was an intra-group transfer of an asset at a commercial (book) loss, (HMRC Capital Gains Manual CG46803).

The *s 31* rules do not apply to trading assets (*TCGA 1992, s 31(9)*).

Asset holding company leaving the group

20.28   *TCGA 1992, s 31A* imposes subsequent conditions (applicable on or after 9 March 1999), which apply even though the third condition in **20.27** is not satisfied because the asset remains in the group. The asset may remain within the group if it is transferred to a non-UK company group member before disposal to a third party. If the UK transferee company ceases to be a member of the group within six years of transfer without a de-grouping charge arising, the value-shifting rules will apply to the transaction. This results in an increase in the gain being brought into charge at the time of the sale of the UK subsidiary company outside the group.

If that company no longer exists or has left the group, HMRC may by notice designate a company to be the chargeable company. This company will have been a group member immediately before the transferor company left the group (*TCGA 1992, s 31A(9)*).

Distributable profits are those profits, computed on a commercial basis, which a company may distribute in accordance with company law and any further restrictions in its own articles of association. A proper provision should be made for any tax payable (*TCGA 1992, s 31(4)*). Distributable profits are chargeable profits if they are within *s 31*. Distributable profits are first identified with non-chargeable profits for value shifting purposes and then with the chargeable profits (*TCGA 1992, s 31(10)*).

Example 20.7

Archer Ltd sold its 100% subsidiary Longfellow Ltd on 1 December 2008.

The substantial shareholdings relief is not available. Prior to sale Longfellow Ltd pays a dividend of £750,000 to Archer Ltd.

The details are as follows:

	£000
Value shifting non-chargeable profits	
—Distributable profits from normal operations.	800
Value shifting chargeable profits	
—Distributable profits from intra-group transfer	900
Pre-sale distribution	1,050

Result

£800,000 is identified with the chargeable profits and an additional £250,000 is added to the consideration on the sale of Longfellow Ltd.

The legislation permits dividend tracing through tiers of companies (*TCGA 1992, s 31(3)*).

Disposals within a group followed by a disposal of shares

20.29   The value shifting provisions of *s 30* do not apply to disposals within *TCGA 1992, s 171(1)* unless particular conditions apply. These conditions are if the underlying asset is disposed of for less than its market value or less than cost unless the disposal was made for bona fide commercial reasons and does not form part of a scheme or arrangements of which the main purpose, or one of the main purposes, is avoidance of liability to corporation tax (*TCGA 1992, s 32(2)*). Cost incurred include all capital expenditure on acquiring and enhancing the value of the asset whilst in the company's ownership (*TCGA 1992, s 32(3)*).

The value shifting provisions do not apply on a disposal resulting from a capital distribution in the course of winding up the company, which has made the intra-group transfer of the underlying asset (*TCGA 1992, s 32(5)*).

Value shifting: reorganisation of share capital

20.30   If a parent company depreciates shares in a subsidiary, which is followed by a company reconstruction to which *TCGA 1992, ss 127, 135(3)* apply (see **15.8**) there is a chargeable gain or allowable loss in relation to the value-shifting portion (*TCGA 1992, s 34*).

Where a company ceases to be a member of a group and there is a deemed disposal of shares or securities at market value under *TCGA 1992, s 178* or *TCGA 1992, s179* the amount of the notional market value consideration for the deemed disposal may be increased under the value shifting provisions. The relevant increase is the amount of any adjustment, which could have been made under the value shifting provisions if the deemed disposal had been an actual disposal (*TCGA 1992, ss 178(7)*, and *179(9)*).

Disposal of shares in another company

20.31   Where a company disposes of shares in, or securities of, another company, the value shifting rules cover a reduction in value, not only of the asset disposed of, but of any 'relevant asset', as defined by *TCGA 1992, s 30(2)*. An asset is a relevant asset if, at the time of the disposal to which *TCGA 1992, s 30* applies, it is owned by a company in the same group as the company making the disposal.

The extension to relevant assets only applies if the following conditions are satisfied.

During the period beginning when the relevant asset was depreciated and ending with the *s 30* disposal, the relevant asset has not been the subject of a disposal, other than a disposal at no gain/no loss under *TCGA 1992, s 171(1)*, or of a deemed disposal under the degrouping provisions in *TCGA 1992, ss 178* and *179*. For this purpose, *TCGA 1992, s 33(2)* disregards disposals of part of the asset. Assuming that all other circumstances had been the same, except that the relevant asset had not been depreciated, the value of the asset disposed of would have been materially greater.

LOSSES ATTRIBUTABLE TO DEPRECIATORY TRANSACTIONS

Depreciatory transactions within a group

20.32   If assets are transferred to group members at below market value this could fictitiously deflate the value of the company. If the shares were later sold, the market price would reflect the deflated price and hence a capital loss would arise. Such a loss will not be an allowable loss for CGT purposes (*TCGA 1992, s 176*).

The depreciatory transactions legislation in *TCGA 1992, ss 176* and *177* restrict the allowable loss on a disposal of shares or securities but do not convert a loss into a gain or increase the amount of a gain. A depreciatory transaction occurs when value is extracted from an asset. The aim of the legislation is to prevent artificial losses for both the shareholder and the company.

TCGA 1992, s 176 deals with depreciatory transactions involving groups of companies. *TCGA 1992, s 177* extends these rules to cover depreciatory distributions to a company with at least a 10% interest in the class of shares or securities to which the distribution relates. The provisions dealing with depreciatory distributions in respect of 10% holdings adopt the same general rules as apply to depreciatory transactions within groups.

For the legislation to apply there must have been a disposal of shares or securities (referred to in the legislation as 'the ultimate disposal') and the value of the shares or securities has been materially reduced, by a depreciatory transaction *TCGA 1992, s 176(1)*.

A depreciatory transaction' is a disposal of assets at other than market value by one group member to another. The adjustment is made on the basis that the allowable loss should not reflect any diminution in the value of the relevant company's assets, which was attributable to a depreciatory transaction. HMRC interpret materially reduced as meaning that the value of the shares or securities is reduced other than by a negligible amount (HMRC Capital Gains Manual CG46540).

Dividend stripping

20.33   This legislation is aimed at situations where a company might hold 10% or more of the same class securities of another company in a non-dealing non-group situation. A distribution is then made, the effect of which reduces the value of the other company dramatically. If the shares are then sold the distribution is not taken into account when calculating the chargeable gain on disposal (*TCGA 1992, s 177*).

Pre-entry losses and gains

20.34   A pre-entry asset is any asset owned by a company before it joined a group. The asset may have been transferred to other group members. An asset derived from a pre-entry asset is deemed to be part of the same asset, eg if the freehold reversion of a leasehold property is acquired (*TCGA 1992, Sch 7A, para 2(8)*).

For changes in ownerships prior to 5 December 2005, restrictions were in place whereby, if a company joined a group it is prevented from utilising its unre-lieved losses arising prior to the time it joined the group against gains on the disposal of assets transferred (or deemed to be transferred) from another group member (*TCGA 1992, Sch 7AA*, repealed by *FA 2006, s 70(4)*).

Similarly, if a company joins a group and in the same accounting period realises a chargeable gain it is prevented from relieving the gain against the loss on sale of group assets transferred to the company during the same accounting period (*TCGA 1992, Sch 7AA*). See **18.18–18.23** for the situation with effect from 5 December 2005.

A realised pre-entry loss belonging to a company on joining a group can be set against a profit on disposal of any asset made before it joined the group or against the profit on disposal of any asset that the company owned when it joined the group and sells after joining. The losses can also be set against the gains on disposal of any assets that it acquired from outside the group and used for the purposes of the trade, which it has continued to carry on since it joined the group (*TCGA 1992, Sch 7A(1)*).

The pre-entry unrealised losses are apportioned accordingly to the time that the company joined the group (*TCGA 1992, Sch 7A(2)*).

Where a company together with all the members of its original group joins a second group the pre-entry losses that it incurred whilst a member of the first group are not available for offset whilst it is a member of a second group (*TCGA 1992, s 1(7)*). See also *Five Oaks Properties Ltd v Revenue and Customs Comrs* (2006) SpC 563.

Chapter 21

The construction industry scheme

INTRODUCTION

21.1 Companies whose trade involves construction or building may find that they are required to comply with the construction industry scheme. Such businesses will include construction businesses, property developers, speculative builders and construction work gang leaders. *FA 2004* introduced the current construction industry scheme, which is effective from 5 April 2007. Legislation is contained in *FA 2004 ss 57–77, Schs 11* and *12*. Secondary legislation is contained within *2005/2045*. The Construction Industry Scheme applies not only to companies but also to individuals and partnerships.

FA 2004 scheme replaced the 6 April 1993 scheme. In brief, the new scheme replaces the CIS4 registration card and CIS6 tax certificates with a verification service. There is also a new employment status declaration. Monthly returns replace the old vouchers and a declaration of the employment status of those engaged is included with the monthly returns.

Sub-contractor companies are now required subject to conditions to register for gross or net payments. Sub-contractors registered under the old scheme are carried over to the new scheme. A contractor company engaging a sub-contractor must verify with HMRC whether to make payment gross or net.

Where a contractor company has a recent connection with the sub-contractor it need not carry out any verification procedures. HMRC will notify any change in the payment status of the sub-contractor to any contractor who has engaged that sub-contractor in the current or previous two years. Each month, the contractor will be required to make a return, including a nil return, of all payments made to sub-contractors in that month.

CONSTRUCTION CONTRACT

Meaning of a construction contract

21.2 A construction contract is a contract relating to construction operations carried out in the UK, which is not a contract of employment (*FA 2004,* *s 57 (2)*). The UK for this purpose consists of England, Scotland, Wales and Northern Ireland and its territorial waters but not the Channel Islands nor the Isle of Man (HMRC Manual CISR 11090 & 12130). For a construction contract to exist there must be a contract and a sub-contractor. Certain payments under construction contracts are to be made under deduction of sums on account of tax (*FA 2004, s 57 (1)*). Reverse premium payments (see **12.18**) are not payments under a construction contract (*SI 2005/2045 reg 20*).

Sub-contractor

21.3   The status of a sub-contractor is determined by the construction contract. If an individual or a company by reason of the construction contract has a duty to the contractor to carry out the operations of the construction contract or to furnish his own labour or to furnish the labour of the employees or officers of the company or indeed to furnish the labour of others or is answerable to the contractor for the work of others that individual or that company is considered to be a sub-contractor for these purposes (*FA 2004, s 58*).

Construction operations

21.4   Activities falling under one of more of the following headings are considered to be construction operations:

1   The construction, alteration, repair, extension, demolition or dismantling of buildings or structures (whether permanent or not), including offshore installations.

2   The construction, alteration, repair, extension or demolition of any works forming, or to form, part of the land, including (in particular) walls, roadworks, power-lines, electronic communications apparatus, aircraft runways, docks and harbours, railways, inland waterways, pipe-lines, reservoirs, water-mains, wells, sewers, industrial plant and installations for purposes of land drainage, coast protection or defence.

3   The installation in any building or structure of systems of heating, lighting, air-conditioning, ventilation, power supply, drainage, sanitation, water supply or fire protection.

4   The internal cleaning of buildings and structures, so far as carried out in the course of their construction, alteration, repair, extension or restoration.

5   The painting or decorating the internal or external surfaces of any building or structure.

6 Operations which form an integral part of, or are preparatory to, or are for rendering complete, such operations as are previously described in this subsection, including site clearance, earth-moving, excavation, tunnelling and boring, laying of foundations, erection of scaffolding, site restoration, landscaping and the provision of roadways and other access works.

(*FA 2004, s 74(2)*).

The following activities are not construction operations:

1 The drilling for, or extraction of, oil or natural gas.
2 The extraction (whether by underground or surface working) of minerals and tunnelling or boring, or construction of underground works, for this purpose.
3 The manufacture of building or engineering components or equipment, materials, plant or machinery, or delivery of any of these things to site.
4 The manufacture of components for systems of heating, lighting, air-conditioning, ventilation, power supply, drainage, sanitation, water supply or fire protection, or delivery of any of these things to site.
5 The professional work of architects or surveyors, or of consultants in building, engineering, interior or exterior decoration or in the laying-out of landscape.
6 The making, installation and repair of artistic works, being sculptures, murals and other

  works, which are wholly artistic in nature.
7 Signwriting and erecting, installing and repairing signboards and advertisements.
8 The installation of seating, blinds and shutters.
9 The installation of security systems, including burglar alarms, closed circuit television and public address systems

(*FA 2004, s 74(3)*).

HMRC offer a CIS helpline 0845 366 7899 for cases of doubt over a particular activity.

Contractors

21.5 A company carrying on a construction operation will be a contractor. Any business or public body, government department or agency or NHS trust will also be a contractor if the average annual expenditure on construction operations in the period of three years ending with the end of the last period of account before that time exceeds £1,000,000 (*FA 2004, s 59(l)*). The business will cease to be a contractor if the construction business annual expenditure is less £1,000,000 for three successive years. Any business will also be a contractor if it was not carrying on the business at the beginning of that period of three years but one-third of the total expenditure on construction operations for the part of that period during which business was carried on exceeds £1,000,000 (*FA 2004, s 59*). The amounts paid will only be treated as contract payments if the property is held for sale of letting or held as an investment property. Incidental use of the property is ignored (*SI 2005/2045, reg 22*). The property may be owned by the company, a fellow group member (see **10.5.**) or another company in which the company in question has a 50% or more holding.

A contractor may elect to be treated as different contractors in relation to different groups of sub-contractors, with the result that for each group the contractor was a different contractor. The election must give information to identify the groups of sub-contractors, and contain a certificate that there are no other sub-contractors besides those identified.

The election must be made before the beginning of the tax year for which it is to have effect. If a contractor company acquires the whole or part of any business from another contractor the company may elect within 90 days of the acquisition to be treated as a different contractor in relation to the acquired sub-contractors and to add some or all of the acquired sub-contractors to existing groups of sub-contractors in respect of whom an election is already in force. The election continues in effect until it is revoked. For a revocation to be effective it must be given before the beginning of the tax year for which it is to apply (*SI 2005/2045 reg 3*).

Transfer of a trade

21.6 If the company transfers the whole or part of a trade to another company to which *ICTA 1988 s 343* applies, the transferee company is deemed to have incurred the expenditure actually incurred by the transferor. Where only part of the trade is transferred a just and reasonable apportionment of the expenditure will be made.

DEDUCTIONS ON ACCOUNT OF TAX FROM CONTRACT PAYMENTS TO SUB-CONTRACTORS

Contract payments

21.7 A contract payment is any payment made by the contractor under a construction contract to either the sub-contractor, a person nominated by the sub-contractor or the contractor, or a person nominated by a sub-contractor under another contract in connection with all or some of the construction operations. A payment is not a subcontract payment if it is treated as employment earnings of an employed person or an agency worker (*FA 2004, s 60*). A payment does not include the cost of materials, VAT or an amount in respect of the Construction Industry Training Board (CITB) levy, but depending on the terms of the contract may include payments for subsistence and/or travelling expenses (Revenue Manual CISR 11100).

Deductions on account of tax from contract payments

21.8   It is necessary to be able to distinguish between the direct cost of materials for the construction operation and all other costs. The contractor must deduct tax when making a contract payment to the sub-contractor, which does not relate to the direct material costs (*FA 2004, s 61*). The sum deducted and payable to HMRC is treated as satisfying the sub-contractor's tax liability either for income tax if an individual or corporation tax if a company (*FA 2004, s 62*).

There is no requirement to deduct tax from a contract payment if the contractor is an approved public body or any company carrying on a business which includes construction operations as highlighted in **21.5** (*FA 2004, s 59(1)(b)*–(*l*)) and the total payments (excluding the direct cost of materials) are lower than or likely to be lower than £1,000 (*SI 2005/2045, reg 18*). Similarly, there is no requirement to deduct tax if the company carrying on a business, which includes construction operations on land, owned by the company and the total payments (excluding the direct cost of materials) are lower than or likely to be lower than £1,000 (*SI 2005/2045, reg 19*).

Rate of tax on deductions from contract payments

21.9   The rate of tax applied to the payment to the sub-contractor depends on the sub-contractor's status. For registered and verified sub-contractors the rate is 20%. For unregistered or unverified sub-contractors the rate is 30%. The rate is nil for those sub-contractors that are registered for gross payment (HMRC Manual CISR 11100 and *SI 2007/46*).

Monthly payment

21.10   The return period is the tax month, ie the fifth day of each month. Payment is due within 17 days of the end of the month if the payment is made electronically and within 14 days if the payment is made by any other means (*SI 2005/2045, reg 7*). If HMRC have not received payment in full within 17 days they may issue a notice requiring a return to be completed (*SI 2005/2045, reg 10*). HMRC may also make an estimation based on past payment criteria (*SI 2005/2045, reg 11*).

If the contractor makes an error in good faith or after enquiry genuinely believed that the scheme did not apply any amounts not deducted by the contractor company can be recovered from the sub-contractor. Also, the contractor may ask HMRC to issue a direction that the contractor is not liable to any excess tax (*SI 2005/2045, reg 9*). If there is a dispute between the contractor and the sub-contractor HMRC may make a determination of the amount due. Both contractor and sub-contractor have the right of appeal (*SI 2005/2045, reg 13*). Interest is charged on unpaid tax for a fiscal year (year ended 5 April) from 19 April until date of payment (*SI 2005/2045, reg 14*). HMRC have the power to bring proceedings against the contractor for unpaid tax and unpaid interest (*SI 2005/2045, reg 16*). A return for 50 subcontractors or less will attract a penalty of £100 for each month that it is outstanding. The monthly penalty is increased progressively by £100 for the addition of 50 subcontractors or less. Therefore a return for 40 subcontractors that is two months late will attract total penalties of £200, and a return for 90 contractors that is also two months late will attract total penalties of £400. See HMRC 4 October 2007, CIS – Penalty regimes.

Overpayments attract interest from the end of the tax year after the tax year in which the payment was made until date of repayment. If a payment was made more than 12 months after the end of the tax year then the repayment interest will run from the end of the tax year in which the payment was made until date of payment (*SI 2005/2045, reg 15*). Any tax overpaid during the year may be reclaimed from HMRC (*SI 2005/2045, reg 17*).

Default surcharge

21.11   If the company fails to pay the tax deducted by the due date it will fall liable to a default surcharge unless there is a reasonable excuse. Inability to pay is not a reasonable excuse (*SI 2005/2045, reg 46*). The company has the right of appeal (*SI 2005/2045, reg 47*).

The surcharge percentage is applied to the difference between the tax deducted from payments under the construction industry scheme and the amounts deducted under the following:

●   *Statutory Maternity Pay (Compensation of Employers) and Miscellaneous Amendment Regulations 1994, regs 4–6,*

●   *Statutory Paternity Pay and Statutory Adoption Pay (Administration) Regulations 2002, regs 3 and 5,* and

- if the company is a sub-contractor against relevant liabilities in the following order in that year:

  — Employee Class 1 NIC contributions

  — Employer Class 1 NIC contributions

  — PAYE

  — Student Loan deductions

  — Construction industry deductions from its sub-contractors.

The default percentage charged depends on the number of defaults and is calculated according to the following table:

Default number (within a surcharge period)	Specified percentage
1st	0%
2nd	0%
3rd	0.17%
4th	0.17%
5th	0.17%
6th	0.33%
7th	0.33%
8th	0.33%
9th	0.58%
10th	0.58%
11th	0.58%
12th	0.83%

A surcharge period begins on the day following the payment date and ends on the last day of the tax year for which there is no default for any specified payment. The surcharge is payable within 30 days after the issue of the surcharge notice (*SI 2005/2045, reg 48*). A contractor has the right of appeal against the notice within 30 days of the issue of the notice (*SI 2005/2045, reg 49*).

Quarterly payment

21.12   A contractor company may pay quarterly if it has reasonable grounds for believing that the average monthly amount will be less than £1,500 and the company chooses to pay quarterly.

The average monthly amount is based on the current year's tax month. The following formula is applied:

$$(P + N + L + S) - (SP + CD)$$

The formula uses the following amounts that would be payable in the circumstances:

P   =   PAYE due for the period less any PAYE repayments as calculated according to the *Income Tax (Pay As You Earn) Regulations 2003, SI 2003/2682, reg 68.*

N   =   Employees' class 1 primary contribution excluding and secondary contributions transferred from the employer to the employee under an *SSCBA 1992, Sch 1, para 3B(1)* election.

L   =   Student Loan repayments less tax credits under *Education (Student Loans) (Repayment) Regulations 2000, reg 39(1)* and *(3)*.

S   =   Tax due by the contractor for the tax month (*SI 2005/2045, reg 7*).

SP =   statutory sick pay, statutory maternity pay, statutory paternity pay and statutory adoption pay under *SSCBA 1992.*

CD =   the amount which others would deduct from payments to the company, in its position as a sub-contractor.

(*SI 2005/2045, reg 8*).

REGISTRATION

Registration of sub-contractors

21.13   HMRC will register a sub-contractor company for gross payment on submission of the relevant information and documentation. In other circumstances the company will be registered for net payment. The company is required to comply with the business, turnover and compliance test conditions in order to be eligible for gross payments:

In turn, the Board may direct that the conditions shall apply to the company directors, the beneficial shareholders if the company is a close company or specified persons as if each were an applicant for gross payment registration (*FA 2004, s 64(5)*).

Information to be supplied to HMRC

A sub-contractor company must supply the following information to HMRC:

- the name, address, national insurance number and unique taxpayer reference of the directors of the company or, if the company is a close company, the persons who are the beneficial owners of shares in the company,

- utility bills,

- council tax bills,

- current passport,

- driving licence,

- company registration number and

- company's memorandum and articles of association.

(*SI 2005/2045, reg 25*).

COMPANY CHANGE OF CONTROL

21.14   If there has been a change in the control of a company that is or that is applying for gross payment registration, HMRC may ask for information regarding the changes in control of the company (*FA 2004, s 65*).

The definition of control for this purpose is *ICTA 1988, s 840*. (See **14.4**.)

Where there is a change of control of a close company by reason of an issue or transfer of shares in the company to a person who was not a shareholder in the company immediately before the issue or transfer, the company must notify HMRC, within 30 days of the issue or of receiving information as to the transfer. The company must supply HMRC with details of the name and address of the person to whom the shares were issued or transferred. (*SI 2005/2045, reg 53*).

CANCELLATION OF REGISTRATION FOR GROSS PAYMENT

Reasons for cancellation

21.15   HMRC may issue a determination stating the reasons to cancel a gross payment registration if at any time it appears to them that:

- if an application to register the person for gross payment were to be made at that time, the Board would refuse so to register him,

- If he has made an incorrect return or provided incorrect information (whether as a contractor or as a sub-contractor) under any provision of this Chapter or of regulations made under it, or

- he has failed to comply (whether as a contractor or as a sub-contractor) with any such provision.

The gross payment cancellation takes effect from the end of a prescribed period after the making of the determination.

On receipt of the determination the sub-contractor company must register for net payment. The sub-contractor company is debarred from re-applying for gross payment registration for a year from cancellation.

Fraudulent conduct

21.16 HMRC may issue a determination stating the reasons, to cancel a company's gross payment registration if at any time if they have reasonable grounds to suspect that the person:

- became registered for gross payment on the basis of information which was false;

- has fraudulently made an incorrect return or provided incorrect information (whether as a contractor or as a sub-contractor) under any provision of this Chapter or of regulations made under it; or

- has knowingly failed to comply (whether as a contractor or as a sub-contractor) with any such provision.

In such circumstances the cancellation takes immediate effect on the issue of the determination. On receipt of the determination, if HMRC thinks fit, the sub-contractor company may register for net payment. Again, the sub-contractor company is debarred from re-applying for gross payment registration for a year from cancellation (*FA 2004, s 66*).

Registration cancellation right of appeal

21.17 The company has the right of appeal to the General Commissioners (or to the Special Commissioners if so elected), against the determination. The appeal must give the full grounds and be made within 30 days after the refusal or cancellation. A refusal or cancellation under appeal does not take effect until the later of:

- the abandonment of the appeal,

- the Commissioners determination of the appeal or
- the determination of the appeal by the appropriate higher court.

(*FA 2004, s 67*).

Verification, returns etc and penalties

21.18 HMRC may make regulations requiring the contractor company to verify the status of the sub-contractor company (*FA 2004, s 69*).

A contractor must verify with HMRC the status of the sub-contractor to whom gross payments are to be made or that person's nominee.

The contractor company must provide details of

- the company name, unique taxpayer reference (UTR), accounts office reference and employer's reference, and
- in relation to the person to whom it is proposing to make the payment and, where that person has appointed a nominee, his nominee:
    - (i) if that person or nominee is an individual, his name, unique taxpayer reference (UTR) and national insurance number;
    - (ii) if that person or nominee is a partner in a firm, the name of the firm and that partner, the unique taxpayer reference (UTR) of the firm, and if the partner is an individual his unique taxpayer reference (UTR) or national insurance number or if the partner is a company the unique taxpayer reference (UTR) or the company registration number;
    - (iii) if that person or nominee is a company, the name of the company, unique taxpayer reference (UTR) and the company registration number.

Verification is not possible until a contract is in place.

Situations where verification is not required

21.19 Verification is not required if:

the sub-contractor has been included in a sub-contract return in the current or previous two tax years;

- the payment is made within two years of 6 April 2007,

- if the person to whom he is proposing has been included in a return of the previous construction industry scheme within the current or previous two years;

- if the company or a company within the same group to whom it is proposed to make the payment has been included in a return of the previous construction industry scheme within the current or previous two years;

- the contractor has elected under *SI 2005/2045 reg 3* (see **21.5**);

- the contractor acquired the contract under which the payment is to be made in a transfer of a business as a going concern in one of the situations as described above.

(*SI 2005/2045 reg 6*).

Record-keeping

21.20   HMRC may make regulations requiring contractor companies that make payments under construction contracts to carry out the following:

- to make returns to HMRC,

- to keep records as prescribed relating to the payments or

- to provide such information as may be prescribed the to persons to whom the payments are made. (*FA 2004, s 70*).

Records must be kept for three years (*SI 2005/2045, reg 51(10)*).

In particular the company making the return must state that none of the contracts to which the return relates is a contract of employment, that the regulations have been complied with, the returns contain in the necessary information and confirmation that the verification status requirements of the sub-contractor have been complied with (SI 2005/2045 para 6). The sub-contractor need not seek verification if the sub-contractor has been included in a monthly return in the current or previous two years of the same company or group company. (A group is defined according to *ICTA 1988, s 413(3)* (see **10.5**)) (*SI 2005/2045, reg 6*).

Inspection of records of contractors and sub-contractors

21.21   A contractor or sub-contractor must produce records for the previous three years to HMRC when required to do so (*SI 2005/2045 para 51*). HMRC may make copies, remove or make extracts from these records. HMRC will issue a receipt for all documents removed and provide copies on request free of charge to the contractor or sub-contractor from whom the documents were removed.

Penalties

21.22 A sub-contractor company may be liable to a £3,000 penalty if it knowingly or recklessly makes a false statement, or provides a false document (*FA 2004, s 72*). An interest payable in connection with the scheme is neither taxable nor deductible for corporation tax purposes (*FA 2004, s 71*).

Since 19 October 2007, HMRC have charged penalties for all CIS returns not received by the due date.

Monthly return

21.23 Contractor companies are required to make monthly returns, either online or manually, within 14 days of the end of each month to HMRC. The contractor company may appoint another company in the same group as the scheme representative (*SI 2005/2045, reg 5*).

The return must show:

- the contractor's name,
- the contractor's unique taxpayer reference (UTR) and Accounts' Office reference,
- the tax month to which the return relates, and
- in respect of each sub-contractor to whom, or to whose nominee, payments under construction contracts were made by the contractor during that month:
    - (i)   the sub-contractor's name;
    - (ii) the sub-contractor's national insurance number (NINO) or company registration number (CRN), if known; and
    - (iii) the information specified in paragraph

Depending on whether the sub-contractor is registered for gross or net payments, details of the relevant payments should be given. The return may be submitted electronically.

Online filing can only be accepted via HMRC's free filing facility or Electronic Data Interchange (EDI). Alternatively third party agent filing is recognised.

The CIS300 and the CIS300(Man) are the only acceptable paper forms. Nil returns may be obtained from the CIS Helpline 0845 366 7899.

HMRC will not accept photocopies, PDFs, computer listings and paper substitute returns of any description. See HMRC Guidance Note 29 August 2007, The contractor monthly return – further guidance on its completion.

Declaration

21.24   The company must declare that none of the contracts to which the return relates is a contract of employment. The company must indicate whether it has verified each sub-contractor status. The contractor must provide the sub-contractor with details of the payments not later than 14 days after the end of the tax month to which the payment relates. Details for a sub-contractor on a net payment basis will include: the contractor's name, the contractor's employer's reference, the tax month to which the payments relate or the date of the payment, the sub-contractor's name, the sub-contractor's unique taxpayer reference (UTR), the total amount of contract payments made by the contractor to the sub-contractor during the tax month, the total amount included in those payments which the contractor is satisfied represents the direct cost to any person other than the contractor of materials used or to be used in carrying out the construction contract to which the contract payment relates, and the total tax deducted. Amount deducted from the payments and the verification reference if the sub-contractor is not registered. If not payments are made, nil returns are still required (*SI 2005/2045, reg 6*).

If the company fails to submit a return there is an automatic penalty of £100 per month for 50 sub-contractors. If the return is made over 12 months late there is a penalty of up to the tax (*SI 2005/2045, reg 4 (TMA 1970, s 98A)*).

GROSS PAYMENT TESTS

21.25   If a company applies for gross payment registration it must satisfy the business test, the turnover test and the compliance test (*FA 2004, Sch 11, para 9*).

The business test

21.26   The company must satisfy HMRC that:

•   it is carrying on a business in the UK, which

- consists of or includes the carrying out of construction operations or the furnishing or arranging for the furnishing of labour in carrying out construction operations, and is substantially carried on through a bank account.

The following evidence must be supplied to HMRC:

- the company's address;
- invoices, contracts or purchase orders for construction work carried out by the company;
- details of payments for construction work;
- the books and accounts of the company;
- details of the company bank account, including bank statements.

(*SI 2005/2045, reg 27*).

The turnover test

21.27   The company must either satisfy HMRC with evidence that it is likely to receive the minimum turnover in the year in which the application is made or satisfy HMRC that the only persons with shares in the company are companies, which are limited by shares and themselves, are registered for gross payment;

The minimum turnover for the period is the smaller of:

- £30,000 × number or relevant persons for the company or
- £200,000.

Company directors are relevant persons. Beneficial owners of shares in a close company are also relevant persons (*FA 2004, Sch 11, para 11*).

The company must be able to supply evidence of turnover and relevant payments together with documentary evidence to demonstrate that operations during the period amounted to construction operations (*SI 2005/2045, reg 29*). In the case of a new business evidence of turnover and relevant persons during the qualifying period should be supplied. Evidence should also be supplied of construction contracts entered into by the company including payment schedules where the aggregate value of these contracts exceeds £200,000 and that payments of at least £30,000 have been made.

If a company's business does not consist mainly of construction operations HMRC will treat the turnover test as met, if not actually met, if the following conditions are met. These conditions are that in the year prior to making the application the total turnover of the business exceeded the relevant turnover threshold, and in the year following making the application the company is likely to receive relevant payments in relation to construction operations which are incidental to the company's main business (*SI 2005/2045 reg 31*).

The compliance test

21.28   Within 12 months of the registration application the company must have complied with all HMRC requests concerning information and documentation (*FA 2004, Sch 11, paras 12* and *14*). HMRC will treat the following prescribed obligations as being satisfied by the following prescribed circumstances:

Prescribed obligations		Prescribed circumstances
Obligation to submit monthly contractor return within the required period.	1	Return is submitted not later than 28 days after the due date, and
	2	the company— (a) has not otherwise failed to comply with this obligation within the previous 12 months, or (b) has failed to comply with this obligation on not more than two occasions within the previous 12 months.
Obligation to pay— (a) the tax deducted from payments made	1	Payment is made not later than 14 days after the due date, and
	2	the company— (a) has not otherwise failed to comply with this obligation within the previous 12 months, or

Prescribed obligations	Prescribed circumstances
during that tax period, or (b) tax liable to be deducted under the PAYE Regulations.	(b) has failed to comply with this obligation on not more than two occasions within the previous 12 months.

Obligation to pay income tax.	1	Payment is made not later than 28 days after the due date, and
	2	the applicant has not otherwise failed to comply with this obligation within the previous 12 months.

Obligation to submit an annual return under the PAYE regulations 73, 74 and 85 within the required period.	Return is submitted after the due date.
Obligation to pay corporation tax for which the applicant or company is liable.	1 Payment is made not later than 28 days after the due date, and 2 any shortfall in that payment has incurred an interest charge but no penalty.
Obligation to submit a self-assessment return within the required period.	Return is submitted after the due date.
Obligations and requests to supply information in support of the compliance test.	The failure to comply occurred before 6 April 2007 but complied with previous requirements.
Obligation to make a payment under the *Tax Acts* or *TMA 1970*	Late or non-payment of an amount under £100.

(*SI 2005/2045, reg 32; SI 2008/1282*).

HMRC will carry out a 'Scheduled Review', also known as an 'Ongoing TTQT (Tax Treatment Qualification Test), to check whether companies holding gross payment status comply with their obligations. See HMRC Technical Note 29 October 2007 – Construction industry scheme – tax treatment qualification test.

APPLICATION OF SUMS DEDUCTED FROM CONTRACT PAYMENTS

21.29   The sums that a contractor company deducts from payments made to a sub-contractor may be applied as follows:

- Employee Class 1 NIC contributions

- Employer Class 1 NIC contributions

- PAYE

- Student Loan deductions

- refunds due to HMRC for statutory sick pay, statutory maternity pay, statutory paternity pay or statutory adoption pay

- Construction industry deductions from its sub-contractors.

HMRC will not repay any tax deducted by a contractor from a sub-contractors payment until after the end of the tax year in which the deduction was made, has ended and the contractor has delivered its annual PAYE return.

Any remaining amount will either be repaid to the contractor or used to off-set any outstanding corporation tax (*SI 2005/2045, reg 56*).

Chapter 22

The year end

CORPORATION TAX COMPUTATION

22.1 Shortly after the year end the company will prepare its annual accounts, whereupon it will be able to prepare its corporation tax computation and self-assessment return. Sample returns have been reproduced in the following pages by kind permission of HMRC.

Adjusted profits

22.2 A master corporation tax computation and capital allowances computation is shown on the following pages that may be adapted to suit individual company needs. The company will commence by adjusting its trading profits in the following manner.

Adjustment of profits under Schedule D Case I

Pro forma

	£	£
Profit before tax per accounts		
Add: Expenditure charged in the accounts, but not allowable as a deduction for Schedule D Case I purposes		
Income which has not been credited in the accounts but which is taxable under Schedule D Case I		
	———	
	———	

536

Less: Income credited in the accounts, but not
taxable under Schedule D Case I

Expenditure not charged in the accounts,
but allowable as a deduction under
Schedule D Case I

Schedule D
Case I

The corporation tax payable will then be calculated. See Chapter 3 for rates and marginal relief computations.Corporation tax computation

22.3 The company will then bring all its income into charge under the various schedule headings to calculate its PCTCT (profits chargeable to corporation tax).

Corporation tax computation for the accounting period of ... months ended on ...

£

Schedule D Case I

Schedule A

Schedule D Case III

Schedule D Case V

Other income

Schedule D Case VI

Chargeable gains

Less: Expenses of management

Charges on income

Profits chargeable to
corporation tax (PCTCT)

Capital allowance computation

22.4 The company will also prepare its capital allowances claim. The following is an outline computation.

Capital allowances—plant and machinery computation for the ... months ended on ...

	Main pool	Special rate allowances	Expensive car	Short-life asset	Allowance given
	£	£	£	£	£
Allowable qualifying expenditure b/f					
Additions not qualifying for FYA					
Annual investment allowance maximum £50,000					
Disposal proceeds					
Balancing allowance/ balancing charge					
WDA (25%/transitional/20%)					
WDA (10%/6%) (restricted)					
Additions qualifying for FYA					
Less: FYA					
Allowable qualifying expenditure c/f					
Total allowances for year					

Capital gains

22.5   A company's chargeable gains incurred during an accounting period are assessed to corporation tax together with its other income for that accounting period. Capital gains legislation is often used as an incentive to provide tax breaks or as an anti-avoidance regulator. See **Chapter 20** for areas discussed.

PLANNING

22.6   A company's accounts and corporation tax computation are based on its transactions for a set period. Once that period has ended, the time has passed to make any changes to the transactions. Hence all planning should ideally take place before the year end.

The minimisation of corporation tax liabilities and the maximisation of reported profits is possibly each and every company's ultimate goal. Under corporation tax self-assessment the company should be aware that planning also looks to ensuring that the company's returns are accurate and timely to avoid interest and penalties and to minimise any adverse consequences arising from an enquiry.

The following list is a summary of some of the areas that a company may wish to turn its attention to with respect to the year end. The list is by no means exhaustive:

- **Accounting dates**. If a company pays corporation tax by quarterly instalments it will pay its first instalment six months and 13 days after the beginning of the accounting period. If the trade is seasonal it might not have sufficient funds to pay the corporation tax. Consider changing the accounting date so that the high-earning period falls at the beginning of the year rather than the end. See **3.10**.

- **Activities**. Consider the type of activities that the organisation carries out and whether it would qualify for charitable or mutual status. See **5.46–5.57**.

- The **annual investment allowance** replaces the FYA with effect from 1 April 2008 onwards. The maximum allowance is £50,000 in a 12-month accounting period. Any balance of unrelieved expenditure qualifies for a writing-down allowance in the period of acquisition. See **6.33, 6.46–6.54**.

- **Apportionment of profits**. If an accounting period is longer than 12 months, taxable profits are normally apportioned pro rata on a time basis. However, an actual basis may be used if this gives a more accurate result. See **2.6**.

- **Assets** may be transferred to group companies without a charge to capital gains tax arising. A deemed transfer may take place to another group company prior to a disposal to a third party, in order to utilise that company's capital losses. An election must be made within two years from end of the vendor's accounting period in which the disposal is made to a third party (*TCGA 1992, s 171A*). See **20.16**.

- **Associated companies**. Associated companies eradicate the benefit of the small companies rate of corporation tax. Prepare a company structure in good time to ascertain whether the separate companies are actually necessary. See **4.27**.

- **Bonus**. If a provision is included in the accounts it must comply with FRS12. There must have been a liability at the balance sheet date. Therefore, if relief is to be given against PCTCT for the accounting period in question, the Board of Directors should formally agree and minute the bonus payment before the end of the accounting period. See **5.16**.

- **Business renovation allowance**. Expenditure on the renovation of unused business premises in a disadvantaged area may qualify for the 100% business renovation allowance. . Check the stamp duty section of HMRC website to carry out a postcode check. See **6.86–6.91**.

- Expenditure on surplus **Business premises** turned into residential accommodation may attract the 100 per cent flat conversion allowance. See **6.102–6.111**.

- **Capital allowance** claims must be made or amended or withdrawn within 12 months after the company's return filing date. If the return is under enquiry, this period may be extended to the later of 30 days after a closure notice is issued on the completion of an enquiry or 30 days after HMRC issues a notice of amendment to a return following the completion of an enquiry or 30 days after the determination of any appeal against an HMRC amendment. Enquiry does not include a restricted enquiry into an amendment to a return (restricted because the time limit for making an enquiry into the return itself has expired) (*FA 1998, Sch 18, para 82*). See Chapter **6**.

- **Cars**. Instead of purchasing a standard model that will only qualify for a reduced writing-down allowance, consider purchasing a low-emission vehicle that will qualify for a 100% first year allowance. See **6.27**.

- **Close investment holding company**. Where a company is making investments in land and property and that property is used by a person connected with the company, the company may be classed as a close investment holding company, liable to pay corporation tax at the full rate. See **4.23–4.26**.

- Assets eligible for capital allowances may be transferred between **connected parties** at tax written-down value. Both parties must submit an election to HMRC within two years from date of sale (*CAA 2001, s 569(1)*). See **15.25**.

- **Companies Act 2006**. The new provisions are being introduced over the period to 1 October 2009. These may have an influence on a company's chosen status. See **1.2**. They may also have an influence on the directors' approach to the management of the company's corporation tax affairs. See **1.11**.

- The **construction of a building** may bring the company within the construction industry scheme. See **Chapter 21**.

- **Contaminated land**. Expenditure on a brown field site may mean that the land is contaminated. Expenditure on contaminated land qualifies for a 150% deduction against PCTCT. See **8.33–8.45**.

- **Controlled foreign companies**. Review interest in overseas companies. The CFC legislation will not apply if a CFC company carries on a genuine economic activity in the country concerned. A formal claim can be made to HMRC. See **13.29**.

- **Corporate venturing scheme**. Gross assets of a qualifying company issuing shares under a CVS must not exceed £7m immediately before the issue and must not exceed £8m immediately afterwards. Similar rules apply for the enterprise investment scheme and venture capital trusts. Companies should take note of their gross assets if considering a share issue under one of these schemes. See **12.33**.

- **Corporation tax rates**. The main rate of corporation tax is decreasing but the small company rate is increasing. Some smaller company director/ shareholders will need to consider whether a company remains a viable option. See **3.2**.

- **Discovery assessment**. The risk of a discovery assessment may be avoided if supporting details of possible contentious items are supplied to HMRC with the corporation tax computation. This may be for instance any analysis of repairs, legal expenses or the like. If a different interpretation of the law is taken from that viewed by HMRC, this should be clearly explained. The Revenue Manuals explain HMRC's interpretation of the law and working practices. See **2.32**.

- **Dividends**. Interim dividends are due and payable on the day they are declared. For this reason they may not be effective in clearing an overdue director's loan account. See **4.18**.

- **Dormant company**. Check to see if any of the associated companies are dormant throughout the accounting period. If so, they will not be included within the count of associated companies. See **4.30**.

- **Enquiries**. For single companies and small groups there is an incentive to file the corporation tax return as soon as possible after the end of the accounting period because the enquiry window is 12 months after the return was delivered to HMRC. This applies to accounting periods ended after 31 March 2008. See **2.15**.

- **Enterprise management incentives**. Ensure the company claims for any outstanding corporation tax relief on shares issued at a discount (*FA 2006, s 93*). See **5.27**.

- **Enterprise Zone** expenditure qualifies for a 100% initial allowance and if not fully claimed any balance of expenditure qualifies for a writing down allowance (*FA 2008, s 86*), but a balancing charge may still arise on disposal. See **6.76** and **6.85**.

- **Enrivonmentally beneficial plant and machinery and energy saving plant or machinery** qualify for a 100% FYA. Loss making companies may claim a repayable tax credit. See **6.24** and **9.29**.

- **Flat conversion allowance** is available on the conversion of business premises into flats. (*CAA 2001, s 393A*). See **6.102–6.111**.

- **Group relief** claims must be made or amended or withdrawn within 12 months after the company's return filing date. If the return is under enquiry, this period may be extended to the later of 30 days after a closure notice is issued on the completion of an enquiry or 30 days after HMRC issues a notice of amendment to a return following the completion of an enquiry or 30 days after the determination of any appeal against an HMRC amendment. Enquiry does not include a restricted enquiry into an amendment to a return (restricted because the time limit for making an enquiry into the return itself has expired) (*FA 1998, Sch 18, para 74*). See Chapter **10**.

- **Group payment arrangements**. Consider whether it would be administratively efficient for one company in a group to attend to the group's corporation tax payments. See **3.21**.

- **HMRC**. A company should ensure that HMRC has been informed that the company is within the charge to corporation tax or has commenced to trade. The company should ensure that HMRC has the correct details for the company. It is the company's duty to keep HMRC informed. See **2.2**.

- **Industrial buildings balancing adjustments** no longer apply from 21 March 2007. On a disposal, the purchaser takes over the balance of the seller's unrelieved expenditure (*FA 2007, s 36*). See **6.82**.

- **Industrial buildings writing down allowances** are to be withdrawn completely for the financial year 2011 onwards and transitional rules apply for the financial years 2008, 2009 and 2010 (*FA 2008, ss 84* and *85*). See **6.75**.

- **Intangible assets** allow debits and credits to follow the accounting treatment. A company might wish to ensure that its depreciation policy is suitable. See **7.10**.

- Corporate **Landlords** may claim an allowance of up to £1,500 per dwelling when installing energy-saving items in residential property. See **12.21**.

- **Large company**. Check if the company is large. If it is large, for one year it will not need to make quarterly payments of corporation tax unless it is large for the second year, subject to conditions. See **3.9–3.10**.

- **Leasing**. Long funding finance lessors do not qualify for capital allowances. See **6.57–6.60**.. Plant leased with an operative will qualify. See **6.31**.

- **Loans to directors**. Outstanding loans to a director at the year end attract a charge under *ICTA 88, s 419* if not repaid within nine months of the year end. Ensure there are no outstanding loans and that they are repaid promptly. See **4.14–4.22**.

- **Long life asset.** The writing down allowance on existing long life assets has been increased from 6% to 10% and included in the special rate pool. See **6.37**.

- Relief for a **non-trading deficit** on a loan relationship must be made within two years from the end of the accounting period in which a deficit arises. If the deficit is to be carried forward the claim must be made within two years from the end of the accounting period following the deficit period, or within such further period as the Board may allow (*FA 1996, s 83(6)*, *(7)*). See **11.17–11.22**.

- **Penalties**. New penalty provisions have been introduced for accounting periods commencing on or after 1 April 2008. So as not to fall foul of these provisions, companies should ensure that they neither carelessly nor deliberately supply a false document to HMRC. See **2.36.**

- **On-line filing**. Consider whether it will be more expedient to file the company's corporation tax on-line for the year. See **2.10**.

- **Pension contributions**. A small company may consider making additional pension contributions on behalf of its directors/shareholders. In applying the spreading rules the company should be aware of the possible business purpose test restriction. See **5.31–5.32**.

- **Plant and machinery writing down allowances** have been reduced to 20% per annum, from 1 April 2008. Relief is therefore spread over a longer period than previously. Transitional rates apply in the interim. See **6.35**.

- **Profits**. The corporation tax computation is based on the reported profits. Certain items of expenditure may be accelerated or sales transactions deferred in order to minimise profits in a period. This may simply be placing orders to meet the company's requirements or considering additional directors' and staff bonuses. See **5.16** regarding bonus payments. The accounts concerned must comply with GAAP. See **Chapter 17.**

- **Professional work in progress** is to be valued at the sales price. See **5.40–5.42** for the adjustments required.

- **Property business**. An investor who purchases a block of flats for sublet should make a claim for capital allowances for building fixtures such as lifts, security systems, emergency lighting, door entry systems, central heating systems etc. Where the fixture covers the whole building a reasonable apportionment should be made to the residential parts but if this is no more than 25% of the whole no apportionment is made. HMRC Capital Allowance Manual CA 20020. See **12.16**.

- **Property developer**. buying a building as trading stock may claim IBAs (until fully withdrawn) if the building is in use for an industrial purpose.

The building is required to be in industrial use but not necessarily by the developer. See **6.71**.

- **Research and development**. An SME can claim an enhanced deduction of 175% of its R&D expenditure against its taxable profits or a repayable tax credit of 14%. See **8.20.** (Previously the rates were 150% and 16% respectively.) A large company can claim an enhanced deduction of 130% on its qualifying expenditure (increased from 125%). See **8.23**. The new rates apply for expenditure incurred on or after 21 July 2008 or later, as announced by Treasury Instrument. Claims must be made within the normal corporation tax timescale two years after the end of the accounting period.

- **Residential property**. HMRC accept that a university hall of residence, accommodation used for holiday letting, a hospital, a nursing home or a prison are not dwelling houses. Substantial capital allowance claims can be made here. See **6.92**.

- **Roll-over relief**. If a company is disposing of tangible assets or intangible assets it is well advised to consider purchasing new assets either 12 months before or within three years after sale to claim roll-over relief to reduce the chargeable gain. See **20.6–20.13** and **7.20–7.22**.

- **Short life assets**. The balance of expenditure may be written off in full if it is less than £1,000. See **6.36**.

- A **special rate allowance** of 10% can be claimed on thermal insulation expenditure, integral fixtures and long life assets brought forward from 1 April 2008. See **6.41**.

- If **stock** is transferred to a connected party on cessation of a trade, the parties may elect for the stock to be valued at the higher of cost or sales price. The valuation applies to both parties. The election must be made within two years from the end of accounting period in which trade ceased (*ICTA 1988, s 100(1C)*). See **19.7**.Transfers out of stock for another purpose are valued at sales price. See **5.43.**

- If a **subsidiary company** with surplus funds is in liquidation, it could invest in quoted shares in UK companies to avoid the 28% corporation tax rate on attaining a CIHC status. The dividends will not be taxable so the 28% CT rate cannot apply. See **4.23–4.24**.

- **Substantial shareholding exemption**. HMRC offer guidance on whether an investor and/or an investee company meet the conditions for the relief. See **12.29**.

- **Surrenderable losses** for group relief purposes may need to be set off against the company's other profits before surrender. The following is a brief summary. See **10.7** for full details.

	Required to be set off against claimant company's profits before used in a group relief claim
Trading losses	No
Excess capital allowances	No
Non-trading loan relationship debits	No
Charges on income	Yes
Schedule A losses	Yes
Management expenses	Yes
Non-trading loss on a loan relationship	Yes

- **Trade**. A trade must continue for *ICTA 1988, s 393* losses to be utilised. See **9.14**. For a carry back the trade must have been in existence at some time during the previous 12 months. For a carry forward the loss continues to be available until the trade ceases. See **9.2**.

- The company's **trading status** is important to retain loss and investment reliefs. Consideration should be given to the company's long-term plans. Restructuring may be seen as necessary to separate the investment and the trading activities. See **15.7–15.24** and **16.13–16.18**.

- **Transfer pricing** rules now apply to all companies entering into transactions with associates. Ensure that documentation is in place to support the inter company arrangement. See Chapter **14**. If a company with which the company trades has a transfer pricing adjustment the company should ensure that it claims the compensating relief. See **14.15**.

- A loss on disposal of shares in an **unquoted trading company** may be set against income of an investment company. The claim must be made within two years from the end of the accounting period in which the loss occurred (*ICTA 1988, s 573(2)*). See **12.25**.

- **Winding-up**. With no formal liquidation procedure a private company may now have funds remaining of up to £4,000 without them being claimed as *bona vacantia*. See **16.32**.

Appendix 1

Retail price index

	Jan	Feb	Mar	Apr	May	Jun
1982	78.73	78.76	79.44	81.04	81.62	81.85
1983	82.61	82.97	83.12	84.28	84.64	84.84
1984	86.84	87.20	87.48	88.64	88.97	89.20
1985	91.20	91.94	92.80	94.78	95.21	95.41
1986	96.25	96.60	96.73	97.67	97.85	97.79
1987	100.00	100.40	100.60	101.80	101.90	101.90
1988	103.30	103.70	104.10	105.80	106.20	106.60
1989	111.00	111.80	112.30	114.30	115.00	115.40
1990	119.50	120.20	121.40	125.10	126.20	126.70
1991	130.20	130.90	131.40	133.10	133.50	134.10
1992	135.60	136.30	136.70	138.80	139.30	139.30
1993	137.90	138.80	139.30	140.60	141.10	141.00
1994	141.30	142.10	142.50	144.20	144.70	144.70
1995	146.00	146.90	147.50	149.00	149.60	149.80
1996	150.20	150.90	151.50	152.60	152.90	153.00
1997	154.40	155.00	155.40	156.30	156.90	157.50
1998	159.50	160.30	160.80	162.60	163.50	163.40
1999	163.40	163.70	164.10	165.20	165.60	165.60
2000	166.60	167.50	168.40	170.10	170.70	171.10
2001	171.10	172.00	172.20	173.10	174.20	174.40
2002	173.30	173.80	174.50	175.70	176.20	176.20
2003	178.40	179.30	179.90	181.20	181.50	181.30
2004	183.10	183.80	184.60	185.70	186.50	186.80
2005	188.90	189.60	190.50	191.60	192.00	192.20
2006	193.40	194.20	195.00	196.50	197.70	198.50
2007	201.60	203.10	204.40	205.40	206.20	207.30
2008	209.80	211.40	212.10	214.00	215.10	216.80

	Jul	Aug	Sep	Oct	Nov	Dec
1982	81.88	81.90	81.85	82.26	82.66	82.51
1983	85.30	85.68	86.06	86.36	86.67	86.89
1984	89.10	89.94	90.11	90.67	90.95	90.87
1985	95.23	95.49	95.44	95.59	95.92	96.05
1986	97.52	97.82	98.30	98.45	99.29	99.62
1987	101.80	102.10	102.40	102.90	103.40	103.30
1988	106.70	107.90	108.40	109.50	110.00	110.30
1989	115.50	115.80	116.60	117.50	118.50	118.80
1990	126.80	128.10	129.30	130.30	130.00	129.90
1991	133.80	134.10	134.60	135.10	135.60	135.70
1992	138.80	138.90	139.40	139.90	139.70	139.20
1993	140.70	141.30	141.90	141.80	141.60	141.90
1994	144.00	144.70	145.00	145.20	145.30	146.00
1995	149.10	149.90	150.60	149.80	149.80	150.70
1996	152.40	153.10	153.80	153.80	153.90	154.40
1997	157.50	158.50	159.30	159.50	159.60	160.00
1998	163.00	163.70	164.40	164.50	164.40	164.40
1999	165.10	165.50	166.20	166.50	166.70	167.30
2000	170.50	170.50	171.70	171.60	172.10	172.20
2001	173.30	174.00	174.60	174.30	173.60	173.40
2002	175.90	176.40	177.60	177.90	178.20	178.50
2003	181.30	181.60	182.50	182.60	182.70	183.50
2004	186.80	187.40	188.10	188.60	189.00	189.90
2005	192.20	192.60	193.10	193.30	193.60	194.10
2006	198.50	199.20	200.10	200.40	201.10	202.70
2007	206.10	207.30	208.00	208.90	209.70	210.90

Appendix 2

Company tax return forms

Company Tax Return form CT600 (2008) Version 2   549

Company – Short Tax Return form CT600 (Short) (2008) Version 2   557

Company Tax Return form – Supplementary Pages – Loans to participators by close companies CT600A (2006) Version 2   561

Company Tax Return form – Supplementary Pages – Controlled foreign companies CT600B (2006) Version 2   565

Company Tax Return form – Supplementary Pages – Group and consortium CT600C (2006) Version 2   568

Company Tax Return form – Supplementary Pages – Charities and CASCs CT600E (2006) Version 2   572

Company Tax Return form – Supplementary Pages – Corporate Venturing Scheme CT600G (2006) Version 2   576

Company Tax Return form – Supplementary pages – Cross-border royalties CT600H (2006) Version 2   580

Company Tax Return form – Supplementary pages – Disclosure of tax avoidance schemes CT600J (2006) Version 2   583

Company Tax Return form
CT600 (2008) Version 2
for accounting periods ending on or after 1 July 1999

Your company tax return

If we send the company a *Notice* to deliver a company tax return (form *CT603*) it has to comply by the filing date or we charge a penalty, even if there is no tax to pay. A return includes a company tax return form, any Supplementary Pages, accounts, computations and any relevant information.

Is this the right form for the company? Read the advice on pages 3 to 6 of the Company tax return guide (the *Guide*) before you start.

The forms in the CT600 series set out the information we need and provide a standard format for calculations. Use the *Guide* to help you complete the return form. It contains general information you may need and box by box advice

Please note that some boxes on form *CT600* are not in order, reflecting changes made since the form was first published in 2004.

Company information

Company name

Company registration number   Tax Reference as shown on the CT603   Type of Company

Registered office address

Postcode

About this return

This is the above company's return for the period
from (dd/mm/yyyy)   to (dd/mm/yyyy)

Put an 'X' in the appropriate box(es) below

A repayment is due for this return period

A repayment is due for an earlier period

Making more than one return for this company now

This return contains estimated figures

Company part of a group that is not small

Disclosure of tax avoidance schemes
Notice of disclosable avoidance schemes

Transfer pricing
Compensating adjustment claimed

Company qualifies for SME exemption

Accounts
I attach accounts and computations
• for the period to which this return relates

• for a different period

If you are not attaching accounts and computations, say why not

Supplementary Pages
If you are enclosing any Supplementary Pages put an 'X' in the appropriate box(es)

Loans to participators by close companies, form *CT600A*

Controlled foreign companies, form *CT600B*

Group and Consortium, form *CT600C*

Insurance, form *CT600D*

Charities and Community Amateur Sports Clubs (CASCs), form *CT600E*

Tonnage tax, form *CT600F*

Corporate Venturing Scheme, form *CT600G*

Cross-border royalties, form *CT600H*

Supplementary charge in respect of ring fence trade, form *CT600I*

Disclosure of tax avoidance schemes, form *CT600J*

Appendix 2: CT600 (2008) Version 2

Company tax calculation

Turnover

1   Total turnover from trade or profession   **1** £

2   Banks, building societies, insurance companies and other financial concerns. *Put an 'X' in this box if you do not have a recognised turnover and have not made an entry in box 1*   **2**

Income

3   Trading and professional profits   **3** £

4   Trading losses brought forward claimed against profits   **4** £

     box 3 minus box 4

5   Net trading and professional profits   **5** £

6   Bank, building society or other interest, and profits and gains from non-trading loan relationships   **6** £

7   *Put an 'X' in box 7 if the figure in box 6 is net of carrying back a deficit from a later accounting period*   **7**

8   Annuities, annual payments and discounts not arising from loan relationships and from which income tax has not been deducted   **8** £

9   Overseas income within Sch D Case V   **9** £

10   Income from which income tax has been deducted   **10** £

11   Income from UK land and buildings   **11** £

12   Non-trading gains on intangible fixed assets   **12** £

13   Tonnage tax profits   **13** £

14   Annual profits and gains not falling under any other heading   **14** £

     total of boxes 12, 13 and 14

15   Income within Sch D Case VI   **15** £

Chargeable gains

16   Gross chargeable gains   **16** £

17   Allowable losses including losses brought forward   **17** £

     box 16 minus box 17

18   Net chargeable gains   **18** £

19   Losses brought forward against certain investment income   **19** £

20   Non-trade deficits on loan relationships (including interest), and derivative contracts (financial instruments) brought forward   **20** £

     net sum of boxes 5, 6, 8, 9, 10, 11,15, & 18 minus sum of boxes 19 and 20

21   **Profits before other deductions and reliefs**   **21** £

CT600 (2008) Version 2

550

Deductions and reliefs

22 CVS loss relief, and losses on unquoted shares under S573 ICTA 1988

22 £ _____

23 *Put an 'X' in box 23 if the entry in box 22 includes CVS loss relief, complete and attach form CT600G*

23 _____

24 Management expenses under S75 ICTA 1988

24 £ _____

25 Interest distributions under S468L ICTA 1988

25 £ _____

26 Schedule A losses for this or previous accounting period under S392A ICTA 1988

26 £ _____

27 Capital allowances for the purposes of management of the business

27 £ _____

28 Non-trade deficits for this accounting period from loan relationships and derivative contracts (financial instruments)

28 £ _____

29 Non-trading losses on intangible fixed assets

29 £ _____

30 Trading losses of this or a later accounting period under S393A ICTA 1988

30 £ _____

31 *Put an 'X' in box 31 if amounts carried back from later accounting periods are included in box 30*

31 _____

32 Non-trade capital allowances

32 £ _____

33 Total of deductions and reliefs

total of boxes 22, 24 to 30 and 32
33 £ _____

34 Profits before charges and group relief

box 21 minus box 33
34 £ _____

35 Charges paid

35 £ _____

36 Group relief

36 £ _____

37 Profits chargeable to corporation tax

box 34 minus boxes 35 and 36
37 £ _____

169 Ring fence profits included

169 £ _____

Appendix 2: CT600 (2008) Version 2

Tax calculation

| 38 Franked investment income | 38 £ |

39 Number of associated companies in this period
or
40 Associated companies in the first financial year

41 Associated companies in the second financial year

42 *Put an 'X' in box 42 if the company claims to be charged at the starting rate or the small companies' rate on any part of its profits, or is claiming marginal rate relief*

Enter how much profit has to be charged and at what rate of tax

Financial year *(yyyy)*	Amount of profit	Rate of tax	Tax	
43	44 £	45	46 £	p
	47 £	48	49 £	p
	50 £	51	52 £	p
53	54 £	55	56 £	p
	57 £	58	59 £	p
	60 £	61	62 £	p

total of boxes 46, 49, 52, 56, 59 and 62

| 63 Corporation tax | 63 £ | p |

| 64 Marginal rate relief | 64 £ | p |

| 65 Corporation tax net of marginal rate relief | 65 £ | p |

| 66 Underlying rate of corporation tax | 66 · % |

| 67 Profits matched with non-corporate distributions | 67 £ |

| 68 Tax at non-corporate distributions rate | 68 £ | p |

| 69 Tax at underlying rate on remaining profits | 69 £ | p |

See note for box 70 in CT600 Guide

| 70 Corporation tax chargeable | 70 £ | p |

Reliefs and deductions in terms of tax

| 71 CVS investment relief | 71 £ | p |

| 72 Community investment relief | 72 £ | p |

| 73 Double taxation relief | 73 £ | p |

74 *Put an 'X' in box 74 if box 73 includes an Underlying Rate relief claim*

75 *Put an 'X' in box 75 if box 73 includes any amount carried back from a later period*

| 76 Advance corporation tax | 76 £ | p |

total of boxes 71, 72, 73 and 76

| 77 Total reliefs and deductions in terms of tax | 77 £ | p |

CT600 (2008) Version 2

Calculation of tax outstanding or overpaid

		box 70 minus box 77
78	Net corporation tax liability	**78** £ _____ p
79	Tax payable under S419 ICTA 1988	**79** £ _____ p
80	*Put an 'X' in box 80 if you completed box A11 in the Supplementary Pages CT600A*	**80** ☐
81	Tax payable under S747 ICTA 1988	**81** £ _____ p
82	Tax payable under S501A ICTA 1988	**82** £ _____ p
		total of boxes 78, 79, 81 and 82
83	Tax chargeable	**83** £ _____ p
84	Income tax deducted from gross income included in profits	**84** £ _____ p
85	Income tax repayable to the company	**85** £ _____ p
		box 83 minus box 84
86	Tax payable - this is your self-assessment of tax payable	**86** £ _____ p

Tax reconciliation

87	Research and Development tax credit, including any vaccines tax credit, or film tax credit	**87** £ _____ p
88	Land remediation or life assurance company tax credit	**88** £ _____ p
170	Capital allowances first-year tax credit	**170** £ _____ p
		box 87 minus box 86
89	Research and Development tax credit payable, including any vaccines tax credit, or film tax credit payable	**89** £ _____ p
		total of boxes 87 + 88 minus boxes 86 and 89
90	Land remediation or life assurance company tax credit payable	**90** £ _____ p
		boxes 87, 88 and 170 minus boxes 86, 89 and 90
171	Capital allowances first-year tax credit payable	**171** £ _____ p
161	Ring fence corporation tax included	**161** £ _____ p
166	Tax under S501A ICTA 1988 included	**166** £ _____ p
91	Tax already paid (and not already repaid)	**91** £ _____ p
		box 86 minus boxes 87, 88, 170 and 91
92	Tax outstanding	**92** £ _____ p
		total sum of boxes 87, 88, 170 and 91 minus box 86
93	Tax overpaid	**93** £ _____ p
94	Tax refunds surrendered to the company under S102 FA 1989	**94** £ _____ p

Indicators

Put an 'X' in the relevant box(es) if, in the period, the company

95	*should have made (whether it has or not) instalment payments under the Corporation Tax (Instalment Payments) Regulations 1998*	**95** ☐
96	*is within a group payment arrangement for this period*	**96** ☐
97	*has written down or sold intangible assets*	**97** ☐
98	*has made cross-border royalty payments*	**98** ☐

CT600 (2008) Version 2

Appendix 2: CT600 (2008) Version 2

Information about enhanced expenditure

Research and Development (R&D) or films enhanced expenditure

167 *Put an 'X' in box 167 if the claim is for films expenditure* | 167

99 *Put an 'X' in box 99 if the claim is made by a small or medium-sized enterprise (SME), including a SME subcontractor to a large company* | 99

100 *Put an 'X' in box 100 if the claim is made by a large company* | 100

101 R&D or films enhanced expenditure | 101 £

102 R&D enhanced expenditure of a SME on work sub-contracted to it by a large company | 102 £

103 Vaccines research expenditure | 103 £

Land remediation enhanced expenditure

104 Enter amount equal to 150% of actual expenditure | 104 £

Information about capital allowances and balancing charges

Charges and allowances included in calculation of trading profits or losses

		Capital Allowances	Balancing Charges
172	Annual investment allowance	172 £	
105-106	Machinery and plant - special rate pool	105 £	106 £
107-108	Machinery and plant - main pool	107 £	108 £
109-110	Cars	109 £	110 £
111-112	Industrial buildings and structures	111 £	112 £
162-163	Business premises renovation	162 £	163 £
113-114	Other charges and allowances	113 £	114 £

Charges and allowances not included in calculation of trading profits or losses

		Capital Allowances	Balancing Charges
173	Annual investment allowance	173 £	
164-165	Business premises renovation	164 £	165 £
115-116	Other non-trading charges and allowances	115 £	116 £
117	*Put an 'X' in box 117 if box 115 entry includes flat conversion allowances*	117	

Qualifying expenditure

118 Machinery and plant on which first year allowance is claimed | 118 £

174 Designated environmentally friendly machinery and plant | 174 £

120 Machinery and plant on long-life assets and integral features | 120 £

121 Other machinery and plant | 121 £

Losses, deficits and excess amounts

		Arising	Maximum available for surrender as group relief
122-123	Trading losses Case I	calculated under S393 ICTA 1988 **122** £	calculated under S393A ICTA 1988 **123** £
124	Trading losses Case V	calculated under S393 ICTA 1988 **124** £	
125-126	Non-trade deficits on loan relationships and derivative contracts	calculated under S82 FA 1996 **125** £	calculated under S83 FA 1996 **126** £
127-128	Schedule A losses	calculated under S392A ICTA 1988 **127** £	calculated under S403 ICTA 1988 **128** £
129	Overseas property business losses Case V	calculated under S392B ICTA 1988 **129** £	
130	Losses Case VI	calculated under S396 ICTA 1988 **130** £	
131	Capital losses	calculated under S16 TCGA 1992 **131** £	
132-133	Non-trading losses on intangible fixed assets	calculated under S29 FA 2002 **132** £	calculated under S403 ICTA 1988 **133** £
		Excess	calculated under S403 ICTA 1988
134	Excess non-trade capital allowances		**134** £
135	Excess charges		calculated under S403 ICTA 1988 **135** £
136-137	Excess management expenses	calculated under S75 ICTA 1988 **136** £	calculated under S403 ICTA 1988 **137** £
138	Excess interest distributions	calculated under S468L(7) ICTA 1988 **138** £	

Overpayments and repayments

Small repayments

If you do not want us to make small repayments please either put an 'X' in box 139 or complete box 140 below. 'Repayments' here include tax, interest, and late-filing penalties or any combination of them.

Do not repay £20 or less **139** Do not repay sums of **140** £ or less. *Enter whole figure only*

Repayments for the period covered by this return

141	Repayment of corporation tax	**141** £		p
142	Repayment of income tax	**142** £		p
143	Payable Research and Development tax credit	**143** £		p
168	Payable film tax credit	**168** £		p
144	Payable land remediation or life assurance company tax credit	**144** £		p
175	Payable capital allowances first-year tax credit	**175** £		p

Surrender under S102 FA 1989 (including surrenders under Regulation 9 of the Instalments Regulations)
Repayments of advance corporation tax cannot be surrendered.

145	The following amount is to be surrendered under S102 FA 1989, and either	**145** £		p
146	the joint Notice is attached or	**146**	*(put an 'X' in either box 146 or box 147)*	
147	will follow	**147**		
148	Please stop repayment of the following amount until I send you the Notice	**148** £		p

Page 8

Bank details (for person to whom the repayment is to be made)

Repayment is made quickly and safely by direct credit to a bank or building society account.
Please complete the following details:

Name of bank or building society
149

Branch sort code
150

Account number
151

Name of account
152

Building society reference
153

Payments to a person other than the company

Complete the authority below if you want the repayment to be made to a person other than the company.
I, as *(enter status - company secretary, treasurer, liquidator or authorised agent, etc.)*
154

of *(enter name of company)*
155

authorise *(enter name)*
156

(enter address)
157

Postcode

Nominee reference
158

to receive payment on the company's behalf.

Signature
159

Name *(in capitals)*
160

Declaration

Warning - Giving false information in the return, or concealing any part of the company's profits or tax payable, can lead to both the company and yourself being prosecuted.

Declaration
The information I have given in this company tax return is correct and complete to the best of my knowledge and belief.

Signature

Name *(in capitals)*

Date *(dd/mm/yyyy)*

Status

CT600 (2008) Version 2

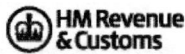
HM Revenue & Customs

Company - Short Tax Return form
CT600 (Short) (2008) Version 2
for accounting periods ending on or after 1 July 1999

Your company tax return

If we send the company a *Notice* to deliver a company tax return (form *CT603*) it has to comply by the filing date, or we charge a penalty, even if there is no tax to pay. A return includes a company tax return form, any Supplementary Pages, accounts, computations and any relevant information.

Is this the right form for the company? Read the advice on pages 3 to 6 of the Company tax return guide (the *Guide*) before you start.

The forms in the CT600 series set out the information we need and provide a standard format for calculations. Use the *Guide* to help you complete the return form. It contains general information you may need and box by box advice.

Company information

Company name

Company registration number   Tax Reference as shown on the CT603   Type of company

Registered office address

Postcode

About this return

This is the above company's return for the period
from (dd/mm/yyyy)   to (dd/mm/yyyy)

Put an 'X' in the appropriate box(es) below

A repayment is due for this return period

A repayment is due for an earlier period

Making more than one return for this company now

This return contains estimated figures

Company part of a group that is not small

Disclosure of tax avoidance schemes

Notice of disclosable avoidance schemes

Transfer pricing

Compensating adjustment claimed

Company qualifies for SME exemption

Accounts
I attach accounts and computations

• for the period to which this return relates

• for a different period

If you are not attaching accounts and computations, say why not

Supplementary Pages
If you are enclosing any Supplementary Pages put an 'X' in the appropriate box(es)

Loans to participators by close companies, form *CT600A*

Charities and Community Amateur Sports Clubs (CASCs), form *CT600E*

Disclosure of tax avoidance schemes, form *CT600J*

CT600 (Short) (2008) Version 2

Appendix 2: CT600 (Short) (2008) Version 2

Company tax calculation

Turnover

1   Total turnover from trade or profession   **1** £

Income

3   Trading and professional profits   **3** £

4   Trading losses brought forward claimed against profits   **4** £

    box 3 minus box 4

5   Net trading and professional profits   **5** £

6   Bank, building society or other interest, and profits and gains from non-trading loan relationships   **6** £

11   Income from UK land and buildings   **11** £

14   Annual profits and gains not falling under any other heading   **14** £

Chargeable gains

16   Gross chargeable gains   **16** £

17   Allowable losses including losses brought forward   **17** £

    box 16 minus box 17

18   Net chargeable gains   **18** £

    sum of boxes 5, 6, 11, 14 & 18

21 Profits before other deductions and reliefs   **21** £

Deductions and Reliefs

24   Management expenses under S75 ICTA 1988   **24** £

30   Trading losses of this or a later accounting period under S393A ICTA 1988   **30** £

31   *Put an 'X' in box 31 if amounts carried back from later accounting periods are included in box 30*   **31**

32   Non-trade capital allowances   **32** £

35   Charges paid   **35** £

    box 21 minus boxes 24, 30, 32 and 35

37 Profits chargeable to corporation tax   **37** £

Tax calculation

38   Franked investment income   **38** £

39   Number of associated companies in this period   **39**
or

40   Associated companies in the first financial year   **40**

41   Associated companies in the second financial year   **41**

42   *Put an 'X' in box 42 if the company claims to be charged at the starting rate or the small companies' rate on any part of its profits, or is claiming marginal rate relief*   **42**

Enter how much profit has to be charged and at what rate of tax

Financial year *(yyyy)*	Amount of profit	Rate of tax	Tax	
43	**44** £	**45**	**46** £	p
53	**54** £	**55**	**56** £	p

    total of boxes 46 and 56

63   Corporation tax   **63** £   p

64   Marginal rate relief   **64** £   p

65   Corporation tax net of marginal rate relief   **65** £   p

66   Underlying rate of corporation tax   **66** · %

67   Profits matched with non-corporate distributions   **67**

68   Tax at non-corporate distributions rate   **68** £   p

69   Tax at underlying rate on remaining profits   **69** £   p

    See note for box 70 in CT600 Guide

70 Corporation tax chargeable   **70** £   p

CT600 (Short) (2008) Version 2

79 Tax payable under S419 ICTA 1988 **79** £   p

80 *Put an 'X' in box 80 if you completed box A11 in the Supplementary Pages CT600A* **80**

84 Income tax deducted from gross income included in profits **84** £   p

85 Income tax repayable to the company **85** £   p

86 **Tax payable - this is your self-assessment of tax payable**   *total of boxes 70 and 79 minus box 84* **86** £   p

Tax reconciliation

91 Tax already paid (and not already repaid) **91** £   p

92 Tax outstanding   *box 86 minus box 91* **92** £   p

93 Tax overpaid   *box 91 minus box 86* **93** £   p

Information about capital allowances and balancing charges

Charges and allowances included in calculation of trading profits or losses

		Capital allowances	Balancing charges
172	Annual investment allowance	**172** £	
105 - 106	Machinery and plant - special rate pool	**105** £	**106** £
107 - 108	Machinery and plant - main pool	**107** £	**108** £
109 - 110	Cars	**109** £	**110** £
111 - 112	Industrial buildings and structures	**111** £	**112** £
113 - 114	Other charges and allowances	**113** £	**114** £

Charges and allowances not included in calculation of trading profits or losses

		Capital allowances	Balancing charges
173	Annual investment allowance	**173** £	
115 - 116	Other non-trading charges and allowances	**115** £	**116** £
117	*Put an 'X' in box 117 if box 115 includes flat conversion allowances*	**117**	

Qualifying expenditure

118 Expenditure on machinery and plant on which first year allowance is claimed **118** £

174 Designated environmentally friendly machinery and plant **174** £

120 Machinery and plant on long-life assets and integral features **120** £

121 Other machinery and plant **121** £

Losses, deficits and excess amounts

122	Trading losses Case I	*calculated under S393 ICTA 1988* **122** £	124	Trading losses Case V	*calculated under S393 ICTA 1988* **124** £
125	Non-trade deficits on loan relationships and derivative contracts	*calculated under S82 FA 1996* **125** £	127	Schedule A losses	*calculated under S392A ICTA 1988* **127** £
129	Overseas property business losses Case V	*calculated under S392B ICTA 1988* **129** £	130	Losses Case VI	*calculated under S396 ICTA 1988* **130** £
131	Capital losses	*calculated under S16 TCGA 1992* **131** £	136	Excess management expenses	*calculated under S75 ICTA 1988* **136** £

Page 4
Overpayments and repayments

Small repayments

If you do not want us to make small repayments please either put an 'X' in box 139 or complete box 140 below. 'Repayments' here include tax, interest, and late-filing penalties or any combination of them.

Do not repay £20 or less **139**   Do not repay sums of **140** £ _____ or less. *Enter whole figure only*

Bank details (for person to whom the repayment is to be made)

Repayment is made quickly and safely by direct credit to a bank or building society account.
Please complete the following details:

Name of bank or building society   Branch sort code
149 _____   **150** ____

Account number   Name of account
151 ____   **152** ____

Building society reference
153 ____

Payments to a person other than the company

Complete the authority below if you want the repayment to be made to a person other than the company.
I, as *(enter status - company secretary, treasurer, liquidator or authorised agent, etc.)*
154

of *(enter name of company)*
155

authorise *(enter name)*
156

(enter address)
157

                          Postcode

Nominee reference
158
to receive payment on the company's behalf.

Signature
159

Name *(in capitals)*
160

Declaration

Warning - Giving false information in the return, or concealing any part of the company's profits or tax payable, can lead to both the company and yourself being prosecuted.

Declaration
The information I have given in this company tax return is correct and complete to the best of my knowledge and belief.

Signature

Name *(in capitals)*   Date *(dd/mm/yyyy)*

Status

CT600 (Short) (2008) Version 2

HM Revenue & Customs

Company Tax Return form - Supplementary Pages
Loans to participators by close companies
CT600A (2006) Version 2
for accounting periods ending on or after 1 July 1999

Company information

Company name

Tax reference as shown on the CT603

Period covered by these Supplementary Pages (*cannot exceed 12 months*)
from (*dd/mm/yyyy*)   to (*dd/mm/yyyy*)

You need to complete these Supplementary Pages if

the company is close and has made a loan (or loans) to an individual participator, or associate of a participator, in this period which has not been repaid within the period. Tax is due under S419 ICTA 1988.

Important points

- These Supplementary Pages, when completed, form part of the company's return.
- These Pages set out the information we need and provide a standard format.
- Complete the boxes with whole figures only, except where pence or decimals are indicated.
- The notes below will help you understand any terms that have a special meaning and notes on these Pages will help with the completion of this form.
- These Pages are covered by the Declaration you sign on back page of form *CT600*.
- The warning shown on form *CT600* about prosecution, and the advice about late and incorrect returns, and late payment of tax also apply to these Pages.

Notes

A 'close company' is one which is under the control of five or fewer participators, or of any number of participators who are directors (S414 ICTA 1988).
A 'loan' within S419 ICTA 1988 includes the situation where a participator incurs a debt to the close company (S419(2)(a) ICTA 1988), for example by overdrawing a current or loan account. There are two exceptions where S419 ICTA 1988 does not apply
- a debt incurred for the supply by the close company of goods or services in the ordinary course of its trade or business, unless the credit given exceeds six months, or is longer than that normally given to the company's customers (S420(1) ICTA 1988), and
- certain loans made to full-time working directors or employees who do not have a material interest in the close company (S420(2) ICTA 1988).

A 'participator' is a person having a share or interest in the capital or income of the company and includes any loan creditor of the company (S417(1) ICTA 1988).

An 'associate' of a participator includes any relative or partner of the participator and the trustees of any settlement of which the participator or their relative is, or was, a settlor (S417(3)(a) and (b) ICTA 1988).

Methods by which a loan can be 'repaid' include depositing money into the company's bank account, crediting the participator's current or loan account with a dividend, director's remuneration or bonus, or book entry.

The term 'release' refers to a formal procedure that normally takes place under seal for a consideration, whereas 'write off' is a wider term that does not necessarily require formal arrangements and could include acceptance by the company that the loan will not be recovered and has given up attempts to recover it.

Appendix 2: CT600A (2006) Version 2

1: Loans made during the return period

You must complete part 1 if the company is close and has made a loan to an individual participator, or associate of a participator, during the return period which has not been repaid within the return period.

Enter in the table below, details of any outstanding loans made to a participator or associate of a participator during the return period. If the participator or associate has a current or loan account with the company, enter details of each participator's or associate's account. The amount you enter in column 2 of the table is the total of all debit entries on the account, less any credit entries and less any credit balance brought forward from the previous return period. In arriving at this figure you must exclude any credit entries that represent repayment, release or write off of loans made in earlier return periods.

A1 *Put an 'X' in this box if loans made during the period have been released, or written off before the end of the period*   **A1** [ ]

A2 Information about loans made during the return period and outstanding at the end of the period

Name of participator or associate	Amount of loan
	£
	£
	£
	£
	£

Total loans within S419 ICTA 1988 made during the return period which have not been repaid, released or written off before the end of the period   Total **A2** £

If a continuation sheet is used, please put an 'X' in box A2A   **A2A** [ ]

A3 Tax chargeable on loans -   box A2 multiplied by 25%
(*Tax due before any relief for loans repaid, released, or written off after the end of the period*) **A3** £   p

2: Relief for amounts repaid, released or written off after the end of the period but *earlier than* nine months and one day after the end of the period - for loans made during the return period

Complete part 2 to obtain relief for loans included in box A2 that were repaid, released or written off if

- the return is for the period in which the loans were made **and**
- the loan was repaid, released or written off after the end of the period but **earlier than** nine months and one day after the end of the accounting period in which the loan was **made**.

Enter in the table details for each participator or associate. If there have been a number of repayments on an account, enter only the total repayments for that account and give the date of the last repayment. **A separate entry must be made for each loan or part loan that has been released or written off.**

Example

A company makes a loan during the accounting period ended 31 December 2004 and it is all repaid to the company on 30 June 2005. The company's tax return for the accounting period ended 31 December 2004 is sent to HM Revenue & Customs on 1 November 2005. Part 2 should be completed because the loan was repaid after the end of the accounting period but earlier than nine months and one day after it.

A4 & A5 Information about loans repaid, released or written off after the end of the period but *earlier than* nine months and one day after the end of the period

Name of participator or associate	Amount repaid	Amount released or written off	Date of repayment, release or write off
	£	£	
	£	£	
	£	£	
	£	£	
	£	£	
	£	£	
Totals **A4** £		£	**A5**

If a continuation sheet is used, please put an 'X' in box A5A   **A5A** [ ]

A6 Total amount of loans made during the return period which have been repaid, released or written off after the end of the period but *earlier than* nine months and one day after the end of the period   total of boxes A4 and A5
A6 £

A7 Relief due for loans repaid, released or written off after the end of the period but *earlier than* nine months and one day after the end of the period   box A6 multiplied by 25%
A7 £   p

CT600A (2006) Version 2

562

Most companies will not need to complete part 3 below

Only complete part 3:
- where the loan was made during the return period, and
- where repayment, release or write off was more than nine months after the end of the period in which the loan was made, and
- the return is submitted after the date on which relief is due (if the return is sent in very late, at least twenty-one months after the end of the return period).

If you are unsure whether or not to complete part 3, apply the following questions to each claim.

Put an 'X' in this box if the loan was made in the return period.
If it was not, then you cannot complete part 3; if it was then go on to the next box

dd/mm/yyyy

End date of accounting period in which the loan was repaid, released or written off   **a**

Enter the date 9 months after the end of that accounting period   **b**

Date you are sending in the company tax return for the period in which the loan was made   **c**

If the date at **c** is earlier than the date at **b** you cannot complete part 3, but can make a separate claim for the relief which is not due until the date in **b**.

If the date at **c** is later than the date at **b** you can complete part 3 below to obtain the relief now.

3: Relief for loans made during the return period repaid, released or written off *more than* nine months after the end of the period and *where relief is due now*

Complete part 3 only if loans made during the return period, that have not been included in part 2, have been repaid, released or written off and where relief is due now (see the notes above under 'Most companies will not need to complete part 3').

Example

A company makes a loan during the accounting period ended 31 December 2004 and it is all repaid on 30 November 2005. The company's return for the accounting period ended 31 December 2004 is sent to HM Revenue & Customs on 1 December 2005. Part 3 of this form **should not** be completed because, although the loan was repaid more than nine months after the end of the return period, the return is sent earlier than nine months after the end of the return period in which the loan was repaid.

Relief for the repayment cannot be given until the due date of the accounting period in which the repayment was made, in this case 1 October 2006 (Ss419(4A) and (4B) ICTA 1988). The company must make a separate claim for relief.

Example

Same as example above except that the return is not sent in until 3 December 2006. Relief for the repayment is due on or after 1 October 2006. In this case part 3 can be completed because the repayment was made more than nine months after the end of the accounting period in which the loan was made, and the relief is due at the time the return is sent in.

A8 & A9 Information about loans made during the return period which have been repaid, released or written off *more than* nine months after the end of the period *and relief is due now*

Name of participator or associate	Amount repaid	Amount released or written off	Date of repayment, release or write off
	£	£	
	£	£	
	£	£	
	£	£	
	£	£	
	£	£	
Totals **A8**	£	£	**A9**

If a continuation sheet is used, please put an 'X' in box A9A   **A9A**

A10 Total amount of loans made during the return period which have been repaid, released, or written off *more than* nine months after the end of the period *and relief is due now*   *total of boxes A8 and A9*   **A10** £

A11 Relief due now for loans repaid, released or written off *more than* nine months after the end of the period. *Put an 'X' in box 80 on form CT600 if you have completed box A11*   *box A10 multiplied by 25%*   **A11** £   p

Appendix 2: CT600A (2006) Version 2

4: Other information

A12	Total of all loans outstanding at end of return period - including all loans outstanding at the end of the return period, whether they were made in this period or an earlier one.	A12 £

5: What S419 ICTA 1988 tax is payable?

A13	Tax payable under S419 ICTA 1988 *Copy the figure in box A13 to box 79 on form CT600*	box A3 minus total of boxes A7 and A11 A13 £ p

---

What to do when you have completed these Supplementary Pages

- Copy the figure from box A13 in part 5 to box 79 of the form *CT600*.
- Put an 'X' in box 80 of form *CT600* if you have completed box A11 in part 3 of these Pages.
- Follow the advice shown under 'What to do when you have completed the return' on page 23 of the *Guide*.

Company Tax Return form - Supplementary Pages
Controlled foreign companies
CT600B (2006) Version 2
for accounting periods ending on or after 1 July 1999

Company information

Company name

Tax reference as shown on the CT603

Period covered by these Supplementary Pages (*cannot exceed 12 months*)
from (*dd/mm/yyyy*)   to (*dd/mm/yyyy*)

You need to complete these Supplementary Pages if

at any time in this period, the company, held a relevant interest of 25% or more in a foreign company which is **controlled** from the UK. No controlled foreign company (CFC) need be included on these pages where it satisfies the **Excluded Countries Regulations**.

A UK company may also include companies which may not be CFCs but which would satisfy one of the exemptions if they were. This applies to foreign companies which may not be subject to a lower level of tax, or may not be controlled from the UK. It also applies where the UK company's relevant interest in the foreign company may be less than 25%. The purpose of this is to save UK companies the cost of working out whether a foreign company is in principle a CFC in cases where it is clear that one of the exemptions would be passed if it were.

Important points

- These Supplementary Pages, when completed, form part of the company's return.
- These Pages set out the information we need and provide a standard format.
- Notes below will help with the completion of this form.
- These Pages are covered by the Declaration you sign on the back page of form *CT600*.
- The warning shown on form *CT600* about prosecution, and the advice about late and incorrect returns, and late payment of tax also apply to these Pages.

Notes

The following information is required on pages 2 and 3:

- **Name of the CFC** Enter the full name of the CFC.
- **Territory of residence** If a residence election is made this should be noted and if a company is conclusively presumed to be resident in a territory in which it is subject to a lower level of tax then this should be indicated by the entry 'S749(5) ICTA 1988'.
- **Exemption due** Companies exempt under the provisions may indicate one (or more) exemptions here. Only one exemption need be noted, and not including an exemption will not prejudice whether it applies. If an exemption applies there is no need to complete page 3 of the supplementary return in respect of the CFC.
- **Percentage measure for apportionment** This will usually be the percentage of ordinary share capital held directly or indirectly by the UK company (but not by associated or connected persons). In all other circumstances the appropriate percentage should be calculated on a just and reasonable basis.
- **Chargeable profits** These are the chargeable profits (after reliefs available under Sch 25 ICTA 1988) apportioned to the UK company.
- **Tax on chargeable profits** This is the amount of tax apportioned on the basis of the company's share of chargeable profits before reliefs are given under Sch 26 ICTA 1988 or relief is given for advance corporation tax.
- **Creditable tax** This broadly represents tax already paid on the chargeable profits and is deductible.
- **Reliefs in terms of tax** Any reliefs available under Sch 26 should be shown at the appropriate rate of corporation tax.
- **ACT as restricted** Unrelieved surplus ACT to the extent not restricted should be shown here.
- **S747 tax chargeable** This is the column J total which is the sum of the figures in column F less the sum of the figures in columns G to I. The net figure should be copied to box 81 of form *CT600*.

What to do when you have completed these Supplementary Pages

- Copy the figure from the Summary box J13 on these Pages to box 81 of form *CT600*.
- Follow the advice shown under 'What to do when you have completed the return' on page 23 of the *Guide*.

Appendix 2: CT600B (2006) Version 2

	A Name of CFC	B Territory of residence for S749 Purposes	C Exemption due (if any)
1			
2			
3			
4			
5			
6			
7			
8			
9			
10			
11			
12			

Put an 'X' in this box if a continuation sheet is used for page 2 ☐

CT600B (2006) Version 2

D Percentage of apportionable profits and creditable tax	E Chargeable profits	F Tax on charge-able profits		G Creditable Tax		H Reliefs in terms of tax		I ACT as restricted		J S747 tax chargeable		
%	£	£	p	£	p	£	p	£	p	£	p	1
%	£	£	p	£	p	£	p	£	p	£	p	2
%	£	£	p	£	p	£	p	£	p	£	p	3
%	£	£	p	£	p	£	p	£	p	£	p	4
%	£	£	p	£	p	£	p	£	p	£	p	5
%	£	£	p	£	p	£	p	£	p	£	p	6
%	£	£	p	£	p	£	p	£	p	£	p	7
%	£	£	p	£	p	£	p	£	p	£	p	8
%	£	£	p	£	p	£	p	£	p	£	p	9
%	£	£	p	£	p	£	p	£	p	£	p	10
%	£	£	p	£	p	£	p	£	p	£	p	11
%	£	£	p	£	p	£	p	£	p	£	p	12
		F		G		H		I		J		
Totals		£	p	£	p	£	p	£	p	£	p	13

Enter this amount in box 81 of form *CT600*

Put an 'X' in this box if a continuation sheet is used for page 3

CT600B (2006) Version 2

Appendix 2: CT600C (2006) Version 2

HM Revenue & Customs

Company Tax Return form - Supplementary Pages
Group and consortium
CT600C (2006) Version 2
for accounting periods ending on or after 1 July 1999

Company information

Company name

Tax reference as shown on the CT603

Period covered by these Supplementary Pages (*cannot exceed 12 months*)
from (dd/mm/yyyy)   to (dd/mm/yyyy)

You need to complete these Supplementary Pages if

- you are claiming or surrendering any amounts under the group and/or consortium relief provisions.
- you are claiming or surrendering eligible unrelieved foreign tax (for accounting periods ending on or after 31 March 2001).

Important points

- These Supplementary Pages, when completed, form part of the company's return.
- These Pages set out the information we need and provide a standard format.
- Complete the boxes with whole figures only, except where pence or decimals are indicated.
- There are notes on these Pages to help you when you complete this form.
- These Pages are covered by the Declaration you sign on back page of form CT600.
- The warning shown on form CT600 about prosecution, and the advice about late and incorrect returns, and late payment of tax also apply to these Pages.

1: Claims to group relief

You need to complete this part if you are claiming group relief in your calculation of corporation tax payable. Attach a copy of each surrendering company's notice of consent to the claim. Include claims made under the consortium provisions and attach a copy of the notice of consent of each member of the consortium. If a simplified arrangement is in force, the claim may be authorised below.

Name of surrendering company	Accounting period [1] of surrendering company	Tax reference [2]	Amount claimed £

[1] Enter the start and end dates of any period that is different from that covered by this return

Total **C1** £   *enter in box 36 of form CT600*

[2] Enter the HM Revenue & Customs office number and taxpayer reference. If you do not know these show whatever information you can that will help us to identify the company, such as the company registration number

Put an 'X' in box C1A if a continuation sheet is used — **C1A**

Put an 'X' in box C1B if a group relief claim involves losses of a trade carried on in the UK through a Permanent Establishment by a non-resident company — **C1B**

Put an 'X' in box C1C if a group relief claim involves losses of a non-resident company other than those covered by box C1B — **C1C**

A claim involves a non-resident if the claimant, the surrendering company, or any other company by reference to which their group relationship is established, is non-resident

Claim authorisation - *complete if simplified arrangements apply and copies of notices of consent are not supplied*

Signature   **Name** (*in capitals*)

Name of authorised company   Date (dd/mm/yyyy)

Any person authorised to sign on behalf of the company that is authorised to act for the companies within the arrangement should sign this authorisation.

Page 2

2: Amounts surrendered as group relief

You need to complete this part if the company is surrendering any amount under the group (or consortium) provisions.
Unless a simplified arrangement is in force
- a notice of consent to each claim is needed
- this part is acceptable as a notice of consent, if the surrendering company details are entered and it is signed by an authorised person in the space below.
- send a copy of the notice of consent to the HM Revenue & Customs office dealing with the claimant company's return before or at the same time as the claimant company submits its return claiming the group relief
- the consent of all the other consortium members is needed for consortium relief.

Surrender as group relief

Trading losses	£
Excess non-trade capital allowances over income from which they are primarily deductible	£
Non-trading deficit on loan relationships	£
Non-trading losses on intangible fixed assets	£
Excess charges over profits	£
Excess of Schedule A losses over profits	£
Excess of management expenses over profits	£
Total	£

Details of surrender

Name of claimant company	Accounting period [1] of claimant company	Tax reference [2]	Amount surrendered £
	Total	C2	£

[1] Enter the start and end dates of any period that is different from that covered by this return

[2] Enter the HM Revenue & Customs office number and taxpayer reference. If you do not know these show whatever information you can that will help us to identify the company, such as the company registration number

Put an 'X' in box C2A if a continuation sheet is used.   C2A ▢

Details of company surrendering relief

You must complete and sign this section if you are using this form as the notice of consent to surrender.

Company name

Tax reference	Accounting period Start date (dd/mm/yyyy)	End date (dd/mm/yyyy)

I certify that all the information I have given on these pages is correct and complete to the best of my knowledge and belief.

Signature *(needed if you are using this form as the notice of consent to surrender)*

Name *(in capitals)*	Status

Except where a liquidator or administrator has been appointed, any person who is authorised to do so may sign on behalf of the company. A photocopy of a signature is not acceptable.

CT600C (2006) Version 2

Eligible Unrelieved Foreign Tax (EUFT)

You need to complete this part if you are claiming EUFT in your calculation of corporation tax payable, or part 4 on page 4 if the company is surrendering any amount of EUFT under the Double Taxation Relief (Surrender of Relievable Tax within a Group) Regulations. These regulations apply to income arising on or after 31 March 2001.

You must attach a copy of each surrendering company's notice of consent to the claim.

Claims to EUFT do not apply to consortium companies and, unlike the claims to and surrenders as group relief covered by parts 1 and 2 of this form, there can be no simplified arrangement for EUFT.

3: Claims to EUFT

You need to complete this part if you are claiming EUFT in your calculation of corporation tax payable.

Remember to include any box C3 figure in your calculation of corporation tax payable on form CT600.

Details of claim

Name of surrendering company	Accounting period [1] of surrendering company	Tax reference [2]	Amount claimed £	p

[1] *Enter the start and end dates of any period that is different from that covered by this return*

[2] *Enter the HM Revenue & Customs office number and taxpayer reference. If you do not know these show whatever information you can that will help us to identify the company, such as the company registration number*

Include in box 73 entry on form CT600

Total **C3** £   p

Put an 'X' in box C3A if a continuation sheet is used

C3A

4: Amounts of EUFT surrendered

You should complete this part if the company is surrendering any amount of EUFT under the Double Taxation Relief (Surrender of Relievable Tax Within a Group) Regulations.
- A notice of consent to each claim is needed.
- This part is acceptable as a notice of consent, if the surrendering company details are entered and it is signed by an authorised person in the space below.
- Send a copy of the notice of consent to the HM Revenue & Customs office dealing with the claimant company's return before or at the same time as the claimant company submits its return claiming the EUFT.

Details of surrender

Name of company claiming	Accounting period [1] of claimant company	Tax reference [2]	Amount surrendered £ p

[1] *Enter the start and end dates of any period that is different from that covered by this return*

Total **C4** £   p

[2] *Enter the HM Revenue & Customs office number and taxpayer reference. If you do not know these show whatever information you can that will help us to identify the company, such as the company registration number*

Put an 'X' in box C4A if a continuation sheet is used **C4A**

Details of company surrendering EUFT
You must complete and sign this section if you are using this form as the notice of consent to surrender.
Company name

Tax reference	Accounting period Start date (dd/mm/yyyy)	End date (dd/mm/yyyy)

I certify that all the information I have given on these pages is correct and complete to the best of my knowledge and belief.

Signature *(needed if you are using this form as the notice of consent to surrender)*

Name *(in capitals)*   **Status**

Except where a liquidator or administrator has been appointed, any person who is authorised to do so may sign on behalf of the company. A photocopy of a signature is not acceptable.

What to do when you have completed these Supplementary Pages

- Copy any figure from box C1 in part 1 to box 36 of form *CT600*.
- Include any figure from box C3 in part 3 in box 73 of form *CT600*.
- Follow the advice shown under 'What to do when you have completed the return' on page 23 of the *Guide*.

Appendix 2: CT600E (2006) Version 2

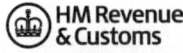 **HM Revenue & Customs**

Company Tax Return form - Supplementary Pages
Charities and Community Amateur Sports Clubs (CASCs)
CT600E (2006) Version 2
for accounting periods ending on or after 1 July 1999

Company information

Company name

Tax reference as shown on the CT603

Period covered by these Supplementary Pages (*cannot exceed 12 months*)
from (*dd/mm/yyyy*)   to (*dd/mm/yyyy*)

You need to complete these Supplementary Pages if

the charity/CASC claims exemption from tax on all or any part of its income and gains.

Important points

- These Supplementary Pages will form the charity's/CASC's claim to exemption from tax on the basis that its income and gains have been applied for charitable or qualifying purposes only.
- Please use the notes on page 2 to help you complete this form.
- Please enter whole figures or '0' where appropriate.
- How often you are asked to make a return will depend on the extent and nature of your activities.
- These Pages, when completed, form part of the company's return.
- These Pages set out the information we need and provide a standard format.
- These Pages are covered by the Declaration you sign on the back page of form CT600.
- The warning shown on form CT600 about prosecution, and the advice about late and incorrect returns and late payment of tax, also apply to these Pages.

Claims to exemption

This section should be completed in all cases

Charity/CASC repayment reference

Charity Commission Registration number, or Scottish Charity number (if applicable)

Put an 'X' in the relevant box if during the period covered by these Supplementary Pages:

- the company was a charity/CASC and is claiming exemption from all tax on all or part of its income and gains.
- all income and gains are exempt from tax and have been, or will be, applied for charitable or qualifying purposes only.

If the company was a charity/CASC but had no income or gains in the period, then put an 'X' in the first box 'claiming exemption from all tax' above.

or
- some of the income and gains may not be exempt or have not been applied for charitable or qualifying purposes only, and I have completed form CT600.
See the note on Restrictions of relief for non-qualifying expenditure on page 2.

I claim exemption from tax

Signature   Date (dd/mm/yyyy)

Name (*in capitals*)

Status

Except where a liquidator or administrator has been appointed, any person who is authorised to do so may sign on behalf of the company. For CASCs the treasurer should sign. A photocopy of a signature is not acceptable.

Page 2

Repayments boxes E1/E1a, E2/E2b and E1a - E4d

Transitional relief only applies on qualifying distributions made on or after 6 April 1999 and before 6 April 2004. The time limit for claims is 2 years after the end of the charity's accounting period in which the distribution was made.

In boxes E1/E1a:

- Enter the amount of income tax and transitional relief claimed on forms *R68(2000)* or *R68(CASC)* for the period covered by these Pages.
- This should relate only to income arising in the period.
- Do not include amounts claimed for earlier periods.

In Box E2/E2b enter the total amount due for income received in the period on which a charity/CASC can claim.

CASCs should leave boxes E1a to E4d blank.

Trading income box E5

Enter details of the turnover of trades, the profits of which will be exempted by

a) S505(1)(e) ICTA 1988, S46 FA 2000 or ESC C4 (for charities), or

b) Schedule 18, Paragraph 4, FA 2002 (for CASCs).

If the charity/CASC has carried on a trade during the return period which falls outside the exemption, complete the *Company Tax Calculation* on form *CT600*. Do not include in the calculation sources of income which are otherwise exempt from tax. Also, complete the *About this return* section on page 1 and *Declaration* on the back page of form *CT600*.

Gifts boxes E11 and E12

Include in box E11 the value of any gifts of shares or securities received under S587B ICTA 1988.

Include in box E12 the value of any gifts of real property received under S587B/S587C ICTA 1988.

Other sources box E13

Enter details in box E13 of income received from sources other than those included in the boxes above where the income is exempt from tax in the hands of a charity/CASC. This will include Case VI income exempted by S505(1)(c)(iic) ICTA 1988.

Investments and loans within Sch 20 ICTA 1988 box E26 charities only

Qualifying investments and loans, for the purposes of S506 ICTA 1988, are specified in Parts I and II of Sch 20 ICTA 1988.

Charities can make claims to HM Revenue & Customs for any loan or other investment not specified in Sch 20 but made for the benefit of the charity and not for avoidance of tax, to be accepted as qualifying.

Put an 'X' in box E26 only if all investments and loans are qualifying investments and loans:

- automatically, because they are specified in Sch 20, or
- because the charity has either claimed (with this return or separately) that they are under Paragraphs 9 or 10 of Sch 20 ICTA 1988, or is prepared to do so on request.

For a claim for qualifying status to succeed, the loan or investment must be made for the benefit of the charity and not for the avoidance of tax (whether by the charity or any other person). Claims should be in writing and specify

- the nature of the item (loans, or shares for example)
- the amount
- the period
- whether the claim is under Paragraph 9 or 10.

It is helpful if a claim includes full details, for example the terms of a loan.

Investments and loans made outside Sch 20 ICTA 1988 box E27 charities only

If the charity has made any investments or loans which do not fall within Schedule 20 ICTA 1988, and no claim is being made with this return, enter the total of such loans or investments in box E27.

Restrictions of relief for non-qualifying expenditure

Relief under S505(1) ICTA 1988 and S256 TCGA 1992 may not be available to some charities.

The charity should attach a calculation of restriction of relief under S505(3) ICTA 1988 and send it with this return. If you need help with this calculation please telephone our helpline on **08453 020203** or email **charities@hmrc.gov.uk**

Where a CASC has incurred non-qualifying expenditure its exemptions from tax may need to be restricted. The CASC should include a calculation of the restriction of relief under Schedule 18, Paragraph 8 FA 2002 with this return. If you need help with this calculation please telephone our helpline on **08453 020203** or email **charities@hmrc.gov.uk**

Further guidance

Further guidance on the reliefs available to charities and CASCs is available on our website at **www.hmrc.gov.uk/charities**

CT600E (2006) Version 2

Appendix 2: CT600E (2006) Version 2

Repayments

Enter details of repayments of Income Tax/payments of Transitional Relief for income arising during the period covered by these Supplementary Pages

		Income Tax	Transitional Relief *Charities only*
E1/E1a	Amount already claimed for period using form R68(2000) or R68(CASC)	**E1** £	**E1a** £
E2/E2b	Total repayment/payment due	**E2** £	**E2b** £
and either			
E3/E3c	Further repayment/payment due *Where E2/E2b is more than E1/E1a*	**E3** £	**E3c** £
or			
E4/E4d	Amounts overclaimed for period *Where E1/E1a is more than E2/E2b*	**E4** £	**E4d** £

If any of the amounts in boxes E3/E3c have been included in any repayment/payment claim on form R68(2000) or R68(CASC) put an 'X' in this box.

Information required

Enter details of any income received from the following sources, claimed as exempt from tax in the hands of the charity/CASC. Enter the figure included in the charity's/CASC's accounts for the period covered by this return
Do not include amounts which are not taxable. Non-exempt amounts should be entered on form CT600 in the appropriate boxes.

Type of income	Amount
E5 Enter total turnover from exempt trading activities	**E5** £
E6 Investment income - exclude any amounts included on form *CT600*	**E6** £
E7 UK land and buildings - exclude any amounts included on form *CT600*	**E7** £
E8 Deed of covenant - exclude any amounts included on form *CT600*	**E8** £
E9 Gift Aid or Millennium Gift Aid - exclude any amounts included on form *CT600*	**E9** £
E10 Other charities - exclude any amounts included on form *CT600*	**E10** £
E11 Gifts of shares or securities received	**E11** £
E12 Gifts of real property received	**E12** £
E13 Other sources	**E13** £

Enter details of expenditure as shown in the charity's/CASC's accounts for the period covered by these Supplementary Pages

Type of expenditure	Amount
E14 Trading costs in relation to exempt activities (in box E5)	**E14** £
E15 UK land and buildings in relation to exempt activities (in box E7)	**E15** £
E16 All general administration costs	**E16** £
E17 All grants and donations made within the UK	**E17** £
E18 All grants and donations made outside the UK	**E18** £
E19 Other expenditure not included above, or not used in calculating figures entered on the form *CT600*	**E19** £

continued on page 4

CT600E (2006) Version 2

Page 4

continued from page 3

Charity/CASC Assets

		Disposals in period (total consideration received)	Held at the end of the period (use accounts figures)
E20/E20a	Tangible fixed assets	E20 £	E20a £
E21/E21b	UK investments (excluding controlled companies)	E21 £	E21b £
E22/E22c	Shares in, and loans to, controlled companies	E22 £	E22c £
E23/E23d	Overseas investments	E23 £	E23d £
E24e	Loans and non-trade debtors		E24e £
E25f	Other current assets		E25f £
E26	Qualifying investments and loans. *Applies to charities only. See note on Page 2*		E26
E27	Value of any non-qualifying investments and loans. *Applies to charities only*		E27 £
E28	Number of subsidiary or associated companies the charity controls at the end of the period. *Exclude companies that were dormant throughout the period*		E28

What to do when you have completed these Supplementary Pages

Follow the advice shown under 'What to do when you have completed the return' on page 23 of the *Guide.*

HM Revenue & Customs

Company Tax Return form - Supplementary Pages
Corporate Venturing Scheme
CT600G (2006) Version 2
for accounting periods ending on or after 1 July 1999

Company information

Company name

Tax reference as shown on the CT603

Period covered by these Supplementary Pages (*cannot exceed 12 months*)
from (*dd/mm/yyyy*)   to (*dd/mm/yyyy*)

You need to complete these Supplementary Pages if

for shares issued **on or after 1 April 2000 but before 1 April 2010** the company is claiming under the Corporate Venturing Scheme (CVS):

- investment relief on the amount subscribed for shares, **or**

- relief against income for losses on certain disposals of shares, whether effect is to be given to the claim in this period or an earlier period, **or**

- postponement of certain chargeable gains where the gains are reinvested in shares under the Corporate Venturing Scheme.

Important points

- These Supplementary Pages, when completed, form part of the company's return.

- They set out the information we need and provide a standard format.

- They are covered by the Declaration you sign on the back page of form *CT600*.

- The warning shown on form *CT600* about prosecution, and the advice about late and incorrect returns, and late payment of tax also apply to these Pages.

- **You are advised to read the relevant notes on page 4 of this form before you complete these Pages.**

What to do when you have completed these Supplementary Pages

- Copy the figure from box G1 to box 71 of the form *CT600*.

- Follow the advice shown under 'What to do when you have completed the return' on page 23 of the *Guide*.

Claims

A company making a claim in its company tax return must do so using these Supplementary Pages.

If a company makes a claim later, but within the time limit for amending its return, it should make the claim on an amended return, giving the same details as are required by forms *CT600* and *CT600G*. (For instance this could be the case if the form CVS 3 to support a deferral relief claim is not received until after the return has been delivered.) No specific form is provided for an amended return, but as long as it is signed by a person authorised to do so and includes a declaration that the information is correct and complete to the best of his or her knowledge and belief, it will be accepted as an amended return.

If the time for amending a return has passed, but the claim is still in time, the company should again give the same details as are required by forms *CT600* and *CT600G*. The claim should be signed by a person authorised to do so and include a declaration that the information is correct and complete to the best of his or her knowledge and belief.

Page 2   *Use this page together with page 3*

If there is not enough space in any section, please continue on a separate sheet and attach it to the form.

Investment Relief

For each issue of shares in respect of which investment relief is claimed, please enter the following details:
All this information, except the actual amount of investment relief claimed, is on the form CVS3 that the issuing company sent to the investing company.

1

Name of qualifying issuing company	Number of shares subscribed for

Relief for losses on disposals of shares

For each disposal in respect of which a claim is being made, please enter the following details:

2

Name of qualifying issuing company	Description of shares disposed of

Deferral relief

For claims to postpone chargeable gains or parts of gains, please enter the details below. Use a separate line for each gain or part of gain.

3

Name of qualifying issuing company whose shares have been disposed of, or in relation to which another chargeable event has occurred	Where the gain was previously postponed under the CVS, enter name of qualifying issuing company on which original gain arose	Date of disposal or of other chargeable event

CT600G (2006) Version 2

577

Appendix 2: CT600G (2006) Version 2

If there is not enough space in any section, please continue on a separate sheet and attach it to the form.

Nominal value of shares subscribed for £	Date of issue (given on form CVS 3)	Amount subscribed for the shares £	Amount of investment relief claimed net of any reduction for value received £	Small Company Enterprise Centre reference

Total investment relief claimed *Copy the figure in box G1 to box 71 of form CT600*   **G1** £

Number of shares disposed of	Date of issue of shares	Date of disposal of shares	Accounting period(s) of claim, and amount of loss relief claimed for (each) period		
			From	To	£

Amount of chargeable gain (or of part of chargeable gain) matched against unused qualifying expenditure on new qualifying shares £	Name of qualifying issuing company that issued the new qualifying shares	Date of issue of new qualifying shares

CT600G (2006) Version 2

578

Page 4

Notes

These notes do not provide a full explanation of the Corporate Venturing Scheme.
More guidance is available on our website at www.hmrc.gov.uk/guidance.htm

Investment relief

A company must not claim the relief on any investment unless it has received a compliance certificate on form CVS 3. You may be asked to produce the certificate relating to that investment.

Investment relief takes the form of a reduction in the investing company's corporation tax liability for the accounting period in which the shares were issued. Except as mentioned below, the amount of that reduction is 20% of the amount of any subscriptions (excluding any associated costs) or, if that would exceed the corporation tax liability, such an amount as will reduce that liability to nil. The amount subscribed will be shown on form CVS 3.

Where the investing company (or any person connected with it) has received value from the issuing company (or from any person connected with that company) so that paragraph 47 of Sch 15 FA 2000 applies, the amount of relief is reduced. The amount of the reduction is usually 20% of the amount of value received, but it will be less where paragraph 51 or 52 of Sch 15 FA 2000 apply. Any amount of value received by the investing company from the issuing company (or any connected person) that was known to the issuing company at the time the form CVS 3 was issued should be shown on that form.

Loss relief

A claim to set an allowable loss on a share disposal against income may be made under the CVS only if

- investment relief was attributable to the shares disposed of at the time of the disposal, **and**
- the investment relief is not withdrawn in full as a result of the disposal, **and**
- the shares were held continuously from the date the shares were issued until disposal, **and**
- the disposal is
  - a disposal by way of a bargain at arm's length for full consideration, **or**
  - by way of a distribution in the course of dissolving or winding up the issuing company, **or**
  - a disposal within S24(1) TCGA 1992, **or**
  - a deemed disposal following a claim under S24(2) TCGA 1992, **and**
- the disposal does not occur in consequence of any company reconstruction or amalgamation for the purposes of tax avoidance.

CVS loss relief may be claimed against income of the accounting period in which the loss arises. Any loss not so relieved may be claimed against income of accounting periods ending in the previous 12 months, subject to the apportionment provision in paragraph 69(2) of Sch 15 FA 2000. To the extent that the loss is not set off against income it may be deducted from chargeable gains in the usual way.

The amount of an allowable loss is calculated according to the rules in TCGA 1992, as modified by paragraph 94, Sch 15 FA 2000.

Deferral relief

A claim may be made to postpone

- a chargeable gain accruing on a disposal of shares to which investment relief was attributable immediately before the disposal, provided that the shares were held continuously from the date they were issued until the disposal, **or**
- a chargeable gain previously postponed under the CVS in respect of an investment in shares which is revived because of a 'chargeable event' (that is a disposal or an event other than a disposal which causes any investment relief attributable to the shares to be reduced or withdrawn).

To be eligible for the relief the company must have subscribed - during the period starting one year before and ending three years after the date on which the gain accrued - for shares to which investment relief is attributable. Before deferral relief can be claimed a form CVS 3 must be held in respect of those shares. If those shares were issued before the gain accrued, the company must have held the shares continuously from the date they were issued until the gain accrued and investment relief must be attributable to them at the time the gain accrued.

However, deferral relief is not available where the gain to be deferred accrues on a disposal of shares and the shares subscribed for are in the same company or in any member of its group. Similarly, deferral relief is not available where the gain to be deferred has been revived because of a chargeable event and the shares subscribed for are in the company whose shares were involved in that event, or in any member of its group.

Appendix 2: CT600H (2006) Version 2

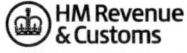 **HM Revenue & Customs**

Company Tax Return form - Supplementary Pages
Cross-border Royalties
CT600H (2006) Version 2
for accounting periods ending on or after 1 July 1999

Company information

Company name

Tax reference as shown on the CT603

Period covered by these Supplementary Pages (*cannot exceed 12 months*)
from (*dd/mm/yyyy*)   to (*dd/mm/yyyy*)

You need to complete these Supplementary Pages if

- the company is a UK company and made cross-border royalty payments after 1 October 2002, and reasonably believed that the recipient of the royalties would be entitled to treaty relief on any tax deducted. The company is entitled to make such payments without deduction of tax or at the rate specified by reference to the double taxation treaty appropriate to the country of residence of the payee. Further information about countries or territories that have double taxation agreements with the UK can be found on our website at **www.hmrc.gov.uk**

and/or

- the company is a UK company or UK permanent establishment of an EU company, and made royalty payments to an associated company in another Member State of the EU on or after 1 January 2004 (1 May 2004 for States joining the EU on that date) and reasonably believed that the beneficial owner of the royalties is exempt from UK income tax on those payments following the implementation of the Interest and Royalties Directive. Such payments should be made without deduction of tax.

In this context 'permanent establishment' is a fixed place of business situated in a Member State through which the business of a company of another Member State is wholly or partly carried on.

Important points

- These Supplementary Pages, when completed, form part of the company's return.
- These Pages set out the information we need and provide a standard format.
- Complete the boxes with whole figures only, except where pence or decimals are indicated.
- These Pages are covered by the Declaration you sign on the back page of form *CT600*.
- The warning shown on form *CT600* about prosecution, and the advice about late and incorrect returns, and late payment of tax also apply to these Pages.
- There are additional penalty provisions for failure to observe the law regarding royalty payments. Details are contained in S349E(1)(7) ICTA 1988, S98(4D) TMA 1970 and S98(4DA) TMA 1970 and there is provision for a Direction to be issued under S349E(1)(3) ICTA 1988 or S96(3) FA 2004, as appropriate.

What to do when you have completed these Supplementary Pages

- Complete box 98 of form *CT600* to show that you have made cross-border royalty payments under reasonable belief.

- Follow the advice shown under 'What to do when you have completed the return' on page 23 of the *Guide*.

Page 2

Details of payments made

	Name of recipient of the royalty	Full address of recipient of the royalty	Type of royalty payment made
1			
2			
3			
4			
5			
6			
7			
8			
9			
10			
11			
12			

Put an 'X' in this box if a continuation sheet is used.

CT600H (2006) Version 2

Appendix 2: CT600H (2006) Version 2

Gross amount of royalty paid £	Agreement under which relief claimed: (a) Interest and Royalties Directive *or* (b) country with double taxation agreement with UK	Rate of tax deducted from payment %	Amount of tax deducted from payment £ p	Additional notes	
	(a)				
	(b)				1
	(a)				
	(b)				2
	(a)				
	(b)				3
	(a)				
	(b)				4
	(a)				
	(b)				5
	(a)				
	(b)				6
	(a)				
	(b)				7
	(a)				
	(b)				8
	(a)				
	(b)				9
	(a)				
	(b)				10
	(a)				
	(b)				11
	(a)				
	(b)				12

Appendix 2: CT600J (2006) Version 2

 HM Revenue & Customs

Company Tax Return form - Supplementary Pages
Disclosure of tax avoidance schemes
CT600J (2006) Version 2

for notifiable arrangements on or after 18 March 2004

Company information

Company name

Tax reference as shown on the CT603

Period covered by these Supplementary Pages (*cannot exceed 12 months*)
from (*dd/mm/yyyy*)   to (*dd/mm/yyyy*)

You need to complete these Supplementary Pages if

you are a party to any notifiable arrangements under S308, 309, 310 Finance Act 2004 (FA 2004) and you have received a reference number.

Under S313(1) FA 2004 you are required to provide HM Revenue & Customs with
- any reference number notified to you in the accounting period covered by this return, **and**
- the time when you obtain or expect to obtain a tax advantage from the notifiable arrangements either in the accounting period covered by this return or in a period covered by a future return.

You should not use this form if
- you are an employer and the notifiable arrangements concerned are arrangements connected with employment. A scheme reference number for employment products should be notified separately using form AIU4.
- you are a party to any notifiable arrangements in the accounting period covered by this return that have not otherwise been notified to HM Revenue & Customs you should do so now by completing form AIU3.

Forms AIU3 and AIU4 are available on our website at **www.hmrc.gov.uk/aiu/index.htm** or from the Orderline by telephoning **0845 300 6555.**

Important points

- These Supplementary Pages, when completed, form part of the company's return.
- These Pages set out the information we need and provide a standard format.
- These Pages are covered by the Declaration you sign on back page of form *CT600*.
- The warning on form *CT600* about prosecution and the advice about late returns and late payment of tax also apply to these Pages. Other penalties that apply are shown overleaf.

Disclosable tax avoidance schemes

See notes overleaf before completing these boxes.

Scheme Reference Number		Accounting period in which the expected advantage arises (*dd/mm/yyyy*)	
J1		J1A	
J2		J2A	
J3		J3A	
J4		J4A	
J5		J5A	
J6		J6A	
J7		J7A	
J8		J8A	
J9		J9A	
J10		J10A	

HMRC 08/06   CT600J (2006) Version 2

Appendix 2: CT600J (2006) Version 2

Scheme Reference Number

Enter the reference number given to you by the promoter or by HM Revenue & Customs (as appropriate) for each notifiable proposal or notifiable arrangement if you

- have received the scheme reference number in the accounting period covered by this return, or
- expect to obtain a tax advantage in the accounting period covered by this return, or
- expect to obtain a tax advantage in an accounting period covered by a later return.

You should enter the reference number even if you have already entered the number on a return covering an earlier period, unless you no longer expect any tax advantage to arise from the notifiable arrangements either in this accounting period or in any later accounting period.

Accounting period in which the expected advantage arises

You should enter the last day of the accounting period in which you currently expect any tax advantage resulting from the notifiable arrangements to arise, using the format dd/mm/yyyy. If you expect the tax advantage to cover more than one accounting period, enter the earliest.

Penalties

If the company fails
- to provide any reference number given to it by the promoter or by HM Revenue & Customs for any notifiable proposal or arrangement, **or**
- to report the last day of the accounting period in which you first expect any tax advantage to arise, as required by S313(1) FA 2004,
the company may be liable to a penalty under S98C(3) Taxes Management Act 1970.

The amount of the penalty will vary as follows:
- £100 for each scheme to which the failure relates unless either of the bullets below applies -
  - £500 for each scheme where the company has previously failed to comply on one and only one occasion during the period of 36 months ending with the date of the current failure, whether or not the failure relates to the same scheme.
  - £1000 for each scheme where the company has previously failed to comply on two or more occasions during the period of 36 months ending with the date of the current failure, whether or not the failure relates to the same scheme.

Glossary

Tax advantage here means
- relief or increased relief from, or repayment or increased repayment of corporation tax, or the avoidance or reduction of a charge to that tax, or an assessment to that tax, or the avoidance of a possible assessment to that tax
- the deferral of any payment of tax or the advancement of any repayment of tax, or
- the avoidance of any obligation to deduct or account for any tax.

Arrangements connected with employment means any notifiable proposal or arrangements which are disclosable under S308, 309, or 310 FA 2004 by virtue of Part 1 of the Schedule to the Tax Avoidance Schemes (Prescribed Descriptions of Arrangements) Regulations 2004 (as amended). A copy of the Regulations giving the prescribed descriptions of arrangements can be seen at **www.hmrc.gov.uk/aiu/index.htm**

Notifiable proposal and **Notifiable arrangements** have the meanings given in S306 FA 2004.

Reference number in relation to the notifiable arrangements, has the meaning given by S311(3) FA 2004.

What to do when you have completed these Supplementary Pages

Follow the advice shown under 'What to do when you have completed the return' on page 23 of the *Guide*.

584

Index

[all references are to paragraph number]

A

Acceptable distribution policy
controlled foreign companies,
  and   13.37

Accounting
deferred tax
  accounts presentation   17.38
  calculation   17.31–17.38
  discounting   17.36
  fixed assets   17.31
  full prevision liability
    method   17.35
  generally   17.30
  pension costs   17.32
  recognition of deferred
    assets   17.37
  tax losses   17.33
  unremitted earnings of
    subsidiaries, etc   17.34
FRS 3: reporting financial
  performance   17.19–17.20
FRS 5: reporting substance of
  transactions   17.18
FRS 10: Goodwill and
  intangibles   17.17
FRS 12: provisions,
  contingent liabilities and
  assets   17.15–17.16
FRS 15: tangible fixed
  assets   17.13–17.14
FRS 16: current tax   17.28
FRS 17: retirement benefits   17.21
FRS 18: accounting policies   17.12
FRS 19: deferred tax   17.30–17.38
FRS 21: post-balance sheet
  events   17.11

Accounting – *contd*
FRS 23: changes in foreign
  exchange rates   17.10
FRS 26: financial
  instruments—
  measurement   17.9
FRSSE
  generally   17.8
  introduction   17.1
generally accepted accounting
  practice (GAAP)
  international   17.6
  UK   17.5
IAS 1: presentation of
  financial statements   17.19
IAS 2: inventories   17.24
IAS 8: accounting policies
  etc   17.20
IAS 10: post-balance sheet
  events   17.11
IAS 11: construction
  contracts   17.24
IAS 12: income taxes   17.29, 17.39
IAS 16: property, plant and
  equipment   17.13
IAS 17: leases   17.22
IAS 19: employee benefits   17.21
IAS 20: government grants   17.25
IAS 21: currency accounting   17.10
IAS 23: borrowing costs   17.14
IAS 36: impairment   17.17
IAS 37: provisions,
  contingent liabilities and
  assets   17.15
IAS 38: intangible assets   17.17

Accounting – *contd*
IAS 39: financial
instruments—
measurement   17.9
IAS 40: investment properties   17.23
IFRS 1: first time adoption of
IFRS   17.26
international accounting
standards (IAS)   17.1
policies   17.2–17.4
SSAP 9: government grants   17.25
SSAP 9: stocks and long-term
contracts   17.24
SSAP 13: research and
development   17.17
SSAP 17: post-balance sheet
events   17.11
SSAP 19: investment
properties   17.23
SSAP 21: leases and
hire-purchase contracts   17.22
SSAP 24: pension costs   17.21
standards   17.1
tax, for   17.27–17.39
taxation principles, and   17.7
UITF Abstracts   17.1
Accounting periods
tax returns, and   2.4–2.6
Accounting principles
income, and   5.3
**Accounting Regulatory
Committee (ARC)**
accounting standards, and   1.9
Accounting standards
company accounts, and   1.9
Accounts
director's duties   1.11
duty to prepare   1.7
format   1.8
GAAP   1.10
groups of companies, and   10.2
HMRC practice   1.13–1.14
legislation   1.12
self-assessment, and   2.1
standards   1.9
Acquisition costs
asset purchases, and   15.3

Acquisition costs – *contd*
purchase of a company, and   15.3
Administration proceedings
administration orders   19.3
administrators   19.4
cessation of trade   19.7
corporation tax   19.6
effect of appointment   19.5
receivers   19.4
Advance pricing agreements
thin capitalisation, and   14.30
transfer pricing, and   14.29
Amalgamations
capital gains tax
bona fide commercial
arrangements   15.9
groups   15.11
reorganisation of share
capital   15.7
share for share exchange   15.8
transfer of business   15.10
EC Mergers Tax Directive   15.26
intangible assets, and   7.26
introduction   15.5
legislative framework   15.6
trading losses
activities of part of trade   15.22
activities of trade   15.21
beneficial ownership   15.16–
  15.18
capital allowances   15.25
carry forward   15.24
change of ownership   15.12
charging condition   15.14
EC Mergers Tax Directive   15.26
effects   15.24–15.25
later events, and   15.23
ownership condition   15.13
relief   15.15
succession   15.20
transfer of trade   15.19
Annual investment allowance
claims   6.48–6.52
exclusions   6.47
first year allowances, and   6.53
group companies   6.49–6.50

Annual investment allowance – *contd*
interaction with capital
    allowances   6.53–6.54
introduction   6.46
multiple accounting periods   6.52
overview   6.33
short chargeable periods   6.51
single companies   6.48
Annual payments
intangible assets, and   7.11
Anti-avoidance
capital gains
    capital losses   18.17–18.25
    international agreements   18.15
    depreciatory transactions   20.32
    dividend stripping   20.33
    pre-entry losses and gains   20.34
    value shifting   20.24–20.31
capital losses   18.17–18.25
case law   18.2
disclosure of tax avoidance
    schemes
    clearance procedure   18.12
    court procedure   18.32
    disclosable arrangements   18.8–
        18.9
    doubt as to notifiability   18.28
    effect   18.16
    hallmarked tests   18.10
    hallmarks   18.11
    HMRC strategy   18.6
    notification   18.7
    order to disclose   18.31
    pre-disclosure enquiry   18.29
    reasons for non-disclosure   18.30
distributions, and   16.7
evasion, and   18.1
finance leases, and   6.61
GAAR, and   18.3
husband and wife companies   18.26
international agreements, and   18.15
introduction   18.1
legislative framework   18.4–18.5
limitation periods   18.27
loans to participators, and   4.22
mitigation, and   18.1
overseas dividends   13.27

Anti-avoidance – *contd*
repos, and   11.43
self assessment
    CT600   18.13
    penalties   18.14
UK approach   18.3
Appeals
general right   2.27
hearing before
    Commissioners   2.29
High Court, to   2.30
information notices, and   2.52
lodgment   2.28
penalties for errors, and   2.44
procedures   2.28–2.29
trading losses, and   9.27
transfer pricing, and   14.17
Tribunals Courts and
    Enforcement Bill   2.31
Apportionment
controlled foreign companies,
    and   13.32
Appropriations of profit
income, and   5.21–5.22
Associated companies
consequences   4.27
exceptions
    non-trading companies   4.30
    partners   4.29
introduction   4.27
rights of attribution   4.31–4.32
status   4.28
tax returns   4.33
Assessment
trading losses, and   9.27
Asset purchases
acquisition costs   15.3
generally   15.2
Asset transfer
capital gains, and
    from trading stock   20.20
    to trading stock   20.18–20.19
companies leaving group   10.29–
        10.30
depreciatory transactions   10.31
dividend stripping   10.32
election   10.24

Asset transfer – *contd*
group structure 10.21–10.22
pre-entry losses and gains 10.33
relief 10.23
roll-over relief 10.28
trading stock, from
generally 20.20
transfer of assets to trading
stock 20.18–20.19
groups 10.27
trading stock, to
generally 20.18–20.19
groups 10.25–10.26
Associates
participators, and 4.12
Attribution, rights of
associated companies, and 4.31–
4.32
Avoidance
and see Anti-avoidance
generally 18.1–18.26

B
**Background plant and
machinery**
capital allowances, and 6.62
Bad debt relief
loan relationships, and 11.33–11.34
'Badges of trade'
income, and 5.5
Balancing adjustments
business premises renovation
allowances, and 6.97
flat conversion allowances,
and 6.111
Balancing events
business premises renovation
allowances, and 6.96
flat conversion allowances,
and 6.110
Balancing payments
transfer pricing, and 14.16
**Bankers' automated clearing
services (BACS)**
payment of tax, and 2.11
Beneficial ownership
trading losses, and 15.16–15.18

Bona vacantia
distributions in winding up,
and 16.30
Bonus issues
redeemable shares, of 16.8
subsequent to repayment 16.6
Buildings
and see Industrial buildings
allowances
and see Plant and machinery
allowances
income, and 5.44
**Business premises renovation
allowances**
balancing adjustment 6.97
balancing events 6.96
demolition costs 6.99
disadvantaged area 6.90
dwelling 6.92
initial allowances 6.94
introduction 6.86
non-qualifying expenditure 6.88
qualifying business premises 6.91
qualifying building 6.89
qualifying expenditure 6.87
relevant interest 6.93
termination of lease 6.101
value added tax 6.100
writing down allowances 6.95
writing off qualifying
expenditure 6.98
Business test
Construction Industry
Scheme, and 21.26

C
Capital allowances
annual investment allowance
claims 6.48–6.52
exclusions 6.47
first year allowances, and 6.53
group companies 6.49–6.50
interaction with capital
allowances 6.53–6.54
introduction 6.46
multiple accounting periods 6.52
overview 6.33

Capital allowances – *contd*
  annual investment allowance – *contd*
    short chargeable periods   6.51
    single companies   6.48
  appropriations of profits, and   5.25
  balancing adjustment   6.33
  business premises renovation
    balancing adjustment   6.97
    balancing events   6.96
    demolition costs   6.99
    disadvantaged area   6.90
    dwelling   6.92
    initial allowances   6.94
    introduction   6.86
    non-qualifying expenditure   6.88
    qualifying building   6.89
    qualifying business
      premises   6.91
    qualifying expenditure   6.87
    relevant interest   6.93
    termination of lease   6.101
    value added tax   6.100
    writing down allowances   6.95
    writing off qualifying
      expenditure   6.98
  cars with low carbon dioxide
    emissions   6.27
  computation
    annual investment
      allowance   6.46–6.54
    disposal proceeds   6.34
    finance leasing   6.55–6.64
    pool   6.32
    special rate allowance   6.41–6.45
    types of adjustment   6.33
    writing down allowance   6.35–6.40
  controlled foreign companies,
    and   13.43
  date incurred   6.5
  disposal proceeds   6.34
  energy services provider   6.26
  environmentally beneficial
    plant and machinery   6.24–6.25
  finance leasing
    accounting treatment   6.55
    anti-avoidance   6.61

Capital allowances – *contd*
  finance leasing – *contd*
    background plant and
      machinery   6.62
    change of company
      ownership   6.64
    funding lease   6.59
    long funding leases   6.57
    non-funding lease   6.60
    plant and machinery leased
      with land   6.63
    short lease   6.58
    taxation treatment   6.40
  first year allowance
    cars with low carbon
      dioxide emissions   6.27
    energy services provider   6.26
    environmentally beneficial
      plant and machinery   6.24–6.25
    excluded expenditure   6.31
    groups   6.23
    introduction   6.21
    natural gas and hydrogen
      refuelling equipment   6.28
    North Sea oil ring-fence
      plant   6.29
    overview   6.33
    owners of fixtures   6.30
    small and medium sized
      enterprises   6.22
    small enterprises   6.22
  flat conversion allowances
    balancing adjustment   6.111
    balancing events   6.110
    high-value flats   6.107
    initial allowances   6.108
    non-qualifying expenditure   6.104
    qualifying building   6.105
    qualifying expenditure   6.103
    qualifying flat   6.106
    relevant interest   6.102
    writing-down allowances   6.109
  generally   6.4
  hire-purchased assets   6.39–6.40

Capital allowances – *contd*
industrial buildings
  construction of building or
    structure 6.65
  disposal of building 6.80–6.82
  enterprise zones, in 6.85
  generally 6.65
  'goods and materials' 6.68
  hotels 6.72
  initial allowance 6.73
  'manufacturing' 6.67
  qualifying expenditure 6.71
  qualifying structures 6.65
  qualifying trade 6.66
  relevant expenditure 6.71
  'storage' 6.70
  'subject to a process' 6.69
  successor company, and 6.84
  temporary disuse 6.79
  writing down allowance 6.74–
    6.78
long-life assets 6.37
natural gas and hydrogen
  refuelling equipment 6.28
North Sea oil ring-fence plant 6.29
overview 5.35–5.36
owners of fixtures 6.30
plant and machinery
  alterations to buildings 6.12
  buildings 6.9
  case law 6.18–6.19
  computer software 6.15
  demolition costs 6.13
  fire safety equipment 6.14
  fixtures, and 6.83
  generally 6.7–6.8
  integral features 6.17
  lighting 6.11
  'plant' 6.10
  qualifying assets 6.9
  rates 6.20
  structures 6.9
  thermal insulation of
    buildings 6.16
pool 6.32
rates 6.20
reduced allowances 6.38

Capital allowances – *contd*
relevant assets 6.6
research and development
  allowances 8.7
  disposal value 8.9
  introduction 8.2
  overview 8.1
  qualifying expenditure 8.6
  reduced claim 8.7
  'research and development' 8.3–
    8.5
  types 8.7–8.8
short life assets 6.36
special rate allowance
  disposal value of assets 6.42
  existing long-life asset
    expenditure 6.45
  integral features 6.43
  intra-group transfers 6.44
  relevant expenditure 6.41
  sale between connected
    persons 6.43
trading losses, and 15.25
transfer pricing, and 14.18
writing down allowance
  hire-purchased assets 6.39–6.40
  long-life assets 6.37
  overview 6.33
  reduced allowances 6.38
  short life assets 6.36
  transitional rate 6.35
year end, and 22.4

Capital expenditure
investment business, and 12.8

Capital gains
anti-avoidance
  depreciatory transactions 20.32
  dividend stripping 20.33
  pre-entry losses and gains 20.34
  value shifting 20.24–20.31
capital losses 20.5
chargeable gains 20.1
companies leaving group 20.22
computation
  capital losses 20.5
  companies leaving group 20.22
  enhancement expenditure 20.3

Capital gains – *contd*
  computation – *contd*
    indexation   20.4
    introduction   20.2
    reliefs   20.6–20.17
    replacement of assets by
      members of group   20.21
    special provisions   20.18–20.22
    transfer of assets from
      trading stock   20.20
    transfer of assets to trading
      stock   20.18–20.19
  corporate venturing scheme
    claims for relief   12.39–12.40
    clearance   12.38
    deferral relief   12.32, 12.41
    form of investment   12.35
    generally   12.31
    group relief   12.43
    investing company's
      interest   12.33
    investment   12.35
    investment relief   12.32
    issuing company   12.34
    loss relief   12.32, 12.42
    qualifying trade   12.37
    reliefs   12.32
    trading activities   12.36
  depreciatory transactions   20.32
  dividend stripping   20.33
  enhancement expenditure   20.3
  indexation   20.4
  intra-group asset transfer
    election to treat disposal as
      if made by another
      member   20.17
    group structure   20.14–20.15
    relief   20.16
  limited companies
    capital losses   12.25
    corporate venturing
      scheme   12.31–12.42
    group relief   12.43
    other reliefs   12.43
    shares in unquoted trading
      companies   12.25

Capital gains – *contd*
  limited companies – *contd*
    substantial shareholdings
      exemption   12.26–12.30
    taper relief   12.43
  pre-entry losses and gains   20.34
  reconstructions and
    amalgamations, and
    bona fide commercial
      arrangements   15.9
    groups   15.11
    reorganisation of share
      capital   15.7
    share for share exchange   15.8
    transfer of business   15.10
  reliefs
    intra-group asset transfer   20.14–20.17
    introduction   20.1
    roll-over relief   20.6–20.13
  replacement of assets by
    members of group   20.21
  roll-over relief
    assets only partly replaced   20.8
    assets owned personally but
      used in the trade   20.13
    conditions   20.7
    depreciating assets   20.9
    introduction   20.6
    land and buildings   20.10
    new assets as depreciating
      assets   20.9
    new assets not brought
      immediately into
      trading use   20.12
    new assets not purchased   20.11
  shares in unquoted trading
    companies   12.25
  substantial shareholdings
    exemption
    conditions   12.28–12.29
    generally   12.26
    substantial shareholding   12.27
    trading activities   12.30
  tangible fixed assets, and
    conditions affecting assets   20.1

Capital gains – *contd*
tangible fixed assets, and – *contd*
  new assets not brought
    immediately into
    trading use   20.12
  new assets not purchased   20.11
  new, depreciating assets   20.9
  partly replaced assets   20.8
  personally-owned assets
    used in trade   20.13
  roll-over relief   20.6
taper relief   12.43
tax avoidance
  capital losses   18.17–18.25
  international agreements   18.16
transfer of assets from trading
  stock   20.20
transfer of assets to trading
  stock   20.18–20.19
transfer pricing, and   14.18
value shifting
  asset holding company
    leaving group   20.28
  disposal of shares in
    another company   20.31
  disposals within group
    followed by share
    disposal   20.29
  distributions within group
    followed by share
    disposal   20.27
  free benefits   20.26
  general application   20.25
  introduction   20.24
  reorganisation of share
    capital   20.30
year end, and   22.5
Capital losses
anti-avoidance, and   18.17–18.25
generally   20.5
investment business, and   12.25
Capital/revenue principles
income, and   5.10
Carry back
loan relationships, and   11.19
overseas dividends, and   13.20–
     13.21

Carry forward
loan relationships, and
  disclaimer   11.21
  generally   11.20
losses, and
  case law   9.3
  charge to tax   9.6
  HMRC enquiries   9.5
  loss claim   9.2
  self-assessment   9.4
overseas dividends, and   13.20–
     13.21
trading losses, and   15.24
**Cars with low carbon dioxide
  emissions**
capital allowances, and   6.27
Cessation of trade
investment business, and   12.10
trading losses, and   9.16
Change of ownership
capital allowances, and   6.64
Construction Industry
  Scheme, and   21.14
investment business, and   12.13
trading losses, and   9.18, 15.12
Chargeable gains
tangible fixed assets, and
  conditions affecting assets   20.1
  new assets not brought
    immediately into
    trading use   20.12
  new assets not purchased   20.11
  new, depreciating assets   20.9
  partly replaced assets   20.8
  personally-owned assets
    used in trade   20.13
  roll-over relief   20.6
transfer pricing, and   14.18
Charge to tax
creditor quasi-repo, and   11.40
creditor repo, and   11.42
debtor quasi-repo, and   11.39
income, and   5.1
liability to tax, and   1.5
Charges on income
non-trade charges   9.15
trade charges   9.8

Charities
benefits received	5.50
cash gifts	5.49
generally	5.46–5.48
non-cash gifts	5.51

Circuitous loans
loans to participators, and	4.21

Clearance procedure
corporate venturing scheme, and	12.38
demergers, and	16.18
disclosure of tax avoidance schemes, and	18.12
purchase of own shares, and	16.23

Close companies
associates	4.12
consequences	4.2
control	4.4
directors	4.8
exceptions	
'director'	4.8
general	4.5
'principal member'	4.7
'public'	4.6
introduction	4.2
investment holding companies	
consequences	4.23
letting land	4.26
letting land to connected person	4.25
status	4.24
loan creditors	4.11
loans to participators	
anti-avoidance	4.22
circuitous loans	4.21
excluded loans	4.17
generally	4.14
indirect loans	4.21
loan accounts	4.18
release	4.20
relevant loans	4.16
self-assessment disclosure	4.15
tax repayment	4.19
overview	4.1
participators	
associates, and	4.12
benefits to	4.13

Close companies – *contd*
participators – *contd*	
loan creditors, and	4.11
loans to	4.14–4.22
meaning	4.10
principal member	4.7
status	4.3
tests	4.9

Close investment holding companies
consequences	4.23
letting land	4.26
letting land to connected person	4.25
status	4.24

Commercial arrangements
reconstructions and amalgamations, and	15.9

Commissioners
appeals, and	2.29

Community amateur sports clubs (CASCs)
conditions	5.54
donor reliefs	5.56
reliefs	5.55
self-assessment	5.57

Community investment tax relief
accreditation	12.47
certificates	12.51
conditions	
loans, as to	12.48
securities, as to	12.49
shares, as to	12.50
eligibility	12.45
excessive returns to investor	12.55
generally	12.46
investment	12.52
reconstructions	12.57
repayments of loan capital	12.54
value received	12.56
withdrawal	12.53

Companies Act 2006
introduction	1.2

Company
definition	1.4

Company accounts
director's duties — 1.11
duty to prepare — 1.7
format — 1.8
GAAP — 1.10
HMRC practice — 1.13–1.14
legislation — 1.12
self-assessment, and — 2.1
standards — 1.9

Company loan stock
investment business, and — 12.44

Company ownership
and see under individual headings
associated companies — 4.27–4.32
close companies — 4.2–4.22
close investment holding companies — 4.23–4.26
introduction — 4.1

Compliance test
Construction Industry Scheme, and — 21.28

Computation of income and gains
generally — 5.2
Schedule D Case I — 5.12

Computer software
plant and machinery allowances, and — 6.15

Connected persons
amortised cost basis — 11.28–11.29
bad debt relief — 11.33–11.34
benefit derived — 11.32
'connection' — 11.25
consequences — 11.28–11.34
creditor relationships — 11.32
discounted securities — 11.31
impairment losses — 11.33–11.34
intangible assets, and — 7.29
meaning — 11.25
post-1 October 2002 — 11.27
pre-1 October 2002 — 11.26
special rate allowance, and — 6.43
unpaid interest — 11.30

Consortia
and see Groups of companies
claims — 10.14

Consortia – *contd*
loan relationships, and — 11.35

Construction Industry Scheme
application of sums deducted — 21.29
business test — 21.26
cancellation of registration
appeals — 21.17
fraudulent conduct — 21.16
reasons — 21.15
change of control of company — 21.14
compliance test — 21.28
construction contracts — 21.5
meaning — 21.2
operations — 21.4
sub-contractor — 21.3
transfer of trade — 21.6
contract payments — 21.7–21.8
contractors — 21.5
declarations — 21.24
deductions on account of tax
application — 21.29
contract payments — 21.7–21.8
default surcharge — 21.11
monthly payment — 21.10
quarterly payment — 21.12
rate of tax — 21.9
default surcharge — 21.11
gross payment tests
business test — 21.26
compliance test — 21.28
introduction — 21.25
turnover test — 21.27
information to be supplied to HMRC — 21.13
inspection of records — 21.21
introduction — 21.1
monthly payment — 21.10
monthly returns — 21.23
penalties — 21.22
quarterly payment — 21.12
rate of tax — 21.9
records
inspection — 21.21
maintenance — 21.20
registration
cancellation — 21.15–21.17

Construction Industry Scheme – *contd*
registration – *contd*
  change of control of
    company 21.14
    generally 21.13
  returns 21.23
  sub-contractors
    inspection of records 21.21
    meaning 21.3
    registration 21.13
  transfer of trade 21.6
  turnover test 21.27
  verification 21.18–21.19

Contingent debts
loan relationships, and 11.8

Control
close companies, and 4.4
controlled foreign companies,
  and 13.35
transfer pricing, and 14.4

Controlled foreign companies
acceptable distribution policy 13.37
apportionment 13.32
capital allowances 13.43
chargeable profits 13.34
claims procedure 13.46
control 13.35
creditable tax and reliefs 13.43
de minimis exclusion 13.40
distributions 13.33
dividends from 13.44
exclusion from profit
  apportionment 13.36
exempt activities test 13.38
genuine economic activities 13.45
group relief 13.43
intangible assets, and 7.33
legislative developments 13.29
loan relationships 13.43
management expenses 13.43
meaning 13.28
motive test 13.41
public quotation condition 13.39
residence 13.30
self assessment 13.31
set-off 13.43
territorial exclusion 13.42

Controlled foreign companies – *contd*
trading losses 13.43

Corporate finance
and see Loan relationships
equity/loan issue 11.1
loan relationships 11.2–11.43

Corporate venturing scheme
claims for relief
  deferral relief 12.41
  generally 12.39–12.40
  loss relief 12.42
clearance 12.38
deferral relief
  claims 12.41
  generally 12.32
form of investment 12.35
generally 12.31
group relief 12.43
investing company's interest 12.33
investment 12.35
investment relief 12.32
issuing company 12.34
loss relief
  claims 12.42
  generally 12.32
qualifying trade 12.37
reliefs 12.32
trading activities 12.36

Corporation tax
basis 1.3
introduction 1.1–1.2
liability 1.4–1.6
rate 1.3

Costs of acquisition
asset purchases, and 15.3
purchase of a company, and 15.3

Court settlements
loan relationships, and 11.8

Credit relief
overseas dividends, and 13.19

Creditor quasi-repo
charge to tax 11.42
generally 11.41
relief 11.42

Creditor repo
charge to tax 11.42
generally 11.40

Creditor repo – *contd*
relief   11.42
CT61
quarterly accounting, and   3.22
CT600
anti-avoidance, and   18.13
generally   2.7
introduction   2.1
Currency contracts
transfer pricing, and   14.22

D

De minimis exclusion
controlled foreign companies,
    and   13.40
Debits and credits
intangible assets, and
    generally   7.10
    non-trading   7.13
    prescribed adjustments   7.14–7.19
loan relationships, and   11.2
Debtor quasi-repo
charge to tax   11.39
generally   11.38
relief   11.39
Declarations
Construction Industry
    Scheme, and   21.24
Deduction of tax
quarterly accounting, and   3.23
Deductions
income, and   5.20
research and development,
    and
    externally provided workers   8.16
    generally   8.10
    intellectual property   8.14
    qualifying expenditure   8.13
    relevant research and
      development   8.12
    'research and development'   8.11
    sub-contracted work   8.17
    subsidised expenditure   8.15
Default surcharge
Construction Industry
    Scheme, and   21.11

Deferred tax
accounts presentation   17.38
calculation   17.31–17.38
discounting   17.36
fixed assets   17.31
full prevision liability method   17.35
generally   17.30
pension costs   17.32
recognition of deferred assets   17.37
tax losses   17.33
unremitted earnings of
    subsidiaries, etc   17.34
Demergers
clearance procedure   16.18
conditions   16.17
generally   16.13–16.15
reliefs   16.16
Demolition costs
business premises renovation
    allowances, and   6.99
plant and machinery
    allowances, and   6.13
Depreciation
income, and   5.21
intangible assets, and   7.12
Depreciatory transactions
asset transfers, and   10.31
capital gains, and   20.32
Derivatives
loan relationships, and   11.36
Determinations
self-assessment, and   2.32
Directors
accounts duties, and   1.11
close companies, and   4.8
Directors remuneration
income, and   5.16
Disadvantaged areas
business premises renovation
    allowances, and   6.90
Disclosure of tax avoidance
  schemes
clearance procedure   18.12
court procedure   18.32
disclosable arrangements   18.8–18.9
doubt as to notifiability   18.28
effect   18.16

Disclosure of tax avoidance schemes –
contd
hallmarked tests   18.10
hallmarks   18.11
HMRC strategy   18.6
notification   18.7
order to disclose   18.31
pre-disclosure enquiry   18.29
reasons for non-disclosure   18.30
Discounted securities
loan relationships, and   11.31
Discovery assessments
self-assessment, and   2.32
Disposal proceeds
industrial buildings
allowances, and   6.80–6.82
plant and machinery
allowances, and   6.34
Distributions
anti-avoidance   16.7
bonus issue
redeemable shares, of   16.8
subsequent to repayment   16.6
controlled foreign companies,
and   13.33
demergers
clearance procedure   16.18
conditions   16.17
generally   16.13–16.15
reliefs   16.16
distribution of assets   16.5
dividends
generally   16.4
small company payments   16.9
ESC 16, and   16.26–16.28
exempt transactions
demergers   16.13–16.18
distributions in
winding-up   16.26–16.32
introduction   16.12
purchase of own shares   16.19–
16.25
income, and   5.21
interest   16.7
introduction   16.1
meaning   16.2
non-qualifying distribution   16.8

Distributions – *contd*
purchase of own shares
'associated persons'   16.24
clearance procedure   16.23
conditions   16.20–16.21
'connected persons'   16.25
generally   16.19
purpose   16.20
shareholder interest in
company   16.22
shareholder residence   16.21
small company payments   16.9
striking off defunct company
ESC 16, and   16.28
generally   16.26
request by private company   16.27
surplus ACT   16.10–16.11
types
bonus issue   16.6
distribution of assets   16.5
dividends   16.4
generally   16.3
interest   16.7
winding up, and
assets and liabilities   16.29
bona vacantia   16.30
generally   16.7
permitted distributions   16.32
striking off defunct
company   16.26–16.28
unauthorised distribution   16.31
Dividend stripping
asset transfers, and   10.32
capital gains, and   20.33
Dividends
and see Distributions
controlled foreign companies,
and   13.44
generally   16.4
income, and   5.21
trading losses, and   9.9
small company payments   16.9
Double tax relief
dual resident companies, and   13.16
Dual resident company
double tax relief   13.16
restrictions   13.15

Dwellings
business premises renovation
  allowances, and   6.92

E

Effective rates
generally   3.6
Employee benefit trusts
income, and   5.30
Employee remuneration
income, and   5.15
Employee share schemes
income, and   5.26–5.29
Energy-saving items
investment business, and   12.21
Energy services provider
capital allowances, and   6.26
Enhancement expenditure
capital gains, and   20.3
Enquiries
affairs of directors, and   2.18
amendment of return   2.22
appeals
  general right   2.27
  hearing before
    Commissioners   2.29
  High Court, to   2.30
  lodgment   2.28
  procedures   2.28–2.29
  Tribunals Courts and
    Enforcement Bill   2.31
completion of
  appeal   2.27
  introduction   2.23
  penalties for periods prior
    to 1 April 2008   2.24
  penalty reduction
    percentages   2.25–2.26
directors' returns, and
  disclosure of directors'
    documents   2.20
  generally   2.19
disclosure of company
  documents   2.17
manner   2.16
penalty reduction percentages   2.25–2.26

Enquiries – *contd*
process   2.21
timing
  accounting periods after
    31 March 2008   2.15
  accounting periods prior to
    1 April 2008   2.14
trading losses, and   9.5
transfer pricing, and   14.26
Enterprise zones
industrial buildings
  allowances, and   6.85
Entertaining
income, and   5.14
**Environmentally beneficial
plant and machinery**
capital allowances, and   6.24–6.25
Errors, penalties for
appeals   2.44
circumstances in which
  payable   2.37
generally   2.36
liability of company officers   2.45
potential lost revenue
  delayed tax   2.41
  losses   2.40
  multiple errors   2.39
  normal rule   2.38
procedures   2.43
reductions for disclosure   2.42
suspension   2.44
Estimation of tax due
self-assessment, and   2.32
Evasion
anti-avoidance, and   18.1
Exempt activities test
controlled foreign companies,
  and   13.38
Expenditure
allowable deductions   5.20
directors remuneration   5.16
employees remuneration   5.15
entertaining   5.14
managed service companies   5.18
personal service companies   5.17

Expenditure – *contd*
  remediation of contaminated
    land, and
    connected sub-contractor   8.42
    contaminated state   8.36
    deduction in calculation of
      profits   8.45
    employee costs   8.38
    entitlement to relief   8.44
    increased expenditure due
      to contamination   8.40
    introduction   8.33
    materials expenditure   8.39
    qualifying expenditure   8.35
    qualifying land   8.34
    relevant activities   8.37
    sub-contractor payments   8.42–
        8.43
    subsidised expenditure   8.41
  research and development,
    and
    externally provided workers   8.16
    intellectual property   8.14
    qualifying expenditure   8.13
    relevant research and
      development   8.12
    'research and development'   8.11
    reverse deduction   8.10
    sub-contracted work   8.17
    subsidised expenditure   8.15
  website development costs   5.19
  'wholly and exclusively'   5.13

F

Filing date
  tax returns, and   2.9
Finance leasing
  capital allowances, and
    accounting treatment   6.55
    anti-avoidance   6.61
    background plant and
      machinery   6.62
    change of company
      ownership   6.64
    funding lease   6.59
    long funding leases   6.57
    non-funding lease   6.60

Finance leasing – *contd*
  capital allowances, and – *contd*
    plant and machinery leased
      with land   6.63
    short lease   6.58
    taxation treatment   6.40
  loan relationships, and   11.8
**Financial Reporting Standard
  for Smaller Entities
  (FRSSE)**
  company accounts, and   1.10
  generally   17.8
  introduction   17.1
  loan relationships, and   11.9
**Financial Reporting Standards
  (FRS)**
  FRS 3: reporting financial
    performance   17.19–17.20
  FRS 5: reporting substance of
    transactions   17.18
  FRS 10: goodwill and
    intangibles
    generally   17.17
    introduction   7.6
  FRS 12: provisions,
    contingent liabilities and
    assets   17.15–17.16
  FRS 15: tangible fixed
    assets   17.13–17.14
  FRS 16: current tax   17.28
  FRS 17: retirement benefits   17.21
  FRS 18: accounting policies   17.12
  FRS 19: deferred tax
    accounts presentation   17.38
    calculation   17.31–17.38
    discounting   17.36
    fixed assets   17.31
    full prevision liability
      method   17.35
    generally   17.30
    pension costs   17.32
    recognition of deferred
      assets   17.37
    tax losses   17.33
    unremitted earnings of
      subsidiaries, etc   17.34

Financial Reporting Standards (FRS)
 – *contd*
 FRS 21: post-balance sheet
  events 17.11
 FRS 23: changes in foreign
  exchange rates 17.10
 FRS 26: financial instruments—
  measurement 17.9
 intangible assets, and 7.6
 introduction 1.10
Fire safety equipment
 plant and machinery
  allowances, and 6.14
First year allowance
 annual investment allowance,
  and 6.53
 cars with low carbon dioxide
  emissions 6.27
 energy services provider 6.26
 environmentally beneficial
  plant and machinery 6.24–6.25
 excluded expenditure 6.31
 groups 6.23
 introduction 6.21
 natural gas and hydrogen
  refuelling equipment 6.28
 North Sea oil ring-fence plant 6.29
 owners of fixtures 6.30
 small and medium sized
  enterprises 6.22
 small enterprises 6.22
Fixed assets (tangible)
 accountancy treatment 6.1
 background plant and
  machinery 6.62
 capital allowances
  business premises
   renovation 6.86–6.101
  computation 6.32–6.39
  date incurred 6.5
  first year allowance 6.21–6.31
  flat conversion 6.102—6.111
  generally 6.4
  industrial buildings 6.65–6.68
  plant and machinery 6.7–6.18
  rates 6.20
  relevant assets 6.6

Fixed assets (tangible) – *contd*
 cars with low carbon dioxide
  emissions 6.27
 chargeable gains
  conditions affecting assets 20.1
  new assets not brought
   immediately into
   trading use 20.12
  new assets not purchased 20.11
  new, depreciating assets 20.9
  partly replaced assets 20.8
  personally-owned assets
   used in trade 20.13
  roll-over relief 20.6
 computation of capital
  allowances
  background plant and
   machinery 6.62
  disposal proceeds 6.34
  finance leasing 6.55–6.64
  funding lease 6.59
  hire-purchased assets 6.39–6.40
  long funding leases 6.57
  long-life assets 6.37
  non-funding lease 6.60
  plant and machinery leased
   with land 6.63
  pool 6.32
  reduced allowances 6.38
  short lease 6.58
  short life assets 6.36
  types of adjustment 6.33
 disposal proceeds 6.34
 energy services provider 6.26
 enterprise zones 6.85
 environmentally beneficial
  plant and machinery 6.24–6.25
 finance leasing
  accounting treatment 6.55
  anti-avoidance 6.61
  background plant and
   machinery 6.62
  change of company
   ownership 6.64
  funding lease 6.59
  long funding leases 6.57
  non-funding lease 6.60

Fixed assets (tangible) – *contd*
finance leasing – *contd*
  plant and machinery leased
    with land — 6.63
  short lease — 6.58
  taxation treatment — 6.40
first year allowance
  cars with low carbon
    dioxide emissions — 6.27
  energy services provider — 6.26
  environmentally beneficial
    plant and machinery — 6.24–6.25
  excluded expenditure — 6.31
  groups — 6.23
  introduction — 6.21
  natural gas and hydrogen
    refuelling equipment — 6.28
  North Sea oil ring-fence
    plant — 6.29
  owners of fixtures — 6.30
  small and medium sized
    enterprises — 6.22
  small enterprises — 6.22
funding lease — 6.59
hire-purchased assets — 6.39–6.40
industrial buildings
  allowances
  construction of building or
    structure — 6.65
  disposal of building — 6.80–6.82
  enterprise zones, in — 6.85
  generally — 6.65
  'goods and materials' — 6.68
  hotels — 6.72
  initial allowance — 6.73
  'manufacturing' — 6.67
  qualifying expenditure — 6.71
  qualifying structures — 6.65
  qualifying trade — 6.66
  relevant expenditure — 6.71
  'storage' — 6.70
  'subject to a process' — 6.69
  successor company, and — 6.84
  temporary disuse — 6.79
  writing down allowance — 6.74–6.78

Fixed assets (tangible) – *contd*
long funding leases — 6.57
long-life assets — 6.37
natural gas and hydrogen
  refuelling equipment — 6.28
non-funding lease — 6.60
North Sea oil ring-fence plant — 6.29
owners of fixtures — 6.30
plant and machinery
  allowances
  alterations to buildings — 6.12
  buildings — 6.9
  case law — 6.18–6.19
  computer software — 6.15
  demolition costs — 6.13
  fire safety equipment — 6.14
  fixtures, and — 6.83
  generally — 6.7–6.8
  integral features — 6.17
  lighting — 6.11
  'plant' — 6.10
  qualifying assets — 6.9
  rates — 6.20
  structures — 6.9
  thermal insulation of
    buildings — 6.16
plant and machinery leased
  with land — 6.63
pool — 6.32
qualifying expenditure
  date incurred — 6.5
  generally — 6.4
  plant and machinery — 6.7–6.20
  relevant assets — 6.6
reduced allowances — 6.38
short lease — 6.58
short life assets — 6.36
tangible fixed assets, and
  conditions affecting assets — 20.1
  new assets not brought
    immediately into
    trading use — 20.12
  new assets not purchased — 20.11
  new, depreciating assets — 20.9
  partly replaced assets — 20.8
  personally-owned assets
    used in trade — 20.13

Fixed assets (tangible) – *contd*
tangible fixed assets, and – *contd*
  roll-over relief 20.6
  tax treatment 6.2
First-year tax credits
amount
  generally 9.33
  PAYE and NIC liabilities,
    and 9.34
clawback
  amount of restored loss 9.41
  claims 9.43
  correction of returns 9.42
  relevant circumstances 9.40
excluded company 9.32
introduction 9.29
PAYE and NIC liabilities 9.34
relevant expenditure 9.31
surrenderable loss 9.30
unrelieved losses, and 9.39
Fixed place of business
permanent establishment, and 13.7
Fixtures
plant and machinery
  allowances, and 6.83
Flat conversion allowances
balancing adjustment 6.111
balancing events 6.110
high-value flats 6.107
initial allowances 6.108
non-qualifying expenditure 6.104
qualifying building 6.105
qualifying expenditure 6.103
qualifying flat 6.106
relevant interest 6.102
writing-down allowances 6.109
Foreign exchange gains and
losses
loan relationships, and 11.36
Fraud
civil investigation procedures 2.34
criminal prosecution 2.35
generally 2.33
Funding lease
capital allowances, and 6.59
Furnished holiday lettings
income, and 5.45

Furnished holiday lettings – *contd*
trading losses, and
  generally 9.35
  overseas business 9.37

G

Generally accepted accounting
principles (GAAP)
company accounts, and 1.10
income, and 5.3
loan relationships, and 11.9
General anti-avoidance rule
(GAAR)
generally 18.3
Going concern
research and development,
  and 8.30
Government investment
written off
trading losses, and 9.21
Government loan stock
investment business, and 12.44
Gross payment tests
business test 21.26
compliance test 21.28
introduction 21.25
turnover test 21.27
Groups of companies
accounting requirements 10.2
annual investment allowance,
  and 6.49–6.50
asset transfer
  companies leaving group 20.22–
    20.23
  depreciatory transactions 20.32
  dividend stripping 20.33
  election 20.17
  group structure 20.14
  pre-entry losses and gains 20.34
  relief 20.16
  roll-over relief 20.06
  trading stock, from 20.20
  trading stock, to 20.18
business structure 10.1
companies leaving group
  asset transfer 20.22
  intangible assets 7.25

Groups of companies – *contd*
consortium relief claim   10.14
controlled foreign companies,
 and   13.43
depreciatory transactions   20.32
dividend stripping   20.33
group relief
 availability   10.8–10.20
 claim   10.13–10.14
 claimant company   10.15
 conditions   10.5
 'consortium'   10.6
 controlled foreign
  companies, and   13.43
 generally   10.7
 'group'   10.5
 group income   10.20
 losses   10.7
 overseas losses   10.9–10.11
 quarterly instalment
  refunds   10.18–10.19
 repayments of tax   10.17
 tax returns   10.16
 transfer of company to
  another group or
  consortium   10.12
 UK losses   10.8
intangible assets, and
 connected persons   7.29
 finance lessor   7.31
 grants   7.30
 intra-group asset transfer   7.24
 leaving   7.25
 meaning   7.23
 reconstructions   7.26
 related parties   7.27–7.28
investment business, and   12.6
joint ventures, and   10.1
loan relationships, and   11.35
overseas dividends, and   13.26
overseas losses   10.9–10.11
partnerships, and   10.1
payment of tax, and   3.21
pre-entry losses and gains   20.34
quarterly instalments, and   10.18–
               10.19

Groups of companies – *contd*
reconstructions and
 amalgamations, and   15.11
reliefs   10.4
repayments of tax   10.17
roll-over relief   20.6
tax returns
 generally   10.3
 group relief   10.16
taxation   10.3
trading losses   10.7
trading stock, and   20.18–20.20

H
High-value flats
flat conversion allowances,
 and   6.107
Hire-purchase
capital allowances, and   6.39–6.40
loan relationships, and   11.8
HMRC practice
company accounts, and   1.13
loan relationships, and   11.15
Hotels
industrial buildings
 allowances, and   6.72
Husband and wife companies
and see Spouses
anti-avoidance, and   18.26

I
Impairment
intangible assets, and   7.15
loan relationships, and   11.33–11.34
Income
accounting principles   5.3
allowable deductions   5.20
appropriations of profit   5.21–5.22
'badges of trade'   5.5
capital allowances
 computation   5.35–5.36
 generally   5.25
capital/revenue principles   5.10
case law   5.6
cessation of trade   5.34
charge to tax   5.1

Income – *contd*

charities
   benefits received 5.50
   cash gifts 5.49
   generally 5.46–5.48
   non-cash gifts 5.51
commencement of trade 5.33
community amateur sports
   clubs (CASCs)
   conditions 5.54
   donor reliefs 5.56
   reliefs 5.55
   self-assessment 5.57
computation of income and
   gains
   generally 5.2
   Schedule D Case I 5.12
deductions 5.20
depreciation 5.21
directors remuneration 5.16
distributions 5.21
dividend payments 5.21
employee benefit trusts 5.30
employee incentives
   employee benefit trusts 5.30
   share schemes 5.26–5.29
employee remuneration 5.15
employee share schemes 5.26–5.29
entertaining 5.14
exempt bodies
   charities 5.46–5.51
   CASCs 5.54–5.56
   members' sports clubs 5.53
   mutual trading 5.52
   self-assessment 5.57
expenditure
   allowable deductions 5.20
   directors remuneration 5.16
   employees remuneration 5.15
   entertaining 5.14
   managed service companies 5.18
   personal service companies 5.17
   website development costs 5.19
   'wholly and exclusively' 5.13
furnished holiday lettings 5.45
GAAP, and 5.3
intangible assets 5.23

Income – *contd*

introduction 5.1
land and buildings 5.44
lease amortisation 5.22
managed service companies 5.18
members' sports clubs
   generally 5.53
   self-assessment 5.57
mutual trading
   generally 5.52
   self-assessment 5.57
pension contributions
   generally 5.31
   spreading rules 5.32
personal service companies 5.17
professional profits 5.4
reliefs 5.2
rent 5.24
returns 5.8
Schedule A
   furnished holiday lettings 5.45
   land and buildings 5.44
Schedule D 5.9
self-assessment
   Schedule D Case I and II
      profits 5.9
   tax returns 5.8
share schemes 5.26–5.29
sources 5.2
stock
   IAS inventories 5.38
   net realisable value/cost 5.39
   SSAP 5.37
   UITF 5.41–5.42
   valuation of transfers to
      and from 5.43
tax returns 5.8
'trade' 5.5
trading income
   'badges of trade' 5.5
   case law 5.6
   generally 5.7
   introduction 5.4
   self-assessment 5.8–5.9
   'trade' 5.4
transfer pricing adjustments 5.23

Income – *contd*
waste disposal restoration
  projects 5.11
website development costs 5.19
'wholly and exclusively' 5.13
work in progress
  IAS inventories 5.38
  net realisable value/cost 5.39
  professional firms 5.40
  SSAP 5.37
  UITF 5.41–5.42
  valuation of transfers to
    and from trading stock 5.43
Indexation
capital gains, and 20.4
Indirect loans
loans to participators, and 4.21
Industrial buildings
 allowances
construction of building or
  structure 6.65
disposal of building
  post-21 March 2007
    regime 6.80–6.81
  pre-21 March 2007 regime 6.82
enterprise zones, in 6.85
generally 6.65
'goods and materials' 6.68
hotels 6.72
initial allowance 6.73
'manufacturing' 6.67
qualifying expenditure 6.71
qualifying structures 6.65
qualifying trade 6.66
relevant expenditure 6.71
'storage' 6.70
'subject to a process' 6.69
successor company, and 6.84
temporary disuse 6.79
writing down allowance
  anti-avoidance 6.77
  introduction 6.74
  pre-condition 6.78
  qualifying enterprise zone
    expenditure 6.76
  transitional period 6.75

Information notices
appeals 2.52–2.53
change of ownership of
  companies 2.54
destruction of documents 2.56
inspection of business
  premises 2.49
inspection of records 2.48
introduction 2.46
offence 2.59
other powers 2.50
penalties 2.55
reasonable excuse 2.57
restrictions on powers 2.51
supplementary information 2.47
Initial allowances
business premises renovation
  allowances, and 6.94
flat conversion allowances,
  and 6.108
industrial buildings
  allowances, and 6.73
Insolvency
administration proceedings
  administration orders 19.3
  administrators 19.4
  cessation of trade 19.7
  corporation tax 19.6
  effect of appointment 19.5
  receivers 19.4
administrative receivers 19.4
distributions, and 16.7
liquidation proceedings
  commencement 19.10
  corporation tax 19.11
  effect of order 19.12
  ESC 16 19.14
  generally 19.8
  liquidator 19.9
  loans to participators 19.13
  tax liabilities of office
    holders 19.15
meaning 19.1–19.2
receivers
  effect of appointment 19.5
  generally 19.4
subsidiary company 19.16

Inspection of records
Construction Industry
  Scheme, and   21.21
Insurance premiums
  investment business, and   12.9
Intangible assets
  annual payments   7.11
  chargeable assets   7.3
  connected persons   7.29
  controlled foreign companies   7.33
  debits and credits
    generally   7.10
    non-trading   7.13
    prescribed adjustments   7.14–7.19
  depreciation   7.12
  excluded assets   7.7–7.8
  existing assets
    generally   7.2
    transitional period   7.4
  finance lessors   7.31
  FRS10, and   7.6
  grants   7.30
  groups
    connected persons   7.29
    finance lessors   7.31
    grants   7.30
    intra-group asset transfer   7.24
    leaving   7.25
    meaning   7.23
    reconstructions   7.26
    related parties   7.27–7.28
  impairment review   7.15
  international aspects
    company ceasing to be UK
      resident   7.32
    controlled foreign
      companies   7.33
  intra-group asset transfer   7.24
  introduction   7.1
  meaning
    excluded assets   7.7–7.8
    FRS10   7.6
    introduction   7.5
    research and development   7.9
  non-trading debits and credits   7.13
  part realisation   7.19
  patent royalties   7.11

Intangible assets – *contd*
  pre-1 April 2002 assets   7.2
  prescribed adjustments
    impairment review   7.15
    introduction   7.14
    part realisation   7.19
    realisation   7.18
    reversal of previous
      accounting gain   7.16
    taxable income   7.17
  realisation   7.18
  reconstructions   7.26
  reinvestment relief   7.21–7.22
  related parties   7.27–7.28
  research and development   7.9
  reversal of previous
    accounting gain   7.16
  roll-over relief   7.21–7.22
  royalties   7.11
  sale
    generally   7.20
    reinvestment relief   7.21–7.22
    roll-over relief   7.21–7.22
  tax treatment   7.10–7.13
  taxable income   7.17
Integral features
  plant and machinery
    allowances, and   6.17
  special rate allowance, and   6.43
Intellectual property
  research and development,
    and   8.14
Interest
  distributions, and   16.7
  late payment of tax, and
    carry back of losses   3.19
    generally   3.14
    not-trading deficit   3.19
  payment of tax, and   2.11
  quarterly instalments, and   3.20
  rate formulae   3.18
  repayments of tax, and   3.17
Interest free loans
  transfer pricing, and   14.20
**International Accounting
  Standards (IAS)**
  company accounts, and   1.9

International Accounting Standards (IAS) – *contd*

IAS 1: presentation of financial statements 17.19
IAS 2: inventories 17.24
IAS 8: accounting policies etc 17.20
IAS 10: post-balance sheet events 17.11
IAS 11: construction contracts 17.24
IAS 12: income taxes 17.29, 17.39
IAS 16: property, plant and equipment 17.13
IAS 17: leases 17.22
IAS 19: employee benefits 17.21
IAS 20: government grants 17.25
IAS 21: currency accounting 17.10
IAS 23: borrowing costs 17.14
IAS 36: impairment 17.17
IAS 37: provisions, contingent liabilities and assets 17.15
IAS 38: intangible assets 17.17
IAS 39: financial instruments— measurement 17.9
IAS 40: investment properties 17.23

International Accounting Standards Board (ASB)

company accounts, and 1.9

International Financial Reporting Standards (IFRS)

accounting standards, and 1.10
IFRS 1: first time adoption of IFRS 17.26

Intra-group asset transfer

election to treat disposal as if made by another member 20.17
group structure 20.14–20.15
intangible assets, and 7.24
relief 20.16
special rate allowance, and 6.44

Investment business

capital expenditure 12.8

Investment business – *contd*

capital losses 12.25
cessation of trade 12.10
community investment tax relief
  accreditation 12.47
  certificates 12.51
  conditions 12.48–12.50
  eligibility 12.45
  excessive returns to investor 12.55
  generally 12.46
  investment 12.52
  reconstructions 12.57
  repayments of loan capital 12.54
  value received 12.56
  withdrawal 12.53
company loan stock 12.44
computation of tax 12.2
corporate venturing scheme
  claims for relief 12.39–12.40
  clearance 12.38
  deferral relief 12.32, 12.41
  form of investment 12.35
  generally 12.31
  group relief 12.43
  investing company's interest 12.33
  investment 12.35
  investment relief 12.32
  issuing company 12.34
  loss relief 12.32, 12.42
  qualifying trade 12.37
  reliefs 12.32
  trading activities 12.36
energy-saving items 12.21
government loan stock 12.44
insurance premiums 12.9
introduction 12.1
lease premiums 12.17
legal fees 12.20
letting income 12.14
limited companies
  capital losses 12.25
  corporate venturing scheme 12.31–12.42
  group relief 12.43

Investment business – *contd*
  limited companies – *contd*
    introduction   12.22
    other reliefs   12.43
    shares in unquoted trading
      companies   12.25
    substantial shareholdings
      exemption   12.26–12.30
    taper relief   12.43
  loan stock   12.44
  management expenses
    capital expenditure   12.8
    cessation of trade   12.10
    change of ownership   12.13
    definitions   12.3
    generally   12.4
    group companies   12.6
    insurance premiums   12.9
    management activities   12.5
    restriction   12.13
    self assessment   12.11
    set-off   12.12
    unallowable purpose   12.7
  property investment
    computation of profit   12.16
    generally   12.15
    introduction   12.14
    lease premiums   12.17
    legal fees   12.20
    repair expenditure   12.19
    reverse premiums   12.18
  repair expenditure   12.19
  reverse premiums   12.18
  Schedule A
    computation of profit   12.16
    energy-saving items   12.21
    generally   12.15
    lease premiums   12.17
    legal fees   12.20
    losses   12.23
    repair expenditure   12.19
    reverse premiums   12.18
  Schedule D Case I   12.22
  self assessment   12.11
  shares in unquoted trading
    companies   12.25

Investment business – *contd*
  substantial shareholdings
    exemption
      conditions   12.28–12.29
      generally   12.26
      substantial shareholding   12.27
      trading activities   12.30
    taper relief   12.43
    trading losses, and   9.38
    trading stock   12.14
    unrelieved losses, and   9.38

J

Joint ventures
  groups of companies, and   10.1

L

Land and buildings
  and see Industrial buildings
    allowances; Plant and
    machinery allowances
  income, and   5.44
Land remediation
  expenditure relief
    connected sub-contractor   8.42
    contaminated state   8.36
    deduction in calculation of
      profits   8.45
    employee costs   8.38
    entitlement to relief   8.44
    increased expenditure due
      to contamination   8.40
    introduction   8.33
    materials expenditure   8.39
    qualifying expenditure   8.35
    qualifying land   8.34
    relevant activities   8.37
    sub-contractor payments   8.42–8.43
    subsidised expenditure   8.41
  tax credit
    amount   8.47
    capital gains, and   8.49
    entitlement   8.46
    payment   8.48
    penalties   8.50
Large companies
  payment of tax, and   3.9

Large companies – *contd*
research and development,
and
contributions to
independent work   8.26
generally   8.23
going concern   8.30
location of work   8.28
qualifying expenditure   8.24
relief   8.23
sub-contracted work   8.25
sub-contracted work to
SME   8.27
time limits for enhanced
deduction   8.29
vaccine research   8.31

Lease amortisation
trading income, and   5.22

Lease premiums
investment business, and   12.17

Legal fees
investment business, and   12.20

Letting income
investment business, and   12.14

Liability to corporation tax
'company'   1.4
extent of tax charge   1.5
introduction   1.3
profits of company   1.6

Lighting
plant and machinery
allowances, and   6.11

Linked enterprises
transfer pricing, and   14.9

Liquidation
commencement   19.10
corporation tax   19.11
effect of order   19.12
ESC 16   19.14
generally   19.8
liquidator   19.9
loans to participators   19.13
tax liabilities of office holders   19.15

Loan creditors
close companies, and   4.11

Loan relationship
accounting treatment   11.9

Loan relationship – *contd*
amortised cost basis   11.28–11.29
bad debt relief   11.33–11.34
carry back previous year
deficit relief   11.19
carry forward deficit relief
disclaimer   11.21
generally   11.20
connected persons
amortised cost basis   11.28–11.29
bad debt relief   11.33–11.34
benefit derived   11.32
'connection'   11.25
consequences   11.28–11.34
creditor relationships   11.32
discounted securities   11.31
impairment losses   11.33–11.34
meaning   11.25
post-1 October 2002   11.27
pre-1 October 2002   11.26
unpaid interest   11.30
consortia, and   11.35
contingent debts, and   11.8
controlled foreign companies,
and   13.43
corporation tax treatment
introduction   11.10
non-trading loan
relationships   11.16
trading loan relationships   11.11
unallowable purposes   11.12–11.15
costs of obtaining finance
generally   11.23
inclusion in accounts   11.24
court settlements, and   11.8
creditor relationships   11.32
current year deficit relief   11.18
debits and credits   11.2
derivatives, and   11.36
discounted securities   11.31
existence   11.5
finance leases, and   11.8
foreign exchange gains and
losses   11.36
FRSSE   11.9

Loan relationship – *contd*
GAAP
    costs of obtaining finance   11.24
    generally   11.9
  groups, and   11.35
  hire purchase, and   11.8
  HMRC advice   11.15
  impairment losses   11.33–11.34
  legislative framework   11.2
  loan guarantees, and   11.8
  meaning   11.3
  money debt
    generally   11.5
    legislative definitions   11.4
    non-loan relationships   11.8
    relevant debts   11.6
    shares   11.7
  non-commercial purpose   11.12
  non-loan relationships   11.8
  non-trading deficit relief
    carry back previous year   11.19
    carry forward   11.20–11.21
    current year   11.18
    manner   11.17
  non-trading loan relationships   11.16
  pre-trading expenditure   11.22
  relevant debts   11.6
  repos
    anti-avoidance   11.43
    creditor quasi-repo   11.40–11.42
    creditor repo   11.40–11.42
    debtor quasi-repo   11.38–11.39
    introduction   11.37
  Schedule D Case I   11.11
  Schedule D Case III   11.16
  shares, and   11.7
  tax avoidance purpose   11.13
  tax returns, and   11.44
  trade debts, and   11.8
  trading loan relationships   11.11
  unallowable purposes
    HMRC guidance   11.15
    non-commercial purpose   11.12
    tax avoidance purpose   11.13
    writing off loans   11.14
  unpaid interest   11.30

Loan stock
  investment business, and   12.44
Loans to participators
  anti-avoidance   4.22
  circuitous loans   4.21
  excluded loans   4.17
  generally   4.14
  indirect loans   4.21
  loan accounts   4.18
  release   4.20
  relevant loans   4.16
  self-assessment disclosure   4.15
  tax repayment   4.19
Long funding leases
  capital allowances, and   6.57
Long-life assets
  allowances, and   6.37
Loss claims
  generally   9.2
  self-assessment   9.22

M
Managed service companies
  generally   5.18
Management expenses
  capital expenditure   12.8
  cessation of trade   12.10
  change of ownership   12.13
  controlled foreign companies,
    and   13.43
  definitions   12.3
  generally   12.4
  group companies   12.6
  insurance premiums   12.9
  management activities   12.5
  restriction   12.13
  self assessment   12.11
  set-off   12.12
  unallowable purpose   12.7
Marginal rates
  generally   3.5
**Matching loans and
  derivatives**
  transfer pricing, and   14.19
Members' sports clubs
  generally   5.53
  self-assessment   5.57

Mergers
And see Reconstructions
EC Mergers Tax Directive 15.26
Mitigation
anti-avoidance, and 18.1
Mixer cap
overseas dividends, and 13.22–13.23
Money debt
generally 11.5
legislative definitions 11.4
non-loan relationships 11.8
relevant debts 11.6
shares 11.7
Monthly payments
Construction Industry
Scheme, and 21.10
Monthly returns
Construction Industry
Scheme, and 21.23
Motive test
controlled foreign companies,
and 13.41
Mutual trading
generally 5.52
self-assessment 5.57

N
Natural gas and hydrogen refuelling equipment
plant and machinery
allowances, and 6.28
Non-commercial purpose
loan relationships, and 11.12
Non-corporation distribution rate
generally 3.3
Non-discrimination clause
transfer pricing, and 14.12
Non-funding lease
capital allowances, and 6.60
Non-qualifying expenditure
business premises renovation
allowances, and 6.88
flat conversion allowances,
and 6.104

Non-trade charges
trading losses, and 9.15
Non-trading companies
associated companies, and 4.30
Non-trading debits and credits
intangible assets, and 7.13
Non-trading deficit relief
carry back previous year 11.19
carry forward 11.20–11.21
current year 11.18
manner 11.17
Non-trading loan relationships
loan relationships, and 11.16
Non-UK resident companies
becoming liable to UK
corporation tax 13.9–13.10
carrying on trade in UK
charge to tax 13.5
fixed place of business 13.7
'permanent establishment' 13.6–13.8
not carrying on trade in UK
but with other UK
income 13.11
permanent establishment
fixed place of business 13.7
generally 13.6
impermanent circumstances 13.8
North Sea oil ring-fence plant
plant and machinery
allowances, and 6.29

O
OECD Model Treaty
transfer pricing, and 14.1
Off-set against profits
trading losses, and 9.11–9.14
Online filing
tax returns, and 2.10
Onshore pooling
overseas dividends, and 13.24
Overseas dividends
anti-avoidance 13.27
carry back 13.20–13.21
carry forward 13.20–13.21
controlled foreign companies,
from 13.25

Overseas dividends – *contd*
credit relief	13.19
group companies, and	13.26
'mixer cap'	13.22–13.23
onshore pooling	13.24
underlying tax	
generally	13.17
relevant profits	13.18
unrelieved tax credits	13.20–13.21

Overseas losses
group relief, and	10.9–10.11

Overseas matters
controlled foreign companies	
acceptable distribution	
policy	13.37
apportionment	13.32
capital allowances	13.43
chargeable profits	13.34
claims procedure	13.46
control	13.35
creditable tax and reliefs	13.43
de minimis exclusion	13.40
distributions	13.33
dividends from	13.44
exclusion from profit	
apportionment	13.36
exempt activities test	13.38
genuine economic	
activities	13.45
group relief	13.43
legislative developments	13.29
loan relationships	13.43
management expenses	13.43
meaning	13.28
motive test	13.41
public quotation condition	13.39
residence	13.30
self assessment	13.31
set-off	13.43
territorial exclusion	13.42
trading losses	13.43
double tax relief	13.16
double tax treaties	13.3
dual resident company	
double tax relief	13.16
restrictions	13.15
fixed place of business	13.7

Overseas matters – *contd*
introduction	13.1
non-UK resident companies	
becoming liable to UK	
corporation tax	13.9–13.10
carrying on trade in UK	13.5–
	13.8
not carrying on trade in UK	
but with other UK	
income	13.11
non-UK resident companies	
carrying on trade in UK	
charge to tax	13.5
fixed place of business	13.7
'permanent establishment'	13.6–
	13.8
overseas dividends	
carry back	13.20–13.21
carry forward	13.20–13.21
controlled foreign	
companies, from	13.25
credit relief	13.19
group companies, and	13.26
'mixer cap'	13.22–13.23
onshore pooling	13.24
underlying tax	13.17–13.18
unrelieved tax credits	13.20–
	13.21
permanent establishment	
fixed place of business	13.7
generally	13.6
impermanent circumstances	13.8
residence of company	13.2
UK company becoming	
non-UK resident	
deemed disposal of	
chargeable assets	13.13
HMRC notification	13.12
outstanding liabilities	13.12
postponement of exit	
charge	13.14
UK resident company with	
overseas income	13.4

Overseas property business
unrelieved losses, and	9.37

P

Part realisation

intangible assets, and	7.19

Participators

associates, and	4.12
benefits to	4.13
loan creditors, and	4.11
loans to	
anti-avoidance	4.22
circuitous loans	4.21
excluded loans	4.17
generally	4.14
indirect loans	4.21
loan accounts	4.18
release	4.20
relevant loans	4.16
self-assessment disclosure	4.15
tax repayment	4.19
meaning	4.10

Partners

associated companies, and	4.29

Partnerships

groups of companies, and	10.1
trading losses, and	9.10
transfer pricing, and	14.10

Patent royalties

intangible assets, and	7.11

Payment

see also Repayments

dates	
introduction	3.7
large companies	3.9
small and medium sized	
companies	3.8
generally	2.11
group arrangements	3.21
late payment interest	3.14
methods	2.11
quarterly instalments	
calculation of tax due	3.12–3.13
generally	3.10–3.11
size of company, and	3.7–3.9

Penalties

Construction Industry	
Scheme, and	21.22
errors, for	
appeals	2.44

Penalties – *contd*

errors, for – *contd*	
circumstances in which	
payable	2.37
generally	2.36
liability of company	
officers	2.45
potential lost revenue	2.38–2.41
procedures	2.43
reductions for disclosure	2.42
suspension	2.44
failure to deliver return by	
filing date, for	2.12
reduction percentages	2.25–2.26

Pension contributions

generally	5.31
spreading rules	5.32

Permanent establishment

fixed place of business	13.7
generally	13.6
impermanent circumstances	13.8

Personal service companies

generally	5.17

Planning

year end, and	22.6

Plant and machinery allowances

alterations to buildings	6.12
buildings	6.9
case law	6.18–6.19
computer software	6.15
demolition costs	6.13
fire safety equipment	6.14
fixtures, and	6.83
generally	6.7–6.8
integral features	6.17
lighting	6.11
'plant'	6.10
qualifying assets	6.9
rates	6.20
structures	6.9
thermal insulation of	
buildings	6.16

Plant and machinery leased with land

capital allowances, and	6.63

Pooling
capital allowances, and 6.32
Potential lost revenue
penalties for errors, and
delayed tax 2.41
losses 2.40
multiple errors 2.39
normal rule 2.38
Pre-entry losses and gains
asset transfers, and 10.33
capital gains, and 20.34
Pre-trading expenditure
loan relationships, and 11.22
Principal member
close companies, and 4.7
Professional profits
trading income, and 5.4
Profits
liability to tax, and 1.6
Property investment
computation of profit 12.16
generally 12.15
introduction 12.14
lease premiums 12.17
legal fees 12.20
repair expenditure 12.19
reverse premiums 12.18
Provision of information
appeals 2.52–2.53
change of ownership of
companies 2.54
destruction of documents 2.56
inspection of business
premises 2.49
inspection of records 2.48
introduction 2.46
offence 2.59
other powers 2.50
penalties 2.55
reasonable excuse 2.57
restrictions on powers 2.51
supplementary information 2.47
Public quotation
controlled foreign companies,
and 13.39
Purchase of a company
acquisition costs 15.3

Purchase of a company – *contd*
generally 15.1
**Purchase of company's own
shares**
'associated persons' 16.24
clearance procedure 16.23
conditions 16.20–16.21
'connected persons' 16.25
generally 16.19
purpose 16.20
shareholder interest in
company 16.22
shareholder residence 16.21

Q

Quarterly accounting
CT61 procedures 3.22
deduction of tax 3.23
Quarterly payments
Construction Industry
Scheme, and 21.12
Qualifying buildings
business premises renovation
allowances, and 6.89
flat conversion allowances,
and 6.105
Qualifying business premises
business premises renovation
allowances, and 6.91
Qualifying expenditure
business premises renovation
allowances, and 6.87
flat conversion allowances,
and 6.103
Qualifying trade
corporate venturing scheme,
and 12.37
Quarterly instalments
calculation of tax due 3.12–3.13
debit and credit interest 3.20
generally 3.10–3.11
group relief, and 10.18–10.19

R

Rates of tax
Construction Industry
Scheme, and 21.9

Rates of tax – *contd*
corporation tax
  effective rates 3.6
  full rate 3.1
  introduction 1.3
  marginal rates 3.5
  non-corporation distribution
    rate 3.3
  small companies rate 3.2
  starting rate 3.3
  table 3.4
Receivers
effect of appointment 19.5
generally 19.4
Reconstructions
capital gains tax
  bona fide commercial
    arrangements 15.9
  reorganisation of share
    capital 15.7
  share for share exchange 15.8
  transfer of business 15.10
community investment tax
  relief, and 12.57
intangible assets, and 7.26
introduction 15.5
legislative framework 15.6
trading losses
  activities of part of trade 15.22
  activities of trade 15.21
  beneficial ownership 15.16–
    15.18
  capital allowances 15.25
  carry forward 15.24
  change of ownership 15.12
  charging condition 15.14
  EC Mergers Tax Directive 15.26
  effects 15.24–15.25
  later events, and 15.23
  ownership condition 15.13
  relief 15.15
  succession 15.20
  transfer of trade 15.19
Records
Construction Industry
  Scheme, and
  inspection 21.21

Records – *contd*
Construction Industry Scheme, and –
  contd
  maintenance 21.20
  self-assessment, and 2.3
  transfer pricing, and 14.25
Reinvestment relief
intangible assets, and 7.21–7.22
Related parties
intangible assets, and 7.27–7.28
**Remediation of contaminated
land**
expenditure relief
  connected sub-contractor 8.42
  contaminated state 8.36
  deduction in calculation of
    profits 8.45
  employee costs 8.38
  entitlement to relief 8.44
  increased expenditure due
    to contamination 8.40
  introduction 8.33
  materials expenditure 8.39
  qualifying expenditure 8.35
  qualifying land 8.34
  relevant activities 8.37
  sub-contractor payments 8.42–
    8.43
  subsidised expenditure 8.41
tax credit
  amount 8.47
  capital gains, and 8.49
  entitlement 8.46
  payment 8.48
  penalties 8.50
Rent
trading income, and 5.24
Repair expenditure
investment business, and 12.19
Repayments
community investment tax
  relief, and 12.54
generally 3.15
group relief, and 10.17
income tax 3.16
interest
  generally 3.17–3.22

Repayments – *contd*
interest – *contd*
    trading losses, and   9.28
    loans to participators, and   4.19
Repos
anti-avoidance   11.43
creditor quasi-repo
    charge to tax   11.42
    generally   11.41
    relief   11.42
creditor repo
    charge to tax   11.42
    generally   11.40
    relief   11.42
debtor quasi-repo
    charge to tax   11.39
    generally   11.38
    relief   11.39
introduction   11.37
Research and development
capital allowances
    disposal value   8.9
    introduction   8.2
    qualifying expenditure   8.6
    reduced allowances   8.7
    'research and development'   8.3–8.5
    types   8.7–8.8
deductions against revenue
    externally provided workers   8.16
    generally   8.10
    intellectual property   8.14
    qualifying expenditure   8.13
    relevant research and
        development   8.12
    'research and development'   8.11
    sub-contracted work   8.17
    subsidised expenditure   8.15
externally provided workers   8.16
going concern   8.30
HMRC claims units   8.32
intangible assets, and   7.9
intellectual property   8.14
introduction   8.1
large companies
    contributions to
        independent work   8.26

Research and development – *contd*
large companies – *contd*
    generally   8.23
    going concern   8.30
    location of work   8.28
    qualifying expenditure   8.24
    relief   8.23
    sub-contracted work   8.25
    sub-contracted work to
        SME   8.27
    time limits for enhanced
        deduction   8.29
    vaccine research   8.31
meaning
    capital expenditure   8.3–8.5
    revenue expenditure   8.11
small and medium sized
    enterprises
    cap on aid   8.22
    definition   8.18–8.19
    relief   8.21
    tax relief   8.20
sub-contracted work
    generally   8.17
    large companies   8.25
subsidised expenditure   8.15
time limits for enhanced
    deduction   8.29
vaccine research   8.31
Residence
controlled foreign companies   13.30
dual resident company
    double tax relief   13.16
    restrictions   13.15
fixed place of business   13.7
introduction   13.2
non-UK resident companies
    becoming liable to UK
        corporation tax   13.9–13.10
    carrying on trade in UK   13.5–13.8
    not carrying on trade in UK
        but with other UK
        income   13.11
non-UK resident companies
    carrying on trade in UK
    charge to tax   13.5

Residence – *contd*
  non-UK resident companies carrying
    on trade in UK – *contd*
    fixed place of business   13.7
    'permanent establishment'   13.6–
                                     13.8
  permanent establishment
    fixed place of business   13.7
    generally   13.6
    impermanent circumstances   13.8
  purchase of own shares, and   16.21
  UK company becoming
    non-UK resident
    deemed disposal of
      chargeable assets   13.13
    HMRC notification   13.12
    outstanding liabilities   13.12
    postponement of exit
      charge   13.14
  UK resident company with
    overseas income   13.3
Returns
  accounting periods   2.4–2.6
  amendment   2.22
  associated companies, and   4.33
  Construction Industry
    Scheme, and   21.23
  CT600   2.7
  enquiries, and   2.16–2.26
  filing date   2.9
  group relief, and
    generally   10.3
    group relief   10.16
  loan relationships, and   11.44
  online filing   2.10
  Supplementary Pages   2.8
  trading income, and   5.8
  trading losses, and   9.26–9.27
Reverse premiums
  investment business, and   12.18
Rights of attribution
  associated companies, and   4.31–
                                     4.32
Roll-over relief
  asset transfers, and   20.14
  assets only partly replaced   20.8

Roll-over relief – *contd*
  assets owned personally but
    used in the trade   20.13
  conditions   20.7
  depreciating assets   20.9
  intangible assets, and   7.21–7.22
  introduction   20.6
  land and buildings   20.11
  new assets as depreciating
    assets   20.9
  new assets not brought
    immediately into trading
    use   20.12
  new assets not purchased   20.11
  partly replaced assets   20.8
  personally-owned assets used
    in trade   20.13
Royalties
  intangible assets, and   7.11

S
Sale of a company
  generally   15.4
Schedule A
  furnished holiday lettings   5.45
  investment business, and
    computation of profit   12.16
    energy-saving items   12.21
    generally   12.15
    lease premiums   12.17
    legal fees   12.20
    losses   12.23
    repair expenditure   12.19
    reverse premiums   12.18
  land and buildings   5.44
Schedule D
  investment business, and   12.22
  loan relationships, and
    Case I   11.11
    Case III   11.16
  trading income, and   5.9
  trading losses, and   9.1, 9.20
Self-assessment
  accounting periods   2.4–2.6
  accounts   2.1
  anti-avoidance, and
    CT600   18.13

Self-assessment – *contd*
anti-avoidance, and – *contd*
  penalties   18.14
appeals
  general right   2.27
  hearing before
    Commissioners   2.29
  High Court, to   2.30
  lodgment   2.28
  procedures   2.28–2.29
  Tribunals Courts and
    Enforcement Bill   2.31
completion of enquiries
  appeal   2.27
  introduction   2.23
  penalties for periods prior
    to 1 April 2008   2.24
  penalty reduction
    percentages   2.25–2.26
contacting HMRC   2.2
controlled foreign companies,
  and   13.31
CT600
  generally   2.7
  introduction   2.1
determination assessments
  generally   2.32
  introduction   2.13
discovery assessments   2.32
enquiries
  affairs of directors, and   2.18
  amendment of return   2.22
  appeals   2.27–2.31
  completion   2.23–2.26
  directors' returns, and   2.19–2.20
  disclosure of directors'
    documents   2.20
  manner   2.16
  penalties   2.25–2.26
  process   2.21
  timing   2.14–2.15
estimation of tax due   2.32
filing date   2.9
fraud, and
  civil investigation
    procedures   2.34
  criminal prosecution   2.35

Self-assessment – *contd*
fraud, and – *contd*
  generally   2.33
income, and
  Schedule D Case I and II
    profits   5.9
  tax returns   5.8
information notices
  appeals   2.52–2.53
  change of ownership of
    companies   2.54
  destruction of documents   2.56
  inspection of business
    premises   2.49
  inspection of records   2.48
  introduction   2.46
  offence   2.59
  other powers   2.50
  penalties   2.55
  reasonable excuse   2.57
  restrictions on powers   2.51
  supplementary information   2.47
introduction   2.1
investment business, and   12.11
loans to participators, and   4.15
online filing   2.10
payment   2.11
penalties
  errors   2.36–2.45
  failure to deliver return by
    filing date   2.12
  reduction packages   2.25–2.26
penalties for errors
  appeals   2.44
  circumstances in which
    payable   2.37
  generally   2.36
  liability of company
    officers   2.45
  potential lost revenue   2.38–2.41
  procedures   2.43
  reductions for disclosure   2.42
  suspension   2.44
provision of information
  powers
    appeals   2.52–2.53

Self-assessment – *contd*
provision of information powers –
 contd
 change of ownership of
  companies 2.54
 destruction of documents 2.56
 inspection of business
  premises 2.49
 inspection of records 2.48
 introduction 2.46
 offence 2.59
 other powers 2.50
 penalties 2.55
 reasonable excuse 2.57
 restrictions on powers 2.51
 supplementary information 2.47
records 2.3
return
 accounting periods 2.4–2.6
 amendment 2.22
 CT600 2.7
 enquiries, and 2.16–2.26
 filing date 2.9
 online filing 2.10
 Supplementary Pages 2.8
tax computation 2.1
trading losses, and
 elections 9.22
 introduction 9.4
 loss claims 9.22
 more than one accounting
  period 9.24
 other claims and elections 9.25
 single accounting period 9.23
transfer pricing, and
 advance pricing
  agreements 14.29–14.30
 enquiries 14.26
 generally 14.23–14.24
 introduction 14.5
 payments of interest
  abroad 14.28
 record keeping 14.25
 thin capitalisation 14.27
Set-off
controlled foreign companies,
 and 13.43

Share capital
reconstructions and
 amalgamations, and 15.7
Share for share exchange
reconstructions and
 amalgamations, and 15.8
Share schemes
trading income, and 5.26–5.29
Shares
loan relationships, and 11.7
**Shares in unquoted trading
 companies**
investment business, and 12.25
Short lease
capital allowances, and 6.58
Short life assets
capital allowances, and 6.36
Size of company
payment of tax, and 3.7–3.9
**Small and medium sized
 companies**
payment of tax, and 3.8
research and development,
 and
 cap on aid 8.22
 definition 8.18–8.19
 generally 8.20
 relief 8.21
transfer pricing, and
 definition 14.8
 election to remain subject
  to rules 14.13
 general exemption 14.7
Small companies rate
generally 3.2
Software
plant and machinery
 allowances, and 6.15
Special rate allowance
disposal value of assets 6.42
existing long-life asset
 expenditure 6.45
integral features 6.43
intra-group transfers 6.44
relevant expenditure 6.41
sale between connected
 persons 6.43

Starting rate
generally   3.3
Statements of Standard
  Accounting Practice
  (SSAP)
introduction   1.10
SSAP 9: government grants   17.25
SSAP 9: stocks and long-term
  contracts   17.24
SSAP 13: research and
  development   17.17
SSAP 17: post-balance sheet
  events   17.11
SSAP 19: investment
  properties   17.23
SSAP 21: leases and
  hire-purchase contracts   17.22
SSAP 24: pension costs   17.21
Stock
asset transfers, and   10.25–10.27
IAS inventories   5.38
net realisable value/cost   5.39
SSAP   5.37
UITF   5.41–5.42
valuation of transfers to and
  from   5.43
Storage
industrial buildings
  allowances, and   6.70
Striking off defunct company
ESC 16, and   16.28
generally   16.26
request by private company   16.27
Sub-contractors
inspection of records   21.21
meaning   21.3
registration   21.13
Substantial shareholdings
  exemption
conditions   12.28–12.29
generally   12.26
substantial shareholding   12.27
trading activities   12.30
Succession
trading losses, and   15.20
Surplus ACT
distributions, and   16.10–16.11

T
Tangible fixed assets
accountancy treatment   6.1
background plant and
  machinery   6.62
business premises renovation
  allowances
  balancing adjustment   6.97
  balancing events   6.96
  demolition costs   6.99
  disadvantaged area   6.90
  dwelling   6.92
  initial allowances   6.94
  introduction   6.86
  non-qualifying expenditure   6.88
  qualifying building   6.89
  qualifying business
    premises   6.91
  qualifying expenditure   6.87
  relevant interest   6.93
  termination of lease   6.101
  value added tax   6.100
  writing down allowances   6.95
  writing off qualifying
    expenditure   6.98
capital allowances
  business premises
    renovation   6.86–6.101
  computation   6.32–6.39
  date incurred   6.5
  first year allowance   6.21–6.31
  flat conversion   6.102–6.111
  generally   6.4
  industrial buildings   6.65–6.68
  plant and machinery   6.7–6.20
  rates   6.20
  relevant assets   6.6
cars with low carbon dioxide
  emissions   6.27
chargeable gains
  conditions affecting assets   20.1
  land and buildings   20.10
  new assets not brought
    immediately into
    trading use   20.12
  new assets not purchased   20.11
  new, depreciating assets   20.9

Tangible fixed assets – *contd*
  chargeable gains – *contd*
    partly replaced assets 20.8
    personally-owned assets
      used in trade 20.13
    roll-over relief 20.6
  computation of capital
    allowances
    background plant and
      machinery 6.62
    disposal proceeds 6.34
    finance leasing 6.55–6.64
    funding lease 6.59
    hire-purchased assets 6.39–6.40
    long funding leases 6.57
    long-life assets 6.37
    non-funding lease 6.60
    plant and machinery leased
      with land 6.63
    pool 6.32
    reduced allowances 6.38
    short lease 6.58
    short life assets 6.36
    types of adjustment 6.33
  disposal proceeds 6.34
  energy services provider 6.26
  environmentally beneficial
    plant and machinery 6.24–6.25
  funding lease 6.59
  first year allowance
    cars with low carbon
      dioxide emissions 6.27
    energy services provider 6.26
    environmentally beneficial
      plant and machinery 6.24–6.25
    excluded expenditure 6.31
    groups 6.23
    introduction 6.21
    natural gas and hydrogen
      refuelling equipment 6.28
    North Sea oil ring-fence
      plant 6.29
    owners of fixtures 6.30
    small and medium sized
      enterprises 6.22
    small enterprises 6.22

Tangible fixed assets – *contd*
  flat conversion allowances
    balancing adjustment 6.111
    balancing events 6.110
    high-value flats 6.107
    initial allowances 6.108
    non-qualifying expenditure 6.104
    qualifying building 6.105
    qualifying expenditure 6.103
    qualifying flat 6.106
    relevant interest 6.102
    writing-down allowances 6.109
  hire-purchased assets 6.39–6.40
  industrial buildings
    allowances
    construction of building or
      structure 6.65
    disposal of building 6.80–6.82
    enterprise zones, in 6.85
    generally 6.65
    'goods and materials' 6.68
    hotels 6.72
    initial allowance 6.73
    'manufacturing' 6.67
    qualifying expenditure 6.71
    qualifying structures 6.65
    qualifying trade 6.66
    relevant expenditure 6.71
    'storage' 6.70
    'subject to a process' 6.69
    successor company, and 6.84
    temporary disuse 6.79
    writing down allowance 6.74–6.78
  long funding leases 6.57
  long-life assets 6.37
  natural gas and hydrogen
    refuelling equipment 6.28
  non-funding lease 6.60
  North Sea oil ring-fence plant 6.29
  owners of fixtures 6.30
  plant and machinery
    allowances
    alterations to buildings 6.12
    buildings 6.9
    case law 6.18–6.19
    computer software 6.15

Tangible fixed assets – *contd*
plant and machinery allowances –
  contd

demolition costs	6.13
fire safety equipment	6.14
fixtures, and	6.83
generally	6.7–6.8
integral features	6.17
lighting	6.11
'plant'	6.10
qualifying assets	6.9
rates	6.20
structures	6.9
thermal insulation of buildings	6.16
plant and machinery leased with land	6.63
pool	6.32
qualifying expenditure	
date incurred	6.5
generally	6.4
plant and machinery	6.7–6.20
relevant assets	6.6
reduced allowances	6.38
short lease	6.58
short life assets	6.36
tax treatment	6.2

Taper relief

investment business, and	12.43

Tax avoidance

capital gains, and	
capital losses	18.17–18.25
international agreements	18.16
depreciatory transactions	20.32
dividend stripping	20.33
pre-entry losses and gains	20.34
value shifting	20.24–20.31
capital losses	18.17–18.25
case law	18.2
disclosure of tax avoidance schemes	
clearance procedure	18.12
court procedure	18.32
disclosable arrangements	18.8–18.9
doubt as to notifiability	18.28
effect	18.16

Tax avoidance – *contd*
disclosure of tax avoidance schemes –
  contd

hallmarked tests	18.10
hallmarks	18.11
HMRC strategy	18.6
notification	18.7
order to disclose	18.31
pre-disclosure enquiry	18.29
reasons for non-disclosure	18.30
distributions, and	16.7
evasion, and	18.1
GAAR, and	18.3
husband and wife companies	18.26
international agreements, and	18.15
introduction	18.1
legislative framework	18.4–18.5
loan relationships, and	11.13
loans to participators, and	4.22
mitigation, and	18.1
self assessment	
CT600	18.13
penalties	18.14
UK approach	18.3

Tax charge

liability to tax, and	1.5

Tax computation

self-assessment, and	2.1

Tax credits

remediation of contaminated land, and	
amount	8.47
capital gains, and	8.49
entitlement	8.46
payment	8.48
penalties	8.50
trading losses, and	
amount	9.33–9.34
clawback	9.40–9.43
excluded company	9.32
introduction	9.29
PAYE and NIC liabilities	9.34
relevant expenditure	9.31
surrenderable loss	9.30

Tax evasion

generally	18.1

Tax mitigation
generally   18.1
Tax planning
year end, and   22.6
Tax repayments
generally   3.15
income tax   3.16
interest   3.17–3.21
loans to participators, and   4.19
Tax returns
accounting periods   2.4–2.6
amendment   2.22
associated companies, and   4.33
CT600   2.7
enquiries, and
   affairs of directors, and   2.18
   amendment of return   2.22
   completion of   2.23–2.27
   directors' returns, and   2.19–2.20
   disclosure of company
     documents   2.17
   manner   2.16
   process   2.21
   timing   2.14–2.15
filing date   2.9
group relief, and
   generally   10.3
   group relief   10.16
loan relationships, and   11.44
online filing   2.10
Supplementary Pages   2.8
trading income, and   5.8
trading losses, and   9.26–9.27
Temporary disuse
industrial buildings
   allowances, and   6.79
Termination of lease
business premises renovation
   allowances, and   6.101
Territorial exclusion
controlled foreign companies,
   and   13.42
Thermal insulation
plant and machinery
   allowances, and   6.16
Thin capitalisation
advance pricing agreements   14.30

Thin capitalisation – *contd*
generally   14.27
Trade charges
trading losses, and   9.8
Trade debts
loan relationships, and   11.8
Trading income
'badges of trade'   5.5
case law   5.6
generally   5.7
introduction   5.4
self-assessment   5.8–5.9
'trade'   5.4
Trading losses
assessment appeals   9.27
carry forward
   case law   9.3
   charge to tax   9.6
   HMRC enquiries   9.5
   loss claim   9.2
   self-assessment   9.4
cessation of trade   9.16
change in conduct or nature
   of trade   9.19
change in situation   9.17
change of ownership   9.18
charges on income
   non-trade charges   9.15
   trade charges   9.8
clawback of first-year tax
   credits
   amount of restored loss   9.41
   claims   9.43
   correction of returns   9.42
   relevant circumstances   9.40
computation
   generally   9.7
   introduction   9.1
   non-trade charges   9.15
   offset against current year
     profits   9.11–9.14
   partnerships   9.10
   relief against interest and
     dividends   9.9
   trade charges   9.8
controlled foreign companies,
   and   13.43

Trading losses – *contd*
first-year tax credits
  amount | 9.33–9.34
  clawback | 9.40–9.43
  excluded company | 9.32
  introduction | 9.29
  PAYE and NIC liabilities | 9.34
  relevant expenditure | 9.31
  surrenderable loss | 9.30
  unrelieved losses, and | 9.39
Government investment
  written off | 9.21
group relief, and | 10.7
HMRC enquiries | 9.5
loss claim | 9.2
meaning | 9.1
non-trade charges | 9.15
offset against current year
  profits | 9.11–9.14
partnerships | 9.10
reconstructions and
  amalgamations, and
  activities of part of trade | 15.22
  activities of trade | 15.21
  beneficial ownership | 15.16–15.18
  capital allowances | 15.25
  carry forward | 15.24
  change of ownership | 15.12
  charging condition | 15.14
  EC Mergers Tax Directive | 15.26
  effects | 15.24–15.25
  later events, and | 15.23
  ownership condition | 15.13
  relief | 15.15
  succession | 15.20
  transfer of trade | 15.19
relief against interest and
  dividends | 9.9
repayment interest | 9.28
restrictions
  change in conduct or nature
   of trade | 9.19
  change in situation | 9.17
  change of ownership | 9.18
Schedule D Case I | 9.1
Schedule D Case IV | 9.20

Trading losses – *contd*
self-assessment
  elections | 9.22
  introduction | 9.4
  loss claims | 9.22
  more than one accounting
   period | 9.24
  other claims and elections | 9.25
  single accounting period | 9.23
tax returns, and | 9.26–9.27
trade charges | 9.8
unrelieved losses
  furnished holiday lettings
   business | 9.35
  lettings business | 9.36
  management of investments | 9.38
  overseas property business | 9.37
  payment in respect of
   first-year tax credit | 9.39
  trades | 9.35

Trading stock
asset transfers, and | 10.25–10.27

Transfer of assets
capital gains, and
  from trading stock | 20.20
  to trading stock | 20.18–20.19
companies leaving group | 10.29–10.30
depreciatory transactions | 10.31
dividend stripping | 10.32
election | 10.24
group structure | 10.21–10.22
pre-entry losses and gains | 10.33
relief | 10.23
roll-over relief | 10.28
trading stock, from
  generally | 20.20
  transfer of assets to trading
   stock | 20.18–20.19
  groups | 10.27
trading stock, to
  generally | 20.18–20.19
  groups | 10.25–10.26

Transfer of business
reconstructions and
  amalgamations, and | 15.10

Transfer of trade
Construction Industry
    Scheme, and   21.6
trading losses, and   15.19
Transfer pricing
advance pricing agreements
    thin capitalisation   14.30
    transfer pricing   14.29
appeals   14.17
application   14.3
balancing payments   14.16
capital allowances   14.18
chargeable gains   14.18
compensating relief   14.15
'control'   14.4
coverage   14.2
currency contracts   14.22
excluded holdings   14.11
general rules   14.2
HMRC enquiries   14.26
interest free loans   14.20
introduction   14.1
linked enterprises   14.9
matching loans and
    derivatives   14.19
non-discrimination clause   14.12
OECD Model Treaty   14.1
partnership enterprises   14.10
pre-existing dormant
    company   14.14
record keeping   14.25
self assessment
    advance pricing agreement   14.29
    enquiries   14.26
    generally   14.23–14.24
    introduction   14.5
    payments of interest
        abroad   14.28
    record keeping   14.25
    thin capitalisation   14.27
small and medium sized
    enterprises
    definition   14.8
    election to remain subject
        to rules   14.13
    general exemption   14.7

Transfer pricing – *contd*
thin capitalisation
    advance pricing
        agreements   14.30
    generally   14.27
    trading income, and   5.23
    'transaction'   14.6
Turnover test
Construction Industry
    Scheme, and   21.27

U
Unauthorised distribution
distributions in winding up,
    and   16.31
Unrelieved losses
furnished holiday lettings
    business   9.35
lettings business   9.36
management of investments   9.38
overseas property business   9.37
payment in respect of
    first-year tax credit   9.39
trades   9.35
Unrelieved tax credits
overseas dividends, and   13.20–
    13.21
**Urgent Issue Task Force
(UITS)**
accounting standards, and   1.10

V
Vaccine research
research and development,
    and   8.31
Valuations
transfers to and from trading
    stock   5.43
Value added tax
business premises renovation
    allowances, and   6.100
Value shifting
asset holding company
    leaving group   20.28
disposal of shares in another
    company   20.31

Value shifting – *contd*
disposals within group
  followed by share
    disposal   20.29
distributions within group
  followed by share
    disposal   20.27
free benefits   20.26
general application   20.25
introduction   20.24
reorganisation of share capital   20.30

W

Waste deposit
restoration payments   5.11
Website development costs
generally   5.19
'Wholly and exclusively'
trading income, and   5.13
Winding up
commencement   19.10
corporation tax   19.11
distributions, and   16.7
effect of order   19.12
ESC 16   19.14
generally   19.8
liquidator   19.9
loans to participators   19.13
tax liabilities of office holders   19.15
Work in progress
IAS inventories   5.38
net realisable value/cost   5.39
professional firms   5.40
SSAP   5.37
UITF   5.41–5.42
valuation of transfers to and
  from trading stock   5.43

Writing down allowances
business premises renovation,
  and   6.95
flat conversions, and   6.109
hire-purchased assets   6.39–6.40
industrial buildings, and
  anti-avoidance   6.77
  introduction   6.74
  pre-condition   6.78
  qualifying enterprise zone
    expenditure   6.76
  transitional period   6.75
long-life assets   6.37
overview   6.33
plant and machinery, and   6.33
reduced allowances   6.38
short life assets   6.36
transitional rate   6.35
**Writing off qualifying
  expenditure**
business premises renovation
  allowances, and   6.98

Y

Year end
adjusted profits   22.2
capital allowances   22.4
capital gains   22.5
computation of tax
  adjusted profits   22.2
  capital allowances   22.4
  capital gains   22.5
  generally   22.3
  introduction   22.1
planning   22.6